Pentaho® Solutions

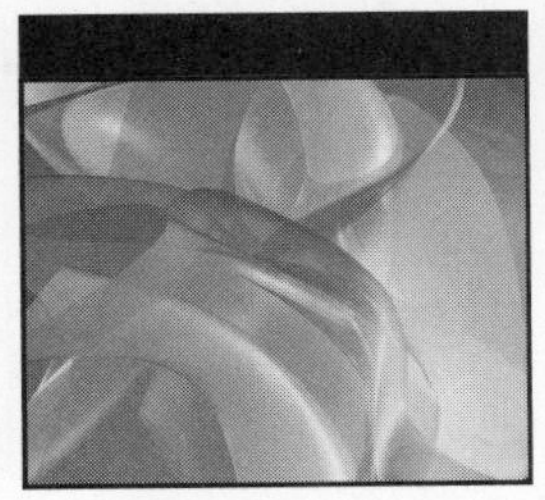

Pentaho® Solutions

Business Intelligence and Data Warehousing with Pentaho and MySQL®

Roland Bouman
Jos van Dongen

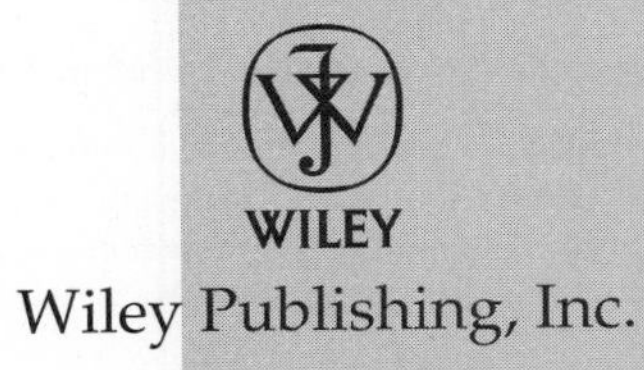

Wiley Publishing, Inc.

Pentaho® Solutions: Business Intelligence and Data Warehousing with Pentaho and MySQL®

Published by
Wiley Publishing, Inc.
10475 Crosspoint Boulevard
Indianapolis, IN 46256
www.wiley.com

Published simultaneously in Canada

ISBN: 978-0-470-48432-6

Manufactured in the United States of America

10 9 8 7 6 5 4 3 2 1

For general information on our other products and services please contact our Customer Care Department within the United States at (877) 762-2974, outside the United States at (317) 572-3993 or fax (317) 572-4002.

Library of Congress Control Number: 2009930282

With love, for Annemarie, David, Roos and Anne.

—Roland

To Yvonne, Thomas and Lisa, for the many evenings and weekends I spent working on this book. Sorry to have missed almost six months of your lives, but I promise to make it up!

—Jos

About the Authors

Roland Bouman has been working in the IT industry since 1998, mostly as a web and database application developer. Over the years, he has focused on open source Web technology, databases, and Business Intelligence. He is an active member of the MySQL and Pentaho communities, and was awarded the MySQL Forum Leader of the Year award in 2006. Roland is regular speaker at conferences. He is also co-author of the MySQL 5.1 Cluster Certification Guide, and technical reviewer of a number of MySQL-related titles. You can follow his blog at `http://rpbouman.blogspot.com/`.

Jos van Dongen is a seasoned Business Intelligence professional and well-known author and presenter. He has been involved in software development, Business Intelligence and data warehousing since 1991. Before starting his own consulting practice, Tholis Consulting, in 1998, he worked for a top-tier systems integrator and a leading management consulting firm. Over the past years, he has successfully implemented several data warehouses for a variety of organisations, both for-profit and non-profit. Jos covers new BI developments for the Dutch *Database Magazine* and speaks regularly at national and international conferences. In addition to this book, he authored another book on open source BI. You can find more information about Jos on `http://www.tholis.com`.

Credits

Executive Editor
Robert Elliott

Project Editor
Sara Shlaer

Technical Editors
Tom Barber
Jens Bleuel
Jeroen Kuiper
Thomas Morgner

Senior Production Editor
Debra Banninger

Copy Editor
Nancy Rapoport

Editorial Manager
Mary Beth Wakefield

Production Manager
Tim Tate

Vice President and Executive Group Publisher
Richard Swadley

Vice President and Executive Publisher
Barry Pruett

Associate Publisher
Jim Minatel

Project Coordinator, Cover
Lynsey Stanford

Proofreader
Josh Chase, Word One
Scott Klemp, Word One

Indexer
J & J Indexing

Cover Image
Ryan Sneed

Cover Designer
Maciej Frolow / Brand X Pictures / jupiterimages

Acknowledgments

This book is the result of the work and ideas of many different people. We, the authors, happen to be the ones that get to put our names on the cover, but we couldn't have done it without the help of these people. Therefore, we'd like to use this opportunity to pay our respects.

One thing that characterizes healthy open source projects is the passion and level of involvement of the developers and software engineers that create the project. Despite their busy schedules, we found the developers from the Pentaho Corporation always willing to make the effort to explain a particular detail of their software. This makes them not only great software developers, but also valuable and respected members of the community. In particular, we'd like to thank Doug Moran, Gretchen Moran, Jens Bleuel, Julian Hyde, Matt Casters, and Thomas Morgner.

Good software never fails to grow a vibrant and lively community. This is even more true for open source software. In a fairly small amount of time, the Pentaho community has matured remarkably, giving rise to a group of Pentaho experts that not only write high quality blogs and help each other on the official Pentaho forums and the (unofficial) ##pentaho IRC channel on `freenode.net`, but also actively participate in and contribute to the development of the Pentaho product. We would like to thank everybody who helped us out on the forums and the IRC channel. In particular, we'd like to thank Daniel Einspanjer, Harris Ward, Nicholas Goodman, Prashant Raju, Tom Barber, and Yassine Elassad for their role in shaping this community. As is to be expected with an open source project like Pentaho, some community members double as product developers. Special thanks goes out to Ingo Klose, and extra special thanks to Pedro Alves. Together, they created the Community Dashboard Framework, and Pedro was very helpful to us explaining its architecture and design. Other people that deserve a special thank you note are Mark Hall, the lead developer of the Weka project, Kasper Sørensen, the architect of eobjects DataCleaner, and Ronald Damhof, for his valuable insights in the Data Vault modeling technique.

Finally, we'd like to thank Sara Shlaer and Bob Elliott for managing this project, and note the great work that both Sara and Nancy Rapoport did with the documents we delivered. We realize it took some extra effort to transform the writings of these two Dutch chaps into readable English text. The collaboration with everyone involved at Wiley has always been very efficient and pleasant; perhaps we will be able to work together again on another project.

—Roland Bouman and Jos van Dongen

First, I'd like to thank Jos, my co-author. Without him, writing this book would have been so time-consuming that I doubt it would have been practically feasible. And of course, I'd like to thank the readers of `http://rpbouman.blogspot.com/`. The idea to write this book developed over time and was fed mainly by the comments I received in response to a number of posts I dedicated to Pentaho. In addition, I received many encouraging comments and emails from my blog's readers during the writing process—there couldn't have been a better incentive to keep working to finish this book.

—Roland Bouman

My open source BI journey started almost three years ago when I published one of my first feature articles in the Dutch *Database Magazine*, titled "Pentaho, Promising Open Source BI Suite". I couldn't imagine back then that this would ultimately lead to writing a complete book on the subject, but somehow we did! So let me thank my co-author Roland for his relentless efforts in getting this project off the ground. Frankly, I don't have a clue how he managed to get all this work done with a full time job and three little children at home to take care of. Special thanks also to Jeroen Kuiper, my good friend and former colleague, for shaping up the data warehouse sections of this book, and for being a very critical reviewer of the material.

—Jos van Dongen

Contents at a Glance

Contents

Introduction

In 1958 IBM Research Fellow Hans Peter Luhn wrote a seminal paper for the *IBM Systems Journal* called ''A Business Intelligence System''. In this paper the term *intelligence* was defined as ''the ability to apprehend the interrelationships of presented facts in such a way as to guide action towards a desired goal.'' Nowadays this paper is generally considered as the spark that started the development of Business Intelligence (BI) systems as we know them today.

For a long time the software market for supporting BI has been the domain of a handful of proprietary vendors who could charge huge sums of money for their specialized solutions. The late nineties marked an important turning point for the worldwide software market when open source solutions started to become viable alternatives for supporting mission-critical systems. First the various flavors of Linux came of age, and in 2001 and 2002 several new projects were initiated, all in the areas of data integration, reporting, analysis and data mining, the typical cornerstones of a modern BI solution. In 2004 both Jaspersoft and Pentaho were founded to offer complete BI suites that leveraged the existing stand-alone BI solutions. Since then, these companies have seen strong growth and market adoption, making open source BI solutions a serious alternative to the established proprietary vendors.

You might ask yourself now, what is Business Intelligence and why does it matter? In fact, the definition given by Luhn is still a valid one, but in 1993, Gartner Analyst Howard Dresner reintroduced the term Business Intelligence and defined it as follows:

> *Concepts and methods to improve business decision making by using fact-based support systems.*

This is a somewhat less abstract definition compared to Luhn's, and one that is still used by most people to explain what BI is. The definition is not primarily technology-focused (''concepts and methods''), but it is the last part—''fact-based support systems''—that is the subject of this book. This book is all about creating a fact-based support system using the toolset delivered by Pentaho. To be able to make better decisions based on facts, you'll need to get this factual information from one or more information systems, integrate this data in a useful way, and present users with reports and analysis that will help them to understand past and present organizational performance.

The real value of BI systems lies in their use to support organizations to make better informed decisions that will lead to increased profitability, lowered costs, improved efficiency, market share growth, higher employee satisfaction, or whatever the goals of your organization might be. The added benefit of using the open source Pentaho solution to accomplish this is the great value for money and flexibility of the software. This allows any organization, for-profit or non-profit, big or small, to implement and use this software to make better decisions.

About This Book

The beginnings of *Pentaho Solutions* go back more than a year ago when we, the authors, noticed an increasing interest in open source and free software solutions, combined with a still-growing awareness that BI software is essential in measuring and improving an organization's performance.

Over the past decade, open source variants of more and more types of software have become commonly accepted and respected alternatives to their more costly and less flexible proprietary counterparts. The fact that software is open source is often mistaken for being free of cost, and though that might be true if you only look at the license costs, a BI solution cannot (and never will) be free of cost. There are costs associated with hardware, implementation, maintenance, training and migration, and if this is all summed up it turns out that licenses make up only a small portion of the total lifecycle cost of any software solution. Open source, however is much more than a cheaper way of acquiring software. The fact that the source code is freely available to anyone ensures better code quality since it is more likely that bugs are found when more people have access to the source than just the core developers. The fact that open source software is built on open standards using standard programming languages (mostly Java) makes it extremely flexible and extensible. And the fact that most open source software is not tied to a particular operating system extends this flexibility and freedom even further.

What is usually lacking, though, is a good set of documentation and manuals. Most open source projects provide excellent quality software, but developers usually care more about getting great software out than delivering proper documentation. And although you can find many good sources of information about each piece of the Pentaho BI solutions, we felt there was a need for a single source of information to help the novice user on his or her way in discovering the Pentaho toolset and implementing the first solution. That is exactly what this book is for—to help you to build your first BI solutions using Pentaho, from the very beginning (discovering Pentaho) to the very end (building dashboards for end users).

Who Should Read This Book

This book is meant for anyone who wants to know how to deliver BI solutions using Pentaho. Maybe you are an IT manager looking for a cost efficient BI solution, an IT professional looking to broaden your skill set, or a BI or data warehouse consultant responsible for developing BI solutions in your organization. Maybe you're a software developer with a lot of experience building open source solutions but still new to the world of Business Intelligence. And maybe you're already an experienced BI or data warehouse developer with deep knowledge of one or more of the existing proprietary tools. In any case, we assume you have a hands-on mentality since this is a hands-on book. We do expect some familiarity with using computers to deliver information, installing software, and working with databases, but most of the topics will be explained right from the start. So if you are not a seasoned SQL expert, don't worry: we'll cover the basics of that query language to get you on your way. Of course the BI and data warehouse concepts are explained as well, but the primary focus is on how to transform these concepts into a working solution. That is exactly why the book is called *Pentaho Solutions*.

What You Will Need to Use This Book

In order to use this book, you only need two things: a computer and an Internet connection. All the software we discuss and use in this book is freely available over the Internet for download and use. The system requirements for the computer you will need are fairly moderate; in fact, any computer that is less than four years old will do the job just fine, as long as you have at least 1 Gigabyte of RAM installed and 2 Gigabytes of free disk space available for downloading and installing software.

The various chapters contain URLs where you can find and download the software being used and the accompanying installation instructions. As for Pentaho, there are, apart from the actual source code of course, three versions of the software that you can use:

- **GA releases**—These are the stable builds of the software, usually not the most recent ones but surely the most reliable.
- **Release candidates**—The ''almost ready'' next versions of the software, possibly with a few minor bugs still in them.

- **Milestone releases**—These are created more frequently and allow you to work with recent versions introducing new features.
- **Nightly builds**—The most up-to-date versions of the software, but also the least stable ones.

When writing this book, we mostly worked with the nightly builds that generally precede the GA releases by three months or more. This means that when you read this book, the software used in this book is at least a milestone release or already GA. This allows you to work through the material using a stable, bug-free product and you can concentrate on building solutions, not fixing bugs.

NOTE **As this book goes to press, the next major release of Pentaho is expected in Fall 2009. The final version number for this release is not yet public knowledge, but the working version is currently designated as "Citrus."**

The complete list with download options is available online at `http://wiki.pentaho.com/display/COM/Community+Edition+Downloads`.

What You Will Learn from This Book

This book will teach you:

- What Business Intelligence is, and why you need it
- The components and products that form the Pentaho Business Intelligence suite, and how these products and components fulfill particular BI needs
- How to install and configure Pentaho, and how to connect it to a data warehouse
- How to design a data warehouse using open source tools
- How to build and load a data warehouse with Pentaho Data Integration (Kettle)
- How to set up a metadata layer to allow ad-hoc and self-service reporting without using direct SQL queries
- How to create reports using the Pentaho Reporting tools
- How to create Pentaho Analysis Services (Mondrian) cubes, and visualize them using the JPivot cube browser
- How to set up scheduling, subscription, and automatic distribution of BI content
- How to get started with Pentaho Data Mining (Weka)
- How to build dashboards using the Community Dashboard Framework for Pentaho

How This Book Is Organized

This book explains BI concepts, technologies, and solutions. We use a fictional online video sales and rental business (think Netflix) that appears throughout the book. For each distinct part, sample implementations are created using Pentaho. When the example relies on a database, we have taken care to ensure the sample code is compatible with the popular and ubiquitous MySQL database (version 5.1).

These samples provide the technical details necessary to understand how you can build BI solutions for real-world situations. The scope of these BI solutions is mainly on the level of the departmental data mart, which we believe is the most common business case for BI/data warehousing.

Part I: Getting Started with Pentaho

Part I is focused on gaining a quick and high-level understanding of the Pentaho software, its architecture, and its capabilities. In addition this part introduces you to a number of supporting open source tools that can help in developing real-world data warehouses and BI applications.

Chapter 1: Quick Start: Pentaho Examples

Business Intelligence is a vast subject, and Pentaho is a complex piece of software. At the same time, it is easy to grasp why you would need it, and how it might apply to you if you follow along with a few examples. This chapter does exactly that: it provides a practical, hands-on demonstration of what you can do with BI and how Pentaho helps you do it.

Chapter 2: Prerequisites

In order to develop BI applications and the supporting architecture such as a data warehouse, you need several software products, such as data modeling tools and a database server. This chapter introduces you to a number of products that are key to the examples developed in this book, as well as a number of supportive tools to increase productivity. Like Pentaho, all products mentioned here are open source/free software. We are confident you'll find a number of valuable additions to your professional toolkit here.

Chapter 3: Server Installation and Configuration

Although this book does not provide a full reference to Pentaho administration and configuration, the most important configuration and installation tasks are described in this chapter. As such, this chapter is not so much about explaining concepts; rather, it is about knowing what configuration files to edit to set things up to your liking. You should at least read through this chapter once before building Pentaho applications. Much of the information here has the character of a reference. As we cover more aspects of Pentaho throughout the book, you may want to revisit this chapter to look up certain details concerning the Pentaho configuration.

Chapter 4: The Pentaho BI Stack

This chapter provides an overview of Pentaho, its components, its capabilities, and its architecture. It introduces you to important Pentaho concepts, such as action sequences and the solution repository. Although there is a fair amount of theory in this chapter, it also provides practical explanations, tying together a lot of material covered in the previous chapters.

Part II: Dimensional Modeling and Data Warehouse Design

Part II introduces you to key concepts and techniques concerning dimensional modeling and data warehousing. These concepts are made tangible by using a single example business case based on a (fictional) online DVD rental business, World Class Movies. By constantly and consciously mixing theory and practical, hands-on examples, we hope to lay a sound foundation for developing BI applications in the remainder of the book.

Chapter 5: Example Business Case: World Class Movies

In this chapter, we introduce the World Class Movies online DVD rental business. We provide a detailed explanation of its business and underlying OLTP database schema.

Chapter 6: Data Warehouse Primer

This chapter introduces and explains fundamental concepts of dimensional modeling and data warehousing. It explains the benefits of using a data warehouse and how a data warehouse differs from other types of databases. The chapter covers the history, current state, and future outlook of data warehouse technology and architecture.

Chapter 7: Modeling the Business Using Star Schemas

This chapter takes the dimensional modeling and data warehousing concepts from the previous chapter and applies them to the World Class Movies business case in order to develop the various parts of the data mart model. This model serves as the cornerstone for BI applications (which are developed in the next part of the book).

Chapter 8: The Data Mart Design Process

In this chapter, the logical design from the previous chapter is further developed, culminating in a series of star schemas that serve to achieve the physical implementation of the World Class Movies data warehouse, which is the basis of virtually all hands-on examples in the remainder of the book.

Part III: ETL and Data Integration

Part III is devoted to the process of filling the data warehouse using Pentaho Data Integration tools and features.

Chapter 9: Pentaho Data Integration Primer

This chapter provides an overview of all the tools that make up the Pentaho Data Integration (PDI) toolkit. It explains the architecture and introduces you to a number of concepts that are fundamental to ETL design within the Pentaho platform. At the same time, it provides you with the basic hands-on skills that will help you to use Pentaho Data Integration tools effectively to build ETL applications.

Chapter 10: Designing Pentaho Data Integration Solutions

Using the concepts and basic skills gained from the previous chapter, this chapter focuses on designing and building a hands-on practical solution to load the Orders data mart of the World Class Movies data warehouse. The example transformations are accompanied by an in-depth description of commonly used transformation steps.

Chapter 11: Deploying Pentaho Data Integration Solutions

This chapter focuses on managing and deploying Pentaho Data Integration solutions. In addition, it explains how individual transformations can be combined to build jobs. Several techniques for managing static resources such as database connections and files are discussed, along with some of the more advanced PDI features such as remote execution and clustering.

Part IV: Business Intelligence Applications

Part IV explains how to use the data warehouse to create BI content the end users care about.

Chapter 12: The Metadata Layer

This chapter introduces Pentaho metadata and the metadata editor. In addition to explaining metadata concepts and the purpose of metadata in BI solutions, this chapter provides detailed instructions for creating a metadata domain that can be used to create self-service reports.

Chapter 13: Using the Pentaho Reporting Tools

This chapter provides an in-depth tutorial about designing and deploying reports using the Pentaho Report Designer. You will learn how to create queries using the visual SQL designer and the metadata query tool, add parameters to the report for interactive analysis, and build great looking and insightful reports using tables, graphs and charts.

Chapter 14: Scheduling, Subscription, and Bursting

This chapter is all about automatic production and delivery of BI content. You will learn how to use Pentaho's built-in scheduler and how it ties into features such as subscription and scheduling.

Chapter 15: OLAP Solutions Using Pentaho Analysis Services

This chapter explains the Pentaho OLAP components. In addition to explaining OLAP and MDX in general, this chapter helps you create Pentaho analysis cubes and views. The last part of this chapter introduces the aggregate designer that helps you to improve the performance of the Pentaho Analysis tool.

Chapter 16: Data Mining with Weka

In this chapter we introduce basic data mining concepts and practices such as clustering and classification using Weka, the Pentaho data mining component. We end this chapter with an example of how you can use a data mining model created with Weka in a Pentaho Data Integration transformation.

Chapter 17: Building Dashboards

This chapter explains the concepts underlying the Community Dashboard Framework. Using a step-by step method, this chapter explains in detail how to combine a number of different Pentaho solution items and bring them together on one dashboard.

On the Website

All the example material used in the book is available for download from the companion website at Wiley (`www.wiley.com/go/pentahosolutions`) and at `www.worldclassmovies.com`. The downloads include the following items:

- Power*Architect data models for the databases in the book
- Data files for customers, products, and employees

- MySQL create scripts for the databases
- MySQL scripts for generating sales transactions
- All PDI jobs and transformations
- Metadata models for building reports
- Sample reports
- Mondrian schemas
- Dashboard definition files
- Action sequence examples

Further Resources

There are numerous books available on the specific topics covered in this book. Many chapters contain references for further reading and links to websites that contain additional information. If you are new to Business Intelligence and data warehousing in general (or want to keep up with the latest developments), here are some good places to start:

- `http://en.wikipedia.org/wiki/Business_intelligence`
- `http://www.kimballgroup.com`
- `http://b-eye-network.com`
- `http://www.tdwi.org`

We also encourage you to visit our websites, `http://rpbouman.blogspot.com` and `www.tholis.com`, where you can find our contact information in case you want to get in touch with us directly.

Pentaho® Solutions

Part I

Getting Started with Pentaho

In This Part

CHAPTER

1

Quick Start: Pentaho Examples

Pentaho is a powerful Business Intelligence Suite offering many features: reporting, OLAP pivot tables, dashboarding and more. In this book you will find a lot of detailed information about Pentaho's components, how they work and interact, the features they deliver, and how to use the Pentaho BI Suite to create solutions for real-world problems. However, it's a good idea to try and grasp the big picture before diving into the details.

This chapter helps you get started by showing you where to get the software and how to install and run it. The Pentaho BI Suite includes many examples demonstrating its features to give new users an idea of what kind of solutions you can build with it. Most of these examples work "out of the box" and are thus ideal for an introduction to the product. By reading this chapter, you'll get acquainted with Pentaho by looking at some examples.

Getting Started with Pentaho

In this section, we describe how to obtain the software, install it, and run it. To run the software, you need a regular desktop or laptop computer running any popular operating system, such as Ubuntu Linux, Mac OS X, or Microsoft Windows 7, XP, or Vista. To download the necessary software you will need an Internet connection with sufficient bandwidth to download tens to hundreds of megabytes.

Downloading and Installing the Software

The Pentaho BI Suite is open source software; you are free to use and distribute its programs, and if you like, you can study and even modify its source code. You may do all of this free of charge.

Pentaho is programmed in the Java programming language. Before you can run Java programs, you need to install Java. For Pentaho, you need at least Java version 1.5. You should also be able to use Java 1.6. We assume you already have a recent version of Java installed on your system. You can find more details on downloading and installing Java in Chapter 2.

You can download all of Pentaho's released software from the SourceForge website. The easiest way to find the software is to navigate to `http://sourceforge.net/projects/pentaho/` and click the Download link. You will see a list of products you can download.

For now, you won't need all of the software—all you're interested in at the moment is the Business Intelligence Server. Click the Download link in the far right column. This takes you to a page containing a list of different versions of the software. Here you should take care to find the latest version of the generally available (GA) release, packaged in a way that is appropriate for your platform. For example, Microsoft Windows users should download the `.zip` compressed package, and users of UNIX-based systems should download the `.tar.gz` compressed package.

> **NOTE** **In Pentaho's download pages on SourceForge, you can usually find at least the latest generally available (GA) release as well as a so-called milestone release of the new, upcoming version. If you really want to be on the bleeding edge of development, you can download nightly builds of the software from `http://ci.pentaho.com/`. For this book, we mostly worked with the nightly builds of the Citrus release, which was still being developed at the time of writing, but which should be available as a milestone or GA release by the time of publishing.**
>
> **It is always a good idea to try out the milestone releases to keep track of future changes and additions. But beware that milestone releases are still in development; they are not intended for production use, and you may find bugs or experience usability issues. However, this is one of the best reasons why you should run milestone releases—by reporting any issues you experience, you can directly influence the improvement of the software for your own benefit (as well as that of all other users).**

After downloading the `.zip` or `.tar.gz` compressed package, you must extract the actual software from the compressed package and copy it to some place you find convenient. Windows users can right-click the `.zip` file and choose Extract Here (in new folder) in the context menu. Alternatively, you can use a third-party program such as Peazip to extract the programs from the compressed package. Users of UNIX-like systems can open a terminal and extract the package from the command line.

Extraction should result in a single folder containing all of the Pentaho BI Server software. Windows users can place this folder anywhere they like, but it makes most sense to put it in the Program Files directory. For UNIX-like systems, the proper location depends on the exact UNIX flavor, but for checking out the examples, it is best to move the Pentaho Server directory to your home directory. In the rest of this chapter, we refer to the directory containing the Pentaho Server software as the Pentaho home directory or simply Pentaho home.

Running the Software

Now that you have downloaded and installed the software, you can start using it.

Starting the Pentaho BI Server

In the Pentaho home directory, you will find a few scripts that can be used to start the server. Microsoft Windows users can double-click the script named `start-pentaho.bat`.

For UNIX-based systems, the script is called `start-pentaho.sh`. You may first need to allow this script to be executed. Modern Linux desktop environments such as GNOME and KDE will let you do this in the file's Properties dialog, which you can invoke from the file browser. For example, in Ubuntu Linux, you can right-click the file and choose Properties from the context menu to invoke the dialog. In the Permissions tab in the dialog, you can select a checkbox to allow the file to be executed, as illustrated in Figure 1-1.

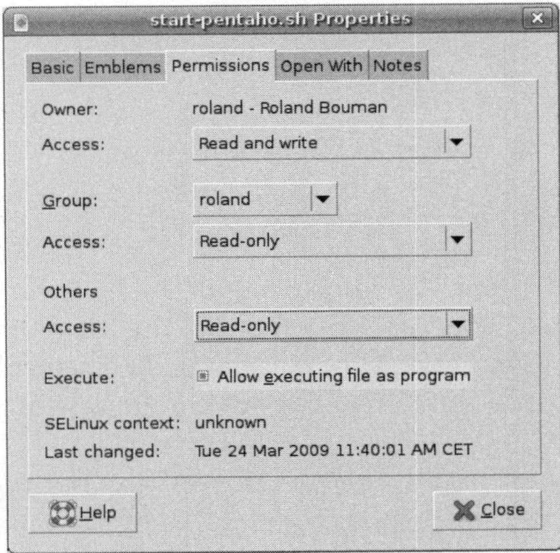

Figure 1-1: Making the start-pentaho.sh script executable

Alternatively, you can open a terminal and change directory (using the `cd` command) to the Pentaho home directory. From there, you can use the following command to make all `.sh` scripts executable:

```
shell> chmod ug+x *.sh
```

Now you can simply start the script by double-clicking it (you may need to confirm in a dialog) or by typing it in the terminal:

```
shell> ./start-pentaho.sh
```

After starting the script, you will see quite some output appearing in the console. You should leave open the terminal window in which you started the script.

NOTE **The `start-pentaho` script does two things.**

First, it starts a HSQLDB database server, which is used by the Pentaho server to store system data, as well as a sample database, which is used by most examples. By default, the HSQLDB database runs on port 9001. You should make sure no other server is running on that port.

Second, it starts a Tomcat server. By default, the Tomcat server listens on port 8080 for web requests. You should make sure no other server is running on that port, or the Pentaho BI Server will not be started successfully.

Logging in

After starting the server you can start your Internet browser to connect to the server. You should be able to use any of the major browsers (such as Mozilla Firefox, Microsoft Internet Explorer, Apple Safari, Opera, or Google Chrome) to do this. Navigate your browser to the following address:

```
http://localhost:8080
```

You are automatically redirected to the following:

```
http://localhost:8080/pentaho/Login
```

Shortly, you should see a Welcome page for the Pentaho user console. From there, you can log in to the server by pressing the large orange Login button. If you press the button, a Login box appears. From there, you can select a username from the drop-down list. For now, log in as the user Joe, as shown in Figure 1-2.

After selecting the username, you can press Login button to actually log in.

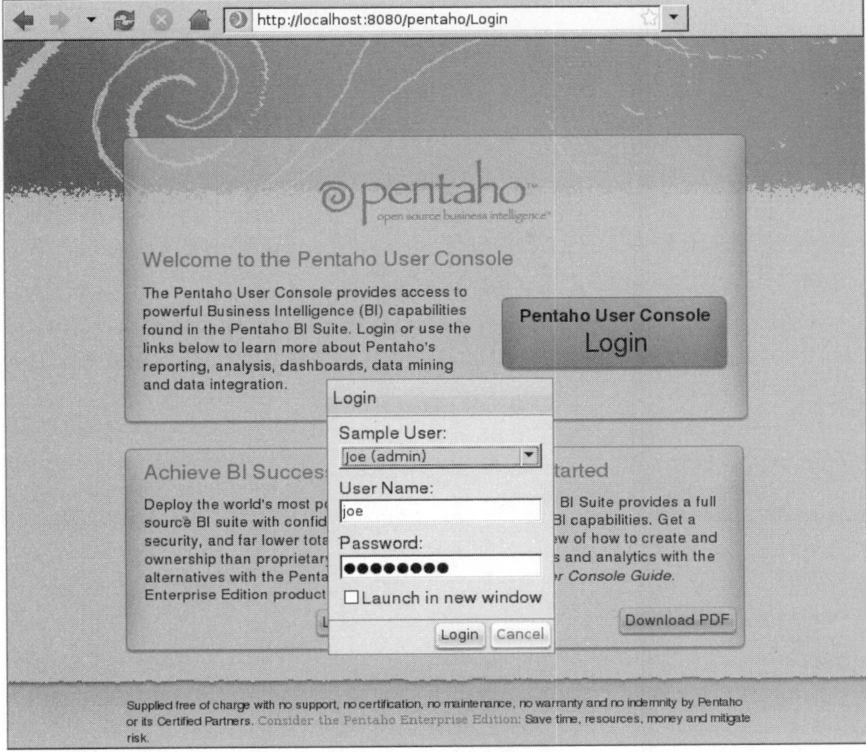

Figure 1-2: The Pentaho welcome screen and login dialog

Mantle, the Pentaho User Console

After confirming the login, you should see the Pentaho user console, as shown in Figure 1-3.

In the user console, you'll find a few elements to control the Pentaho BI Server:

- A menu bar, which is located at the top of the page and spans the page horizontally. Here you can find some standard menu items: File, View, Tools and Help.
- A toolbar containing several buttons, located immediately beneath the menu.
- A side pane, located on the left of the page, can be dynamically resized using the gray vertical bar at the far right of the pane. The pane can also be hidden/displayed in its entirety using the Toggle Browser button, which is the rightmost button on the toolbar.

- The tree view that is visible in the upper half of the side pane is called the Repository Browser. In Figure 1-3, this is labelled Browse. You can use this to browse through all BI content available in the Pentaho BI Server.
- A folder contents pane is located in the side pane, right beneath the solution repository browser. In Figure 1-3 this is labelled Files. It shows any contents of the selected folder in the solution repository (such as reports, dashboards and OLAP pivot tables) as a list of items. You can open an item by double-clicking it.
- A workspace. This is the larger pane on the right. When you double-click an item in the folder contents pane, it will be displayed here using a tab interface.

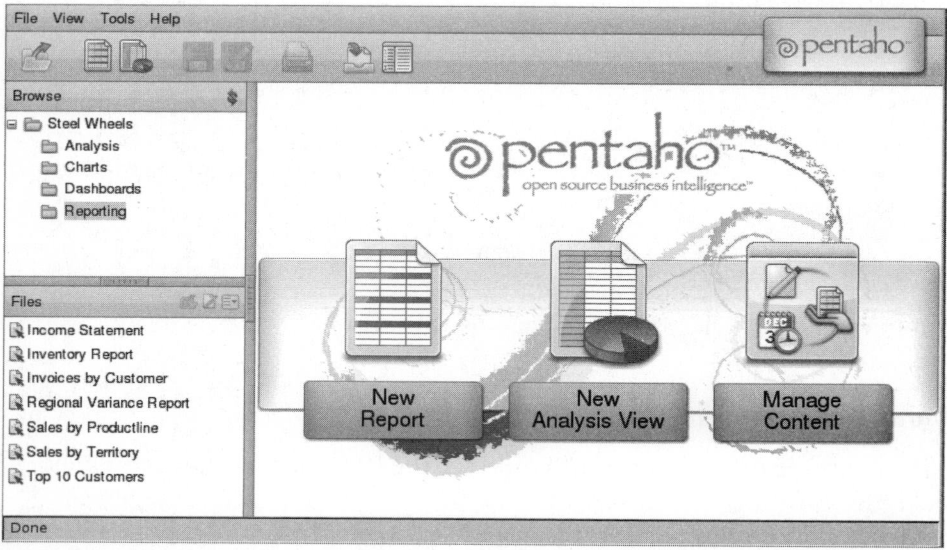

Figure 1-3: The Pentaho user console, also known as Mantle

Working with the Examples

The community edition of the Pentaho BI Server comes with two sets of examples:

- BI Developer Examples
- Steel Wheels

Each set of examples resides in its own Pentaho solution and is visible in the solution repository browser (see Figure 1-4).

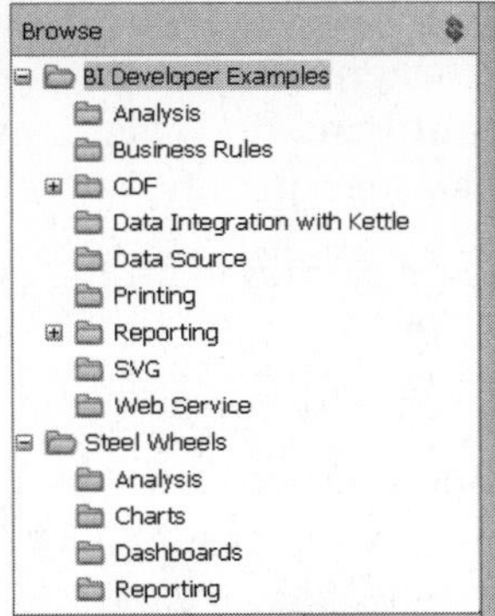

Figure 1-4: Two example solutions included in the Pentaho BI Server

Both of these Pentaho solutions contain good examples to demonstrate the types of reports you can create with Pentaho. Both solutions use the same sample data set. The BI Developer Examples focus more on the technical aspect of accomplishing a particular task, whereas the Steel Wheels examples illustrate how to combine techniques to build an application to support a classic cars business. The Steel Wheels examples also pay more attention to customizing look and feel.

Using the Repository Browser

You can access all of the examples using the repository browser. (This is the top pane of the left side bar in the user console, labelled Browse.) The repository browser offers a tree view that can be used to open and close the folders in the repository. To open a folder and reveal its subfolders, simply click once on the plus icon immediately on the left side of the folder icon. The folder's subfolders will become visible right beneath the parent folder, and the icon left of the folder icon changes to display a minus, indicating the folder is currently expanded. To close a folder and hide its subfolders, click on the minus icon.

To view the contents of a folder, click the folder icon or the folder name that appears directly on the right of the folder icon. The folder title will display a gray highlighting and its contents will become visible in the folder contents pane directly beneath the repository browser (in Figure 1-3, this is labelled Files).

To open an item that appears in the Files pane, double-click it. This will open a new tab page in the workspace, showing the output created by the item.

Understanding the Examples

Although you can learn a lot from the examples by simply running them, you can learn even more if you can see how they were built. Especially if you are a

Business Intelligence developer, you should consider examining the examples more closely using Pentaho Design Studio.

You'll learn the details about Pentaho Design Studio in Chapter 4, but you can follow these steps to get started quickly:

1. Download Pentaho Design Studio from the Pentaho downloads page at SourceForge.net.
2. Unzip the download to some location you find convenient.
3. Start Pentaho Design Studio. Microsoft Windows users can double-click `PentahoDesignStudio.exe`; users of UNIX-based systems can execute the `PentahoDesignStudio` binary file.
4. Use the main menu (File ➢ Switch Workspace) to change the workspace to the directory where you installed the Pentaho BI Server. The program will restart. In the opening splash screen, choose Workbench.
5. Create a new project by choosing File ➢ New ➢ Project. In the dialog, expand the General folder and choose Project to create a plain project. Click Next.
6. In the next dialog, enter `pentaho-solutions` for the project name. Make sure that whatever you type here corresponds exactly to the name of the `pentaho-solutions` directory located in the home directory of the Pentaho BI Server. The Use Default Location checkbox should be selected, and the location should automatically point to the Pentaho BI Server home directory.
7. Confirm the dialog.

In the Navigator tab page in the left side pane in Pentaho Design Studio, you should now see the `pentaho-solutions` project folder (which corresponds exactly with the actual `pentaho-solutions` folder). You can expand this folder and browse through the Pentaho solution repository.

Double-clicking on any items inside the folders will usually load the file in a new tab page in the Pentaho Design Studio Workspace. You can learn a lot, especially from opening the `.xaction` files that are present throughout the repository. Refer to Chapter 4 for more details on these files.

Beware that the items that show up in the repository browser in the user console of the Pentaho BI Server usually have a label that is distinct from the actual file name. This complicates things a bit in case you're looking for the corresponding item in Pentaho Design Studio, as the navigator there only displays file names. To discover the corresponding file name for any item shown in the repository browser, right-click the item and choose Properties in the context menu. This will pop up a dialog with a few tabs. The actual file name is shown in the General tab.

NOTE **The `.xaction` extension indicates an *action sequence*. Action sequences are Pentaho-specific lightweight processes to run or deliver BI content. In this particular case, the action sequence simply calls a Pentaho report. Action sequences are coded in a specific XML-format and typically stored in `.xaction` files. Action sequences are discussed in more detail in Chapter 4.**

Running the Examples

In the remainder of this chapter, we discuss a few items from these examples to give you a feel for what you can do with Pentaho solutions. For each item, we include references to the chapters of this book that relate to the example. We hope this will allow you to quickly get an overview of Pentaho's features and see how this book can help you master them.

Reporting Examples

Reporting is often one of the first requirements of any BI solution. Reporting is covered in detail in Chapter 13. Most of the reports discussed here are invoked from an action sequence; you can find more details on action sequences in Chapter 4.

The following sections examine a few of the reporting examples.

BI Developer Examples: Regional Sales - HTML

The Regional Sales - HTML example is one of the most straightforward reporting examples; as you would assume, it shows the sales figures for an example company broken down by region. You can find it in the Reporting folder in the BI Developer Examples set. The corresponding file name is `JFree_Quad.xaction`.

When you run the example, the report output is immediately shown in the workspace (see Figure 1-5).

In the report output you see an organization detailed by region (Central), department (Executive Management, Finance) and then position title (SVP Partnerships, CEO, and so on). For the position title level, you see the actual data. In this case, the data pertains to sales and shows the actual and projected (budgeted) sales numbers in the first two columns and the variance in the third column. You also see a totals line that sums up the figures for the department level, and if you could scroll down further you would also see the totals for the regional level, followed by the figures for another region. All the way down at the bottom of the report you would see totals for the entire business.

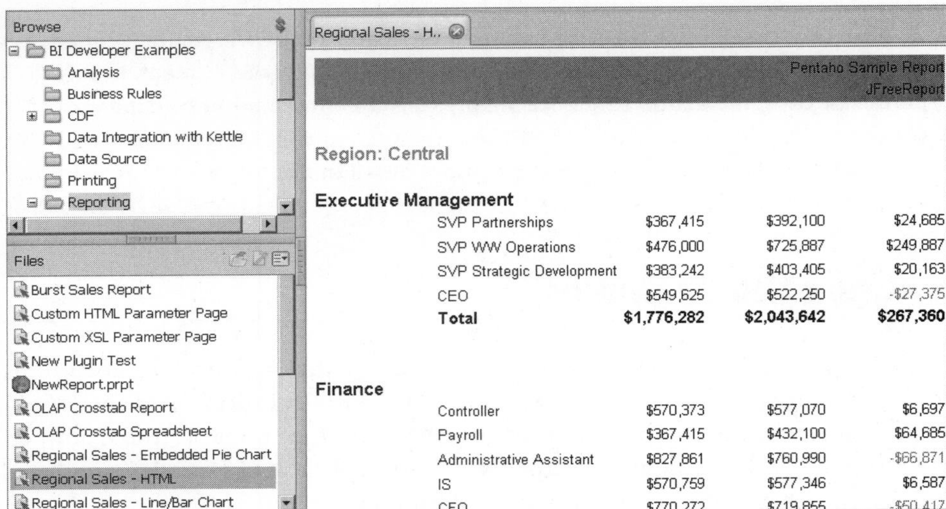

Figure 1-5: The Regional Sales - HTML sample report

Steel Wheels: Income Statement

The Income Statement example report from the Steel Wheels example set is another typical report with a self-explanatory name. You can find it in the Reporting folder beneath the Steel Wheels solution, and the corresponding file name is `Income Statement.xaction`. Figure 1-6 shows the report.

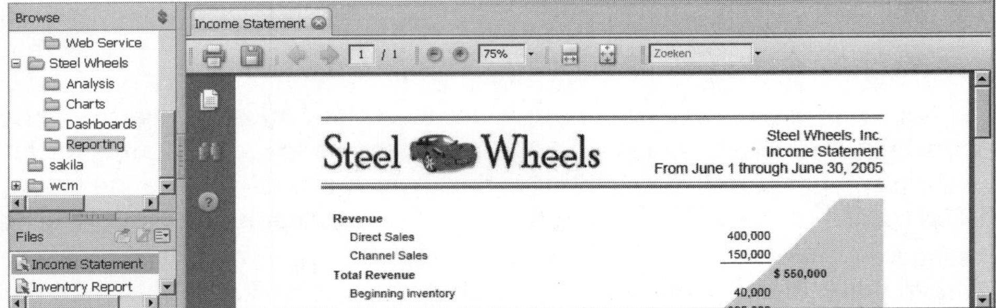

Figure 1-6: The Steel Wheels Income Statement report

A few differences from the Regional Sales report in the previous example are the styling and the output format. Although both reports were created with the Pentaho Report Designer, and both are rendered by the Pentaho reporting engine (which is the component responsible for interpreting reports and generating report output), they look quite different. Whereas the Regional Sales report outputs an HTML page, this report delivers a PDF file as output. In addition, this report shows adornments using a picture for a logo and a page background picture.

Steel Wheels: Top 10 Customers

In the previous section, we mentioned that the Income Statement report delivers output in the form of a PDF file, whereas the Regional Sales example outputs a plain web page. The Top 10 Customers report illustrates two more important features of the report output format. You can find this report also in the reporting folder in the Steel Wheels example set, and its file name is `Top Ten Customer ProductLine Analysis.xaction`. Running this example does not immediately show the report output, but displays the dialog shown in Figure 1-7 instead.

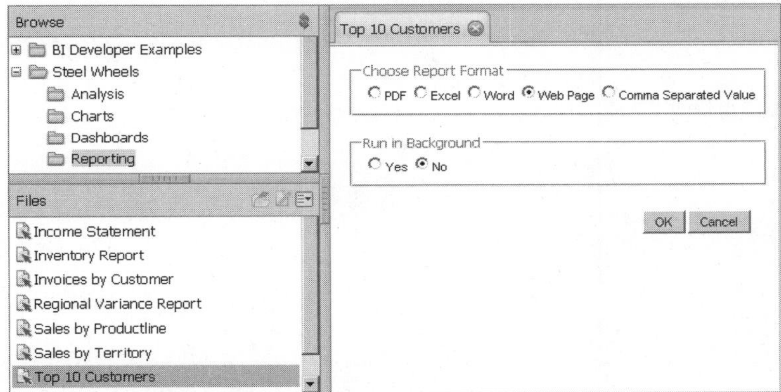

Figure 1-7: The Top 10 Customers report

As indicated by the dialog, you can choose from as many as five different output formats. In the previous reporting examples, the desired output format was stored as part of the report, but there is nothing in the reporting engine that forces this. This allows users to choose whatever format is most appropriate for the purpose at hand.

The dialog shown in Figure 1-7 illustrates another important feature of Pentaho reporting. The user can choose to wait for the report output now, or to have the Pentaho BI Server run the report in the background. The latter option will execute the report, but does not wait for the output to be returned. Rather, the output will be stored in the user's personal storage space on the server. This feature is especially useful for long-running reports.

You can find more on background execution and related features such as scheduling and subscription in Chapter 14.

BI Developer Examples: button-single-parameter.prpt

The previous example reports were all called from action sequences. In the upcoming Citrus release, reports can also be called directly. Examples using this feature are all located in the Reporting folder in the BI Developer Examples set.

This example takes a closer look at the `button-single-parameter.prpt` example. When you start it, the report loads immediately in the workspace. However, the actual report output won't show until you press one of the Region buttons that appear in the Report Parameters section at the top of the page. Figure 1-8 illustrates what you might see after you press the Central button.

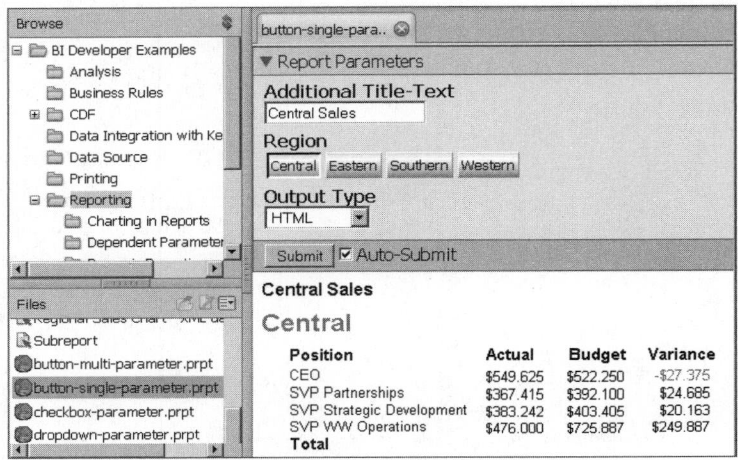

Figure 1-8: The button-single-parameter.prpt example

This example shows yet another feature of Pentaho, namely report parameters. Through parameters, the user can interact with the report and specify values to influence report behavior. Generally, this feature is used to allow the user to select only a portion of all possible report data.

In this example, there are two parameters. The Additional Title-Text parameter allows the user to specify a title that appears above all remaining report output. There is another parameter for Region, which allows the report to render output pertaining to only the specified region.

There are many more things you can do with report parameters, and these examples, as well as Chapter 13 of this book, should offer enough guidance for you to use this feature in a meaningful way.

Charting Examples

Whereas reports are great to communicate detailed information, they are less suitable for obtaining an overview of the data as a whole. For this purpose, charts and graphs usually work better. Charts are also better suited than reports to display trends over time.

The Pentaho BI Server ships with two different charting solutions:

- JFreeChart—A 100% Java chart library.
- Pentaho Flash Charts—A charting solution based on open flash charts (which requires Adobe Flash).

Pentaho reporting offers full integration with JFreeChart, and you will find detailed information on integrating charts with your reports in Chapter 13. You can find more information about JFreeChart charts and how to integrate them with dashboards in Chapter 17.

Steel Wheels: Chart Pick List

The Chart Pick List example is located in the Charts folder in the Steel Wheels example set. The corresponding file name is `ChartComponent_ChartTypes.xaction`. Executing the item loads a dialog in the workspace that allows you to choose a particular chart type. After picking the chart type, you can press the Run button to actually display the chart. Figure 1-9 shows how this works for a Pie Grid.

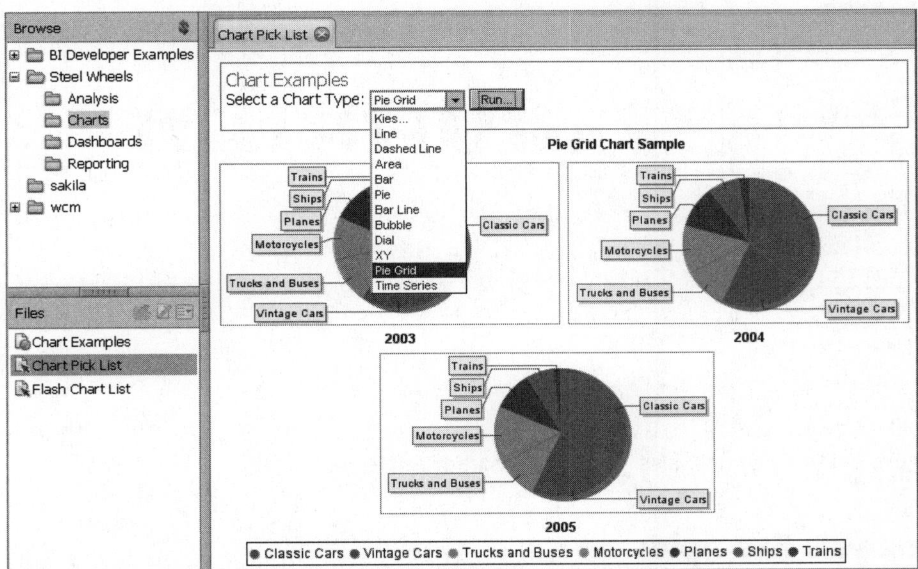

Figure 1-9: Pentaho charting using the JFreeChart Chart Pick List

Steel Wheels: Flash Chart List

Functionally, the Flash Chart List example is similar to the Chart Pick List example (which is based on JFreeChart). The difference is that the JFreeChart

Pick List example is based on the Open Flash Chart project. You can find the Flash Chart List also in the Charts folder within the Steel Wheels example set. The corresponding file name is `pentahoxml_picker.xaction`.

BI Developer Examples: Regional Sales - Line/Bar Chart

The Regional Sales - Line/Bar Chart example is located in the Reporting folder in the BI Developer Examples solution. The corresponding file is `JFree_SQLQuery_ComboChart.xaction`.

This example report displays a chart on the top of the page, and below that, a more detailed report shows the actual figures. In this case the chart is embedded into the report. The example report is shown if Figure 1-10.

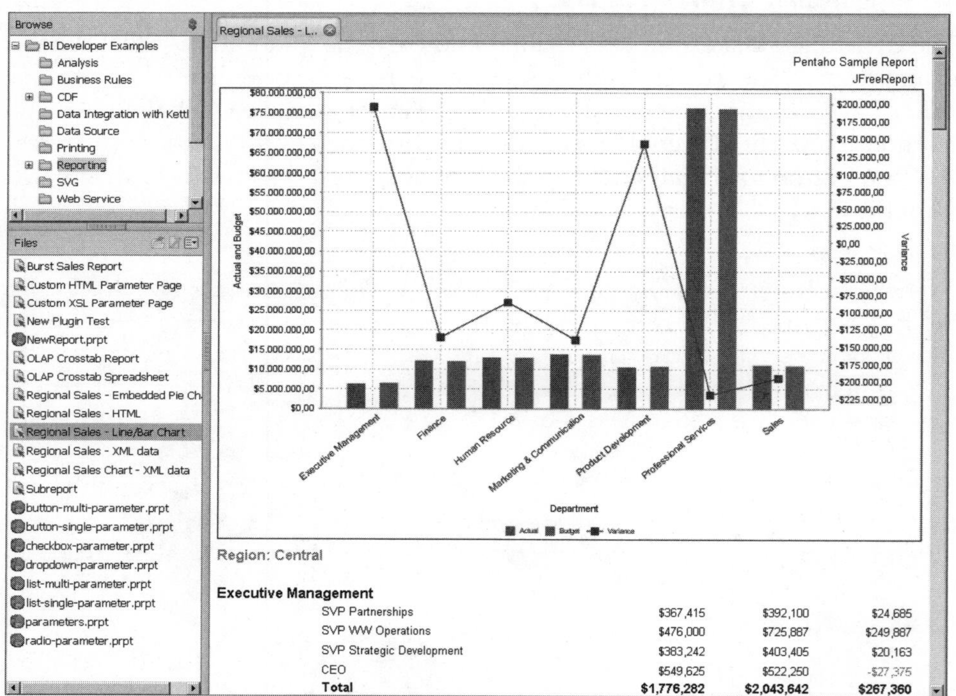

Figure 1-10: Regional Sales - Line/Bar Chart example

Analysis Examples

Like reporting, analysis is another essential feature of all BI solutions. Reports are typically static (save for parameters) and mainly used to support decisions that affect the business at the operational level. Analysis tends to be a lot more dynamic, and is typically used by managers to support decisions at the tactical and strategic level.

One of the typical elements in analytical solutions is that they allow the user to dynamically explore the data in an ad-hoc manner. Typically, the data is first presented at a highly aggregated level, say, total sales per year, and then the user can drill down to a more detailed level, say, sales per month per region. Any interesting differences between regions and/or months can then be used to drill into a new direction until a new insight or understanding of the business is obtained, which could then be used to affect plans for new promotions, next season's product catalog, or development of new products. This, in a nutshell, is what analysis is for.

Closely related to typical analytical questions and solutions is the dimensional model. Ultimately, this is what allows viewing data in aggregated form and features such as drill up/down. You will find detailed information about the dimensional model in Chapters 6, 7, and 8 of this book. In Chapter 15, we discuss the practical implementation of analytical applications using Mondrian and JPivot. All analytical examples presented in this chapter are based on Mondrian/JPivot.

BI Developer Examples: Slice and Dice

The Slice and Dice example is located in the Analysis folder in the BI Developer Examples. Its corresponding file is called `query1.xaction`.

The Slice and Dice example is the most basic analysis example included with the Pentaho BI Server. Running it produces a dynamic crosstab, also known as a *pivot table*. The pivot table shows actual and budgeted sales figures, as well as actual versus budget variance. In the context of Analytics, figures like these are called *measures* or *metrics*. The measures can be split according to Region, Department, and Position. These headings are shown at the left side of the pivot table and represent *dimensions*, which are aspects that describe the context of the metrics.

A typical feature is that the pivot table not only shows the figures themselves but also totals, and that the totals can be computed at several levels of the dimensions (see Figure 1-11).

In Figure 1-11, you can see the columns for Region, Department, and Positions. The first row in the pivot table shows the results for All Regions, Departments, and Positions, and the figures are aggregated or "rolled up" along these dimensions. This represents the highest level of aggregation. Below that, you see that the data is split; in the first column, All Regions is split into Central, Eastern, Southern, and Western, forming the second-highest level of aggregation for the Region dimension. In the first row for each individual region, you see the data rolled up only across Department and Positions. For the Central region, the data is again split, this time showing all individual departments. Finally, for the Executive Management department, data is again split according to position.

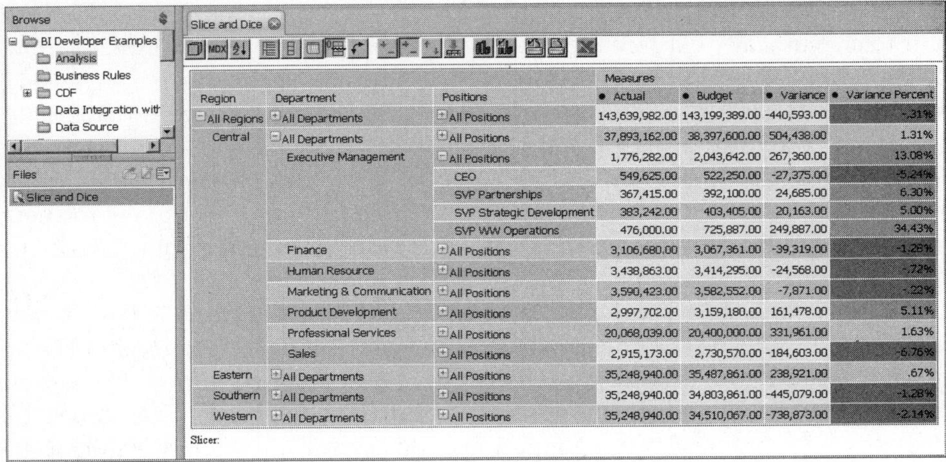

Figure 1-11: The Slice and Dice pivot table example

The splitting and rolling up is achieved dynamically by clicking on the plus and minus icons that appear next to the labels identifying Region, Department, and Positions. For example, by clicking on the plus icon next to any of the All Departments labels appearing in the second column, you can drill down and see how the rolled-up total value for any of the Sales metrics can be split up. Clicking a minus icon will roll the values back together into the total again, thus drilling up.

Steel Wheels Analysis Examples

In addition to the basic Slice and Dice example, you can find other interesting Analytics examples in the Analysis folder in the Steel Wheels example set. There you will find two examples:

- Market Analysis By Year
- Product Line Analysis

Like the basic Slice and Dice example, these examples display a pivot table, showing aggregated sales figures. In these examples, sales figures can be sliced along Product, Market (region), and Time.

Whereas the Slice and Dice example displayed only the measures on the horizontal axis, these examples show some more variety by placing the market on the horizontal axis. The Product Line Analysis example also places Time on the horizontal axis, beneath the Markets.

If you like, you can use alternative ways to set up the axes using the OLAP Navigator. You can invoke the OLAP Navigator by pressing the button with the cube icon on the toolbar that appears in the very top of the pages showing the analysis examples. The OLAP Navigator and a part of that toolbar are shown in Figure 1-12.

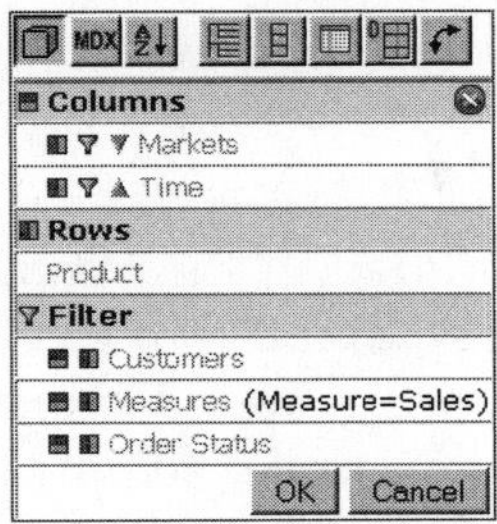

Figure 1-12: The OLAP Navigator

The OLAP Navigator shown in Figure 1-12 was taken from the Product Line Analysis example. In the top of the OLAP Navigator, you can see the caption Columns, and below that are two rows, Markets and Time. This corresponds directly with the Markets and Time shown along the horizontal axis of the pivot table. In the section below that, you see a Rows caption, with one row below it, Product. This corresponds with the products that are listed along the vertical axis of the pivot table. You can move the items in the Columns section to the Rows section and vice versa by clicking the small square in front of it.

There's a third section in the OLAP navigator labelled Filter. In this section, you find Customers, Measures, and Order Status. These items do not currently appear along one of the axes of the pivot table. You can move items from the Rows and Columns sections to the filter by clicking the filter icon. Moving items from the filter to either one of the axes is done by clicking the little square icon that corresponds to the axis to which you want to move the item.

We discuss the OLAP Navigator in detail in Chapter 15.

Dashboarding Examples

Dashboards are discussed in detail in Chapter 17. If you are interested in dashboards, you are strongly encouraged to check out the Community Dashboard Framework (CDF) dashboards examples included in the Pentaho BI Server. You can find them in the CDF folder in the BI Developer Examples solution.

A good way to start with Pentaho Dashboards is by navigating to the Samples subfolder of the CDF folder in the BI Developer Examples solution. Here you will find examples to use Charts, Reports, Analytic Pivot tables, and Maps in a dashboard, and see how you can tie these elements together.

Once you have a taste for what you can do with dashboards, you can read Chapter 17 and follow the detailed steps described there to build your own dashboard. When you are in the process of building your own dashboards, you will find the documentation included with the CDF examples indispensable. You can find detailed documentation in the Documentation subfolder of the CDF folder. The documentation found in the Component Reference folder will be an especially invaluable companion.

Other Examples

Many more examples are included in the Pentaho BI Server. These include examples to start ETL processes, to call web services, to send report output to a printer or by e-mail, and much more. However, we will not discuss these examples here. Many of these examples require additional setup, and others are not particularly instructive unless you have need for that particular feature. However, readers are encouraged to experiment with the remaining examples.

Summary

This chapter provided an introduction to the Pentaho software and walked you through some of the examples that are shipped with it. After installing the software and exploring the examples, you should have a good idea of what you can do with Pentaho. The rest of this book will teach you how to work with each part of Pentaho to create your own Pentaho solutions.

CHAPTER

2

Prerequisites

The intention of this book is to let you, the reader, develop a Business Intelligence solution from start to finish (and even beyond because BI solutions need maintenance as well). In order to do this, you will need some additional tools that are not part of the Pentaho BI platform. These are primarily database-related tools used to design and create a database, validate the quality of the data in the source systems, and perform maintenance tasks such as making backups, creating users, and setting up data access restrictions. How to use the different tools is described in the respective chapters—for example, the subject of data profiling is covered in Chapter 8 and a hands-on tutorial of the tool we use for that task is included there as well. This chapter explains where to get the software and how it can be set up on a developer system.

NOTE **If you already have a running system with Java enabled and MySQL installed, you can probably skip most of this chapter. Its aim is to get the novice user up and running with the tools required to design, build, and manage databases in a Pentaho/MySQL installation.**

Software release cycles, especially in the open source world, are relatively short. Since the time this book was finalized in July of 2009, new versions of the software we used may already have become available. In order to avoid possible confusion we list the version numbers of the software packages we used in the book:

- Ubuntu 9.04 (64 and 32 bit)
- Windows XP Pro SP3
- Sun Java 6.0.13

- MySQL Server 5.1.34
- MySQL GUI Tools 5.0.12
- Power*Architect 0.9.13
- Squirrel 3.0.1
- eobjects DataCleaner 1.5.1

Basic System Setup

Before you can set up anything at all there are some very basic things to take care of, such as making sure that you have set up Java correctly on your machine. For some tasks, you will need to work with the terminal. If you're not familiar with that, don't worry; we explain the basics to get you going. We assume that most of our readers will be familiar with using a Windows-based computer, but hope you will take this opportunity to explore the option of using Pentaho on a Linux installation. All the Linux examples we provide here will be based on Ubuntu Linux with a GNOME desktop, but using other Linux distributions shouldn't be very different in most cases.

Installing Ubuntu

If you are among the readers that view this book as a good opportunity to start experimenting with Linux as well as the Pentaho BI Suite, you might appreciate some quickstart notes about how to go about doing this. There are several options to get an Ubuntu system up and running, depending on what system you want to install it on and whether you want to replace or augment a running Windows system. This section is not a complete step-by-step installation guide, but points out the different options and where to get started.

First, you'll need to get the software. It can be freely downloaded from `http://www.ubuntu.com`, where you will find different versions for different hardware architectures. The website displays both a desktop and a server edition, but unless you want to take a really deep dive into Linux, do not start with the server edition. This has only a character-based terminal interface (no GUI) and not all the bells and whistles you might expect. The next choice is the one between 32 and 64 bit. Most modern computers will be able to run the 64-bit version of Ubuntu, and if you want to use Ubuntu as your primary operating system that's probably your best choice. All other choices, for instance which language you want to use, are part of the installation itself. The downloaded file is an ISO image and you'll need an image burner to create a bootable CD from the downloaded file. Most CD burning programs are capable of doing that, but if you use Windows and don't have such a program, you can download and install the free Active@ ISO Burner from `http://www.ntfs.com/iso_burner_free.htm`.

Using Ubuntu in Native Mode

By *native* we mean that you will install the software on a computer so the machine can boot and run Ubuntu directly from the hard drive. If you're not sure yet about whether or not Ubuntu is the way to go, just insert the disk and wait for the welcome screen. The first option is to run Ubuntu in Live mode, meaning that you don't install anything but run the software from the CD. If you like it, click the install button to start the installation process; if you don't like it, just eject the CD and continue using Windows.

The installation process will ask you a couple of questions. Most are fairly easy to answer, such as language, time zone, and location, while for others you might need a little help. The most important one is about the disk configuration. Ubuntu will happily let you keep your existing operating system, resulting in a dual-boot configuration. In that case, each time you switch on your computer you can select to run either Windows or Ubuntu.

TIP **If you have a new computer and would like to create a dual-boot system, first install Windows, then Ubuntu. If you first install Ubuntu the Windows installer will overwrite the boot-partition of your hard drive.**

A step-by-step set of instructions on how to install Ubuntu can be found in the online help on `https://help.ubuntu.com/community/GraphicalInstall`.

Using a Virtual Machine

Most modern computers have ample processing power and memory, so it might be an option to use a virtual machine to run Ubuntu. In that case, Ubuntu operates as a *guest* system, whereas your regular operation system acts as the *host*. There are many solutions available for running Ubuntu as a virtual machine; most of them can be found in the online help at `https://help.ubuntu.com/community/VirtualMachines`. We work a lot with VirtualBox from Sun (`http://www.virtualbox.org`), in fact, half of this book was written on a virtual Windows XP machine using VirtualBox on a Ubuntu 64-bit host system. The interesting part of using virtualization software is that there is also a large collection of ready-to-run virtual machine images available for download, which means that there is hardly any installation required to get a new system up and running. In case of Pentaho, the best option available is created by InfoBright, an analytical database vendor. You can download a complete image from `http://www.infobright.org/Downloads/Pentaho_ICE_VM` that contains the following:

- Ubuntu 8.04 server operating system
- InfoBright Community Edition
- Pentaho BI Suite Community Edition

The image is a `.vmdk` file, the native VMware file format, but VirtualBox can open this file type as well without any problems.

Working with the Terminal

A Linux terminal is basically the equivalent of the Windows command screen and can be used as such. There are a couple of small differences to take into consideration, such as the fact that in Linux there are no drive letters and the path names contain forward slashes. There are also bigger differences such as the fact that most Linux commands are totally different from their Windows counterparts, and that, in Linux, everything is case-sensitive. Moving to a directory with `cd /opt/Pentaho` can return an error message telling you that there is no such file or directory, while `cd /opt/pentaho` will work just fine. Remember that in Linux, `pentaho` and `Pentaho` are two completely different words!

There are two ways to start a terminal screen, or to put it more precisely, there are two types of terminal screens: the basic X terminal and the GNOME terminal. The X terminal looks very much like a Windows command screen; it has a black background with white characters and there are no menu options. You can start an X terminal by pressing Alt+F2 and typing the command `xterm`. The Run Application dialog appears, displaying the command line ready to accept your command. Unlike a Windows terminal, however, the dialog cannot return anything; it just executes your command when you press Enter.

The second terminal screen is the GNOME terminal, which has a menu and a white background with black characters. This is the one we'll refer to from here on. You can start the GNOME terminal by selecting Applications ➤ Accessories ➤ Terminal or by pressing Alt+F2 and using the command `gnome-terminal`.

We cannot cover the complete set of commands, but the ones you'll need most are provided in the following sections.

NOTE **For a useful reference on using the command line on a Linux system, try *Ubuntu Linux Toolbox*, by Christopher Negus and Francois Caen, Wiley Publishing, 2008.**

Directory Navigation

You can use the following commands to navigate through the directory structure:

`cd`—Change directory, same as in Windows.

`cd ..`—Move one level up (`cd ../..` moves two levels up, and so on).

`cd ~`—Go to your home directory.

`cd /`—Go to the root (system) directory.

The operating system "knows" the paths so when you enter the first characters of a directory and press the Tab key, the full name is completed automatically. For example, type `cd /o`, press the Tab key, and the path is autocompleted to `cd /opt/`. Add a `p` and press Tab again to obtain the `cd /opt/pentaho/` command. Of course these directories have to exist, so if there is no `/opt/pentaho` directory, it's obvious that the operating system cannot find it.

When you want to clear your screen and have the prompt displayed at the top of the window again, just enter the command `clear` and press Enter.

Command History

By using the up and down arrows, you can browse through previously issued commands. All commands are stored in a command *history file*, which can be viewed by typing `history` at the command line. If the list is long, you can use `history | more` and page through the list with the spacebar (CTRL+C to end). If you want to reuse a specific command from history, you can type an exclamation mark followed by the history file line number (for example, !174) and the command will be executed again. A more flexible option is to use the CTRL+R key combination, which starts a `reverse-i` text search in the history file, meaning that the most recently issued command containing the string will be found first. Note that you can continue typing the search string, which will dynamically change the argument for the search. For example, pressing CTRL+R and entering `e` displays the following:

```
(reverse-i-search)`e': clear
```

Adding `c` displays the following:

```
(reverse-i-search)`ec': echo $JAVA_HOME
```

The command can be simply accepted (and executed) by pressing Enter, but if you want to modify the command first, press the left or right arrow, which will open the command on the command line for editing.

Using Symbolic Links

Most programs go directly to your home directory when you want to open or save a file. Sometimes it is not possible to change the default path where the application should look for folders and files. The Pentaho design tools like the Report Designer or the Mondrian Schema Workbench mostly work from the home directory of the user who started the program. This isn't always a convenient location to start, especially when the last location used isn't remembered by the program either. Opening a different path each time you want to open or save a file takes time, so the capability to open the right folder directly from your home directory would be a welcome convenience. This is where *symbolic links* come in handy.

Creating Symbolic Links in Ubuntu

A symbolic link in Linux looks like a shortcut in Windows, but creating them is a bit different.

NOTE **Windows shortcuts are regular files that can be resolved only by Windows and Windows Explorer. Windows Vista supports "true" symbolic links.**

There are two ways of creating symbolic links (or *symlinks* as they are usually called): by using the GNOME file browser Nautilus, or by entering commands at the command line. When using Nautilus, just right-click on the file or folder for which you want to create a link, select Make Link from the drop-down menu, and copy the resulting link to the desired location after which it can be renamed. Using the command line requires knowledge of the syntax, which is pretty straightforward. The command is a simple `ln`, followed by options, the location to link to, and the name of the link. To create a symlink in your home directory that points to the Pentaho solutions directory, the following command can be entered:

```
ln -s /opt/pentaho/biserver-ce/pentaho-solutions ~/pentaho
```

The `-s` option denotes that you are creating a link to a directory, not a single file. Now any reference to `~/pentaho` (pentaho subdirectory in the current user's home folder) is automatically translated to the target folder.

Creating Symlinks in Windows Vista

Creating symlinks in Vista works in a similar way as in Linux when the command line is used, but the command and parameters differ. To make things more confusing, the argument order is reversed: in Windows the link is specified before the target. The same symlink as in the preceding example can be created with the following command:

```
mklink /D C:\Documents and Settings\Administrator\My Documents\pentaho
 C:\Program Files\pentaho\biserver-ce\pentaho-solutions
```

Java Installation and Configuration

All Pentaho programs are developed in Java and require a Java Virtual Machine to be present on the computer that will run Pentaho. Installing Java has been made very easy on both Linux and Windows, thanks to Sun Microsystems. Besides installing Java, one important configuration step is left—setting the environment variable `JAVA_HOME`. Without this, Java programs don't know where to look for the Java libraries and your Java software still won't run. (You can skip this section if you've already installed Java and set your environment variable.)

Installing Java on Ubuntu Linux

You can install Java on a Linux machine in two ways. The first option is to do it manually, by going to `www.java.com`, downloading the installer, and running it on your system. The second and better option is to use the Synaptic Package Manager. The Java packages are part of the regular Ubuntu repositories, so open the System-Administration menu and select Synaptic Package Manager. Enter the `su` (superuser) password to start Synaptic. In the quick search box, type `java6`, which will display all available Java packages from Sun. Select the sun-java6-jdk package (Java Development Kit), which has a couple of required packages that will be automatically selected by Synaptic. Click Apply to download and install the software. This will install Java in the subdirectory `/usr/lib/jvm/`.

Alternatively, you can use the command line to install the Java SDK. Open a terminal screen and type the following commands:

```
shell> sudo apt-get update
shell> sudo apt-get install sun-java6-jdk
```

The first command ensures that all repository information is up to date; the second command will install the Java packages after you've confirmed the installation by typing Y. During the installation you'll have to agree to the terms of the license agreement.

When you open the installation directory `/usr/lib/jvm` you'll notice two new entries: the actual Java directory with a version number postfix, and a symbolic link that points to this first directory. The symbolic link is the one that you'll use for the environment variable. First check whether the installation succeeded by opening a terminal screen and entering the `java -version` command. This should give you an output similar to the one listed here:

```
java version "1.6.0_13"
Java(TM) SE Runtime Environment (build 1.6.0_13-b03)
Java HotSpot(TM) Client VM (build 11.3-b02, mixed mode, sharing)
```

The environment variable can be set by adding an extra line to the file `/etc/environment`, but you need root privileges to do so. In the same terminal screen, enter the command `sudo gedit /etc/environment`. This will start the editor with the file opened. Just add the following line to this file:

```
JAVA_HOME="/usr/lib/jvm/java-6-sun"
```

Save the file and close the editor. You can check whether the variable is set correctly by issuing the echo `$JAVA_HOME` command, but you'll notice that nothing is returned yet. If you want to activate the variable in the terminal session, you can use the command `source /etc/environment`, but to activate the variable for all sessions, just log off and log on again (there is no need to reboot the system).

Installing Java on Windows

For installation, just open a browser, go to `www.java.com`, and click on the Free Java Download button. Follow the instructions on the site to install Java. The next step is to set the environment variable. Environment variables can be added by opening System Properties in the control panel and choosing the Advanced tab and selecting System Settings (or from the Advanced System Settings directly in Vista). Add a new system variable named `JAVA_HOME` that points to the Java install path, as shown in Figure 2-1 (the path may be different on your own system).

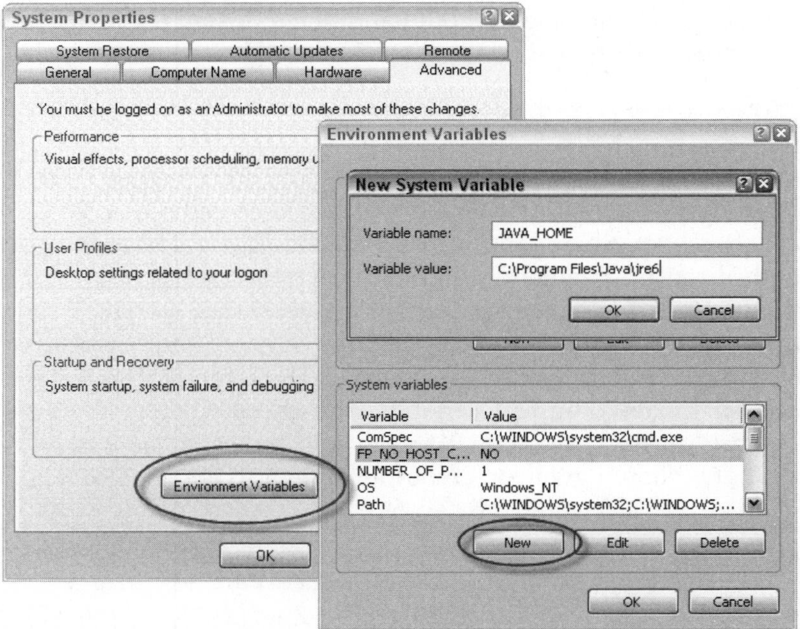

Figure 2-1: Setting the JAVA_HOME variable

Reboot your machine to activate the setting. If you don't want to reboot your machine right away, it is possible to set a temporary system variable by opening a command screen and using the SET command to set the environment variable:

```
SET JAVA_HOME=C:\Program Files\Java\jre6
```

You can verify the setting with the ECHO command, followed by the variable whose value should be returned enclosed in percentage signs. This will display the path if it has been set correctly, or the name of the variable if this is not yet specified:

```
shell> echo %FOO%
%FOO%

shell> echo %JAVA_HOME%
C:\Program Files\Java\jre6
```

MySQL Installation

This book will make extensive use of MySQL so next to having Java enabled, this is the second important prerequisite to following along with all the examples and tutorials. Whether you use Windows or Linux, installing MySQL is pretty straightforward and, in the case of Ubuntu, almost automatic.

Installing MySQL Server and Client on Ubuntu

You can install MySQL on Linux in two ways: manually, by downloading the installation files and doing all the configuration yourself, or by using the Package Manager. The MySQL database packages are part of the Ubuntu repositories, and since the release of Ubuntu version 9.04, MySQL version 5.1 is available from the repository as well. You might choose to do a manual install, for example, to try the latest features or to have full control over the installation. If you need to do a manual install, check the MySQL website for installation instructions.

To install MySQL using Synaptic, open the Synaptic Package Manager from the System-Administration menu and search for mysql. Browse to the msql-server-5.1 package and mark it for installation. Note that all required additional packages are automatically selected; just confirm by selecting Mark and select Apply to start downloading and installing the packages.

TIP **You can simultaneously select the mysql-admin package and skip the separate GUI install step.**

The Debian configurator will ask for a new password for the MySQL "root" user. This is a new password for a new user that will be created for starting and managing the MySQL instance. Unfortunately, setting a password is not required but we strongly advise you to set one (and don't forget it!). For the mail server settings, just accept the given defaults. When the installation is finished, you'll get a "Changes applied" message. Close this and the Package Manager as well—the MySQL server has been installed.

You can check the installation by connecting to the MySQL instance from the command line. Open a terminal screen and type the `mysql` command followed by `-uroot -p<your_password>`. This should open the MySQL command prompt:

```
shell> mysql -uroot -pPassWord
Welcome to the MySQL monitor.  Commands end with ; or \g.
Your MySQL connection id is 43
Server version: 5.1.31-1ubuntu2 (Ubuntu)

Type 'help;' or '\h' for help. Type '\c' to clear the buffer.

mysql>
```

Exit the client with the `quit` command followed by a semicolon:

```
mysql> quit;
Bye
```

Congratulations, the server is running!

Installing MySQL Server and Client on Windows

The Windows installers for MySQL 5.1 can be found at `http://dev.mysql.com/downloads/mysql/5.1.html`. Select the MSI installer and download this to your computer. After starting the installer, you're presented with three install options: Typical, Complete, or Custom. The first option will do, but will install your data files in the directory `C:\Documents and Settings\All Users\Application Data\MySQL\MySQL Server 5.1`. If you prefer to have the data files located somewhere else, select the Custom install and change the MySQL Data Files path. After displaying some commercial MySQL Enterprise information screens, the MySQL configuration is started; select the Standard Configuration and accept all the defaults in the next screen. Now the root password screen appears. Although you can leave the root password blank, we strongly advise against it. If you want to be able to manage the database from machines other than localhost, you'll have to mark the root access checkbox as well. The final screen lets you execute the configuration settings and starts the MySQL service on your computer.

MySQL GUI Tools

The MySQL client is merely a piece of software to connect to a MySQL server. To work with the database you'll need to add two more tools, the MySQL Administrator and the MySQL Query Browser. Both are included in the GUI tools, which can be found at `http://dev.mysql.com/downloads/gui-tools/5.0.html`.

Ubuntu Install

The GUI tools download site enables you to download the Linux binary installers, but the tools are also available in the Ubuntu repositories. Because this is a more convenient way of installing the software, open Synaptic Package Manager again, search for mysql-admin, and mark it for installation. Note that the packages `mysql-query-browser` and `mysql-gui-tools-common` are automatically included. Select Apply to install the tools. Your menu will now be enriched with a new main entry called Programming, with two items: the Administrator and the Query Browser.

Windows Install

Just download the Windows installer from `http://dev.mysql.com/downloads/gui-tools/5.0.html`. It's a simple Windows installer, which doesn't require any special settings. Accepting the defaults will do just fine. The program shortcuts can be found in the Windows Start menu under the MySQL entry.

Database Tools

Working on BI solutions often means working with data and databases. Each database comes with its own database management and query tools, but what if you need to access multiple databases or need a tool to develop a new database in a visual way? This section introduces three of our favorite tools for designing, developing, and querying databases. All tools are written in Java so they will run on any platform as long as a JVM is installed.

Power*Architect and Other Design Tools

Pentaho does not provide the design tools needed to develop a data warehouse because there are many databases out there and in a lot of cases organizations already have one or more design tools available. For supporting the full design lifecycle, from business to logical to technical modelling, including model comparisons, version and lifecycle management, auto documentation features, and team support, there are (as far as we're aware of) no open source solutions available. But if there are, please let us know! To design database schemas, you have a couple of options, both freeware and open source. The following is a small, but far from complete list:

- **Power*Architect** (`http://www.sqlpower.ca/page/architect`) — Our tool of choice for this book. Chapter 8 contains further instructions about installation of Power*Architect and how to use the tool to create database diagrams and data marts.
- **MySQL Workbench** (`http://dev.mysql.com/downloads/workbench/5.1.html`) — Standard database design tool from MySQL and the successor to the popular DBDesigner.
- **Mogwai ERDesigner** (`http://mogwai.sourceforge.net`) — Eclipse-based, but there's also a Squirrel plugin available (see next section).
- **ERMaster** (`http://ermaster.sourceforge.net`) — Still with some Japanese help texts here and there.
- **Azzurri Clay** (`www.azzurri.jp`) — Widely used Eclipse plugin. The core edition is free.

Squirrel SQL Client

Squirrel is an open source SQL query tool that allows you to open and query just about any database that's ever been developed, as long as a JDBC driver is available. Installing Squirrel is easy: go to `www.squirrelsql.org/` and follow the instructions in the Download and Installation section for downloading the file.

Ubuntu Install

We will modify the installation instructions from the site slightly, although the defaults will work as well. If you follow the defaults, the tool will be installed in the directory `/usr/local/SQuirreL SQL Client`. Because we don't like installing anything in `/usr/local`, let alone using a mixed case folder name with spaces in it, we recommend installing it as follows:

1. Open a terminal and navigate to the folder where you downloaded the installer file. Use the following command to start the installer:

   ```
   sudo java -jar squirrel-sql-<version>-install.jar
   ```

   In the preceding command, `<version>` should be replaced with the current version number.
2. The third screen in the installer asks for an installation path. Change this into `/opt/tools/squirrel`, press Next, and then click OK to accept the creation of the new folder.

3. The following screen shows a long list of plugins that can be installed. Depending on the databases and languages you'd like to use, you can make your selection. Just make sure to select the MySQL checkbox and to leave the Standard plugins checkbox selected because that one contains the Code Completion feature. To get a description of all available plugins, go to `http://www.squirrelsql.org/index.php?page=plugins`.
4. The last screen of the installer asks for a location for the shortcut. That's for Windows and won't help very much on a Linux machine, so just press Next to finish the installation.

Squirrel can now be started by executing the `squirrel-sql.sh` script from a command line, but for more convenience we'll create a Launcher to add it to the menu. Open the menu editor by right-clicking the left part of the standard panel and select Edit Menus. A new entry can be added to any of the default main menu options or you can create a new one. Click New Item to add a menu item and enter the available fields, as shown in Figure 2-2.

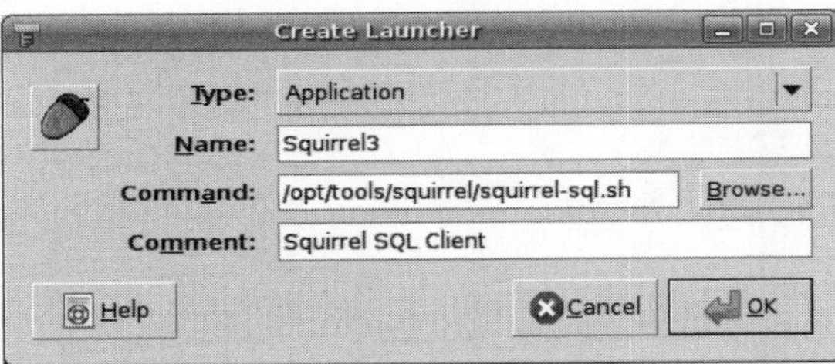

Figure 2-2: Squirrel launcher

The comment field is optional, and the icon can be changed by clicking it and navigating to the `/opt/tools/squirrel/icons` folder.

Windows Install

Installing Squirrel on Windows takes even less effort than on Linux; just double-click the downloaded installation jar and the installer starts. The tool will be installed in `C:\Program Files\SQuirreL SQL Client`. If you prefer a different location you can, of course, change it here. Now the selections for shortcuts in the last screen will create the additional menu entry automatically.

SQLeonardo

The last tool you might want to consider is SQLeonardo, a SQL query tool that can do something that is not yet available in Squirrel: graphical query design. The software can be downloaded from `http://sourceforge.net/projects/sqleonardo` in a zip file with only one `.jar` file inside. Extract the zip file to the desired location (in our case, `/opt/tools/sqleonardo`) and create a Launcher (Linux) or Menu shortcut (Windows). Don't forget to set the permission for the file to ''Allow executing file as program.'' Otherwise, it will not start. Figure 2-3 shows the interface for designing queries with the Pentaho sample database opened.

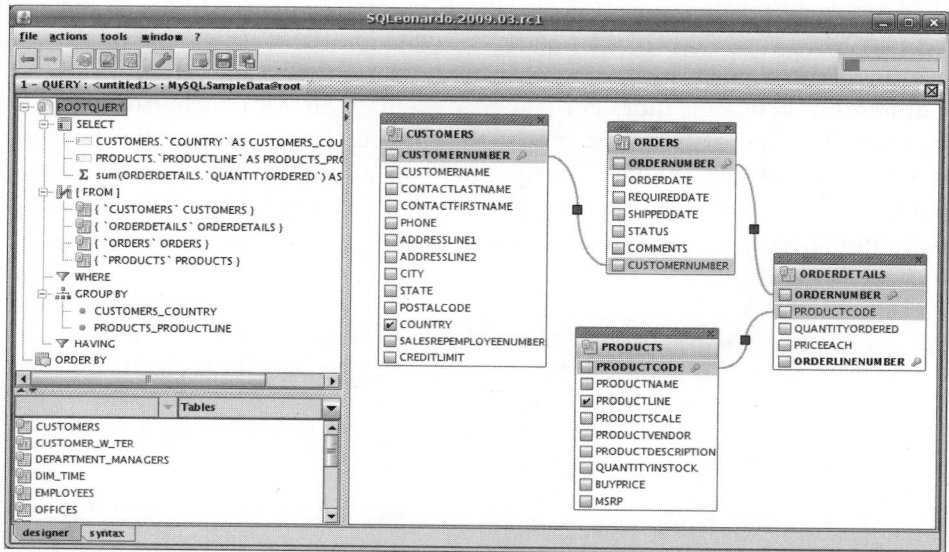

Figure 2-3: SQLeonardo query interface

We cover SQLeonardo in more depth in Chapter 13 because it is also the graphical query tool in the Pentaho Report Designer.

Summary

This chapter introduced the supplemental tools needed to develop and manage a BI solution. In fact, you can hardly call MySQL a supplemental tool because it forms the basis of the solution we will develop during the course of this book. We covered the following in this chapter:

- Working with the command line in Ubuntu or other Linux distributions
- Setting up Java and the `JAVA_HOME` environment variable
- Installation of MySQL and the MySQL GUI tools

- Introduction to database design tools
- Installation of Squirrel, a universal database query tool
- Installation of SQLeonardo, a convenient graphical query builder

Installation of the tools described in this chapter is just a prerequisite for setting up the sample databases and examples we will use throughout the book. All the database creation scripts, data files, and setup instructions we use in the examples can be found on the book's website at `www.wiley.com/go/pentahosolutions`.

CHAPTER

3

Server Installation and Configuration

In this chapter, you learn the basic tasks involved in configuring the Pentaho BI Server. In addition, we introduce you to setting up and working with the Pentaho Administration Console (PAC).

Server Configuration

As we illustrated in Chapter 1, you can run the Pentaho BI Server immediately after downloading and unzipping the software. However, the default configuration is typically not sufficient for production purposes for the following reasons:

- The BI Server is not configured to start automatically when the operating system reboots.
- Initially, the BI Server will be accessible only from port 8080, which might conflict with another service running on your machine.
- Some features, such as e-mail messaging and publishing BI content, require extra configuration in order for them to work at all.
- By default, an in-memory HSQLDB database is used for all system databases, and you might want to use an RDBMS that you are more familiar with instead.
- You may need to supply extra JDBC drivers in order to connect to a particular RDBMS.

In this chapter, we describe how to alter the default configuration of the Pentaho BI Server. Although we do not provide an in-depth guide to Pentaho Server administration and configuration, this chapter covers how some of its major components are controlled.

Installation

We already described how to download and extract the Pentaho BI Server. If necessary, see Chapter 1 for detailed instructions. The unpacked directory contains two subdirectories:

- `administration-console`—This is an administrative service to manage and configure the actual Pentaho BI Server. This is also known as PAC (for Pentaho Administration Console).
- `biserver-ce`—This is the actual Pentaho BI Server (Community Edition).

Installation Directory

In Chapter 1, we also mentioned that you can install the Pentaho Server at any location you desire. However, depending on your operating system, there are some locations that (by convention) make more sense than others. For the purpose of the remainder of the book, we will assume the following locations:

- `C:\Program Files\pentaho` for Windows systems
- `/opt/pentaho` for UNIX-based systems

You should create this directory and move both the `administration-console` and the `biserver-ce` directories (including their contents) to this directory. In the remainder of this book, we will refer to the `biserver-ce` directory as the Pentaho home directory, and the `administration-console` directory as the PAC home directory.

NOTE You need root privileges to create a subdirectory in `/opt`. For example, on Ubuntu Linux, you can use `sudo` to temporarily obtain these privileges:

```
shell> sudo mkdir /opt/pentaho
```

User Account

For security considerations, you should consider creating a separate user account to run server applications such as Pentaho. Typically, the user account would also be made owner of the directory containing the software. In addition, this user account would be locked out of the remainder of the system. This is a matter of damage control: a bug in the software or a hacked server simply cannot do any harm outside its own software directories—that is, provided the user account reserved for Pentaho does not have any permissions outside the Pentaho tree. Listing 3-1 shows one possible way of setting this up in Linux:

Listing 3-1: Setting up a user account, group, and directory for Pentaho on UNIX-based systems

```
# create a group for the pentaho user
shell> sudo addgroup pentaho
Adding group 'pentaho' (GID 1001) ...

# create a system user for pentaho
shell> sudo adduser --system --ingroup pentaho --disabled-login pentaho
Adding system user 'pentaho' (UID 115) ...
Adding new user 'pentaho' (UID 115) with group 'pentaho' ...
Creating home directory '/home/pentaho' ...

# create software directory, and unpack the software there
shell> sudo mkdir /opt/pentaho
shell> sudo cd /opt/pentaho
shell> sudo tar -zxvf ~/downloads/biserver-ce-CITRUS-M2.tar.gz

#...lots of output...

# grant ownership of software directories to the pentaho user
shell> sudo chown -R pentaho:pentaho /opt/pentaho
```

After setting up the user account and granting ownership to the Pentaho software, you can start Pentaho from the command line using a command like this:

```
shell> sudo -u pentaho JAVA_HOME=usr/lib/jvm/java-6-sun ./start-pentaho.sh
```

Note the `-u pentaho` in the command: this ensures the command will be executed with the permissions of the `pentaho` user. If you omit that, the server will run with root permission, which is exactly what you want to avoid! In the next section, you see how you can set things up so the Pentaho BI Server starts automatically when the operating system boots.

Configuring Tomcat

The Pentaho BI Server is preconfigured based on the Apache Tomcat Servlet container. The Tomcat software resides in the `tomcat` directory, which resides within the Pentaho Server home directory. By default, Tomcat listens on port 8080. This means that Pentaho, too, is accessible through this port. For example, if the Pentaho Server is started on your local machine, the web address of the Pentaho home page is `http://localhost:8080/pentaho`.

NOTE **There are other server products that use port 8080 by default, in particular other Java Servlet containers like JBoss and GlassFish but also Oracle Application Express (APEX), which is installed as part of the Oracle Express Database Server. Multiple servers cannot use the same port number simultaneously. For this reason, you may need to configure server software to ensure each of them is assigned a unique port.**

Things such as the server port as well as basic logging features are configured at the Tomcat level. Most of Tomcat's configuration is controlled through XML files that reside in the `tomcat/conf` directory. For example, if you want to change the port that is used by Tomcat, you can edit the following snippet from `tomcat/conf/server.xml`:

```
<Connector port="8080" maxHttpHeaderSize="8192"
           maxThreads="150" minSpareThreads="25" maxSpareThreads="75"
           enableLookups="false" redirectPort="8443" acceptCount="100"
           connectionTimeout="20000" disableUploadTimeout="true" />
```

So, changing the `port` attribute causes Tomcat to listen on another port. If you decide to change the port number here, you also need to change the port number in the `web.xml` configuration file which is located in the `tomcat/webapps/WEB-INF` directory. You should look for a snippet that looks like this:

```
<context-param>
    <param-name>base-url</param-name>
    <param-value>http://localhost:8080/pentaho/</param-value>
</context-param>
```

NOTE **A full discussion of Tomcat configuration is beyond the scope of this book. However, you can find good online resources and books on the subject. The obvious starting point to learn more about Tomcat is the manual, which you can find at `http://tomcat.apache.org/tomcat-5.5-doc/`.**

Automatic Startup

The Pentaho BI Server, as well as the Administration Console, are server applications, and typically you'd like them to start automatically after booting the operating system.

Automatic Startup in UNIX/Linux Systems

Users of UNIX-based systems need to create an init script (sometimes called an rc file) that starts the Pentaho Server. Listing 3-2 shows a very basic, but fully functional, init script called `pentaho-init.sh`. You should be able to figure out what it does by reading the code and comments.

Listing 3-2: A very basic pentaho-init.sh script

```
#!/bin/sh
# go to the pentaho home
cd /opt/pentaho/biserver-ce
# set up command for pentaho user, set java environment
cmd="sudo -u pentaho JAVA_HOME=usr/lib/jvm/java-6-sun
JAVA_OPTS=-Djava.awt.headless=true"

case "$1" in
start)
# run the original pentaho start script
$cmd ./start-pentaho.sh >> pentaho-demo.log &
;;
stop)
# run the original pentaho start script
$cmd ./stop-pentaho.sh >> pentaho-demo.log &
;;
restart)
$0 stop
$0 start
;;

*)
echo "Usage: $0 {start|stop|restart }"
exit 1
esac

exit 0
```

NOTE **Note that the script in Listing 3-2 is not intended to be a great example of UNIX scripting. It simply is a minimal approach that gets the job done. If you are interested in writing these scripts yourself, you should refer to the numerous resources on UNIX/Linux scripting and system administration.**

The `pentaho-init.sh` script must be placed in the `/etc/init.d` directory. (Note that this requires root privileges, and you must use `sudo` to copy or move the script to that location.) You should then test it and verify that you can use it to start and stop the Pentaho BI server, as shown here:

```
shell> cp pentaho-init.sh /etc/init.d
shell> cd /etc/init.d
shell> sudo ./pentaho-init.sh
Usage: ./pentaho-init.sh {start|stop|restart|status}
```

```
shell> sudo ./pentaho-init.sh start
shell> sudo ./pentaho-init.sh stop
```

For Debian-based Linux distributions, including Ubuntu, you can then use the `update-rc.d` utility, which sets up a number of symbolic links, causing the script to be used at boot time to start up Pentaho (and to stop it at system shutdown):

```
shell> sudo update-rc.d pentaho-init.sh defaults
update-rc.d: warning: /etc/init.d/pentaho-init.sh missing LSB style header

 Adding system startup for /etc/init.d/pentaho-init.sh ...
   /etc/rc0.d/K20pentaho-init.sh -> ../init.d/pentaho-init.sh
   /etc/rc1.d/K20pentaho-init.sh -> ../init.d/pentaho-init.sh
   /etc/rc6.d/K20pentaho-init.sh -> ../init.d/pentaho-init.sh
   /etc/rc2.d/S20pentaho-init.sh -> ../init.d/pentaho-init.sh
   /etc/rc3.d/S20pentaho-init.sh -> ../init.d/pentaho-init.sh
   /etc/rc4.d/S20pentaho-init.sh -> ../init.d/pentaho-init.sh
   /etc/rc5.d/S20pentaho-init.sh -> ../init.d/pentaho-init.sh
```

You can use the same `update-rc.d` utility to remove an existing service using a line such as this:

```
shell> sudo update-rc.d -f pentaho-init.sh remove
```

Another tool that comes in handy to manage Linux init scripts is the graphical boot-up manager `bum`. You can install it using the Synaptic Package manager, or using the following command:

```
shell> sudo apt-get install bum
```

After installation on Ubuntu Linux, you can start `bum` from the System ➤ Administration ➤ Boot-up Manager. This provides you with a graphical user interface to perform tasks like starting, stopping, enabling, and disabling init scripts.

NOTE **For Red Hat–based Linux distributions, including Fedora, the `chkconfig` utility can be used to achieve something similar. The following snippet will install and enable the `pentaho-init.sh` script:**

```
shell> chkconfig pentaho-init.sh --add
shell> chkconfig pentaho-init.sh on
```

After setting up the init script, you should restart the computer to verify that the Pentaho BI Server indeed starts up as part of the boot sequence.

Automatic Startup in Windows Systems

For Windows, you should create a service to enable automatic startup of the Pentaho Server. The easiest way to do this is to use the `service.bat` script. This is distributed along with the Tomcat server that is used to ship the Pentaho BI Server, so it is already included in your Pentaho download. To use this script, open a command shell and `cd` into the Pentaho home directory, and from there into `tomcat\bin`. Then, simply run the following:

```
C:\Program Files\pentaho\biserver-ce\tomcat\bin>service.bat install Pentaho
Installing the service 'Pentaho' ...
Using CATALINA_HOME:     C:\Program Files\pentaho\biserver-ce\tomcat
Using CATALINA_BASE:     C:\Program Files\pentaho\biserver-ce\tomcat
Using JAVA_HOME:         D:\Libraries\java\jdk-1_5_0_15
Using JVM:               D:\Libraries\java\jdk-1_5_0_15\jre\bin\server\jvm.dll
The service 'Pentaho' has been installed.
```

NOTE **In the previous example, we used `Pentaho` as the name of the service. You may omit the name, in which case the default name `Tomcat5` will be used.**

You can now browse your service using the Service Manager (Start ➢ Control Panel ➢ Administrative Tools ➢ Services) and configure it to start automatically. Note that the new service is labeled "Apache Tomcat Pentaho" rather than simply "Pentaho." Uninstalling the service is similarly easy; simply run the following command:

```
C:\Program Files\pentaho\biserver-ce\tomcat\bin>service.bat uninstall Pentaho
The service 'Pentaho' has been removed
```

NOTE **The `service.bat` script is actually a wrapper around the `Tomcat5.exe` program, and you can exert more control using that directly. You can also use that to modify the already installed Tomcat service. For example, instead of browsing for the service in the service manager you could also run the following:**

```
shell> tomcat5.exe //US//Pentaho --Startup auto
```

to modify the service to start up automatically. The following example illustrates how to change the display name of the service to Pentaho BI Server:

```
shell> tomcat5.exe //US//Pentaho --DisplayName="Pentaho BI Server"
```

This final example illustrates how to configure Java Virtual Machine memory usage for the service. In this case, the initial heap memory is set as follows:

```
shell> tomcat5.exe //US//Tomcat5 --JvmMs=256M --JvMx=1024 --JvmSs=64
```

You can find more information on the `service.bat` script and `tomcat5.exe` in the Tomcat documentation here at `http://tomcat.apache.org/tomcat-5.5-doc/windows-service-howto.html`.

Managing Database Drivers

All Pentaho applications, including the Pentaho Server, use Java Database Connectivity (JDBC) for database communication. In order to connect to a particular RDBMS, Pentaho needs to load the appropriate Java driver. By default, the Pentaho Server ships with JDBC drivers for the following databases:

- **HSQLDB**—`hsqldb-x.x.x.jar`
- **MySQL**—`mysql-connector-java-x.x.x.jar`
- **PostgreSQL**—`postgresql-x.x-xxx.jdbc3.jar`

NOTE **The occurrences of `x.x.x` and `x.x-xxxx` in the `.jar` file names do not appear literally, but indicate a specific version number.**

So, if you want to connect to any other RDBMS, you need to obtain an appropriate driver and ensure that it can be used by the Pentaho BI Server. The remainder of this section describes how to do this.

Driver Location for the Server

The JDBC drivers are located in the `tomcat/common/lib` directory beneath the home directory of the Pentaho Server. If you need to connect to another type of RDBMS, you must copy the appropriate `.jar` files to this location. The server needs to be restarted in order for the new drivers to be loaded.

Driver Location for the Administration Console

Copying the driver `.jar` files to the `tomcat/common/lib` directory only allows the server to connect to the corresponding database system. However, the PAC is typically used to configure new named database connections. So, in order to correctly configure and test database connections, the PAC also needs to load the new JDBC driver.

The JDBC driver `.jar` files for the PAC are stored in the `jdbc` directory. This directory resides immediately beneath the installation directory of the Administration Console software.

Managing JDBC Drivers on UNIX-Based Systems

On UNIX-based systems, you can use symbolic links to make it easier to manage JDBC drivers across multiple programs. With this method, you can upgrade a driver with a single action.

To do this, you should keep all your JDBC driver `.jar` files in a single directory (say, `/lib/jdbc`). In addition, this directory would contain one symbolic link for each distinct RDBMS, pointing to the preferred version of the `.jar` file. This symbolic link serves to create a generic file name that will be used to refer to the driver `.jar` file for that RDBMS type, regardless of the version. For example, a symbolic link called `mysql-connector-java.jar` could point to either `mysql-connector-java-5.1.7.jar` or `mysql-connector-java-5.0.8.jar`, depending on what version you prefer for most applications.

Instead of copying any `.jar` files to application directories (such as `/tomcat/common/lib`), you can place a symbolic link there, pointing to the generic symbolic link in the `/lib/jdbc` directory. Whenever you want to upgrade (or downgrade) a driver, you can simply place the new `.jar` file in the `/lib/jdbc` directory and recreate the generic symbolic link to point to the new `.jar` file.

A slightly simpler approach is to directly rename the `.jar` file to something more generic, but this makes it harder to keep track of exactly which version you are currently using.

System Databases

The Pentaho platform relies on a number of system databases:

- `hibernate`—This database is used to store the user authentication and authorization data, BI content (solution repository), and named data sources.
- `quartz`—This database acts as the repository for the Quartz scheduler, which is one component that makes up the Pentaho Server.
- `sampledata`—This is the sample data that is mostly used by the `examples` discussed in Chapter 1. Strictly speaking, this is not a system database because it does not affect the normal operation of the Pentaho BIServer.

By default, the system databases are all managed by a HSQLDB RDBMS. In this section, we describe how to migrate these to a MySQL database. We assume you have already set up the MySQL database software, and we assume this uses the default MySQL port (3306) and resides on the same host machine as the Pentaho Server. For this particular setup, all MySQL JDBC connect strings should have this form:

```
jdbc:mysql://localhost:3306/<database-name>
```

Here, ***<database-name>*** stands for a particular schema (database) managed by the MySQL instance. In the remainder of this chapter, we will always use JDBC connect strings like this. You are free to use another host, or another port, or both, but you'll need to change the connect strings as they appear in the following sections accordingly. Of course, the same goes if you want to deploy this on another RDBMS. For details on setting up MySQL, please refer to Chapter 2.

The steps for migrating from the preconfigured HSQLDB database are largely the same, regardless of the specific RDBMS. By default, the Pentaho BI Server already provides some resources (such as schema creation scripts) to set this up for MySQL, Oracle, and PostgreSQL. This means you'll have to adjust those scripts yourself in case you want to set up the Pentaho system databases for any other RDBMS.

Setting Up the MySQL Schemas

Before you can configure anything concerning the databases at the Pentaho BI Server's end, you must first create a couple of things on the MySQL server that will replace the HSQLDB database. You can find the SQL scripts to do so in the `data/mysql5` directory, which resides beneath the Pentaho BI Server home directory. The following scripts must be run in order:

- `create_repository_mysql.sql`—Creates the `hibernate` database, which is used to store the solution repository as well as user credentials and permissions.
- `create_sample_datasource.sql`—Adds a data source for the sample data on which all examples that ship with Pentaho are based. Data source definitions are also stored in the `hibernate` database. For now, this will still point to the HSQLDB database, but we will modify it later on when we also migrate the sample data itself to MySQL.
- `create_quartz_mysql.sql`—Creates the repository for the Quartz scheduler.

You can use any tool you like to run these scripts, such as the MySQL command-line client or Squirrel. When using the MySQL command-line tool `mysql`, you can use the SOURCE command to run a script from disk:

```
mysql> SOURCE /opt/pentaho/biserver-ce/data/mysql5/create_repository.sql
```

Alternatively, you can run it directly from the shell:

```
shell> mysql -h localhost --u root -p \
     > < /opt/pentaho/biserver-ce/data/mysql5/create_repository.sql
```

NOTE **Note the less than sign (`<`). This causes the contents of the script file to be executed by the `mysql` command-line tool.**

Configuring Quartz and Hibernate

In this section, you will learn to edit the Pentaho configuration files in order for the Quartz and Hibernate components to connect to the MySQL database.

Quartz

Quartz is a job scheduler. Pentaho uses it to automate tasks and to implement content subscription. Quartz stores job definitions in a relational database. To allow Quartz to connect to MySQL, you need to open `/tomcat/webapps/pentaho/META-INF/context.xml`, which resides in the Pentaho Server home directory. Look for the section that reads:

```
<Resource name="jdbc/Quartz" auth="Container"
    type="javax.sql.DataSource"
    factory="org.apache.commons.dbcp.BasicDataSourceFactory"
    maxActive="20" maxIdle="5" maxWait="10000"
    username="pentaho_user" password="password"
    driverClassName="org.hsqldb.jdbcDriver"
    url="jdbc:hsqldb:hsql://localhost/quartz"
    validationQuery="
        select count(*)
        from INFORMATION_SCHEMA.SYSTEM_SEQUENCES
    "/>
```

You need to change the values of following properties:

- `driverClassName`—the value of this property must be set to the Java class name of the MySQL JDBC driver, which is `com.mysql.jdbc.Driver`.
- `url`—this must be set to the JDBC connect string. It should be changed to the appropriate MySQL JDBC connect string, which is `jdbc:mysql://localhost:3306/quartz`.
- `ValidationQuery`—this is used to verify that the connection can be created. This must be changed to `SELECT 1`.

After modification, the snippet should look like this:

```
<Resource name="jdbc/Quartz" auth="Container"
    type="javax.sql.DataSource"
    factory="org.apache.commons.dbcp.BasicDataSourceFactory"
    maxActive="20" maxIdle="5" maxWait="10000"
    username="pentaho_user" password="password"
    driverClassName="com.mysql.jdbc.Driver"
    url="jdbc:mysql://localhost:3306/quartz"
    validationQuery="SELECT 1"/>
```

Hibernate

Hibernate is an object-relational mapping layer that is used by Pentaho to access (and cache) the following:

- Objects from the solution repository
- Named data sources, which are used by items such as reports to gather data from JDBC databases
- User authentication and authorization data

You should modify the relevant Pentaho configuration files to point them to the MySQL database instead of the HSQLDB database. First, modify the section corresponding to Hibernate in /tomcat/webapps/pentaho/META-INF/context.xml. In the previous subsection, you already changed this file to configure the connection for Quartz. This time you need to perform the same task for Hibernate, and change this snippet:

```
<Resource name="jdbc/Hibernate" auth="Container"
    type="javax.sql.DataSource"
    factory="org.apache.commons.dbcp.BasicDataSourceFactory"
    maxActive="20" maxIdle="5" maxWait="10000"
    username="hibuser" password="password"
    driverClassName="org.hsqldb.jdbcDriver"
    url="jdbc:hsqldb:hsql://localhost/hibernate"
    validationQuery="
        SELECT COUNT(*)
        FROM INFORMATION_SCHEMA.SYSTEM_SEQUENCES"/>
```

to this:

```
<Resource name="jdbc/Hibernate" auth="Container"
    type="javax.sql.DataSource"
    factory="org.apache.commons.dbcp.BasicDataSourceFactory"
    maxActive="20" maxIdle="5" maxWait="10000"
    username="hibuser" password="password"
    driverClassName="com.mysql.jdbc.Driver"
    url="jdbc:mysql://localhost/hibernate"
    validationQuery="SELECT 1" />
```

Then, cd into the pentaho-solutions/system/hibernate directory in the Pentaho Home directory. You need to modify two files here:

- hibernate-settings.xml
- mysql5.hibernate.cfg.xml

First, edit hibernate-settings.xml. In this file, you'll find one line that reads:

```
<config-file>system/hibernate/hsql.hibernate.cfg.xml</config-file>
```

The value in the <config-file> element is the name of a file that also resides in this directory. As you can see, it still refers to a HSQLDB-specific configuration file. You need to change this to mysql5.hibernate.cfg.xml, which contains the MySQL-specific configuration. This is all you need to change in hibernate-settings.xml. There are two things you might need to change in mysql5.hibernate.cfg.xml:

- This file contains the JDBC connect string to connect to the hibernate database, so if you are using a different host, port, or both you'll need to adjust the JDBC connect string here accordingly.

- You might want to add robust connection pooling. Database connections are not created willy-nilly. Rather, the server maintains a pool of connections, which remain opened as long as the server is running.

The JDBC connect string is configured in the line that reads:

```
<property name="connection.url">jdbc:mysql://localhost:3306/hibernate
</property>
```

(As we just mentioned, you needn't change this unless you know you set up MySQL differently from what we suggested.)

To add a connection pool, add the following snippet, right below the `<session-factory>` opening tag:

```
<property name="hibernate.c3p0.acquire_increment">3</property>
<property name="hibernate.c3p0.idle_test_period">14400</property>
<property name="hibernate.c3p0.min_size">5</property>
<property name="hibernate.c3p0.max_size">75</property>
<property name="hibernate.c3p0.max_statements">0</property>
<property name="hibernate.c3p0.timeout">25200</property>
<property name="hibernate.c3p0.preferredTestQuery">select 1</property>
<property name="hibernate.c3p0.testConnectionOnCheckout">true</property>
```

This snippet causes the c3p0 connection pool to be used. You'll need to ensure that this is loaded by the server in advance. To do that, you need to put the `c3p0-x.x.x.x.jar` file in the `tomcat/common/lib` directory. In addition, you also need to place it into the `lib` directory beneath the PAC home. (Note that `x.x.x.x.` represents the version number.) You can obtain it from `http://sourceforge.net/projects/c3p0`. You only need to download the c3p0-bin package. Windows users should get the `.zip` archive, and there is a `.tgz` archive for UNIX-based operating systems.

NOTE **c3p0 is a free JDBC-compliant connection pool implementation. If you like, you can use an alternative connection pool implementation, such as dbcp, which is provided by Apache (see `http://commons.apache.org/dbcp/`). For more information on using dbcp for the Pentaho Hibernate configuration, read this article on Tom Barber's blog: `http://pentahomusings.blogspot.com/2008/05/pentaho-server-fails-every-night-we.html`.**

Strictly speaking, you don't need to set up a connection pool like this—things will still work most of the time without it. However, it happens to solve a problem that is often encountered when running Pentaho on top of MySQL. The problem is that Hibernate always attempts to keep the MySQL connection opened. However, MySQL connections automatically expire after a certain period of inactivity. This can be configured at the MySQL end by setting the value of the `wait_timeout` server variable. By default, inactive connections expire after 8 hours. If this happens on a production system, Hibernate stops working properly, which essentially requires you to reboot the Pentaho Server before it becomes usable again. Typically, you start noticing this problem on a production server: during the night time, it's possible for the server to sit idle, and the next morning you'll notice things don't work anymore. Setting up the connection pool as just described solves that problem.

NOTE **To learn more about the specific problems you might encounter when running Pentaho on top of MySQL in absence of a connection pool, please read this thread on the Pentaho forums:** `http://forums.pentaho.org/showthread.php?t=54939`.
For more info on the MySQL `wait_timeout` **variable, see** `http://dev.mysql.com/doc/refman/5.1/en/server-system-variables.html#sysvar_wait_timeout` **and** `http://dev.mysql.com/doc/refman/5.1/en/gone-away.html`.

Configuring JDBC Security

You'll also need to adapt the user authentication and authorization configuration to the new `hibernate` database. To do so, edit `applicationContext-acegi-security-jdbc.xml`. This file resides in `pentaho-solutions/system` inside the Pentaho BI Server home directory. You need to look for the following snippet:

```
<bean id="dataSource"
    class="org.springframework.jdbc.datasource.DriverManagerDataSource">
    <property name="driverClassName" "value="org.hsqldb.jdbcDriver" />
    <property name="url"
    value="jdbc:hsqldb:hsql://localhost:9001/hibernate" />
    <property name="username" value="hibuser" />
    <property name="password" value="password" />
</bean>
```

Modify this to match the MySQL database, like so:

```
<bean id="dataSource"
    class="org.springframework.jdbc.datasource.DriverManagerDataSource">
    <property name="driverClassName" value="com.mysql.jdbc.Driver" />
    <property name="url" value="jdbc:mysql//localhost:3306/hibernate" />
    <property name="username" value="hibuser" />
    <property name="password" value="password" />
</bean>
```

In the same directory is a file called `applicationContext-acegi-security-hibernate.properties`. Its contents are as follows:

```
jdbc.driver=org.hsqldb.jdbcDriver
jdbc.url=jdbc:hsqldb:hsql://localhost:9001/hibernate
jdbc.username=hibuser
jdbc.password=password
hibernate.dialect=org.hibernate.dialect.HSQLDialect
```

You'll need to edit this to and adjust the database properties to match the MySQL `hibernate` database, as follows:

```
jdbc.driver=com.mysql.jdbc.Driver
jdbc.url=jdbc:mysql: //localhost:3306/hibernate
jdbc.username=hibuser
jdbc.password=password
hibernate.dialect=org.hibernate.dialect.MySQLDialect
```

Sample Data

If you also like to move the sample data from HSQLDB to MySQL, you should first download a script to load the sample data into MySQL. This script is kindly provided by Prashant Raju, and you can download it from `www.prashantraju.com/pentaho/downloads/sampledatamysql5.sql`.

NOTE Prashant Raju also provides good guides to configure Pentaho for MySQL. You can find them here: **`http://www.prashantraju.com/pentaho/guides/biserver-2.0-final/`.**

After setting up the database, you still need to update the `SampleData` data source definition that is stored in the `hibernate` database. Later in this chapter, we discuss how to edit data sources using the Pentaho Administration Console. For now, we'll use a slightly more direct method, and directly update the database record that stores the data source definition:

```
UPDATE hibernate.DATASOURCE
SET    DRIVERCLASS = 'com.mysql.jdbc.Driver',
       URL = 'jdbc:mysql://localhost:3306/sampledata',
       QUERY = 'SELECT 1'
WHERE NAME = 'SampleData'
;
```

Modify the Pentaho Startup Scripts

If you worked through the previous subsections, you can discard the HSQLDB database altogether. The Pentaho startup and shutdown scripts contain a line to explicitly start and stop the HSQLDB database respectively. You should remove these lines. It saves you some memory, and it also provides a good test to see if you correctly moved all databases to MySQL.

Here's a summary of the scripts and the lines to remove:

- `start-pentaho.bat`:

```
start start_.bat
```

- `stop-pentaho.bat`:

```
start stop_.bat
```

- start-pentaho.sh:

```
sh start_.sh &
```

- stop-pentaho.sh:

```
start stop_.bat
```

NOTE **Instead of removing the lines, you can turn them in to comment lines—this makes it easier to undo the change later on. For the `.bat` scripts, you create a comment line by setting the keyword `REM` followed by a space character immediately at the start of the line. For the `.sh` scripts, you can set the hash sign (#) immediately at the start of the line.**

E-mail

The Pentaho BI Server has SMTP (Simple Mail Transfer Protocol) e-mailing capabilities. E-mail can be used to distribute BI content (such as reports) to the appropriate recipients in bursting scenarios, or for sending monitoring messages. Specifically, Pentaho uses the JavaMail API to act as an SMTP client to send mail through an existing SMTP server. Note that you need to have a running STMP server before you can use this—Pentaho does not implement a mail server itself.

E-mail will not work out-of-the-box in the default configuration. In order to use e-mail, you need to configure a few things. The e-mail configuration is controlled through the file `email_config.xml`, which resides in the `smtp-email` directory inside the `system` Pentaho solution.

Basic SMTP Configuration

Listing 3-3 shows the contents of a basic `email_config.xml` file.

Listing 3-3: The contents of email_config.xml

```
<email-smtp>
  <properties>
    <mail.smtp.host>smtp.wcm.com</mail.smtp.host>
    <mail.smtp.port>25</mail.smtp.port>
    <mail.transport.protocol>smtp</mail.transport.protocol>
    <mail.smtp.starttls.enable>false</mail.smtp.starttls.enable>
    <mail.smtp.auth>true</mail.smtp.auth>
    <mail.smtp.ssl>false</mail.smtp.ssl>
    <mail.smtp.quitwait>false</mail.smtp.quitwait>
  </properties>
```

```
  <mail.from.default>joe.pentaho@pentaho.org</mail.from.default>
  <mail.userid>joe.pentaho@gmail.com</mail.userid>
  <mail.password>password</mail.password>
</email-smtp>
```

As you can see in Listing 3-3, there is a `properties` section that contains the configuration for communicating with the SMTP Server. The most important properties are as follows:

- `mail.smtp.host`—The name of the host or IP address where the SMTP server is running.
- `mail.smtp.port`—The port where the SMTP server is listening. The default SMTP port is 25.
- `mail.transport.protocol`—The protocol used to communicate with the SMTP server. By default, this is `smtp`.
- `mail.smtp.starttls.enable`—By default, false. If true, the `STARTTLS` command is used to switch to a secure TLS-protected connection.
- `mail.smtp.auth`—By default, false. If true, the AUTH command will be used to authenticate the user. Many SMTP servers require authentication, so this should normally be set to true.
- `mail.smtp.ssl`—By default, false. If true, a secure socket is used to communicate with the server.
- `mail.smtp.quitwait`—By default, true, which means the client will wait for a response to the `QUIT` command. If false, the connection is closed immediately after the `QUIT` command.

Outside the `properties` section there are a few configuration parameters that are used for authenticating the SMTP request:

- `mail.from.default`—The default e-mail address of the sender. The SMTP protocol requires the sender to be specified, and this e-mail address will be used if no from address is explicitly specified when sending the e-mail.
- `mail.userid` and `mail.password`—The credentials of the sender. This is required when the STMP server requires authentication (which is the case when the `mail.smtp.auth` property is true). Typically, the mail sender's e-mail address and credentials are associated and SMTP servers will require the sender's e-mail address to correspond to the user identified

by the credentials. Although by default the SMTP protocol does not require authentication, in practice almost all SMTP servers are set up to use it.

NOTE **You can find more information on JavaMail and its configuration properties in the Java API documentation at `http://java.sun.com/products/javamail/javadocs/com/sun/mail/smtp/package-summary.html`.**

Secure SMTP Configuration

More and more often, mail servers require you to use a secure communication protocol. A well-known example is Google Gmail. In order to send mail using such a mail server, you'll need a slightly different mail configuration:

- `mail.smtp.port`—The default port for secure SMTP is 465. Sometimes 587 is used. Contact your administrator to obtain the proper port number.
- `mail.transport.protocol`—This should be `smtps` rather than `smtp`.
- `mail.smtp.starttls.enable`—You may need to set this to true rather than false.

Testing E-mail Configuration

To test your email configuration, you can use the Burst Sales Report, which resides in the Reporting section of the BI Developer Examples solution. You can find directions on working with the predefined Pentaho examples in Chapter 1.

Publisher Password

Pentaho design tools are used to create definitions for BI content such as reports, OLAP cubes, and metadata. The BI content files that are created by these tools can be deployed manually, by copying the files directly to the appropriate solution directory on the file system of the Pentaho Server host. However, the typical and preferred way to deploy BI content is through a process called *publication*.

To publish, the design tools call upon a web service implemented by the Pentaho Server, which authenticates the user as well as checking his or her permissions. When this is successful, the client tool sends the content data to the server, which stores it at a desired location in some location inside the solution repository.

To enable publishing, you first have to explicitly set the publisher password. This password must be supplied to the web service in addition to the user's credentials when publishing BI content. There is one publisher password for the entire server, and it is configured in the `publisher_config.xml` file, which resides in the `pentaho-solutions/system` directory beneath the Pentaho home directory. The contents of the configuration file are shown here:

```
<publisher-config>
    <publisher-password>publish</publisher-password>
</publisher-config>
```

In the preceding example, the password is set to `publish`.

NOTE By default, no publisher password is specified, which prevents the design tools from publishing any content to the server.

Administrative Tasks

In this section, we describe how to perform common administrative tasks using the Pentaho Administrative Console (PAC).

The Pentaho Administration Console

The PAC software is shipped in the same package as the Pentaho BI Server. We mentioned before that it resides in the `administration-console` directory.

PAC is implemented as a lightweight web server based on Jetty. Technically, there is no reason why PAC could not also run inside the Tomcat server on which the Pentaho BI Server is based, except that now it is possible to easily separate the administrative capabilities from the BI application. For example, you can easily run PAC on a physically distinct server, which may make it easier to manage security.

NOTE Jetty is a web server and Java servlet container, just like Apache Tomcat. The important difference is that Jetty provides a very minimal lightweight implementation that makes it especially suitable for embedding it. Jetty is also used by Pentaho Data Integration to implement clustering.You can find more about the Jetty project at `http://www.mortbay.org/jetty/`.

Basic PAC Configuration

Before using PAC, you may need to configure a few things. Open the `console.xml` file located in the `resource/config` directory beneath the PAC home. Its contents are as follows:

```
<?xml version="1.0" encoding="UTF-8"?>
<console>
  <solution-path></solution-path>
```

```
    <war-path></war-path>
    <platform-username>joe</platform-username>
    <biserver-status-check-period-millis>
         30000
    </biserver-status-check-period-millis>
    <homepage-url>http://www.pentaho.com/console_home</homepage-url>
    <homepage-timeout-millis>15000</homepage-timeout-millis>
    <!-- comma separated list of roles (no spaces) -->
    <default-roles>Authenticated</default-roles>
</console>
```

You need to modify the `<solution-path>` and `<war-path>` elements inside the `<console>` element to point to the location of the solution repository and the Pentaho web application, respectively. You can use relative paths, so assuming a default location as described in the installation section of this chapter, these elements should read:

```
<solution-path>../biserver-ce/pentaho-solutions</solution-path>
<war-path>../biserver-ce/tomcat/webapps/pentaho</war-path>
```

Starting and Stopping PAC

Start and stop scripts are located directly inside the `administration-console` directory. Windows users can start PAC by executing `startup.bat`; users of UNIX-based systems should use `start.sh`. Similarly, Windows users can use `stop.bat` to stop PAC, whereas `stop.sh` should be used on UNIX-based systems.

The PAC Front End

The PAC front end is a web page. You can access it with any modern JavaScript-enabled browser. By default, PAC listens for requests at port `8099`. For example, when running PAC on the local machine, you can access the console by navigating to `http://localhost:8099/`.

When navigating to the page, you are first prompted for your credentials. The default username is `admin`, and the default password is `password`. After logging in, you will see a page like the one shown in Figure 3-1.

The PAC home page offers little more than some seemingly static textual information about the Pentaho Enterprise Edition. However, the information on the home page is downloaded live from the Internet, so it can be used to show up-to-date information.

Notice the large green Administration button at the left side of the PAC home page. Clicking it gives you access to the actual administrative console.

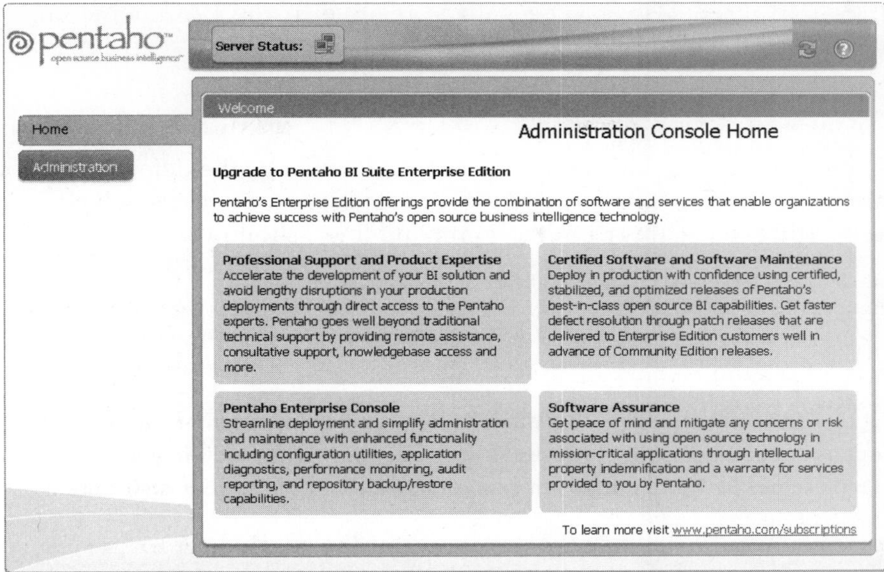

Figure 3-1: The Pentaho Administration Console home page

Configuring PAC Security and Credentials

Jetty features its own pluggable authentication. This is separate from the Pentaho Platform security system. PAC security is configured through the `login.conf` configuration file. This file defines the type of security by specifying a so-called *login module*. Jetty ships with a number of standard login modules, such as a properties file login module or a JDBC login module.

The default contents of the `login.conf` file are as follows:

```
PropertiesFileLoginModule {
    org.mortbay.jetty.plus.jaas.spi.PropertyFileLoginModule required
    debug="true"
    file="resource/config/login.properties";
};
```

As you can see, PAC uses the properties file login module by default (which is implemented by the `org.mortbay.jetty.plus.jaas.spi.PropertyFileLoginModule` Java class). With this type of authentication, the usernames and passwords are stored in a properties file. In this case, the file is `resource/`

`config/login.properties`. The path is relative to the PAC home and the contents of that file are shown here:

```
admin: OBF:1v2j1uum1xtv1zej1zer1xtn1uvk1v1v,server-administrator,
content-administrator,admin
```

If you want to add additional entries here, or change the default password, you can use the `org.mortbay.jetty.security.Password` class, which is part of Jetty. You can use this from the command line, as follows:

```
shell> cd /opt/pentaho/administration-console/lib/
shell> java -cp jetty.jar;jetty-util.jar org.mortbay.jetty.security.Password
Usage - java org.mortbay.jetty.security.Password [<user>] <password>
If the password is ?, the user will be prompted for the password
```

NOTE **In reality, the `.jar` file names include a version number—for example, `jetty-6.1.2.jar` and `jetty-util-6.1.9.jar`. Please look in your `resource/lib` directory to figure out which version numbers apply to your distribution.**

So, if you want to change the password for the admin user to "secret," you can do the following:

```
shell> java \
     > -cp jetty-6.1.2.jar:jetty-util-6.1.9.jar \
     > org.mortbay.jetty.security.Password \
     > secret
```

This command generates the following output:

```
secret
OBF:1yta1t331v8w1v9q1t331ytc
MD5:5ebe2294ecd0e0f08eab7690d2a6ee69
```

You can now modify the `resource/config/login.properties` file and change the occurrence of `OBF:1v2j1uum1xtv1zej1zer1xtn1uvk1v1v` to `OBF:1yta1t331v8w1v9q1t331ytc`.

NOTE **For more information on PAC pluggable authentication, please refer to the Pentaho documentation. You can find it at `http://wiki.pentaho.com/display/ServerDoc2x/Configuring+Security+with+Pentaho+Administration+Console`.**

User Management

By default, the Pentaho BI Server uses a simple authorization system consisting of users, roles, and permissions that is stored in a relational database. PAC enables you to create roles and users, and make user/role associations. The actual permission can be controlled from the Pentaho User Console (that is, from the Pentaho BI Server's end). Here, the current user can grant or revoke permissions to items from the solution repository to individual users or to roles (thereby bestowing the permission to all users to which that particular role is assigned).

The user management console is shown in Figure 3-2. It can be invoked by clicking the Users & Roles tab at the top of the management console.

Figure 3-2: The user management console

If you want to add a new user, be sure to activate the Users mode by clicking the User toolbar button. At the left side of the console, you'll see the list of existing users. Click the + button at the top right of the list to open a dialog where you can enter the data describing the new user (see Figure 3-2).

You can click any entry in the user list to select that user. Clicking the little x button at the top right of the user list will remove the selected user. Alternatively, you can update the data of the selected user in the form at the left side of the user management console. At the bottom of this form, there's a list that shows the user's assigned roles.

You can invoke the user/role assignments dialog by clicking the + button at the top right of the assignments list. This dialog is shown in Figure 3-3. You can add assignments by selecting one or more roles in the Available list at the left side of the dialog, and then clicking the > button. Similarly, you can revoke roles by selecting them in the Assigned list and clicking the < button.

Use the Update button at the bottom of the form to confirm any changes you made to the user's data or role assignments.

If you want to create a new role, click the Roles toolbar button. This provides an interface similar to the one shown in Figure 3-2, but from the other end: On the left side, this screen provides a role list instead of a users list, and instead of an assigned roles list, it provides a list of users that were assigned the selected role.

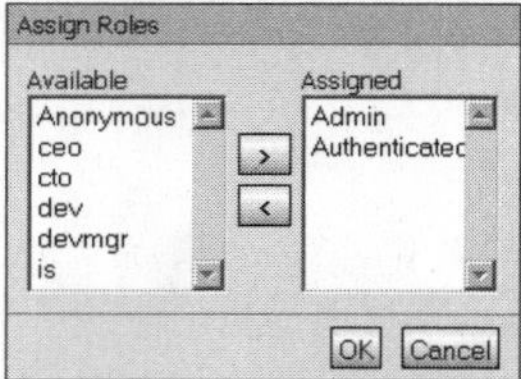

Figure 3-3: Assigning roles to the selected user

NOTE **The Pentaho platform is not limited to the default authentication and authorization system stored in a relational database. The Pentaho platform taps into the Spring Security system (formerly known as ACEGI). This is a flexible security system that provides access to a wide range of authentication and authorization back ends, such as LDAP.**

For more information on Spring Security, see: `www.springsource.com/products/springsecurity`. For more information on how to apply Spring Security concepts to Pentaho, please refer to the Pentaho documentation at `http://wiki.pentaho.com/display/ServerDoc2x/Security`.

Data Sources

PAC allows you to create and edit named JDBC data sources (JNDI data sources). You can access the data source console by clicking the Data Sources tab at the top of the management console. The Data Sources management console is shown in Figure 3-4.

The list of available data sources is at the left of the console. If you select an item in the list, you can change its properties in the form on the right. Data sources have the following properties:

- Name—The JNDI name for the data source. This can be used in the reports and other BI content to refer to this connection.
- Driver Class—The name of the Java class that implements the JDBC driver. For MySQL, you can use `com.mysql.jdbc.Driver`.
- User name—The name of the database user.
- Password—The password of the database user.
- URL—The connect string. The format of the connect string is dependent upon the driver, and you should refer to the driver documentation to figure out what format to use. For MySQL, the format is:

```
jdbc:mysql://<hostname>[:<port>]/<schema_name>
```

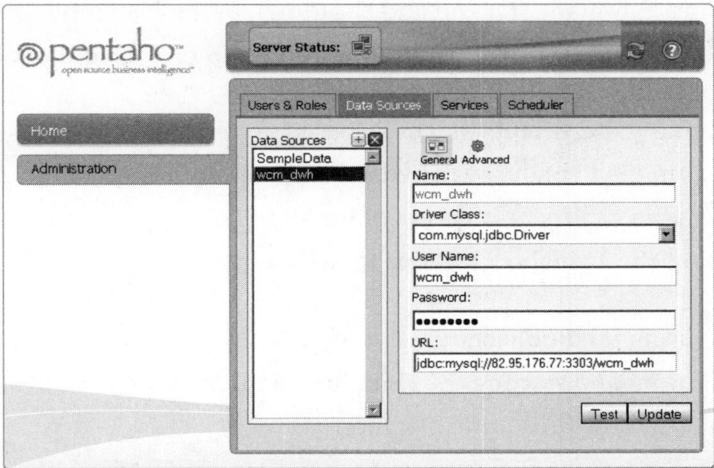

Figure 3-4: The data source management console

When using a local database called `wcm_dwh` that listens on the default port, the URL should be:

```
jdbc:mysql://localhost:3306/wcm_dwh
```

When done modifying the properties, you can use the Test button to confirm the connection is working properly. Use the Update button to store the modifications.

You can add a new data source by clicking the + button that appears at the top right of the data source list. This opens a dialog where you can edit the data source properties. Confirming the dialog will add the data source to the list on the left side of the console.

NOTE **For more information on creating data sources with PAC, see the Pentaho documentation at `http://wiki.pentaho.com/display/ServerDoc2x/.04+Configuring+Data+Sources`.**

Other Administrative Tasks

PAC also allows you to manage schedules and subscriptions. This topic is explored in detail in Chapter 14.

Summary

In this chapter, you learned a few basics concerning Pentaho Server installation, configuration, and administration, including the following:

- The preferred installation directory
- Setting up a separate user account to run the Pentaho Server

- Enabling automatic start up and shutdown of the Pentaho BI Server
- Enabling database connectivity to an RDBMS of choice by adding new JDBC drivers
- Managing JDBC drivers on UNIX-based systems using symbolic links
- Setting up the Pentaho system databases on MySQL
- Setting up a c3p0 connection pool for Hibernate
- Enabling the Pentaho platform to send e-mail using an existing SMTP server.
- Configuring the Publisher password
- Configuring and starting the Pentaho Administration Console (PAC)
- Managing basic PAC authentication
- Managing Pentaho BI Server users and roles with PAC
- Managing data sources with PAC

CHAPTER 4

The Pentaho BI Stack

Pentaho is a business intelligence suite rather than a single product: it is made up of a collection of computer programs that work together to create and deliver business intelligence solutions. Some of these components provide functionalities that are very basic, such as user authentication or database connection management. Other components deliver functionality that operates at a higher level, such as visualizing data using charts and graphs.

Often, but not always, the components that offer high-level functionality rely on other components offering low-level functionality. As such, the collection of programs that forms the entire suite can quite literally be viewed as a *stack* of components, each level bringing functionality closer to the end user. The Pentaho BI stack is shown in Figure 4-1, where all the components that make up the complete solution are shown.

In this chapter, we describe the different components, their functions, and, where applicable, the relationships that exist between them. In Figure 4-1, the main layers of the stack are clearly identified, with the presentation layer at the top and the data and application integration layer at the bottom. Most end users will interact with the presentation layer, which can take many forms. Pentaho can be accessed by a simple web browser, but the components can also be embedded in an existing portal such as LifeRay or a content management system such as Alfresco. Perhaps the most common form of presentation is sending Pentaho content as a PDF file to a user's Inbox via e-mail.

The main functional areas of the BI stack—reporting, analysis, dashboards, and process management—constitute the middle layer of the stack, whereas the BI platform itself delivers basic features for security and administration. Data integration completes the stack and is needed to get data from various source systems into a shared data warehouse environment.

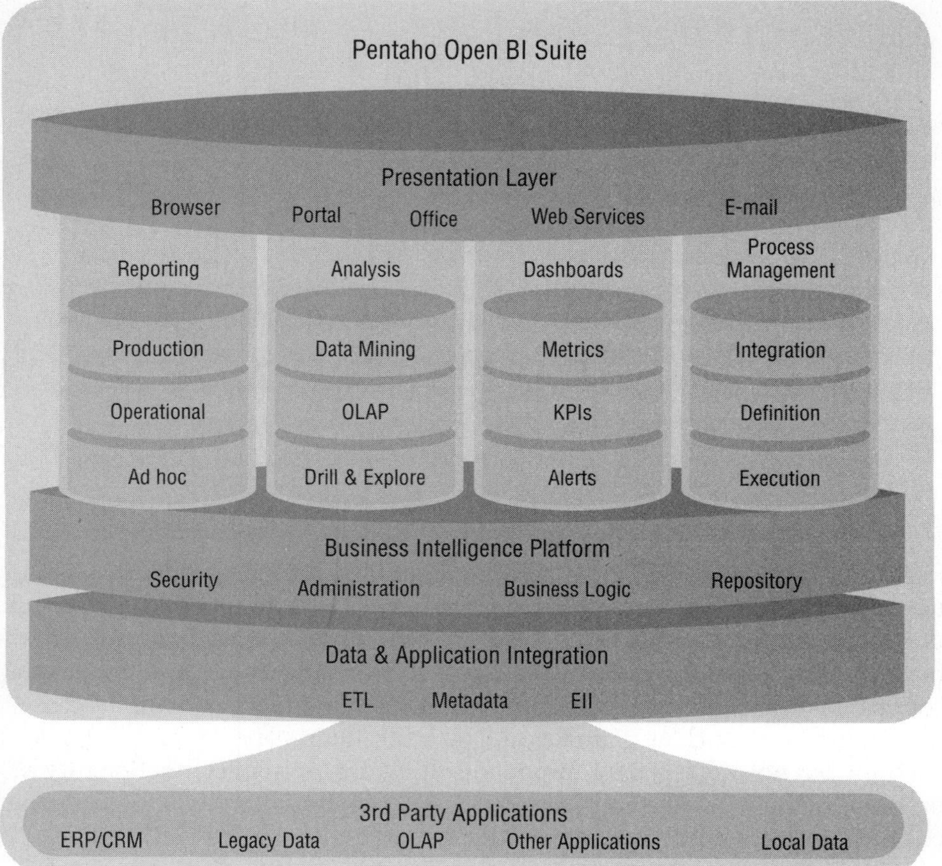

Figure 4-1: Pentaho BI stack

In a sense, the diagram not only displays the Pentaho BI stack at a high level, but the Pentaho BI architecture as well. An architecture defines the structure and outline of a solution, but doesn't exactly prescribe *how* the structure should be built. In the case of Pentaho, the architecture defines the layers and building blocks but doesn't necessarily force you to use everything from the stack, or, to take this one step further, from Pentaho. Although there are several advantages in using Pentaho software to build the stack, you're free to mix in other components as well. For instance, Pentaho has two ways of creating reports, the web-based Ad Hoc Query and Reporting component and the Pentaho Report Designer, but the platform can run both Jasper and BIRT reports as well. Even in the Pentaho world, a multitude of alternatives are available, mostly initiated by community projects and later adopted by the company. We'll cover all the currently available options but you should be aware of the fact that new projects are started regularly, sometimes covering a missing part of the Pentaho functionality, sometimes replacing or augmenting an existing part of the stack. The Pentaho BI stack is therefore an evolving entity, like a city where new buildings are created and older ones are restored, expanded, or replaced on a continuous basis.

Pentaho BI Stack Perspectives

We can classify the programs that make up the Pentaho BI Suite according to a number of criteria. The following sections offer different lenses for viewing the components in the stack.

Functionality

One way of categorizing the components in the Pentaho stack is by *functionality*. By functionality we mean the task or tasks that a particular program was designed to perform. From the user's perspective, the functionality is what defines the purpose of the program.

Some of Pentaho's components offer typical BI functionalities, such as ETL, Reporting, and OLAP. The components that provide these typical BI functionalities are supported by a number of components that offer functionality at a considerably lower level. Collectively, these supporting components are known as the Pentaho Platform.

The functionalities offered by the platform are not all BI-specific, but offer a basic software infrastructure. Tasks such as user authentication and authorization, database connection pool management, and execution of scheduled tasks are all part of the platform.

Server, Web Client, and Desktop Programs

Another criterion is whether the program can be classified as a client, a server, or a desktop program. Some Pentaho programs are easily recognized as server programs. These are typically executed on a central computer that is accessed by web-based clients through a network (intranet or Internet). Non-server programs in the Pentaho Suite can best be classified as desktop programs. These are typically installed on the user's local computer. These desktop programs will in most cases be used by designers and developers to issue requests to a (Pentaho) server program to which they are connected. A good example of the division between server, desktop, and client is the design, publication and execution of a report. The desktop Report Designer is used to create the report, which is published to the Pentaho Server. The Pentaho Server can execute the report on request using the built-in Report Engine, and output is displayed via the Pentaho Web Portal, which serves as the client.

Front-Ends and Back-Ends

Another way to distinguish the programs is front-end versus back-end. Front-end programs are those programs that provide a friendly user interface that allows human users to interact with the program. Back-end programs are typically not designed to support direct human interaction. Rather, they receive commands from some front-end tool that knows how to translate the actions of the user into commands on which the back-end can operate to perform the actual task.

The front-end/back-end aspect is related to, but distinct from the difference between server, desktop, and client programs. Although desktop and client programs are often also front-end programs, it is possible to implement a front-end as a server program. It is equally possible to implement the back-end as a desktop program.

There is also a relationship between the functionality aspect and the front-end/back-end aspect: Most of the platform components do not have any front-end at all. By contrast, programs that offer BI-specific functionality usually have a clearly distinguishable front-end.

Underlying Technology

Virtually all programs in the Pentaho stack are programmed in the Java programming language. Some of the server-side components implement web applications based on AJAX technology, but this is still achieved by a Java program.

From the perspective of the end user, the programming languages and technology upon which Pentaho is built are quite irrelevant. However, it is hugely important from a system administrator's or developer's point of view.

One of the most notable properties of the Java platform is that Java programs are extremely portable across hardware architectures and operating systems. As a consequence, Pentaho is available for many different operating systems.

From a system administrator's point of view, managing Pentaho is much like managing other Java applications. There are a few things about Java that may require some effort from a system administrator:

- Java applications are usually designed to be compatible with a particular minimal version of the Java platform, and sometimes one specific major version.
- Another issue may be the particular implementation of the Java platform. The Java specifications have always been rather open, and there are many different implementations of both the Java virtual machine as well as the standard class libraries. Java programs generally run fine when using Sun's reference implementations.

- Java programs are executed by a virtual machine, which usually is a native program. Sometimes it is necessary to adjust the virtual machine's parameters to effectively run the program.

The Pentaho Business Intelligence Server

The Pentaho Server is a collection of programs that work together to provide a number of core functions of the Pentaho BI Suite. These programs are implemented as Java *servlets*. Servlets do not run standalone, but are executed inside a so-called *servlet container*, which is itself an HTTP Server (a web server), or part thereof.

Typically, the servlet container runs on a remote, centralized computer, where it responds to requests from client programs that are connected to the server through a network. The Java Servlet Technology is discussed in more detail later in this chapter.

On a functional level, the Pentaho server can be divided into three layers:

- The platform
- BI components
- The presentation layer

The Platform

The collection of components collectively known as *the platform* offers the following services:

- Solution repository and solution engine
- Database connection pool management
- User authentication and authorization services
- Logging and auditing services
- Task-scheduling
- E-mail services

The functionality offered by these services is relatively low-level and constitutes the basic infrastructure of the BI platform. A number of components in this layer could appear equally well in other types of application servers.

In the remainder of this section, we briefly describe the function of each component.

The Solution Repository and the Solution Engine

The Pentaho platform organizes BI content into so-called solutions. A Pentaho solution can be thought of as a file system folder with all the BI content to solve some business problem. A Pentaho solution can contain folders and items called *action sequences*.

Folders simply serve to provide a general organization of BI content. Folders can contain other folders and action sequences (AS). Action sequences are services that can be invoked to deliver some BI content. They can be invoked directly through user interaction, or addressed as a web service from another application. The latter property allows integration of Pentaho with other applications

Action sequences can contain multiple steps, sometimes called *action definitions*. In the simplest form, an action sequence contains just one step, for example to execute a report. A slightly more advanced action sequence could consist of one step to prompt a user for input, and a second step to execute a report, using the input from the first step as parameter values. By adding more steps, advanced action sequences can be built—for example, execute a database query to find all warehouses that are running low on stock, loop over the found warehouses to execute a stock details report, and distribute the report output via e-mail to the relevant warehouse managers.

Action sequences are represented using XML and are stored in plain text files with an *.xaction* extension. Action sequences are therefore also called *xactions*, after the file extension. In principle, you could create them with a simple text editor. Some of Pentaho's front-end tools, such as the Report Designer, can generate simple, single-step action sequences. More advanced action sequences are best created using Pentaho Design Studio, or using Eclipse with the Pentaho action sequence plugin. These provide a graphical *action sequence editor* as well as control over the action XML source.

Action sequences are executed by the platform component known as the *solution engine*. Whenever some client invokes an action sequence, the engine reads the definition of the action sequence, and then executes its steps.

Logically, Pentaho solutions are stored and maintained in the *solution repository*. Applications that connect to the Pentaho server can browse solutions and folders, and store new action sequences, a process called *publishing*.

Physically, the solution repository can be stored as files on the file system, or stored in a relational database. For basic action sequence execution, both methods suffice. However, the file-based solution repository does not currently support authorization. So, for precise control over which users can access which content, the solution repository needs to be stored in a database.

Database Connection Pool Management

In the vast majority of cases, data presented in business intelligence applications is stored in a (relational) database. In order to access data in the database, the application needs to establish a database connection. The connection is then used to send requests (queries) to the database server, which sends back the data as a response.

Establishing a connection to a database may be a relatively expensive task. Some time is required to look up the database host, and some time may be spent on negotiating protocols, authenticating the user, and setting up a session. In many cases, the connection is needed to perform only very few queries. For example, many reports are based on only one database query, and many queries will use the same database to retrieve their data from.

To avoid the overhead of establishing a new connection for each query or batch of queries, database connections can be opened once and stored in a pool. Whenever a client needs a database connection, a free connection can be picked from the pool, used to do some work, and is then released back into the pool again.

Database connection pooling is also an easy way to limit the number of simultaneous open database connections. By insisting that applications always pick a free connection from a fixed-size pool rather than establishing a new connection directly, the database can be protected from being flooded with connection requests.

JDBC connection pooling is common in most Java application servers, and many different implementations are available. Pentaho does not offer its own connection pool implementation.

User Authentication and Authorization

The Pentaho platform uses Spring Security (formerly known as the Acegi Security System for Spring) to handle user authentication and authorization. This is the standard security solution of the Java Spring framework.

Spring Security provides many different components to implement all kinds of different authentication schemes. It provides the logic that keeps track of whether a user needs to be authenticated, and it can delegate authentication requests to an external authentication mechanism, such as a database server, an LDAP directory, or NTLM authentication on a Windows network.

Task Scheduling

The Pentaho platform uses Quartz as a task scheduling component. Quartz is created and maintained by the OpenSymphony project and released under an Apache 2.0 license (see www.opensymphony.com/quartz for detailed project information).

The task scheduler is used for a number of things:

- Periodical execution of maintenance tasks
- Background execution of reports
- Scheduling ETL jobs

The scheduling capabilities of the platform are covered in Chapter 14.

E-mail Services

The BI platform includes the capability to send e-mail by using a standard SMTP server. A configuration file for using a Gmail account is also included. Before mail can be sent, the server must first be configured. The mail configuration must be entered in the file `email_config.xml`, which is located in the directory `<install-path>/pentaho-solutions/system/smtp-email`. The config files have excellent inline comments and it should be simple to set this up. Restarting the server after changing the config file is not required; the new entries will be picked up automatically when the values have been entered correctly.

BI Components

The platform forms the foundation for a number of components that offer typical business intelligence functionality. In this layer, we find the following components:

- Metadata layer
- Ad hoc reporting service
- ETL engine
- Reporting engine
- OLAP engine
- Data mining engine

The Metadata Layer

The function of the Pentaho Metadata Layer (PML) is to shield end users from the complexity of SQL and databases. The PML is based on the Common Warehouse Metamodel specification of the Object Management Group (www.omg.org/cwm) and is able to generate SQL from a query written in the Metadata Query Language (MQL). The MQL query in turn is created by an end user by building the desired selection from a set of objects exposed in a metadata model. The metadata layer consists of three layers, as specified by the CWM:

- **Physical layer**—This is where the database connection is stored and where the physical representation of the database objects is created. When generating SQL, this is the layer from which PML ultimately gets the database attribute information.
- **Business layer**—The intermediate translation layer where translations from technical database attributes to more user-friendly descriptions are made. This is also the layer where relationships between tables and additional formulas and calculations are created.
- **Business view**—Exposes and re-organizes the business layer for end users and end user groups.

Figure 4-2 displays a graphical representation of the preceding description.

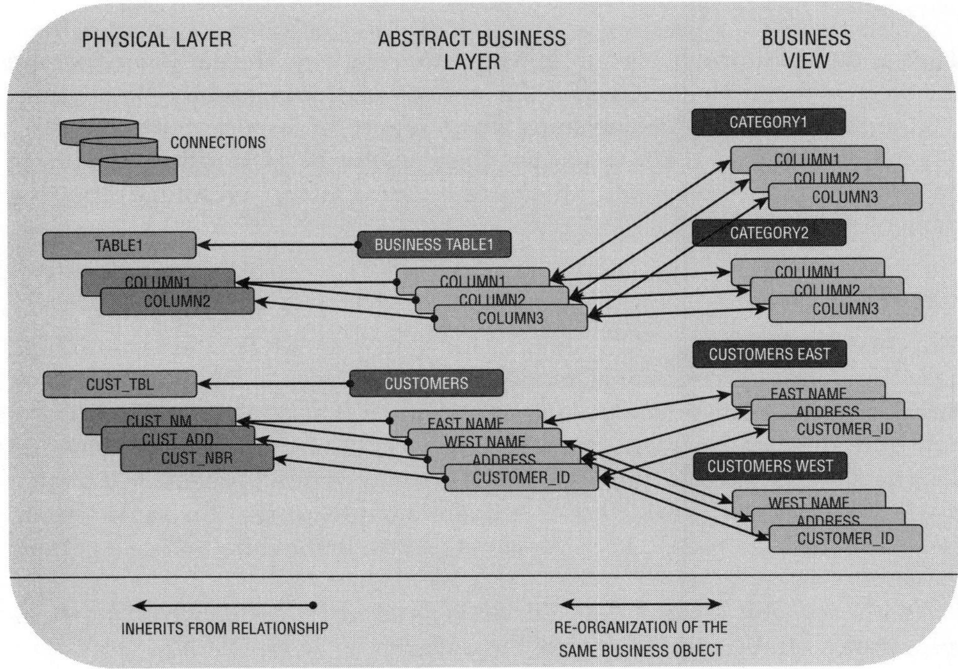

Figure 4-2: Metadata model layers

The right side of the diagram in Figure 4-2 is the only part of the metadata layer that is visible to end users when they work with one of the report design tools. The other layers are there to correctly translate the user-exposed model object back to the correct query for the database on which the metadata layer operates.

Ad hoc Reporting Service

The Web Ad Hoc Query and Reporting service, or WAQR, offers end users an easy way to create reports by using the metadata layer. The WAQR (pronounced "wacker") is a separate service from the full-fledged reporting engine and is able to create a simple grouped list report. WAQR is covered in more detail in Chapter 13.

The ETL Engine

Pentaho's ETL engine is the workhorse for data integration tasks and executes the jobs and transformations created with the Pentaho Data Integration tools. The ETL engine is part of the BI stack but can also run on a different server or even multiple servers in a clustered mode.

Reporting Engines

The Pentaho platform hosts multiple reporting engines. The native engines are the already mentioned engine for the ad hoc query tool, and the JFreeReport engine. Additionally, Pentaho ships with support for JasperReports and BIRT already embedded. This means that the Pentaho BI platform is capable of handling all reports created for the three most popular open source reporting tools.

The OLAP Engine

Mondrian is Pentaho's OLAP engine and translates MDX queries into SQL based on a multidimensional model. Mondrian does a lot more than just translating from one query language to another; it also takes care of caching and buffering intermediate and previous results to optimize performance. This means that the first time an analysis is run on a multidimensional model, it will take more time than the subsequent analysis during the same session because Mondrian tries to keep previous results, hierarchies and calculations in memory.

Another notable feature of Mondrian is its security model, which supports roles. Roles can be used to restrict the data that is accessible by a user, thus limiting the number of different OLAP views and reports that need to be developed.

The Data Mining Engine

Pentaho's data mining engine is arguably one of the most powerful yet lesser used parts of the platform. It is actually the Weka data mining engine that has been adopted by Pentaho that handles the data mining tasks. It consists of a comprehensive collection of data mining algorithms such as the ones needed for clustering, decision trees, regression, and neural networks. Parts of the Weka algorithms can be called from a Kettle transform to enable, for instance, direct scoring of incoming data during a Kettle transformation. Chapter 16 covers the different Weka tools and shows a step-by-step example of how Weka and Kettle can be used together to develop a data transformation that automatically scores new customers.

The Presentation Layer

Pentaho comes with a built-in web interface called the *user console*. The user console forms a front-end that allows a human user to interact with the server. The presentation layer can be used for browsing and opening existing content (reports, dashboards, analysis) but to some extent can also be used to create new BI content. Figure 4-3 shows the Pentaho user console where on the left side a folder tree is used for organizing content that is listed in the panel at the bottom left. Opened documents are displayed in the main screen and by using tabs, the user console can have multiple dashboards, analysis, and reports opened at the same time.

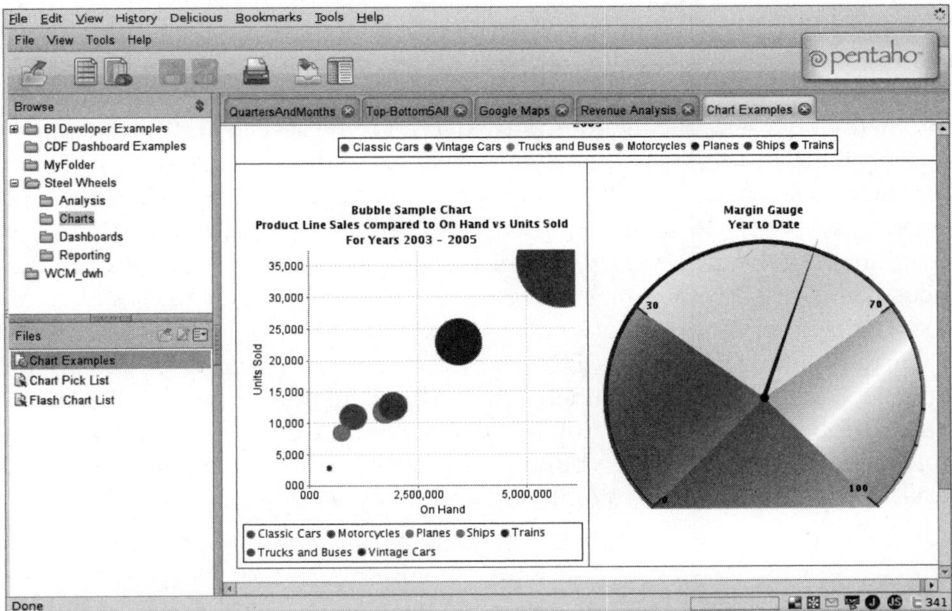

Figure 4-3: Pentaho user console

New content in the form of reports and analysis views can be created using the Web Ad Hoc Query and Reporting component (WAQR) and the JPivot analysis front-end. The WAQR is covered in depth in Chapter 13, and Chapter 15 contains a detailed treatment of JPivot and the underlying Mondrian technology.

Underlying Java Servlet Technology

Although the term ''The Pentaho Server'' may suggest otherwise, there is not one program that can rightfully be called by that name. Rather, Pentaho provides a number of programs called *servlets* that perform some specific task, a service, for any client that requests it. Servlets are Java programs that do not run standalone on the local computer. Instead, they are executed within another program, the *servlet container*.

Typically, the servlet container is itself a web server (that is, an HTTP server), or a part thereof. The servlet container is responsible for accepting HTTP requests and routing them to an appropriate servlet. The servlet then processes the request, and generates an appropriate response, which is transferred to the container to eventually route it back to the requesting client.

The organization of a Java program in a servlet container and several servlets that perform the actual service is called *Java Servlet Technology*. The Java Servlet Technology is the de facto standard for implementing Java web applications. The ways in which the servlet and its container may interact are precisely defined by the Java Servlet API. This specification for this API was initially created by Sun Microsystems, and further developed by the Java community process.

Pentaho does not offer its own servlet container. Rather, Java servlets can run in any Java servlet container, provided both the servlet and the container support the same version of the Java Servlet API, which is the usual situation. The guarantee that a servlet will run in any compatible servlet container allows servlet developers to focus on what they do best, which is adding useful functionality to web servers. Conversely, creators of web server software can focus completely on their task without worrying that any changes will break servlet-based server extensions.

Currently, the Community Edition of the Pentaho BI server is actually an Apache Tomcat servlet container with all the Pentaho servlets pre-installed. However, all servlets can be downloaded separately and installation instructions are available for other popular servlet containers too, such as JBoss, Glassfish, Websphere, BEA WebLogic, and many more.

Desktop Programs

As pointed out in the introduction of this chapter, most of Pentaho's non-server programs can best be classified as desktop programs. Some of them can only act as a client and need to interact with a Pentaho server, but many can be used standalone as well. The desktop programs mainly serve as design tools or aids because most of the end user experience is delivered in the Pentaho web portal. The desktop tools will therefore be mainly used by developers, although some, such as the Report Designer, could be used by power users. All desktop programs have a BI component or server component for which they are intended. Table 4-1 shows the available tools with their counterpart server components.

Table 4-1: Desktop tools and server components

DESKTOP TOOL	SERVER/BI COMPONENTS
Design Studio (PDS)	BI Platform
Metadata Editor (PME)	Metadata layer, Ad Hoc Reporting component
Schema Workbench (PSW)	OLAP Engine
Aggregate Designer (PAD)	OLAP Engine
Report Designer (PRD)	Reporting engine
Spoon (PDI)	ETL engine
Weka	Data Mining Engine

Each of these tools is covered in a later chapter, with the exception of the Pentaho Design Studio (PDS), which makes up the last part of this chapter. PDS is not a tool for creating new content, but is used for creating workflows and actions that work with existing BI content. PDS is also in another way a different kind of tool; it is the only part of the BI suite that is not a standalone Java program but a plugin for an existing development environment (the Eclipse IDE). The following list is a brief overview of the different desktop tools and their position in the BI suite:

- **Pentaho Metadata Editor (PME)**—With PME, designers can build metadata layers that serve as an abstraction layer between a relational database and an end user. The metadata layer can take user objects such as Customer Name, Country, and Revenue and translate this selection into the correct SQL statement needed to retrieve this information from a database. More on PME in Chapter 12.
- **Pentaho Schema Workbench (PSW)**—This is the tool for building multi-dimensional schemas to be used by the Mondrian Engine.
- **Pentaho Aggregate Designer (PAD)**—A separate tool for (automatically) designing aggregate tables that are used by Mondrian to enhance the performance of OLAP cubes. PSW and PAD are covered in-depth in Chapter 15.

- **Pentaho Report Designer (PRD)**—The front-end for building reports for the Pentaho platform and arguably the only of the available desktop tools that can be put in the hands of a knowledgeable end user. PRD is covered in Chapter 13.
- **Pentaho Data Integration (PDI)**—The desktop tool for building ETL jobs and transformations is called Spoon. PDI contains more than just Spoon but this is the most visible part of the ETL solution. PDI is covered in Chapters 10 and 11.
- **Weka**—The well-known open source data mining solution and the only tool not provided with a three-letter Pentaho abbreviation because it is not maintained by Pentaho and not available from the regular Pentaho download sites. Weka is a project initiated and still maintained by the University of Waikato in New Zealand but has been adopted by Pentaho as its standard data mining tool. Data mining with Weka is the subject of Chapter 16.

All of these tools have a few things in common: They are written in Java and will run on any platform that contains a Java Virtual Machine. They are all provided with a startup script or batch file but can also be started directly from the command line with the `Java -jar` command. The second important commonality is that none of them creates or works with proprietary file formats. All definitions created with the various desktop tools are XML based, thus open to any editor and any person. As a consequence, you are not bound to use any of the design tools but are free to create and/or modify the XML files directly with a simple text editor. Some people find it even easier to work with the XML files than with the GUI tools.

Pentaho Enterprise Edition and Community Edition

Pentaho offers two versions of the Pentaho BI Suite. The main distinction is made between the commercially licensed Enterprise Edition and the full open source Community Edition. This distinction has more to do with the kind of support offered than with actual software differences, but the Enterprise Edition (EE) offers a few components that are not available in the community version. Although we will not cover EE-specific components in this book, we mention them here for completeness.

- **Enterprise Console**—The larger part of the EE additions are aimed at extending the Community Edition with functionality needed in a corporate environment, such as security configuration, application diagnostics and performance monitoring, auditing and logging, lifecycle management (migrating content from development to test to production), content expiration, and backup/restore of the Pentaho repository. Most of these tasks can be executed with the Enterprise Console. This doesn't mean that you cannot do these things with the Community Edition, but it will require major efforts to set up—for example, lifecycle management without the EE tools.

- **PDI Extensions**—Pentaho Data Integration EE adds an Enterprise Console for performance monitoring, remote administration, and alerting. There is also an extra plugin for data mining, the KnowledgeFlow plugin.
- **Single Sign-On with LDAP & AD integration**—Although the Pentaho Community Edition has its own authentication and authorization component, it is not integrated with an external authentication provider such as LDAP or Active Directory. The advantage of having this integration is twofold: users only need to be entered and maintained once in a central location, and users don't have to log on separately and remember another password.
- **Dashboard Builder**—The most visible component of the EE is the Dashboard Builder, which enables users to easily populate a BI dashboard with various content types such as charts, reports, and maps. Creating dashboards using the Community Dashboard Framework (CDF) is covered in Chapter 17.
- **Services and support**—In addition to enhanced functionality, Pentaho Enterprise Edition provides support, indemnification, software maintenance, and additional technical resources.

Other than this list, there is no difference between the Community and Enterprise Edition in the products making up the BI stack. This means that there are virtually no limits to what you can do and build with the individual BI tools because there is no Enterprise Edition report builder that lets you do more than you could do with the standard Community Edition. In fact, this is what sets Pentaho apart from many other (even open source!) vendors.

Creating Action Sequences with Pentaho Design Studio

Pentaho Design Studio (PDS) is based on the Eclipse integrated development environment (IDE), and can be downloaded as a complete, ready-to-use solution that includes Eclipse. If you already have a version of Eclipse running, PDS can be added to an existing environment as a plugin. (Basically, PDS is just the plugin, but Pentaho offers a complete working package for convenience.) PDS has one purpose—creating and maintaining *action sequences*. As the name implies, an action sequence is a predefined set of actions that can be executed on the Pentaho BI server. Execution of an action sequence can be triggered by a user action, a schedule, or any other event, including another action sequence. Action sequence complexity ranges from very simple, for example, "execute a report" or "display a message onscreen" to fairly complex, for example, "find all customers with overdue items and send them a reminder in the customer preferred format (XLS, PDF, HTML) containing a description of the overdue items." Action sequences are the real workhorses of a Pentaho solution and because they tie all other components together the last part of this chapter is targeted at explaining what action sequences are and how you can build and deploy them on the Pentaho platform.

From the introduction, you might have gathered that action sequences (AS) are only used for creating output in one form or another. Although this is an important AS feature, that is only part of the story. An AS can be used for very low-level system activities as well, for instance to set session variables the moment a user logs in, or to create global lists of parameters that can be used by another process or AS. Suppose, for instance, that you want to restrict access to your data based on the user that is logging in, and suppose that each user is only allowed to view data from his or her own department, region, or any other criterion you can think of. With a system AS, you can set the department name that belongs to the logged in user and use this name in other action sequences as a parameter to filter the data on. It is beyond the scope of this book to explain system ASes, but you can find a detailed instruction on the Pentaho wiki at `http://wiki.pentaho.com/display/ServerDoc2x/Using+System+Actions+to+Control+Data+Access`.

Pentaho Design Studio (Eclipse) Primer

PDS is, as we already explained, a plugin component written for the widely used Eclipse IDE. Although we cannot offer a complete Eclipse tutorial here, we can cover the basics to get you started with PDS to be able to create your own solutions. For the remainder of this chapter, we will use the PCI examples and the Steel Wheels database; later on in the book, we will use the World Class Movies database to show some of the power of xactions combined with reports and dashboards.

Installation and configuration of Eclipse and PDS are covered in Chapter 3. For the examples in this chapter we assume that you have a working Pentaho system with the examples ready at hand. When you start Eclipse/PDS, the Eclipse Welcome screen is displayed and the BI Platform option appears in the top menu. The BI Platform menu has only one suboption: New Action Sequence.

The basic Eclipse components and terminology that you need to get started boil down to the following:

- **Workspace**—This is the highest level container of the solutions you will create; a workspace is used to keep a collection of Eclipse projects logically grouped together. You can have only one workspace open at a time, and for most Pentaho implementations, using a single workspace will do just fine. The (default) workspace needs to be defined when you first start Eclipse; after this first time, the default workspace is opened automatically each time you start the program.

- **Project**—The collection of files and folders that together make up a solution. Projects can be created within the workspace (which is a folder on your system) but that is not mandatory. Figure 4-4 shows a newly created project called My Pentaho. For the project folder, an existing Pentaho-solutions folder is selected. Now it is easy to open and modify existing xactions like the report bursting sample, which is open in the screenshot.

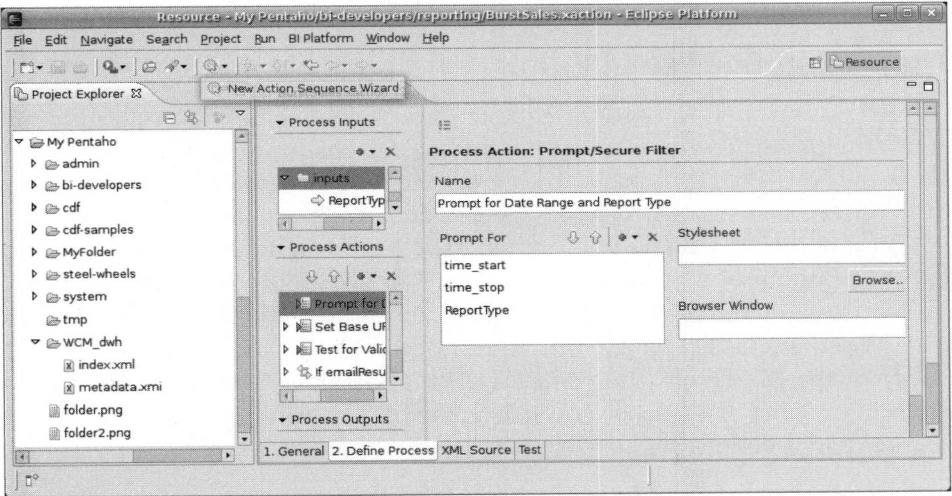

Figure 4-4: Pentaho Design Studio with action sequence editor

- **View**—In Eclipse, a *view* is a window within the IDE that displays some specific content such as the project structure, data sources, or a Java package explorer. The screenshot in Figure 4-4 shows the default Project Explorer view on the left side. Eclipse contains a huge collection of other views as well; they can be opened via the Window ➢ Show View menu or by using the little Fast View icon in the lower left corner of the screen (the small blue-white icon with the little superscripted plus sign).

- **Editor**—This is where you actually write code or, in the case of using PDS, define your action sequences. The Pentaho action editor is shown in Figure 4-4. To start the editor, just double-click on one of the existing sample xactions or create an empty one by selecting the New Action Sequence option from the BI Platform menu.

- **Perspective**—Probably the most powerful feature of Eclipse is the ability to completely change its behavior and available options by changing to a different *perspective*. A perspective transforms the general purpose Eclipse IDE into a specific tool tailored to a certain task. When you develop Java code, you will use the Java perspective to have the built-in editors, debuggers, code outline, and so on at your disposal. When you develop BIRT reports, you will use the Report Design perspective, which suddenly transforms Eclipse into a powerful reporting environment. For working with PDS, the simple Resource perspective will do just fine. Other perspectives are opened by selecting the Open Perspective option from the Window menu.

For more information about working with Eclipse, visit the project's website at `www.eclipse.org`.

The Action Sequence Editor

Before you can create an action sequence, you'll need to define a project to put your new file in. To create a project, select File ➤ New ➤ Project. Eclipse now starts the New Project Wizard, asking for the type of project to create. For the BI platform, just select Project in the General tab. You will need to give the project a name (any name will do; we used My Pentaho as an example) and select a location for your new project. You'll notice that the default location of a new project is the open workspace but you can select any other location as well. When you select an existing folder (for example, the Pentaho-solutions folder of the BI server), the contents of this folder will be displayed in the Project Explorer as soon as you click Finish. You can create a new Action Sequence in several ways:

- Use the New Action Sequence item from the BI Platform menu. This will create a new, empty xaction file, but you will have to define the location for the file (the Container) first.
- Right-click on an existing folder in the Project Explorer and select New Action Sequence from the BI Platform menu. Note that the container is now automatically filled in.
- Use the New Action Sequence Wizard from the shortcut icon menu. (The Tooltip for the icon is displayed in Figure 4-4). Again, the location (container) needs to be selected.

In all three cases the Action Sequence Wizard opens so you can enter a name for the new action sequence and select a template to help you jump-start building a new action sequence. Templates predefine inputs and actions for the specific tasks such as a new Analysis view or a burst action.

The xaction editor consists of four panels or tabs, which you can see along the bottom of the screen. An important part of the General tab, shown in

Figure 4-5, is the Title, which will be displayed in the user console. You can also find the icon that will accompany the Action title in the browser, the Version, the logging level, and the Author on the General tab. The Visible checkbox hides the xaction from the user console when selected, which makes it possible to create "helper" xactions that are not visible to end users.

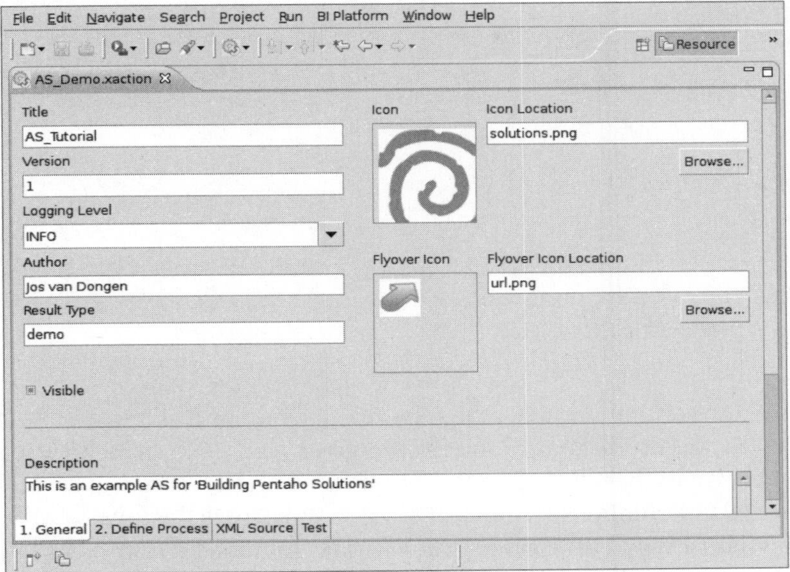

Figure 4-5: Action sequence editor, General tab

The Define Process tab shown in Figure 4-6 is the actual editor where you can add inputs, actions and outputs. To verify the generated XML code, you can open the XML Source tab, which some people will claim is the real action editor. The Test tab at the end lets you run the action directly from the Design Studio, although the Pentaho server is used for the actual execution of the code.

Before starting to build new action sequences, it is a good idea to test whether you can run actions from the Test screen. The easiest way to do this is to open the `HelloWorld.xaction` file, which is located in the folder bi-developers ➢ getting-started. On the Define Process tab shown in Figure 4-6, one process action is defined.

When you click on that, the process action Hello World is displayed, which has just two fields: the Name and Message of the action. Now you can change the message to something like `It is working!` Otherwise, the default `%string` message will be displayed. After saving the changes you can move to the Test tab to check whether your platform is working.

NOTE **A Pentaho server should be started before running a PDS test; otherwise, nothing will happen.**

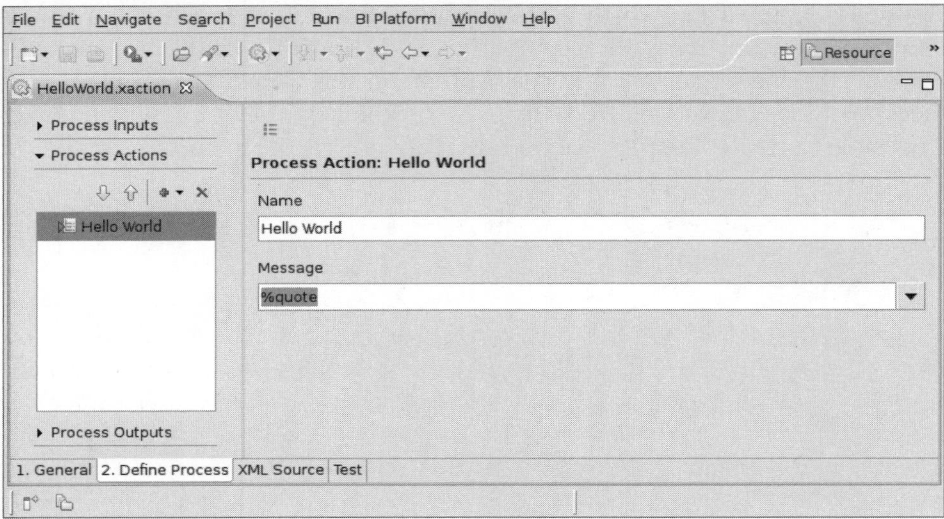

Figure 4-6: The Define Process tab

There are two text fields on the Test tab, as shown in Figure 4-7—one for entering the server URL, and one for the generated URL, which includes the xaction call. If you have the default Pentaho installation running on your local computer, the Pentaho Server URL is `localhost:8080/pentaho`. When you enter this and press Test Server, the Pentaho login screen appears. First log in and refresh the repository cache by selecting Tools ➤ Refresh ➤ Repository Cache (otherwise the existing xaction with the default text will be displayed). Click on Generate URL and then press the Run button at the right of the generated URL. You should see the result displayed in Figure 4-7.

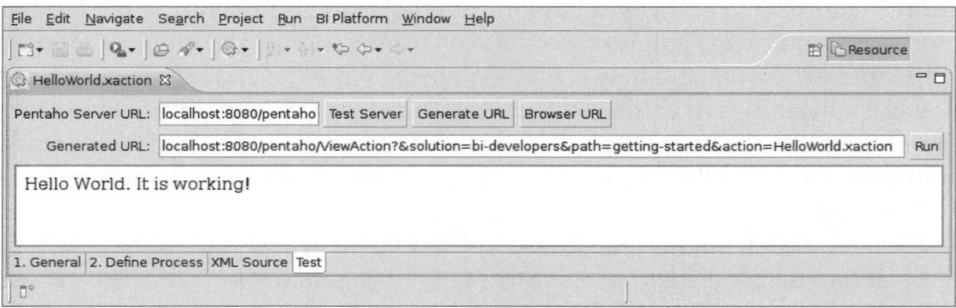

Figure 4-7: Hello World executed

Now that we've covered the basics of Eclipse and the Action Sequence Editor, it's time to get some real work done using these tools.

Anatomy of an Action Sequence

Action sequences (ASes) all have a similar structure, consisting of the following four building blocks:

- Inputs
- Resources
- Actions
- Outputs

When you open the Define Process tab of the AS editor you will notice that it looks like there are only three blocks that need to be defined: Process Inputs, Process Actions, and Process Outputs. This is where there is a slight difference between the designer and the created XML files; the XML files make a distinction between Inputs and Resources, whereas the designer treats both as different input types. The rationale behind this is that you will rarely need to manually add resources yourself because they will be managed by PDS. If, for instance, you add a report action, the file location is added as a resource automatically.

Inputs

Process inputs for action sequences are the parameters that can be used in process actions. The simplest form of an input is a hard-coded parameter. Each process input should at least have a name and a type (string, integer, and so on) that can be given a default value—for instance, a text string that can be passed into the Hello World action for display. An AS can read parameters from different sources, making it possible to pass information from outside the AS to a process input. The following sources of input are available:

- **Request**—These are name-value pairs that can be read directly from the URL. Using the same Hello World example, you can add an input named `RequestText` of type `string`, and add a new `two words` with an origin `request`. The default name given for the `input source` is the same as for the process input itself, but that can be changed. The process input name is the internal parameter reference; the input source name is the external reference. Figure 4-8 shows an example of this. Using this example, you can now select the Hello World process action and select the `<RequestText>` parameter from the Message drop-down list. When you now save the AS, refresh the repository cache and add the text `&req=This is great fun!` to the URL; the text `Hello World. This is great fun!` will be displayed. Note that in this case, the AS doesn't need to be altered and saved anymore to display new output. You can try this by entering a different text after `req=` and pressing Run again.

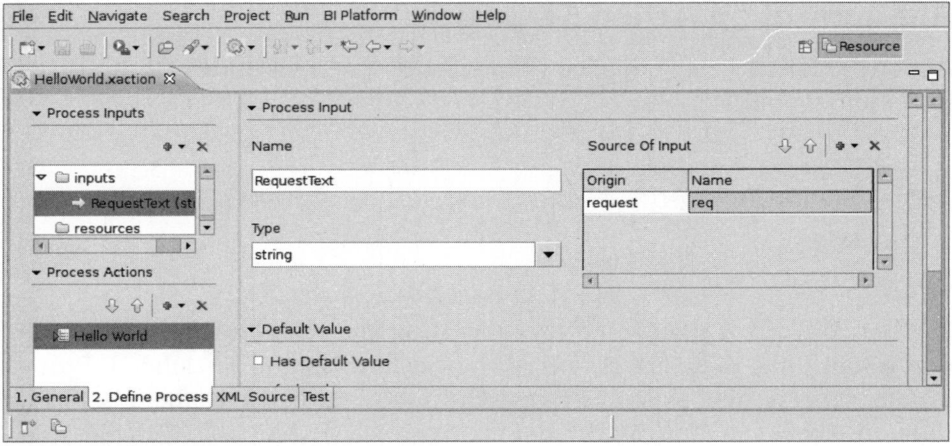

Figure 4-8: Request input source

- **Session**—These are variables that live for the duration of the user session. Interestingly, session, global, and runtime variables can be set using a system action that in turn is created with PDS. There are also a couple of default session variables that can be accessed, with the username of the current user the most frequently used one. This can be tested using the same Hello World xaction by changing the input source of the RequestText process input to `session` and the Name to `name`. After saving the AS and running it, it should now display `Hello World. <username>`, where `<username>` is the name used to log in to the Pentaho server.
- **Global**—Similar to session variables, but these have a global scope, which means that the values of these variables are the same for everyone using the BI server. The lifetime of a global variable is bound to the application, meaning that as long as the application runs (the BI server is `up`), the variables can be accessed.
- **Runtime**—Global variables but their lifetime is infinite, meaning that when you shut down the BI server (not the machine, but the application!), the runtime variable remains in memory. Because this somehow limits the control you have over these variables, it is better to use global variables instead.
- **Security**—Enables the retrieval of security (session) variables. The following parameters are available (note that these names are all case-sensitive!):
  - `PrincipalName (string)`—The name of the currently authenticated user. Similar to the session variable `name`.
  - `PrincipalRoles (string-list)`—The roles that the currently authenticated user is a member of.

- `PrincipalAuthenticated (string)`—`true` if the user is authenticated, otherwise `false`.
- `PrincipalAdministrator (string)`—`true` if the authenticated user is an Administrator, otherwise `false`.
- `systemRoleNames (string-list)`—All the known roles in the system. Handle with care because this list can become quite large.
- `systemUserNames (string-list)`—All the known users in the system. Handle with care because this list can become quite large.

Outputs

Outputs are what an action sequence can pass to the outside world, which could be other action sequences as well. They can have roughly the same destinations as an input can have origins, but there are a few differences. Instead of a request, an output can pass a response. Outputs can also save to a file or `vfs-ftp`.

Actions

Process Actions come in all sorts and sizes. There are actions to retrieve data, create or open reports and charts, schedule jobs, execute workflows or data integration jobs, and to send output to e-mail or a printer. Although we cannot cover all available actions and combinations of actions, we will give a few examples to help you on your way to building your own action sequences. Remember that Chapters 14 and 17 contain additional examples of ASes, more specifically for report bursting and dashboarding.

A collection of process actions will be executed in the order in which they are listed on the screen. By selecting an action and using the up and down arrows, the execution order can be altered. This is not the only control available here; two options are at your disposal for branching (`if`) and looping (`loop`) actions. Combined with the Prompt/Secure Filter action with which a user can be asked for input, these options allow for fairly complex execution logic. Basically there are two types of xactions: the ones that users will see in the folders they can access and can be run on demand by clicking on them, and the ones that will be scheduled and run in the background. A good example of the latter is report bursting, which generates personalized content for each user or user group. But because one AS can start another one (by adding a Pentaho BI Process in the process action list) the possibilities are virtually limitless.

WARNING **Be careful when calling one xaction from another one; deleting the "child" process is not prevented so you could easily break the main process.**

We could take the sample burst action template and explain how this works, but grasping the true power of PDS is best accomplished by starting with an empty action sequence and extending it step by step. First, let's explain what we want to accomplish:

1. Create a list of managers with their names, regions and e-mail addresses from the sample database.
2. Loop through this list and send an e-mail with the region revenue, budget, and variance to the respective region managers.
3. When the loop encounters the manager of the region 'Central', send him an additional overview of the total revenue for all regions.

This example uses many of the available features and is an excellent introduction if you want to build your own action sequences. The following steps walk you through the example.

1. First, create a new empty AS by selecting the Action Sequence Wizard. Select a container, a blank template and type in a file name. This is shown in Figure 4-9.

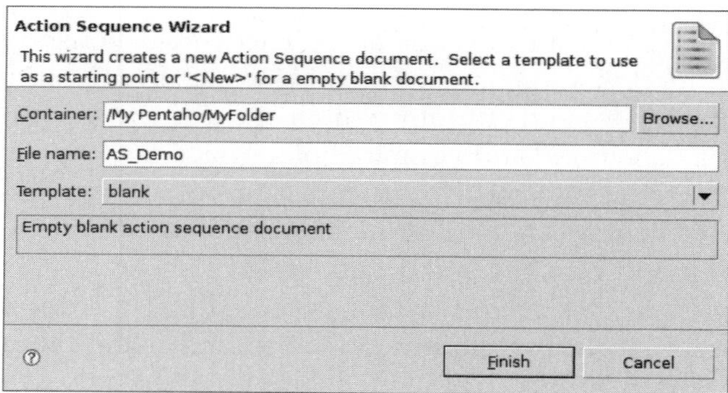

Figure 4-9: Create a new action sequence

2. On the General tab, type in the Title (required) and other fields (optional).
3. Now move to the second tab to define the process. First, you need to define where the mail is coming from, so create a new process input. Name the input parameter `from` and make sure the request origin is removed from the Source of Input.
4. Now you can add your first process action to retrieve the data list. Add a new process action and select Get Data From ➢ Relational. This is

probably the most frequently used process action so we explain this in a little more detail:

a. The Name of the action is displayed in the Process Action list and should reflect the function of the action. In this case, a name like `GetManagerInfo` will do fine.

b. To be able to retrieve data from a database, a connection is needed. Here you can use the simple JNDI type with the name `SampleData` (you need to type this in; it is not available in the drop-down list). Also, the Result Set Type should be set to In-Memory.

c. The Query itself retrieves the data. For this example, we'll use the query `select distinct REGION, MANAGER_NAME, EMAIL from DEPARTMENT_MANAGERS`. This query should run immediately.

d. Finally the Result Set Name should be entered; this is the name by which the list will be referenced later, so use a meaningful name again, such as the name LoopList we used. Because the query columns are not automatically translated into referenceable variables, the Result Set Columns need to be explicitly entered. In this case, you add the columns `REGION`, `MANAGER_NAME`, and `EMAIL`, all of type `string`.

5. Notice that the `GetManagerInfo` action now contains four action outputs: the three column names plus the name of the result set. Now you add a loop to be able to handle all rows from the result set sequentially. The Loop On drop-down list contains only one option, the LoopList. After selecting this, you can continue by adding the inner actions for the loop.

6. With the Action Loop selected, add another Relational action. A pop-up screen will ask whether the action should be created within or after the selected action; you need to add it within the loop. Name this action `GetResults`, use the same JNDI connection, and enter the following query:

```
SELECT  SUM(ACTUAL) ACTUAL, SUM(BUDGET) BUDGET, SUM(VARIANCE) VARIANCE
FROM    QUADRANT_ACTUALS
WHERE   REGION = '{REGION}'
```

Note that we use `{REGION}`, which is a reference to the region name of the current iteration of the loop. There are four regions so this query will be executed four times.

WARNING **All aliases and result set column names (parameters) in a Relational action should be in the same case or Pentaho will generate an error message.**

7. Before you can create the actual e-mail, you need to take a few steps. First, add the result set columns to the second Relational action if you haven't done this yet.

8. Now note that even if this result set retrieves only a single row, you still need to add another loop because PDS cannot know that you retrieved only a single row. This second loop will, of course, execute only once for each iteration of the outer loop. Inside this inner loop, you need to prepare the subject and message text by using a Message Template. Within this action, a mix of fixed text and parameters can be used, resulting in a dynamically generated text.

   Add a Message Template and name this `FormatSubject`. Use Text as the template source and enter `Results for region {REGION}` as Text. The Output name is the name by which this text can be recognized in the following actions, so we'll use `MailSubject` here.

9. Now add another Message Template. Call this one `FormatText`, and use `MailText` as the output name. The text you enter here is the full mail body text, including the parameters of the retrieved results, which can be seen in Figure 4-10.

10. Finally you can add an Email action, which can be found under the Send To actions. Name this one `Send Region Email` and use the `<from>` string input parameter you created first in the From field. In a real-life scenario, you would use the `<EMAIL>` parameter in the To field but because these are fake addresses in this case, use your own e-mail address or select the `<from>` parameter if you entered your own e-mail address there. In the Subject field, select `<MailSubject>` and in the Text Message, select `<MailText>`. Now the action can be saved and run. If everything was entered correctly, you should receive four e-mails with different results.

11. To complete the scenario you need to add a couple of extra steps. First, add an `If` statement to check for the Central region. The condition to add (`REGION=='Central'`) is shown in Figure 4-10. Then you can add the GetTotals Relational Action to retrieve the overall results. And just like you added an action loop for the region results, you add another loop here as well with a separate Message Template and Email message. The completed flow is displayed in Figure 4-10. The screenshot also shows that the `If` statement uses the Java-style comparison operators `==` for equality and `!=` for non-equality.

TIP **You can create and add your own action sequences as templates for Design Studio by saving the *.xaction file to the PDS template directory. It is located at `<eclipse install directory>/plugins/org.pentaho.designstudio .editors.actionsequence_<version number>/templates`.**

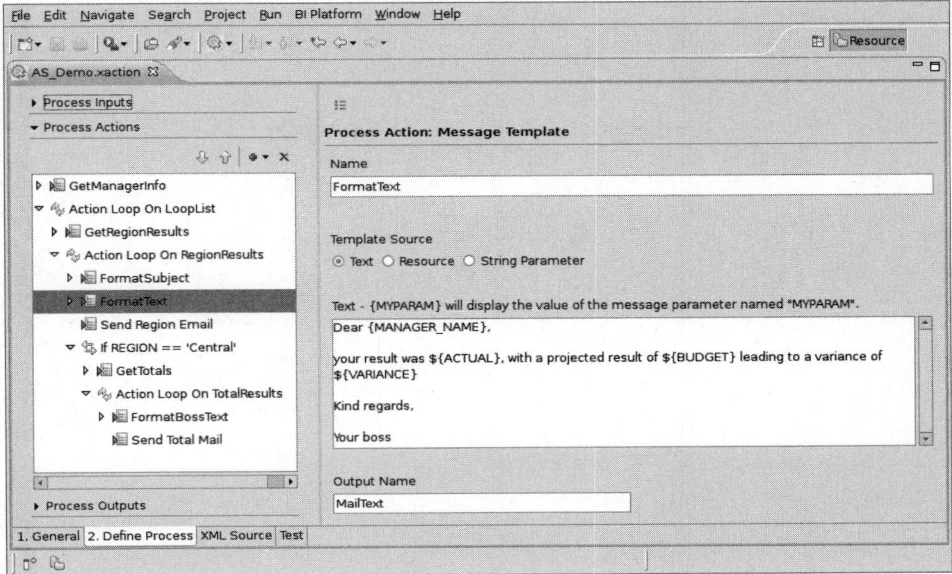

Figure 4-10: Completed workflow

Summary

This chapter offered a bird's-eye view of the complete Pentaho BI stack and all the constituent components. Topics covered in this chapter included the following:

- The open nature of the platform, allowing for non-Pentaho tools to be integrated
- Server, client, and desktop programs to be used by designers, administrators, and end users
- The Java servlet–based server architecture of the platform
- The Community Edition of Pentaho and the extra capabilities of the Enterprise Edition
- An overview of and introduction to Eclipse and the Pentaho Design Studio

The final part of the chapter consisted of a step-by-step tutorial for creating a report bursting action sequence.

Part

II

Dimensional Modeling and Data Warehouse Design

In This Part

CHAPTER

5

Example Business Case: World Class Movies

The examples in the remainder of this book are based on a fictitious company named World Class Movies (WCM). WCM is an online retail firm offering both movie sales and rentals; this combination sets the company apart from online retailers such as Amazon that only sell items, and companies such as Netflix, where movies can only be rented or viewed online.

Why did we choose an online movie store? First, it's an example that most people can easily relate to: we love movies, we read about new movies, we follow ''news'' about the actors that star in the movies, and watch movie review programs on television. And, of course, we're all familiar with ordering all kinds of stuff off the web. Second, the technical benefit of using an online retail example is that all transactions can be tied to a named or identified customer, so we can avoid the challenges presented by ordinary outlet sales selling items to anonymous clients. Finally, a reasonable amount of data is needed to illustrate some of the concepts related to data warehousing, business intelligence and analytics. This means we need many customers, many individual products, and a lot of transactions, which coincides wonderfully with the chosen example.

NOTE **An example like this can never cover all the intricacies of a real company or organization, so be prepared to run into several other types of departments and business processes in the real world. Departments such as finance, production, quality control, IT, and HR all have their own business processes and supporting systems and interact with one another and with the outside world in their own particular ways. Also be prepared to encounter industry-specific processes such as claims processing (insurance), environmental, health, and safety practices (chemical, manufacturing) or risk management (banking), each presenting its own**

challenges when it comes to process and data modeling and information management.

World Class Movies: The Basics

World Class Movies started selling and renting DVDs online in April 2000 and has shown a steady growth since then.

The WCM business model includes two tightly integrated processes: *customer order fulfillment* and *inventory replacement*, as evident from the following description of WCM's business.

A customer can order a DVD from a WCM web catalog and view it whenever he likes. If the DVD is returned within a specified amount of time, it's considered a ''rental'' transaction, whereas if the DVD is kept or not returned on time, it's considered a ''buy'' transaction. The key to the model lies in the fact that the DVD is initially paid for as if it was purchased, and upon returning the movie on time, the difference between the sales and rental price is added to the customer's account balance for subsequent orders. Customers are required to become members and pay an entry fee before they are allowed to order a movie. If a customer returns a DVD after the rental period, the movie is already booked as a purchase but the acquired item is again at a WCM warehouse and needs to be sent back to the customer. In this case the entry fee is used to cover the extra shipping and handling costs.

To stimulate customers to buy/rent more products, WCM uses various kinds of promotions.

WCM operates different websites targeted at different customer groups so that a more refined assortment can be offered to each market segment, although customers can acquire products via multiple channels:

- **World Class Movies Portal**—This is the company's main website, with a broad offering of blockbusters and all-time favorites, excluding the latest releases from the major studios.
- **WCM Premium**—Premium is a high-end website where customers are charged extra but are guaranteed to receive a new shrinkwrapped DVD. The site contains only the latest movies and the biggest blockbusters.
- **WCM Outlet**—The Outlet is the bargain site, where customers can get ''used'' movies that might have been rented multiple times already but are available at a discount.

- **WCM Cool**—This site is aimed at a younger and trendier audience.
- **WCM Exclusive**—The Exclusive site offers special editions and imported items.

This division into multiple channels, each with its own target audience and price plans, enables WCM to keep its stock moving briskly.

The back office of the business consists of a series of warehouses spread across the country. When a customer order is placed, the ordered items are sent from the nearest warehouse to minimize distribution cost and shipping times. WCM started out with a single warehouse but, because the business has grown steadily over the years, it was deemed more economical to add multiple distribution points.

The company's headquarters are still located in the same location as the California warehouse where WCM started out. All purchase orders placed at the different distributors originate from this head office, where each order specifies the warehouse the goods should be delivered to.

The two main business processes for the company can be summarized as follows:

- *Customer order fulfillment* handles individual customer orders and ships/receives DVDs from and to different warehouses.
- *Inventory replenishment* covers centralized ordering and decentralized receipt of goods in different warehouses.

And of course, to make the company actually do something, people are needed as well, so employees and job descriptions complete the roundup of the high level business description.

The flow of orders and products between distributors, WCM, and customers is illustrated in Figure 5-1.

The WCM Data

Whenever you embark on a business intelligence project, it is imperative that you understand the source and nature of the data that will be used in the data warehouse. Without this knowledge, it is nearly impossible to design and build a system that will support the business in analyzing and reporting on the data to improve business performance.

World Class Movies uses two databases to support its business, one for the operation of the back office (warehouse management, purchasing, HR) and one for the various websites (customer registration, sales). Product management is tied to both processes and WCM takes an interesting approach to this. Instead of having employees manually enter information about each product the company offers, WCM uses an external data feed for the company's product catalog. The only thing that WCM adds to this data is its own internal product IDs to link the information in the internal systems to the data from the external source. In addition to the movie catalog, which contains details on each piece of inventory, WCM uses the ISO 639 and 3166 tables for the code and name of language, country, and state (region).

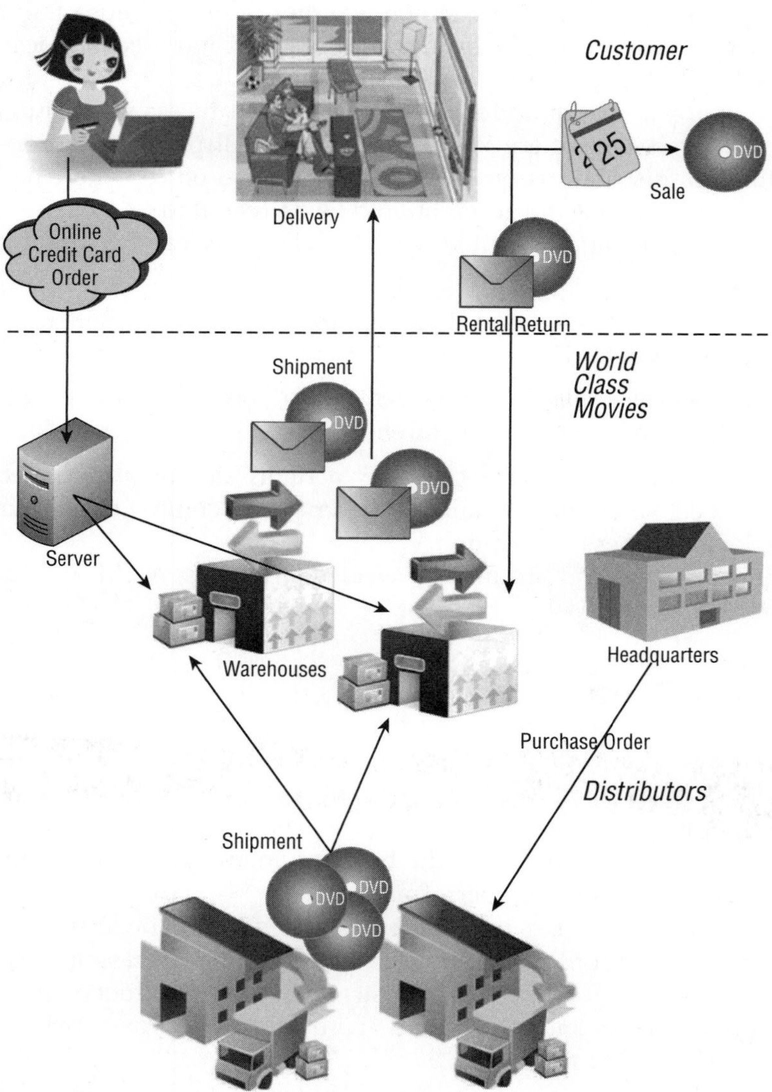

Figure 5-1: Main process flows in World Class Movies

ISO: INTERNATIONAL ORGANIZATION FOR STANDARDIZATION

ISO defines and manages standards on a large variety of topics, most notably the ISO 9000 family of quality management standards. Over 17,000 international standards have been developed thus far and more than 1,100 are added every year. Among the most well-known standards are ISO 9660, which defines the ISO Image archive format that is used to burn CDs and DVDs, and ISO 12232:2006, which defines the film speed in digital still cameras. The biggest advantage of using a standard for data values such as dates or country names is the conformity of the entries between various systems, which ensures compatibility and easy translation from one system to another. Best practice is to use data that conforms to an ISO standard in your source systems whenever possible. The more the source system is standardized and makes use of uniform data definitions, the easier the task of building a data warehouse will be.

Obtaining and Generating Data

There aren't a lot of good sample databases available, and most of them can't be used without restrictions or are part of a commercial database offering. People familiar with MySQL might know the Sakila sample database, which served as a starting point for the WCM database but is a bit too simple and contains too little data to illustrate the concepts in this book. For this reason, we decided to develop a freely available, LGPL-licensed sample database with enough complexity and a realistic amount of data in it to be useful as a source for a data warehouse project.

While developing an instructive data model is a challenge in itself, this challenge is dwarfed by creating meaningful data for it. Luckily, there are some publicly accessible data sources such as the U.S. Census, the Fake Name Generator, and the Home Theater Info DVD catalog that we can use for customer, employee, product, and external information. All other data in the database is either created by hand or generated using scripts. The base data sets and the scripts to create the schema and create the transaction data can be downloaded from the companion website of this book.

WCM Database: The Big Picture

Before explaining the individual parts of the WCM data model, we present a global overview here of the database that will be used for the examples in the remainder of the book. The fastest and easiest way to get acquainted with the data model is to sum up the different entities, relations, and roles played by each entity, which is the purpose of the following list. The diagram in Figure 5-2 can be used as a reference.

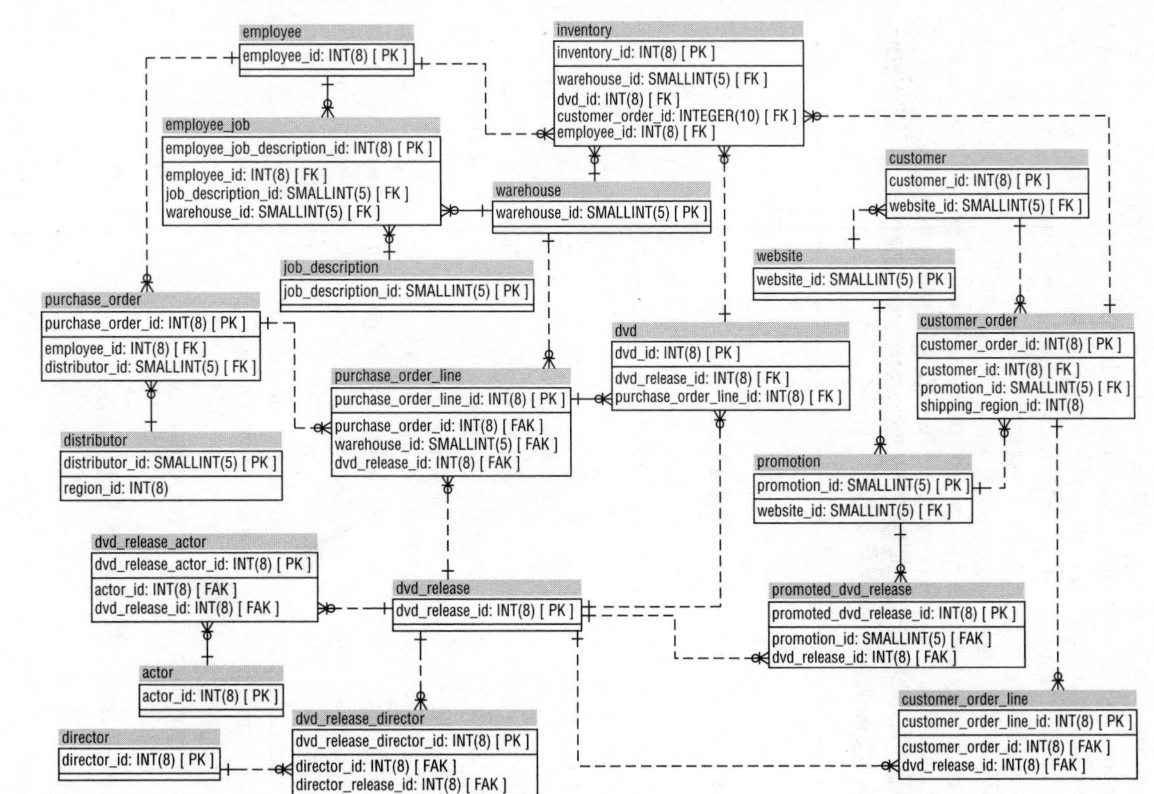

Figure 5-2: Global database diagram

- The cornerstone of the database is made up of customers, products, and orders.
- There are two types of orders: purchase orders and customer orders.
- Products are purchased from distributors and received in a warehouse where they are checked in by employees.
- Each purchase order is placed by an employee at a certain distributor and can have one or more purchase order lines.
- A purchase order line consists of the item, quantity, and price of the acquired product and also denotes the destination warehouse of the products.
- Employees have a job description and work at a specific warehouse.
- Warehouses, employees, customers, and distributors have an address.
- Each address is located in a certain region, and a region is part of a country.
- Customer orders are placed on a website and can have a promotion attached to them.
- Promotions pertain to certain products (DVD releases) and can either have a lower sales price, a lower rental price, an extended rental period, or a combination of these.
- A customer order consists of one or more order lines where an order line is created for each individual product.

Not all entities are visible on the diagram; all tables that contain address information are linked to `region` and `country`. Both tables are left out for clarity but can be found in the detailed customer diagram. Two other tables not visible in the diagram are `lookup_type` and `lookup_value`, which contain different combinations of key/value pair information such as status code and transaction type. Constructs like these (multiple non-related lists in a single lookup table) are common in an Enterprise Resource Planning (ERP) system.

The next sections provide additional information on each part of the database schema, including the data model and content.

DVD Catalog

There are several options for obtaining cinematic information from the Internet, with the Internet Movie Database (`www.imdb.com`) being probably the most well known and widely used source of movie information. WCM investigated the use of the IMDB as the source for the DVD catalog but found the information contained in the IMDB Laserdisc list to be far from useful. The best and most complete source of this information turned out to be the Home Theater Info site (`www.hometheaterinfo.com`), where information for all DVDs available from the various studios can be found, including actor and director information. WCM has decided to license this database for internal use as well as for the web catalog.

Every title is considered a *DVD release*, and although there is a distinction between the concept of a movie and a DVD, only the latter is available in the WCM database. A *movie* is the artifact describing the Hollywood production, and when this movie is released on DVD, WCM creates a DVD release, which can be ordered by customers via the web store. The customers are then sent a physical DVD, which is picked from the inventory. So theoretically speaking, there is a three-layered data model (movie ➢ DVD release ➢ DVD), which denotes a master-detail-detail relationship among the three entities. In this theoretical case attributes such as title, actors, and director would be linked to the movie and attributes such as release date and rental price would be related to a DVD release. However, the WCM catalog has no `movie` entity and therefore stores all the available movie information at the DVD release level.

Added to the DVD information is data about actors and directors, which is also obtained from the Home Theater Info database. This enables WCM customers to look for movies featuring a specific actor or movies that are directed by a specific director. The complete movie catalog schema is displayed in Figure 5-3.

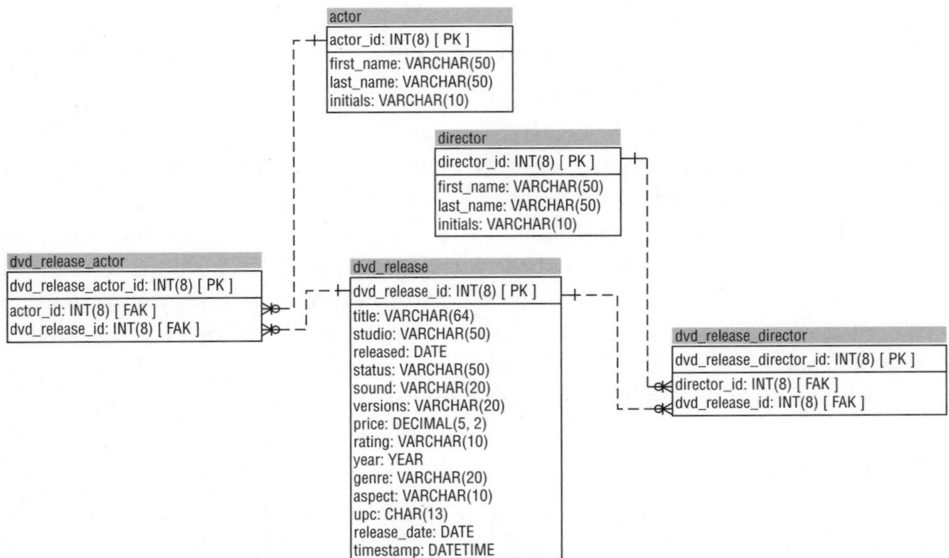

Figure 5-3: Movie catalog data model

NOTE Because this data is loaded from an external source, the data model is adopted as well, resulting in a less elegant model. A better solution would be to

merge actors and directors into a `Person` table and add a link table between `DVD release` and `Person`. This link table could then be extended with flag fields such as `is_actor` and `is_director` (and in the future perhaps `is_producer`, `is_music_composer`, etc.)

Customers

Like most commercial organizations, WCM has customers. And because products need to be shipped to an address and paid for by a credit card, WCM has quite a lot of information about its customers. This information includes address, zip code, date of birth, and gender, which makes the customer data very suitable for all kinds of analysis. The WCM database to date contains information on over 145,000 customers who subscribed to the different webstores over the past eight years. Of course, this is not exactly true: the real story is that this collection of customer data is randomly generated by the online Fake Name Generator (`www.fakenamegenerator.com`) where customer data can be generated for a number of countries in free batches with a maximum size of 40,000, or can be bought in batches of a million names. The interesting aspect of the generated names is that they are not really random, but representative of certain demographic patterns. For example, you'll see more people living in New York city than in Zwolle, Louisiana, which makes the data perfectly suitable for the WCM demo database. The `customer` table also references the `country` and `state` tables because (new) customers are only allowed to select from a fixed list of values to prevent data entry errors. The last reference concerns the website where the customer originally applied for an account at WCM. Figure 5-4 shows the complete customer data model.

Employees

The employee data model is kept simple but allows for switching jobs within the company and even for reallocation of employees to different warehouses. Figure 5-5 shows the employee diagram.

WCM has a separate HR system that includes all other staff-related information such as salaries, contract types, absence, education plans, and the like. HR systems are notoriously complex to retrieve data from and are not covered in this book. The source of the used employee information is the same as for customers and consists of a subset of the generated fake name set.

Purchase Orders

The purchasing process is fairly simple at WCM: a purchase order is placed at a distributor by a certain employee and contains one or more purchase order lines. Each purchase order line contains a number of DVD releases ordered for a specific warehouse. The Entity Relationship Diagram (ERD) is shown in Figure 5-6.

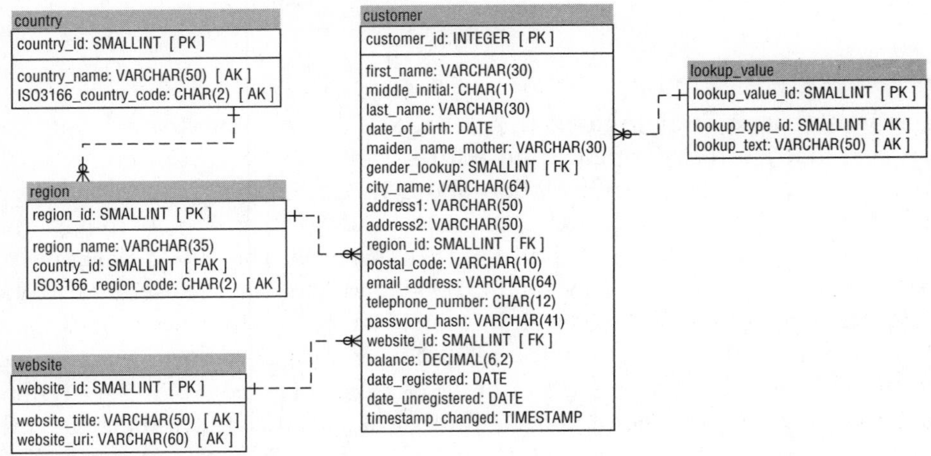

Figure 5-4: Customer data model

The purchase order line also contains the purchase price obtained from the `DVD release` table at the time of ordering, the cost of shipping, and the dates for shipping, expected delivery, and actual delivery. Price history is not maintained in the DVD release data but the price merely updated there. The price history, however, can always be obtained from the purchase order lines. Note that any intermediate price changes are lost this way, for instance when no order exists at a certain price point. Also note that this is a simplified model that ignores the fact that in the real world multiple distributors can offer the same product at different prices.

Customer Orders and Promotions

Customers order DVDs online and the web application makes sure that these orders are entered into the `customer order` and `customer order line` tables. Promotions are used by WCM to stimulate additional sales or to clean up redundant stock. Active promotions are automatically translated to banners and ads on the various websites. When a promotion is selected directly or DVDs are ordered that belong to a promotion, the correct customer order lines with the discounted DVD releases are added to the database by the web application. In other cases, customers might order a single DVD that belongs to a current promotion and at this time the option is offered to select the complete promotion (which can consist of multiple DVDs).

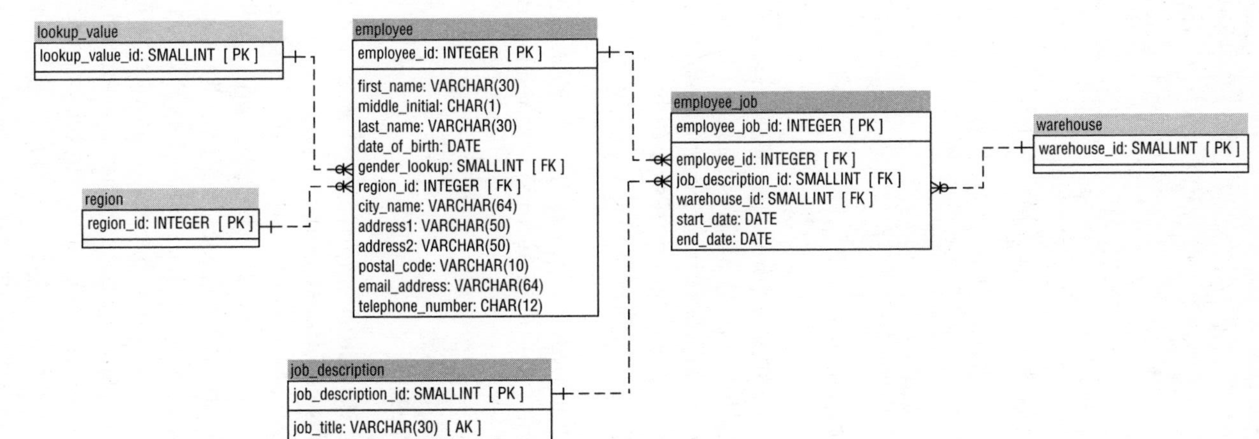

Figure 5-5: Employee data model

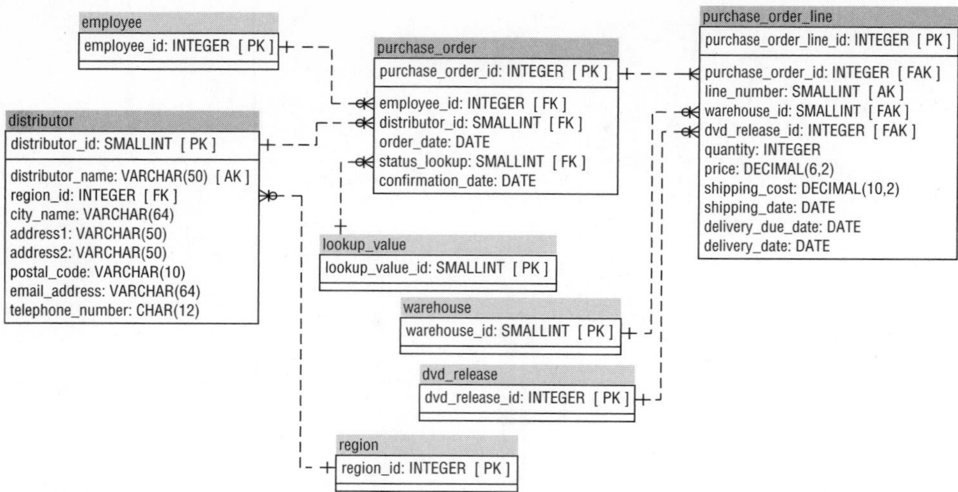

Figure 5-6: Purchase order data model

What might seem strange initially is the duplication of customer name and address data. This ensures that WCM always has a fully traceable history of customer data. The customer address might be updated in the `customer` table, but the orders will always reflect the address an item has been shipped to. The customer order and promotion part of the database schema is displayed in Figure 5-7.

Note that in this model an order quantity field is not available, leading to the limitation that only one item of a specific DVD release can be ordered at the same time.

Inventory Management

WCM needs to control its inventory and wants to record all product history as well. This information is combined in the `warehouse`, `DVD`, and `inventory` tables. Each physical DVD that is received from a distributor is registered and added to the `DVD` and `inventory` tables. The DVD entry gets the status `new`, meaning that it is available for sale or rent. The inventory entry gets the same `new` status, meaning that the new DVD is added to WCM's stock. After this event, the `inventory` table reflects the history of each individual transaction. A DVD can be `shipped`, `returned`, or `sold`. When a returned item turns out to be damaged, it gets the status `trashed`. Although the current status of an item can be retrieved from the `inventory` table, the choice is made to duplicate the current status in the `DVD` table for easy reference. This way, WCM is able to report on both current and historical stock levels. Figure 5-8 shows the part of the entity relationship diagram with the inventory management submodel.

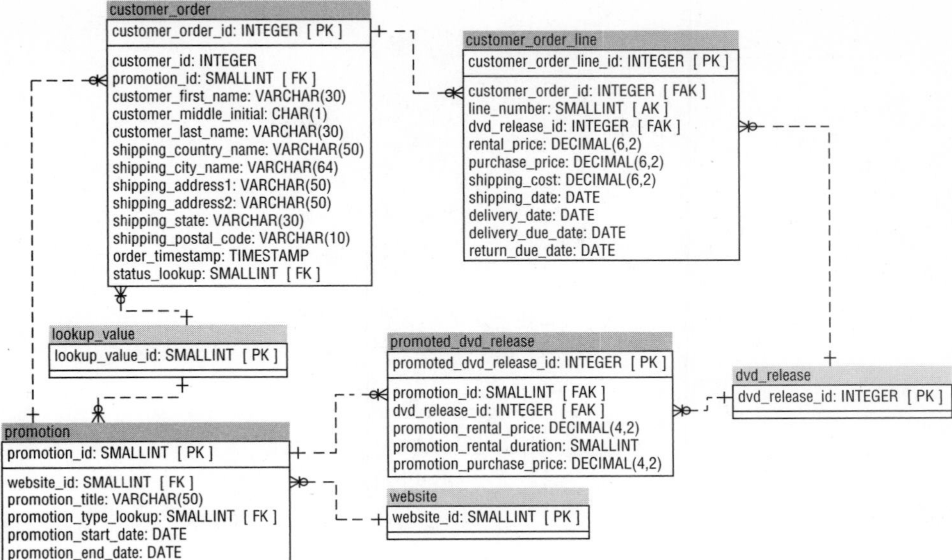

Figure 5-7: Customer order data model

Each DVD has a physical location at each point in time, denoted by the ID of the warehouse where the item is shipped from or returned to. Usually a product is shipped from the same warehouse as it is returned to but this doesn't necessarily have to be the case. Other information that can be obtained from the `inventory` table is:

- `Customer (customer_order_id)`—Shows the customer the item is shipped to, sold to, or returned from.
- `Employee (employee_id)`—Shows the warehouse staff member that shipped or received the DVD.
- `Timestamp`—The exact date and time the information is entered into the system.

Managing the Business: The Purpose of Business Intelligence

Managing a business is actually very simple when you take a mission-oriented view. WCM was founded because there was an obvious need for a convenient way to buy and rent DVDs without having to go out to a store. The mission is to become the biggest online DVD distributor in the country, and various intermediate steps have been defined to ultimately reach that goal (establish the business in one state, expand the customer base, add different sales channels).

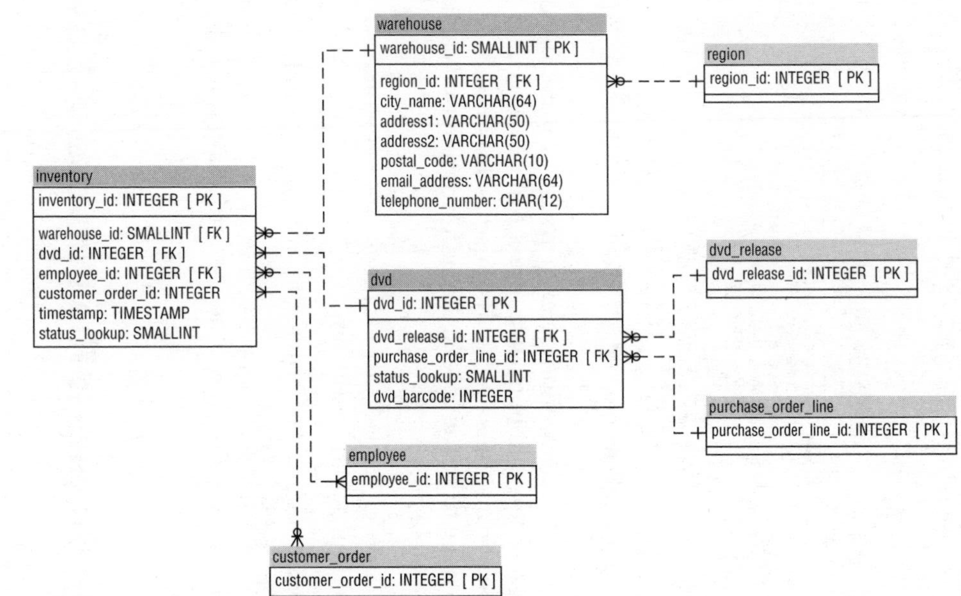

Figure 5-8: Inventory diagram

Along the way, WCM needs to monitor and analyze its performance to see what factors are contributing to success and which are detracting from it, and that's where business intelligence kicks in.

BUSINESS INTELLIGENCE

Howard Dresner, a long-time senior analyst of the Gartner Group, is often credited with defining the term *business intelligence* (BI). Although Dresner popularized the term, he wasn't the inventor. In fact, the term business intelligence was first used as early as 1958 by Hans Peter Luhn in the *IBM Journal*. Nevertheless, it's Dresner's definition of BI that is used most often nowadays: "Concepts and methods to improve business decision making by using fact-based support systems." This definition describes in a very elegant way that BI is much more than technology alone (a fact that is often overlooked by many of the BI practitioners) and that BI is a means to an end, not the goal itself.

Typical Business Intelligence Questions for WCM

For the sake of argument, let's assume that World Class Movies runs a very efficient organization but corporate management lacks the necessary insight to take the company to the next level. WCM's organization contains departments such as Finance & Sales, Logistics & Purchasing, Customer Service, and Marketing & Product Management and, of course, has some kind of general management and a CEO. These people and departments all have different needs in order to run their part of the business better and have some questions in common as well. Typical questions might include:

FINANCE & SALES

- How much revenue do we generate by region, month, and movie category?
- Which movie categories generate the highest revenue and is this constant over time?
- How does our performance compare to the total entertainment market?
- Are we growing faster or slower than our main competitors?

LOGISTICS & PURCHASING

- How do our distributors score in terms of product assortment, price, and delivery performance?
- How can we further optimize our distribution costs?

CUSTOMER SERVICE

- How many complaints do we handle?
- What kind of complaints do customers usually have?
- What's the average case load by service rep?

NOTE Customer service is added as an extra example and is not covered by the sample data models

MARKETING & PRODUCT MANAGEMENT

- How does the lifetime value of the top 100 customers compare to the bottom 100?
- How can we segment our customers based on RFM (recency, frequency, monetary) analysis?
- Do we have customer data that can be used to indicate future profitability or churn?
- Can we predict future revenues for a new customer based on existing customer profiles and characteristics such as zip code, age, or gender?
- How do we keep track of the lifecycle of a product and which sales channels are to be used (product market combinations)?
- Which DVD releases are most likely to generate high revenue based on product characteristics such as actor, director, or movie genre?

From these examples, it is obvious that some questions (and their answers) relate to multiple business areas. And again, these examples are typical for a commercial organization selling products to consumers, but are probably not applicable to other industries—for instance, a healthcare organization such as a hospital.

Data Is Key

No business intelligence system can exist without data, and the sample questions provided might already have illustrated that internal data alone doesn't suffice to get a good understanding of the performance of an organization. Most BI systems start with an internal focus, reporting on past sales data. This is great for getting your feet wet, as you will see in the next couple of chapters, but is hardly enough in a competitive environment. Take, for example, an organization that celebrated a 10 percent growth in net sales revenue over the past year but overlooked the fact that the overall market growth was 20 percent. They actually did a very bad job, but remained unaware because the external data that could have disclosed this information was not used. For full insight into the real performance of a company, external data is mandatory. World Class Movies therefore uses two extra sources of information. The first one is the 2000 Census Zip Code data set, which allows the company to relate internal customer data to overall demographic data and trends.[1] The second source of information is the historical e-commerce revenue data obtained from the E-Stats site of the U.S. Census, which can be found at `www.census.gov/eos/www/ebusiness614.htm`.

Summary

This chapter introduced the fictitious company World Class Movies that we created for this book. Based on this example we described the following:

- The main business processes of the World Class Movies company
- An overall data model of the database supporting the processes
- The detailed data model for each main business entity (customers, products, orders, inventory, employees)

The last part of the chapter illustrated the purpose and value of using Business Intelligence solutions in general and the answers that a BI solution can provide for a company like World Class Movies.

[1]The 2000 Census Zip Code data set is reused with permission from *Data Analysis Using SQL and Excel*, by Gordon S. Linoff, Wiley Publishing, Inc., 2008

CHAPTER

6

Data Warehouse Primer

A data warehouse is nothing new; in fact, data warehousing was being practiced for years even before the term was coined by Bill Inmon in his seminal work *Building the Data Warehouse*.[1] Although Inmon is often referred to as the "father of data warehousing," this is not entirely the case. To give credit where credit's due, it was the Irish IBM architects Barry Devlin and Paul Murphy who, in 1988, laid the foundations for what we today call a data warehouse. It's interesting to see that the concept of the *Business Data Warehouse* (BDW) Devlin and Murphy described in their original article hasn't changed that much over the past decades. They define the BDW as "the single logical storehouse of all the information used to report on the business," which is still exactly what it is.

NOTE **Feel free to just skim over this chapter or even skip it if you're already familiar with the basics of data warehousing.**

To get a better understanding of the nature of a data warehouse we will add Inmon's original description as well. He defined a data warehouse as being:

- **Subject oriented**—All entities and events relating to a specific subject (e.g., "sales") are linked together.
- **Time variant**—All changes to the data are tracked to enable reporting that shows changes over time.
- **Non-volatile**—When data is entered into the data warehouse, it is never overwritten or deleted.

[1]See *Building the Data Warehouse*, 4th Edition, by W. H. Inmon, Wiley Publishing, Inc., 2005.

- **Integrated**—The data warehouse contains data from multiple source systems after being cleaned and conformed.

Over the years, these descriptions (especially the "non-volatile" aspect) have been challenged and adapted by other authors and practitioners, leading to different architectures and ways of modeling the data warehouse. It is, however, good to keep in mind that all authors still agree on the reasoning behind a separate data store for business analysis and reporting as was originally defined by Devlin and Murphy:

- Ensuring that the performance of the production systems is not disrupted by ad hoc queries or analyses
- Requiring that information needed by end users does not change while they use it, i.e., point-in-time data

Why Do You Need a Data Warehouse?

People who have never been exposed to the concept of a data warehouse are often confused about the need and purpose of a specialized database for decision support purposes. Even after the obvious benefits—integrated data from different systems, query performance, relieving source systems from long running queries, and the tracking of history—have been explained, it's still not always clear why building a data warehouse is a good idea. Quite often, these users have grown accustomed to retrieving or obtaining data from various sources, including data sent to them by e-mail, which they then import into a spreadsheet application that they use for further analysis and reporting. No data warehouse needed, right? Not so right, actually. Let's try to explain why a data warehouse is useful, from a user's perspective:

- **All information is in one place**—No more hunting down several disparate sources of information or trying to find older files in a cluttered e-mail system or folder structure. No need either for combining all this data yourself: it's already integrated and ready for use.
- **Up-to-date information**—Data in the data warehouse is automatically loaded and updated on a regular basis, which means you are never out of date or looking at old information.
- **Quick access**—The data warehouse is optimized for speedy retrieval of information. The data warehouse answers your queries a lot quicker than local file stores or e-mail archives.
- **No size limits**—Spreadsheets can store only a limited amount of data and often need to be split in pieces to accommodate all required information. A data warehouse can store a virtually unlimited amount of data so no

more offloading of data to a local database or yet another spreadsheet is required.

- **All history available**—The data warehouse not only contains current information but also data from last week, last month, last year, and several years back as well. This means that any trend analysis or comparison over time is supported by the data warehouse. In fact, if you never delete data from the data warehouse, it will often contain much more historical information than the source systems. The available history is not only "older data," but offers additional value when changes are tracked as well. This allows you to look at the data as it actually was during the time it was originally processed. When someone lives in Boston in 2008 but moves to New York in 2009, you will still see the 2008 results for this customer attributed to Boston, not to New York.
- **Easy to understand**—The data warehouse is modeled in business terms and reflects the way you look at your organization. You don't need to decipher three-letter acronyms that no one understands, but can have clear names for all data elements.
- **Clear and uniform definitions**—No more discussions about what data means or what the definition of "revenue" is. Everyone in the organization uses the same definitions, which greatly simplifies communication.
- **Standardized data**—All data conforms to standards, which means there is only one definition and one set of values for each piece of information. A good example of this is the coding of gender. Some systems use 0 and 1, some use male/female and other use M/F/U (for unknown). All translations into a single standardized definition have been taken care of.

This list points out the advantages of a data warehouse but is based on an important assumption: that the data warehouse is designed and built properly. Even when the implementation is top-notch from a technical perspective (first five bullet points), it can still be considered a failed project from a user perspective (last three bullet points). The "easy to understand," "clear and uniform definitions," and "standardized data" advantages are often overlooked, especially when the data warehouse is implemented by an IT department without enough user involvement.

METADATA: NAMING AND DESCRIBING YOUR DATA

If the last three arguments for building a data warehouse are reversed, it's also possible to look at the purpose of the data warehouse in a different way: as the vehicle to arrive at standardized data and clear and uniform definitions. This is not entirely a data warehouse–related subject but has a much broader

(continued)

METADATA: NAMING AND DESCRIBING YOUR DATA *(continued)*

applicability which is often referred to as *metadata*. A simple and widely used definition of metadata is *data about data*. Lots of misconceptions exist about what metadata is or should be, but without wanting to oversimplify it, it all boils down to one question: how do you name and describe the information in an organization in such a way that everyone immediately understands the meaning of it and this meaning is the same to everyone involved? If you can overcome this hurdle early on in your data warehouse project, you'll be paid back threefold. If you take it one step further, you'll see that metadata covers a whole lot more than just descriptions of data (e.g. what is meant by 'revenue'?). The following items are also considered metadata and are of imminent importance in a data warehouse environment:

- Data Lineage—The information about origin and destination of the data in each step of the data transformation process. Data lineage information provides a full audit trail of the data in a data warehouse, which is essential for meeting compliancy regulations such as the Sarbanes-Oxley Act.
- Data Timeliness—The information about when data has changed and how 'old' the data is a user is looking at. Often, multiple timestamps are used when information is presented: the time a report is run or printed, the time the data was loaded or changed in the data warehouse, and the time the data was last changed in the source system.
- Data Model—The models used in the book are also a form of metadata, usually called *structural metadata* as it does not provide a description (as in the previous items) but only the structure of the data. The text explaining the data model is the descriptive metadata in this case.

The Big Debate: Inmon Versus Kimball

There is general agreement on the basic idea of using a special data store for supporting analysis and reporting. It is how this data store should be structured and organized that has been the subject of many heated debates over the years.

In the beginning there were basically two approaches to modeling the data warehouse. It all started when the two industry giants, Ralph Kimball and the aforementioned Bill Inmon, started publishing and evangelizing their data warehousing ideas. Each got a loyal (and sometimes even fanatical) group of followers, which contributed to even more discussion around the two schools of thought. While Inmon popularized the term *data warehouse* and is a strong proponent of a centralized and normalized approach, Kimball took a different perspective with his *data marts* and *conformed dimensions.*

The main differences between the Inmon and Kimball approach center on three points. An understanding of these points of difference will help you gain a greater understanding of data warehousing in general. (You'll get plenty of data mart examples in this book so don't worry if these descriptions don't sink in immediately.)

- **Data warehouse versus data marts with conformed dimensions**—We have already presented Inmon's definition of the Business Data Warehouse: "the single logical storehouse of all the information used to report on the business." In contrast, a data mart contains information pertaining to a specific business function such as sales or employee headcount. This information can be viewed from different perspectives, called *dimensions*. Each dimension contains all information related to a certain business object, such as a calendar, customers, or products, and can be linked to one or more *fact tables* containing measurable items (revenue, cost, number of employees, and so on). The end effect is that users can retrieve information about sales by department, by customer for a specific period from a data mart, but from the same data mart it is not possible to retrieve tangentially related information such as employee headcount. This requires a separate data mart, which can reuse some of the same dimension information (in this case: employee and calendar) already used in the sales data mart. Because the dimensions *employee* and *calendar* have an applicability that extends beyond a single data mart, they are called *conformed dimensions*. The concept of dimensional modeling is covered in depth in Chapter 7.
- **Centralized approach versus iterative/decentralized approach**—As mentioned, a data mart contains only data for a specific purpose, whereas a data warehouse contains all information in an integrated fashion. The main difference between a Kimball- and Inmon-style data warehouse is the fact that Kimball organizes his data warehouse as a combination of integrated data marts, whereas Inmon considers a data warehouse as one integrated, normalized data model that contains all data needed for reporting and analysis and uses data marts just for end user access. This sounds like an extra layer of complexity, but keep in mind that in an Inmon-style data warehouse all problems relating to conformation of data and securing historical correctness of data are solved in the central warehouse, whereas in a Kimball-style architecture these issues need to be solved inside the data marts.
- **Normalized data model versus dimensional data model**—If the combined data marts versus the central warehouse were the only source for debate, the discord would have been resolved long ago, but there's

another and maybe even more striking contrast between the two: the issue of normalization versus de-normalization. Kimball introduced the technique of *de-normalization* for the dimension tables. Now a product can have a product group related to it, which in a normalized database would be stored in a separate table and linked via foreign keys. For an example of this, take a look at the WCM `customer` table, which contains a link to region which in turn contains a link to country (see Figure 6-1). In a normalized database schema, customer, region, and country are stored in three different tables to ensure the integrity of the region and country names (which are stored only once). A de-normalized schema, on the other hand, stores all information in a single table, thus creating redundant information, which is a curse to the strictly normalized camp. Figure 6-1 shows the difference between a normalized and a de-normalized database schema.

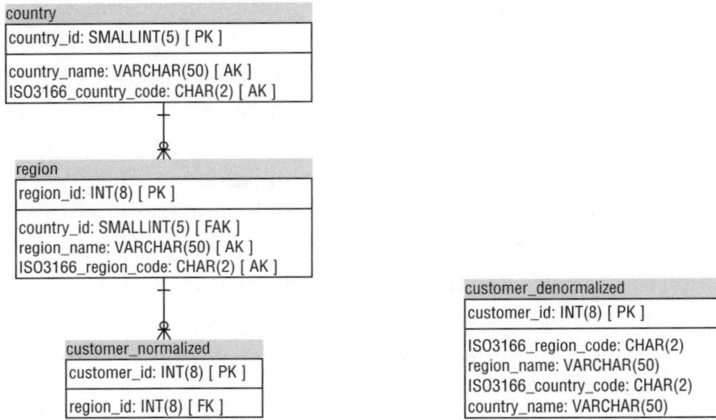

Figure 6-1: Normalization versus de-normalization

Contrary to popular belief, de-normalizing data *in a dimension* is not prone to the usual problems related to not normalizing a transaction database for the simple reason that it's not used for transactions. Dimension tables only get updated through the use of an extract, transform, and load (ETL) process that eliminates the risks otherwise involved with updating non-normalized data. We cover the dimension loading process in Chapter 10 and will cover dimensional modeling techniques in Chapter 7. The subsequent parts of this chapter focus on architecture and technology used for data warehousing.

Data Warehouse Architecture

An *architecture* is a set of rules to adhere to when building something, and because a data warehouse can become quite large and complex, using an architecture is essential for success. Several data warehouse architectures exist, but before exploring this subject in depth we will introduce a general framework and explain some of the terms you'll encounter further on.

The framework is illustrated in Figure 6-2. In the diagram, you can see:

1. One or more source systems (files, DBMS, ERP);
2. A process for Extracting, Transforming, and Loading the data (ETL). Often this process contains a staging area used as a landing place for extracted data and for doing initial data transformation and cleansing. For staging data both a database and flat files can be used. In many cases using flat files allows for faster processing.
3. The data warehouse, consisting of the central warehouse database and zero or more data marts.
4. The end user layer (EUL) with the various tools for working with the data (reports, dashboards, spreadsheets, and published documents).

Usually the combination of the central warehouse and the data marts is considered to be *the data warehouse*, and the term *data warehousing* is used to denote the complete process of building, loading and managing the data warehouse (DWH).

NOTE **The diagram in Figure 6-2 is a logical structure but not a required physical structure. Some ETL processes transfer the data "straight through" from the source systems to the data warehouse tables, and some data warehouses do not contain data marts at all or only contain data marts and no central warehouse.**

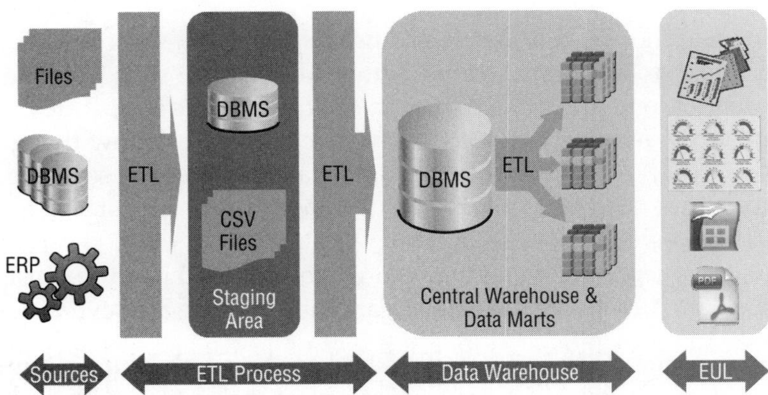

Figure 6-2: Generic data warehouse architecture

Some other terms generally used when talking about data warehousing are *back office* and *front office*. In Kimball's definition, the back office encompasses all technology and processes used to build and maintain the data warehouse, whereas the front office is the area where end users use the data in the DWH. In

Figure 6-2, the front office is the combination of all the reporting and analysis tools available to gain access to the data. The back office is comprised of ETL processes and the data warehouse.

Of course, this diagram is a very abstract and simplified version of most DWH implementations. The most important part of the process is the automated periodic loading of new data into the data warehouse. This is where the ETL (for Extract, Transform and Load) tool is used. ''Periodic'' may mean ''daily,'' but more frequent or sometimes even more infrequent loads are common. Periodical data loading is also referred to as *batch-wise* ETL, as opposed to *real-time* ETL. In the former, multiple records are transformed in a single batch; in the latter a transaction in the source system is immediately captured and loaded in the data warehouse. Currently, most data warehouses are loaded using batch-wise ETL but also with batch loading a near–real-time frequency can be necessary. Consider, for instance, the load of budget data; when this data changes only once a month or once a quarter, it is quite useless to load the budget every day. On the other hand, when the data warehouse is used for operational reporting as well, the data needs to be as current as possible.

When using batch-wise ETL this could mean running the process every five minutes. ETL is not only used for extracting data from source systems and loading the data warehouse, but also for maintaining relational data marts or moving data from one source to another.

The Staging Area

Every data warehouse solution should use a *staging area* where extracted data is stored and possibly transformed before loading the data into the central warehouse. Implementing this part of the architecture as a separate part of the data warehouse architecture is common practice so we follow this guideline here as well. The World Class Movies data warehouse uses a separate staging catalog (*catalog* is the MySQL term for database) called `wcm_staging` but CSV files are used as well.

What is the purpose of a staging area when we could just use our ETL tool to load the data directly into the data warehouse? There are several reasons:

- Source system load times should be kept to an absolute minimum, so when data is extracted from source system tables, it is a best practice to copy the data ''as is'' to the staging tables as quickly as possible.
- Using a separate staging area enables you to work on a specific subset of the data, or to be more specific, just the data that's required for the current run.
- A dedicated schema allows for specific sorting or indexing to further optimize and support the ETL process.

- The staging area is a safety net: a process can fail before completing. Because a staging area contains all data to be processed, a process can be restarted from the beginning or halfway point without requiring the data to be extracted again. Furthermore, the data set in the staging area doesn't change during a single run; loading again from the source system imposes the risk of data being changed since the previous load.

Remember that the staging area only contains the current extracted data, meaning that after a successful load or before running the ETL process all tables are being truncated again. Sometimes an historical archive is added to the architecture containing all extracted data with a load timestamp added but this is a separate database, not a staging area.

Modeling a staging area is a very straightforward process, especially when tables are truncated each time. Just duplicate the definition of the source tables without all the keys and indexes and you're done. Removing foreign key constraints does impose some risks of data inconsistency but this can be tackled with a carefully crafted ETL job. If indexes are used at all in the staging tables, their only purpose should be to help speed up the transformation process, nothing else.

The Central Data Warehouse

Strict rules for how to architect a data warehouse do not exist, but over the last 15 years a few common architectures have emerged. To help you decide which one is best for your purposes, it's always a good idea to look for benchmarks and case studies of DWH implementations, as The Data Warehousing Institute (TDWI) did in 2006. The research TDWI conducted distinguished five possible ways to architect a data warehouse and scored them based on the success of the different architectures. The diagram in Figure 6-3 shows the five alternatives.

We describe these architectures here briefly and explain some of the advantages and disadvantages of each before we explain the choices made for the example cases in this book.

- **Independent data marts**—Each data mart is built and loaded individually; there is no common or shared metadata. This is also called a *stovepipe* solution.
- **Data mart bus**—The Kimball solution with conformed dimensions.
- **Hub and spoke (corporate information factory)**—The Inmon solution with a centralized data warehouse and dependent data marts.
- **Centralized data warehouse**—Similar to hub and spoke, but without the spokes; i.e. all end user access is directly targeted at the data warehouse.
- **Federated**—An architecture where multiple data marts or data warehouses already exist and are integrated afterwards. A common approach

to this is to build a virtual data warehouse where all data still resides in the original source systems and is logically integrated using special software solutions.

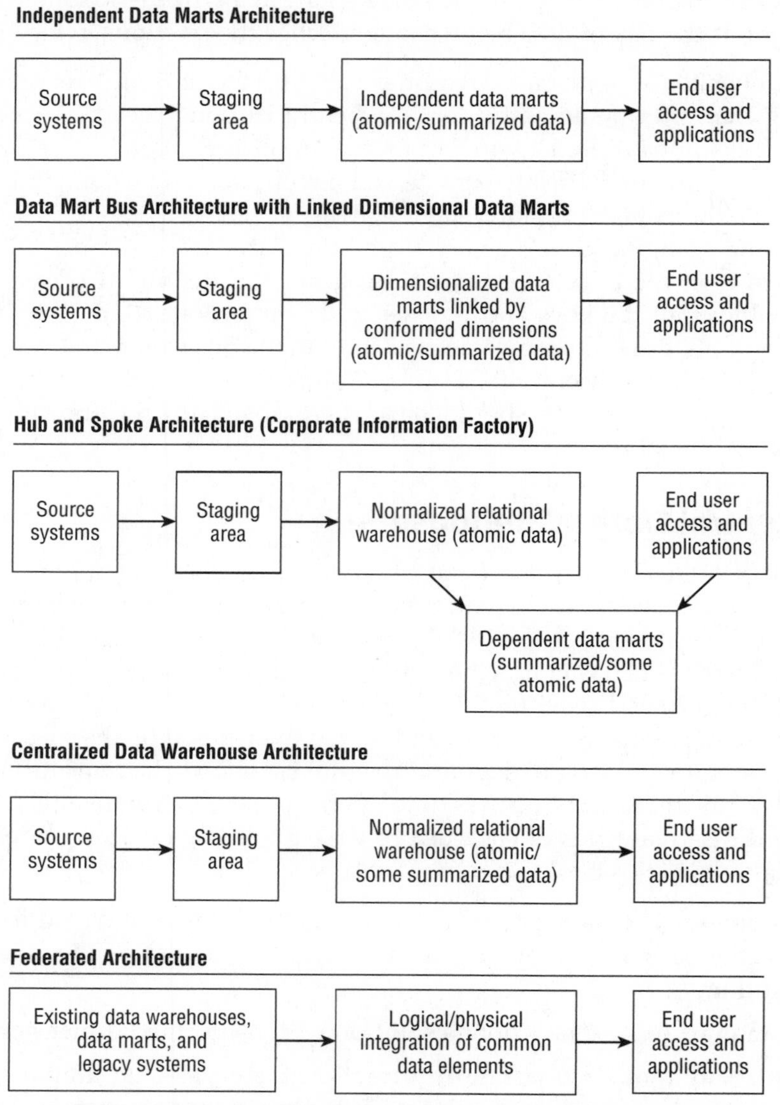

Figure 6-3: Data warehouse architecture alternatives

Of the five approaches both independent data marts and federated architectures were given a significantly lower score by TDWI than the other three, but what's most interesting is the fact that bus, hub and spoke, and centralized architectures score about equally well.

The difference between hub and spoke and centralized architectures is not that big; dependent data marts are added as spokes merely for performance reasons. There are still quite a few so-called hub and spoke data warehouse implementations that use only views to define those data marts, which results in a logical data mart without any performance gain. The major difference, however, between centralized or hub and spoke on the one hand and the bus architecture on the other is the cost and time of building the first *increment*, or useable part of the data warehouse. As might be expected, this cost is considerably higher in a hub and spoke solution. Furthermore, the information in the data warehouse is preferably exposed in the form of dimensional data marts anyway since this model is easier to understand for developers building end user solutions or even power users who can access the data marts directly. This is the reason we'll base our data warehouse example solutions on the bus architecture.

We heartily recommend reading the full report, which is still available online at `http://www.tdwi.org/Publications/BIJournal/display.aspx?ID=7890`.

Data Marts

From the discussion in the previous section, it may seem like a data mart contains only a limited set of data. In order to meet the specific needs of an organization, a data mart may indeed cover only a specific process and be limited to the boundaries of that process. You won't find employee absence information in a sales data mart, for example, because a sales analyst doesn't need that information.

From a technical or database viewpoint, however, there is no limitation to the amount or type of data that may be included in a data mart. For instance, consider a telecommunication company that wants to analyze average call duration by type of subscription, customer group, and period. Such a detailed analysis will require that all call detail records be included in the data mart, which could easily add up to billions of records in the fact table. In fact, companies even buy specialized hardware for these kind of analyses that can crunch terabyte-size data collections within seconds.

OLAP Cubes

As you've already seen, a data mart can be defined as a set of views on a central warehouse (virtual data mart) but in the case of using the bus architecture, the data warehouse consists of an integrated set of data marts that do not need an extra layer on top of them. This isn't the end of the story, however. To complete the picture, we have to introduce another type of storage which is often used for data marts, and that's the OLAP engine. OLAP is an acronym for OnLine Analytical Processing and has been around for decades, although the term OLAP was only introduced in 1993 by E.F Codd[2]. Probably the best known OLAP database in the world is Analysis Services, originally developed by the Israeli software company Panorama but later acquired by Microsoft who now bundles the product with its database. The idea of an OLAP database is to use an optimized storage format for analyzing data in a multi-dimensional format to offer the user flexibility and very fast access. The speed offered by OLAP databases is caused by the fact that most totals and subtotals (a.k.a. *aggregations*) are precalculated and stored in the OLAP *cube*. Although an OLAP cube can have many more than three dimensions, an OLAP database is often visualized as a Rubik's cube, hence the name *cube*.

Storage Formats and MDX

Three variations of OLAP databases exist, each named based on the storage format that is used:

- **MOLAP (Multidimensional OLAP)**—The original OLAP format in which the data is stored in a proprietary multidimensional format. All detail data and aggregates are stored inside the cube file. A good example of an open source MOLAP database is PALO, developed by the German company Jedox.
- **ROLAP (Relational OLAP)**—In this case, the data and all aggregates are stored in a standard relational database. The ROLAP engine translates multidimensional queries into optimized SQL and usually adds caching capabilities as well to speed up subsequent analytical queries. Pentaho Mondrian is a perfect example of a ROLAP engine.
- **HOLAP (Hybrid OLAP)**—In HOLAP, aggregates and navigational data are stored in a MOLAP structure but detailed data is kept in the relational database. To date, there is no open source HOLAP solution available, but some of the advantages have been incorporated in Mondrian with the addition of automatically generated aggregate tables to speed up queries.

All these solutions have the MultiDimensional eXpressions or MDX query language in common. MDX provides a specialized syntax for querying data stored in OLAP cubes, just like SQL does for relational tables. The language was first introduced by Microsoft in 1997 as part of the OLE DB for OLAP specification but was quickly adopted by the majority of the OLAP vendors. The reason for developing a specialized language for analyzing data in OLAP data stores is that SQL wasn't very well suited to do that. Although over the

[2]For an overview of the history of OLAP engines see `http://olapreport.com/origins.htm`.

years the SQL language has been extended with analytical features, MDX is still the de facto standard in the OLAP world. For those eager to get started right away: Chapter 15 covers the basics of MDX for using it in conjunction with Mondrian. In the year 2000, the XML for Analysis (XML/A) specification was introduced, which is now a de facto standard for querying OLAP databases. XML/A extends the MDX language with standardized XML tags to enable execution of query statements over HTTP using SOAP methods.

The Mondrian OLAP server supports both MDX and XML/A, which makes it a very versatile solution for all kinds of scenarios, but keep in mind that Mondrian is neither a data storage (data resides in the underlying relational database) nor an analysis tool (you'll still need a front end for analyzing data). So when you're using Mondrian as the (R)OLAP solution in your data warehouse environment, the components will look like the diagram in Figure 6-4.

Figure 6-4: Data warehouse with Mondrian

This concludes the description of data marts from a more technological and conceptual perspective; Chapters 7 and 8 will cover the design challenges involved with developing data marts.

Data Warehouse Challenges

Describing the different architecture components of a data warehouse merely serves as a starting point and to explain common terminology. The next few sections cover the major challenges involved with data warehousing: data quality, data volume and performance, capturing changed data, and changing requirements. It is tempting to look at data warehousing as a technical challenge, but as we already described in "The Purpose of the Data Warehouse" section earlier in this chapter, organizational challenges are probably even more important and harder to tackle. This is especially true in regard to data quality management, the topic of the next section, which takes the top spot in hard-to-address problems that often have only a limited relation to technology.

Data Quality

One of the biggest challenges in any data warehouse project is to ensure data quality (DQ). According to leading analyst firm Gartner Group, there isn't an organization in the world that does not have a data quality problem, so be prepared to fight some internal battles before going live with any reporting or analysis solution. DQ problems come in a variety of forms that are impossible to cover completely, but the most important ones usually fall into one or more of the following categories:

- **Duplicate data**—The same entity is entered multiple times in a single system, or the same entity exists in multiple systems but cannot be linked for the lack of missing keys or references.
- **Incomplete data**—The entities are there but some of the information is missing—for example, a house number in an address, a phone number, or any other property of a business entity (a business entity can be anything here, ranging from an insurance policy to an airplane). A properly designed system should prevent users from entering incomplete data, but there are still a lot of improperly designed systems out there. And even when a company uses an ERP system such as SAP or Oracle, it's likely that data from older systems has been migrated to these systems, which again is a cause for incomplete or inconsistent data.
- **Incorrect data**—All data is available and complete but has errors due to misspelled or mistyped entries. The most common source of incorrect data is call center agents that have to manually enter names, addresses, and other information given to them over the phone. Typing and listening speeds differ, and there you go.
- **Conflicting data**—The same data is stored in different source tables (in the same system) or in different source systems and contradicts each other.
- **Unclear metadata**—Definitions of the data in a system are not clear, leading to ambiguity in the data itself. As an example, think of a utility company defining its customers as connection points with an address, resulting in sending bills to lampposts.
- **Missing data**—This is an extreme version of incomplete data where complete records that should be in the system or were there earlier have gone missing. This is obviously the hardest category of problems to tackle because in most cases it's not even clear that there is a problem.
- **NULL values**—Fields in a database that have no value at all. The problem is that this can mean different things: not applicable, unknown, or missing.

Many tools are available, both proprietary and open source, that can help solve one or more of these problems, but there isn't a tool in the world that solves the real issue, which is lack of standards, procedures, and proper processes. Solving data quality issues is not a technical problem; it's an organizational problem. And although we will show you some workarounds using data profiling and data quality tools, including the validation steps available in Kettle in Chapters 9 and 10, you will need to be very careful in applying these.

In many data warehouse projects improving data quality is included as one of the project goals because the data warehouse needs to contain valid and correct data. Or does it? We like to think differently. The proper route to take, in our view, is to first put all the right procedures surrounding data quality in place as part of the primary business process, then clean up the source systems, and only after all this work has been done start loading the data. Because from this point on the DQ process is guarding the source of data, the data warehouse team can focus on delivering actionable information to end users and analysts. This is part of a broader topic called *data governance*, which, just like finance or production, treats its managed object (in this case, data) as a corporate asset. And just like any other business process involving assets like money, physical resources, or employees, a proper control framework needs to be in place.

Unfortunately, this is still utopia for most organizations. Data warehouse projects usually take a shortcut by including data cleansing steps as part of the load process without feeding the exceptions back to the business or source systems. And because this is a book about building BI solutions with Pentaho, we'll show you how to set this up. Just keep in mind that this is a solution to only part of the problem!

Data Vault and Data Quality

There is a new school of thinking based on a concept called the *data vault*. Data vault (DV) is a database modeling technique that's radically different from the conformed dimensional model we're using in this book. DV models are based on the concept that any data belongs to one of three entity types: hubs, links, and satellites. In short, the hubs contain the key attributes of business entities (such as orders, products, and customers), links define the relations between the hubs (for example, customer orders or product categories), and satellites contain all other attributes related to hubs or links, including all attribute change history. Figure 6-5 displays a partial example of how the World Class Movies data warehouse would look when translated into a data vault model.

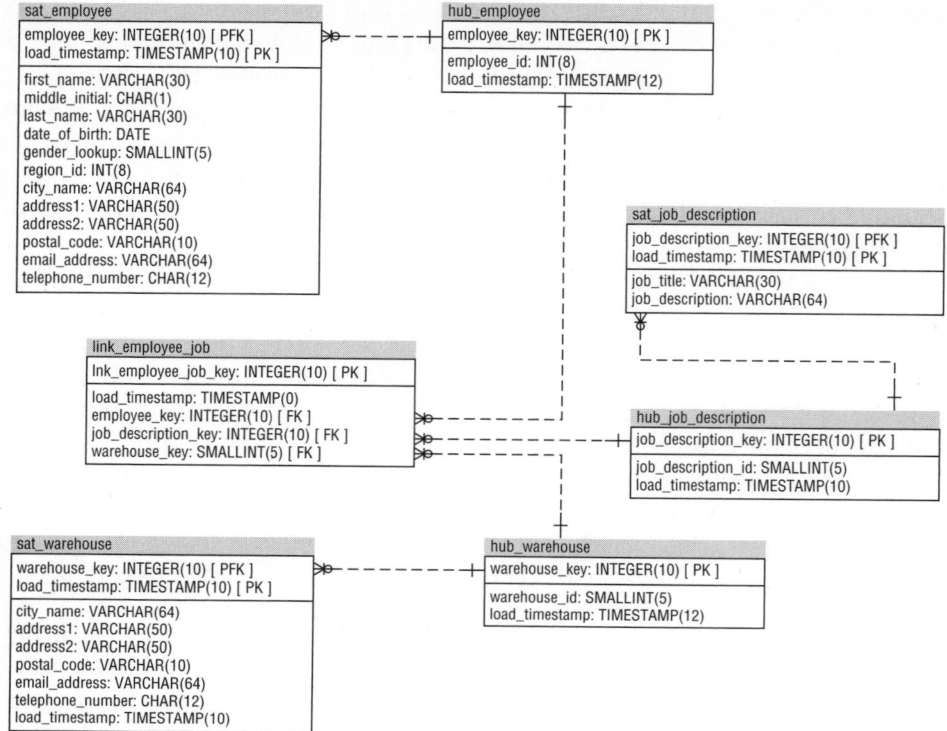

Figure 6-5: Data vault example

The big advantage of the technique is its ultimate flexibility. Adding attributes or new transaction types is relatively straightforward; there's no need to rebuild any of the existing parts of the database. On the other hand, a data vault is not accessible by any end user, not even an experienced analyst. Only after building data marts from the data vault, which includes processes for cleaning up and conforming possibly dirty data, can the information be made available to end users. Another possible drawback is the fact that the number of tables in the data warehouse will be large compared to a traditional normalized or data bus architecture, making the DV harder to manage.

From a data quality point of view, using a data vault has one major advantage: data in the DV is loaded from the source systems "as is," so if the data is dirty in the source system, it's dirty in the data vault as well. If a correction is made in the source system, the corrected data is *added* to the data vault as a new version. If there are multiple source systems, the system of record is included in the key of the stored data. The result of all this is that a data vault can always reproduce the information as it was stored in a source system at any point in time, which makes it an ideal solution in cases where auditability and traceability of data and transactions are mandatory, as in banking or insurance companies. All cleaning, merging, and conversion of data that usually takes place between the staging area and data marts in a bus architecture now takes place between the data vault and data mart. And because all history is available in the data vault, data marts can easily be disposed of or rebuilt in another way to answer different business questions.

In the BI community, one of the biggest buzzwords over the last couple of years has been *Single Version of the Truth*, meaning that the data in a data warehouse (no matter how it is modeled) means the same thing to all different people who work with the data. Data vault practitioners look at this slightly differently: their take is that the only truth is the source data (Single Version of the Facts), which should not be transformed in any way when entered in the data warehouse. From that point on, each user or department can have its own "version of the truth" created in the data mart: backtracking to the real "truth" is always possible then.

If you're interested in learning more about using the data vault, please visit the inventor's site at `www.danlinstedt.com/`.

Using Reference and Master Data

The term *master data management* (MDM) is used to describe all processes and technologies needed to enforce uniform data definitions and data content across an organization. Master data management is an area adjacent to data warehousing with its own range of concepts, books, practitioners, and conferences covering the topic. In the context of a data warehouse, it is necessary to cover the basic principles of MDM because the absence of a proper MDM process might heavily impact the success of a business intelligence project.

MDM has to do with managing information pertaining to business entities such as customers, products, vendors, and locations. One of the initial goals of any MDM initiative is to identify the *system of record* of an entity. In many organizations there are multiple systems containing one of the aforementioned items, with the "customers" entity having the reputation of being the most notoriously complex to handle. A customer system of record identifies the "gold copy" of customer data and shouldn't be mistaken for the *system of entry* where the data is initially entered or maintained afterwards. Ideally, these two systems are the same but that's not necessarily the case, especially when there are many systems of entry and only one system of record.

An example of this last situation is an organization that uses a product such as SugarCRM for maintaining all customer interactions via phone and e-mail, and Compiere as an ERP system that handles ordering, shipping, and invoicing from and to the same customers. In addition, customers can also enter and maintain their own data in a separate database through a custom web application as front end, so you have three systems with customer data, each with the ability to update this information. The problem gets even worse at banks, where most systems are product-oriented instead of customer-oriented, meaning that each product system has its own customer data.

An MDM initiative shares many characteristics with a data warehouse project: data needs to be analyzed, integrated, and cleansed. And just like data warehousing, MDM is a *process*, not a project. There are, however, also some notable differences. The most important difference is that unlike a data mart or data warehouse, MDM can never be a departmental initiative, run only within a customer service department, for example. And of course proper master data is initially intended to support the transactional systems to ensure that orders are being shipped to the correct address and that customer inquiries can be directed to the correct phone number and contact person.

Master data doesn't need to originate within an organization: sometimes it's even better to use the same external data that everyone else is using. Good examples of these are the ISO region and country tables we use in the World Class Movies database, or the North American Industry Classification System (NAICS) to identify in which line of business a company operates. In this case, a standardization organization takes care of the management of the data. Sometimes this external master data is called *reference data* to distinguish it from internal master data, which is simply called *master data*.

From this brief introduction, it's hopefully immediately clear why MDM is so important with respect to data warehousing and data quality: if there is one identified system that contains the correct copy of a business entity, that's probably the best source to feed your dimension tables from.

Data Volume and Performance

As you learned earlier, two reasons for using a separate physical environment for a data warehouse is the performance gain, compared to querying a regular transaction system, and the inability of systems to support both transactional and analytical queries. Another thing that's easily overlooked at first is the fact that data warehouses tend to get very large as a result of storing data from multiple systems over a long period of time. Usually transaction data can be archived after a certain amount of time, for instance after all required external reporting to tax authorities has been finalized. This frees up space and speeds up the transaction system, but also makes the database useless for trend analysis over an extended period of time. For this reason, the data warehouse retains all historical data, preferably at the most detailed level, resulting in huge data collections of sometimes several hundred Terabytes in size. The largest data warehouses at the time of this writing contain more than a Petabyte (1024 Terabytes = 1 Petabyte) of user data.

The biggest challenge when trying to analyze these amounts of data is to achieve an acceptable query performance for end users. Several techniques have been developed over the years to attain this performance, but unfortunately some of these techniques are only available in expensive proprietary database management systems such as Oracle, SQL Server, or DB2. The following list helps in determining which techniques might be useful in a data warehouse to enhance query performance:

- **Indexing**—With no special measures taken, any table in a database is just an unordered list with rows of data. Any query needs to read all data in the table (a.k.a. a *full table scan*) to find the correct answer. This process can be accelerated by storing pointers to the correct data in special index files. Indexes in a database are similar to indexes in a book where you can look up a keyword and find all pages that reference this keyword. A special kind of index is the *primary key* index, which is the unique identifier for a row. If you are using InnoDB as the MySQL storage engine, the primary key also denotes the physical sort order of the records in a table. This might come in handy because a lot of queries will have a reference to date. When the date key is the first column in a fact table and part of the primary key, the column can be put in a descending sort order, resulting in the most recent rows being the first physical rows as well. Retrieving last week's sales revenue won't be a very time consuming undertaking.
- **Bitmap indexing**—A special form of index is the *bitmapped* or *bitmap index*. Bitmap indexes are an optimal choice for indexing so-called low cardinality columns (columns with a relatively small number of unique values, like gender or movie genre). The basic idea is that for the distinct number of values in the column, a bit projection is created that enables very fast access to the indexed values. Figure 6-6 contains a simple example of this—a column with three possible values with the accompanying bitmap index values. Unfortunately, support for bitmap indexing is planned for a future version of MySQL but is not available yet.
- **Partitioning**—One of the most exciting new features in MySQL 5.1 is *partitioning*, which is the capability to slice a table into multiple physical vertical pieces. The advantage of this technique is that when a query can be satisfied by the data in one or a limited amount of partitions, the other partitions don't need to be looked at. In this sense, a partition is a kind of super index. Suppose, for instance, that a very large table is partitioned by year-month and you have 36 months of data stored. A query referencing the last quarter is then automatically restricted to the last three partitions, which saves you the effort of looking at the other 33. Another advantage of using partitions is the ability to drop and (re)create partitions, for instance when designing a ''round robin'' scheme where the most recent 36 months of data are always available. In this case, the oldest partition can simply be dropped while a new one for the current month can easily be added for loading current data.

Table data		Bitmap Index		
ID	COLOR	Ix1	Ix2	Ix3
1	Red	1	0	0
2	Green	0	1	0
3	Yellow	0	0	1
4	Green	0	1	0
5	Yellow	0	0	1
6	Yellow	0	0	1
7	Green	0	1	0

Figure 6-6: Bitmap index example

- **Aggregation**—All performance enhancement techniques aim to limit the amount of data to be searched for answering a specific query. This can also be achieved by using aggregate tables where precalculated results are being made available. To answer the question, ''What was our total sales revenue by month by website?'', the query doesn't need to query detailed data and summarize it but can get the data directly from an aggregate table where these results are readily available. Of course, the data warehouse load process needs to rebuild or update the aggregate tables each time new data is added, which can make this a time-consuming and challenging task, especially when multiple aggregate tables have been created. At this point, the Mondrian Aggregate Designer comes to the rescue (see Chapter 15) to create these tables automatically for you.
- **Materialized views**—A *materialized view* is a ''view with data.'' Unfortunately, this feature is not currently available in any open source database. A regular database view is just a definition mimicking a table but not containing real data. So when a view with the total revenue by month by movie genre is created (with ''sum'' and ''group by''), the database needs to calculate these results from the views base tables each time the view is queried. A materialized view not only stores these calculated values but also updates these automatically when the base tables are being loaded or updated.

  Now if that were the only advantage, it would still be possible to create a similar solution in any database using update triggers and queries. The part that would still be missing in that case is the real beauty of materialized views: *query redirection*. This feature parses the query targeted at the detail tables and redirects the query to the materialized view when the required data is in there or otherwise retrieves the data from the detail tables. Materialized views can dramatically increase the performance of a data warehouse but are sadly enough only available in the enterprise editions of the leading proprietary databases.

Even though there is no open source database with this support available, that doesn't mean that there is no solution at all. Again, Mondrian needs to be mentioned here since it works in a similar way when aggregate tables have been defined. Mondrian can then calculate the cost of resolving the query, and when using an aggregate table scores better, it is used by the engine.

- **Window functions**—For analytical purposes, the SQL 2003 standard is extended with so-called *window functions*. This allows a query to perform calculations over (part of) a result set. The advantage is that a table only needs to be scanned once to generate multiple outputs such as averages or subtotals. Two important SQL additions take care of this functionality: the `Over` and `Partition By` clauses. Window functions work in conjunction with regular aggregate functions such as `Sum`, `Avg`, and `Count` but also allow for special functions such as `Rank()` and `Row_number()`.

WINDOW FUNCTIONS EXAMPLE

The following statement is a simple example of a table with three columns: `ORDERID`, `PRODUCTID`, and `REVENUE`. The table contains five rows with two distinct product IDs:

```
SELECT ORDERID, PRODUCTID, REVENUE,
  SUM(REVENUE)OVER(PARTITION BY PRODUCTID) AS
  PRODUCTTOTAL, SUM(REVENUE) OVER() AS GRANDTOTAL
FROM SQLWINDOW
ORDER BY 1
```

The query results are shown in Table 6-1.

Table 6-1: Window Function Result Set

ORDERID	PRODUCTID	REVENUE	PRODUCTTOTAL	GRANDTOTAL
1	A	3	9	19
2	A	3	9	19
3	B	5	10	19
4	B	5	10	19
5	A	3	9	19

(continued)

WINDOW FUNCTIONS EXAMPLE *(continued)*

Open Source Database Window Support

PostgreSQL supports window functions as of version 8.4, but MySQL does not have this capability yet, nor is it part of the MySQL roadmap. MySQL has only a Rollup function to allow for adding totals and subtotals within the SQL result set. A MySQL version of the preceding query looks like this:

```
SELECT IFNULL(PRODUCTID,"ALL") AS PRODUCTID,
SUM(REVENUE) AS REVENUE
 FROM SQLWINDOW
GROUP BY PRODUCTID WITH ROLLUP
```

which results in the data shown in Table 6-2:

Table 6-2: MySQL Rollup Results

PRODUCTID	REVENUE
A	9
B	10
ALL	19

Please note that the rolled up results are labeled `NULL` if no special measures have been taken. In the preceding example, the statement `IFNULL` takes care of translating the `NULL` value into the text `ALL`.

- **Archiving**—Remember when we said all historical data should be available in the data warehouse at the lowest detail level? Well, we lied (just a little bit). Sometimes it suffices to retain historical data at an aggregated level, which can still be perfectly acceptable for supporting trend analysis (for example, for analyzing daily sales trends by product group it suffices to store data at the product group/day level). A possible scenario would be to keep detailed data online in a moving timeframe of 24 or 36 months; after this, only the daily, weekly, or monthly aggregates will be available. Of course in special cases the detailed data can be brought back in from the archive to support detailed analysis.

The preceding list shows a number of ways to increase performance in a data warehouse but depending on the actual database being used some of these features might not be available. The Pentaho BI suite is database independent, and while we're using MySQL as the sample database in this book there will be cases where other database systems might be a better alternative. Selecting a database for data warehousing is always a matter of required functionality versus available budget.

Changed Data Capture

The first step in an ETL process is the extraction of data from various source systems and the storage of this data in staging tables. This seems like a trivial task and in the case of initially loading a data warehouse it usually is, apart from challenges incurred from data volumes and slow network connections. But after the initial load, you don't want to repeat the process of completely extracting all data again, which wouldn't be of much use either, since you already have an almost complete set of data that only needs to be refreshed to reflect the current status. All you're interested in is what changed since the last data load, so you need to identify which records have been inserted, modified, or even deleted. The process of identifying these changes and only retrieving records that are different from what you already loaded in the data warehouse is called *Changed Data Capture* or *CDC*.

Basically there are two main categories of CDC processes, *intrusive* and *non-intrusive*. By intrusive, we mean that a CDC operation has a possible performance impact on the system the data is retrieved from. It is fair to say that any operation that requires executing SQL statements in one form or another is an intrusive technique. The bad news is that three of the four ways to capture changed data are intrusive, leaving only one non-intrusive option. The following sections offer descriptions of each solution and identify their pros and cons.

Source Data-Based CDC

Source data–based CDC is based on the fact that there are attributes available in the source system that enable the ETL process to make a selection of changed records. There are two alternatives here:

- **Direct read based on timestamps (date-time values)**—At least one update timestamp is needed here but preferably two are created: an insert timestamp (when the record was created) and an update timestamp (when the record was last changed).
- **Using database sequences**—Most databases have some sort of auto-increment option for numeric values in a table. When such a sequence number is being used, it's also easy to identify which records have been inserted since the last time you looked at the table.

Both of these options require extra tables in the data warehouse to store the data regarding the last time the data is loaded or the last retrieved sequence number. A common practice is to create these parameter tables either in a separate schema or in the staging area, but never in the central data warehouse and most certainly not in one of the data marts. A timestamp or sequence-based solution is arguably the most simple to implement and for this reason also one of the more common methods for capturing changed data. The penalty for this simplicity is the absence of a few essential capabilities that can be found in more advanced options:

- **Distinction between inserts and updates**—Only when the source system contains both an insert and an update timestamp can this difference be detected.
- **Deleted record detection**—This is not possible, unless the source system only logically deletes a record, i.e. has an end or deleted date but is not physically deleted from the table.
- **Multiple update detection**—When a record is updated multiple times during the period between the previous and the current load date, these intermediate updates get lost in the process.
- **Real-time capabilities**—Timestamp or sequence-based data extraction is always a batch operation and therefore unsuitable for real-time data loads.

Trigger-Based CDC

Database triggers can be used to fire actions upon using any data manipulation statement such as `INSERT`, `UPDATE`, or `DELETE`. This means that triggers can also be used to capture those changes and place these changed records in intermediate change tables in the source systems to extract data from later, or to put the data directly into the staging tables of the data warehouse environment. Because adding triggers to a database will be prohibited in most cases (it requires modifications to the source database, which is often not covered by service agreements or not permitted by database administrators) and can severely slow down a transaction system, this solution, although functionally appealing at first, is not implemented very often.

An alternative to using the triggers directly in the source system would be to set up a replication solution where all changes to selected tables will be replicated to the receiving tables at the data warehouse side. These replicated tables can then be extended with the required triggers to support the CDC process. Although this solution seems to involve a lot of overhead processing and requires extra storage space, it's actually quite efficient and non-intrusive since replication is based on reading changes from the database log files. Replication is also a standard functionality of most database management systems, including MySQL, PostgreSQL, and Ingres.

Trigger-based CDC is probably the most intrusive alternative described here but has the advantage of detecting all data changes and enables near–real-time data loading. The drawbacks are the need for a DBA (the source system is modified) and the database-specific nature of the trigger statements.

Snapshot-Based CDC

When no timestamps are available and triggers or replication are not an option, the last resort is to use snapshot tables, which can be compared for changes. A snapshot is simply a full extract of a source table that is placed in the data warehouse staging area. The next time data needs to be loaded, a second version (snapshot) of the same table is placed next to the original one and the two versions compared for changes. Take, for instance, a simple example of a table with two columns, `ID` and `Color`. Figure 6-7 shows two versions of this table, Snapshot 1 and Snapshot 2.

Snapshot_1

ID	COLOR
1	Black
2	Green
3	Red
4	Blue

Snapshot_2

ID	COLOR
1	Grey
2	Green
4	Blue
5	Yellow

Figure 6-7: Snapshot versions

There are several ways to extract the difference between those two versions. The first is to use a full outer join on the key column ID and tag the result rows according to their status (I for Insert, U for Update, D for Delete, and N for None) where the unchanged rows are filtered in the outer query:

```
select * from
(select  case
                when t2.id is null then 'D'
                when t1.id is null then 'I'
                when t1.color <> t2.color then 'U'
                else 'N'
            end as flag
,           case
                when t2.id is null then t1.id
                else t2.id
            end as id
,           t2.color
from            snapshot_1 t1
full outer join snapshot_2 t2
on                t1.id = t2.id
) a
where flag <> 'N'
```

That is, of course, when the database supports full outer joins, which is not the case with MySQL. If you need to build a similar construction with MySQL there are a few options, such as the following:

```
Select 'U' as flag, t2.id as id, t2.color as color
from snapshot_1 t1 inner join snapshot_2 t2 on t1.id = t2.id
where t1.color != t2.color
union all
select 'D' as flag, t1.id as id, t1.color as color
from snapshot_1 t1 left join snapshot_2 t2 on t1.id = t2.id
where t2.id is null
union all
select 'I' as flag, t2.id as id, t2.color as color
from snapshot_2 t2 left join snapshot_1 t1 on t2.id = t1.id
where t1.id is null
```

In both cases the result set is the same, as displayed in Figure 6-8.

FLAG	ID	COLOR
U	1	Grey
D	3	NULL
I	5	Yellow

Figure 6-8: Snapshot compare result

Most ETL tools nowadays contain standard functionality to compare two tables and flag the rows as `I`, `U`, and `D` accordingly, so you will most likely use these standard functions instead of writing SQL. Pentaho Kettle, for instance, contains the `Merge rows` step. This step takes two *sorted* input sets and compares them on the specified keys. The columns to be compared can be selected, too, and an output flag field name needs to be specified.

Snapshot-based CDC can detect inserts, updates, and deletes, which is an advantage over using timestamps, at the cost of extra storage for the different snapshots. There can also be a severe performance issue when the tables to be compared are extremely large. For this reason we added the SQL illustration because for this kind of heavy lifting, the database engine is often better suited than an engine-based ETL tool.

Log-Based CDC

The most advanced and least intrusive form of changed data capture is to use a log-based solution. Every insert, update, and delete operation run in a database can be logged. In cases using a MySQL database, the binary log has to be enabled explicitly in the Administrator tool (Startup variables ➢ Logfiles). From that moment on, all changes can be read in near–real-time from the database log and used for updating the data in the data warehouse. The catch here is that this sounds simpler than it actually is. A binary log file needs to be transformed first into an understandable form before the entries can be read into a subsequent process.

The MySQL installation contains a special tool for this purpose, *mysqlbinlog*. This tool can read the binary format and translates it into a somewhat human-readable format and can output the read results to a text file or directly into a database client (in case of a restore operation). Mysqlbinlog has several other options, with the most important one for our purposes being the fact that it can accept a start and/or end timestamp to read only part of the logfile. Each entry also has a sequence number that can be used as an offset, so there are two ways of preventing duplicates or missing values when reading from these files.

After the mysqlbinlog output is written to a text file, this file can be parsed and read, for instance by a Kettle input step that reads the data and executes the statements on the corresponding staging tables. For other databases there are similar solutions, and some offer a complete CDC framework as part of their data warehouse solution.

The drawback of using a database-specific set of tools is obvious: it only works with a single database. Whenever there is a need to use a log-based solution in a heterogeneous environment, several commercial offerings are available on the market.

Which CDC Alternative Should You Choose?

As we've shown in the previous sections, each of the described options for identifying and selecting changed data have their strengths and weaknesses. Some alternatives require adaptations to the source database by a database administrator (DBA), some can support real-time loading of data, and others only support a partial discovery of changes. Table 6-3 summarizes these points to help you decide which option is most applicable in your situation.

Changing User Requirements

This might seem an odd place to talk about changing user requirements since this usually involves the analysis and design part of a data warehouse, which is covered in the next chapter. It's not as odd as it might seem, however. A new user requirement often means enhancing the data warehouse and the load process in some way or another. New or changed user requirements might lead to changes in your data warehouse ranging from simply adding a new column or an extra calculation to adding an entire new source system. User requirement changes can not only be demand-driven (from the perspective of the data warehouse), but can also be driven by changes in the operational systems. One of the most challenging projects you can embark on is having a complete replacement of one or more source systems, for instance migrating from financial application A to financial application B from a different vendor. Now imagine that the user requirements don't change at all, meaning you'll have to change all ETL processes without breaking the existing reporting environment including the data warehouse.

Table 6-3: CDC Options

	TIMESTAMP	SNAPSHOT	TRIGGERS	LOG
Insert/update distinction?	N	Y	Y	Y
Multiple updates detected?	N	N	Y	Y
Deletes identified?	N	Y	Y	Y
Non-intrusive?	N	N	N	Y
Real time support?	N	N	Y	Y
DBMS independent?	Y	Y	N	N
No DBA required?	Y	Y	N	N

It's impossible to cover all changes that might occur during the lifetime of a data warehouse, but there is one guiding principle that should be clear and agreed upon from day one of the inception of a possible solution:

A data warehouse is a process, not a project.

So now that we have that out of the way, we can start making plans to accommodate this process with some general guidelines. Just be aware of the fact that everything will (eventually) change; be it reports, source systems, people and departments who use the system, basically everything related to the data warehouse will change at some point in time. Make sure that these changes can be accommodated by following these rules:

- **Design your data warehouse as a set of independent (but interrelated) building blocks that can easily be replaced by alternative solutions.** For instance: suppose that your precious data warehouse gets replaced with a data warehouse appliance of another vendor. How much non-standard SQL did you use in ETL processes or queries used for reporting?
- **Use the right tools and use them right.** All too often organizations spend buckets of money on fancy BI dashboarding and reporting tools and hire expensive consultants to implement them but turn down a request for a

$5,000 tool for modeling and managing the data warehouse. Instead, they use spreadsheets to store definitions and manually create databases and tables using the standard tools that came with the database product. This is fine for quickly building a prototype but that's as far as it should go.

- **Standardize.** Pick a solution and stick with it (unless there are compelling reasons to switch components: see the first bullet point for that). How does this help accommodate changes? Simple: Almost any BI or data warehouse tool that you can buy (or download) will do the job. Some may have a fancier interface or have support for Flash speedometers while others don't, but basically the business value is in the information, not in the presentation. A standard you stick with enables an organization to build deep skills around a product. Then, when a new requirement pops up, it can quickly be implemented because all skills are already available. This book helps you achieve that goal for the Pentaho BI Suite but the same message applies to all other solutions as well.

Data Warehouse Trends

We conclude this chapter by highlighting some of the ongoing and recent developments in data warehousing: virtual data warehousing, real time data warehousing, analytical databases, data warehouse appliances, and on-demand data warehouses.

Virtual Data Warehousing

This book covers a classic approach to data warehousing, which means designing and building a newly architected data store and physically moving the data into this data store by making use of ETL tools. This approach is also referred to as *physical* data warehousing. And when there is a physical solution, there probably is a virtual solution as well. As you might already have guessed, a virtual data warehouse does not store a replica of the data extracted from source systems, but the data remains in the operational data stores. From a user point of view, however, there is a special layer created that translates the transactional data into a data warehouse view. Virtual data warehouse solutions can also integrate data from different source systems, offering a live view into the data as it is at the moment of executing a query. This is probably the most notable advantage of using this kind of solution: it is real time, current data you'll be looking at, and you don't need a lot of big iron to store data before being able to analyze and report on it. Of course, there are many drawbacks as well: data is not cleansed, conformed, and validated. It can drain the performance of the source systems; and there is no notion of history—all data is presented in its current form, which makes it hard to use for trending and historical comparisons.

In a lot of cases, virtual and physical solutions are used side by side, where a query directed at the data warehouse retrieves historical data from the physical data warehouse and complements this with current data from the source systems. This requires a very intelligent metadata layer, which is not yet available within the Pentaho framework. One option to consider in this case is the LucidDB analytical database, which can be used to ''wrap'' views around any source system (including, for instance, text files) and then behaves as a federated solution (see the section that follows on ''Analytical Databases''). Queries are then targeted at the LucidDB database, which in turn redirects the queries to the respective source systems. Note that this is only a lightweight alternative to various proprietary solutions on the market that also contain intelligent caching and indexing mechanisms, which LucidDB lacks. A full-fledged open source data federation solution hasn't been available for long, but early in 2009 Red Hat made its acquired MetaMatrix solution available as an open source project called *Teiid* (`http://www.jboss.org/teiid`).

CROSS-REFERENCE **For more information about virtual data warehousing, see the following sources:**

- **`www.tdwi.org/Publications/WhatWorks/display.aspx?id=7305`**
- **`www.b-eye-network.com/channels/5087/view/9752/`**
- **`www.b-eye-network.com/channels/1138/view/663`**
- **`www.ebizq.net/topics/eii/features/8153.html`**

Real-Time Data Warehousing

In the early days of data warehousing, weekly and even monthly loads were common practice. Nowadays, daily loads are considered standard and there is a trend towards moving to intraday or even near–real-time data loads. This trend coincides with another one, which is aimed at bringing business intelligence (BI) to the operational level of the organization, also called Operational BI. A good example of this is customer service representatives needing up-to-date information about their accounts, including all historical information related to their customers. Operational BI is about lots of small decisions to be made by many people as part of their daily job, as opposed to tactical or strategic BI, which leaves more time for thorough review. The diagram in Figure 6-9 shows the relation between the time needed to make a decision and act on it, and the value lost when the latency between the original business event and the decision made is too high.

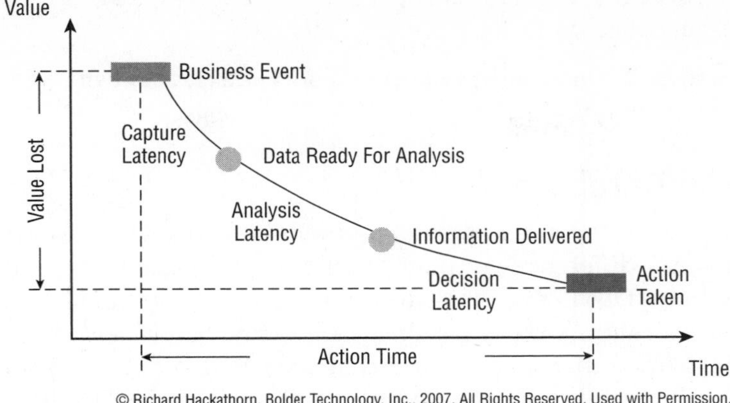

Figure 6-9: Action-value diagram

From this diagram, you can see that getting the data into the data warehouse in real time is only part of the story. Data still needs to be analyzed and acted upon. There are several ways to implement a solution that loads data in near–real-time, as covered earlier in the "Changed Data Capture" section, and several commercial solutions are on the market that can simplify the setup of such an alternative. One solution that wasn't mentioned there because it is not part of CDC is the use of *message queues*. In that case, each business event and the resulting data is immediately passed on as a message that can be picked up and transformed by the data warehouse environment. In all cases, however, this real-time refresh needs to be tightly linked to the next steps in the process, which can also be automated. For instance, analysis can be done by using business rules that automatically fire when a certain threshold is reached, which then initiates corresponding actions as well. There are a couple of very good open source business rules engines available, with Drools (`www.jboss.org/drools`) and OpenRules (`http://openrules.com`) probably being the most mature and well known. Pentaho's *action sequences* (covered in Chapters 4, 13, and 17) can also be used for this purpose.

Real-time message-based solutions that can apply business rules and do calculations on the fly are usually addressed as *complex event processing* (CEP). An open source CEP solution is Esper (`www.espertech.com`), which is a message-based solution that can handle large volumes of streaming data. These tools can complement data warehouse environments but are not a replacement for the ETL processes as described earlier.

CROSS-REFERENCE **For more information about real-time data warehousing, see the following sources:**

- **`www.tdwi.org/Publications/WhatWorks/display.aspx?id=8913`**

- **www.ebizq.net/topics/operational_bi/features/10604.html**
- **www.information-management.com/issues/20040901/1009281-1.html**

Analytical Databases

In this chapter, we've already explained why a data warehouse needs to be architected in a different way than an operational system. Yet still in most cases the same RDBMS that is used for the transaction system is also selected as the data warehouse database. In recent years many new products have entered the market that challenged this approach by offering capabilities that are specifically tailored to handle analytical workloads. The use of OLAP databases for data marts has already been mentioned, but one of the most radical new approaches is the emergence of so-called *columnar databases* or *columns stores*. Columnar databases do not store data sequentially in rows but horizontally in columns. This results in a number of advantages:

- **Pruning**—Most analytical queries pertain only to a few columns. Queries on row-based databases always read complete rows from disk, even when only two columns are selected. In a column store, only the selected columns need to be read. This characteristic heavily influences disk I/O, which is one of the major speed limiters.
- **No need for indexing**—Because a column store already stores the data column by column in the correct order, each column is automatically its own index.
- **Compression**—Because a column always contains data of one particular data type, the data can be compressed very efficiently, further reducing disk I/O.

Added to these advantages, most commercial column stores such as Vertica, ParAccel, and XASOL can be run on a massive parallel processing (MPP) cluster, which further enhances the performance of these solutions.

When considering open source alternatives, there are three products worth looking at:

- MonetDB (www.monetdb.com) is a Dutch product developed at the Free University of Amsterdam. It has a very small footprint (about 5 MB) and is designed to run mostly in main memory, which explains the impressive benchmark results, even for somewhat larger datasets of 10 and 20GB. MonetDB is recommended for use when requiring fast response times on smaller (<10GB) datasets.
- LucidDB (www.luciddb.org) is a columnar database designed from the ground up with data warehousing and business intelligence in mind.

It also includes ETL capabilities with special SQL extensions to build transformations. The developers of Pentaho and LucidDB work closely together, which makes this a viable alternative for smaller data warehouse or data mart implementations. LucidDB is a preferred data store for Mondrian and has built-in support for the Pentaho aggregate designer. In addition, Pentaho Data Integration contains a native LucidDB connector and bulk loader.

- Infobright (`www.infobright.com`) released a community edition of its analytical database in September 2008 under a GPL license. The most notable feature of Infobright is that it acts as a MySQL storage engine, so you can use the product to enhance the data warehousing capabilities of MySQL without having to implement or learn new tools. Infobright is capable of handling data volumes of up to 30 Terabytes and thus is a great companion to the Pentaho BI suite. One point of caution, however: the open source version does not support the SQL data manipulation `INSERT`, `UPDATE`, and `DELETE` statements. Data needs to be reloaded every time if you need to make updates, making it hardly usable as a data warehouse solution. The commercial version does not have these limitations.

None of the three products mentioned here have parallel processing (MPP) capabilities; hence there can be scalability limitations. Nevertheless, data warehouses beyond the 10 Terabyte range are still not very common so in most cases these alternatives can help you in setting up a high performance data warehouse architecture using open source solutions.

Data Warehouse Appliances

The final noticeable development in the data warehouse market is the rise of the so-called *appliances*. We all know appliances such as toasters or radios that have only to be plugged into a power outlet and you're up and running. A *data warehouse appliance* is a plug-and-play solution consisting of hardware and software and aims to make data warehousing as easy as toasting a slice of bread. Because this is an emerging market with only a few established vendors and a lot of companies who recently entered the marketplace, you should take special care when considering one of these solutions.

Several companies who started as analytical database vendors now partner with hardware companies such as Sun (now Oracle) or Hewlett Packard to deliver a full-fledged appliance. An interesting phenomenon is the adoption of open source technology within these appliances. PostgreSQL, especially the SQL parser, is used by many of the new vendors. Greenplum, for instance, not only based their entire solution on PostgreSQL but also embeds the open source statistical library *Project R* for advanced analytics and in database data mining.

One of the latest new entrants to the market is the Kickfire appliance (`www.kickfire.com`), which is of particular interest because it is architected as a MySQL pluggable storage engine. This allows data warehouses developed for MySQL with an InnoDB or MyISAM storage engine to be migrated seamlessly to a Kickfire appliance. The company is one of the few appliance vendors to have published performance benchmark results on `www.tpc.org` and is a price/performance leader in the 100 and 300 Gigabyte TPC-H benchmark. TPC-H is an industry benchmark measuring query performance of typical BI queries such as for determining market share or reporting sales volume for a specific period.

On Demand Data Warehousing

With the advent of so-called *cloud computing* solutions [with Amazon's Elastic Cloud Computing (Ec2) infrastructure probably being the best known but hardly the only solution on the market], it is becoming feasible to host a data warehouse or even a complete BI solution outside the corporate firewall. Solutions for hosting applications in an off-site data center have been available since the late nineties and were offered by *Application Service Providers* (ASPs). To distinguish the latest developments from the original ASP concept, the term *Software as a Service* or *SaaS* has been introduced, and sometimes people even talk about *Database* or *Data Warehouse as a Service* (*DaaS*, *DWaaS*[3]). The big difference is the shared architecture where all customers of a serviced solution share a common infrastructure, not only at a technical but also at the application level. By dividing the available resources in a smart way (also called a *multi-tenant* solution) many users can share the same servers, applications, and licences, making this a very cost effective mode of operation. Developments in this area are progressing extremely fast so we cannot cover any specific vendor or offering here (there are simply too many of them), but in striving for a complete overview we needed to point out the availability of these solutions as well.

Summary

This chapter introduced a broad range of concepts and technologies related to data warehousing. We showed you the following things which we will build on for the rest of the book:

- What a data warehouse is and how it can help you in achieving your business goals

[3]Which is kind of funny since the Dutch word "Dwaas" means "Fool."

- The global architecture of a data warehouse and all constituting building blocks that can be identified within this architecture
- The purpose of each of the data warehouse building blocks
- The main challenges you face when building a data warehouse: data quality, data volume, performance, capturing changed data and adapting to changing requirements

We also highlighted the main difference between two of the leading authorities in data warehouse modeling, Ralph Kimball and Bill Inmon, and pointed out why we picked dimensional modeling and the bus architecture for our example data warehouse.

Finally, we highlighted the major trends in data warehousing and illustrated how the Pentaho BI Suite, the MySQL database, and other related open source technologies fit in.

CHAPTER

7

Modeling the Business Using Star Schemas

When working with data from the data warehouse, it's likely that star schemas are used to deliver the data to the end user. Not directly, however; typically, a reporting or analysis tool is used to access the data, while more advanced users might use a query tool directly. Nevertheless, it's important to note that star schemas are the vehicle of choice whether working with a Kimball-style data bus architecture or an Inmon-style corporate information factory.

NOTE **There is one exception to this rule. An advanced analyst or data miner often needs access to the complete set of data in the data warehouse, thereby circumventing the created star schemas in an Inmon-style data warehouse solution. This discussion, however, will be limited to star schema access.**

What Is a Star Schema?

The first thing you might ask is: Why are these database models called ''star schema''? Probably because the entity-relationship diagram of this kind of schema resembles a star. The center of the star consists of a large fact table and the points of the star are the dimension tables. Most users first encounter a star schema in a sales data mart with customers, products, stores, promotions, and time, as displayed in Figure 7-1.

NOTE **Although we use five points to make the model resemble a star, it is by no means required to use five points. In fact, even a fact table with only one or two dimension is also called a star schema.**

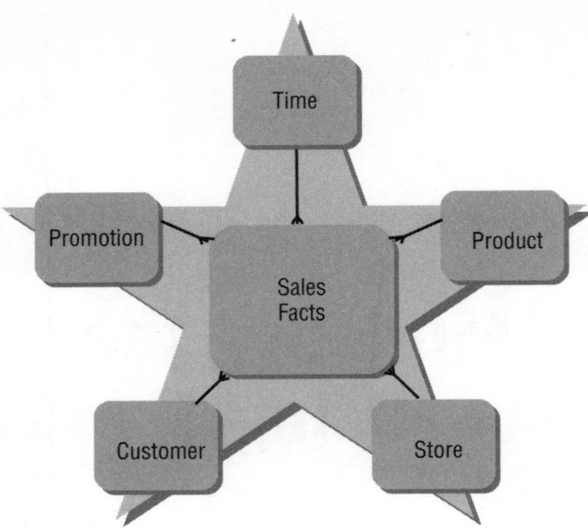

Figure 7-1: Star schema diagram

It's the modeling technique that counts, not the number of dimension tables used. One of the obvious benefits of using a schema like this is its simplicity and understandability for end users. Very often during the design phase of a data warehouse, star schemas are used to draw the initial translation of business questions into logical database diagrams.

NOTE **A simple logical diagram might still lead to a more complex technical design that results in a model that's less understandable to the end user than the initial white board design.**

Dimension Tables and Fact Tables

The next question is, of course: What's the difference between dimension and fact tables, and what makes something a fact table? As you will see later, the distinction is not always clear, and there are even occasions when a dimension table in one star schema can become a fact table in another star schema. A simple explanation is that dimension tables contain information about business entities (customers, products, stores) and fact tables about business events (sales, shipments, orders). The most notable difference is in the measureable columns such as revenue, cost, and items, which are part of the fact tables. Also, all of the different angles and attributes that are required to summarize these facts are stored in the dimension tables. It's actually pretty simple if you translate a typical report request such as ''Show me the total order value per month per product group'' into a dimensional model, as displayed in Figure 7-2. The calculated item of interest (sum of order value) is a fact, month is a ''time'' attribute belonging to the time dimension, and "product group" is a product attribute belonging to the product dimension. A fact table therefore contains only foreign keys pointing to the dimension tables and attributes that can be aggregated (*quantitative* elements). Dimension tables contain all attributes that describe a certain organization perspective (*qualitative* elements).

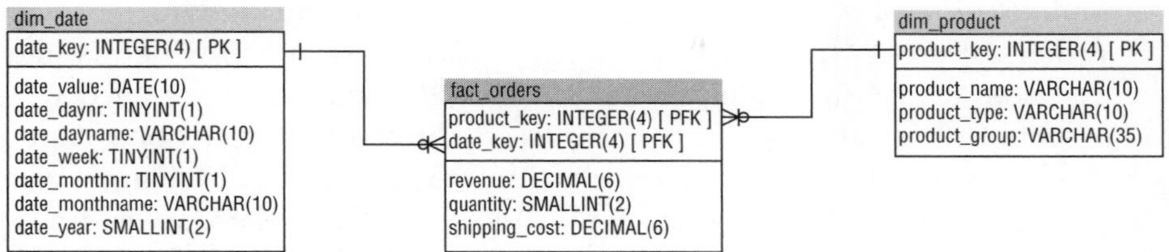

Figure 7-2: Star schema example

This data mart gives you very little information because it contains only a few measurements and two dimensions. Nevertheless, it's a good starting point to illustrate how exactly a dimensional model works:

- All fact rows are stored at the lowest possible *granularity* level. By granularity, we mean the grain of the data; a fact table at the date level has a lower granularity than a fact table at the month level.
- The granularity of the fact table is determined by the combination of the granularity of the dimension tables. In the example, this means that for each combination of product and date there is a *possible* fact row. Not all combinations need to be present, of course!
- All measures in the fact table can be rolled up or grouped by the elements of the dimension tables, so this little data mart can calculate revenue by year, month and product group, or by year and product type, or any other desired combination.

You could argue that an order is also a business entity and only the order lines with the individual transactions are facts. In a way, that assumption is correct. This is a case where special attention is needed in modeling the data marts. Later in this chapter we'll explain what special attention is needed and describe other more advanced dimensional modeling topics. For now, it suffices to keep the simple definition in mind.

Fact Table Types

Fact tables are not always based on transactions alone. Transactional fact tables are the most commonly used type, but there are a couple of variations you need to be aware of. The first one is the *accumulating periodic snapshot* table. This sounds more complicated than it actually is; the only difference between a regular fact table and this one are the date fields tied to a specific process that need to be updated when new events occur. Take, for instance, World Class Movie's rental process where DVDs are ordered on an order date, shipped on a ship date, and returned on a return date. Because we don't want to wait until the process is completed to begin entering the data, we start by adding the fact row to the data warehouse when the order is placed and subsequently accumulate this row with the correct dates as they become known.

A rather different type of fact table is the *periodic snapshot*, which is like a picture taken every day, week or month. Periodic snapshots are used when you need to freeze data that are only indirectly linked to transactions. A good example in the WCM data warehouse is the DVD inventory. Inventory levels change constantly and there is no way to keep track of these over time by using a transactional fact table. The only option here is to periodically take a snapshot that enables you to report on inventory level increase or decrease over time.

Another way of looking at transaction and snapshot fact tables is by the types of measures that they contain. Measures in a regular transaction table, like sales revenue, can be summarized across all dimensions, including time. These are referred to as *additive facts* or measures. The measures in a periodic snapshot table cannot be easily summarized, at least not when multiple periods are involved. Summarizing the weekly DVD stock levels does not give you a total yearly stock! These measures are called *semi-additive*, meaning that you can add them together (for example, the total inventory of all movies starring Tom Cruise) but need to include a time or period filter to slice the data.

The last type of measure is the *non-additive fact*. A good example of this is room temperature. It doesn't make sense to summarize the temperature of different rooms or different periods, although you can always calculate averages.

NOTE **The SQL language does not support semi-additive and non-additive measures, but some OLAP servers can be configured to accommodate for exception aggregation. Pentaho Mondrian (covered in Chapter 15) does not have built-in support for non- and semi-additive measures.**

The next part of the chapter covers the basic SQL needed for getting data out of star schemas with transactional and accumulating fact tables. Because both of these fact table types contain transactions, you can safely summarize the numbers that are in there.

Querying Star Schemas

So far, you've seen diagrams linking dimension and fact tables together, but in a database these are just tables. The relations in the diagrams are *foreign key constraints*, which means that it will not be possible to insert a product key into the orders fact table if this key does not exist in the dim_product dimension table. Getting data out of the database is another thing. For this, you need a query language called Structured Query Language, or SQL. If you're not familiar with SQL, don't worry—the SQL you need for retrieving information from a star schema is not very complicated. And although this book is not a SQL text, we cover enough of the basics here to enable you to start writing queries to retrieve data from dimensional data marts. All we need for this is the SELECT statement, a way of *joining* the different tables together, and an understanding of how to *group* the results from the query. For starters, have a look at the basic SQL building blocks for selecting data:

- SELECT—A list of the columns, constants, and expressions you want to retrieve from the database.
- FROM—The tables and views that contain the data you need, including the relationships between those tables and views.
- WHERE—The restrictions you want to apply to the data in the selected tables, views, and expressions, excluding the aggregations.
- GROUP BY—Specifies the summary level of the query. All non-aggregate columns and expressions in the SELECT list should be part of the GROUP BY statement.
- HAVING—Contains conditions on summarized expressions, e.g., having sum (revenue) > 100,000.
- ORDER BY—Denotes the order in which the results will be displayed.

If only the total revenue is needed from the fact table, there's no need to use JOINS or GROUP BY clauses, just the following:

```
SELECT SUM(revenue)
FROM   fct_orders
```

This little query doesn't tell you very much, so you can add the date dimension to calculate the revenue by year:

```
SELECT   date_year, SUM(revenue)
FROM     fct_orders
JOIN     dim_date
ON       fct_orders.date_key = dim_date.date_key
GROUP BY date_year
```

Now you have a simple query that is the basis for all other possible queries that can be executed against a dimensional data model. The first line with the SELECT clause tells the database what the result set will look like. Next, you need to tell where the data is retrieved from by using the FROM clause.

You also want to JOIN another table and you need to tell the database which columns the join will be based on—in this case, the date_key in the dimension and fact tables. Finally, the results are grouped by all elements of the SELECT statement that are not part of an aggregate function. For example, when the SELECT statement looks like this:

```
SELECT date_year, product_type, product_name, SUM(revenue), SUM(quantity)
```

the GROUP BY statement needs to be

```
GROUP BY date_year, product_type, product_name
```

To complete this query all you need to add are the FROM and JOIN parts:

```
SELECT   date_year, product_type, product_name,
         SUM(revenue), SUM(quantity)
FROM     fct_orders
JOIN     dim_date
ON       fct_orders.date_key    = dim_date.date_key
JOIN     dim_product
ON       fct_orders.product_key = dim_product.product_key
GROUP BY date_year, product_type, product_name
```

The SQL examples used so far still lack the use of aliases. An *alias* is another name you can use to refer to a table, column, or expression. Although they are not always required, it's good practice to always use them. Adding the alias total_revenue to the expression SUM(revenue) gives more meaning to the result column, and using aliases for table names enables a shorthand notation of the join conditions. Compare the following JOIN clauses to understand what we mean by that:

```
FROM fct_orders
JOIN dim_date ON fct_orders.date_key = dim_date.date_key
```

versus

```
FROM fct_orders AS f
JOIN dim_date AS d ON f.date_key = d.date_key
```

There are cases in which the use of aliases is not optional but required. The first practical case where aliases are at least very helpful is when the same column name appears in more than one table of the set used in the query. Suppose that in the previous example you wanted to include date_key in the result set. Because this column is part of both the fact and the dimension table, the SQL parser cannot determine which table to pick the column from, so you need to include the table reference in your SELECT statement—for example, SELECT dim_date.datekey. Now it's immediately obvious that the use of a short alias such as d will save a lot of typing. The complete query statement, including the use of aliases, now looks as follows:

```
SELECT   d.date_year, p.product_type, p.product_name,
         SUM(f.revenue) AS total_revenue, SUM(f.quantity) AS total_quantity
FROM     fct_orders AS f
JOIN     dim_date AS d ON    f.date_key    = d.date_key
JOIN     dim_product AS p ON f.product_key = d.product_key
GROUP BY d.date_year, p.product_type, p.product_name
```

The second case where aliases are not only practical but required is when the same table is used in different roles. An example is a query that asks for all revenue by product type with an order date in 2007 and a ship date in 2008:

```
SELECT   p.product_type, SUM(f.revenue) AS total_revenue
FROM     fct_orders AS f
JOIN     dim_date AS od ON f.order_date_key = od.date_key
JOIN     dim_date AS sd ON f.ship_date_key  = sd.date_key
JOIN     dim_product AS p ON f.product_key  = d.product_key
WHERE    od.year = 2007
AND      sd.year = 2008
GROUP BY d.date_year, p.product_type, p.product_name
```

The WHERE part of this query is covered in more detail shortly.

Join Types

In the examples used so far, we've used the clause JOIN to combine different tables. Although this is technically correct, JOIN is shorthand for the complete statement INNER JOIN. The term *inner* means that the column entries should have a match in both columns. This isn't always the case; there are perhaps products that haven't been sold yet. Using an INNER JOIN between products and orders will therefore generate a result set that contains only products for which an order exists. To work around this limitation, you can also use *outer joins,* which will return empty rows as well. The three OUTER JOIN types are LEFT, RIGHT, and FULL, and there is also a special CROSS JOIN that will combine any value from the joining tables column with any value from the joined table. The result set of a CROSS JOIN is also known as a *Cartesian product.* To better understand the different types of joins, you can use the following examples as a reference. All examples are based on two tables, table_a and table_b, each with two columns, id and value.

```
table a
+----+-------+
| id | value |
+----+-------+
|  1 | A     |
|  2 | B     |
|  3 | C     |
|  4 | D     |
+----+-------+

table b
+----+-------+
| id | value  |
+----+-------+
|  1 | Red    |
|  3 | Blue   |
|  5 | Yellow |
+----+-------+
```

A regular `INNER JOIN` between the two tables will produce a result set with only the common values from both tables:

```
SELECT     a.value AS a, b.value AS b
FROM       table_a AS a
INNER JOIN table_b AS b ON a.id=b.id

+-------+-------+
| a     | b     |
+-------+-------+
| A     | Red   |
| C     | Blue  |
+-------+-------+
```

A `LEFT OUTER JOIN` will display all values from the left table in the join statement and displays a `NULL` value for the values in the right table with no matching `id`:

```
SELECT          a.value AS a, b.value AS b
FROM            table_a AS a
LEFT OUTER JOIN table_b AS b ON a.id=b.id

+-------+-------+
| a     | b     |
+-------+-------+
| A     | Red   |
| B     | NULL  |
| C     | Blue  |
| D     | NULL  |
+-------+-------+
```

A RIGHT OUTER JOIN displays all values from the right table in the join clause and displays a NULL value for the values in the left table with no matching id:

```
SELECT           a.value AS a, b.value AS b
FROM             table_a AS a
RIGHT OUTER JOIN table_b AS b ON a.id=b.id

+-------+--------+
| a     | b      |
+-------+--------+
| A     | Red    |
| C     | Blue   |
| NULL  | Yellow |
+-------+--------+
```

The FULL OUTER JOIN statement is not available in MySQL but other databases such as MS SQL Server and Oracle would produce the following output from a FULL OUTER JOIN:

```
+-------+-------+
| a     | b     |
+-------+-------+
| A     | Red   |
| B     | NULL  |
| C     | Blue  |
| D     | NULL  |
| NULL  | Yellow|
+-------+-------+
```

The last option, the CROSS JOIN, does not require join columns at all:

```
SELECT     a.value AS a, b.value AS b
FROM       table_a AS a
CROSS JOIN table_b AS b

+-------+--------+
| a     | b      |
+-------+--------+
| A     | Red    |
| A     | Blue   |
| A     | Yellow |
| B     | Red    |
| B     | Blue   |
| B     | Yellow |
| C     | Red    |
| C     | Blue   |
| C     | Yellow |
| D     | Red    |
| D     | Blue   |
| D     | Yellow |
+-------+--------+
```

Cross joins are great to create cross tab reports in which you want to have a complete grid with all product groups on the y axis, and all months on the x axis, regardless of whether data for a specific combination exists or not.

TIP **We recommend that you always use the complete join clauses; use `INNER JOIN` instead of `JOIN` and `LEFT OUTER JOIN` instead of `LEFT JOIN`.**

Applying Restrictions in a Query

In most cases, a business question is more specific than the revenue of all products, all customers, and all years. And when data marts contain millions of rows of data, it's also impractical to select data without putting some restrictions in the query. This is why the `SELECT` statement can also be extended with a `WHERE` clause to filter only the data of interest. The simplest `WHERE` condition is just a filter on a certain value, for example, `date_year = 2008` or `date_year >= 2008`. Most comparison operators you're already familiar with can be used for defining selections, such as `=`, `<`, `>`, `<=`, `>=` and `<>` or `!=`. These operators compare the content of the restricted column or expression with a single value. Suppose you need to filter all customers who have a last name with three or fewer characters. Then you can use the `CHAR_LENGTH` function to calculate the number of characters in a string and compare this to the value `3`:

```
WHERE CHAR_LENGTH(c.last_name) <= 3
```

The last options we'll present here are the `IN` and `BETWEEN...AND` operators. By using `IN`, the left part of the restriction can be compared to more than a single value on the right, for instance to select all customers whose names begin with an `A`, `E`, `I`, or `Q`:

```
WHERE SUBSTRING(c.last_name,1,1) IN ('A','E','I','Q')
```

The right side of the `IN` comparison doesn't need to be a predefined list but can be a new query as well, which in that case is called a *subquery*. Subqueries can, of course, also be used in combination with all other comparison operators.

A `BETWEEN...AND` operator can be used to define a lower and upper limit to a restriction. `BETWEEN...AND` does not exactly behave the way you might expect so be careful when using this one. When `BETWEEN...AND` is used, as in the condition `P.PRODUCT_PRICE BETWEEN 1 AND 5`, the values 1 and 5 are both included in the restriction.

`WHERE` clauses cannot be placed anywhere in the `SELECT` statement; there are very strict rules for their use. The conditions should be placed right after the

FROM but before GROUP BY, as in the following example:

```
SELECT      d.date_year, p.product_type, p.product_name,
            SUM(f.revenue) AS total_revenue, SUM(f.quantity) AS total_quantity
FROM        fct_orders AS f
INNER JOIN dim_date AS d ON    f.date_key    = d.date_key
INNER JOIN dim_product AS p ON f.product_key = d.product_key
WHERE       CHAR_LENGTH(c.last_name) <= 3
GROUP BY    d.date_year, p.product_type, p.product_name
```

Combining Multiple Restrictions

If you want to use more than one condition in a WHERE clause, you can combine these with AND and OR operators. To apply more complex logic or group certain statements together, opening and closing brackets are required. You've already seen the BETWEEN...AND operator, which is actually a shorthand notation of using two comparisons using >= and <=. In such complex cases, you'd probably want to use brackets to group them as well. The following is an example in which the use of parentheses is mandatory:

```
(d.year = 2007 AND d.month_nr = 12) OR (d.year = 2008 AND d.month_nr = 1)
```

Without the parentheses, the result set would be empty because there isn't a single row that satisfies D.MONTH_NR = 12 AND D.MONTH_NR = 1. When the parentheses are used, the result set includes the data from December 2007 and January 2008.

Restricting Aggregate Results

So far we've been using restrictions to filter the data as it was stored in the database. The WHERE clause can only filter constants, expressions, and columns, not aggregates. There are situations in which the resulting aggregate values need to be filtered after the GROUP BY clause has been applied. For instance, when you're interested only in customers who have total revenue of at least $100, it's necessary to summarize first and filter later. This can be achieved by using the HAVING clause:

```
SELECT      c.first_name, c.last_name, SUM(f.revenue) AS total_revenue
FROM        fct_sales AS f
INNER JOIN dim_customer AS c ON c.customer_id = f.customer_id
GROUP BY    c.first_name, c.last_name
HAVING      SUM(f.revenue) >= 100
```

Ordering Data

Unless you apply a specific sort order, the returned data is displayed as a list without any ordering, which makes it hard to navigate through a result set. Ordering data is quite simple—just add an extra ORDER BY clause to the query and add the columns you want to order the data by. Ordering is applied from left to right in the order statement. The default sort order is ascending, but data can be ordered descending as well by adding the DESC ordering specification:

```
SELECT     c.first_name, c.last_name, sum(f.revenue) AS total_revenue
FROM       fct_sales AS f
INNER JOIN dim_customer AS c ON c.customer_id = f.customer_id
GROUP BY   c.first_name, c.last_name
HAVING     SUM(f.revenue) >= 100
ORDER BY   SUM(f.revenue) DESC,c.last_name
```

NOTE **MySQL lets you use the alias names in the HAVING and ORDER BY clauses as well, but most databases don't support this.**

That's it. You've gained enough knowledge of SQL to be able to query the data marts we'll present in the remainder of the book. If you want to learn more about SQL, there is an abundant set of books and websites available. More information about the specific MySQL SELECT syntax can be found in the online reference guide at http://dev.mysql.com/doc/refman/5.1/en/select.html.

The Bus Architecture

The data warehouse bus architecture was developed by Ralph Kimball and is extensively described in his books *The Data Warehouse Toolkit* and *The Data Warehouse Lifecycle Toolkit*. Both books are published by Wiley Publishing and cover the complete lifecycle of modeling, building, and maintaining data warehouses. The term *bus* refers to the fact that the different data marts in the data warehouse are interlinked by using *conformed dimensions*. A simple example can explain this. Suppose you have dimension tables for customers, suppliers, and products dimensions and want to analyze data about sales and purchase transactions. In case of the purchasing transactions, the customer is still unknown so it's not very useful to include the customer dimension in the purchase star schema. For sales transactions the situation is slightly different: You need information about the customer who purchased a product and the

CH 5, 6, 7, 8

	2				9		5	
			2					
1		8				9	3	
4	1		5					
			3					
		3	4		1	8		9
	4					5	8	
			6					
	8	5					2	7

2	4	8	9	3	5	1	6	7
5	3	9	6	1	7	8	2	4
7	1	6	8	2	4	3	9	5
9	7	4	5	6	3	2	1	8
3	5	1	2	9	8	4	7	6
8	6	2	7	4	1	9	5	3
6	2	3	4	7	9	5	8	1
1	8	7	3	5	2	6	4	9
4	9	5	1	8	6	7	3	2

TUESDAY JULY 14

supplier the product was purchased from. The resulting diagram for this small example data warehouse is shown in Figure 7-3.

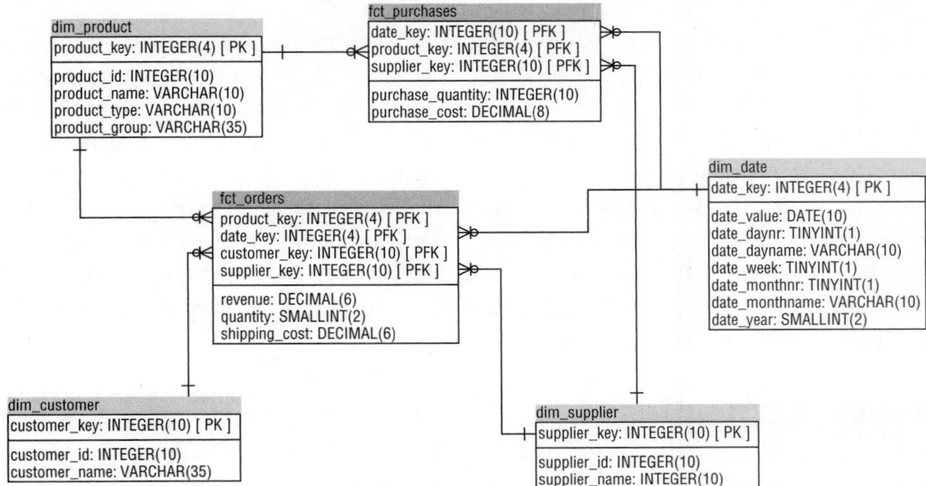

Figure 7-3: Example bus architecture

It's best to start with a high-level bus architecture matrix before the data mart's design process is started. Figure 7-4 shows an example matrix, where all identified business facts are placed in the rows and all identified dimensions in the columns. The "bus" is formed by the main business process or the natural flow of events within an organization. In our case, that would be ordering from suppliers, storing and moving inventory, receiving customer orders, shipping DVDs, and handling returns. Within such a main business process it's easy to check off all relationships between dimensions and facts, which makes the design process easier to manage and can also be used to communicate with the business users about the completeness of the data warehouse.

	Date	Time	Customer	DVD Release	Distributor	Warehouse	Employee	Promotion	Website
Purchase orders	X	X		X	X		X		
Inventory	X	X		X	X	X	X		
Customer orders	X	X	X	X		X	X	X	X
Returns	X	X	X	X		X	X	X	

Figure 7-4: Bus matrix sheet

Using the bus architecture with conformed dimensions is what enables the collection of data marts to be treated as a true Enterprise Data Warehouse. Each dimension table is designed and maintained in only one location, and a single process exists to load and update the data. This contrasts sharply with a collection of independent data marts where each individual data mart is designed, built, and maintained as a point solution. In that case, each data mart contains its own dimensions and each individual dimension has no relation to similar dimensions in other data marts. As a result of this way of working, you might end up having to maintain five or more different product and customer dimensions. We strongly oppose this type of ''architecture''! Our advice here is to always start with developing and agreeing upon the high-level bus matrix to identify all the entities of interest for the data warehouse. Only after completing this step can the detailed design for the individual dimension and fact tables be started.

Design Principles

As soon as you start working with star schemas to support common business questions you will quickly adapt to the underlying design principles. It's like driving a car with a stick shift, which seems complicated in the beginning but feels very natural once you get the hang of it. Adapting to the basic design principles of star schema modeling might be even simpler than learning to drive a stick shift. The next sections introduce the following design principles that enable you to design enterprise-grade data marts:

- Surrogate keys
- Name and type conventions
- Granularity and aggregation
- Audit columns
- Date and time
- Unknown dimensions keys

Using Surrogate Keys

Each table in a database usually has a *primary key*, which is the unique identifier of a record. This key can consist of one or more columns, and any data type can be used for these columns. The databases used as a source system for a data warehouse often contain primary keys consisting of multiple columns. These primary keys come in all sorts and are either database-generated or user-supplied. The term used to refer to these source system keys is *natural key*, as opposed to the term *artificial* or *surrogate* key used in a data warehouse. Natural keys often contain information about the nature of the record they're referring to. A product key might therefore consist of multiple parts indicating things like department, model number revision number, and product type. When a key comprises a combination of such parts and the key alone is enough to reveal to a user what the data is about, it is also referred to as a *smart key*.

From a data warehouse point of view, there's nothing smart about a smart key; they take up unnecessary space and are hard to build and maintain indexes on. In a data warehouse, *surrogate keys* should be used, which is perhaps the most important design principle when building a data mart using star schemas. A surrogate key is a database-generated identifier without any inherent meaning. Its sole purpose is to uniquely identify a dimension record using the smallest possible data type. The primary key of a dimension table therefore always consists of a single column. This is important because fact records can usually be identified by the combination of the primary keys of the dimension tables.

When you look at the diagram in Figure 7-1, you will see that each sales fact (an individual sales transaction) has five foreign keys, to time, product, customer, store, and promotion. Now suppose that for "time" you use a datetime data type and for all the other keys their original source system primary key. Suppose also that these other keys are "smart" and occupy 15 characters, which translates to 15 bytes. You end up with a 68 byte key for the fact table (4 × 15 plus 8 bytes for the datetime). With 100 million fact rows, you need approximately 6.5 gigabytes to store this information. Using surrogate keys, this can be slimmed down to 20 bytes per key (5 integers) resulting in 1.9 GB. That's 4.6 GB less disk space to occupy and also (which is more important) less disk I/O when a query is executed.

Surrogate keys have other advantages as well:

- There's always only a single column key for each dimension table so the resulting primary key index will be smaller.
- Integer indexes are usually a lot faster than character or datetime indexes.
- They enable the storage of multiple versions of an item where the item retains its original source key but is allotted a new surrogate key.
- They allow for dealing with optional relations, unknown values and irrelevant data, so therefore you can avoid using outer joins in your queries.

Surrogate keys can be generated in two ways: by using database functionality (auto-increment values or sequences) or by using the ETL tool to generate next key values. We prefer the latter because some ETL tools need special configuration for handling database-generated keys.

Naming and Type Conventions

A production data warehouse can contain many tables and views, all with many columns of different sizes and types. As a best practice, use meaningful names, prefixes, and postfixes for all database objects. Furthermore, set up guidelines for the data types used in the data warehouse to enforce standardization and prevent possible data loss due to conversion or truncation of values. Most organizations already have a set of database design guidelines readily available and you can either enhance those or develop your own. At a minimum, you should adhere to prescribed naming conventions if they are available.

For our demo data mart projects, we will use the following set of rules:

- All tables get a prefix (followed by an underscore) indicating their role and function in the data warehouse:
  - `STG_` for staging tables
  - `HIS_` for historical archive tables
  - `DIM_` for dimension tables
  - `FCT_` for fact tables
  - `AGG_` for aggregate tables
  - `LKP_` for lookup tables
- All dimension key columns are named after the table they belong to without the postfix and get a `_key` postfix (so the key column of `dim_product` is named `product_key`, and so on).
- All dimension key columns are of the smallest unsigned integer type possible. MySQL has five different integer types, ranging from tiny to big. Integers can be defined as `SIGNED` or `UNSIGNED`, indicating whether they take negative and positive values, or positive values alone. For key columns, use unsigned integers.
  - `TINYINT`—1 byte, 2 ^ 8 values (0–255)
  - `SMALLINT`—2 bytes, 2 ^ 16 values (0–65532)
  - `MEDIUMINT`—3 bytes, 2 ^ 24 values (0–16,777,215)
  - `INT` or `INTEGER`—4 bytes, 2 ^ 32 values (0–4,294,967,295)
  - `BIGINT`—8 bytes, 2 ^ 64 values (0–18,446,744,073,709,551,615)

- Use meaningful names for the columns. We try to prefix all column names with the table name, unless it becomes impractical to do so due to extremely long column names.
- Use standard names for *audit* columns. These are the columns indicating when and who or which process inserted the record or did the last update.
- Avoid the use of reserved words for database objects as tables, columns, and views. Using reserved words such as `group`, `time`, `view`, `order`, `field`, `update`, and so on makes it harder to work with these objects in queries because they must be quoted to distinguish them from the same words in the SQL language.

NOTE **Integers in a MySQL database are `SIGNED` by default, which means they take negative values as well. Make sure to explicitly define integers for key columns as `UNSIGNED` to accommodate for a larger range of values. If you omit the `UNSIGNED` keyword, a `TINYINT` will accept values from −128 to 127. Because we usually start (auto-)numbering at 1, almost half the values will then remain unused.**

Granularity and Aggregation

By *granularity*, we mean the level of detail at which the data is stored in the data warehouse. The golden rule here is to store the data at the lowest level of detail possible. For a retail company, this means the individual sales transaction level; for a mobile operator, it is the call detail record level. In the early days of data warehousing, disk space was expensive and computer power limited, but with today's state of technology storing and querying, terabytes of data are within reach of most organizations.

One of the misconceptions about star schemas is that the fact tables must always be pre-aggregated. *Aggregation* can be a good thing for increasing query performance, but only after loading the data at the lowest level of detail. It's very easy to see whether this lowest level is actually loaded: If you need to do a `sum()` function when loading the fact records, you're not loading the lowest level of detail. The reasoning behind designing the data warehouse to capture the lowest level of detail is very simple. You can always aggregate data when the details are available, but when the details aren't available it's impossible to add them without having to rebuild the entire data warehouse.

Aggregation can have a dramatic impact on performance. A table that aggregates data by month, region, and product category to display in a management report contains probably more than 1,000 times less data than the lowest level transaction fact table. We've witnessed query speed increases from an average of 30 minutes to a couple of milliseconds by using aggregate techniques. Although these results are spectacular, you shouldn't forget that the data model exposed to the outside world (the end users) is the detailed granular one. The existence of aggregate tables should be invisible to end users, while the redirection of queries from the detail tables to the aggregates should be handled by an intelligent *query governor*.

As explained in Chapter 6, this query-governing mechanism is not yet available in open source databases, but fortunately you can use the aggregate designer of Mondrian to at least partly benefit from the automated creation and usage of aggregate tables in your data warehouse solution. Using the aggregate designer along with a columnar database such as LucidDB or Infobright, you can achieve very good query results combined with the availability of detailed fact data.

Audit Columns

We highly recommend including *audit columns* in the data warehouse. These columns enable you to trace back data to its original source, and tell you when a certain row was inserted or modified and who or which process executed the operation. Under normal operation, the ETL process takes care of all modifications to the data in the data warehouse, but sometimes it might be necessary to manually correct something. When this occurs in a carefully constructed dimension table, it's important to have the table record these modifications automatically. For auditing reasons we recommend using the following four columns (at least in the dimension tables):

- Insert timestamp
- Insert batch process
- Update timestamp
- Update batch process

Usually data in a data warehouse is loaded and updated in *batches*. For those situations, we also recommend using a separate batch table, which stores information about the start and end time of the batch, number of records processed, the machine the process ran on, the name and version of the ETL tool that processed the data, and the system profile (development, test, and production) used. Pentaho Data Integration enables you to create these log tables on both the job and the transformation level.

The combination of audit columns and a batch ID helps you find and correct data problems in the data warehouse more easily. They can also be used to prove the correctness of data or, even more important, the correct loading of incorrect data from the source systems. In 99 percent of the cases, data problems are due to errors in the source system, not to errors in the ETL process or the data warehouse itself. When faced with the inevitable discussions about the reliability of the data in the data warehouse, audit columns are your safety net.

Modeling Date and Time

Date and time seem trivial subjects at first, but when you think about it for a couple of seconds there's a lot more to it. For instance, think about how you would account for different time zones your organization operates in. Or think about how to handle fiscal years that are out of sync with the regular calendar year. The week numbering in Europe is based on ISO 3306, whereas in the U.S. week numbering starts at 1 on January 1, causing possible differences in results when an EU subsidiary reports weekly results to a U.S.-based head office. ISO also has a different year calculation, which means that the ISO year for a date can differ from the calendar year of the same date. And how would you model date and time? What granularity do you want to use? We give you our thoughts on the subject here and a couple of hints and best practices to get you started, but ultimately the design decisions should be made by you based on the case at hand.

Time Dimension Granularity

Sometimes when people start with designing a dimensional model, they think that date and time should be stored in a single dimension table. This assumption is perhaps not entirely wrong, but usually not the best one to make. Suppose you want to be able to reference a date-time dimension by seconds. There are 24 × 60 × 60 seconds in each day. For a year consisting of 365 days, you would need 31,536,000 rows in the dimension table, and because you usually store 10 or more years, that adds up to over 315 million rows. Doesn't look like a sensible approach. The most extreme alternative is to create a dimension table per date-time part. In that case, you'd have to create dimension tables for year, month, day, hour, minute, and second. These tables would all be very small but would require six foreign keys in the fact table. This is also not a very good approach. It's best to stay somewhere in the middle between these two extremes by creating one date and one time dimension. Even in the case where you would need your transactions to reference a specific second, the `dim_time` table would only contain 86,400 rows. Our sample WCM data warehouse uses a time dimension by minute, which is only 1,440 rows.

Local Versus UTC Time

When dealing with time, you must also consider the challenges presented when your organization covers multiple time zones. In that case, it might be beneficial to add both local and UTC time to the time dimension table so any transaction can always be looked at from different perspectives.

UTC TIME

UTC is an international standard time and time notation governed by the ISO 8601 standard. The acronym is a compromise between the French TUC (Temps Universel Coördonné) and the English CUT (Coordinated Universal Time). Anyone familiar with military terminology might have heard of "Zulu time," which is the same as UTC. International time zones are indicated as UTC plus or minus a number of hours. This offset can even vary over time when countries change the daylight savings start or end date, or when a government (for example, Venezuela) decides to deviate from international standards. The fixed offset in our time dimension table is therefore a simplification of the real world.

Smart Date Keys

There is one exception to the use of meaningless surrogate keys—the key for the date dimension. We prefer to use an integer in the form YYYYMMDD for two reasons. First, this key can be easily generated from an incoming date and therefore saves a lookup operation on the date dimension table. Second and probably more important is the fact that this numbering scheme can be used to partition your fact tables. Table partitions can also get a name with a date number extension to easily identify, such as P_200808 for all the August 2008 transactions. Other than these two reasons, the use of a smart date key is prohibited and can under no circumstances be used directly in queries on the fact table without joining the corresponding date dimension table.

Handling Relative Time

In many cases, we are not interested in a specific time period such as a week or a month, but want to know what a specific time period looks like compared to another one. The question is how to set up the time dimension to handle relative time, such as last week, last month, or same month last year. Of course, you can write SQL to retrieve the corresponding rows from the database but then you either need to adjust the statement for each new period, or need to use functions and expressions to make a statement dynamic. The examples in the following query blocks show what we mean. The first query retrieves the result from the current and last month, but the statements are hard coded:

```
SELECT     d.year4, d.month_number, f.sum(revenue) AS revenue
FROM       fact_sales AS f
```

```
INNER JOIN dim_date d ON f.order_date_key = d.date_key
WHERE      d.year4 = 2008 AND d.month_number BETWEEN 7 AND 8
```

A dynamic version might look something like this:

```
SELECT     d.year, d.month, f.sum(revenue) AS revenue
FROM       fact_sales AS f
INNER JOIN dim_date d ON f.order_date_key = d.date_key
WHERE      d.year4 = EXTRACT(year from NOW())
AND        d.month_number
BETWEEN    EXTRACT(month FROM NOW())-1
AND        EXTRACT(month FROM NOW())
```

This will work fine, except when the current month is January. To avoid complex coding like this it's better to add additional columns to the time dimension table that can be updated during the ETL process. As an example, we'll use two columns: `current_month` and `last_month`. When applicable, they will contain the value 1, otherwise 0. The same technique can be applied to indicate year to date, month to date, and so on.

Another technique we'd like to mention is the use of offsets to be able to perform date arithmetic in a simple way. A good example of this is the use of Julian dates, which are consecutive integer values. This makes it very easy to filter on the last 30 days or 30 days prior to a chosen date. Again, you can expand this to weeks, months, and years as well. By setting the current week, month, or year to 0 and counting backwards, it's possible to have both a current period indicator and a means of filtering on the last three months, last six quarters, etc.

Table 7-1 shows a partial collection of rows and columns from the time dimension to illustrate this technique. The current date in this example is July 1, 2009 with a week starting on Monday.

In this table, you can see three ways of handling relative time:

- Sequence number—The Julian date is an integer that allows for simple arithmetic, e.g., "last 30 days." Any date can be used as the offset (starting point).
- True/false indicators—The current and last week columns are updated each week. Retrieving the current week is a matter of adding `current_week = 1` to a query.
- Sequence with offset 0—This combines the first two options in one column. Current week is always 0, last week −1, and so on.

The third option might appear to be the ideal solution to handle all relative time issues, but there's a catch. The extra current and last week columns with just 1 and 0 enable you to do calculations as well. In many cases, you need to see current and last week's revenue side by side, and this can easily be accomplished by using a statement like the following:

```
SELECT      p.product_type,
            SUM(f.revenue*d.current_week) AS current_week,
            SUM(f.revenue*d.last_week) AS last_week
FROM        fact_sales AS f
INNER JOIN dim_date d ON f.order_date_key = d.date_key
INNER JOIN dim_product p ON f.product_key = p.product_key
WHERE       d.week_sequence BETWEEN -1 AND 0
```

Table 7-1: Relative time columns

date_key	date_value	date_julian	current_week	last_week	week_seq
20090620	20-Jun-09	2455002	0	1	-2
20090621	21-Jun-09	2455003	0	1	-2
20090622	22-Jun-09	2455004	0	1	-1
20090623	23-Jun-09	2455005	0	1	-1
20090624	24-Jun-09	2455006	0	1	-1
20090625	25-Jun-09	2455007	0	1	-1
20090626	26-Jun-09	2455008	0	1	-1
20090627	27-Jun-09	2455009	0	1	-1
20090628	28-Jun-09	2455010	0	1	-1
20090629	29-Jun-09	2455011	1	0	0
20090630	30-Jun-09	2455012	1	0	0
20090701	1-Jul-09	2455013	1	0	0
20090702	2-Jul-09	2455014	1	0	0
20090703	3-Jul-09	2455015	1	0	0
20090704	4-Jul-09	2455016	1	0	0
20090705	5-Jul-09	2455017	1	0	0
20090706	6-Jul-09	2455018	0	0	1

Unknown Dimension Keys

In addition to the already-mentioned advantages for using surrogate keys (and the upcoming explanation in this chapter of handling history in the data warehouse), there is another good reason to use surrogate keys. Sometimes data will be loaded in a fact table and no corresponding dimension key can be found based on the natural key and/or the validity of the dimension record. For those cases, you need a mechanism that stores the facts anyway to make sure that no data is omitted during processing. For this reason, we recommend having an unknown record in each dimension table. Key generation in a dimension usually starts at 1, so that leaves the number 0 as a perfect candidate for the unknown dimension record key. This record should have a value of "unknown" in all attribute fields. Table 7-2 shows a partial example of the unknown record in a customer dimension table.

Table 7-2: Unknown dimension record

key	source_id	name	address	phone
0	0	Unknown	Unknown	Unknown

We use the value `Unknown` to inform our business users that this data is not available. This is a much better alternative than allowing `NULL` values, which often confuses users. Besides, when `NULL` values are used in a calculation they may cause erroneous results. A simple test will illustrate this; just start the MySQL query browser and type in `SELECT 'result'`. This will return the text '`result'`. Now alter the statement into `SELECT 'result'+NULL` and see what happens.

In some cases, a single unknown indicator is not enough. Sometimes the dimension is not relevant for a specific fact. This can occur when the fact table contains different kinds of facts. An example of this is a click stream fact table. We'd like to store all clicks together to be able to easily calculate total page views, but not all clicks are the same. Some are just navigational clicks, some confirm a transaction, and others download a file. In case of a navigational click, a reference to a download file is not relevant, but because we don't allow `NULL` values in our fact table foreign key columns we add a special surrogate key with the value `not relevant` to the dimension table in addition to the `unknown` key.

Handling Dimension Changes

Dimensional data changes constantly. Customers move, new products are introduced, employees get a salary raise, warehouses get new managers, and so on. One of the main challenges when building a data warehouse is how to adapt to these changes in such a way that all relevant history is captured and all transactions are linked to the correct historical dimension records. Some of these changes occur frequently, others only occasionally. Some changes affect a single record, and some involve complete tables, such as introducing a new customer classification. And some changes are relevant to store in a historically correct way for the organization, while others can simply replace old data. For all of these situations, a different strategy can be applied, and together they form the different ways of handling *slowly changing dimensions* (*SCD*s). In his first edition of *The Data Warehouse Toolkit*, Ralph Kimball introduced three different SCD strategies: overwrite, stack, and add. These strategies are now respectively called SCD type 1, 2, and 3 and will be described shortly. Over the years, many other people from the database modeling community added new types and variations to the original SCD types; the current approach covers the handling of all possible changes that can be applied to source data and how to handle these changes most effectively in a data warehouse.

The term slowly changing dimensions is slightly misleading in the sense that you might get the impression that these types should be applied to the complete dimension table. This is an incorrect assumption which we'd like to address before we go on. Each column in a dimension table should be treated individually. So it is possible that for some columns a type 1 is used, while for others the type 2 approach will be more appropriate. Other strategies or combinations can also be used, but identifying which strategy should be applied to each column is an important part of the design process. We'll give some design tips in the next chapter on how to do this and document it.

The story doesn't begin with type 1, however. There is also a type 0, meaning either "do nothing" or "replace completely." In both cases, this is not an advisable strategy, unless it concerns static dimension tables. The most prominent example of these are the Date and Time dimensions. It's highly unlikely that the Year value of the date Jan. 20, 2008 will ever change. What can change, however, is a Fiscal Year classification but in that case values usually get overwritten (type 1) or stored in an additional column (type 3).

NOTE Not all dimension attributes will be used for analytical purposes and thus not all are of interest for historical correctness. Which attributes are analytical and which are details differs per industry and organization. In some cases, a phone number is just a customer dimension detail that can be overwritten when a new value is extracted from the source system. In other cases, the phone number is being used for analytical purposes and changes need to be tracked. When we analyze sales, it's usually sufficient to group by city, not necessarily by street or address. In that case, the column `city` is an analytical attribute and the column `address` is a plain detail.

SCD Type 1: Overwrite

A type 1 slowly changing dimension is the most basic one and doesn't require any special modeling or additional fields. SCD type 1 columns just get overwritten with new values when they come into the data warehouse. Figure 7-5 shows what a dimension record looks like before and after applying a type 1 dimension change. In this case, the customer moved to a new address on a certain date.

Existing situation

Customer_key	Customer_id	Customer_Name	Customer_City
1	22321	Humphries	Toronto

New situation

Customer_key	Customer_id	Customer_Name	Customer_City
1	22321	Humphries	Vancouver

Figure 7-5: SCD type 1 example

Without additional knowledge, you have no way of identifying when this change happened, and even if you insert an extra column with a last modified timestamp you only know that something changed inside the record, not in which column this change took place. A type 1 overwrite approach is used for columns that are of interest for our users (otherwise the columns wouldn't have been there in the first place), but only the current status of the data is relevant, even when looking at older transactions. Remember that when you overwrite a column like this and run a query, all results will show the content of the column as it is now, not the earlier value.

SCD Type 2: Add Row

Type 2 is not ''the next step'' in terms of functionality or complexity but is actually a category of its own. All ETL vendors went out of their way to support type 2 SCDs with wizards, macros, and other add-ins over the last couple of years so nowadays you'll be hard-pressed to find a tool without this support. Of course, Kettle/PDI also has this functionality in the Dimension Lookup/Update step. But what exactly does it do? SCD type 2 is about history preservation and enables an organization to capture changes to a dimension table to retrieve historical correct data when querying the data warehouse. Figure 7-6 shows the same example as in the previous paragraph, but now you can track changes through time by adding a few extra fields. There are multiple ways of modeling this or storing multiple versions; the most basic one is to add only a `valid_from` timestamp to the dimension record. Omitting the corresponding `valid_to` timestamp adds extra complexity when trying to retrieve the correct version of the dimension entry, so mark this as a mandatory field for this type of change as well. Two other extra columns can often be found in type 2 supporting tables: a current_record column indicating the current version of the dimension record, and a sequence or version number that is incremented each time a new version of the record is added.

Now you can do lots of interesting things with this data. Suppose Mr. or Mrs. Humphries is a regular customer and orders something every month. What happens in your fact table when these transactions are loaded is that the ETL process looks at the valid customer record for each particular customer at the time of loading. This means that all order fact rows for the customer with ID 22321 (the source system customer number) will store customer_key 1 until May 1, 2008, and use customer_key 2 from that day on until the next change for this customer is applied. The example fact table is displayed in Figure 7-7.

Existing situation

Customer_key	Customer_id	Customer_Name	Customer_City	Valid_from	Valid_to	Current_record
1	22321	Humphries	Toronto	1900-01-01	9999-12-31	1

New situation

Customer_key	Customer_id	Customer_Name	Customer_City	Valid_from	Valid_to	Current_record
1	22321	Humphries	Toronto	1900-01-01	2008-04-30	0
2	22321	Humphries	Vancouver	2008-05-01	9999-12-31	1

Figure 7-6: SCD type 2 example

Sales facts

Customer_key	Date_key	Product_key	Items	Revenue
1	20080123	123	1	5
1	20080208	221	2	10
1	20080315	332	1	5
1	20080421	334	1	5
2	20080511	221	2	10
2	20080609	432	3	15
2	20080729	554	1	5
2	20080817	101	2	10

Figure 7-7: Facts with SCD type 2

Now when you want to know how much revenue was generated in Toronto in 2008, and you run this query in September, the condition is where customer_city = 'Toronto'. The dimension record with the value 1 for customer_key is the only record satisfying this condition. And because the join is on customer_key, only the first four rows of the fact table are retrieved for this customer. When the condition is where customer_name = 'Humphries', both customer_id 1 and 2 satisfy the condition and all the fact rows will be returned.

PROCESSING TYPE 2 SCD DATA

An ETL process, whether hand coded or coded with a tool, needs to have several capabilities for handling type 2 dimension changes. First of all, the incoming data must be compared to the data that already exists in the dimension table. The output of this process is the incoming data set with flags added for new rows (I for Insert) to be inserted, existing rows that need to be updated (U for Update), and possibly even deleted rows that don't exist anymore in the source system (D for Delete). Based on the I, U, or D flags, the process then needs to assign new surrogate keys in case of inserts or updates. Inserts are easy: the new row can be added with the default settings for `valid_to` and `current_record`. For an update, additional processing is required: the existing row needs to be detected (that's why the `current_record` indicator is so useful), the `valid_to` timestamps need to be set to the correct value, and the `current_record` flag has to be set to a value of 0, N, or whatever logic you have designed for it. Then a new record with the updated data has to be created, a surrogate key generated, and the appropriate timestamps and `current_record` flag need to be set. Because deleting dimensional data is out of the question (it probably still is referenced by existing facts) the records with a delete flag get their `valid_to` timestamp set. In addition, another indicator can be used to mark the record as deleted. A possible solution is to use a value other than 0 or 1 for the `current_record` flag.

Of course there is more to capturing history in a data warehouse; this is just the plain version of historical correctness. For instance, think about the following issue: what point in time do we use for the `valid_from` and `valid_to` timestamps? Is it the time the change was entered in the source system? The time the data was loaded in the data warehouse? The actual time in the real world when the event took place? Or the time when we were notified of this event? The third option might seem the most appropriate version and the best representation of the actual event, but how do we track this? In some industries, such as the insurance business, all these timestamps need to be stored and the data warehouse should have a full account for the *history of history*, as it is called, as well. Further discussion of this problem is beyond the scope of this book, but we wanted to raise the issue for completeness here.

For the remainder of this book, we will use the standard version of history preservation as shown in the examples shown in Figures 7-6 and 7-7. We will also add an extra version column to capture the number of changes made to a particular source record.

SCD Type 3: Add Column

The type 3 strategy requires at least one extra column in the dimension table. When the data for a type 3 column changes, the existing value is copied to the extra `_old` column while the new value is placed in the regular column. Figure 7-8 shows an example of this.

Existing situation

Customer_key	Customer_id	Customer_Name	Customer_City	Customer_City_Old
1	22321	Humphries	Toronto	Toronto

New situation

Customer_key	Customer_id	Customer_Name	Customer_City	Customer_City_Old
1	22321	Humphries	Vancouver	Toronto

Figure 7-8: SCD type 3 example

This might seem an odd way of keeping previous values at first, and in most cases it is. It's only possible to handle one previous version. Storing additional changes requires an extra column for each version you want to keep. But imagine that your organization structure changes completely, or a completely new product group structure is introduced. In those cases, where all records change at the same time, it makes sense to use an extra column. Handling these massive changes with a type 2 scenario doubles the number of records in your dimension table and in most cases, only the new structure of the data is relevant. The old version is just kept for reference purposes or as a translation table.

SCD Type 4: Mini-Dimensions

Kimball's dimensional modeling introduces the term *mini-dimension*. Some sources claim this to be a type 4 scenario; others use the term ''type 4'' for other purposes. The notions of type 4 and 5 SCDs were introduced in 1998 by Michael Schmitz, a renowned expert in data warehousing and dimensional modeling. We conform to this classification here, in contrast to other sources such as Wikipedia, which uses a different categorization.

Mini-dimensions solve two particular problems with changing dimension tables. One problem occurs when dimension tables get really big, say a customer dimension with 150 million rows (they exist!). The second problem occurs when changes happen very frequently, causing the dimension table to double or triple in size each year. The trick here is to first identify which analytical attributes change very frequently and put these as a group in one or more separate dimension tables. The result of this is one or more extra dimension keys in the fact table.

Here's an example. Suppose you have a large customer dimension table with the attributes `city`, `region`, `country`, `gender`, `birth_date`, and `income`. The first three fields can be categorized as geographic data; the latter three have a more demographic nature. Of course, the gender description doesn't change very often but is probably one of the key attributes for analytical purposes. These six fields can therefore be put in two different mini dimensions, a `dim_geography` and a `dim_demography`.

Mini-dimensions do honor to their name: They usually are very small, not only in number of records but also in number of attributes, as in this example. There is, however, a tradeoff involved in order to keep this number of records as small as possible. When an attribute such as income is used in a mini-dimension, it's impossible to store all possible different values so you need to work with *banded values* or *ranges*. Remember that when using fields A, B, and C for a mini-dimension, the number of records is determined by multiplying the number of possible values of A, B, and C. So if each age from 0 to 100 is used, the multiplier is already 101. It makes more sense to define age and income ranges, maybe 10 of each, resulting in 100 records. Multiplied by the three possible values for gender (male, female, and unknown) the number of rows in the mini-dimension will be 300, which is really small by any standard. Mini-dimensions with 100,000 rows are not uncommon and with the current state of technology also not a problem. If the mini-dimensions get any larger than that, it's advisable to redesign the dimension table and maybe split it up again into smaller dimensions. Figure 7-9 shows an example data model with a fact table and three dimension tables of which two are mini-dimensions.

In order to make this work you need to identify the correct mini-dimension key when loading the facts, which requires extra overhead. For instance, to determine the age group a customer belongs to, you need to calculate the age based on the load date and the customer's birth date. The same goes for income band and all other attributes needed to determine the correct mini-dimension key. The payoff, however, is huge. Suddenly, many fewer changes can occur to your "main" dimension table. History is perfectly covered in the fact tables using the mini-dimension foreign keys, and to top it off, you also added the current mini-dimension key to the main dimension table. This last addition enables the user to use the mini-dimensions in conjunction with the main dimension without the need to query the fact table. In fact, this model serves two purposes: It gives the current dimension record value, which is very useful for selecting target groups—for example, for direct marketing campaigns—while retaining the full history of the analytical attributes in the fact table.

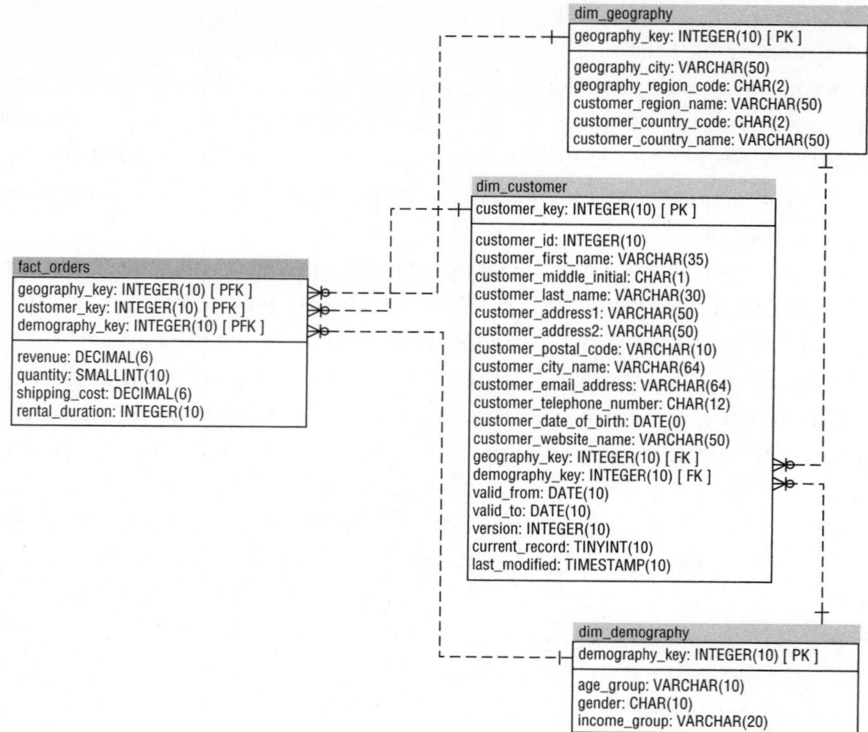

Figure 7-9: Mini-dimensions

SCD Type 5: Separate History Table

So far, the dimension changes have affected the way you look at your query results with respect to the corresponding fact rows. The different strategies enable you to identify which version of a dimension record was valid at the time of a transaction, be it a sale, an inventory movement, or some other business event. Type 5 is a little bit different because it cannot be used to run analytical queries that use the fact table as well. With type 5, a separate history table is created for a dimension table with the sole purpose of correctly capturing all changes to all attributes in the dimension table. A type 5 strategy is therefore an addition to the existing SCD types and should be used in conjunction with one or a combination of the other strategies. Type 5 history tables should therefore not be used for analytical queries involving fact tables. Figure 7-10 shows an example of this type of table together with the parent dimension table.

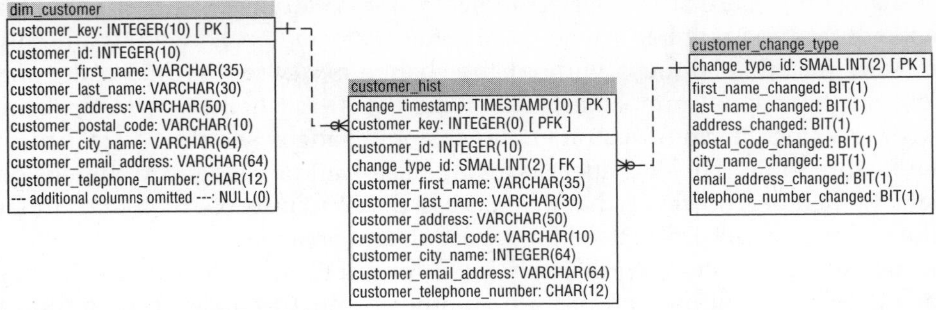

Figure 7-10: Type 5 history table

This almost looks like a fact table, and indeed it has some of the same characteristics as a fact table. However, there are no real facts: There's nothing to summarize because there are no measurable items. The only available option is to count the number of customers or changes, but that could be an interesting enough activity: How many times do customers get a new e-mail address? What's the average moving rate?

Also note that the diagram in Figure 7-10 contains a change type table that serves as a lookup table that indicates exactly what values have changed. Table 7-3 shows the first few rows of this table so that you can get a feeling of what this data is all about.

Table 7-3: Customer change type table

change_type_id	first_name_changed	last_name_changed	address_changed	postal_code_changed	city_name_changed	email_address_changed	telephone_number_changed
1	false	false	false	false	false	false	true
2	false	false	false	false	false	true	true
3	false	false	false	false	false	true	false
4	false	false	false	false	true	false	false

Change types are also a perfect indicator for data quality issues. Look, for instance, at type number 4 where only the city name is changed. It's highly unlikely that this happens without the change of address, postal code, and possibly telephone number as well. Regardless of whether you overwrite existing values in your customer dimension, changes should be tracked in the history table. The end effect is a full audit trail of changes to dimension data. Remember, however, that this serves a different purpose than the regular dimension and fact tables used for reporting and analysis.

The example described previously is only one of the many possible solutions for modeling a full data audit trail. Another common approach is to mimic the change or log tables used by many database management systems for replicating and synchronizing data between two or more databases. Besides the changed data, these change tables contain the record key, change timestamp, and the change type indicator I, U, or D for Insert, Update, and Delete. Sometimes *before* and *after* images are both present in these tables, comparable to a type 3 SCD scenario.

SCD Type 6: Hybrid Strategies

Type 6 doesn't really exist but is sometimes described as 1+2+3=6, indicating that it is a mix of different strategies applied to a single dimension table. Kimball gives an example of this in *The Data Warehouse Lifecycle Toolkit*. A common business request is ''I want to see all product revenue according to the current version of the product group.'' This query cannot be answered if a product group is handled as a type 2 attribute, which is usually the case. One way to solve this is to add an extra product attribute to the dimension table where the current version of the product group is stored for all versions of the product. Table 7-4 illustrates this feature.

Table 7-4: Hybrid SCD strategy

product_key	product_id	product_name	product_group	product_group_curr	valid_from	valid_to	current_record
101	ABC	Acidrip	Software	Open Source	1-1-1900	12-3-2002	false
102	ABC	Acidrip	Freeware	Open Source	13-3-2002	31-12-2008	false
103	ABC	Acidrip	Open Source	Open Source	1-1-2009	31-12-9999	true

By using this modeling technique, you can still store the correct version of the product in your fact table for historical correctness, but this technique also enables a user to look at this information as if all history were based on the current product group classification. This is, however, not a very flexible solution and works only for one or a few attributes. Another way of solving this problem is joining the same dimension table on the source ID, and restricting the extra joined table on the current record. By doing this, all attributes can be used ''as is'' while at the same time retrieving the full history from the fact table based on the SCD keys. The last option is to add an additional dimension table with only the current values in it. This current dimension table will then get its own key in the fact table. A drawback of this solution is that you need an extra key column in the fact table for each current dimension you add this way.

Advanced Dimensional Model Concepts

Designing a data warehouse can be a daunting task, especially when it seems that none of the techniques described thus far solve your specific problem. What should you do when, for instance, your customer dimension is really, really big, like 150 million records? That's the issue of monster dimensions. Or what if multiple values can exist for a single dimension entry? The WCM database has a `dim_dvd_release` product dimension, but each movie has multiple actors playing in it. How do you model this? And what about when you have finished modeling and there are some leftover attributes that don't seem to fit anywhere? The next sections show you the advanced concepts needed to solve these problems and fully exploit the dimensional modeling technique.

Monster Dimensions

We mentioned the 150 million record customer table before. Maybe your customer dimension isn't that big, but even with 5 million records, maintaining the dimension table in a limited batch window can be challenging enough. We've shown one of the solutions to make a monster dimension better manageable and optimize query performance: the mini-dimensions. Still, when your monster dimension contains a lot of detail columns that will not be used for analytical purposes anyway, it might be a good idea to split them into a separate table, also called *vertical partitioning*. The query speed in a row-based database like MySQL is not only determined by the number of rows, but also by the total byte size of each row. When a column-based database such as Infobright, LucidDB or MonetDB is used, this penalty is eliminated by the fact that the data is already stored in a column-by-column fashion, thereby eliminating the need to partition the table yourself.

A third option is to partition the table horizontally. This is a quite common technique for fact tables that are usually partitioned by time period, but is not used very often for dimension tables. The problem with horizontal partitioning is that a partition key needs to be defined in such a way that the partitioning makes sense. The benefit of horizontal partitioning lies in the fact that when a query is parsed, the optimizer can determine which partitions to use and which not, based on the partition key. Most queries involve a date/time attribute, so when using a time-based partitioning scheme, this is easy. If your data is partitioned by month and the query affects only last month's sales, the optimizer can select a single partition to retrieve the data from.

With customer data it's not that simple. You cannot use a date field to partition by because no available date is relevant to your analytical queries. Other attributes that can serve as a candidate partitioning key might be geographic or demographic entities, but choosing one of these entities only allows for one way of slicing the data, which might not be relevant in most cases. Added to this, you have to take into account that developing and maintaining a partitioning schema is not a trivial task. It requires advanced database administration skills to set this up and integrate the partitioning scheme with the data loading processes for the data warehouse. For taming monster dimensions, the combination of vertical partitioning and the use of additional mini-dimensions seems, therefore, the best available alternative. To determine which columns to split off for the mini-dimension(s) you'll need to look at a couple of things:

- **Similarity**—Which columns contain similar information or information that is logically grouped together, such as demographic attributes.
- **Cardinality**—How many different values can occur in a single column? Columns of low cardinality (such as gender) are ideal candidates for mini-dimensions.
- **Volatility**—How often do values in a column change over time? Names don't change very often; demographic attributes such as age or income group do.

Junk, Heterogeneous, and Degenerate Dimensions

When developing the dimensional model, you'll probably end up with some attributes that don't really fit in one of the agreed upon dimension tables. This is usually the case with attributes that have a meaning in a process such as order or shipment status flags, order type, or payment terms. The possible solutions for these attributes, such as leaving them in the fact table, moving them to separate dimensions, or leaving them out altogether all have their specific disadvantages. A fact table should be as narrow as possible so adding text columns is a bad idea. Modeling each attribute as a separate dimension is an equally bad idea, and omitting these attributes means that they cannot be used for any analysis. The best solution is to group these attributes in a separate dimension table called a *junk dimension*—not junk in the literal sense but as a collection of leftovers that need to be handled in an elegant way. Actually you've already seen several examples of the way these dimensions are modeled in the SCD type 4 paragraph. The only difference between a mini- and a junk dimension is the fact that the latter contains often unrelated attributes whereas the attributes in a regular mini-dimension have a relation of some sort and can be named accordingly.

Heterogeneous dimensions are a variation on this theme where different kinds of items are grouped together in a single dimension table. Because our demo company, World Class Movies, has only a single type of product in stock it doesn't serve as a good example. For this case, however, we can easily find a good example in the local supermarket. Products in a supermarket can belong to different categories such as food, non-food, and beverages. Food can also be categorized into multiple categories with very different characteristics. When these products are stored in a single product dimension, you end up with a table where most of the attributes will be irrelevant to an individual product. Indicating the expiration date or caloric value of a broom simply doesn't make a lot of sense. The challenge here is to find the right balance between the single product table with many useless attributes and tens of different product dimension tables that are perfectly tailored for a specific product category. In this case, there is no best answer; it all depends on the situation at hand.

Degenerate dimensions are a slightly different kind of breed. These are dimensions that do not really exist but should get a place in the dimensional model anyway. A good example is the order number. Order numbers can help to trace some of the information in the data warehouse back to the source system, but there is no real order dimension. All attributes of order and order line are modeled at the lowest level of granularity, which is the order line fact. The attributes that are part of an order, such as order date and customer, are already moved to the order facts. At the end of this process, what do you do with the order number then? There's no point in creating an order dimension because all of the relevant attributes are already pushed down into the fact table and related dimensions. In these cases where you end up with a single attribute, just add the attribute to the fact table. This attribute is not a measure object and is also not a foreign key to a dimension table; hence it is called a *degenerate dimension*.

Role-Playing Dimensions

This isn't about dimensions performing Romeo or Juliet, but is meant to indicate that the same dimension can be used to act as multiple, similar dimensions. The obvious example is the time dimension, which can be used, or better, *must* be used to accommodate multiple occurrences of time and date. Looking at a typical sales fact table, you see order date, ship date, receive date, return date, and payment date—five dates, one dimension. Physically speaking, all these dates link to the same date dimension table; logically, of course, they don't because you would end up with an empty result set in most of the cases where multiple date restrictions apply. Take for instance the query for retrieving the total order value of DVDs ordered in December 2007 that were not returned within five days after shipment. This query involves three types of dates, and when all the required date restrictions are being set on the same date dimension table, you end up with an empty result set, or at least a result set that doesn't correctly answer the question. The SQL to illustrate the correct solution for this looks similar to the query we used when discussing table aliases (which is basically the same):

```
SELECT     SUM(f.revenue) AS ordervalue
FROM       fact_sales AS f
INNER JOIN dim_date AS o ON f.order_date_key = o.date_key
INNER JOIN dim_date AS s ON f.shipping_date_key = s.date_key
INNER JOIN dim_date AS r ON r.return_date_key = r.date_key
WHERE      o.year4 = 2007
AND        o.month_number = 12
AND        r.julian_date > s.julian_date + 5
```

Now it's easy to see that if you apply the last two restrictions to the same table, this would cause an empty result set; it's not possible for a date to be bigger than the same date plus 5 days.

Another example related to the WCM database is the actor and director information. We could combine these two entities in a single role-playing `artist` or `movie_person` dimension. A lot of actors become directors later in their career and sometimes even the opposite occurs. Take for instance Quentin Tarantino, who started his career as a director and could later be found acting in his own movies as well.

Multi-Valued Dimensions and Bridge Tables

One of the hardest to solve problems in dimensional modeling is the multi-valued dimension. Again, the actor table is a perfect example: Our customers buy or rent a single DVD but this item usually has multiple actors appearing in the movie. Depending on the kind of information we'd like to retrieve from the data warehouse, there are two possible solutions to solve this problem. The first one is to list the actors in a text field at the movie level, as in Table 7-5.

Table 7-5: Actor list as attribute

dvd_key	dvd_id	dvd_name	dvd_actors
101	AA332	Lizard Wars	Harry Protz; Neill Pine; Will Grant

This is fine for informational purposes and answers the question ''Which actors played in movie X?'' but cannot be used for other, more interesting, questions as ''In which movies did actor Y play?'' or ''Which are the top 10 actors based on rental revenue?'' To solve this last problem, you need a way to relate multiple facts to multiple dimension values. And because you cannot directly create many-to-many relationships in a database you need a bridge table to perform the task. Figure 7-11 shows the part of the data warehouse model with the `dvd_actor` bridge table.

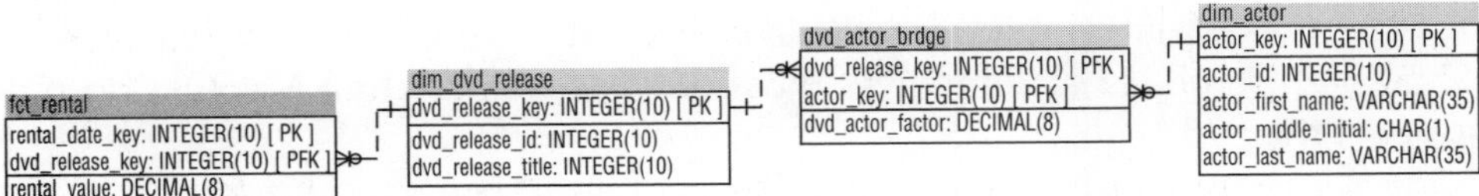

Figure 7-11: dvd_actor bridge table

Note that in this diagram, the table `dvd_actor_bridge` contains a `dvd_actor_factor` field. This is a necessary addition to the bridge table to force SQL to return the correct results. If we omit the factor in our calculations involving actors, the revenue will be multiplied by the number of actors linked to a specific DVD. Debate is, of course, open to whether this should be an equal division (10 actors, factor 0.1) or that the leading actor gets a higher factor (10 actors of which one is Brad Pitt; Brad counts for 0.55, the others for 0.05 each). This poses a problem when you want an answer to the question ''How much revenue did we generate with the movies starring Brad Pitt?'' In that case, only one actor is selected causing the factor to return a value that's too low so the calculation factor should be either omitted or set to the value 1 in this case. Things get really messy when we want to know our top 10 movie stars based on the total revenue of the movies they played in. Some of these actors might have co-starred in one or more movies in the past, causing incorrect results. The message here is: Be careful when modeling these kinds of relationships and make sure that you provide access only to bridged relations when the user or analyst working with the data knows exactly what he or she is dealing with. It is also possible to use an abstraction layer such as the Pentaho metadata layer where multiple calculation objects can be created, one for each particular case with a narrowly documented definition. Chapter 12 will show you how to set this up.

Building Hierarchies

Hierarchies are very useful instruments for navigating though your data. A hierarchy enables a user to start at a high aggregation level (for example, product category) and supports drilling into the details of a particular dimension. Most hierarchies will be implicitly modeled inside the dimension tables. Good examples of this can be found inside the date dimension with the time hierarchies year-quarter-month-date or year-week, or the customer dimension with country-region-zipcode-address. Those are simple, fixed hierarchies where all leaves in the hierarchy have the same "depth." It gets interesting when you need to model hierarchies of variable depth as well. The common way of building hierarchies of various depth in a source system is to have the records in a table reference other records in the same table. Think, for instance, of an employee table where each employee record points to a manager, which is also an employee. In that case, the table references itself; hence it is mostly referred to as a *self-join*. Oracle's SQL contains a *connect by prior* statement, which can traverse these relationship trees. This is also called *recursion*, but this isn't an ANSI SQL standard statement so most databases, including MySQL, do not support this.

Luckily, you can also use bridge tables here. Using the bridge table for unbalanced hierarchies is optional; without the bridge table, the dimension table can be joined to the fact table as usual. The bridge table is just there to assist in navigating additional hierarchies. This is why these tables are still sometimes referred to as *helper* tables. Figure 7-12 shows the resulting database diagram when using a hierarchy bridge table.

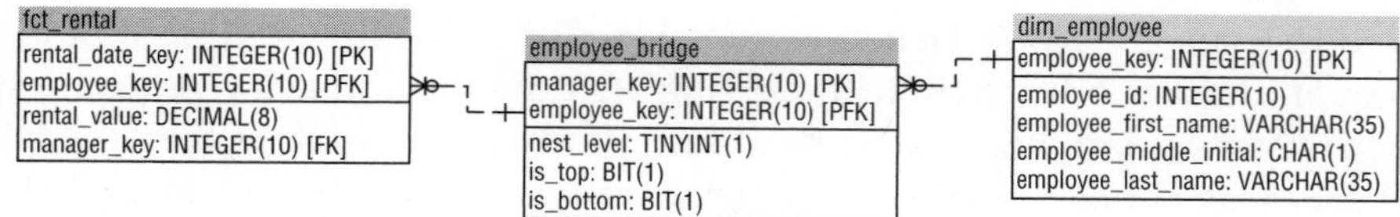

Figure 7-12: Hierarchy bridge

Table 7-6 shows what the data in this table looks like when the data for the manager-employee relationships is added, as shown in Figure 7-13.

This bridge table enables you to roll up the data based on any question you'd like to ask. Care is necessary, however; if you don't add all needed restrictions, there's a risk of double counting some of the values. Suppose you want the total revenue of employee 2 by filtering the employee key. Without additional filters on `nest_level` the result set is doubled because `employee_key` 2 is entered twice. This is also the major disadvantage of a hierarchy bridge table: Each path from each item to any other item in the same tree is stored in a separate record. As a result, the bridge table gets much larger than the dimension table it belongs to.

Table 7-6: Employee bridge table content

manager_key	employee_key	nest_level	is_top	is_bottom
1	1	0	Y	N
1	2	1	N	N
1	3	1	N	N
1	4	2	N	Y
1	5	2	N	Y
2	2	0	N	N
2	4	1	N	Y
2	5	1	N	Y
3	3	0	N	Y

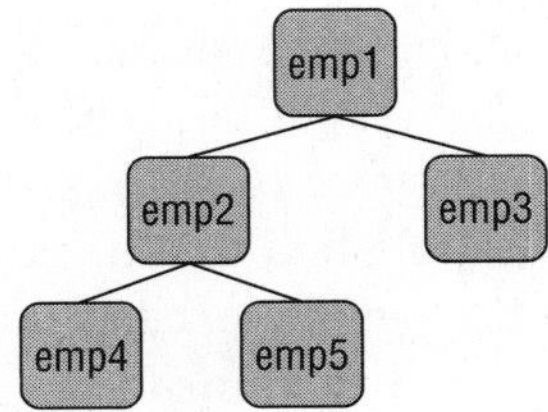

Figure 7-13: Unbalanced hierarchy

An alternative to using bridge tables to model unbalanced hierarchies is to force the flattening of the hierarchy. The blank spots in the diagram are simply filled in by repeating the values of the level above. Table 7-7 shows this principle.

Table 7-7: Flattened unbalanced hierarchy

employee_key	manager_id	boss_id
1	1	1
2	1	1
3	1	1
4	2	1
5	2	1

You can now create a navigation structure from the boss to the employee level where all levels contain a relation to the level above. The number of columns you need depends on the number of levels in the hierarchy; there is no need for the additional overhead of a bridge table. There is a potential risk involved here: A flattened hierarchy assumes a fixed number of levels. If another level is added to the data, the resulting hierarchy table has to be restructured again.

No matter which construct is used to model the hierarchy, the transformation of the data from a self join relationship into the correct placement in bridge or hierarchy tables is not a trivial task.

Snowflakes and Clustering Dimensions

So far, we've been mostly talking about denormalizing the data in the data mart dimensions. As a result, the query join paths to the fact table are only one level deep. The only exception thus far has been the use of bridge tables for multi-valued dimension columns. You've seen that the general rule of thumb when modeling data marts is to denormalize the dimension tables. When you take this to the extreme, you can denormalize even further. The ultimate denormalized data model consists of a single table, at least from the user's point of view. Dutch author and consultant Dr. Harm van der Lek described this as the *One Attribute Set Interface* (OASI) concept, in which all non-key attributes in a star schema are published to the end user and/or query tool as a single list. At the other end of the scale, you can find the completely normalized data models that are mostly used in transaction systems. Dimensional data marts are positioned somewhere in the middle between these two extremes.

Using normalization in a star schema is usually called *snowflaking*, to indicate the resemblance of this kind of schema with an actual snowflake. Figure 7-6 in the previous chapter showed an example of this for the customer-region-country relationship. As with any data warehouse modeling technique, there are advocates and opponents of using snowflakes in dimensional data marts. Ralph Kimball strongly opposes using snowflakes with only one exception, explained in the following section. We'd like to list another exception, which is called *clustering*. This concept is described in a paper by Dr. Daniel Moody, which can be downloaded at `http://ftp.informatik.rwth-aachen.de/Publications/CEUR-WS/Vol-28/paper5.pdf`.

The original paper is from 2000, and in the summer and fall of 2003 Moody wrote two subsequent articles for The Data Warehouse Institute (TDWI), which are still worthwhile reading. These latter articles drop the term *clustering* and introduce the term *starflake*, which boils down to the same thing. The issue at hand is caused by multiple references to the same normalized table in a data mart. In our WCM example, we have this situation with customers, warehouses, employees, and suppliers all of whom reference the same region and country table in their address fields. In a strictly enforced star schema, we need to build four denormalization transformations, one for each dimension. In this case, Moody advises to cluster the region/country table and make this a shared subdimension for all four dimension tables. The rule of thumb is that as soon as a so called *fork* appears in the data model, the lookup table is not denormalized but used as a cluster table. A fork means that two candidate dimension tables reference the same lookup table, as you can see in Figure 7-14. The diagram shows an example of a strictly normalized solution on the left and a clustered star or starflake schema on the right.

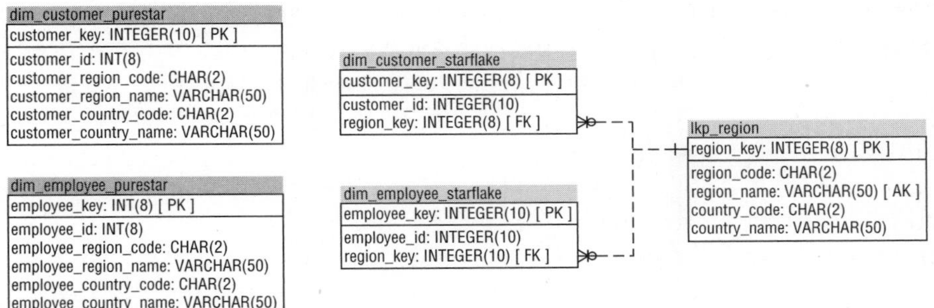

Figure 7-14: Starflake schema

This approach has several advantages. First of all, it's a minor issue, but the dimension table gets a little smaller. Of more importance is the maintenance of starflake tables: Changes occur only in one table and the ETL process only has to refresh one table instead of two or more. There are disadvantages as well, of course. You need to create extra views (when you model the solution in advance) or use extra aliases in your queries because you cannot reference the same lookup table in a query where customers and employees are involved. The biggest drawback, however, is that you are creating dependencies in your ETL process. You need to make sure that the region/country lookup table is processed before the dimensions that use this table or you run the risk of inconsistencies in your data warehouse.

If you want to adhere to a strict star schema model, which means a maximum level of 1 for the joins between facts and dimensions, there's also another solution. Instead of snowflaking the clustered tables, you can treat them as regular dimensions. This means that the dimension keys will be part of the fact table as well. Drawbacks to this way of modeling are that you always need to traverse the fact table to get to the region/country of a customer, and of course that you need extra keys in your fact table, which can make it unnecessarily wide.

Outriggers

There is, in Kimball's opinion, only one permissible case for using the snowflake technique. He uses the term *outrigger* tables to describe this particular type of snowflaking, so we kindly adopt the same word for this to avoid any confusion. First, let's explain what we mean by an outrigger: Suppose you have a set of attributes that are all dependent on one of the dimension's higher level attributes. An example is the Zipcensus data, which contains a large set of analytical attributes. Zip code is a higher level attribute than customer (you can have multiple customers sharing the same zip code) and all Zipcensus attributes are dependent on zip code. If you store all these additional columns in the customer table, you are denormalizing a lot of data and cluttering the dimension table with a lot of extra attributes—in this case, 112 extra attributes besides the zip code itself. Figure 7-15 shows an example of the Zipcensus outrigger table in combination with the customer dimension.

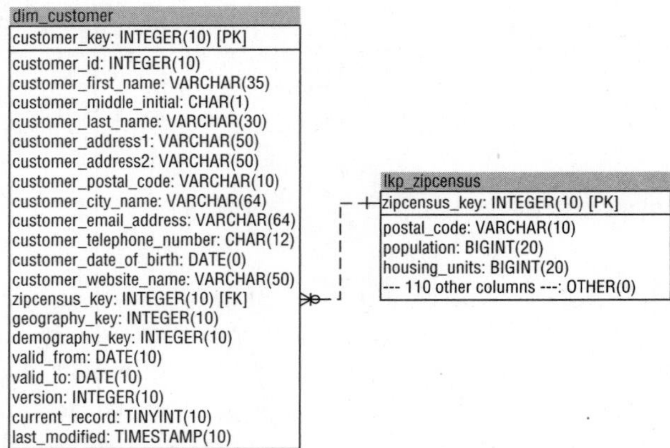

Figure 7-15: Outrigger example

Consolidating Multi-Grain Tables

The last modeling issue is slightly different from the ones described thus far since it does not address modeling a single dimension. The case is this: suppose you have a fact table containing transaction level data and you want to compare these actuals to a budget or forecast. Most organizations do not create budgets on the individual customer and product level, but do this, for instance, at the month and product group level, while omitting the customer and other dimensions. So how do you accommodate for this difference in granularity? One thing is very clear: you cannot compare a monthly value to a daily one without first summarizing the daily values to the month level. So the first thing needed is a summarized fact table which can be done both in a physical (extra table plus load process) or a virtual way (view). The latter is easier to create but might be prohibitive due to performance issues. The accompanying dimension tables need to be available at the same level as well, either by creating a separate table or by creating a view. (Remember that when you join a fact table at the month level with a dimension table at the day level, the results are multiplied by the number of days in the month!)

Figure 7-16 shows an example based on the WCM data warehouse that contains both budget and actual data at a consolidated level of granularity. This is why Ralph Kimball calls this *consolidated fact tables*.

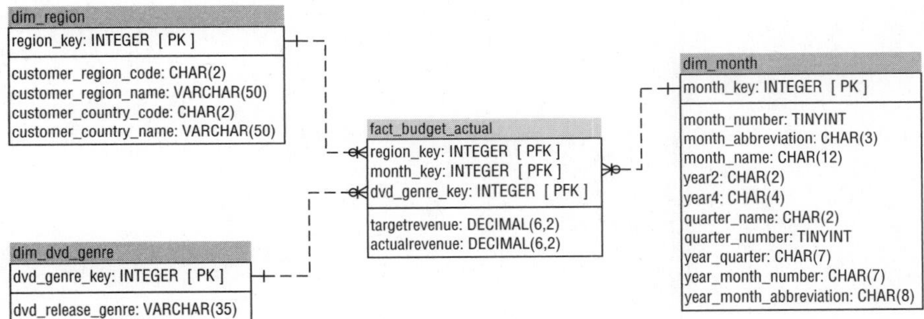

Figure 7-16: Actual and budget consolidated

The tables in Figure 7-16 can be created directly from the existing tables in the data warehouse. Also note that when data is available in a dimension table at a higher level of granularity, it is kept in the derived dimension table as well. This is the case for the quarter and year columns in the month dimension, and the country information in the region dimension.

Summary

This chapter introduced a large collection of modeling techniques for working with dimensional data. We covered the following subjects:

- Basic star schema terminology and modeling
- An introduction to the SQL needed for querying star schemas
- Applying the bus architecture to glue all data marts together to form a dimensional enterprise data warehouse
- A set of design principles to use when building a data warehouse
- The various strategies for capturing history in the dimensional model

- Advanced concepts that can be used for building dimensional data warehouses

As mentioned, we recommend the *Data Warehouse Toolkit* series by Ralph Kimball and company on this subject, and also heartily recommend a visit to the website `www.kimballgroup.com`, where you can find many more tips on dimensional design.

CHAPTER 8

The Data Mart Design Process

Chapters 6 and 7 introduced you to data warehousing, the available technology and the predominant modeling techniques used. These chapters laid a solid theoretical foundation you can build on once you actually start designing and creating your first real solutions. Now it's time to explain the steps needed to get these solutions in place. As we explained in Chapter 6, a data warehouse is a process, not a project. A process consists of more than just technology and especially in the case of a business intelligence solution, involving your end users in the process is essential for its success.

Before you can start building a data warehouse or the first data mart for the data warehouse, you need to know what you want to put into it. In most cases there is an existing demand for a solution that will deliver the insights and reports needed to better manage an organization. The first step in the design process is to identify these often latent demands and convert them into concrete requirements for the business intelligence solution. With the requirements identified, you can begin to design and build a data warehousing solution that can meet those demands that provide your organization with real value.

Requirements Analysis

The starting point of any data warehouse project is to clearly define the requirements from a business point of view. How much data will be coming in to the organization, from what sources, and in what condition? What kind of information, in what formats, does your organization need? Which departments will run reports, how often, and on what data? How much technical knowledge do your business users have—do they need packaged reports or will they run ad hoc queries? And most importantly, which information will help the users to identify whether the business is still on track in achieving the goals set out in the corporate strategy? Based on these requirements, a proper business case should be developed. The business case is ultimately the justification for starting the data warehouse project in the first place. Without a business case, there is obviously no apparent reason for embarking on an often costly and time-consuming project such as developing a data warehousing solution for your organization. So how do you gather requirements and develop a business case (BC) for a data warehouse project?

First, as we explained in the previous chapters, a data warehouse and the accompanying business intelligence solution are a means to end. This ''end'' is what it's all about and should be described in the BC in terms of business benefits from a business perspective. In other words, you don't want to justify an investment in technology for technology's sake, but for the value it can bring to the organization. The best way to start is to involve one or more key stakeholders and jointly create the business case and reporting requirements.

This brings us to one of the most important aspects, or maybe *the* most important aspect, of a data warehouse project team. The team should be *multi-disciplinary* and consist of both technically skilled people and business users. Needless to say, in all cases the IT department must be involved as well because you're going to need an IT infrastructure to run the databases and reports on. The next section helps you identify the business users who will be most helpful in identifying your requirements.

Getting the Right Users Involved

A *user* is anyone in the organization who will work with the Pentaho front-end tools for dashboarding, reporting, and analysis. Typically, there are four kinds of users:

- **One-click user (consumer)**—Can only consume information that's being pushed in a pre-formatted form, usually by e-mail or via a portal.
- **Two-click user (refresher)**—Uses a portal to browse a dashboard or opens predefined reports. Can open and refresh documents on demand, but filling in prompts is the only interactivity involved.
- **Multi-click user (builder)**—Can work interactively with the presented information and can create additional reports and analysis views with the Ad-Hoc Report component and the Mondrian JPivot front end.
- **Power user (analyst)**—Can build reports using the Report Designer and creates new Mondrian models. The most advanced users can also work with the Weka data mining workbench.

Interestingly, these user types map to different parts and levels in the organization. For the success of your project, your first priority is to get the one-click users on board. These are the people that allocate budgets and can pull the right strings to get you going. They're also called *managers*, and because a data warehouse project tends to require a considerable budget and has a high impact and visibility within the organization, your challenge is to convince at least one C-level executive to sponsor the data warehouse project. With this sponsorship, it's easy to attract other key users to get involved. Without it you'll have a hard time convincing the company that all the effort and expense is worthwhile.

The second group of people is usually the largest. They have the ability to pull required information on demand from a portal or special software client application. Only a little training is required for using these tools; usually a short introduction suffices to get the users going. Typically, the combination of the one- and two-click users is called *end users*.

The third group and the ones you'll be working with on a more frequent basis can be found in the multi-click user group. These users can help you in defining the "what" of the data warehouse in terms of the output. This group usually consists of the people who already deliver information to the organization in the form of Excel spreadsheets or similar formats, and usually work in departments such as finance or marketing. It's no coincidence that most data warehouse projects start from either a financial, sales, or marketing perspective, and these people can explain to you what the end result should look like.

The fourth group consists of the advanced users or analysts. They can make your life very easy because they probably know where the data comes from, what the quality of the data is, and how it can be integrated. They can also make your life complicated because they have high demands that are usually not covered during the first iteration of the data warehouse. You need them on the team but have to manage their expectations in advance. Also, be very careful in making promises to this group about what will and will not be possible in the first phase of the data warehouse.

Collecting Requirements

The process of gathering requirements calls for the availability of a so-called *business analyst*. In many cases this job falls to an outside consultant. As much as we would like you to hire external consultants, there's a possible pitfall here that you should be aware of. No matter how experienced these people are, they do not know all the nooks and crannies of the organization and the corporate culture. The most successful business intelligence projects work with insiders, at least in a supporting role. A business analyst must not only understand the business but also needs to be able to translate business requirements into the right solution. He or she should also be able to do this translation the other way around, to explain technical issues in business terminology.

A common way of collecting requirements is to interview potential users, managers, and staff members. These interviews should be conducted by two people, where the business analyst has the lead role and is usually accompanied by someone from the data warehouse team who has insight in the available data and functionality of the tools that will be used. Explaining the interview process in depth is beyond the scope of this book, but the already-mentioned *Data Warehouse Lifecycle Toolkit* by Ralph Kimball is an excellent resource for this topic.

In many cases, there is already some form of reporting in place and these existing reports often make an excellent set of requirements, or at least a good starting point. If this is the case, it's still a good idea to conduct interviews to affirm the user's involvement in the project, and to determine the strengths and weaknesses of the current reports.

Whether interviews or other means of gathering information is used, the end result should be a clear set of requirements, written down in plain English. The requirements should be grouped by main business processes because your data warehouse will be built around main business processes such as sales, customer retention, warehouse management, and finance. The document should at least contain the following entries:

- **Topic**—The main area or process the requirement pertains to.
- **Audience**—Who is the solution for?
- **Owner**—Who will be the business owner of the solution?
- **User demand**—Text explaining what the users need and how they will use the described solution.
- **Questions answered**—The business questions that will be answered by the solution. Chapter 5 contains several examples of these questions.
- **Business benefits**—What will the organization gain from building this specific part of the data warehouse?
- **Delivery mechanism**—How will the information be made accessible to the users? This can be anything from a simple list sent by e-mail to an interactive analysis dashboard.
- **Information sources**—Where is additional information on this requirement available; which persons can be asked?
- **Data sources**—What systems or databases can be used to obtain the data from?
- **Data coverage**—Indication of the completeness of the available data to answer the business questions.

- **Cost estimation**—A rough indication of the time and investments needed to develop this solution.

Each of these documents serves as a small business case on its own and should fit in the overall business case of the data warehouse project. By filling in all the topics in the list, the collection of requirements can also be used to prioritize project increments.

Data Analysis

The source for every data warehouse solution is data. Data can be obtained from many sources and each source can have specific challenges in retrieving and transforming the data to be of use in the data warehouse. The following list serves as a guide to help you select the right data sources and address some of the challenges involved:

- **ERP systems**—Most organizations nowadays run one or even multiple *Enterprise Resource Planning* (ERP) systems like SAP, Oracle Financials, Compière or OpenERP (to name a few). These systems strive to support the complete business process and encompass anything from accounting to purchasing to manufacturing to HR. This also means that these systems are notoriously complex; the widely used ERP system SAP R/3 contains over 70,000 tables! These tables often cannot be accessed directly but expose their content via an API or other metadata layer. As a consequence, it is not enough to be able to connect to the database, which is often prohibited by licenses anyway. You need specialized software to be able to read the metadata of the system and, as you may have guessed already, very few open source solutions are available today that offer this functionality. For Pentaho Data Integration, a commercial plugin from the German company ProRatio is available. The French ETL solution Talend Open Studio has a native open source SAP connector, but if you run Oracle's E-Business Suite, JD Edwards EnterpriseOne, or any of the other major ERP suites, you face some challenges in getting to the right data.
- **Home-grown systems**—If your organization developed its own supporting systems, you might have an advantage over pre-built solutions because knowledge about the underlying data structures is already available. Beware, however, that in these cases documentation might not be up-to-date, the people who initially developed the system might have left the company, or you are simply not allowed to access the systems data directly.
- **Mainframe systems**—Large corporations such as banks or insurance companies still rely heavily on the mainframe for their core information

processing needs. This means that you'll need to get data from the mainframe, which can be a challenging task. The easiest way to obtain this data is to have it delivered to the data warehouse load area in a standard character-separated ASCII file.

- **Spreadsheets**—The only good advice when an organization wants to use spreadsheets as a data source is: don't! Spreadsheets are often used as complete subsystems, especially in finance and accounting departments. Their big advantage is the flexibility and ease of use, and that's exactly why you should refuse to accept spreadsheets as a source. They also use display formats that shows the data in a formatted way but when reading the data directly contains something completely useless. So even if PDI is capable of reading spreadsheets, don't make them part of the process. If no alternative source is available (typical for budgets and forecasts), have the spreadsheet owner export the data in a predefined and agreed-upon format as an ASCII text file.
- **Desktop databases**—See the preceding entry for Spreadsheets. There is a very simple rule for which data sources can be accepted for the data warehouse and which can't: If the system is not supported by the IT department or there's only one user maintaining the system, don't waste much energy on it.
- **Structured external data**—Structured means that the data is delivered in a well-defined format by a third party who makes this data available, be it online or in any other form. Good examples of these data sources are the Zipcensus data sets we use for WCM or the retail market data that can be obtained from Nielsen.
- **Online data**—More and more information can be obtained directly from the web and consumed in the form of a web service or RSS feed. Pentaho Data Integration contains all the features to work with online data.
- **Weblogs**—This is a special case of structured data because you will need quite a bit of custom regular expressions to rip the log lines apart and make useful information out of it.
- **XML**—The Extensible Markup Language (XML) has become the lingua franca of the computer world. All Pentaho products store their (meta) information in an XML format, and many other products are able to export data in an XML format as well. The delivery of the information is not limited to files; most message- or queue-based systems deliver their messages in XML format as well. The big advantage of XML is that it's basically a text file, just like a regular comma- or tab-delimited ASCII file. This means that XML files can be opened with any text editor to view the contents. The challenge with XML files, however, is that it is so flexible that it can be hard to transform the nested structure to a usable

relational format used in the data warehouse. Luckily, unlike many other data integration tools, PDI has a very powerful XML input step and can also read RSS feeds directly (which is an XML format).

We've been involved in data warehouse projects since the early 90s and found that each assignment and case is different. Any reasonable-sized organization has a mix of all the described data sources. Sometimes the ERP part of the equation is filled in by just a single financial or HR system, and several home-grown or custom-made systems surround this. In none of the projects so far could all the required information be found in a single integrated system. All structured data is commonly stored in a relational database, which makes it easily accessible, at least from a technical point of view. The most common additional data not stored in databases consists of budgets, estimates, forecasts, and account plans and is usually maintained in spreadsheets. The challenge is to decipher the content, structure, quality, and meaning of all this data, and that's what you need documentation (if available—otherwise it needs to be created) and data profiling for.

Data Profiling

Data profiling is the process of collecting statistics and other information about the data available in different source systems. The obtained information is invaluable for the further design of your data warehouse and ETL processes. Data profiling is also an important part of any data quality initiative; before quality can be improved, a baseline has to be established indicating what the current state of the data is. Profiling can be performed at three different levels:

- **Column profile**—Collects statistics about the data in a single column
- **Dependency profile**—Checks for dependencies within a table between different columns
- **Join profile**—Checks for dependencies between different tables

The starting point for profiling is always the column-level profile, which generates useful information about the data in a column, including but not limited to:

- **Number of distinct values**—How many unique entries does the column contain?
- **Number of NULL and empty values**—How many records have no value or an empty value?
- **Highest and lowest values**—Not only for numeric but also for textual data.

- **Numeric sum, median, average, and standard deviation**—Various calculations on the numeric values and value distribution.
- **String patterns and length**—Are the values correctly stored? (For example, German postal codes should contain five digits.)
- **Number of words, number of upper and lowercase characters**
- **Frequency counts**—What are the top and bottom *N* items in a column?

Most data profiling tools can deliver this information and sometimes even more. It gets trickier when you look at the profiling within a single table to identify correlations and interdependencies. Examples of this are combinations of postal code-to-city, city-to-region, and region-to-country. Obviously, a city name is dependent on a postal code, the region name on the city, and the country on the region. The existence of these dependencies violate the third normal form, so when finding these relationships in a third normal form source system, you should take extra care, especially regarding the address information. Sometimes the relations are not very clear or are even confusing, which makes it hard to distinguish correct from incorrect entries. This is exactly the reason that so many expensive address matching and cleansing solutions exist. Take, for instance, the city-region combination: There are more than ten states in the United States with a city named Hillsboro. Without additional knowledge of the country or zip codes, it's hard to tell whether a record contains erroneous information or not. For these cases, you'll need external information to validate the data against.

Inter-table relationships are easier to profile; it is simply a matter of evaluating whether a relationship is correctly enforced. In an order entry system, it shouldn't be possible to find a customer number in the order table that does not exist in the customer table. The same relationship test can be used to find out how many customers are in the customer table but not (yet) in the order table. The same applies to products and order details, inventory and suppliers, and so on.

Using eobjects.org DataCleaner

Currently, the Pentaho BI Suite does not contain data profiling capabilities, so we will use a tool named DataCleaner developed by the open source community eobjects.org. The software can be obtained from `http://datacleaner.eobjects.org` and is very easy to install. On Windows, you simply unzip the package and start `datacleaner.exe`. On a Linux machine, after unpacking the `tar.gz` file you first need to make the `datacleaner.sh` shell script executable to start the program. If you are using the GNOME desktop environment, this is very easy: Just right-click the file and open the properties. Then go to the Permissions tab and mark the checkbox before Allow executing file as program. Now you can double-click on the `datacleaner.sh` file and the program will start. If you want a more convenient way to start the program next time, you can create a shortcut (in Windows) or a launcher (in GNOME).

DataCleaner provides three main tasks:

- **Profile**—All the column profiling tasks described earlier. The idea here is to gain insight into the state of your data. You can thus use the profiling task whenever you want to explore and take the temperature of your database.
- **Validate**—To create and test validation rules against the data. These validation rules can then later be translated (by hand) into Pentaho Data Integration validation steps. The validator is useful for enforcing rules onto your data and to monitor the data that does not conform to these rules.
- **Compare**—To compare data from different tables and schemas, and check for consistency between them.

From these descriptions, it's immediately clear that DataCleaner does not provide intra-table profiling capabilities as a direct option, but there are other ways to accomplish this with the tool, as we'll show later.

The first thing you need, of course, is a connection to the database you want to profile. For each type of database, DataCleaner needs the corresponding driver, which enables the communication between the tool and the database. Before we explain how to add drivers and connections, let's take a first look at the available functions. DataCleaner starts with the New task panel open, which allows you to choose one of the three main options: Profile, Validate, and Compare. Click on Profile to start a new profiling task. You'll see an almost empty two-pane screen with some options and the No data selected indication in the left pane (see Figure 8-1).

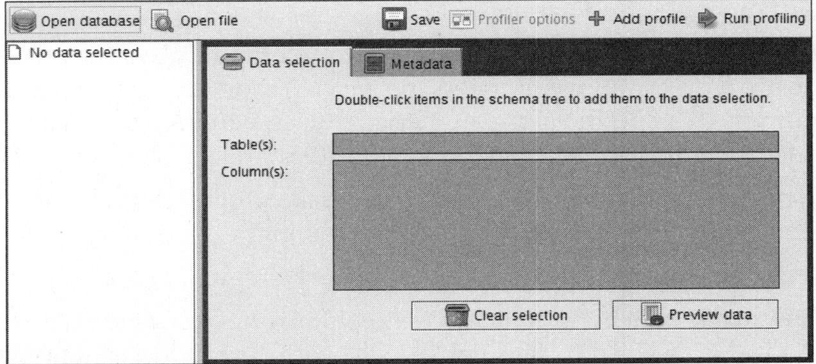

Figure 8-1: Profiling task

Now select Open database, select the DataCleaner sampledata entry from the Named connection drop-down list, and click Connect to Database. All other fields have been set already. When you open the PUBLIC tree node on the left by clicking on the + sign, the list with tables appears. Each table can be opened individually, which displays the available columns. To add a column to the data selection, just double-click it. You'll notice that the table name is added to the Table(s) field, and the column to the Column(s) field. To remove a column from the selection, double-click it again or use Clear Selection to completely remove the selected tables and columns. The Preview option shows a sample of the selected data; the number of rows to be retrieved can be adjusted after clicking the button. The default value often suffices to get a first impression of the content of the data. Each table gets its selected columns displayed in a separate window.

Next to the Data selection tab is the Metadata tab. When you click this, the technical metadata of the selected columns is displayed. The field type, field length, and especially the Nullable indication give you a first impression of the kind of data to be expected.

Adding Profile Tasks

After selecting some columns to profile, you can add different profiles. DataCleaner contains the following standard profile options:

- **Standard measures**—Row count, number of NULL values, empty values, highest and lowest value.
- **String analysis**—Percentage of upper and lowercase characters, percentage of non-letter characters, minimum and maximum number of words, and the total number of words and characters in the column.
- **Time analysis**—Lowest and highest date value, plus number of records per year.
- **Number analysis**—Highest, lowest, sum, mean, geometric mean, standard deviation, and variance.
- **Pattern finder**—Finds and counts all patterns in a character column. Mostly used for phone numbers, postal codes, or other fields that should conform to a specific alpha-numeric pattern. Pattern examples are 9999 aa (4 digits, space, 2 characters), aaa-999 (3 characters, hyphen, 3 digits).
- **Dictionary matcher**—Matches the selected columns against the content of an external file or another database column (a "dictionary").
- **Regex matcher**—Matches columns against a regular expression.
- **Date mask matcher**—Matches text columns against date patterns; this cannot be used with date fields, only with text fields containing date and/or time information.

- **Value distribution**—Calculates the top and bottom N values in a column based on their frequency, or ranks the number of occurrences and calculates the frequency percentage for each value. The value for *N* can be any number between 0 and 50; the default is 5.

The collection of profiles in a task is very flexible; it's possible to add profiles of the same type to a single task. Each task can be saved as well, but this will only save the connection and task profiles, not the profiler results. This last option is a separate function and saves the results in an XML file, which is unfortunately a one-way street; DataCleaner cannot read these files back. Persisting profile results is part of the roadmap for future releases.

Adding Database Connections

One of the first things to do when setting up the data profiling environment is to add the correct database drivers and store the connections to your own databases for easy selection. The first task is pretty straightforward; in the main DataCleaner screen, select File, Register database driver. There are two ways to add a new driver. The first is to automatically download and install them. This option is available for MySQL, PostgreSQL, SQL Server/Sybase, Derby, and SQLite. The second way of doing this is to manually register a `.jar` file with the drivers. To help you find the drivers, DataCleaner contains the option to visit the driver website for the most common database drivers, such as those for Oracle or IBM DB2. After downloading a driver, you'll need to reference it by selecting the file and the correct driver class. For MySQL, we will use the Automatic download and install option.

TIP **If you already installed the MySQL JDBC driver, there's no need to download it again; just register your existing `.jar` file.**

Adding the connection so you can select it from the drop-down list in the Open Database dialog box is a bit more complicated. For that we need to alter the DataCleaner configuration file, which can be found in the DataCleaner folder and is called `datacleaner-config.xml`. To edit XML files, it's best to use a plain-text editor that understands the XML syntax. For the Windows platform, the open source Notepad++ can be used; on a Linux machine, just right-click the file and open with Text editor. Look for the part in the file that says:

```
<!-- Named connections. Add your own connections here. -->.
```

Below this line there's an empty entry for the drop-down list; just leave that where it is. The second entry is the connection to the sample data. Copy the sample data part that starts with `<bean` and ends with `</bean>`, including the start and end `bean` tags. Paste it right below the closing tag of the sample data entry and adjust the information to reflect your own settings. Below is the entry as it should look for the connection to the WCM database on your local machine:

```
<bean class="dk.eobjects.datacleaner.gui.model.NamedConnection">
   <property name="name" value="WCM MySQL database" />
   <property name="connectionString" value="jdbc:mysql://localhost:
       3306" />
   <property name="username" value="yourusername" />
   <property name="password" value="yourpassword" />
   <property name="tableTypes">
     <list>
         <value>TABLE</value>
     </list>
   </property>
</bean>
```

To have DataCleaner also connect to the correct catalog, in our case the WCM catalog, an extra line should be added below the password property line, like this:

```
<property name="catalog" value = "wcm" />
```

We don't recommend storing passwords in plain-text files; in fact, we strongly oppose doing so, and in this case you can leave the password field empty as well. In that case, you'll need to provide the password each time you create a new profiling task.

To use DataCleaner with sources other than our WCM database, you can find examples of the XML bean-element for other popular databases in the online DataCleaner documentation.

Doing an Initial Profile

The DataCleaner profiler has been optimized to allow you to do a rather quick and at the same time insightful profile with little effort. To get started with profiling, you can add the Standard Measures, String Analysis, Number Analysis, and Time Analysis profiles by repeatedly clicking the Add Profile button in the top-right corner of the Profile task window. You can apply these profiles to all the columns of your database to get the initial insight.

Working with Regular Expressions

Regular expressions, or regexes, are a way of masking and describing data, mainly for validation purposes but also to find certain patterns in a text. Several books have been written about working with regular expressions, so we refer to existing information here. Additionally, Chapter 11 contains a few examples of how you can use regular expressions to parse data from websites. DataCleaner contains both a regex matcher as one of the profiles as well as a regex validation as part of the validator. Before you can use regular expressions, you'll need to add them to the Regex catalog in the main DataCleaner screen. Initially, this catalog is empty, but it's easy to add regexes. When you click New regex, three options appear. The first one is to create a new regex manually and the last one is to get a regex from the `.properties` file. The second option is the most interesting: When you select Import from the RegexSwap, an online library is opened with a large collection of existing regexes to pick from. It is also possible to contribute your own regexes to the RegexSwap at `http://datacleaner.eobjects.org/regexswap` for others to (re)use. After importing a regex from the RegexSwap, you can open it to change its name and the expression itself, and there's an option to test the expression by inputting strings you want to validate. If the RegexSwap doesn't fulfill your needs, a vast number of regular expressions are available on other Internet websites as well. The site `http://regexlib.com`, for example, contains regexes for U.S. phone numbers and zip codes. Another great site, especially if you want to learn the regular expression syntax, is `www.regular-expressions.info`. Use the following steps to try one for the telephone numbers in our WCM customer base.

1. An expression that will match most numbers with or without extension looks like this:

   ```
   ((\(\d{3}\) ?)|(\d{3}[- \.]))?\d{3}[- \.]\d{4}(\s(x\d+)?){0,1}$
   ```

   Click New regex in the main DataCleaner screen and create a new expression. Give the expression a name and type in the expression above, or copy it from the WCM samples on the companion site.

2. Save the expression (you can, of course, test it first with a real phone number) and start a New task. Open the WCM database and double-click on the `telephone_number` field in the customer table.

3. Add a Regex matcher profile, activate the Regex matcher tab, and select only the name of the expression you just created. DataCleaner, by default, selects all available regexes so if this is the only one available it's already selected. Otherwise, click Select none first and then activate the U.S. Phone Number. If the telephone number is the only column in this task, there's no difference between applying the match to all selected data, but it's better to explicitly select the `telephone_number` column as a subset of data.

Your screen should now look like the example in Figure 8-2.

If you don't select the telephone number as a data subset and add additional columns later, they will be automatically scanned with the same regular expression, which doesn't make a lot of sense in most cases.

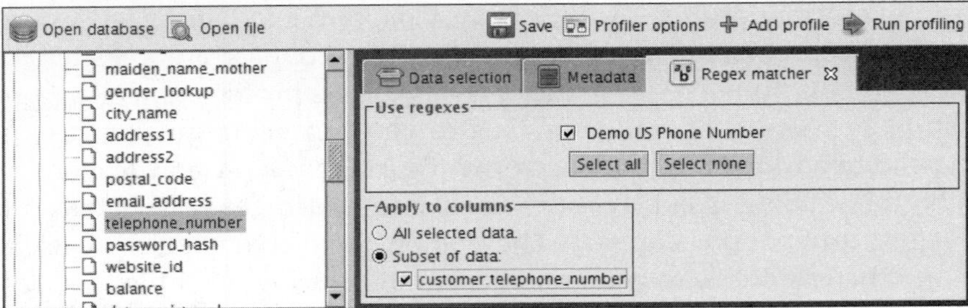

Figure 8-2: Regex matcher setting

Profiling and Exploring Results

You're now ready to profile the telephone numbers, so click Run profiling to start the process. DataCleaner will display a status screen where you can also monitor the progress of the profile process. When the profiler is finished, a results tab is added to the screen, one for each table that contained profiled columns. Open the customer tab, and the result screen should look something like Figure 8-3.

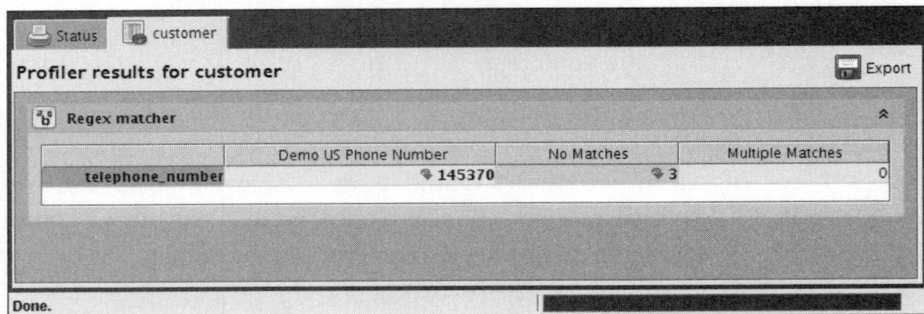

Figure 8-3: Profiler results

We deliberately altered a few phone numbers here to get some exceptions and to be able to show another nice DataCleaner feature: drilling down to the details. Clicking on the green arrow next to the three found exceptions opens the screen shown in Figure 8-4.

customer_id	first_name	middle_initial	last_name	date_of_birth	maiden_name_mother	gender_lookup	city_name	address1	address2	postal_code	email_address	telephone_number
45	Columbus	C	Gardner	1984-03-...	Henry	1	Saint Pete...	3401 Bad...	<null>	33716	Columbus.C...	727-208-819
121	Teodoro	B	King	1974-08-...	Schuman	1	Lanai City	2745 Arr...	<null>	96763	Teodoro.B.K...	80?-565-2773
138	Melissa	J	Jenkins	1968-03-...	Laguerre	2	Carbondale	3243 Ros...	<null>	62901	Melissa.J.Jen...	618-3031292

Figure 8-4: Exceptions

This isn't the end, however. When you right-click, you'll get two export options: one for selected cells and one for the entire table. The latter option will also add the column headers to the clipboard; the first one just copies the selected data. Selected cells don't have to be adjacent. By using the Ctrl key, you can, for instance, select the customer ID and telephone number and just copy those columns to the clipboard. After that, you can easily paste the data into a spreadsheet or other file for further exploration.

Validating and Comparing Data

Validation works in a similar fashion as the profiling task but adds some capabilities. You can check for null values or do a value range check to find out whether entries in a column fall between a lower and upper value bound. The most advanced feature is the JavaScript evaluation, which lets you use any JavaScript expression for evaluating data. The difference is the output: The validation task will only display the entries that do not pass the tests with a count of the records. The DataCleaner roadmap includes future plans to integrate the profile and validation tasks and offer a single integrated interface for both tasks.

Data comparison enables you to compare data from different databases or schemas, or compare data against a file. Therefore, this task can be used to check whether all customers in the `orders` table also exist in the `customer` table and similar comparison tasks.

Using a Dictionary for Column Dependency Checks

DataCleaner does not provide an out-of-the-box solution to verify combinations of columns or whether one dependent column contains an invalid entry based on the information in another column. There is, however, a way to do these analyses by using a dictionary combined with database views. A DataCleaner dictionary is a text file containing values that can be used to validate data in a database table. For example, you can download the ISO country table, store the values in a text file, and use this text file as a catalog to verify the entries in a country column. If you take this one step further, it's also possible to store multiple concatenated fields per row and create a view in the database, which concatenates the columns to be validated in the same way. Now the view can be profiled using the dictionary with the concatenated entries; each row that does not correspond to the correct values in the text file will be recognized by DataCleaner. As an alternative to using text files, it's also possible to use a "real" database dictionary. This database dictionary needs to be added to the DataCleaner configuration file as explained in the "Adding Database Connections" section.

Alternative Solutions

Very few open source alternatives exist for standalone or embedded data profiling. The data modeling tool from SQLPower, which we introduce shortly, has some basic profiling capabilities, and Talend offers a Data Profiler as well. If any of these tools work for you, just use them. Another frequently used alternative for data profiling is creating custom SQL scripts for data profiling purposes. We would recommend this only if you have very specialized requirements that are not provided out-of-the box by DataCleaner. Although it's outside the scope of this book, it is possible to extend DataCleaner's functionality with your own customer profiling tasks, which gives you a faster, more reliable, and more flexible solution than completely starting from scratch.

Developing the Model

After the requirements are clear, the correct data sources have been identified, and the data profiling process has provided you with enough detailed information about the content and quality of the source data, you can start by developing the global data mart data model. Before you can create the actual detailed data model in a data modeling tool, you first need to identify which subjects and measures you will create in your initial data mart. That's where the requirements created earlier come into play. A requirement that covers "customer product sales analysis" clearly needs to have the subjects `customer`, `product`, and `time` added with the measures `sales revenue` and `number of items`. Without describing these entities in detail, it's already feasible to draw the high-level model as displayed in Figure 8-5.

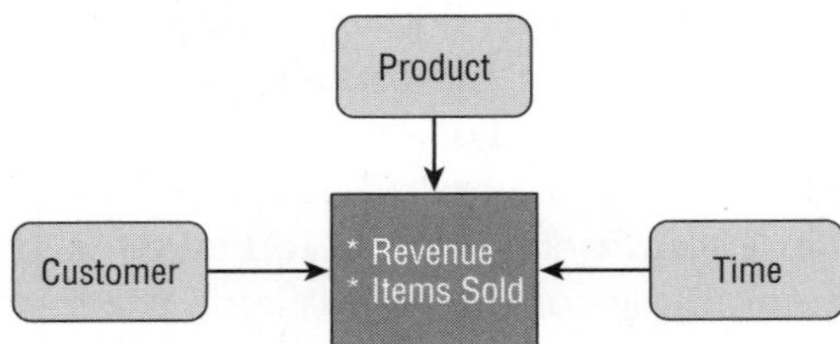

Figure 8-5: High-level star model

This is a perfect starting point for further specifying the exact content of your dimension and fact tables because this model is easy to understand, even for a non-technical business user. The next step in refining the model is determining which attributes need to be part of each dimension. It helps to differentiate between analytical and detail attributes. An analytical attribute is a field that will be used to report or group the data on, such as customer group, city, genre, and month. Detail attributes are mostly descriptive elements such as customer names, telephone numbers, and address information. You might even consider leaving the detail attributes out of the data warehouse altogether. This isn't always a good idea, however. Suppose you want to generate mailing lists directly from the data warehouse based on some analysis or selection process; you'll need the detailed address information, telephone numbers, and e-mail addresses.

TIP **In small dimension tables the distinction between detail and analytical attributes is negligible, but when the dimension table gets very large, this distinction helps in determining which attributes can be moved into a mini-dimension.**

For each attribute, you need to define what the data type and length will be. It's also a good idea to add a description for each field; this might seem cumbersome at the start but this added metadata is very helpful for both end users and people who will be maintaining the system. Table 8-1 contains a partial example of a customer dimension. A very important column is the one with the title SCD (for Slowly Changing Dimension type). This determines how updates to these columns will be handled by the ETL process.

Table 8-1: Customer dimension

FIELD	ANALYTICAL	TYPE	LENGTH	SCD	DESCRIPTION
Customer_key	N	INT	4		Surrogate dimension key
Customer_id	N	INT	4		Original source system key
Customer_name	N	VARCHAR	63	2	Full name (first + middle + last)
Customer_city	Y	VARCHAR	64	2	Name of city
Customer_phone _number	N	CHAR	12	2	Telephone number
Customer_register _date_key	Y	INT	4	1	First registration date of customer

Later in this chapter, we will extend this table with source and transformation information as well, but for initially discussing and documenting the data mart tables, the arrangement shown here works well.

A final remark on field lengths: It may turn out that your source system schema tells you that the city name field is 64 characters wide. When you profile the data, you find something else, namely that the largest city name is only 30 characters (which is true for the WCM sample database: STE MARTHE DU CAP LA MADELEINE). Please do not fall into the trap of cutting the city name field in the dimension table to 30 characters in such a case. The same applies to other descriptive fields such as job description, DVD title, and so on. Even though the current entries are all smaller than the specified length doesn't mean that at some point someone won't enter a value that exceeds that number. This might lead to either an incomplete entry or a failure in the ETL process, which needs to be handled. Always take the length of the source table fields as a minimum for the target table field lengths.

Special attention needs to be given to the fact table and especially the granularity (level of detail) of the facts. The business users should agree on the meaning of a single record. When we look at the order facts in our example, the order line is the lowest level of detail and thus the granularity of the model.

Data Modeling with Power*Architect

So far we've analyzed data and worked with office applications to document our design. Now it's time to translate this information into a real data model in a database. Because Pentaho is a BI suite and not a data modeling tool, we will use a third-party solution here as well. There are a few open source data modeling tools available but most of them have limited capabilities. Sometimes the limitation is in functionality—for example, you cannot reverse engineer existing databases—and sometimes the limitation is the databases the tool can work with. For these reasons we will not use the MySQL Workbench. It can be used only in conjunction with MySQL and the open source version is a stripped down edition of the commercial one.

TIP **We assume a basic understanding of data modeling concepts and theory. If this is not the case, the book *Mastering Data Warehouse Design* by Claudia Imhoff et al. (Wiley, 2003) has an excellent introduction on the subject and also provides a deeper dive into some of the modeling concepts we introduced in this and the previous chapter.**

When looking for a data modeling tool, make sure that at least the following functionality is available:

- **Multi-database support**—Perhaps you want to reverse engineer an existing Oracle database and generate a MySQL database from an adapted model. Later you may decide to switch to PostgreSQL, but if the tool doesn't support this, you have a problem.
- **Forward engineering**—Generate new database objects from a model.
- **Reverse engineering**—Generate a model from an existing database.

- **Model comparison**—Compare the model with the database schema (or vice versa) and generate modification scripts.

The more advanced tools on the market also offer features such as version management and version comparison, division between business, logical and physical database models, collapsing and expanding graphical elements, and documentation features. Prices for commercial tools with one or more of these advanced features range from $200 to $5,000, but if you're designing a mission-critical database system for a large company, those costs might not be a problem. We will be using the open source Power*Architect (P*A) tool from SQLPower (`www.sqlpower.ca`) because it is one of the few or maybe even the only open source tool available that supports the four functions in the preceding list. Power*Architect is available for Linux, Windows, and Mac and can be downloaded from the SQLPower site. The Windows version is an executable installer just like any other Windows program; setting the program up in Linux takes a little more effort (but not much). Download the `tar.gz` file and extract it to a directory of choice. The program is a Java archive (`Architect.jar`), which can be started with the command `java -jar architect.jar` from the command line from within the Architect folder. You can also easily create a launcher or a new menu item for the program.

We can add very little to the excellent Power*Architect user guide provided by SQLPower. As you will find out very quickly, the tool also includes a data profiling option. For a basic insight into data, this functionality suffices but there are no regex or domain validators, as in DataCleaner. One other point of caution here: The profiler can work on a complete table only, not on individual columns. Profiling very large tables might therefore take a long time to complete.

MORE PROS AND CONS OF POWER*ARCHITECT

Some features you might find in other tools but not in P*A is a selection of view options that let you view only the table name, or only the primary key fields, or all fields. And although there is a zoom in and out facility, this works for the entire model, not for a selected area. But these are all minor points and didn't stop us from using and recommending this tool. In fact, there are a couple of unique features not available in any other tool, such as the ETL and OLAP options. One very nifty gadget (which might actually prove to be very useful) is the possibility to copy tables from one database to another. Imagine you have an Oracle database and want some tables copied to a MySQL instance. Simply create a connection to both databases and use the Copy table data option from the Tools menu to select a table from a source database, click a destination schema, and click OK.

Building the WCM Data Marts

After you've consulted the Power*Architect user guide and made yourself familiar with the tool, it's time to start building the WCM data marts. You will need two connections to do this, one to the source database WCM, and one to a new database WCM_DWH, which will serve as the data warehouse.

In many cases your data warehouse will pull data from more than one source system. Sometimes you will not even have direct access to these databases, or at least not when you're designing the data marts. This makes it hard to build your model based on one or more source systems. If you can make and use connections directly to the source databases, there are a few advantages when working with P*A. The tool "remembers" the mappings you make when you drag a column from a source connection to your project panel. You can also see this in the column property editor, where the first two lines right above the column name display the source databases name and the name of the source table column. A column that is added by hand will display the text "None Specified" for both database and column name.

TIP **To quickly open the properties for a table or column, right-click the table or column name and press Enter.**

You probably saw the Create Kettle Job menu option in the ETL menu and wondered whether this is a quick way to build transformation jobs. The answer to this is: It depends. If all your columns are mapped from a source database, you might consider generating Kettle jobs as a quick start for your transformations. In all other cases, this option is useless because a job can only be created if there is an actual mapping.

TIP **With Power*Architect it is easy to migrate part of or an entire database from one platform to another using the Create Kettle Job option. The Kettle job can be created as a collection of files (one job file plus a transformation file for each table) or directly in the Kettle repository. An even faster solution is to use the Copy Tables Wizard in Pentaho Data Integration (Spoon) directly.**

The diagram in Figure 8-6 displays the Orders data mart schema, which is most likely the first that will be created. Using this data mart, a multitude of business questions can be answered:

- Which movie genres or websites generate the most revenue?
- How effective are the promotions we launch?
- Who are our most profitable customers?
- How is our revenue evolving over time?
- What is the relationship between our websites and demographic groups?
- At which time of day do customers place the most orders?

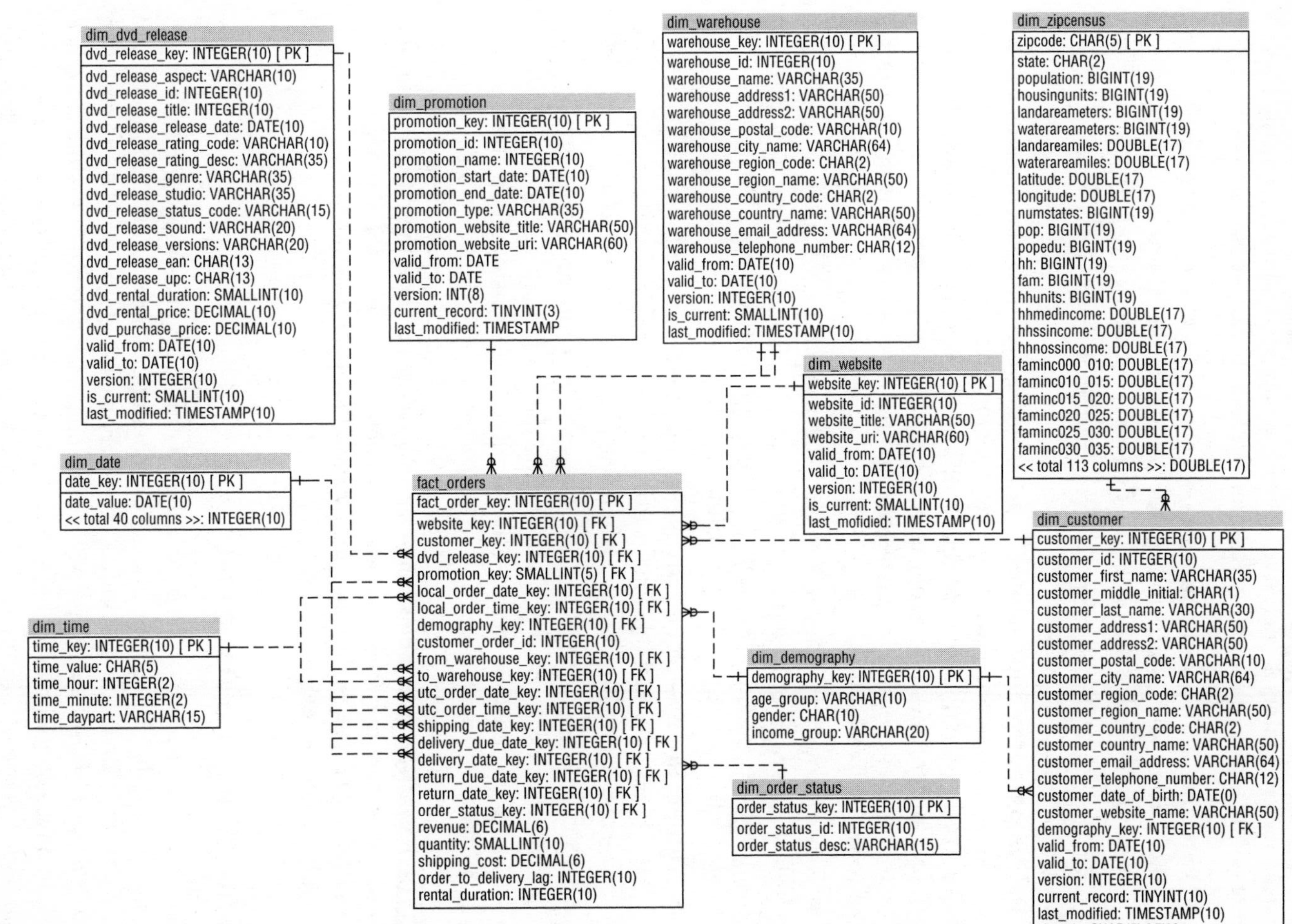

Figure 8-6: Orders data mart

The diagram contains the complete Orders data mart but, for clarity, we abbreviated the `date` dimension, which is covered in the next paragraph. The `dim_zipcensus` table is included as well in an abbreviated form. First, let's have a look at the diagram and explain some of the choices we made.

- **Fact table**—To avoid duplicates, we explicitly added a database-generated fact_order_key as a primary key for the table. There are also a couple of calculated entries: order_to_delivery_lag and rental_duration. These calculations are not defined in the database but are part of the ETL process.
- **Demography dimension**—This is a regular dimension table but we need the customer data during the loading process to determine the correct value. Please note that there are two possible join paths between fact_orders and dim_geography: one directly and one via dim_customer. In the final user model we need to create an extra alias for dim_geography to work around this.
- **Region/country**—Based on our discussion in Chapter 7 regarding starflakes we could have snowflaked `region` and `country` as they occur in both `dim_warehouse` and `dim_customer` but we decided to make the star schema as "pure" as possible.
- **Audit columns**—For clarity we left out the audit columns `batch_insert`, `batch_update` (which batch inserted or updated the record?), and `dt_insert` and `dt_update` (when was the record inserted and updated?).
- **SCD2 columns**—The dimension tables for time, order status, date, and demography do not contain the fields for managing slowly changing type 2 dimensions because these tables are considered to be static or fully type 1 (overwrite).

TIP Power*Architect tables can be given their own color in the title bar. You can use this feature to distinguish between dimension and fact tables and make special tables such as the demography mini-dimension and the Zipcensus outrigger table easily recognizable.

Generating the Database

With P*A, the creation of the physical data model is very simple. First you need to make sure that the target catalog or schema exists and add a connection to this catalog. With the menu option Tools ➤ Forward Engineer, P*A can generate the SQL for the creation of the tables and indexes in several SQL dialects. Click OK, to have the tool generate the script and display it in a preview pane. Now you have two options: execute the script directly using the selected connection information, or copy the content of the pane to the clipboard for use in an external tool. If you want to modify the script before execution, you'll have to use the copy option because it is not possible to alter the script in the preview pane.

Generating Static Dimensions

Our initial data mart design contains two static tables that do not get their data from the source systems but will be generated using scripts. The first one is the time dimension, which contains a row for each minute in a day (1440 records).

The date dimension is special and can be set up to accommodate for answering many time-related questions as you saw in Chapter 7. Although there are no strict rules for which columns should be present in a date dimension, Table 8-2 shows the structure of a date dimension that will give you a great deal of flexibility when working with time-related questions. The date dimension displayed has a granularity of one day, so each day on the calendar translates to a single record. Also note that the table is not really static as the relative date columns need to be updated every night. So it is true that generating the table is a one-time process, another process is needed to keep the table up to date.

You may have noticed that the table title contains the ''US-EN'' addition. Names and abbreviations for days, months and quarters may vary for each language, and you need a way to accommodate this in your solution. There are two alternatives to implement this. The first is to add additional fields for each language in the same date table, and the second is to create separate tables which contain only the descriptive columns for each language. We prefer the latter since that offers the most flexibility. The relative date columns only need to be stored and maintained once since they remain the same regardless of the language used.

It's not only a matter of different names in different languages; some parts of the date can differ as well. The first day of the week is different in European countries (Monday) than in the United States (Sunday), and most European countries adhere to the ISO 8601 standard for numbering weeks and year. This means that a week number in the U.S. might differ from the same week in the U.K. For this reason, we included the `_iso` columns for week, year, and year-week. It is important when you are building a data warehouse for a multinational organization to take these differences into account and try to agree upon a standard way of using these numbers. Other columns that you might need in your own situation are fiscal period indicators. Not all organizations use the calendar year as their fiscal year, and when this is the case you should include fiscal year, fiscal month, and fiscal quarter in your date dimension as well. The list with possible entries is almost limitless; we've seen indicators for working day and number of working days in month and week, indicators for holidays with references to tables that contain descriptions of international and religious holidays, and so on. We've limited our design to the standard calendar fields and the corresponding relative time columns but feel free to experiment with other concepts in your own data mart.

Table 8-2: Date dimension (US-EN)

FIELD	TYPE	LENGTH	DESCRIPTION	EXAMPLE
date_key	INT	4	Surrogate dimension key	20091123
date_value	DATE	4	Date value for the day	23-11-2009
date_julian	INT	4	Rounded Julian date	2455159
date_short	CHAR	12	Short text value for date	11/23/09
date_medium	CHAR	16	Medium text value for date	Nov 23, 2009
date_long	CHAR	24	Long text value for date	November 23, 2009
date_full	CHAR	32	Full-text value for date	Monday, November 23, 2009
day_in_week	TINYINT	1	Number of day in week	2
day_in_month	TINYINT	1	Number of day in month	23
day_in_year	SMALLINT	2	Number of day in year	327
is_first_day_in_month	TINYINT	1	1 for first day, 0 for other	0
is_first_day_in_week	TINYINT	1	1 for first day, 0 for other	0
is_last_day_in_month	TINYINT	1	1 for last day, 0 for other	0
is_last_day_in_week	TINYINT	1	1 for last day, 0 for other	0
day_name	CHAR	12	Full name of day	Monday
day_abbreviation	CHAR	3	Short name of day	Mon
week_in_year	TINYINT	1	Week number	47
week_in_month	TINYINT	1	Week number in month	3
week_in_year_iso	TINYINT	1	Week number	47
is_weekend	TINYINT	1	1 for Sat-Sun	0
is_weekday	TINYINT	1	1 for Mon-Fri	1

FIELD	TYPE	LENGTH	DESCRIPTION	EXAMPLE
month_number	TINYINT	2	Number of month in year	11
month_name	CHAR	12	Full name of month	November
month _abbreviation	CHAR	3	Short name of month	Nov
year2	CHAR	2	Short year indicator	09
year4	CHAR	4	Long year indicator	2009
year2_iso	CHAR	2	Short ISO year indicator	09
year4_iso	CHAR	4	Long ISO year indicator	2009
quarter_number	TINYINT	1	Number of quarter	4
quarter_name	CHAR	2	Text value of quarter	Q4
year_quarter	CHAR	7	Year-quarter value	2009-Q4
year_month	CHAR	7	Year-month value	2009-11
year_week	CHAR	7	Year-week value	2009-47
year_week_iso	CHAR	7	ISO year-week value	2009-47
current_week_cy	TINYINT	1	*	1
current_month_cy	TINYINT	1	*	1
last_week_cy	TINYINT	1	*	0
last_month_cy	TINYINT	1	*	0
current_week_ly	TINYINT	1	*	1
current_month_ly	TINYINT	1	*	1
last_week_ly	TINYINT	1	*	0
last_month_ly	TINYINT	1	*	0
ytd_cy_day	TINYINT	1	*	0
ytd_cy_week	TINYINT	1	*	0
ytd_cy_month	TINYINT	1	*	0
ytd_ly_day	TINYINT	1	*	0
ytd_ly_week	TINYINT	1	*	0
ytd_ly_month	TINYINT	1	*	0

Continued

Table 8-2 (*continued*)

FIELD	TYPE	LENGTH	DESCRIPTION	EXAMPLE
current_year	TINYINT	1	*	1
last_year	TINYINT	1	*	0
week_sequence	INT	4	0 for current week, −1 for previous, 1 for next, and so on	0
month_sequence	INT	4	0 for current month, −1 for previous, 1 for next, and so on	0

*See the section "Special Date Fields and Calculations" later in this chapter.

A final remark on generating the date and time tables: It might be tempting to include the definition of these tables directly in a Pentaho Data Integration SQL transformation but then you'll have to create database-specific code to generate the table. By using a database-independent data modeling tool for this, you keep the design generic, which makes it easier to switch to another database when required.

Special Date Fields and Calculations

Chapter 7 already introduced the `current_week` and `last_week` columns. In Table 8-2 and our sample data warehouse we extended this construction with additional fields that are great for comparing different time periods. These fields are all of type `TINYINT` and can only have values 0 or 1, which means that we can use them in calculations. The abbreviations `cy` and `ly` are for current year and last year, `ytd` is for year to date, and the last part—`day`, `week`, or `month`—indicates the completed periods to compare.

In this case, it's Monday of week number 47, which means that all dates with a week number of 46 or less will get the value 1 for `ytd_cy_week`. The column `ytd_ly_week` will contain a value 1 for all days of the previous year (in this example, 2008) that have a week number of 46 or less. To report on revenue of this year up to the last week compared to the same period last year can be easily accomplished with the following query:

```
SELECT  p.product_type
,     SUM(f.revenue*d.ytd_cy_week) AS ytd_current_year
,     SUM(f.revenue*d.ytd_ly_week) AS ytd_last_year
,     ROUND(SUM(f.revenue*d.ytd_cy_week) /
        SUM(f.revenue*d.ytd_ly_week)*100,0) AS index
FROM    fact_sales AS f
INNER JOIN dim_date  AS d ON f.order_date_key = d.date_key
INNER JOIN dim_product AS p ON f.product_key  = p.product_key
```

What happens in the preceding query is that for each row in the fact table, the value of revenue is multiplied by the values of the fields `ytd_cy (week)` and `ytd_ly (week)`. Then the outcomes of these calculations are summarized and grouped by product type. Tables 8-3 and 8-4 show an example of how this actually works.

Table 8-3: Relative date calculations

PRODUCT_TYPE	REVENUE	YTD_CY	YTD_LY	YTD_CY VALUE	YTD_LY VALUE
Blu-ray	30	1	0	30	0
DVD	40	1	0	40	0
DVD	25	0	1	0	25
Blu-ray	33	0	0	0	0
Blu-ray	21	1	0	21	0
DVD	56	0	0	0	0
Blu-ray	45	0	1	0	45
DVD	35	0	1	0	35

Table 8-4: Relative date result set

PRODUCT_TYPE	YTD_CY	YTD_LY	INDEX
Blu-ray	51	45	113
DVD	40	60	67

The big advantage of using these special fields is that you don't need to combine multiple queries, each with their own filters, to generate the required reports. In fact, it is possible to get all period results and comparisons from the data warehouse in a single query, which greatly simplifies building the queries and the reports. Other common elements in sales and revenue analysis are *moving totals* and *averages*. For this type of calculation, the total of the last 12 months (for a moving annual total or *MAT*) is compared to the total of the 12 months prior to the last 12. For a month-to-month comparison, you can also calculate the MAT per month to eliminate seasonal influences from the calculations and get a better insight into the real sales trend. To calculate a MAT, the month sequence is a great help but the SQL needed is a bit more complex because you'll need a `case` statement to determine whether a period should be included in the end result. The following statement will calculate the MAT and MAT - 1 year:

```
SUM(f.revenue * CASE WHEN d.month_sequence BETWEEN -12 AND -1
          THEN 1 ELSE 0 END) AS mat1,
SUM(f.revenue * CASE WHEN d.month_sequence BETWEEN -24 AND -13
          THEN 1 ELSE 0 END) AS mat2
```

Chapter 13 provides several other examples of how you can use the date and time dimension to simply analyze results without having to rely on complex formulas in the report itself. In most cases, it's easier to model these constructions directly in the database, which saves time later on in building the meta model or the reports.

Source to Target Mapping

The last design step before we can start building the actual ETL processes is to identify the mappings from the source system(s) to the target data warehouse. A good way to start is by first drawing the high-level data flows at the table level without bothering too much about the details. Figure 8-7 shows an example of this high-level mapping, where we pretend the country and region tables come from another source (the master database). The diagram shows only a part of the complete data warehouse, of course, and displays the logical mapping, not the physical one. The physical mapping most likely will include intermediate staging tables that are used to store the data extracted from the source systems to be transformed and loaded into their final destination dimension tables.

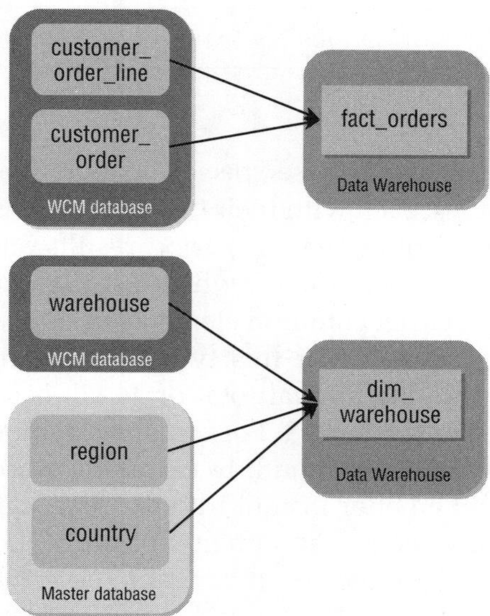

Figure 8-7: High-level mapping

Now we have determined what our data mart will look like and made a global mapping from the source system to the data mart tables. The next step is to create the detailed field-level mapping. This process is not from source to target but actually the other way around. We already know what our target should look like, so now it's time to find the right sources and transformations to get the data. You work from target to source because it's possible that there is no source available for certain target fields. When you work "backwards" from the target tables, these gaps are trapped earlier than when working "forward" from the sources. For each target field (see Figure 8-1 for an example) we need to identify the following elements:

- **System**—In our case, most fields originate from the WCM database, but the generated keys and audit columns do not have a source system. They are filled from the *ETL process*, which can be entered as the source system for these columns.
- **Schema**—When applicable, enter the name of the database schema or catalog.
- **Object**—When applicable, enter the name of the table, view, or stored procedure that serves as the source for the column.
- **Field**—The name of the field in the source object.
- **Data type**—The data type of the column.
- **Length**—The length of the column.
- **Transformation**—Describes the steps needed to convert the value from the source system to the correct value in the target. This can (and should!) include lookups to other tables as well.
- **Comments**—Additional remarks that might help the ETL developer to build the correct data transformations.

TIP With DataCleaner, you can easily select the source tables and copy the generated table from the metadata tab into a spreadsheet. This will give you the schema, object, field, data type, and length, which you can then use to extend the mapping information.

After you've completed the global and detailed mapping, you should verify the completeness of your modeling efforts with the key business users. It doesn't hurt either to have a technical review by a DBA if you have one around. The most important check is whether the generated model can be used to answer the business questions that were initially brought forward by the user community. If not, you should identify the missing parts and go back to the drawing board to adjust the model and mapping. Just make sure that your initial model is able to handle the top priorities of the business stakeholders. If your logical and physical design turns out to be complete, you're ready to move on with the development of the ETL processes.

Summary

This chapter introduced you to two important pieces of software in your toolbox: eobjects DataCleaner and SQLPower Data*Architect. DataCleaner enables you to analyze the source data and report on the quality issues that might arise, and Data*Architect helps you in building the physical data model for the data marts, and ultimately, the data warehouse. As such, this chapter acts as a bridge between the more theoretical previous chapters and the more practical chapters that follow. We covered the following items to get you on your way with your first data mart:

- The different user groups you need to understand and work with
- Data analysis and the challenges involved with accessing different sources of data
- The purpose of data profiling, with an introduction to using a data profiling tool to assess data structure, content, and quality
- An introduction to data modeling with Data*Architect
- The design of the order facts data mart that we will use in the remainder of the book for the ETL, reporting, and analysis examples
- A further refined model of the date dimension with the additional benefit of advanced date arithmetic and simplification of the reporting process
- The final mapping information needed to create the ETL transformations

Part III

ETL and Data Integration

In This Part

CHAPTER

9

Pentaho Data Integration Primer

When the data warehouse design is stabilized, a process must be designed to fill the data warehouse with data. We use the general term *data integration* to describe the collection of activities that result in or contribute to filling of the data warehouse. Pentaho offers a collection of tools collectively known as *Pentaho Data Integration* that are designed to support this task.

This chapter provides some background information about the data integration process in general. We provide an overview of the Pentaho Data Integration tools, and explain in detail how these tools can be used to design and create a data integration solution to load the data warehouse.

Data Integration Overview

In a general sense, the word ''integration'' denotes a process that forms a whole out of multiple parts. The term ''data integration'' is usually understood as the process that combines data from different sources to provide a single comprehensible view on all of the combined data. A typical example of data integration would be combining the data from a warehouse inventory system with that of the order entry system to allow order fulfilment to be directly related to changes in the inventory. Another example of data integration is merging customer and contact data from separate departmental customer relationship management systems into a corporate customer relationship management system.

In the introduction to this chapter we stated that data integration comprises those activities that result in filling a data warehouse. This is a considerably simplified notion of data integration with regard to its general definition, but it can be justified when assuming that a properly designed data warehouse automatically provides a unified view of the data from different systems.

In this section, we explain some of the key characteristics of the data integration process and its components to provide the necessary context for those readers that are completely new to the topic. A detailed discussion of data integration is beyond the scope of this book. Fortunately, many good books are available that cover this subject, such as *The Data Warehouse ETL Toolkit* by Ralph Kimball and Joe Caserta (Wiley, 2004).

Data Integration Activities

One way of understanding data integration is to decompose the process of filling the data warehouse into a number of distinct activities. In this subsection we describe a number of essential types of data integration activities.

On a very high level, the problem of filling a data warehouse consists of only three major types of activities:

- *Extraction*—Acquiring data from one or more source systems. For example, obtaining and loading all customer records that were added or changed since the last loading data.
- *Transformation*—Changing the form and/or content of the data to fit it into the structure of the target data warehouse. For example, looking up state and country names for numerical key values.
- *Loading*—Actually storing data in the target data warehouse.

These three activities—Extraction, Transformation, and Loading—are often referred to by the abbreviation *ETL*.

In some cases, the term ETL is understood quite literally, and taken to mean that the individual activities of extraction, transformation, and loading are actually performed in that sequence. From this school of thought, the related terms *ELT* (extract, load, transform) and *ETLT* (extract, transform, load, transform) have been keyed to do justice to the fact that data-transforming activities can be implemented by either an RDBMS (ELT), or by a specialized tool outside the RDBMS (ETL), or both (ETLT).

Although there may be some contexts where it is advantageous to use these different terms, the distinction is not explored any further in this book. Instead, we prefer to use only the term ETL without limiting in advance what software components are occupied with transforming the data. As you shall see, Pentaho Data Integration is perfectly capable of offloading certain tasks to the RDBMS, and does nothing to prevent the RDBMS from taking part in data transformation. Therefore, we treat ETL as an umbrella term that may imply rather than exclude ELT and ETLT.

ETL is only a very broad categorization of data integration activities. Within each of the main processes Extraction, Transformation, and Loading, we can identify a number of supportive activities. A few of these are listed below:

For extraction we can discern:

- *Change data capture*—In many cases extraction is limited to the portion of source data that has changed since the last extraction. The process of identifying the changed data is called *change data capture*.
- *Data staging*—It may not always be possible or efficient to immediately transform extracted data. Often, the extract is temporarily stored until it enters the transformation process. This is called *data staging*.

Transformation is a broad and varied process. It is not possible to provide an exhaustive list of detailed activities, but a few typical activities are:

- *Data validation*—*Data validation* is the process of verifying the source data is correct, and possible filtering out invalid data.
- *Data cleansing*—*Data cleansing* is the process of correcting invalid data.
- *Decoding and renaming*—In many cases, raw data from the source system is not suitable for reporting purposes because it contains obscure names and codes. A large portion of the transformation process is occupied with converting this to more descriptive and user-friendly names and labels.
- *Aggregation*—Typically, BI applications present aggregated data to the end-users. Sometimes, aggregates are calculated in advance as part of the transformation process.
- *Key generation and management*—New dimension rows are uniquely identified by surrogate keys, which need to be generated. In order to store new fact data, these keys need to be looked up.

In the loading process, we can discern two main activities:

- *Loading fact tables*—Typically, fact tables grow by adding new rows. Sometimes existing rows are updated to reflect a new status.
- *Loading and Maintaining dimension tables*—New fact rows may give rise to new dimension rows.

We will look at these activities in more detail in the following subsections.

NOTE **This is not an exhaustive list, although these activities are quite typical. You can find quite a thorough overview of ETL activities in Ralph Kimball's article "The 38 Subsystems of ETL" at** `http://www.intelligententerprise.com/showArticle.jhtml?articleID=54200319`.

Extraction

The first step in the entire data integration process is the acquisition of data. This process is usually called *extraction*.

Often, the data source is a relational database system that forms the back end of some operational application. In these cases, it might be possible to access the source data directly through a database connection. In this case, extraction can be a relatively easy task. However, it may not always be feasible to gain direct access to the back-end database system.

There may be policies in place that prohibit database access beyond the operational application. Operational systems are increasingly expected or required to be always available, and the impact of a data acquisition process may simply be incompatible with these requirements. In these cases, the data may need to be extracted from system backup data or database log files.

Another factor that may complicate extraction is the fact that often, not all source data can be acquired at the same location. There may be multiple operational systems in use from which data needs to be acquired. In fact, the requirement to report across multiple information systems is often the driving force behind BI and data warehousing projects.

Change Data Capture

Change data capture (CDC) is the process of tracking data changes in the source systems in order to update the data warehouse accordingly. On the one hand, CDC is a process that drives extraction because data needs to be acquired only up to the extent that it makes a difference with regard to the current state of the data warehouse. On the other hand, CDC also has functional and logical facets because it determines to what extent the data warehouse is capable of recording business history.

There are a number of methods to practically implement CDC:

- Recording "natural" event data in the operational systems. In many cases, key events are recorded as part of the operational business process. For example, customer registration, order placement, and order shipment are typically recorded on date level in the operational system.
- Using sequential key data in the source systems.
- Journaling with database triggers. In many database systems, it is possible to add database triggers to the schemas of operational applications.
- Database log reading.

Data Staging

Extracting data may have considerable impact on the performance and availability of the operational source system. Often, there is a strict requirement to keep the amount of time spent on extraction to a minimum in an attempt to lessen the impact on normal operations such as data entry. Typically, these time constraints do not leave enough time to completely process all data before storing it in the data warehouse.

Apart from the actual duration of the extraction process, the matter of timing may also come into play. In quite a few cases, data from several distinct operational systems may need to be combined before it is fed into the data warehouse. Often one cannot rely on all source systems to be simultaneously available for extraction.

To cope with these problems, data is usually temporarily stored in a so-called *staging area* immediately after extraction. This approach allows extraction activities to be performed in the smallest possible time frame because no time is spent waiting on subsequent processing. It also allows synchronization of processes that combine data from distinct sources arriving at different times.

In most cases, the data staging area is simply a relational database that is specifically designed to serve as a buffer between the source systems and the data warehouse. This leads us to another advantage of data staging. Because the data is stored in a distinct database system, indexes that can help improve the performance of the subsequent data processing can be freely added without altering the source system.

Data Validation

Once the data is acquired (and possibly stored in a staging area), there is usually some process in place to assess the validity of the data. Invalid data must be treated differently than valid data, because it may taint the reliability of the data warehouse. Detecting invalid data is a prerequisite for treating it differently.

In the context of ETL and data validation, data is considered invalid when it contains logical errors. This occurs when source records are encountered that could never have been entered if all constraints implemented by the source application (and its underlying database system) had been enforced. For example, data for required fields may be missing, or values in one field may contradict values in another field, such as when a delivery date falls before the corresponding order date.

It may seem unnecessary to check for logical errors when data is acquired from applications and database systems that are known to rigorously enforce constraints. However, the reality is that there is no way of assessing data validity other than actually checking it. If invalid source data accidentally ends up in the data warehouse, it may be discovered by the end user. This may lead to general distrust of the data warehouse and supporting data integration processes.

Making data validation a part of the data integration process results in immediate benefit. If no invalid data is caught, it provides the peace of mind that the source system can be trusted. On the other hand, if invalid data is caught it may solicit extra support for the data integration project because it offers a unique opportunity to improve the source system.

Data Cleansing

In many cases, possible issues with the source data are known in advance, and processes may be in place to help correct data that would otherwise be invalid. This is referred to as *data cleansing*.

The simplest solution to deal with invalid data is to discard it. Although this prevents the invalid data from tainting reliability of the known correct data this is usually not an acceptable option. A better solution is to keep known invalid data aside, and if possible to correct it.

Keeping invalid data, provided that it is marked and classified accordingly, has many advantages. In the future, some way may be found to correct or otherwise reconcile the invalid data so it can be loaded after all. It may be worthwhile to use the invalid data as evidence in an attempt to convince any responsible parties to repair or improve the source system. For example we may get phone numbers from a CRM system in all kinds of different formats: some may contain a country code, whereas others may omit it. Some may contain an area code, and others may omit it. Country codes may be denoted using a +, others may use a leading 0. Sometimes phone numbers contain parentheses, dashes, or space characters for readability. In many of these cases we can parse the phone numbers and standardize the notation. In some cases, we can make an educated guess based on customer's address to fill in an omitted country code or area code.

Another possibility is to load the invalid data after properly tagging it. Because the invalid data is tagged as such, it can be included or excluded from analyses at the user's discretion. It also allows end users to inspect the nature of the invalid data, and enables them to make an informed judgment with regard to data quality. This approach may also act as a lever to fix the data quality problem at the source because all stakeholders can now see the impact of the invalid data on their reports for themselves.

Decoding and Renaming

Renaming and decoding are among the most basic transformation activities. Although humble in nature, these are perhaps the most ubiquitous types of transformations.

Decoding occurs when the values of a field in the source system are mapped to other values in the target system. For example, a source field containing the values `1` and `0` may be decoded into the more comprehensible values `Yes` and `No` in the target system.

Renaming occurs when the name of a particular field in the source is given a new name in the target system. For example, a field that is named `zip` in the source system may end up as `postal_code` in the target system.

It is important to realize that normally, neither decoding nor renaming add any information in the formal sense. However, these activities can help to make data more accessible to the end user. This is particularly true when the source system uses cryptic abbreviations for field names or field values.

Key Management

Chapter 6 explained that tables in the data warehouse do not use natural primary keys. All dimension tables have surrogate primary keys, and fact tables are joined to dimension tables using only references to these surrogate keys. The values for these keys must not be derived from the source systems that feed the data warehouse (with the possible exception of the date dimension table). Instead, they must be generated as part of the data integration process.

Aggregation

There are several cases where the data integration process involves aggregating data.

Dimension tables may contain attributes that are derived by aggregation. For example, a Customer dimension table may contain attributes such as `total amount spent`. Loading aggregate tables with precalculated, aggregated metrics may be required to improve performance of certain reports and ROLAP cubes.

The Pentaho Analysis Server (Mondrian) is a ROLAP server that can take advantage of aggregate tables. Pentaho also provides the Pentaho Aggregate Designer, which is especially tailored to creating and maintaining aggregate tables for this purpose. For this reason, we discuss aggregation in Chapter 15 rather than in this chapter.

Dimension and Bridge Table Maintenance

Most dimension tables are not static. Their contents need to adapt according to additions and changes occurring in the source systems.

There are simple examples, such as new products that need to be added to the product dimension table. More complex examples include handling various types of slowly changing dimension. Even more complex examples occur when the dimension table needs support for browsing along a recursive parent-child relationship.

Storing the changes in the dimension tables is one of the prime responsibilities of the data integration process.

Loading Fact Tables

Loading the fact tables is the most important activity of the data integration process. The data integration process needs to overcome a number of challenges when loading the fact tables.

In many cases, the sheer amount of fact data is in itself a challenge. Dimension keys need to be looked up for each row that will be stored in the fact table, and performance is often an issue, especially when many dimension tables are involved that tend to be large themselves (such as Product and Customer tables). Metrics need to be accurately stored, and sometimes, additional metrics need to be calculated, too. To complicate things even more, some types of fact tables require existing rows to be updated to reflect status changes in the source systems.

Pentaho Data Integration Concepts and Components

Pentaho Data Integration solutions are built out of two different types of objects:

- Transformations
- Jobs

The heart of the Pentaho Data Integration product is formed by the Pentaho data integration engine. This engine is a software component that is capable of interpreting and executing jobs and transformations, thereby performing the actual data integration tasks accordingly. In addition to the engine, Pentaho Data Integration offers a number of tools and utilities to create, manage, and launch transformations and jobs.

All Pentaho Data Integration tools and components are available for download as a single `.zip` file. This file can be found in the download area of the Pentaho project page at `sourceforge.net/projects/pentaho`. Pentaho data integration does not require a separate installation procedure other than unzipping the download.

For a high level overview of the Pentaho data integration components, see Figure 9-1.

The components are outlined in the following sections.

Tools and Utilities

Pentaho Data Integration comprises the following set of tools and utilities:

- **Spoon**—A graphical data integration IDE for creating transformations and jobs
- **Kitchen**—A command-line tool for running jobs
- **Pan**—A command-line tool for running transformations

- **Carte**—A lightweight server for running jobs and transformations on a remote host

NOTE **As you can see, a culinary theme was used in naming the tools. This naming scheme goes back to the days when the software that is now known as Pentaho Data Integration was first created. The original product was called Kettle (or actually K.E.T.T.L.E., which is a recursive acronym for Kettle Extraction, Transformation, Transportation, and Loading Environment). The terms kettle, K.E.T.T.L.E., and Pentaho Data Integration can all be used interchangeably.**

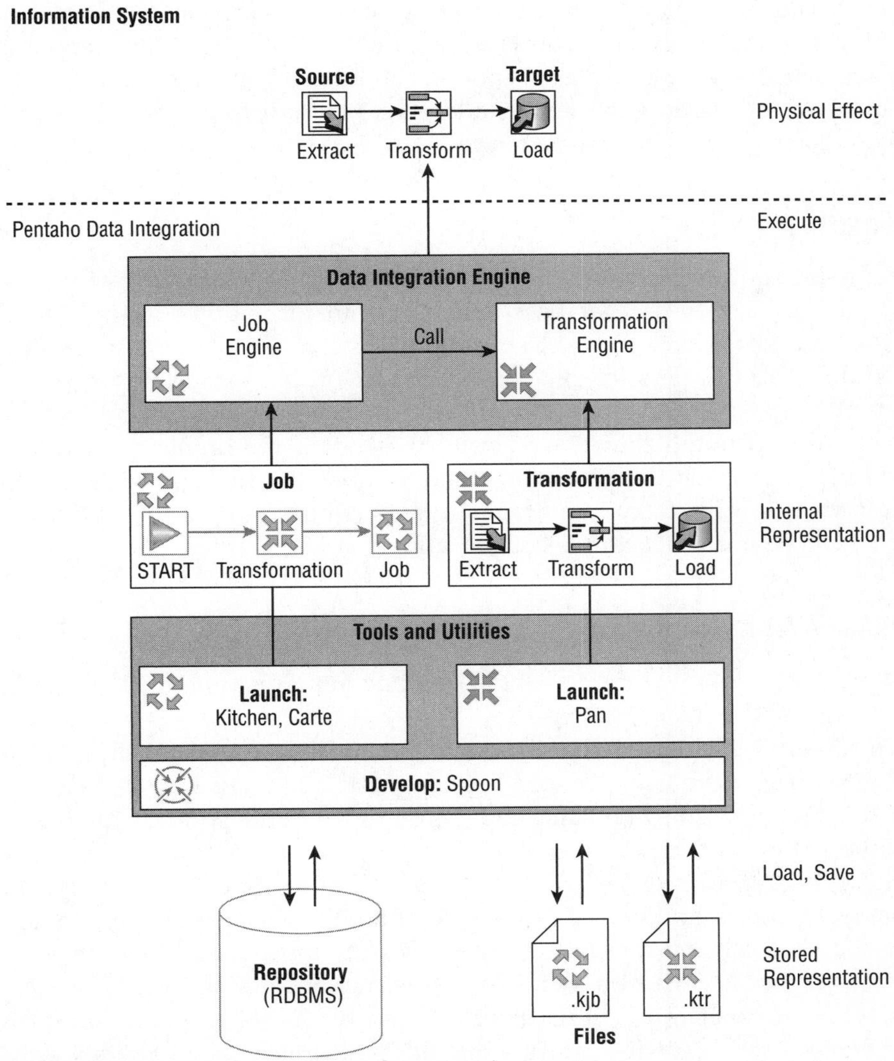

Figure 9-1: Pentaho data integration tools and components

The Data Integration Engine

The data integration engine is responsible for interpreting and executing data integration jobs and transformations. Jobs and transformations are actually handled by different parts of the engine. However, because jobs can contain transformations and executing a job may result in execution of one or more transformations, it is usually more convenient to consider the job engine and the transformation engine as a whole (the data integration engine).

The data integration engine is physically implemented as a Java library. The front-end tools use a public API to have the engine execute jobs and transformations on their behalf in response to user interaction.

Using the engine in this way is not confined to the front-end tools: The engine can be used by any application. The data integration engine is also included in the Pentaho BI server, allowing jobs and transformations to be executed as part of an action sequence.

Repository

Jobs and transformations may be stored in a database repository. The front-end tools can connect to the database and load transformations and job definitions stored in the repository. Using the repository also offers an easy way for multiple developers to collaborate when working on a data integration solution.

It should be noted that the repository is not a requirement. When not working with the repository, transformations and jobs are stored as files in an XML format. In this case, an external version control system like subversion or CVS can be used to facilitate collaboration.

Jobs and Transformations

Now that we explained the tools and components, it is time to take a closer look at jobs and transformations.

We already mentioned that the data integration engine interprets and executes jobs and transformations. This suggests a likeness between jobs and transformations on the one hand and computer program source code files on the other. However, there are good reasons to reject this notion.

Typically, a computer program's source code is made up of a set of rather literal instructions, and it is up to the programmer to make sure these instructions together achieve the desired effect. For the most part, transformations and jobs do not consist of a literal set of instructions. Rather, jobs and transformations are declarative in nature: they specify a particular result that is to be achieved, and leave it up to the engine to figure out a way of achieving that result. Another way to put it is to say that the data integration engine is *metadata-driven*: transformations and jobs contain information about the data, the source system, and the target system, and when executing a job or transformation, this information is used to perform the necessary operations to achieve the result. This is done without generating intermediate program code.

The difference between computer program source code and jobs and transformations is also apparent in the way these are developed. Source code is typically text-based, and developed by typing statements according to the grammar of the programming language (*coding*). In contrast, jobs and transformations are developed in a highly graphical manner. They are created by dragging and dropping elements on a canvas and connecting them together to form a graph or diagram. This process is akin to drawing a flow chart. Transformations and jobs can contain elements that may involve scripting, but this is an exception rather than the rule.

Transformations and jobs both consist of a collection of items that are interconnected by *hops* (see the following section). In this respect, there is a similarity between transformations and jobs. This likeness becomes especially apparent in the visual representation, as both transformations and jobs are depicted as graphs.

However, a closer look at transformations and jobs reveals that the similarities are actually few in number and rather superficial in nature. There are important differences in the concepts underlying jobs and transformations, and the semantics of their constituent elements and hops are quite different from one another. We hope this will become clear by reading the following sections.

Transformations

A Pentaho transformation represents an ETL task in the narrow sense. Transformations are data-oriented, and their purpose is to extract, transform, and load data.

A transformation consists of a collection of *steps*. A step denotes a particular operation on one or more *record streams*. Steps may be connected by *hops*. A hop is like a pipeline through which records can flow from one step to another step.

A record stream is a series of *records*. A record is a collection of values that is structured in such a way that each value is associated with exactly one *field*. The collection of fields associated with all values in a record is called the *record type*. All records in a record stream must be of the same record type.

Every field has a name that must be unique within the record type. Fields define properties such as data type and format that collectively describe the nature of any value associated with the field. These properties form the value's *metadata* ("data about data"). In a similar manner, the record type forms the metadata of the record. See Figure 9-2, for a graphical representation of these concepts.

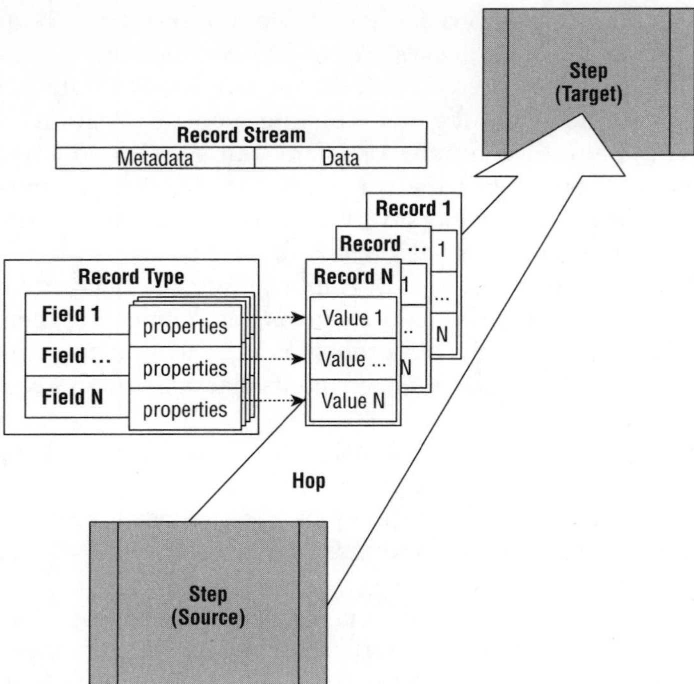

Figure 9-2: Steps, hops, and record streams

Transformation steps produce records in a continuous fashion. Records travel through the step's outgoing hops immediately after they are produced until they arrive at the step at the other end of the hop. There, the arriving records are queued and wait to be consumed by the receiving step. For each incoming record, the receiving step performs some predefined operation. Typically, this generates output records that are then pushed into the step's output record stream.

An important thing to realize about the entire process is that steps work simultaneously and asynchronously. When executing a transformation, steps that know how to generate rows based on some external data source will simply start generating rows until the data source is exhausted. Records will immediately flow to any downstream steps, where they are processed as fast as possible as they arrive: downstream steps do not wait for the upstream steps to finish. This way, the records trickle through the transformation.

The operation performed by a transformation step depends on the type of the step and the way it is configured. There is quite a bit of variety in step types. Some types of steps generate a single output record for each input record. Other types of steps aggregate a group of input rows into a single output row. Yet other types of steps can split a single input row into a collection of output records. For some types of steps, the output streams have the same record type as the input streams, yet other step types may add, remove, or rename fields from the input records.

A few of the available transformation steps are discussed in detail in Chapter 10.

Jobs

Typically, jobs are composed of one or more transformations. For example, to load a star schema, you would typically build one transformation to do the actual extraction, and build one transformation for each dimension table, and one transformation to load the fact table. The *job* would be used to put all these transformations in the proper sequence (first extract, then load all dimension tables, and then load the fact table). Like transformations, jobs consist of a number of interconnected items, but the likeness ends there.

Jobs are procedural and task-oriented rather than data-oriented. The items appearing in jobs are called *job entries*, and denote the execution of a particular task. A connection between the steps in a job denotes the sequential ordering of these tasks.

Execution of a job entry always results in an exit status. This is used to convey whether the underlying task was successfully executed. Depending on the value of the exit status, job execution continues with the appropriate subsequent job entry.

When comparing the nature of job entries to transformation steps, the key difference is that transformation steps operate on streams of data. Job entries operate on the exit status resulting from task execution.

Job entries are typically used to execute transformations, but they can also be used to perform other supportive tasks, such as emptying database tables, initiating file transfer from a remote host, or sending an e-mail message.

Pentaho jobs are discussed in more detail in Chapters 10 and 11.

Plug-in Architecture

Pentaho Data Integration features a *plug-in architecture*. Steps as well as job entries can be implemented separately from the core product as software components called plug-ins. Plug-ins can be dynamically loaded without recompiling the core.

Currently, there are quite a few third-party plug-ins for Pentaho Data Integration. Some of them are closed source and available under the terms of a commercial license. Many others are licensed under some form of open source license.

Getting Started with Spoon

Spoon is the name of the graphical Pentaho Data Integration development environment. It can be used to create transformations and jobs.

In this section, you will learn how to use Spoon. After starting the application, and briefly discussing some of the user interface's main elements, you will quickly start building a "Hello, World!" transformation to become acquainted with the user interface. We will then introduce you to some timesaving functionalities that can help you to troubleshoot issues efficiently. You'll then learn how to work with database connections, and enhance the "Hello, World!" example to put that knowledge into practice.

Launching the Spoon Application

Spoon can be started by executing the spoon startup script in the Pentaho integration home directory. For Windows systems, the script is called `Spoon.bat`. On Windows systems you can also start `Kettle.exe`. For UNIX-based systems, this script is called `spoon.sh`.

NOTE Users of UNIX-based systems will need to enable execute permissions for the script before they can execute it:

```
$ chmod ug+x spoon.sh
```

All Pentaho data integration tools are started using a script, so you might as well enable execute permissions for all of them:

```
$chmod ug+x *.sh
```

After Spoon starts, you will see a splash screen. Some time after that, a dialog appears, prompting for repository credentials. We will explore the possibilities of the repository in Chapter 11. For now, you will work without a database repository. To continue, click the button with the caption No Repository. Optionally, you can clear the Present this dialog at startup checkbox to prevent the dialog from appearing the next time you open Spoon.

The main application window should now appear. You might see a Spoon tips window showing a tip of the day, and optionally, you can clear the Show tips at startup? checkbox to prevent it from showing up the next time you open Spoon. Press Close to close the Spoon tips window.

The Spoon application window, shown in Figure 9-3, is divided into a main workspace on the right and a side pane on the left. The main workspace provides a tab/page interface to work with all opened transformations and jobs.

Initially, a special Welcome page may automatically appear in the workspace right after the application starts. It's also possible that the Welcome page pops up in your Internet browser. The Welcome page contains useful links to the official Pentaho data integration documentation as well as to community resources and developer blogs.

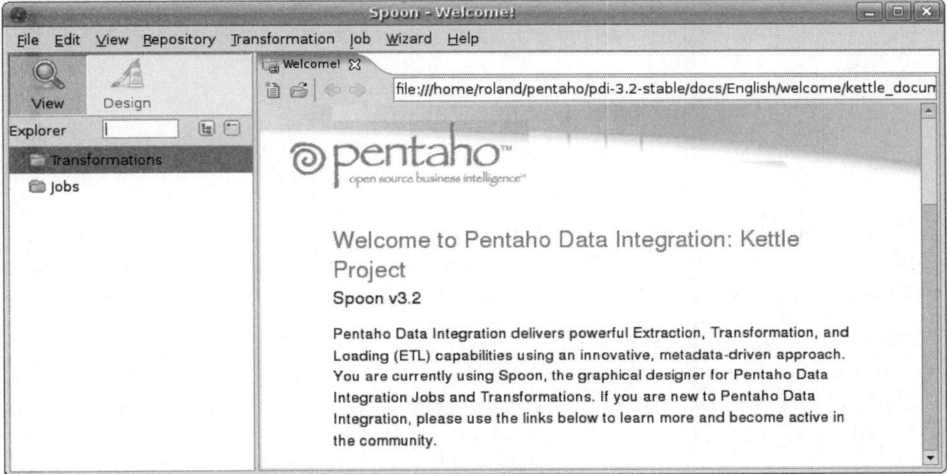

Figure 9-3: The Spoon main window

If you like, you can prevent the Welcome page from showing up by clearing the Show welcome page at startup checkbox in the Options dialog. The Options dialog can be opened using the main menu (Menu ➤ Edit ➤ Options).

A Simple "Hello, World!" Example

Spoon offers a single user interface to create and design both jobs and transformations. Although jobs and transformations are quite different kinds of things, there are many similarities in the way they are visually represented, and this is reflected in a nearly identical user interface for designing them.

The best way to become familiar with the user interface is to start building a very simple ''Hello World!'' example, ETL style. This is described in detail in the remainder of this section.

Building the Transformation

The following instructions describe in detail how to build a transformation that extracts people's names from a text file to generate a ''Hello, World!'' message. Finally, the messages are stored in a new text file.

1. Using an ordinary text editor such as notepad (Windows) or vi (UNIX-based systems), create a text file with the text in Listing 9-1. Name

the file `hello_world_input.txt` and save it in some location you find convenient.

Listing 9-1: The contents of hello_world_input.txt

```
Name
George Clooney
Daniel Lay Lewis
Johnny Depp
Tommy Lee Jones
Viggo Mortensen
```

2. Start Spoon (if it is not already running) and create a new transformation by choosing File ➤ New ➤ Transformation from the main menu. A new page is automatically opened in the workspace, and the transformation is also added to the tree view in the side pane, as shown in Figure 9-4.

   In addition to using the main menu, you can create a transformation by using the keyboard shortcut Ctrl+N, or by using the toolbar: Toolbar ➤ New ➤ Transformation. The toolbar button is shown in Figure 9-4.

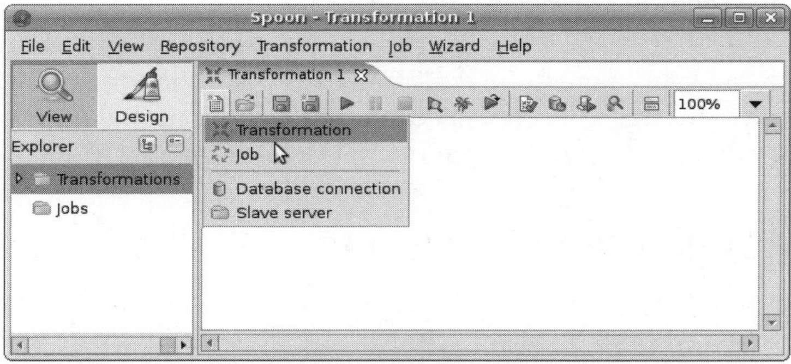

Figure 9-4: Using the toolbar to create a new transformation

3. In the side pane, switch from View mode to Design mode by clicking the Design button. In Design mode, the side pane displays a tree view containing a number of folders representing step type categories. Expand the folder labeled input that sits in the top of the tree view.

4. Drag the item labeled Text file input from the input folder and drop it on the transformation page to create a new step, as shown in Figure 9-5.

   Almost all steps require some form of configuration to control their behavior. Steps are configured through their configuration dialog, which can be brought up by double-clicking the step, or by choosing Edit step from the step's context menu.

STEPS: TYPES, CREATING, MOVING, AND REMOVING

Note that the icon you dragged from the tree view was a *step type*, rather than an actual step. By dropping the step type onto the canvas, you created an actual step of that type.

Steps can also be created using the transformation context menu. For example, the Text file input step can also be added by right-clicking in the transformation page and choosing New step ➢ Input ➢ Text file input.

Once a step is created, it can be placed anywhere on the transformation page using drag-and-drop. Simply place the mouse pointer on the step, and then press and hold the left mouse button. Moving the mouse pointer will now drag the step along until the mouse button is released.

To delete a single step, right-click it to bring up the step's context menu; then choose Delete step.

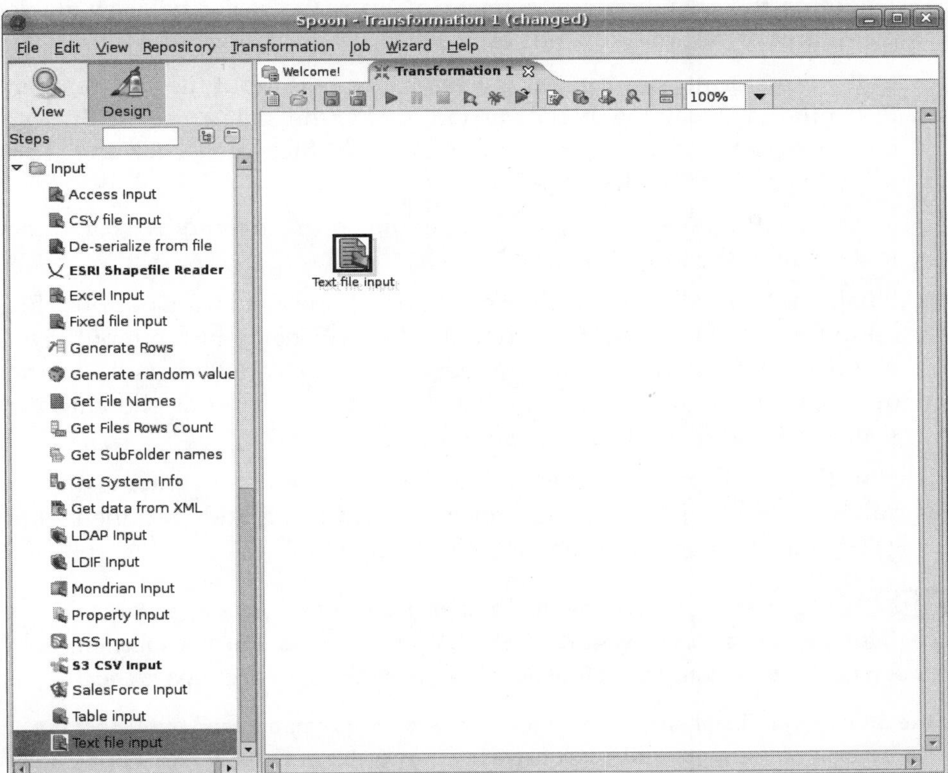

Figure 9-5: The transformation page with its first step

One thing that can be configured for all steps is the name. Every step has a name that must be unique within the transformation. The name is also used as a caption for the step in the transformation page. In the configuration dialogs, the step name always appears before any other configuration options.

By default, the name of the step is the name of its step type, possibly followed by a number to ensure the name is unique. For now, you can leave the default name (Text file input), but typically the default name would be changed to reflect the purpose of the step within the transformation (as opposed to a label that only describes what operation is performed). Specifying a descriptive name for steps is key to designing maintainable transformations.

Other configuration elements that recur frequently in steps of different types are tab pages to group related options and grids to configure the fields for the step's data streams. However, the majority of available configuration options depends on the step type.

5. In the transformation page, double-click the Text input file step to open its configuration dialog. In the File tab page of the dialog, use the Browse button to select the `hello_world_input.txt` file. Then click the Add button to assign the file to the Selected files grid.

   Next, click the Content tab page and set the Format drop-down list in the lower half of the form to Mixed.

6. Finally, activate the Fields tab page, and click the Get Fields button. This button tells Spoon to scan the data to discover fields in the input. You will first be prompted for the number of rows to scan. You can leave the default number (100) for now. After confirming, a window showing the scan results appears. This is all shown in Figure 9-6.

   Note that one field was discovered, and note the minimum and maximum values. Close that dialog, and notice the field being added to the Fields grid. Close the configuration dialog by clicking OK.

NOTE **After creating and configuring a step, you can always re-open the configuration dialog and review its properties. However, for quick inspection, Spoon offers more convenient functionalities from the step's context menu.**

The Show input fields and Show output fields options can be used to inspect the record type of the input and output streams respectively. These options bring up a window that displays a grid containing one row for each field in the stream showing the field's name, data type, and name of the step where the field was originally created.

The Text file input step does not expect an input stream, and this is properly indicated in the pop-up window. The window for the Show output fields option is shown in Figure 9-7.

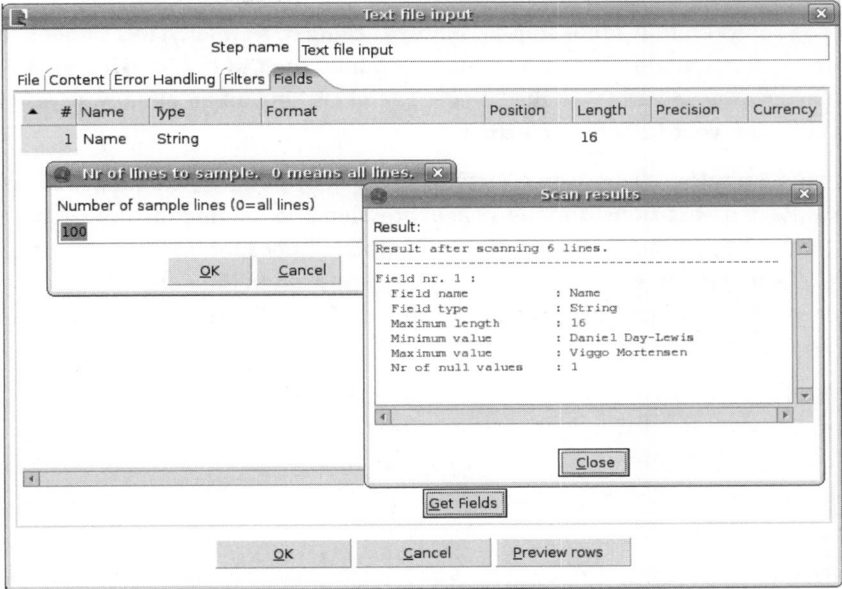

Figure 9-6: Defining fields with the Get Fields button

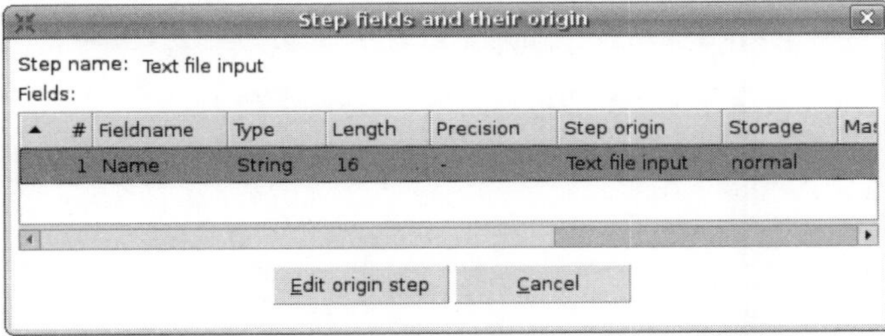

Figure 9-7: The output fields for the Text input file step

7. Find the Add constants step type in the Transform category, and add one to the transformation near the Text file input step. Open its configuration dialog and enter the following two rows in the Fields grid (see Figure 9-8):

```
Name: message; Type: String; Value: Hello
Name: exclamation; Type: String; Value:!
```

NOTE Spoon supports creating selections of one or more steps. This greatly facilitates working with multiple steps because this allows you to move or remove all steps included in the selection at once. Selected steps are recognizable by their thick black border.

You can select an individual step by simply clicking it. Normally, this undoes the previous selection. However, if you press and hold the Ctrl key, clicking on an unselected step will add it to the selection, and clicking on an already selected step will remove it from the selection.

You can also select all steps in a rectangular area by pointing the mouse to an empty place on the transformation page, pressing and holding the mouse button, and then dragging the mouse pointer to another empty spot below and to the right of the starting point. A "rubber band" appears and when the mouse button is released, all steps that fall between the boundaries of the rubber band become the new selection.

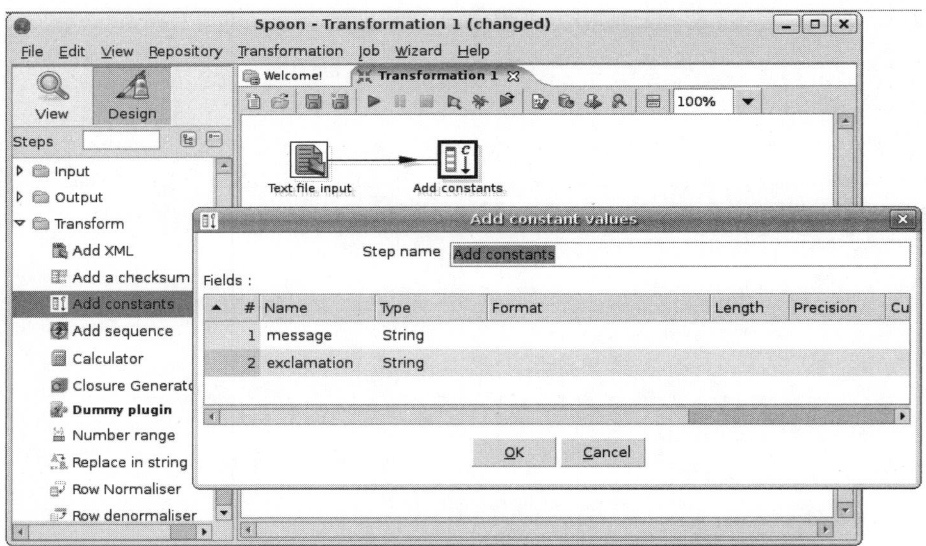

Figure 9-8: The Add constants step

Hops can be created to direct the output stream of one step to the input stream of another. In this example, you want to create a hop from the Text file input step to the Add constants step to add the fields from the Add constants step to the records of the output stream of the Text file input step.

To create a hop, hold the Shift key, and drag the source step onto the destination step. The Shift key can be released after dropping the step. When not holding the Shift key, the step is only moved, but no connection is made. Alternatively, if you have a middle mouse wheel, simply press it at the source step, keep it pressed and move it to the target step. There is yet another way to create a hop: activate the View mode in the side pane and make sure the tree view node corresponding to the transformation is expanded. Then, right-click the Hops node to bring up the context menu. In the context menu, click New to bring up the Hops dialog. In this dialog, you can connect steps simply by selecting the source and target steps in the list boxes.

A hop is displayed as a line drawn from the source step to the destination step. The line has an arrowhead slightly beyond the center of the line, pointing away from the source step and to the destination step.

8. Add a hop from the Text file input step to the Add constants step by dragging the Text file input step onto the Add constants step while holding the Shift key. This is also shown in Figure 9-8.

TIP **Typically, as you add more and more steps and hops, the transformation can start looking a bit messy. To prevent that, you can horizontally or vertically align steps. To vertically align multiple steps, select the steps and then press the up arrow key (to align the tops of the selected steps to the top of the step that is closest to the top of the canvas) or the down arrow key (to align the bottom of the selected steps to the bottom of the step that is closest to the bottom of the canvas). Similarly, you can align steps horizontally using the left and right arrow keys.**

9. Next, create a Text file output step (from the Output category) and add a hop to it from the Add constants Step. The result is shown in Figure 9-9.

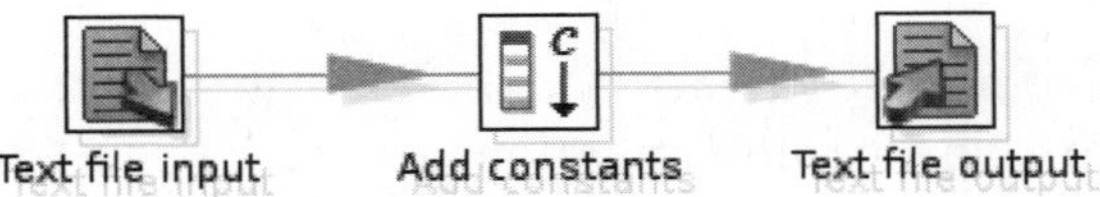

Figure 9-9: The three-step transformation example

10. Open the configuration dialog for the Text file output step and set the Filename property to a file named `hello_world_output` in the same directory as the `hello_world_input.txt` file. (Note the Extension property is set by default to `txt`, which is why we did not include the `.txt` extension when specifying the Filename property.)

    Activate the Fields tab page, and press the Get Fields button to automatically fill the Fields grid. After that, press the Minimal Width button and adjust the lengths of the fields to generate more compact variable length output. Note the order of the fields corresponds exactly to the sequence of the steps from where they originate: first the `Name` field generated by the Text file input step, then the `message` and `exclamation` fields added by the Add constants step.

Right-click on the row that defines the `Name` field and from the pop-up menu choose the Move down item so that the final order of the fields is `message`, then `Name`, and then `exclamation`. Alternatively, you can select the row in the grid corresponding to the `Name` field and press the cursor down key. Click OK to close the configuration dialog.

The Text file output step and its fields dialog are shown in Figure 9-10.

FIELD GRIDS

Many transformation steps require multiple fields to be configured. In many cases the configuration dialog provides a grid like you just saw in the Fields tab of the Text file output step. Usually a Get Fields button is present to automatically populate the grid. When populating a non-empty grid in this manner, you are prompted to make a choice to deal with the existing fields. The choices are Add new, Add all and Clear and add all, with obvious behavior for each choice.

Rows in the grid can be selected by clicking on them, and multiple selections can be made by holding the Ctrl key while selecting rows. Rows are added by simply typing in a new row after the last existing one. Deleting selected rows is done using the Del key. Keeping selected rows (deleting all unselected rows) is done using Ctrl+K.

The list given here is not exhaustive—it is just here to give you an idea. If you want a full overview of the possibilities, right-click on a grid to see its context menu.

11. You are now done with the actual building of the transformation. This is a good time to save the transformation, using the File ➢ Save item from the main menu. Save the transformation as `hello_world_transformation` in the same directory as you saved the input file. The file should automatically get the `.ktr` extension, which is short for "Kettle Transformation."

NOTE Note that a Save button is also available on the toolbar. Alternatively, you can also use the keyboard shortcut Ctrl+S.

Running the Transformation

You can run the active transformation from within Spoon through the main menu using the Menu ➢ Transformation ➢ Run option. Alternatively, you can use the keyboard shortcut F9 or the Run toolbar button (the green-filled arrowhead pointing to the right).

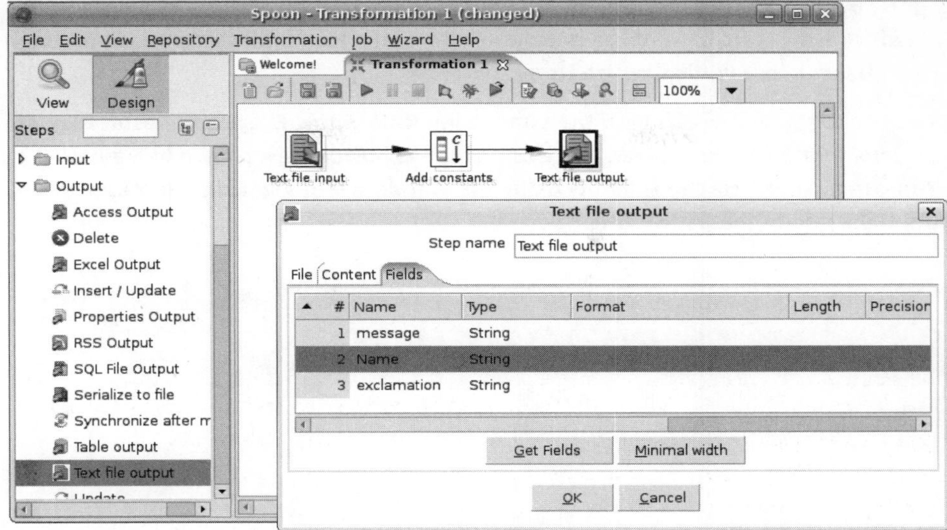

Figure 9-10: The Text file output step and its fields dialog

When running the transformation, a dialog with the title Execute a transformation pops up first. We will discuss this dialog in more detail later on in this chapter and again in Chapter 11, but for now you can simply press the Launch button at the bottom of the dialog.

The Execution Results Pane

After launching the transformation, the Execution Results pane becomes visible at the bottom of the workspace. This panel provides a number of tab pages that offer useful functionality to monitor a transformation. By default, the Step Metrics tab page is activated, and for now, we'll mostly limit ourselves to using this tab page as well as the Logging page. All of these tab pages will be discussed in more detail in Chapter 11.

If everything worked like it should, the Execution pane should now look similar to Figure 9-11. In the Step Metrics grid, you should see exactly three lines (one for each step in the transformation).

All of the lines should indicate that they are Finished in the Active column (on the right side of the grid). If one or more lines in the grid have a red background, and the Active column shows the status Stopped, an error occurred while executing the transformation. The section "Verifying the Transformation" later in this chapter may give you some clues as to what went wrong.

NOTE The height of the Execution Results pane can be adjusted by dragging its top in the vertical direction. To do so, place the mouse pointer exactly between the top of the title bar of the pane and the bottom of the workspace. You can find the

"grip" by placing your mouse pointer right in the text of the pane's title bar and slowly moving it up toward the bottom of the workspace until the mouse pointer icon changes to a vertical resize icon.

You can toggle the visibility of the pane using Hide/Show Execution Result toggle buttons found on the toolbar. The icons of these buttons are shown in Figure 9-12. You can also control the visibility using the standard window icons that appear on the right side in the pane's title bar.

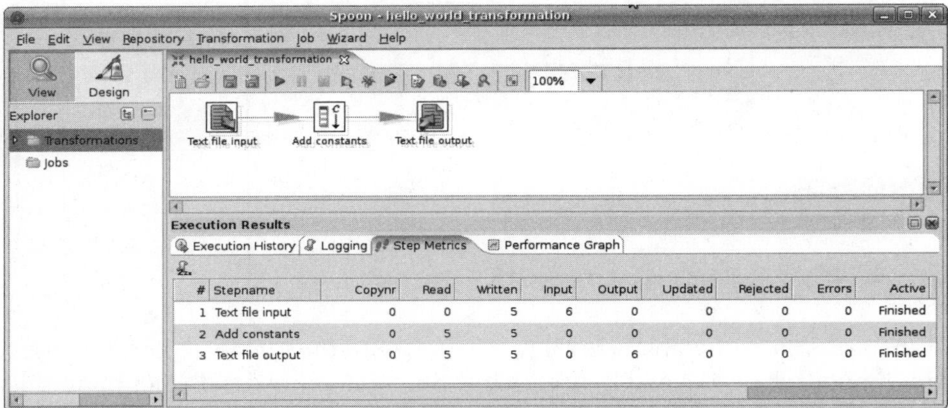

Figure 9-11: The finished transformation

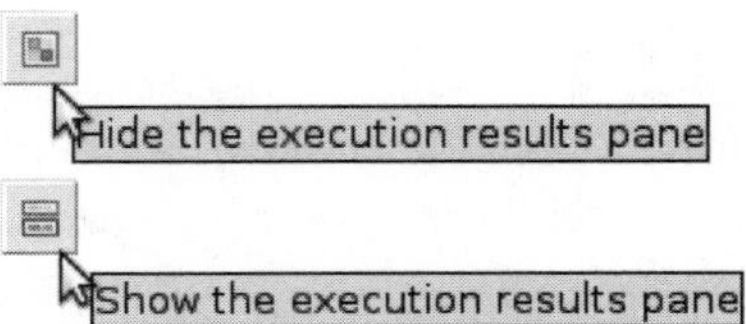

Figure 9-12: Toggling visibility of the Execution Results pane

The Output

The `hello_world_output.txt` file you created earlier should now contain `Hello,<name>!` messages like those shown in Listing 9-2.

Listing 9-2: The contents of hello_world_output.txt

```
messageNameexclamation
Hello,George Clooney!
Hello,Daniel Day-Lewis!
Hello,Johnny Depp!
Hello,Tommy Lee Jones!
Hello,Viggo Mortensen!
```

Checking Consistency and Dependencies

You just made a most capricious move by immediately running your transformation without even performing the most basic checks. Granted, the transformation is a very simple one, but even so, there is a staggering number of things that could go wrong. The following sections present some basic checks you should always run.

Logical Consistency

The most basic thing to check is whether the transformation is logically consistent. For example, if a step operates on a particular field, it follows that that field must be present in the incoming data stream, and it is considered an error if this is not the case. Another type of error occurs when record streams with incompatible layouts are "mixed." This occurs when two record streams having a different record layout are connected to the same step. There are more varieties of logical issues such as steps with neither incoming nor outgoing hops and steps that are connected in a circular manner.

Resource Dependencies

Another thing to check is whether all resources that are used by the transformation are actually available. For example, our "Hello, World!" example refers to an input file and an output file. Real-world transformations are likely to depend on database connections and on the availability of database objects such as tables and perhaps sequences or stored procedures. Obviously, there will be a problem executing such a transformation if these resources are not available.

Verifying the Transformation

The Verify option in the Transformation menu can be used to check for logical errors as well as for the availability of resources such as files and database tables. Choosing this option pops up a window titled Results of transformation checks showing each potential issue as a row in a grid.

Rows use traffic light colors to indicate severity of the issue: green rows indicate the check is okay, red rows indicate errors, and yellow rows indicate warnings. Selecting the Show successful results checkbox in the bottom of the result window reveals the results of all checks that passed with no issue, providing a nice overview of everything that could have gone wrong. There may also be remark rows in the result, which do not have any special color at all. These rows are reported for checks that currently cannot be performed.

See Figure 9-13 for an example of what the validation result for the "Hello, World" transformation might look like.

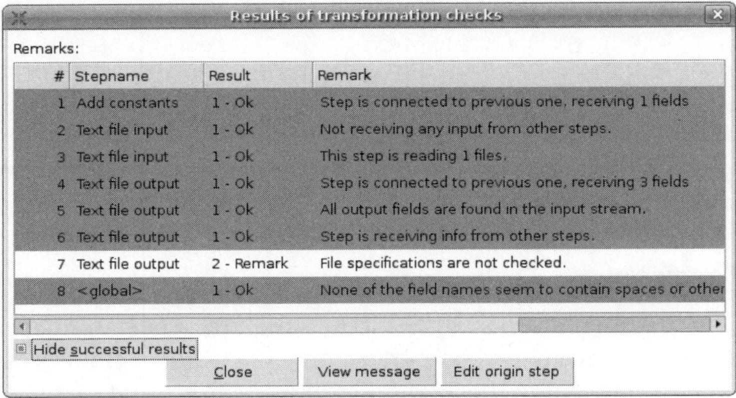

Figure 9-13: Verifying the transformation

When verifying the ''Hello, World!'' example transformation, you may find one remark row in the report, as shown in Listing 9-3.

Listing 9-3: A remark in the verification result

```
Stepname          Result      Remark
Text file output  2 - Remark  File specifications are not checked.
```

This result occurs if the output file does not yet exist at the time of validating the transformation. Spoon would like to check if it is possible to write to the output file, but it cannot complete that check until the file actually exists.

Working with Database Connections

RDBMS access is one of the basic functionalities of any data integration product. Pentaho Data Integration offers built-in support for more than 30 different database products. This includes all well-known RDBMS products, such as IBM DB2, Microsoft SQL Server, MySQL, Oracle and PostgreSQL, and many lesser known ones such as Kingbase, Gupta, MonetDB and others.

JDBC and ODBC Connectivity

Throughout the Pentaho BI Suite, database connectivity is based on JDBC, and Pentaho Data Integration is no exception. In addition to bare JDBC support, Spoon offers additional support for a large collection of RDBMS products, shielding the user from driver-specific details such as the exact format of the JDBC connect string, and presenting often-used options in a friendly manner. Even if there is no direct built-in support for a particular RDBMS it is still possible to connect to it using a generic JDBC connection, providing a JDBC-compliant driver is available for that particular RDBMS.

JDBC is quite a well-established standard, and most RDBMS vendors provide JDBC drivers for their RDBMS. But even if no JDBC driver is available, it is often still possible to connect using ODBC connectivity.

ODBC connectivity is provided through a JDBC-ODBC bridge, which is essentially a JDBC driver that can act as proxy for an ODBC-compliant driver. This enables access to any RDBMS for which there is an ODBC driver available. Because ODBC connectivity adds an extra layer, it should be avoided if possible. That said, it may be the only choice in case there simply does not exist a JDBC driver.

By default, Pentaho Data integration uses Sun's JDBC-ODBC bridge for ODBC connectivity. This driver is included in the standard edition of Sun's JDK. However, it is always possible to use any third-party JDBC-ODBC bridge. Any JDBC-compliant driver can always be utilized with a generic JDBC connection, and this includes any third-party JDBC-ODBC bridges.

Creating a Database Connection

Database Connections are defined inside transformations and jobs. To create a connection from the toolbar, click New and choose the Connection option. The Database Connection dialog appears.

NOTE There are a couple of ways to create a database connection besides using the toolbar.

To create a connection using the side pane, ensure the side pane is in View mode and bring up the context menu of the Connections folder beneath the node that represents the current transformation. In the context menu, choose New.

Connections can also be created from within the configuration dialogs of any database-related transformation steps. These steps contain a list box for choosing an existing connection, and you can use the New and Edit buttons to respectively create or modify the configured connection.

Finally, you can use the keyboard shortcut F3 to start a database connection wizard, which offers a step-by-step procedure to fill in database connection properties.

The left side of the Database Connection dialog contains a list of categories of types of things that can be configured. Actually specifying these properties is done in the fill-in form on the right side of the dialog. The contents of this form are synchronized according to the selected category in the left side of the dialog. The categories are:

- **General**—Basic properties such as the type of database, host name, port number, and the like are configured here. The connection's name must also be specified here.

- **Advanced**—This category can be used to specify a few options that affect how database identifiers are treated by any steps using this connection. It can also be used to specify some custom action whenever this connection is initialized.
- **Options**—The JDBC standard defines a common way to configure JDBC driver-specific properties. These can be specified here.
- **Pooling**—Connection pooling options.
- **Clustering**—These options can be used to create a group of connections that are used in a clustered environment and also with partitioning.

See Figure 9-14 for an example of the Database Connection dialog.

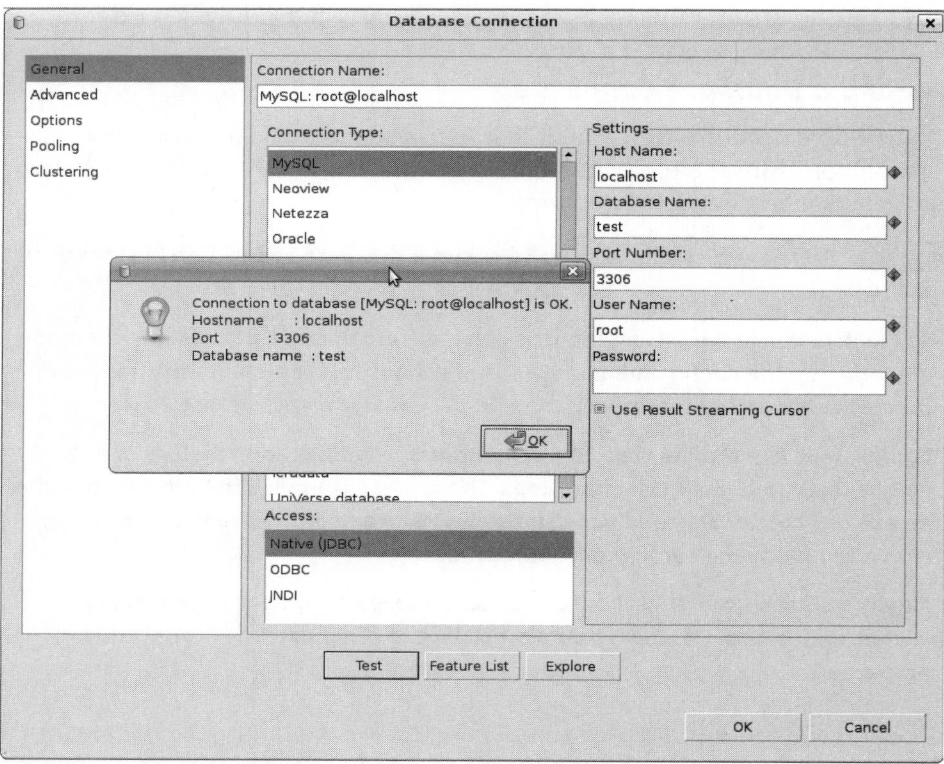

Figure 9-14: Typical configuration options for JDBC connections

By default, the General category is selected. The properties in this category are sufficient for all common use cases. We will describe the other categories later in this chapter. The following items are found on the left side of the general properties form, and must be filled in for every connection:

- **Connection Name**—In this textbox, a name must be specified that uniquely identifies this connection within the transformation. Steps that require a database connection refer to one using this connection name.
- **Connection Type**—This list is used to choose one of the many database products to connect to.
- **Access**—After you specify the Connection Type, this list provides the available connection methods for the specified RDBMS. In most cases, a JDBC and an ODBC option is shown. For all Connection Types that support JDBC, this list also contains a JNDI option. The JNDI option will be explained in Chapter 11.

The right side of the properties form displays a Settings frame that contains configuration options that are specific for the specified connection type and access method. JDBC connections to an RDBMS that is directly supported usually require the following properties:

- **Host Name**—The domain name or IP address of the computer where the database server resides. For a local database server, this should normally be localhost or 127.0.0.1, but you can also try leaving the field blank.
- **Port number**—The host's TCP/IP where the database server is listening for connection requests. In many cases, the value for the RDBMS's default port is automatically filled in.
- **User Name and Password**—The credentials for logging in to the database server.

For many RDBMSs, this is all that is required to establish a JDBC connection. Pentaho Data Integration uses this information to load the appropriate driver, and to generate the proper JDBC connect string to establish the connection.

For ODBC connections, properties such as host and credentials are already configured in the ODBC data source. Therefore, ODBC connections require only the name of an existing ODBC data source (DSN).

Sometimes, extra options are available for a particular connection type. For example, for an Oracle connection, the form also provides textboxes to specify which tablespaces to use for tables and indexes. Another example appears in Figure 9-14, which shows the Use Result Streaming Cursor checkbox right below the password textbox.

Testing Database Connections

After configuring the connection, it is a good idea to test it. The Test button in the bottom of the Database Connection dialog can be used to find out if it is at least possible for Pentaho Data Integration to connect to the specified database. After pressing the Test button, a message box pops up. If the test is successful, the message box should look like the one shown in Figure 9-14. If the test is not successful, the message box will display a large stacktrace, which can be used to analyze the problem.

Although the stacktrace can be daunting, problems usually boil down to spelling errors in the credentials or typos in the host name or port number. Usually, the top of the stacktrace displays a useful message providing a fair chance of solving the problem.

How Database Connections Are Used

Database connections are referred to by all transformation steps or job entries that need to work with a database. The configuration dialogs of these steps and job entries provide some means of specifying the connection, exploring its associated database or even creating a new one.

Database connections specified in Pentaho Data Integration are actually more aptly referred to as database *connection descriptors*. This is an important point because one such "connection" can very well translate to multiple, sometimes many, actual connections from the database server's point of view. For example, there may be many steps in one transformation that refer to the same connection descriptor. When such a transformation is executed, all these steps would normally open their own instance of the connection, each of which corresponds to one "real" connection at the RDMBS level. This means that by default, you cannot rely on state changes within one connection. A typical example are database transactions: you cannot simply commit or rollback a transformation, because each step opens its own connection, and each will use its own transaction which is completely independent from the transactions maintained by the connections opened by the other steps.

Now that we have identified the difference between Pentaho Data Integration connections and "real" database connections, we won't be picky in our terminology. We will use the term "connection" to refer to a connection descriptor object in Pentaho Data Integration, and we will make an explicit distinction only if it makes sense to do so for the topic at hand.

USING TRANSACTIONS

In principle, Pentaho Data Integration connections are just descriptors—recipes that may be used over and over by multiple steps to establish a real, physical connection to the database. This means that one transformation can be connected many times simultaneously using the same connection descriptor. Multiple connections allow work to be parallelized, which is good for performance.

Sometimes, multiple physical connections are not desirable. For example, having a separate physical connection for each step means that session state (such as transaction status) does not translate across multiple steps: each step, or rather, each physical connection, has its own state (and thus its own transaction).

If you really need to, you can ensure that each connection descriptor really corresponds to exactly one physical connection. To do so, check the Make the transformation database transactional checkbox in the Miscellaneous tab page of the Transformation Properties dialog. To open it, select Menu ➤ Transformation ➤ Settings.

A Database-Enabled "Hello, World!" Example

Now that you have learned how to create a database connection, you can enhance the ''Hello, World!'' transformation and add some database support. To keep things simple, you will simply add a step that writes the ''Hello'' messages to a database table in addition to the output file.

1. Open the ''Hello, World!'' example transformation if it's not already open. Choose Menu ➤ Transformation ➤ Settings to open the Transformation Properties dialog. In the Transformation Name text box, type `hello_world_transformation_with_db`. Then, choose Menu ➤ File ➤ Save As and save the transformation as `hello_world_transformation_with_db.ktr` in the same directory where the original transformation is stored.

NOTE **Strictly speaking, we could have created the copy of the transformation without editing the name in the transformation configuration dialog. That said, it is a good idea to do so because Spoon uses the name entered here as the display title for the transformation. By editing the name, you can avoid any confusion as to which transformation you are currently modifying.**

2. Create a database connection called Target Database. Choose SQLite as the connection type, and Native (JDBC) as the access method. In the

Settings frame, type `<path>/hello_world.sqlite` where `<path>` stands for the file system path where the transformation is stored. Specify `-1` for the Port. Leave the Host Name, User Name and Password fields blank. Click the Test button to verify the database connection works correctly.

NOTE We chose to create a SQLite database connection for this example. SQLite is a lightweight embedded relational database. The main reason for this choice is to allow a quick setup for those readers that do not have a database server set up. SQLite requires only the ability to create and modify a file.

If you do have a database server set up, you can try to connect to that instead.

Note that we used the forward slash to separate the path from the database filename `hello_world.sqlite`. Even though the forward slash is normally not used on Windows paths, this does, in fact, work.

3. Drag the Table Output step type from the Output category in the side pane and move it over the hop between the Add constants and Text file output steps. If positioned right, the line used to represent the hop will thicken, as shown in Figure 9-15, and you'll be asked if you want to split the hop. Drop the step there. This will insert the Table Output step between the Add constants and Text file output steps. The outgoing hop from the Add constants step is automatically connected to the input of the Table Output step, and the incoming hop of the Text file output step is likewise attached to the output of the Table Output step, thus splitting the original hop. Confirm that you want to split the hop, and optionally check the Don't ask again checkbox to avoid being prompted in the future.

NOTE The step's context menu contains the Detach option, which is the exact opposite of splitting hops: it detaches the step from its hops without discarding the hops themselves.

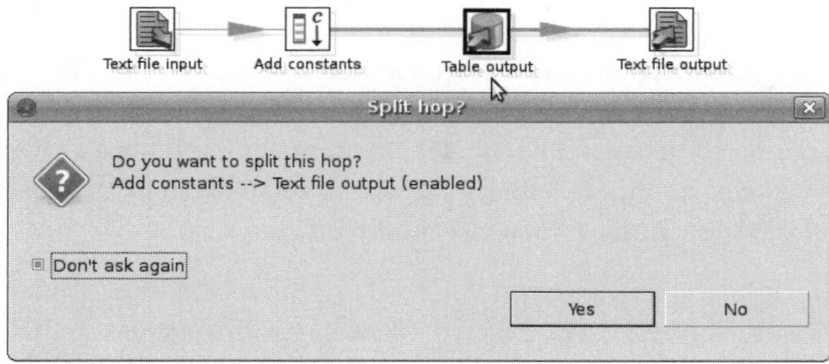

Figure 9-15: Splitting an existing hop

4. Open the configuration dialog of the new Table Output step. Note that the Connection list box is already set to the name of the database

connection. In the Target Table textbox, type `hello_world_output`. Then, press the SQL button in the bottom of the configuration dialog. The Simple SQL Editor opens containing an SQL `CREATE TABLE` statement, as shown in Figure 9-16, to create the `hello_world_output` table. Note that you can edit the generated statement to your heart's content. Press the Execute button to create the table. Another window opens, which should indicate the statement executed successfully. Close it, and also close the SQL editor window.

TIP You can also invoke the SQL editor directly from the connection's context menu, which can be brought up by right-clicking the connection entry in the sidebar.

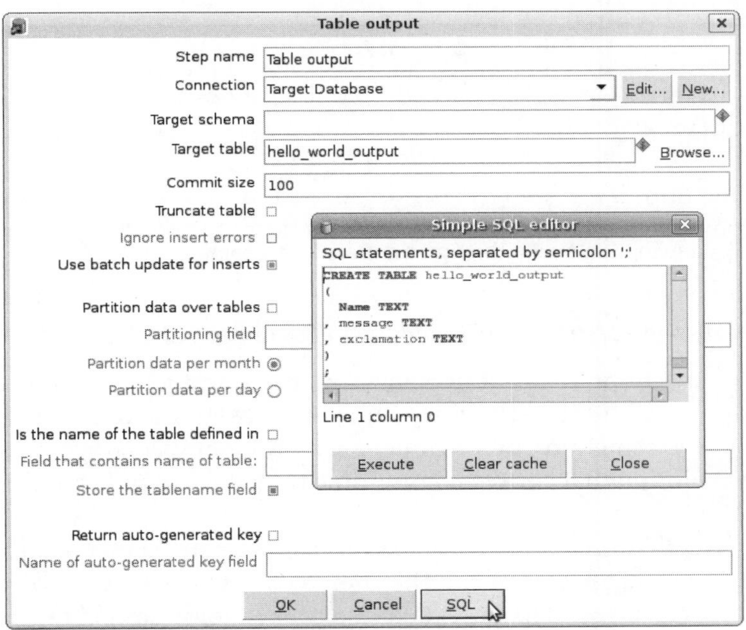

Figure 9-16: Generating CREATE TABLE statements

5. Run the transformation. Check the Execution Results Pane for any errors. The table should now contain rows.
6. In the sidebar, switch to the View mode and right-click the Target Database connection. From the context menu, choose the Explore option. This opens the Database Explorer window. In the tree view, open the Tables node and click the `hello_world_output` table to select it. Then, click the Preview first 100 rows button to examine the contents of the table. A preview window opens, and you should see something similar to what is shown in Figure 9-17.

TIP **The SQL Explorer can also be invoked from within the step configuration dialogs of all database related steps.**

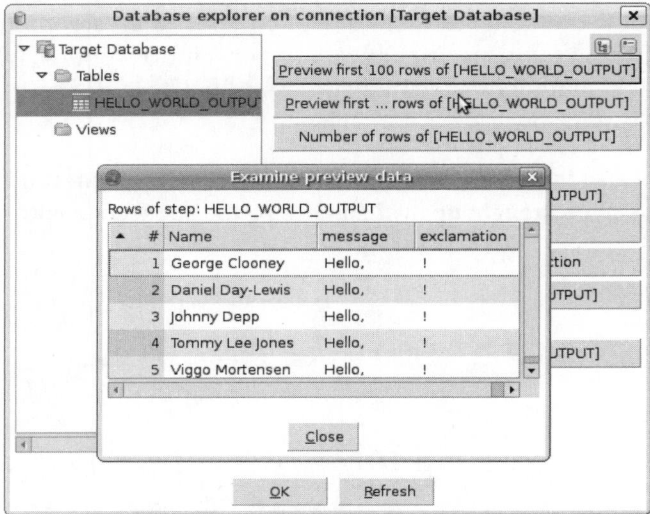

Figure 9-17: Viewing table data through the Database Explorer

Database Connection Configuration Management

Database connections are part of transformations and jobs. This means that a connection can be reused within, but not across transformations and/or jobs. This poses something of a maintenance problem when designing a data integration solution that consists of multiple transformations and jobs (which is almost always the case).

Fortunately, there is a way to cope with this. Transformations and jobs are associated with a *shared objects file*. The shared objects file is stored on the local machine, and can be used to store database connections (among other things). All objects in the shared objects file are automatically available for all jobs and transformations.

NOTE **By default, Spoon uses a single shared objects file per OS user. This file is called `shared.xml` and stored in the `.kettle` directory beneath the user's home directory. The shared objects file can be configured in the Misc tab page of the Transformation properties or Job properties dialog respectively.**

To store a database connection in the shared objects file, open the connection's context menu and choose the Share option. The connection name now appears in a bold font in the sidebar. At this point, you must save the transformation.

WARNING **Unfortunately, the act of sharing the connection is itself not regarded as a change. This means that if there are no unsaved changes before sharing the connection, immediately saving the transformation after sharing it will not store the connection to the shared objects file.**

You can see if Spoon thinks the job or transformation has changed. One way to find out is to look at the application title bar. If that displays the text "(changed)" after the document caption, changes will be saved. Another way is to check whether the label in the page's tab is shown in a bold font.

If you are using the database repository, the problem is moot. The repository stores database connections globally. All transformations and jobs in one repository can automatically access all connections, even if they were created for another job or transaction.

Generic Database Connections

If you want to connect to an RDBMS for which no built-in support is available in Spoon, you can try to establish a generic database connection. In this case, you must first obtain a JDBC driver for the RDBMS. These can usually be obtained from the database vendor, often at no extra cost.

JDBC drivers are usually distributed as `.jar` files (Java archives). Before you can use the `.jar` file (or rather, its contents), you must ensure Pentaho Data Integration can load it. This is achieved by copying the `.jar` file to the `libext/JDBC` directory, which is located beneath the installation directory of Pentaho Data Integration.

To create the connection, open the Database Connection dialog in the usual manner. Select the Generic database entry in the Connection Type list, and select Native (JDBC) in the Access list. The following properties are now available in the Settings frame:

- **Customer Connection URL**—This is where you specify the JDBC connect string (called an URL in JDBC terminology). The format of this URL is `jdbc:<driver specific string>`. Refer to the documentation of the particular driver you want to use to find out exactly what the format is of the driver-specific string.
- **Custom Driver Class Name**—The actual JDBC driver is a Java class. The fully qualified name (package name, followed by a dot, followed by the class name) of this class must be specified here. Like the format of the URL, this information is also driver-specific. You should look for it in the documentation supplied with the driver.
- **User Name and Password**—Credentials for logging on to the RDBMS. These data are not driver-specific. They correspond to an account on your database system.

Figure 9-18 depicts an example of a generic JDBC connection to LucidDB.

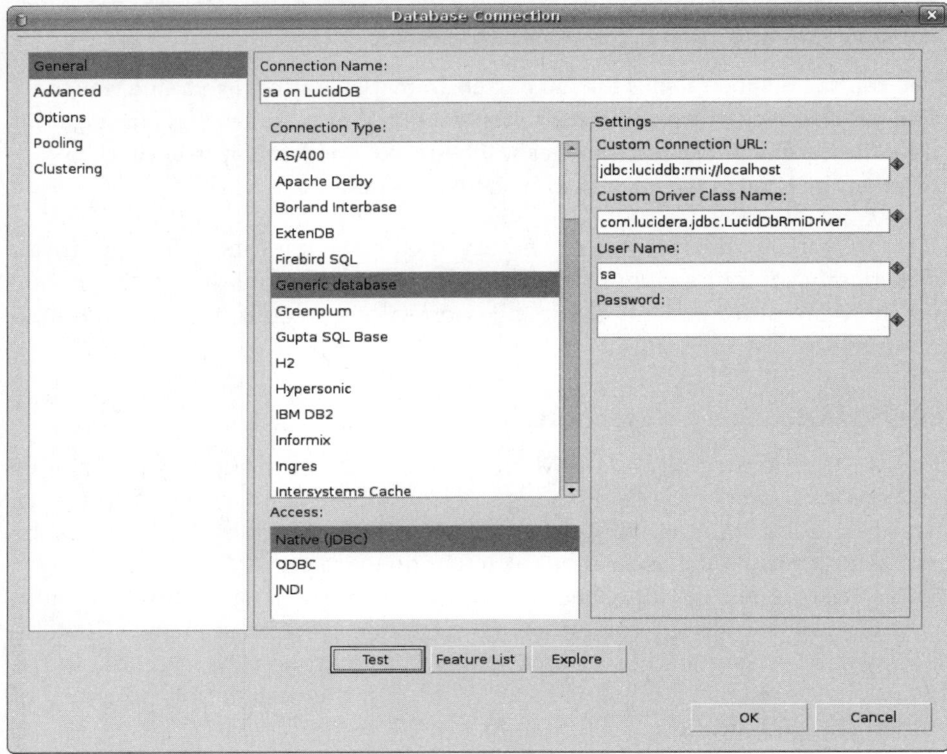

Figure 9-18: A generic JDBC connection to LucidDB

It is also possible to use ODBC as an access method for the generic database connection. This requires only the name of an already-configured ODBC data source.

Summary

In this chapter, you learned about the ETL processes and activities involved in filling the data warehouse. In addition, you learned about a number of supporting activities, such as change data capture, data validation, and decoding and renaming.

We also introduced Pentaho Data Integration tool, also known as Kettle. You learned that PDI consists of a data integration engine that can execute jobs and transformations. In addition, PDI features a number of tools and utilities to create and execute jobs and transformations.

Transformations are data-oriented and consist of steps, which are operated on record streams. Transformation steps can be connected through hops, allowing records to stream from one step to the other. Jobs are procedural in nature, and consist of Job entries, which are sequentially executed tasks. Typically, jobs contain transformations, among other types of steps.

You also learned the basics of using Spoon, which is the PDI tool to create jobs and transformations. You built your first "Hello, World!" transformation in Spoon. After that, you learned about database connections, and extended the "Hello World!" transformation to store the result in a database.

You should now have a reasonable foundation for Chapter 10, in which you will learn how to use this knowledge and skills to fill the World Class Movies data warehouse.

CHAPTER

10

Designing Pentaho Data Integration Solutions

In the previous chapter, we introduced a set of tools and utilities that make up Pentaho Data Integration (PDI). We gave some extra attention to the data integration design tool Spoon, and provided two walkthroughs to familiarize the reader with its user interface. In this chapter, you learn how to put these skills to use to build the transformations and jobs that are used to fill the World Class Movies data warehouse.

This chapter offers a hands-on approach, focusing on common problems and practical solutions. Although we use the World Class Movies data warehouse as an example, we believe most of the problems encountered are common to most data warehouses. The methods used in this chapter are by no means the only possible solution. Rather we have chosen a number of approaches to acquaint you with the most often needed features of Pentaho Data Integration.

The best way to read this chapter is to download all PDI transformations and jobs from this book's website at `www.wiley.com/go/pentahosolutions` so you can easily open them, check any details, run a preview, or more.

NOTE In addition to the samples and exercises discussed in this chapter, you are encouraged to take a look at the samples included with PDI. You can find them in the `samples` directory which is located in the PDI home directory. The `samples` directory itself contains a `jobs` and a `transformations` subdirectory containing sample jobs and transformations. The `samples` directory also contains a `mapping` directory which illustrates the usage of subtransformations.

In addition to these samples, you should also take a look at the Pentaho Data Integration documentation. The Step reference at `wiki.pentaho.com/display/EAI/Pentaho+Data+Integration+Steps` and the Job entry reference at

`wiki.pentaho.com/display/EAI/Pentaho+Data+Integration+Job +Entries` are especially great resources to obtain new ideas for building PDI solutions.

Generating Dimension Table Data

Almost every data warehouse design contains a few dimension tables that can, to a large extent, be populated with generated data. A well-known example is the date dimension. Also well known but less commonly used are the time and demography dimensions.

In this section, we first briefly discuss the practice of using database stored procedures to load these types of dimension tables. We then quickly move on and explain how to go about this using Pentaho Data Integration for this task. This provides a great opportunity to get better acquainted with Spoon and a few of its basic transformation steps. This will lay an important foundation for the subsequent sections.

Using Stored Procedures

A common method to generate data for a date dimension is to create a database stored procedure that uses the date functions of the target RDBMS.

NOTE **One drawback to using a database stored procedure is that it needs to be written over and over for each different target RDBMS, as there are usually syntactic differences with regard to both the stored procedure language and the built-in date and time functions. For this reason (and others explained later in this chapter), we actually do not recommend this approach, but for the sake of completeness we include this topic anyway.**

By way of example, a simple MySQL stored procedure to load a date dimension is shown in Listing 10-1. In this case, the built-in function `DATE_FORMAT` (shown in bold) is used to generate multiple representations of the date value.

Listing 10-1: A simple (partial) MySQL stored procedure to load a date dimension

```
CREATE PROCEDURE p_load_dim_date (
    p_from_date DATE
,   p_to_date   DATE
)
BEGIN
    DECLARE v_date DATE DEFAULT p_from_date;
    WHILE v_date < p_to_date DO
        INSERT INTO dim_date(
            date_key
        ,   date
```

```
        ,   date_short
        ,   ...
        ) VALUES (
            v_date + 0
        ,   v_date
        ,   DATE_FORMAT(v_date, '%y-%c-%d')
        ,   ...
        );
        SET v_date := v_date + INTERVAL 1 DAY;
    END WHILE;
END;
```

Loading a Simple Date Dimension

All compatibility problems caused by using database stored procedures can be overcome by simply avoiding them. This may sound easier than it really is, but for loading a date dimension the process is actually quite straightforward and easy to implement directly in Pentaho Data Integration.

To avoid unnecessary complexity, we will first use a slightly simplified version of the date dimension table. Its `CREATE TABLE` statement is shown in Listing 10-2. As you can see, this date dimension table simply provides a number of different formats for a date.

Listing 10-2: CREATE TABLE statement for a simplified date dimension table

```
CREATE TABLE dim_date (
  date_key                INTEGER      NOT NULL,
  date_value              DATE         NOT NULL,
  date_short              VARCHAR(12) NOT NULL,
  date_medium             VARCHAR(16) NOT NULL,
  date_long               VARCHAR(24) NOT NULL,
  date_full               VARCHAR(32) NOT NULL,
  day_in_week             SMALLINT     NOT NULL,
  day_in_year             SMALLINT     NOT NULL,
  day_in_month            SMALLINT     NOT NULL,
  is_first_day_in_month   VARCHAR(10) NOT NULL,
  is_last_day_in_month    VARCHAR(10) NOT NULL,
  day_abbreviation        CHAR(3)      NOT NULL,
  day_name                VARCHAR(12) NOT NULL,
  week_in_year            SMALLINT     NOT NULL,
  week_in_month           SMALLINT     NOT NULL,
  is_first_day_in_week    VARCHAR(10) NOT NULL,
  is_last_day_in_week     VARCHAR(10) NOT NULL,
  is_weekend              VARCHAR(3)   NOT NULL,
  month_number            SMALLINT     NOT NULL,
  month_abbreviation      CHAR(3)      NOT NULL,
  month_name              VARCHAR(12) NOT NULL,
  year2                   CHAR(2)      NOT NULL,
```

```
  year4                      CHAR(4)      NOT NULL,
  quarter_name               CHAR(2)      NOT NULL,
  quarter_number             SMALLINT     NOT NULL,
  year_quarter               CHAR(7)      NOT NULL,
  year_month_number          CHAR(7)      NOT NULL,
  year_month_abbreviation CHAR(8)         NOT NULL,
  PRIMARY KEY (date_key),
  UNIQUE KEY (date_value)
);
```

Figure 10-1 shows such a simple transformation. The transformation is divided into four distinct parts: Prepare, Input, Transformation and Output, and in Figure 10-1 you can see a few notes to indicate that.

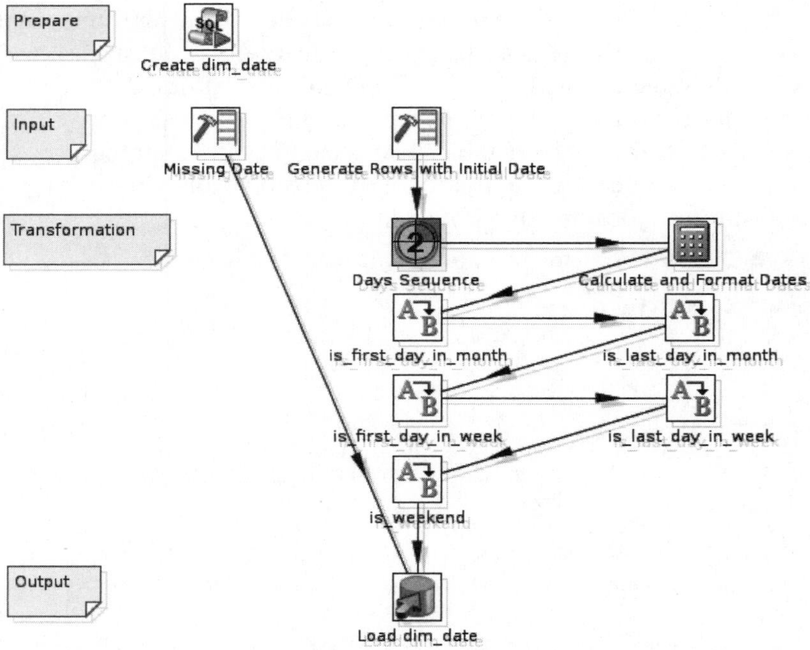

Figure 10-1: A simple transformation to load a date dimension table

NOTE **You can place notes anywhere on the transformation or job canvas. Although notes are not a substitute for documentation, they are a convenient means to clarify the intent of the transformation.**

To add a note, right-click on the canvas to open the context menu. Choose New Note in the context menu. A dialog box appears in which you can enter the text for your note. When done editing, click OK to close the dialog and place the note on

the canvas. Once the note is placed on the canvas, you can use the mouse to drag it to a new location. To edit an existing note, double-click it. To remove it, right-click on the note and choose Delete note from the context menu.

Here's a summary of what happens in this transformation:

1. Create dim_date: Issues the necessary SQL statements to the target database to create the `dim_date` dimension table.
2. Missing Date: Generates one row that represents a special date that is used to represent all missing or inapplicable dates.
3. Generate Rows with Initial Date: Generates one row per calendar day. The rows have one field that specifies the initial date.
4. Days Sequence: Adds an incrementing integer field to the rows generated by the previous step.
5. Calculate and Format Dates: The incrementing integer is added to the initial date, resulting in a sequence of calendar days.
6. is_first_day_in_month, is_last_day_in_month, is_first_day_in_week, is_last_day_in_week and is_weekend: These steps map numerical data to the text that is to be stored in the dimension table.
7. Load dim_date: The rows from the input stream are inserted into the `dim_date` table.

The following sections examine the transformation steps and their configuration in more detail.

CREATE TABLE dim_date: Using the Execute SQL Script Step

In Figure 10-1, the Create dim_date step is of the type *Execute SQL script*. This step type can be found in the Scripting category; its icon (shown at the top of Figure 10-1) appears as a scroll with a SQL label.

The step works by executing the SQL statements specified in the script property against the specified connection. You can use the script property to specify one or multiple SQL statements, separated by semicolons. There is no restriction with regard to the form or type of the SQL statements that make up the script, as long as they are syntactically valid according to the RDBMS underlying the specified connection. Steps of the Execute SQL type are primarily useful for executing DDL statements.

Figure 10-2 shows how the step was configured for the sample transformation shown in Figure 10-1. As you can see in the figure, the script contains two statements: a `DROP TABLE` statement to drop the table in case it already exists and a `CREATE TABLE` statement to define the table. The rationale behind dropping and then (re-)creating the table is that this makes it easier to add or remove columns.

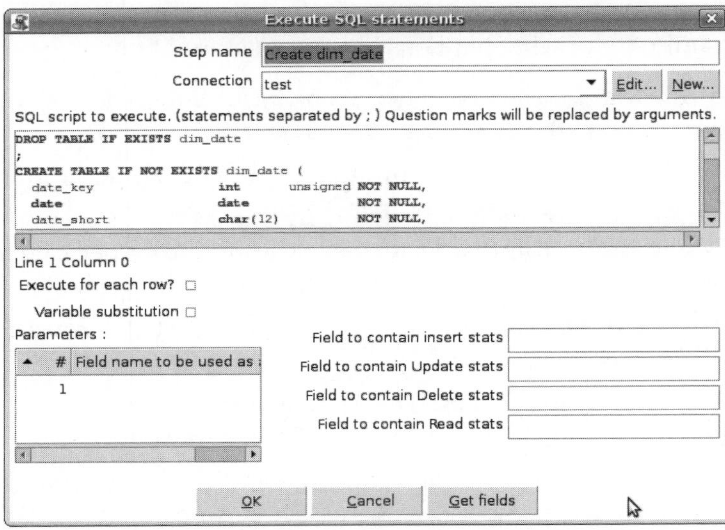

Figure 10-2: Configuring the Execute SQL step to execute multiple SQL statements

The Execute SQL script step is a bit of an odd duck when compared to other types of transformation steps because it is not particularly data-oriented. By default, the steps of this type execute only once before any of the other steps are executed.

NOTE **When running a transformation, all steps are first initialized. This is called the *initialization phase*. Preparatory actions like opening files and database connections, but also substituting variables (see Chapter 11 for more information about variables) and preparing database statements are typically executed in the initialization phase. After all steps have been initialized, the steps enter the running phase and start processing rows.**

By default, the Execute SQL step executes SQL statements just once in the initialization phase. For this reason, the sample transformation shown in Figure 10-1 does not need any hop to connect it to the remainder of the transformation: the SQL will be executed before the other steps in the transformation start processing rows anyway. It is possible to drive SQL execution using data from an input stream. A scenario like this is discussed in detail later on in this chapter in the section "Staging Lookup Values".

Note that steps enter the initialization phase asynchronously, and in no particular order. This means that you must ensure that the work done in the initialization phase of a particular step does not rely on completion of the initialization phase

of another step. For example, the `DROP` and `CREATE` statements in the Create dim_date step in Figure 10-1 cannot each be executed separately in their own Execute SQL steps, because there would be no guarantee that the `DROP` statement would be executed prior to the `CREATE` statement.

Missing Date and Generate Rows with Initial Date: The Generate Rows Step

In Figure 10-1, the steps Missing Date and Generate Rows with Initial Date are of the *Generate Rows* step type. This type is found in the Input category and its icon appears as a hammer next to a ladder (see the Input row of Figure 10-1).

Unsurprisingly, the purpose of this step is to generate rows. Steps of this type are typically configured by setting a value for the Limit property to specify the number of rows to generate. Optionally, a number of fields having constant values can be specified. Figure 10-3 shows how the Generate Rows with Initial Date step from the transformation shown in Figure 10-1 was configured.

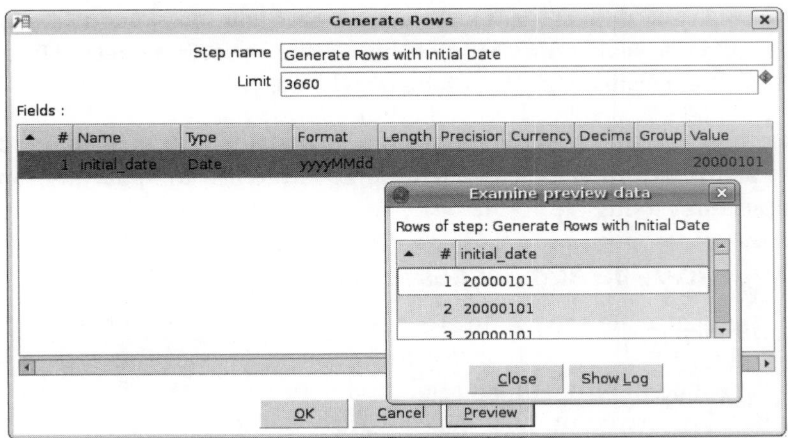

Figure 10-3: Configuring the Generate Rows step to get 10 years worth of days

For the Generate Rows with Initial Date step, we specified a Limit of 3660 (which is slightly more than 10 years worth of days). In the Fields grid, we specified a single field called `initial_date`, which serves as the starting date for the date dimension. Note that we specified the `Date` as Type, the Value `20000101`, and the Format `yyyyMMdd`. The value represents the calendar date of January 1, 2000. The Type and Format are necessary to explain to Spoon how to interpret this date. You will encounter many more examples of date formatting in the subsection ''The Select Values Step'' later on in this section.

For the Missing Date step, we specified a Limit of 1 (one). Rather than specifying only a field for the initial date, we added fields that represent a missing or inapplicable date. For the `date_value` and `date_key` fields, we used the values `0001-01-01` and `10101` respectively. When you load your fact tables, you should remember to use this key for any `NULL` dates. For the textual fields of this special date we used the label `Not Applicable`, `N/A`, or `NA` depending on the available space.

TIP **Typing all the fields for the Missing Date step can be a bit tedious. You can save yourself some time and effort by first creating the generic part of the transformation and then adding the steps to insert these special rows.**

Once you have set up the final Load dim_date target step, you can right-click on it and choose the Show input fields option from the context menu. A grid will appear with the fields of input stream. Click the first row in the grid to select it, and then select all rows using the Ctrl+A keyboard shortcut. Next, copy the grid to the clipboard using Ctrl+C. You can then paste that in the Fields grid of the desired Generate Rows step using Ctrl+V.

This method will at least help you fill in the field names and types. You may need to remove some pasted data from the remaining columns and you still need to type the field values. However, it will generally save you some time and effort, and more importantly, avoid errors because this method ensures the record layout of the output stream will match that of the target step.

After configuring the Generate Rows step, you can click the Preview button to view a sample of the rows that will be generated in the Examine preview data dialog (refer to Figure 10-3).

Days Sequence: The Add Sequence Step

The Days Sequence step in Figure 10-1 is of the *Add sequence* type. This type of step can be found in the Transform category. Steps of this type work by adding a new incrementing integer field to the rows from the input stream. Its icon appears as a circled number 2 (see Figure 10-1).

In the sample transformation, the purpose of this field is to generate the data to calculate a sequence of calendar dates. (The actual calculation is discussed in the next subsection.) The Add sequence step can be configured to work in either of the following two ways:

- To draw the next value from a database sequence. Some RDBMSs (such as Oracle and PostgreSQL) offer a special sequence schema object that is designed especially for providing surrogate key values, which can be used by the Add Sequence step.
- To increment a counter maintained by the transformation engine.

Our usage of the Add sequence type, the Days Sequence step, uses the latter option. The configuration of the Days Sequence step is shown in Figure 10-4.

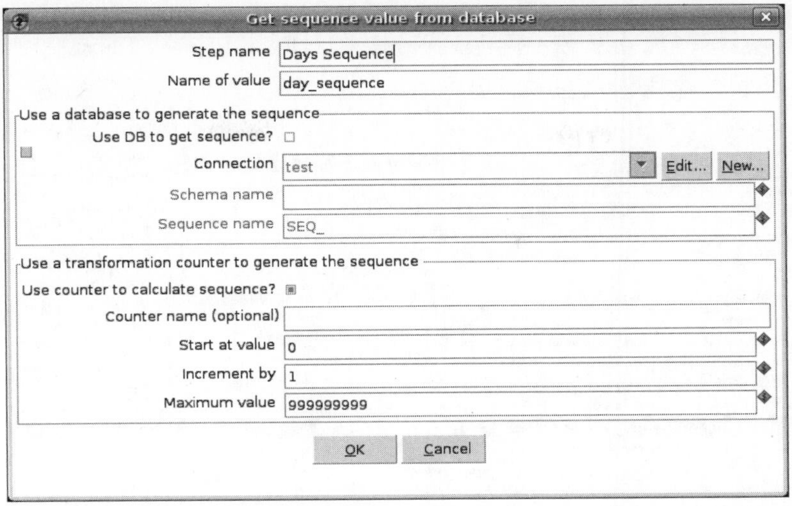

Figure 10-4: Configuration of the Days Sequence step

In the Name of value property, the name `day_sequence` is provided for the field that will hold the sequence number. The Use counter to generate the sequence checkbox is selected to use a counter maintained by the transformation engine. In the sample transformation, the optional Counter name property is left blank. If required, this can be filled in to force multiple Add sequence steps to draw from one and the same counter. For the Start at value, the value `0` (zero) was explicitly specified (instead of the default of one) to ensure that the initial date specified in the Generate Rows step is indeed the starting date for the date dimension.

Calculate and Format Dates: The Calculator Step

In Figure 10-1, the Calculate and Format Dates step uses a *Calculator* step to generate all the date representations to load the date dimension. The Calculator step is found in the Transformation category. Unsurprisingly its icon depicts a hand-held calculator.

The Calculator step allows you to choose from a number of predefined calculations. Depending on the type of calculation, it uses up to three fields as arguments, generating one new field for the result, which is added to the output stream. The argument fields can be taken from the input stream, but also from the output fields generated in the same calculator step, enabling you to stack calculations on top of each other.

In the sample transformation, the Calculator step is configured as shown in Figure 10-5.

In the Fields grid, a number of expressions are set up to compute various representations of the calendar date.

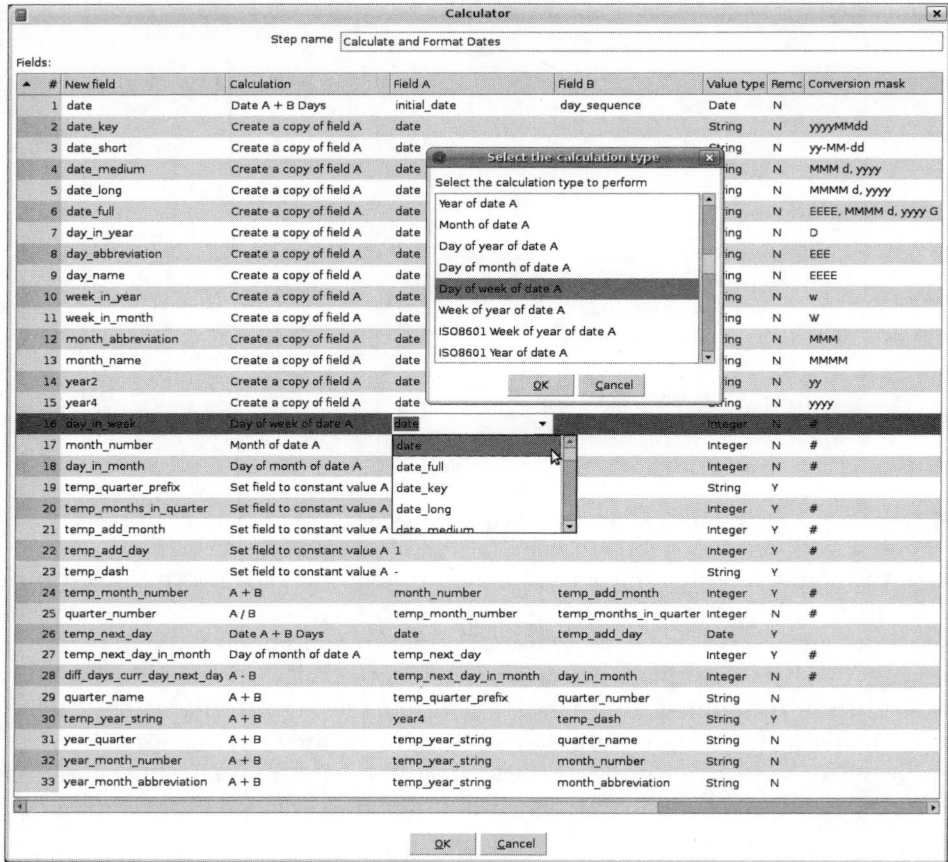

Figure 10-5: Using the Calculator step to compute calendar days

Calculation #1 uses the expression `Date A + B Days` to add the value of the `day_sequence` field generated by the Add Sequence step to the `initial_date` field that was specified in the Generate Rows step. This yields a new field called `date`, which represents the calendar date. This `date` field is used by the following calculations to generate alternate date representations. For completeness, Listing 10-3 shows how this calculation was configured.

Listing 10-3: Adding the sequence to the initial date to obtain calendar days

```
New field   Calculation       Field A          Field B          Type
---------------------------------------------------------------------
date_value  Date A + B Days   initial_date     day_sequence     Date
```

Calculations #2 through #15 do not actually perform a proper calculation. Rather, these use the `Create a copy of field A` expression to duplicate the `date_value` field that is the result of calculation #1 and apply a particular format to convert it to a String value. This yields a number of alternative representations of the calendar date, which are all given a name according to the target column name. The format string is entered into the Conversion mask column of the Fields grid. For date-to-string conversions, the mask should be specified using the notation also used for the `java.text.SimpleDateformat` Java class. The configuration of these fields is shown in detail in Listing 10-4.

Listing 10-4: Using format strings to format dates

```
New field                Calculation                  Fld A        Conversion mask
----------------------------------------------------------------------------------
date_key           Create a copy of field A  date_value  yyyyMMdd
date_short         Create a copy of field A  date_value  yy-MM-dd
date_medium        Create a copy of field A  date_value  MMM d, yyyy
date_long          Create a copy of field A  date_value  MMMM d, yyyy
date_full          Create a copy of field A  date_value  EEEE, MMMM d, yyyy G
day_in_year        Create a copy of field A  date_value  D
day_abbreviation   Create a copy of field A  date_value  EEE
day_name           Create a copy of field A  date_value  EEEE
week_in_year       Create a copy of field A  date_value  w
week_in_month      Create a copy of field A  date_value  W
month_abbreviation Create a copy of field A  date_value  MMM
month_name         Create a copy of field A  date_value  MMMM
year2              Create a copy of field A  date_value  yy
year4              Create a copy of field A  date_value  yyyy
```

TIP For more information on notation of the date format masks, take a look at `http://java.sun.com/j2se/1.5.0/docs/api/java/text/SimpleDateFormat.html`.

Calculation #16 uses the `Day of week of Date A` expression to calculate an integer value corresponding to the weekday to generate the values for the `day_in_week` column of the date dimension table. To ensure the result is formatted as an integer, we set the Conversion mask to the hash symbol (`#`). It would make sense to compute this by simply applying an appropriate format string, just as we did for expressions #2 through #16. Unfortunately, the appropriate formatting pattern string does not seem to exist, which is why we use a calculation to do the job.

Calculation #17 calculates the `month_number` field by using the expression `Month of Date A` on the `date` field. Although this value could have been obtained by converting to the String type and applying the format string `M`, the `Month of Date A` expression retrieves the value as an integer expression, which allows us to use it to calculate the quarter number in calculations #24 and #25. It would be nice to calculate quarters, too, using a format string but just like the `day_in_week` number, this is not supported.

Calculation #18 calculates the `day_in_month` field using the expression `Day of month of date A`. Like calculation #17, we could have done this by simply converting to String and applying the `d` format string, but by using this expression we obtain the value as an Integer, which allows us to (indirectly) find out if the current day happens to be the last day of the month in calculations #26 through #28.

The configuration of calculations #16, #17, and #18 is shown in Listing 10-5.

Listing 10-5: Obtaining the day of the week and month number using predefined calculations

```
New field      Calculation              Field A     Type     Conversion mask
--------------------------------------------------------------------------
day_in_week    Day of week of date A    date_value  Integer  #
month_number   Month of date A          date_value  Integer  #
day_in_month   Day of month of date A   date_value  Integer  #
```

The "calculations" #19 through #23 use the `Set field to constant value A` expression to define a number of constant values that are used in the final few calculations. Because we only need these calculations temporarily, we set the `Remove` property to `Y`, which prevents the result fields of these calculations to be added to the output stream. You can review the configuration of these calculations in Listing 10-6.

Listing 10-6: Defining constants in the Calculator step

```
New field                Calculation                   Fld A  Type     Rmv
---------------------------------------------------------------------------
temp_quarter_prefix      Set field to constant value A  Q     String   Y
temp_months_in_quarter   Set field to constant value A  3     Integer  Y
temp_add_month           Set field to constant value A  2     Integer  Y
temp_dash                Set field to constant value A  -     String   Y
```

Calculations #24 and #25 together make up the calculation of the quarter number. Calculation #25 does the actual calculation by performing an Integer division of the `temp_month_number` by `temp_months_in_quarter`. The `temp_month_number` field was obtained by adding the constant 2 to the `month_number`. So, in January, this will evaluate to `(1 + 2) / 3 = 1`, in February this will be `(2+2) / 3 = 1`, and so on until April where we get `(4+2) / 3 = 2` and so on. Note that there is no separate predefined calculation for whole number division. Whole number division is performed automatically when applying the `A / B` expression on integer arguments and setting the result type also to integer. The configuration of calculations #24 and #25 is shown in detail in Listing 10-7.

Listing 10-7: Calculating the quarter number using integer division

```
New field          Calculation  Field A            Field B
-----------------------------------------------------------------------
temp_month_number  A + B        month_number       temp_add_month
quarter_number     A / B        temp_month_number  temp_months_in_quarter
```

Calculations #26 through #28 make up a calculation that can be used to see if the current value of the `date` field happens to be the last day of the month. This is done by subtracting the value of the day in month of the current date from that of the following day. If the two consecutive days happen to be in the same month, the difference will be 1 (one). If the next day happens to lie within the next month, the result will be a negative number between 27 (1–28) and 30 (1–31). Calculation #26 calculates the next day by adding the constant 1 to the value of the `date` field. In calculation #27, the day in month of that next day is computed, and finally, in calculation #28, the difference is calculated. The results of calculations #26 and #27 are intermediate and are discarded by specifying `Remove = Y`. The final result is kept in the `diff_days_curr_day_next_day` field, which will used outside this step to compute the actual column value. The configuration of these calculations is shown in detail in Listing 10-8.

Listing 10-8: Calculating the last day in the month

```
New field           Calculation              Field A          Field B
-----------------------------------------------------------------------
next_day            Date A + B Days          date_value       add_day
next_day_in_month   Day of month of date A   next_day
diff_days           A - B next_day_in_month  day_in_month
```

The calculations #29 through #33 use the `A + B` expression to concatenate a few of the previously computed strings to gain representations for `quarter_name`, `year_quarter`, `year_month_number`, and `year_month_abbreviation`. As with integer division, there is no separate string concatenation operator, but applying the expression `A + B` to fields of the String data type has exactly that effect. The details of the final calculations #23 through #29 are shown in Listing 10-9.

Listing 10-9: Calculating the quarter and concatenating strings

```
New field                Calc.   Field A               Field B
------------------------------------------------------------------------
quarter_name             A + B   temp_quarter_prefix   quarter_number
temp_year_string         A + B   year4                 temp_dash
year_quarter             A + B   temp_year_string      quarter_name
year_month_number        A + B   temp_year_string      month_number
year_month_abbreviation  A + B   temp_year_string      month_number
```

The Value Mapper Step

The following steps are all based on the *Value Mapper* step type:

- is_first_day_in_month
- is_last_day_in_month

- is_first_day_in_week
- is_last_day_in_week
- is_weekend

The Value Mapper step can be found in the Transformation category. Its icon shows an arrow connecting the letters A and B (refer to Figure 10-1).

The Value Mapper step translates values from a field in the input streams to the values specified in a list. The translation value can either be used to replace the original value from the field in the input stream or written to a new field, which is added to the input stream. Optionally, a default value can be specified in case none of the values in the list matches the value from the input stream. A very simple example is shown in Figure 10-6, which depicts the configuration of the step labeled is_first_day_in_month.

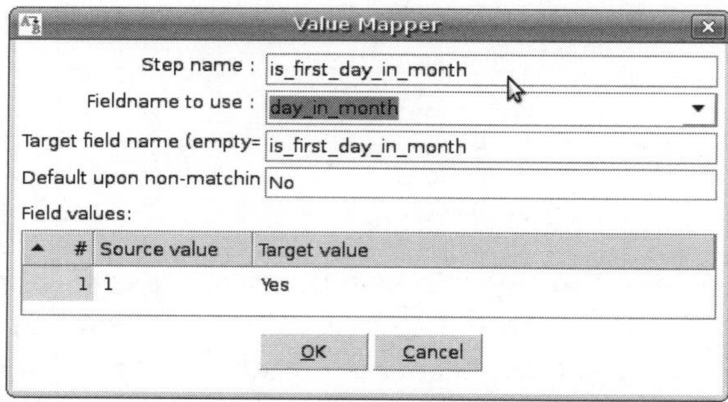

Figure 10-6: Mapping integer data to text labels with the Value Mapper step

As shown in Figure 10-6, this step takes the value from the `day_in_month` field from the input stream and creates a new `is_first_day_in_month` field to hold the translated values. There is only one value to map: Only when the `day_in_month` field happens to have the value 1 (one) should the string `Yes` be returned. By specifying the value `No` in the Default upon non-matching property, the value `No` will be returned in any other case.

The configuration of the is_first_day_in_week and is_last_day_in_week steps is entirely analogous to that of the is_first_day_in_month step. Both these steps use the `day_in_week` field from the input stream and return the value `Yes` in case a specific value (1 and 7 for is_first_day_in_week and is_last_day_in_week respectively) is matched, and `No` in any other case. Again, both steps write the value to a new field of the output stream (`is_first_day_in_week` and `is_last_day_in_week` respectively).

The configuration of the is_weekend step is almost exactly the same. This step translates the values from the `day_in_week` field from the input stream to a new `is_weekend` field in the output stream, but this time, two values are mapped: both values 1 and 7 are mapped to `Yes`, and again `No` is returned by default.

Load dim_date: The Table Output Step

The final step in the transformation shown in Figure 10-1 is labeled Load dim_date and based on the *Table Output* step. This step works by inserting the records from the input stream into a database table. You can find the Table Output in the Output category. Its icon is an arrow pointing at a green drum cylinder (see Figure 10-1).

In the Load dim_date step, the Table Output step is used to insert the data created in this transformation into the `dim_date` table that was created in the very first step of the transformation, the Execute SQL step. You already encountered the Table Output step in our database transformation walk-through from the previous chapter. There, we didn't bother configuring the mapping between the fields from the input stream and the table columns because the fields in the input stream already matched the table columns. In this transformation, things are a bit different. The input stream still contains a few fields that do not correspond to any table columns, such as `initial_date`, `day_sequence`, and `diff_days_curr_day_next_day`. Another thing is that the `date` field from the input stream should be mapped to the `date_value` column of the `dim_date` table. Figure 10-7 shows part of the configuration.

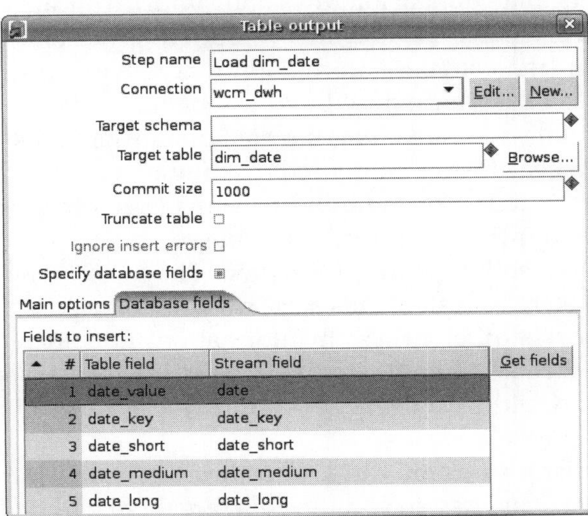

Figure 10-7: Mapping specific columns from the input stream to table columns

In order to map fields to columns, you first have to select the Specify database fields checkbox. You can then activate the Database fields tab page and use the Get fields page to fill the grid with all the fields present in the input stream. You can then select and remove the fields you don't need, and type the matching column name in the Table field column as required.

More Advanced Date Dimension Features

Now that you've learned how to fill a simple date dimension, you can extend the design and add more steps to customize the date dimension to your liking. The date dimension design from Chapter 8 mentions a couple of possible enhancements, such as including ISO year and week numbers, special date fields, and calculations to facilitate comparing the current year with the previous year, and to support different locales and languages.

ISO Week and Year

The Calculator step (shown in Figure 10-5) provides the `ISO8601 Week of Date A` and `ISO8601 Year of Date A` expressions. Using these, it is trivial to extend the date dimension table with ISO week and year attributes.

Current and Last Year Indicators

Maintaining the current and last year indicators discussed in Chapter 8 involves regularly updating the date dimension table. Alternatively, you can incorporate the necessary extra calculations directly in the transformation that generates the date dimension rows and simply truncate and then refresh the date dimension table in its entirety. Updating the table makes sense if your date dimension contains information that is hard to generate (such as holidays). In this case, you would build a separate transformation to do the updates. Truncating and refreshing the date dimension in its entirety is more straightforward, because you only need to maintain one transformation.

Calculating the values for the indicators involves a few extra steps. First, you need a step to introduce the current date so you can compare that to the dates being generated by the transformation. The easiest way to do that is by adding a Get System Info step. This step lets you define new fields. It offers a list box with a host of different system information items, including the current date. In this particular case, the item you need is called system date (fixed), which will fill the field with the system date/time as determined in the step's initialization phase.

Using a Calculator step, you can dissect the system date into date parts like year, month, week, and day so you can compare them with the corresponding fields in the date dimension table. Likewise, you can use the Calculator step to calculate the previous year, month and week.

To finally calculate the values for the flag fields you can use the Formula step, found in the Scripting category. The Formula step lets you use formulas with a syntax similar to that used in spreadsheet programs like Microsoft

Excel or OpenOffice.org's Calc. For example, to calculate the value of the `current_year` column, you would create a new field in the Formula step called `current_year` and specify a formula like this:

```
IF([year4]=[current_year_number];1;0)
```

Note that the formula is not preceded by an equals sign as would be the case in spreadsheet programs. In this example, `year4` is the `year4` column from the `dim_date` table, and `current_year_number` is the year part of the system date as calculated by the preceding calculator step. Note that you need to enclose fields in square brackets. `IF()` is one of the built-in functions provided by the Formula step. This function takes three arguments: first a Boolean expression (in our case, the year comparison); second, the value to return if the first argument is true; and finally, the value to return if the first argument is false. Note that function arguments are separated using semi-colons.

Using this technique, you can add as many fields as you like to calculate the flags.

Internationalization and Locale Support

Java offers built-in locale support. Because PDI is programmed in Java, it is relatively easy to tap into the Java locale system and use it to format dates and numbers in a locale-dependent manner. We describe the method here in a nutshell.

PDI offers the Modified Javascript Value step type in the scripting category. Using this type of step, you can use JavaScript to process dates generated by your transformation. The Modified Javascript Value step is based on the Mozilla Rhino JavaScript engine, which allows you to instantiate and access Java objects. In this manner, you can create a `java.util.Locale` object for the desired locale and use that to format dates using the `java.text.SimpleDateFormat`.

The procedure is described in detail in `http://rpbouman.blogspot.com/2007/04/kettle-tip-using-java-locales-for-date.html`.

Loading a Simple Time Dimension

The time dimension appears in the Customer and Orders star schemas of the World Class Movies data warehouse. Just like the date dimension, most of the data of the time dimension can be generated, either with a database stored procedure or a Pentaho Data Integration transformation. We already discussed the disadvantage of using database stored procedures for this kind of work. For this reason, we prefer to do this using a PDI transformation.

A simple transformation to load the `dim_time` table in the `wcm_dwh` database is shown in Figure 10-8.

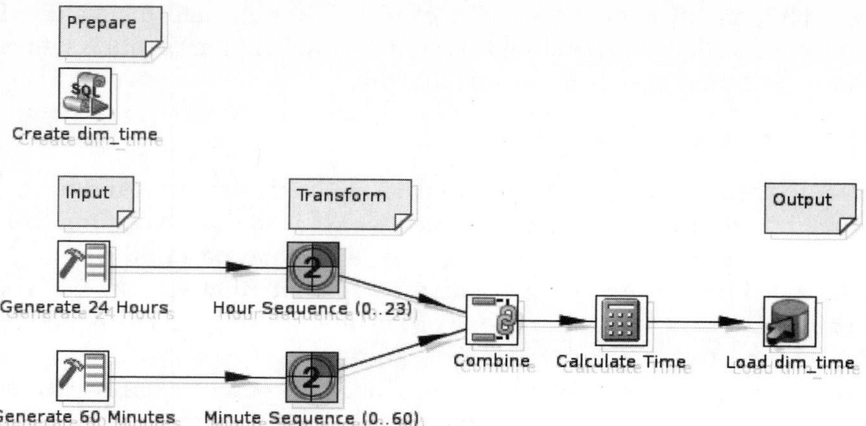

Figure 10-8: A simple transformation to load the time dimension

Here's a summary of the workings of this transformation:

1. Create dim_time: This is an Execute SQL script step to create the target time dimension table.
2. Generate 24 Hours and Generate 60 Minutes: These are both Generate Rows steps that create the rows that make up the hours and minutes of the time dimension. The Limit of the Generate 24 Hours step is set to 24 because there are 24 hours per day. Similarly, the Limit of the Generate 60 Minutes step is set to 60 because there are 60 minutes per hour.
3. Hour Sequence (0..24) and Minute Sequence (0..60): These are both Add Sequence steps, which add an incrementing integer field to the input rows to represent the hours and minutes respectively. In both cases, the Start at value is set to 0 (zero) and the increment is left to the default of 1 (one).
4. Combine: This is a Join Rows (Cartesian product) step. This step combines the hour rows and minute rows from its input streams.
5. Calculate time: In this Calculator step, the hour/minute combinations are parsed into a Date value, which is then converted to a String value using a format string to retain only the time part.
6. Load dim_time: This is a table output step to insert the generated rows into the `dim_time` target table.

When looking at Figure 10-8, you see that, except for the Join Rows step, this transformation uses the same basic elements as the transformation to load the date dimension shown in Figure 10-1.

As compared to the transformation to load the date dimension, there is something radically different about the way this transformation generates its data. The transformation to load the date dimension was completely linear, and the calendar day that drove the transformation was obtained by adding days to the initial date. In this transformation, the Generate Rows and Sequence steps are independent of one another. The actual time of day is obtained by combining the data from the two streams and then parsing a date out of the combined hour/minute value. This approach would be less practical to load a date dimension: although you can set up separate streams to generate years and months, this is not so easy for the day part of the date because the number of days is dependent upon the month and whether or not the year is a leap year.

Combine: The Join Rows (Cartesian product) Step

The Combine step in Figure 10-8 is of the *Join Rows (Cartesian product)* type. This is found in the Joins category. Its icon, visible in Figure 10-8, is a set of chain links.

The Join Rows (Cartesian product) step is functionally analogous to the `INNER JOIN` operation in SQL, the difference being that it operates on record input streams and not database tables.

> **NOTE** **Although the Join Rows (Cartesian product) step is functionally analogous to a database join operation, one should be very careful not to consider it as a replacement. As a general rule, you should not use this step to avoid writing SQL—rather, you should consider using this step in case you cannot use SQL. For example, when you want to join the rows from two tables that are available within the same connection, you should probably use a Table input step and specify the appropriate SQL to solve the problem.**
>
> **A typical use case for the Join Rows (Cartesian product) step is when you want to create a cross-product of data sets across database servers or data sources. Although you can configure a join condition for the Join Rows (Cartesian product) step, you should consider using the Merge Join step in case you want to use complex join types and/or conditions.**

The step works by combining the records from all of its input streams into a new composite record, which is sent to the output stream. The particular manner in which the records are combined is known as the *Cartesian product*. For two input streams, the result is created by pairing each of the records coming in from the Hours Sequence (0..23) step with all of the records coming in from the Minute Sequence (0..60) step. The resulting output stream has both an `hour` and a `minute` field, and contains 24 × 60 (=1440) rows, which together make up all possible hour/minute combinations, starting from 00:00 through 23:59.

For this particular usage of the Join Rows (Cartesian product) step, only a small amount of configuration is required, but for completeness, the configuration dialog is shown in Figure 10-9.

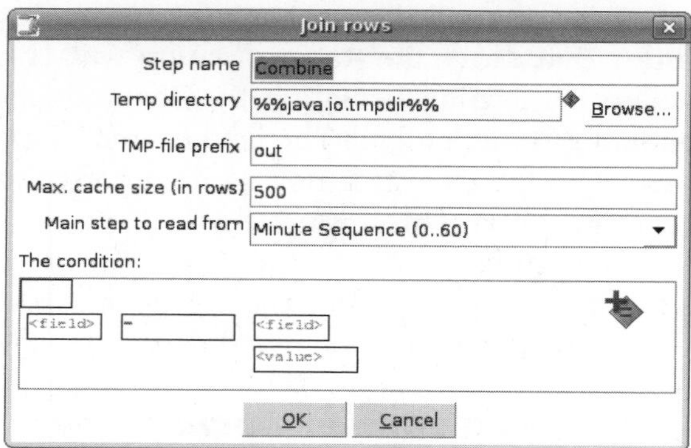

Figure 10-9: The configuration dialog of the Join Rows (Cartesian product) step

The Join Rows (Cartesian product) step always assumes that one input stream is the ''main'' stream. You can specify this step in the Main step to read from property. This stream ''drives'' the step: the step consumes one record from the main stream, and then creates combination records with each of the records from the other input streams. When all combinations are created, the step proceeds with the next record from the main stream.

To improve performance, the Join Rows (Cartesian product) step uses in-memory caches for all input streams, except the main input stream. The size of the input stream caches can be specified by setting the number of rows to `cache` in the Max. cache size property. If the number of rows in an input stream exceeds the size of its cache, the rows are written to a temporary file. The default for the Max. cache size property is 500, which exceeds the number of records from either input stream in our transformation, so we can be confident no temporary files will be needed.

NOTE The records from the main stream do not need to be cached because the Join Rows (Cartesian product) step always looks at exactly one record from that stream at any point in time. For this reason, you should always specify the stream that contains most of the rows as the Main step to read from. In our transformation, we set the Main step to read from to the Minute Sequence (0..60) step accordingly.

If necessary, you can specify in which directory any temporary files are to be stored by setting the Temp directory property. The default for this property is `%%java.io.tmpdir%%`, which denotes the value of a built-in variable referring to the standard Java temporary file directory. (For more information about variables, see the section "Using Variables" in Chapter 11). If you like, you can also specify the prefix for the temporary file names, which is useful mainly for debugging purposes.

Although it is possible to specify a join condition for the Join Rows (Cartesian product) step, we recommend using a Merge Join step instead as this allows better control over the join condition and join type.

Calculate Time: Again, the Calculator Step

In the transformation shown in Figure 10-8, the Calculate Time step is based on the Calculator step. We already discussed this type of step extensively in the subsection "Calculate and Format Dates: The Calculator Step" earlier in this chapter. For completeness, we show the particular configuration used to calculate the time in Figure 10-10.

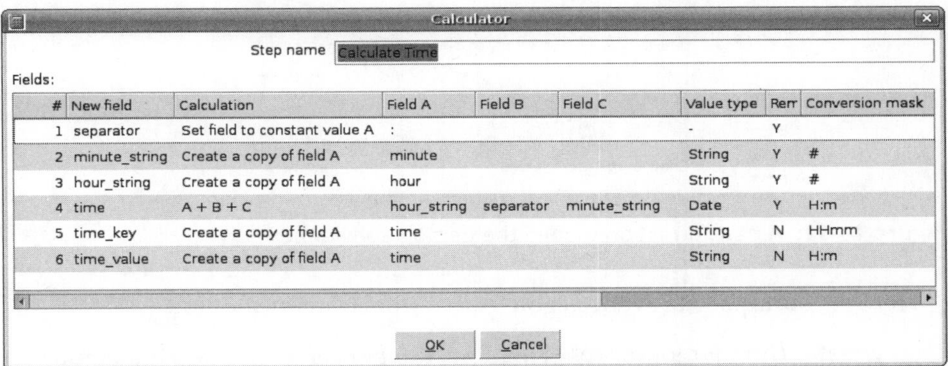

Figure 10-10: Using the Calculator step to calculate the time of day

Calculation #4 is the most important one, as it concatenates string representations of the `hour` and `minute` fields and converts the result to a field of the Date type using the format `H:m`. By reformatting this again, the `time_key` and `time_value` fields are generated, which correspond directly to the `time_key` and `time_value` columns in the `dim_time` table.

Loading the Demography Dimension

The World Class Movie database uses a demography mini-dimension for managing the large customer dimension. The transformation to load the demography dimension is shown in Figure 10-11.

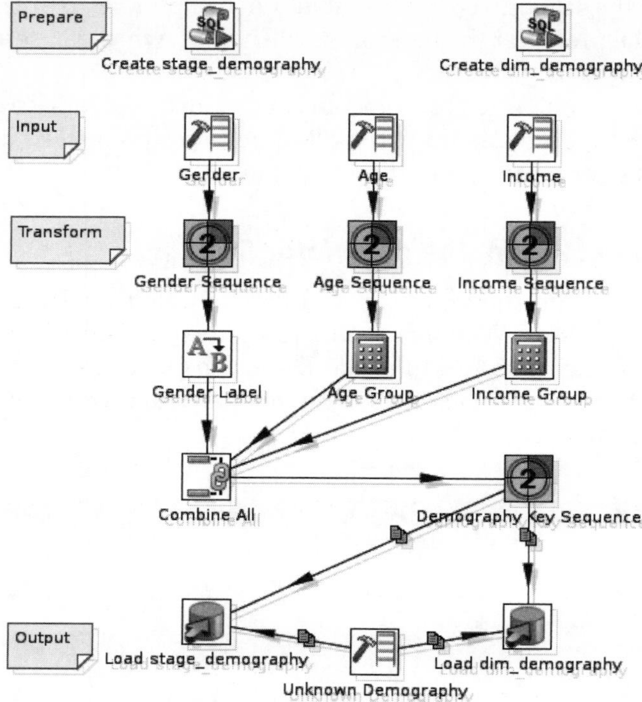

Figure 10-11: A transformation to load the demography dimension

Here's a summary of what is going on in this transformation:

1. Create dim_demography: This Execute SQL step creates the actual `dim_demography` dimension table in the `wcm_dwh` database.
2. Create stage_demography: This Execute SQL step creates a `stage_demography` table in the `wcm_staging` database. We describe the purpose of this table in detail in the next section.
3. Gender and Gender Sequence, Age and Age Sequence, and Income and Income Sequence: These pairs of Generate Rows and Add Sequence steps generate the raw data that forms the possible values for gender, age group and income group respectively.
4. Gender label: This Value mapper step converts the values from the Gender Sequence step into `Male` and `Female` labels, which are to be stored in the `gender` column of the target tables.
5. Age Group and Income Group: These Calculator steps generate the appropriate boundary values for the Age and Income group, and also create nicely human-readable labels to identify the group.

6. Combine All: Just as we did when loading the `dim_time` dimension, we use a Join Rows (Cartesian product) step to make all possible combinations of the records from all input streams.
7. Demography Key Sequence: This Add Sequence step is used to generate key values that will be used to identify the rows in the `dim_demography` table.
8. Unknown Demography: This Generate Rows step creates a single row that can be used whenever the appropriate demography row cannot be found.
9. Load stage_demography and Load dim_demography: These Table Output steps run in parallel to load the demography data from the input streams incoming from the Demography Key Sequence and Unknown Demography steps.

Understanding the stage_demography and dim_demography Tables

The transformations you've seen so far always used a single target table. This transformation acts on two tables:

- The `dim_demography` table in the `wcm_dwh` database, which is the actual demography dimension table. This table is created in the Create dim_demography step and loaded in the Load dim_demography step.
- The `stage_demography` table in the `wcm_staging` database, which serves as a lookup table to lookup the key of the dimension table. This table is created in the Create stage_demography step and loaded in the Load stage_demography step.

The reason for requiring two tables will hopefully become clear when we look at the definition of the `dim_demography` dimension table. The `CREATE TABLE` statement for the `dim_demography` table is shown in Listing 10-10. In the listing, you see that in addition to the `demography_key`, only the human-readable labels for the `gender`, `age_group` and `income_group` are stored in the `dim_demography` table.

Listing 10-10: The CREATE TABLE statement of the dim_demography dimension table

```
CREATE TABLE  dim_demography (
  demography_key  SMALLINT     NOT NULL,
  age_group       VARCHAR(10) NOT NULL,
  gender          VARCHAR(10) NOT NULL,
  income_group    VARCHAR(20) NOT NULL,
  PRIMARY KEY (demography_key)
);
```

Now, suppose you want to load customers into the dim_customer or fact_customer tables. In both cases, you need to store the appropriate value for the demography_key as part of the customer row. But assuming you have the customer's age, income, and gender, it is quite a challenge to use these data to search the dim_demography table.

To overcome our inability to use the dim_demography table directly to look up the demography_key, we introduce the stage_demography table in the wcm_staging database. The stage_demography table stores the demography_key and the gender label as well as the actual integer values that form the boundaries of the age and income groups. The CREATE TABLE statement for the stage_demography table is shown in Listing 10-11.

Listing 10-11: The CREATE TABLE statement of the dim_demography dimension table

```
CREATE TABLE  stage_demography (
  demography_key    SMALLINT     NOT NULL,
  gender            VARCHAR(10)  NOT NULL,
  min_age_group     SMALLINT     NOT NULL,
  max_age_group     SMALLINT     NOT NULL,
  min_income_group  INTEGER      NOT NULL,
  max_income_group  INTEGER      NOT NULL,
  PRIMARY KEY (demography_key),
  UNIQUE (
     min_age_group, max_age_group,
     min_income_group, max_income_group,
     gender
  )
)
```

Given a value for gender, income, and age, it is fairly straightforward to look up the demography_key in this stage_demography table. In addition to demanding a matching value in the gender column, we need to require that the value for age be equal to or larger than the value in the min_age_group column, but less than the value in the max_age_group column. Similarly, the value for income must lie between the values in the min_income_group and max_income_group columns respectively. We will discuss the lookup process in further detail later in this chapter when we describe loading the dim_customer and fact_customer tables.

Generating Age and Income Groups

The age and income groups are generated by using an Add Sequence step with a modified value for the Increment by property. The increment is set to 1 by default. For generating income groups, we use an increment of 10,000. For age groups, we use an increment of 5, and an initial value of 15. (World Class Movies does not rent or sell DVDs to minors.)

In the subsequent Calculator steps, the value used for the increment is used to compute the upper (exclusive) boundary of the group, taking the sequence value itself as the lower (inclusive) boundary. The Calculator steps also generate a human readable label for each group. For example, the income group from $10,000 to $20,000 is labeled as `$10,000 - $20,000`. For completeness, the configuration of the Income Group Calculator step is shown in Figure 10-12.

Calculator

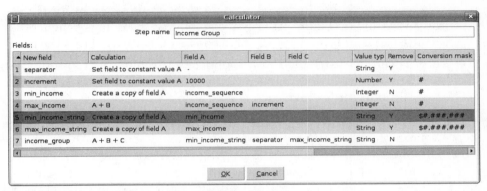

Step name: Income Group

Fields:

	New field	Calculation	Field A	Field B	Field C	Value typ	Remove	Conversion mask
1	separator	Set field to constant value A	-			String	Y	
2	increment	Set field to constant value A	10000			Number	Y	#
3	min_income	Create a copy of field A	income_sequence			Integer	N	#
4	max_income	A + B	income_sequence	increment		Integer	N	#
5	min_income_string	Create a copy of field A	min_income			String	Y	$#,###,###
6	max_income_string	Create a copy of field A	max_income			String	Y	$#,###,###
7	income_group	A + B + C	min_income_string	separator	max_income_string	String	N	

OK Cancel

Figure 10-12: Calculating and formatting income groups

Multiple Incoming and Outgoing Streams

The transformation in Figure 10-12 shows an interesting PDI feature. The Demography Key Sequence and Unknown Demography steps each have two outgoing hops. For both of these steps, the outgoing hops are led to the Table Output steps Load stage_demography and Load dim_demography, which consequently have two incoming hops.

You already saw an example of a step that could accept multiple input streams when we covered the Join Rows (Cartesian product) step. However, there is a difference as compared to the incoming hops of the Table Output steps. The nature of the Join Rows (Cartesian product) operation simply assumes at least two input streams. A Cartesian product of a single input does not make sense because the operation is defined by combining data from two or more streams. But for the Table Output step, a single input stream makes perfect sense, and we can rightfully ask ourselves what the significance is of an extra input stream in this case.

Most transformation steps can handle a single kind of input stream. But there is nothing wrong with accepting records from multiple input streams provided they have identical record layouts. Another way of putting it is that for most steps it doesn't matter where the input records originate as long as they all have the same properties. The incoming hops simply dump their records in the input buffer of the receiving step regardless of origin.

The same goes for output streams. Most step types generate output records that all have the same layout. There is no reason why all these records should be sent down a single outgoing hop. They could just as well be sent down multiple streams. Note that this is not entirely symmetrical as compared to multiple input streams. In the case of multiple outgoing hops, there are two different ways to send records out:

- Records may be copied, sending all output records to all outgoing hops. This is useful for sending the same data along multiple paths for parallel transformation. In Figure 10-11 you can tell that the data is being copied because this is indicated by the small copy icon halfway across the hop.
- Records can be distributed in a round-robin fashion over all outgoing hops. This essentially partitions the output stream, sending only a portion of all output records down each hop.

The distribution method can be configured through the context menu of the step. In the context menu, find the Data movement submenu. There, choose either Distribute data to next steps or Copy data to next steps.

In the transformation shown in Figure 10-11, the Demography Key Sequence and Unknown Demography steps are both configured to copy all data to all output streams. This makes sense because we need all data to be available in both the data warehouse as well as the staging area.

Loading Data from Source Systems

So far, we've only loaded dimension tables based on generated data. However, most tables in the data warehouse are filled using data coming from various database tables in a source system, and sometimes, multiple source systems.

In this section we take a closer look at some of the considerations, issues, and solutions that come into play when loading data warehouse tables with data coming from source systems. We start by introducing a few concepts and then continue to describe Pentaho Data Integration solutions to load the World Class Movies data warehouse.

Staging Lookup Values

The World Class Movies database features a single `lookup_value` table that serves as reference for relatively small and fixed lists of predefined values. All values that belong to one list have the same lookup type. The `lookup_type` table is used to store the name of the table and column to which the list of values applies.

In the data warehouse design, most of the references to the `lookup_value` table reappear as de-normalized dimension attributes. For example, in the `dim_promotion` table, the `promotion_type` column is loaded from those rows in `lookup_value` that are referred to using the `promotion_type_lookup` column in the `promotion` table.

The data in the `lookup_value` and `lookup_type` tables almost never changes. Changes are to be expected only if the source system is upgraded to a new version.

We need the lookup values so frequently, and the changes occur so seldom that it makes sense to pull all the data from the `lookup_value` table for permanent storage in the staging area. While we are at it, we might just as well store the values for each lookup type in its own table. Each individual list of lookup values will be very small, which should make lookups and joins as fast as possible.

The stage_lookup_data Job

To load the lookup values into the staging area, we created a Pentaho Data Integration job. Creating a new job is much like creating a new transformation. You can create a new job from the menu (by choosing File ➢ New ➢ Job) or from the toolbar. Alternatively you can use Ctrl+Alt+N.

The job to load the lookup values into the staging area is shown in Figure 10-13.

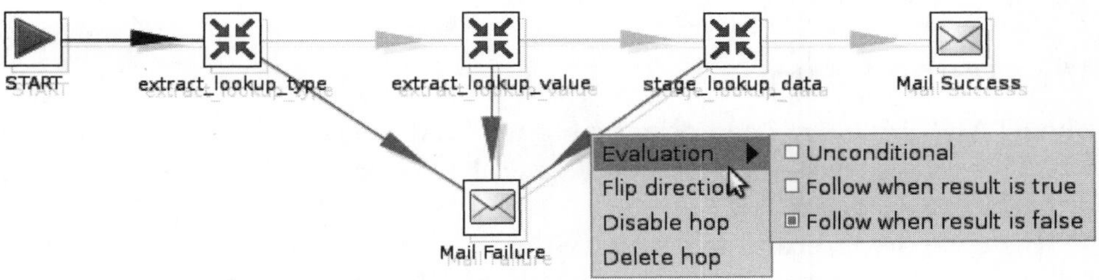

Figure 10-13: A job to load the lookup values into the staging area

NOTE **In Chapter 9 we discussed the most important differences between jobs and transformations. We won't repeat that discussion, but we would like to stress again that transformations and jobs may look similar but are very different kinds of things. The main difference to keep in mind is that jobs consist of *job entries,* which represent the execution of a task, whereas transformations consist of *transformation steps* that represent an operation on record streams. Hops connecting job entries represent an execution sequence, whereas hops connecting transformation steps represent a stream of records.**

Here's a summary of what is going on in this job:

- **START**—This is the entry point for job execution.
- **extract_lookup_type and extract_lookup_value**—By executing these transformations, data is read from the `lookup_value` and `lookup_type` tables in the source system and temporarily stored.

- **stage_lookup_data**—This transformation reads the data from the temporary storage and loads it into the tables in the staging area.
- **Mail Success and Mail Failure**—These job entries send notification e-mail messages to report whether the job failed or succeeded.

The job entries are connected to one another with hops. The green hops (those connecting the five job entries along the top row) indicate the normal execution path: if a job entry completes successfully, execution is resumed at the job entry found at the other end of the outgoing green hop. In Figure 10-13, the normal execution path forms a sequence of job entries that begins at the job entry labeled START and ends with the job entry labeled Mail Success.

All but the first and last job entries also have a second, red-colored outgoing hop to the job entry labeled Mail Failure. The red hops indicate an error execution path. The error execution path is entered whenever a job entry does not execute successfully. If a job entry does not have an outgoing error hop, unsuccessful execution of that job entry will cause the job as a whole to be aborted with an error.

You can change the properties of a hop by right-clicking it and choosing an action from the context menu. To modify whether the hop will be followed in case of success or failure, choose the appropriate option in the Evaluation submenu. This is also shown in Figure 10-13.

The START Job Entry

The START job entry is a special job entry that denotes the entry point of a job. This job entry is found in the General category, and its icon is a green arrowhead (see Figure 4-13).

This type of step can have only one outgoing hop that is unconditionally followed. Job execution commences with the job entry found at the other end of the outgoing hop of the START job entry. Every job must have exactly one job entry of this type.

The configuration dialog of the START job entry contains a number of options for scheduling job execution. Details about job scheduling are discussed in Chapter 14.

Transformation Job Entries

The job entries extract_lookup_type, extract_lookup_value, and stage_lookup _data are all *Transformation job entries*. This type of job entry is found in the General category. Its icon (visible in Figure 10-13) shows four arrows aimed at a central point.

In the configuration dialog, the transformation file that is to be executed can be specified in the Transformation filename field. Alternatively, if you are connected to a repository, you can use the Transformation name and Repository Directory fields to specify a transformation stored in the repository.

(Using the repository is covered extensively in Chapter 11.) In both cases, a button is available on the right to browse for transformations. To quickly open the specified transformation, right-click the step and choose the Open transformation option.

Figure 10-14 shows the configuration dialog of the Transformation job entry labeled extract_lookup_type.

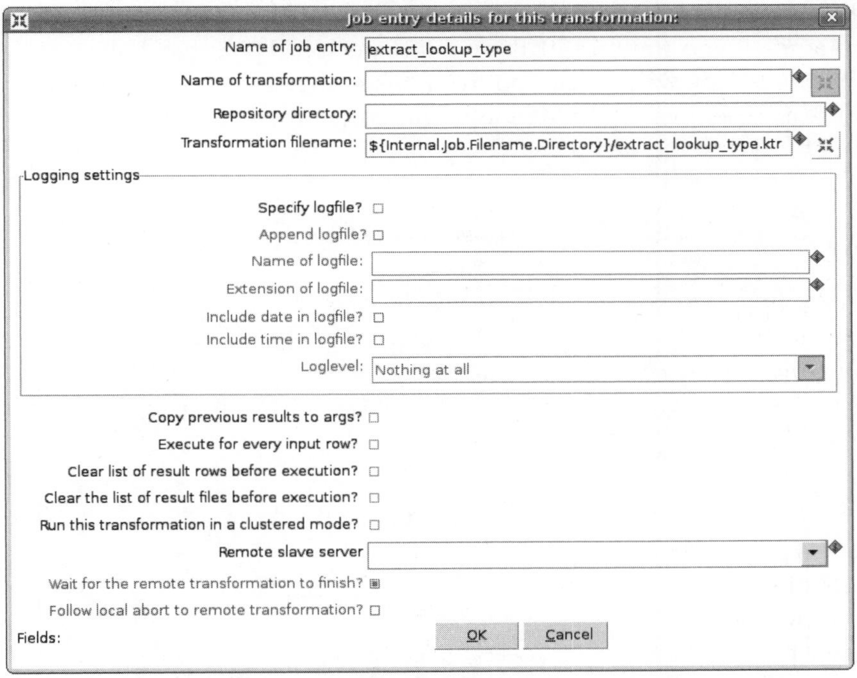

Figure 10-14: The Transformation job entry configuration dialog

In Figure 10-14 the transformation's file name is specified as `${Internal.Job.Filename.Directory}/extract_lookup_type.ktr`. This denotes the file `extract_lookup_type.ktr` residing in the same directory as that of the job file itself, as explained in detail in Chapter 11.

The configuration dialog contains many more properties that could be configured. You will encounter some of them later on in this chapter.

Mail Success and Mail Failure

In Figure 10-13, the job entries labeled Mail Success and Mail Failure are of the type Mail, denoted by an envelope icon. This can be found in the Mail category.

The Mail job entry is designed to send an e-mail message using the Simple Mail Transfer Protocol (SMTP). Its primary purpose is to provide basic notification of job execution status (success, failure, or progress).

Configuration of the Mail step is not particularly difficult, although the number of configuration options may be a bit daunting at first. The configuration dialog contains four tab pages. In the Addresses page, shown in Figure 10-15, you must specify at least one valid e-mail address in the Destination address property. Optionally you can also configure CC and BCC addresses. In addition to the destination address, the Sender name and Sender address properties are required by the SMTP protocol and must be specified. You can optionally specify a Reply-To address and some additional contact data such as the name and phone number of the contact person. For typical success/failure notifications, one would send notifications to the IT support staff, and specify details of a member of the data integration team as the sender. Figure 10-15 shows the Addresses tab page.

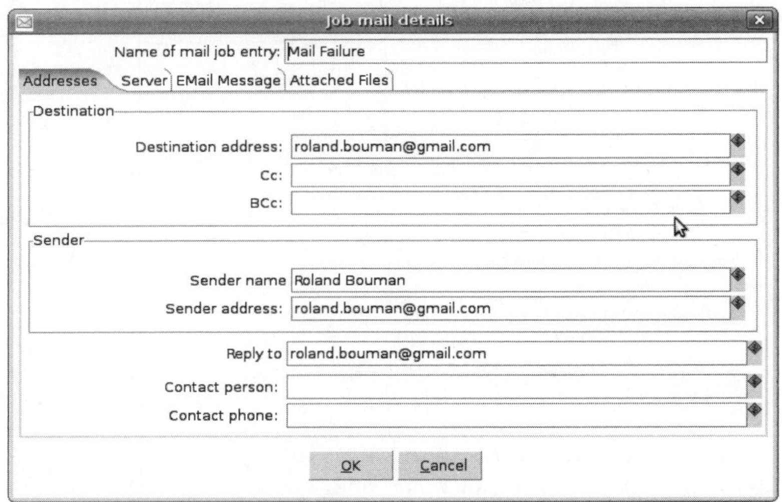

Figure 10-15: The Addresses tab page in the configuration dialog of the Mail job entry

You must specify the details of the SMTP server in the Server tab page, shown in Figure 10-16.

You are required to provide at least the host name or IP address of your SMTP server. Optionally, you can provide the port to use. By default, port 25 (default for SMTP) is used. In most cases, SMTP servers require user authentication. To enable authentication, check the Use authentication checkbox and provide the username and password in the Authentication user and Authentication password fields respectively. More and more often, SMTP servers require secure authentication using a protocol such as SSL (Secure Sockets Layer) or TLS (Transport Layer Security). You can specify secure authentication by selecting the Use secure authentication checkbox and choosing the appropriate protocol in the Secure connection type list box. Note that network communication for a secure authentication protocol generally employs another port. For SSL, the default port is 465. Contact your local network or system administrator to obtain this data.

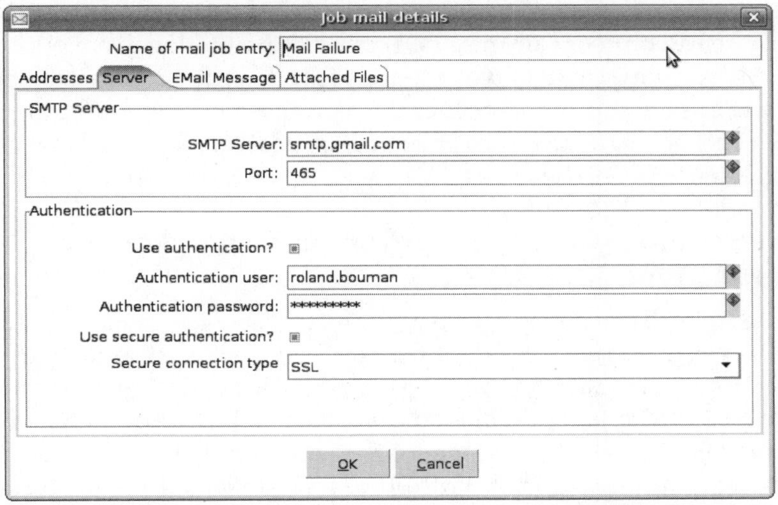

Figure 10-16: The Server tab page in the configuration dialog of the Mail job entry

You can specify the actual message content on the Email Message tab. This tab page is shown in Figure 10-17.

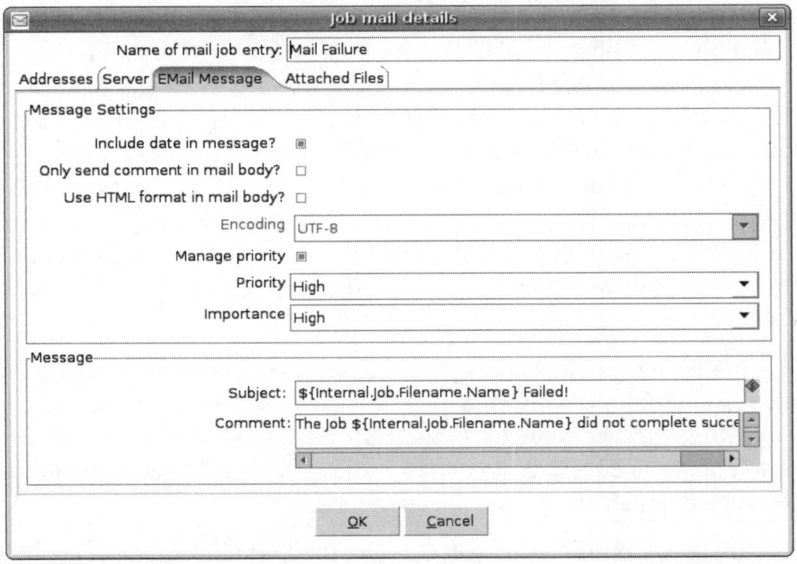

Figure 10-17: The EMail Message tab in the configuration dialog of the Mail job entry

The message subject and body are specified in the Subject and Comment properties respectively. You can use text and freely include variable references for these properties. By default, PDI includes a brief status report of the transformation in the message body, right after the content provided in the Comment property. To prevent this status report from being included, select the Only send comment in mail body checkbox. Optionally, you can select Use HTML format in mail body to send HTML formatted e-mail. Some e-mail clients use message priority headers. If you like you can select the Manage priority checkbox to enable this. When this is enabled, you can set the Priority and Importance properties.

The extract_lookup_type and extract_lookup_value Transformations

The purpose of the `extract_lookup_type` and `extract_lookup_value` transformations is to retrieve the data from the `lookup_type` and `lookup_value` tables in the source system. The design of both of these transformations is extremely simple: a table input step executes a SQL `SELECT` statement on the respective table. The output stream of the table input step is led immediately to a Text file output step that writes the data to file. Figure 10-18 shows the design of the `extract_lookup_type` transformation.

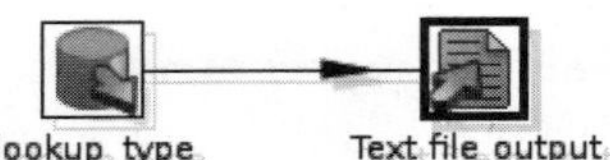

Figure 10-18: The design of the extract_lookup_type transformation

The objective of these transformations is to extract the data as quickly as possible from the World Class Movies database. Although it is possible to have the transformation store the data directly in the `wcm_staging` database, we prefer to dump the data into a text file because this is faster. One may argue that for these amounts of data, writing directly to a table in the staging area should still offer good performance. This may be true enough, but write performance is not the primary concern of this extraction. The amount of time we need to occupy the source system is the main concern, which is why we opt for the fastest possible solution.

NOTE **In this design, the data is pulled across the network and stored in a file on the file system of the staging area host. This may not be the best solution when dealing with large data volumes. If there is a risk of network congestion, it may be better to dump the data to a file on the source system's file system and compress the file before transfer to the staging area host.**

This is a trade-off: compression will increase the CPU load on the source system. In addition, this scenario adds complexity to the deployment of the data integration

solution because it becomes distributed. However, it is good to know that you can do it. Tools for distributing Pentaho Data Integration solutions are discussed in Chapter 11.

The stage_lookup_data Transformation

The purpose of the `stage_lookup_data` transformation is to load the lookup data into the tables in the `wcm_staging` database. The transformation is shown in Figure 10-19.

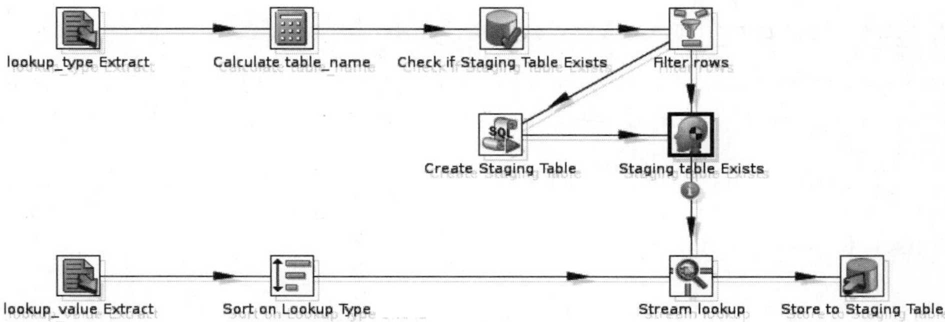

Figure 10-19: The stage_lookup_data transformation

Here's a summary of what is going on in this transformation:

1. lookup_type Extract and lookup_value Extract: These Text file input steps parse the text files created by the extract_lookup_type and extract_lookup_value transformations into a stream of records.
2. Calculate table_name: This Calculator step uses the data from the lookup_type Extract to generate a table name for the staging table. The table name is added to the output stream in the `table_name` field.
3. Check if Staging Table Exists, Filter rows, and Staging table Exists steps: The Check if Staging Table Exists step uses the `table_name` field to see if the staging table exists. The result of the check is fed into the Filter rows step. If the staging table exists, execution continues directly with the Staging table Exists step. Otherwise, the transformation takes a detour and continues with the Create Staging Table step. This is an Execute SQL step that will create the target staging table, and then continues at the Staging table Exists step.
4. Stream Lookup and Sort on Lookup Type steps: The Stream Lookup step essentially joins the data streams coming from both Text file input steps based on the `lookup_type_id` field, which is present in both extracts. This adds the `table_name` field to each of the rows incoming from the lookup_value Extract. The Sort on Lookup Type is required for the

correct operation of the Stream Lookup step, which assumes the main data stream (the one coming from the lookup_value Extract) is sorted on key value.

5. Store to Staging Table: This Table Output step inserts the lookup values in the appropriate staging table specified by the `table_name` field.

We already discussed the Text file input, Calculator, and Table Output steps from the earlier sections in this and the previous chapter. We will now briefly discuss the steps we did not encounter before.

Check If Staging Table Exists: The Table Exists Step

In Figure 10-19, the step labeled Check if Staging Table Exists is of the Table Exists type. This step is found beneath the Lookup category and its icon is a drum with a checkmark.

As implied by its name, the Table Exists step can check if a table is accessible on the specified database connection. The configuration dialog of the Table Exists step is shown in Figure 10-20.

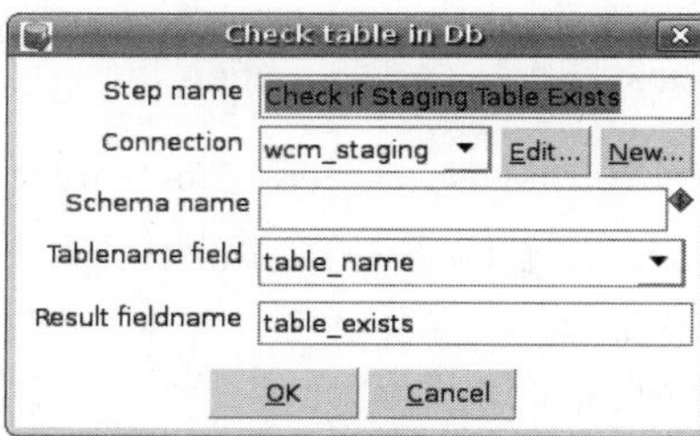

Figure 10-20: The configuration dialog of the Table Exists step

The database connection is specified by the Connection property. The value for the property called Tablename field is the name of the field in the input stream that conveys the table name. In this case, the field is called `table_name` and originates in the Calculate table_name step. The Result fieldname property is used to specify the name of the field that will hold the result of the check. This Boolean field is added to the output stream of the step.

The Filter rows Step

The Filter rows step is used to choose appropriately between two alternative paths according to the outcome of the Table Exists step. The Filter rows step is found in the Transformation category and its icon is a funnel (see Figure 10-19).

The Filter rows step provides basic If-Then-Else functionality. The configuration of the step is shown in Figure 10-21.

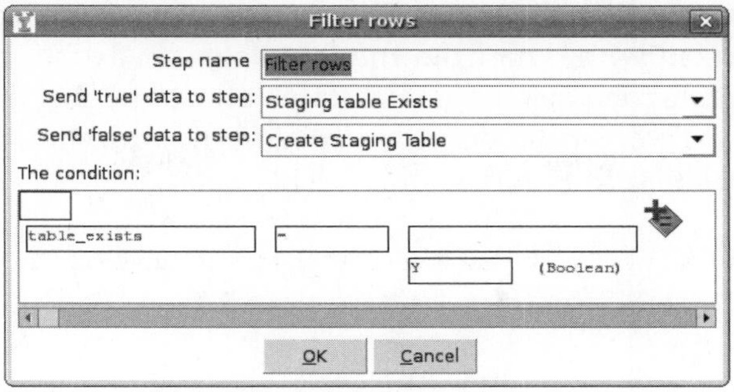

Figure 10-21: The configuration of the Filter rows step

In the Filter rows step, you can specify a condition by adding one or more comparisons. In Figure 10-21, only one comparison is added, which checks if the value of the `table_exists` field (which originated from the Table Exists step) is equal to the Boolean constant `Y`.

NOTE **In Pentaho Data Integration, Boolean values are represented using the string constants `Y` and `N` for TRUE and FALSE respectively.**

If required, multiple comparisons can be combined with the usual logical operators. To add more than one comparison, click the plus icon in the upper-right part of the condition area. You can then click the newly added comparison to edit it, and choose a logical operator like AND or OR to combine the comparisons.

The Filter rows step must have two outgoing hops. The steps at the other end of the outgoing hops can be selected in the drop-down list boxes to configure branching. The Send 'true' data to step will be executed in case the condition evaluates to TRUE, and the Send 'false' data to step will be executed otherwise. In this example, we choose to continue with the Create Staging Table step in case the `table_exists` field is FALSE.

Create Staging Table: Executing Dynamic SQL

The Create Staging Table step is of the Execute SQL type. We described this type of step earlier in this chapter in the section "CREATE TABLE dim_date: Using the Execute SQL Script Step".

So far, all of the transformations we have discussed used the Execute SQL step to create the target table, and this transformation is no exception. There is, however, one important difference in the way this step takes part in the transformation. In all prior transformations, the Execute SQL step appeared detached from the remainder of the transformation, as it was not connected to any of the other steps. In this transformation, the Execute SQL step is part of the data flow, and has an incoming and outgoing hop just like the other steps.

In the transformation shown in Figure 10-18, the SQL script is dynamic and parameterized with data from the input stream. To be specific, the SQL script is a template for a `CREATE TABLE` statement containing a placeholder for the table name. The placeholder is denoted with a question mark. The SQL statement template is shown in Listing 10-12.

Listing 10-12: A CREATE TABLE statement template with table name placeholder

```
CREATE TABLE ? (
    lookup_value_id          INT
,   lookup_text              VARCHAR(50)
,   lookup_type_id           INT
,   lookup_type_table_name   VARCHAR(64)
,   lookup_type_column_name  VARCHAR(64)
,   PRIMARY KEY(lookup_value_id)
,   UNIQUE(lookup_text)
)
```

The configuration of the Create Staging Table step is shown in Figure 10-22. In the configuration dialog, the Execute for each row checkbox is selected. This allows the SQL script to be executed for each row arriving through the input stream rather than just once in the initialization phase of the transformation. In addition, the `table_name` field is specified in the parameters grid. When handling a row from the input stream, the placeholder(s) in the SQL script are substituted with the value(s) of the field(s) specified in the grid. The resulting `CREATE TABLE` statement is then executed, creating a new table.

The Dummy Step

The Staging table Exists step is a Dummy step. The Dummy step can be found in the transformation category and its icon (visible in Figure 10-19) is a dummy's head.

The Dummy step passes the data from its input streams to its output stream(s) and does nothing else. Although it does not represent a true operation, it is useful for joining and splitting record streams. This deserves some explanation.

When we discussed the transformation for loading the `dim_demography` dimension, we explained that most steps can have multiple incoming and outgoing records streams of the same type because the type of operation performed by the step is not influenced by the origin or destination of the records. But some steps are designed to operate on multiple different input streams, and some steps generate multiple different output streams. Often this implies the streams can have different record layouts, but the defining characteristic is that the step is designed to attach different meaning to different streams.

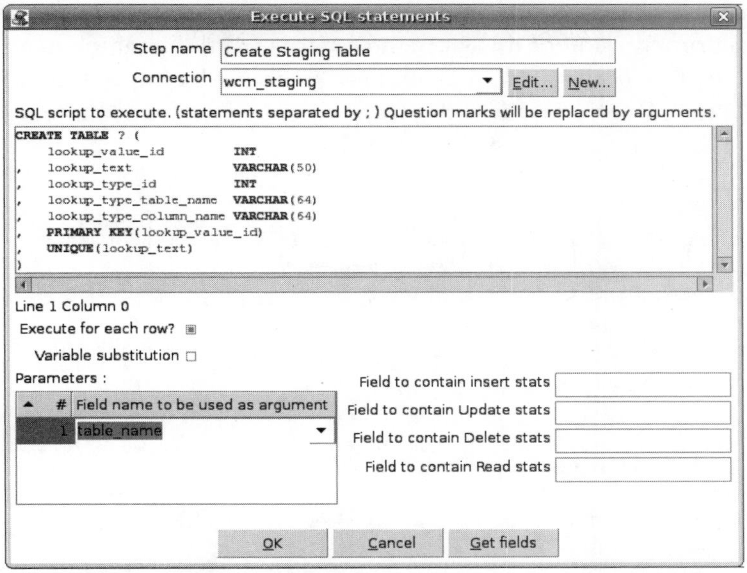

Figure 10-22: Configuring the Execute SQL step to accept a parameter and execute once for each row

For example, in the transformation shown in Figure 10-19, the Filter rows step generates two output streams with different semantics: the 'true' branch and the 'false' branch. As you will learn in detail in the next subsection, the Stream Lookup accepts two different input streams, namely one main data stream and one lookup stream. Look again at Figure 10-19. Notice the small ''information'' (i) icon halfway down the hop going out of the Dummy step to the Stream lookup step. This icon indicates that this is indeed a special input stream, which is considered to have a role distinct from that of the main input stream.

As it happens, the two branches coming out of the Filter rows step together form the source of the lookup data for the Stream Lookup step. So, in order to allow the Stream Lookup step to use all data from both branches, they have to be brought together somehow so the data can be treated as a single stream again. This is where the Dummy step comes into play. Leading the two streams to the Dummy step is the functional equivalent of a SQL `UNION` operation.

The Stream Lookup Step

The Stream Lookup step is found in the Lookup category and its icon is a magnifying glass.

The Stream Lookup step accepts two different input streams. One stream is considered to be the main stream, and the other stream is the lookup stream. The step works by looking up a record from the lookup stream for each row in the main stream based on the outcome of a comparison of field values. For the correct functioning of this step, the records from the main stream must be sorted according to the fields that are used to do the lookup. The configuration for the stream lookup used in the transformation to load the lookup values into the staging area is shown in Figure 10-23.

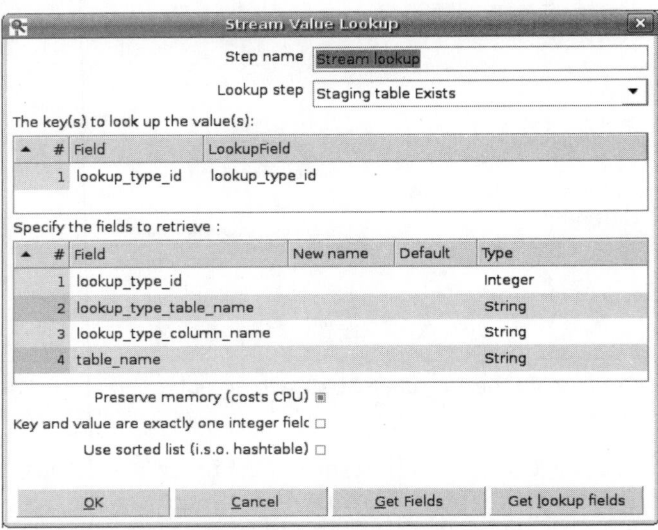

Figure 10-23: The configuration of the Stream Lookup step

Using the Lookup Step drop-down list, you can select which step provides the lookup input stream. By clicking the Get Fields button, you can fill the key(s) to look up the value(s) grid. In the Field column of this grid, you can specify the fields from the main stream. In the LookupField column, you can specify the corresponding fields from the lookup stream. With the Get lookup fields button, you can fill the Specify the fields to retrieve grid. This fills the grid with all fields from the lookup stream. Fields in this grid will be added to the input stream to generate the output stream. The checkboxes beneath this grid may be used to optimize the lookup algorithm. Selecting the Preserve memory checkbox ensures that the rows from the lookup stream will be compressed. This decreases the memory requirements for the step, but will demand more CPU cycles to compress (and decompress) the data.

The Key and value are exactly one integer field checkbox can be enabled in case the key that links the main stream and the lookup stream consists of a single Integer field and only one Integer field is retrieved from the lookup stream. This checkbox enables an optimization that allows the lookup data to be stored more efficiently, which saves memory and increases performance. If the record size of the lookup records is large, you can enable the Use sorted list checkbox to save memory.

Sort on Lookup Type: The Sort Rows Step

In Figure 10-19, the Sort on Lookup Type step is of the Sort rows step type. This step is found in the Transformation category. You can see the corresponding icon in Figure 10-19.

This step takes an unsorted input stream and creates a sorted output stream based on the specification of a set of fields. Optionally, you can specify that only unique (based on key values) rows should be passed to the output stream. The configuration dialog is shown in Figure 10-24.

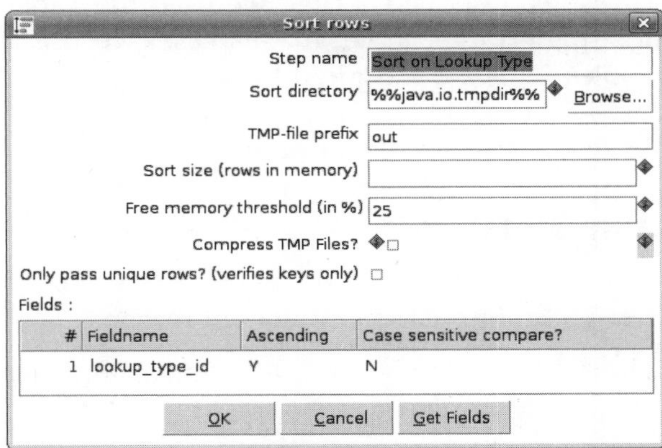

Figure 10-24: The configuration dialog of the Sort rows step

You can quickly fill the Fields grid using the Get Fields button. If you wish, you can configure the sorting direction (ascending or descending). For fields of the String type, you can specify whether to honor or ignore differences in letter case.

Pentaho Data Integration tries to perform an in-memory sort. By default, 5,000 rows can be sorted in-memory. Beyond 5,000 rows, the algorithm writes intermediate sorting results to temporary files to save memory. If you want to sort more than 5,000 rows and you know the set will fit in memory, you can set the Sort size property to the maximum number of rows you want to sort.

You can also use the Free memory threshold (in %) property to control memory usage. Here you can specify the amount of memory that will be used for sorting before storing sorted rows to a temporary file. The amount of memory is specified as a percentage of the total amount of memory available to the Java Virtual Machine.

You can configure the location where temporary files are written by specifying the Sort directory property. You can also specify the TMP-file prefix, which will be used to prefix the names of any temporary files written by this step. This is mainly useful for debugging purposes. If you find that the temporary files are growing very large, you could consider selecting the Compress TMP Files checkbox. This may help save disk space, and potentially increase performance (due to reduced I/O). Compression will come at a cost of increased CPU load.

Store to Staging Table: Using a Table Output Step to Load Multiple Tables

The final step of the transformation shown in Figure 10-19 is a Table Output step. We've discussed this type of step in detail in the subsection ''Load dim_date: The Table Output Step'' earlier in this chapter.

In all transformations described earlier, we used the Table Output step to insert data into a single target table. In this case, we use the step to load multiple target tables. This is configured by selecting the Is the name of the table defined in a field checkbox and specifying the `table_name` field in the Field that contains the name of table property.

The Promotion Dimension

This section demonstrates how to load the `dim_promotion` dimension table. This process is relatively simple for a number of reasons:

- The dimension table is quite small: it does not contain many columns, nor does it contain many rows.
- Promotions are static and do not change over time. Therefore, we don't need to keep track of a promotion's history. This simplifies the loading process considerably.
- Promotions are in effect for a fixed period of time. This makes it easy to capture data changes.
- In the case of World Class Movies, the promotion dimension table maps to only a few source tables that are all available in the same system.

When developing a plan to load a dimension table, the following considerations come into play:

- **Mapping**—In which tables and columns of the source system does the dimension data originate? How are these tables related to each other? The mapping should be known in advance as a secondary product of the data warehouse design. However, the data integration developer may not have been involved in the database design process, necessitating a review of the intended mappings.

- **Data changes**—What kind of changes do you expect to see in the source tables, and which changes should be reflected in the dimension data? How many changes do you expect to be dealing with, and what are the estimated data volumes?
- **Synchronization**—How often do you want to synchronize the data in the dimension table with the source system? How does this relate to the actual availability of the source system and the data warehouse?

Answering these questions does not provide a ready-made solution, but doing so does help you gain an understanding of the problem. That understanding is a prerequisite for developing a solution that can meet the requirements of the data warehouse design.

Promotion Mappings

You can find details concerning the mappings for the `dim_promotion` table in Chapter 8. For the `dim_promotion` table, you see that there are three source tables:

- `promotion`—This table forms the main source of data for the `dim_promotion` dimension. For each row in the `promotion` table, there will be exactly one row in the `dim_promotion` table.
- `website`—In the source system, the `promotion` table has a foreign key to the `website` table to point out the website that features the promotion. However, in the data warehouse, descriptive attributes from the `website` table are folded into the `dim_promotion` table, which is an example of de-normalization.
- `lookup_value`—This is quite like the `website` table: the `promotion` table has a foreign key to this table to point out the type of promotion, and the textual description of the type is folded directly into the de-normalized `dim_promotion` table.

Promotion Data Changes

Now that it's clear from which table we will be loading data, we should analyze what kind of data changes (additions, modifications, removals) will affect the promotion dimension. We should also estimate how many changes we expect to see over time, and what data volumes are involved.

- For the `promotion` table, we expect to see mainly additions. The volume of changes is expected to be quite low: even if we assume a new promotion is started on each World Class Movies website on a daily basis, we would still be dealing with only 1,500 rows per year.
- We should also expect some updates on existing promotions. It is not unlikely that a successful promotion might be extended to last longer than

originally planned. Even if we can dismiss that possibility, we should still take the possibility into account that a mistake entered into the source system is corrected afterwards. For example, if a wrong ending date was accidentally specified when creating the promotion, it is likely that the error is corrected afterwards by updating the ending date. Another possibility is that a wrong promotion row may be replaced by a correct one, or even removed altogether.

Despite all these scenarios, we do expect to see a certain level of stability. For example, we do not expect a promotion that has already ended to change or be removed. In addition, it seems reasonable to assume that the starting date of promotions that have already started remains fixed and that these promotions are not suddenly removed. Of course, whether we can make these assumptions is up to the business and the source system, but these are the assumptions we will make for the World Class Movies database.

- For the website table, we expect to see a very small number of rows at all times. Over a period of a year or so, a new website may be added. Modifications of existing rows could occur on a very infrequent basis due to occasional changes in the website's title, and perhaps the URI.
- We assume the lookup data to remain static at all times. We expect very few rows here.

Synchronization Frequency

Come what may, you must always ensure that promotions that occurred in the past as well as promotions that are currently active are loaded into the dimension table. If you fail to do that, you won't be able to load fact tables such as `fact_customer` and `fact_order` because we may not be able to lookup the key for `dim_promotion` dimension table.

Considering that promotions may be added or corrected during every working day, it seems sensible to ensure that promotions are loaded on a daily basis.

The load_dim_promotion Job

We created a job called load_dim_promotion to load the promotion dimension. It is shown in Figure 10-25.

The job consists of two main transformations:

- `extract_promotion`—Isolates and extracts the set of promotions from the promotion table in the source system that may have changed since the last load.
- `load_dim_promotion`—Actually loads the data into the dim_promotion dimension table in the data warehouse.

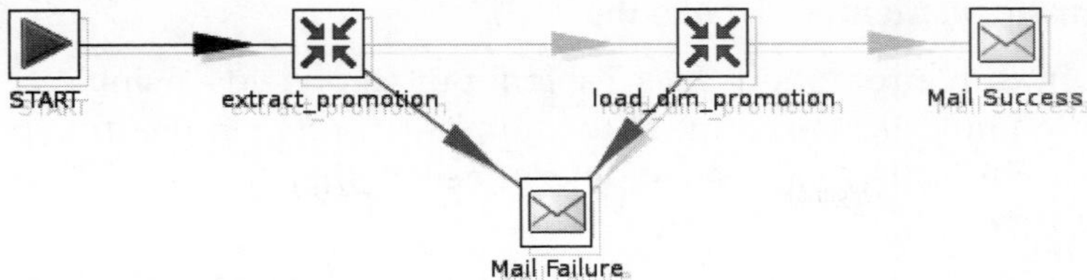

Figure 10-25: The load_dim_promotion job

As in the job to load the lookup tables, we use the Mail job entries for notification purposes.

The extract_promotion Transformation

The extract_promotion transformation is the first transformation in the load-_dim_promotion job. Its purpose is to extract those promotion rows from the source system that may have changed since the last time we loaded the dim_promotion dimension. The extract_promotion transformation is shown in Figure 10-26.

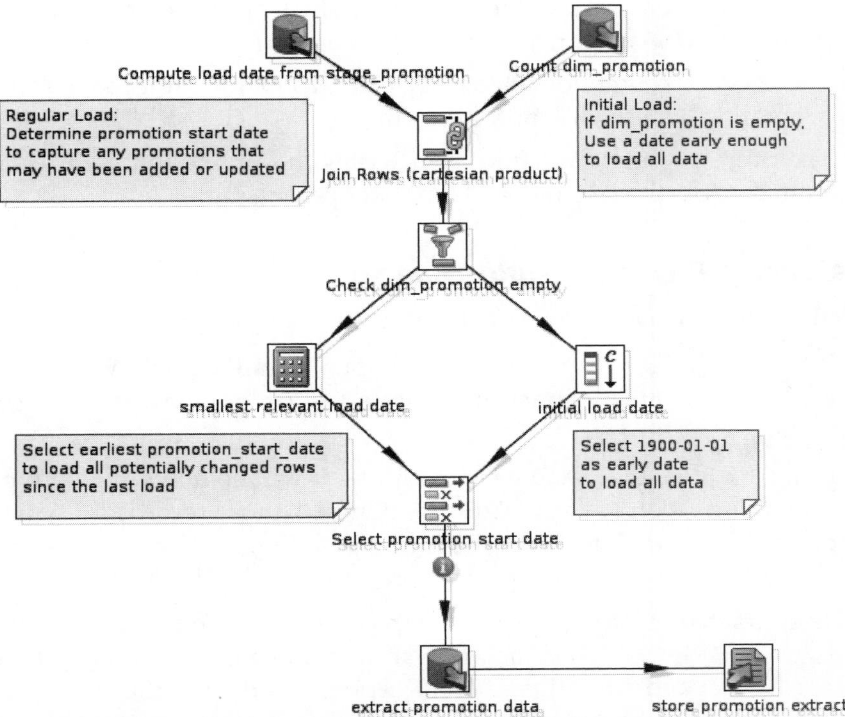

Figure 10-26: Extracting promotion data with the extract_promotion transformation

The transformation works like this:

1. Count dim_promotion: This Table input step yields a single row with a column holding the count of the number of rows in the dim_promotion table. This is used later on to determine whether an initial load should be performed.
2. Compute load date from stage_promotion: This table input step computes a value for promotion_start_date that can be used to select all promotion rows from the source system that may have changed since the last time we synchronized the dim_promotion table.
3. Join rows: This is used to create a single record of the input data created by the prior two steps.
4. Check dim promotion_empty: This Filter rows step uses the count on dim_promotion to determine whether we need to do an initial or a regular load.
5. Smallest relevant load date and initial load date: One of these dates is chosen to determine the set of rows that will be pulled from the source system.
6. Select promotion start date: Discards any unnecessary fields from the stream in order to be able to pass a single parameter to the extract promotion data step.
7. The Extract promotion data step actually extracts the data from the promotion table in the source system.
8. The Store promotion extract step writes the promotion data extracted from the source system to a file for later processing.

Determining Promotion Data Changes

To determine which rows to extract, we reason as follows:

- If the `dim_promotion` table is empty, then we are dealing with an initial load, and we must extract the entire set of promotions from the source system.
- If the `dim_promotion` table is not empty, it will be filled by two types of promotion records: ''active'' promotions, i.e. those records for which the promotion_end_date lies in the future and ''finished'' promotions, those promotions for which the promotion_end_date lies in the past.

To keep track of changing promotion records, we introduce a staging table called `stage_promotion`. For each transformation run, we will load the rows from the extract and store them here. Keeping this data in the staging tables allows you to trace back any changes in the dimension table to the source, which is a great aid in troubleshooting. The `CREATE TABLE` statement for the `stage_promotion` table is shown in Listing 10-13.

Listing 10-13: The CREATE TABLE statement for the stage_promotion table

```
CREATE TABLE  wcm_staging.stage_promotion (
    promotion_id           SMALLINT     NOT NULL,
    website_id             SMALLINT     NOT NULL,
    promotion_title        VARCHAR(50)  NOT NULL,
    promotion_type_lookup  SMALLINT     NOT NULL,
    promotion_start_date   DATE         NOT NULL,
    promotion_end_date     DATE         NOT NULL,
    extract_filename       VARCHAR(255)NOT NULL,
    extract_linenumber     INTEGER      NOT NULL,
    load_timestamp         TIMESTAMP    NOT NULL
                                DEFAULT CURRENT_TIMESTAMP
);
```

Note that the structure of this table is much like that of the original `promotion` table. The difference is that this table has three extra columns:

- `Extract filename`—The name of the file used to load the data again.
- `Extract linenumber`—This is used to store the linenumber in the extract. This makes it easier to load a portion from the extract should we need to do so in the future.
- `Load_timestamp`—An automatically generated timestamp.

Listing 10-14 shows the SQL used to determine the load date.

Listing 10-14: Using SQL to determine promotions that may have changed

```
SELECT MIN(promotion_start_date) start_date
FROM   stage_promotion
WHERE  promotion_end_date > load_timestamp
```

The heart of the query shown in Listing 10-14 is formed by the `WHERE` condition. All rows that have a higher end date than the last load date could have changed in the meanwhile, so we must process them.

Now consider what would happen if the `stage_promotion` table is empty. Well, it would return a NULL value. Now consider what happens in case we run this query right after we finished loading the `dim_promotion` and `stage_promotion` tables. In this case, we are up-to-date for the moment and the query also returns zero rows.

Because we cannot easily distinguish between these two cases of zero rows, we explicitly check whether the dimension table is empty. This is done using a simple `SELECT COUNT(*) ...` script. If the outcome is zero, we can be sure nothing was loaded, and we use 1900-01-01. Otherwise, we use the date determined by the script shown in Listing 10-14, and use it as a parameter for the actual extraction step. Figure 10-27 shows how the date field is used as a parameter.

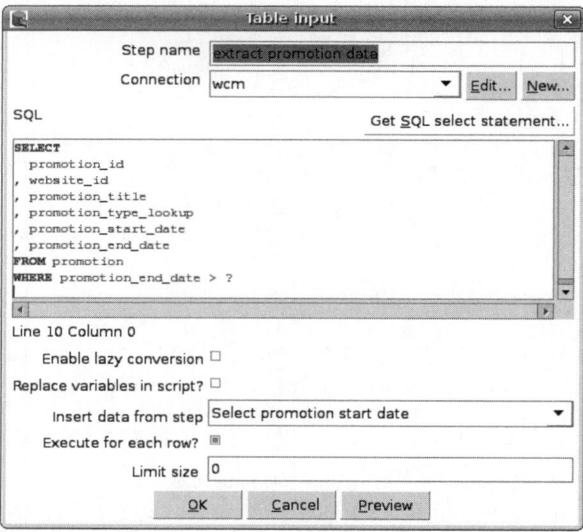

Figure 10-27: Using the date as a parameter for a Table input step

As shown in Figure 10-27, a question mark is used in the SQL statement where the value must be inserted. In addition, the Insert data from step list box must be used to point out exactly which step data will be received from.

Saving the Extract and Passing on the File Name

The extracted rows are saved to disk using an ordinary Text file output step. To gain better control over the extract and to achieve better maintainability of the job as a whole, we use a few PDI features for working with files. The configuration of the Text file output step is shown in Figure 10-28.

Note that we selected the Include date in filename and Include time in filename checkboxes. This ensures we will have fairly unique names for extracts. We also selected the Add filenames to result checkbox. This allows the file name to be passed between two or more transformations in a job.

Picking Up the File and Loading the Extract

The load_dim_promotion transformation immediately follows the extract_promotion job. The purpose of this job is to read the extract into the staging area and load the dim_promotion table. Figure 10-29 shows the entire transformation.

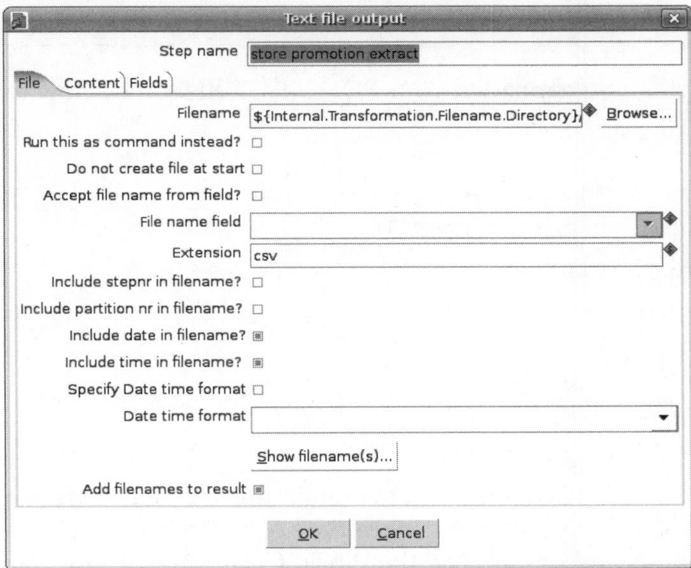

Figure 10-28: Configuring file names with date and time and passing the file to the result

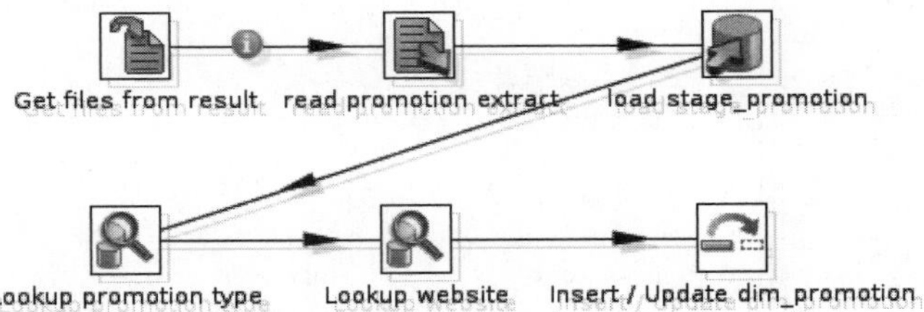

Figure 10-29: Loading the extract into dim_promotion

Here's a quick summary of what is going on in this transformation:

1. The Get files from result step: This step is mandatory to pick up the file that was created by the extract_promotion transformation.
2. read promotion extract: This is an ordinary text input that we configured to pick up the file created by the previous transformation.
3. load stage_promotion: This loads the extract into the stage_promotion table.
4. Lookup promotion type and Lookup website: These steps are used to find and add fields from the related website and lookup value tables.
5. Insert/Update dim_promotion: This step is used to actually load the `dim_promotion` table. If a promotion row is new, it will be added. If a promotion row already existed, its values are overwritten with the current values.

Summary

In this chapter, you expanded your PDI skills. You learned how to:

- Execute SQL
- Generate rows
- Format numbers and dates
- Perform calculations
- Join streams
- Split streams
- Create jobs
- Pass files between transformations

In addition to the many things covered in this chapter, there are even more things we didn't cover. Please refer to the book's website to download all the transformations and jobs to load the World Class Movies data warehouse.

CHAPTER

11

Deploying Pentaho Data Integration Solutions

As you learned in the preceding chapters, during the design and development phase, the Pentaho Data Integration (PDI) solution is executed mainly using Spoon. After the development phase, the data integration solution is typically moved to a server environment, either for further testing or for production purposes.

On the server, transformations and jobs are usually not launched using a graphical user tool such as Spoon. Instead, steps are taken to provide automated execution. Depending on the requirements of the data integration solution, execution may be scheduled or driven in a continuous manner by some background process. At any rate, the administrator must act to take the solution out of the development environment to put it to work on its target platform. We refer to this process as *deployment*.

There is more to deployment than installing the software and setting up automated execution. Measures must be put in place to allow system administrators to quickly verify, and if necessary, diagnose and repair, the data integration solution. For example, there must be some form of notification to confirm whether automated execution has taken place. In addition, data must be gathered and examined to measure how well the processes are executed. We refer to these activities as *monitoring*.

In this chapter, we provide an overview of the features and tools you can use to organize deployment, and to monitor your PDI solution. The aim of this chapter is not to dictate how you should manage your PDI solutions. Rather, this chapter should provide you with sufficient information to make informed decisions on which tools and strategies best meet your needs.

Configuration Management

Jobs and transformations rely on resources such as file system directories, files, and database servers. During development, these resources are typically also reserved for development purposes. For example, instead of pointing a transformation to the actual source systems, a development or test version of the source system is used. Likewise, output of the transformation is directed to a development or test version of the target system.

For deployment, all elements that are specific to the development environment must also work correspondingly on the target system. In some cases, it may be possible to do this without altering the solution. For example, in the case of file resources, it may be possible to consistently use relative paths, which are then dynamically resolved at runtime. In other cases, something must happen to point the components of the data integration solution to the right resources for the target environment.

One way to provide the right resources for the target platform is to modify the transformation or job accordingly. However, this is not a very good solution. It may simply be too much work to replace all references to database servers and the like throughout the solution. More important, there is a distinct possibility that modifying a job or transformation will introduce errors.

A better way to provide the right resources is to somehow parameterize all components that are dependent upon the environment. This way, this data can be supplied at runtime without changing the job or transformation itself.

We refer to all environment-dependent data as the *configuration*. The process responsible for maintaining this data and providing it to the solution is called *configuration management*. There are a few constructs that allow configuration management:

- Variables for configuring jobs and transformations
- JNDI connections for managing database connections
- A repository to manage multiple developers working on the same data integration solution, and also to manage database connections

These topics are discussed in detail in the remainder of this section.

Using Variables

Most properties of steps, job entries, and database connections can be parameterized using *variables*. Variables are placeholders for values. At runtime, the actual values for these variables becomes known, and the occurrence of each variable is replaced by its runtime value. To be more precise, the actual substitution of the variable with its value takes place in the step's initialization phase, and remains fixed during the running phase (the initialization and running phases are explained in Chapter 10 in the section ''CREATE TABLE dim_date: Using the Execute SQL Script Step'').

NOTE **Transformation steps often allow properties to be parameterized by specific fields from the input stream. Although this device can sometimes be used for configuration management, it is often better to keep a clear separation between the actual data transformation (which is the domain of fields) and the environment-specific configuration (which is best done with variables).**

Variables in Configuration Properties

In configuration dialogs, a tiny red dollar sign icon appears on the right side of those properties where variables may be entered. This icon is shown in Figure 11-1.

Figure 11-1: The variable icon

To refer to a variable, you can use a syntax similar to that for UNIX or Windows environment variables. The following code shows two alternative ways of referring to a variable named `foo`:

```
${foo}
%%foo%%
```

It is perfectly valid to embed variable references within a literal property value. For example, Figure 11-2 shows the configuration dialog of a Text file output step that uses the variable `os_user` to parameterize part of the file system path to the output file.

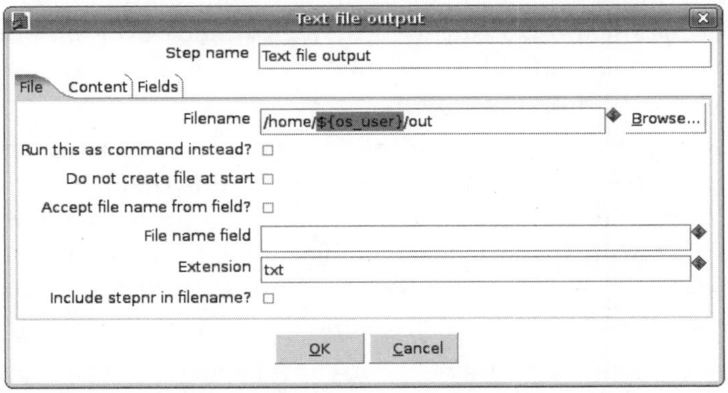

Figure 11-2: Embedding variable references in property values

NOTE **If you don't want to type the variable, you can also use the keyboard shortcut Ctrl+Spacebar, which brings up a list where you can select the desired variable. For example, Figure 11-3 shows the picklist of all available variables. Notice the tooltip displaying the current value for the variable.**

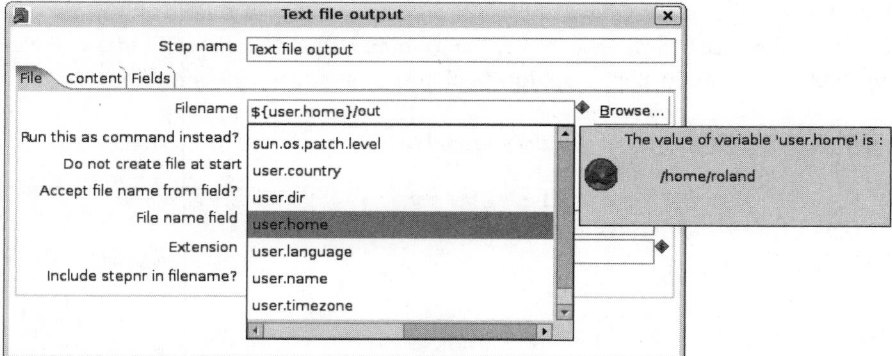

Figure 11-3: Picking variables from a list

User-Defined Variables

As the name implies, *user-defined variables* are created by the user. The `os_user` variable shown in Figure 11-2 is a typical example of such a user-defined variable. User-defined variables obtain their value in one of the following ways:

- Transformations can create and/or change the value of variables using a Set Variables step.
- A Set Variables job entry is available to set variables from within a job.
- In Spoon, you can set default variable values per job and per transformation in the grid that appears in the right bottom of the Execute a transformation and Execute a job dialogs. In the development phase, this allows you to use variables even when executing the job or transformation stand-alone from within Spoon.
- In Spoon, you can create and assign global variables in the Set Environment variables dialog. You can invoke this dialog via Menu ➢ Edit ➢ Set Environment Values. Using Menu ➢ Edit ➢ Show Environment Values, you can inspect all available variables and their values. Both of these dialogs are useful when developing or testing multiple jobs or transformations that rely on a common set of variables.
- Variables can be entered as a `<NAME>=<VALUE>` pair in the `kettle.properties` file. This file resides in the `.kettle` directory beneath the user's home directory.

NOTE **For UNIX-based systems, the location of `kettle.properties` is `/home/<user>/.kettle`.**

For Windows, this is usually `C:\Documents and Settings\<user>\.kettle`.

User-defined variables that are defined in the `kettle.properties` file have global scope. This means they are accessible in all jobs and transformations. For the Set Variables step and job entry, the scope can be defined in the Variable scope type column, as shown in Figure 11-4.

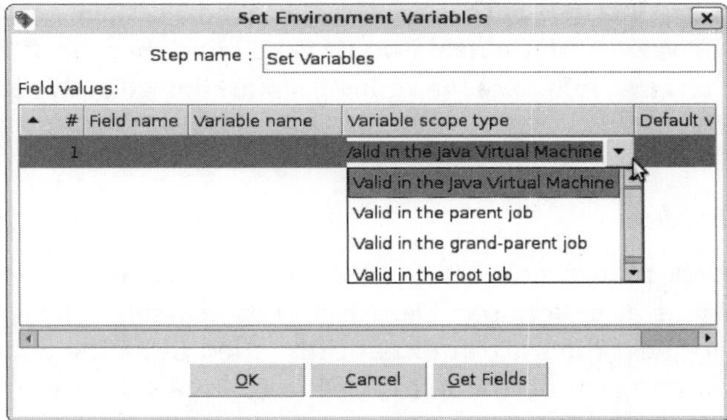

Figure 11-4: Choosing variable scope in a Set Variables step

The available scopes are:

- **Valid in the parent job**—This scope is available for both the Set Variables transformation step as well as the job entry. Variables with this scope are available in the job that contains the transformation or job entry respectively. Other transformations contained in that job can also refer to the variable.
- **Valid in the current job**—This scope is available for the Set Variables job entry. Variables with this scope are available in the containing job and the transformations and jobs therein. Functionally this scope is equivalent to the Valid in the parent job scope available in the Set Variables transformation step.
- **Valid in the grand-parent job**—This scope is available for the Set Variables transformation step. Variables with this scope are available in the job that contains this transformation (the parent) and also in the job that contains that job (grand-parent). All jobs and transformations contained by the grand-parent job can reference the value, too.
- **Valid in the root job**—Variables with this scope are available in the top-level job and all the jobs and transformations directly or indirectly

contained therein can reference the variable. This scope is supported by both the transformation step and the job entry.

- **Valid in the Java Virtual Machine (JVM)**—The variable is a true global variable and is visible to all jobs and transformations that happen to run in the same instance of the Java Virtual Machine. This scope is supported by both the transformation step and the job entry.

WARNING **Use variables with virtual machine scope with caution. In scenarios where one Java Virtual Machine is used to run multiple instances of the PDI engine, such as when running inside the Pentaho BI server, all running jobs refer to the exact same instance of the variable. This almost certainly excludes any use case where the value of the variable would need to be changed. If the value is changed, all jobs that reference the variable almost immediately see the new value of the variable.**

Built-in Variables

Built-in variables reflect properties of things that have to do with the runtime environment and Pentaho Data Integration itself. These variables are predefined, and the values are automatically filled in by the engine.

Built-in variables include the name of the current transformation step, the location of the current transformation, and the name of the operation system.

Variables Example: Dynamic Database Connections

To illustrate how to actually use variables, let's look at a practical example that illustrates how you can use variables to manage database connection configuration. In the example, the variables are used to configure a MySQL connection, but the same principles apply to any database connection.

1. Create a new transformation and store it as `set_variables` in a directory on the file system. Add a Generate Rows step from the Input category. Configure the step by adding the `HOST`, `DB`, `PORT`, `USER`, `PASSWORD`, and `TABLE` variables, as shown in Figure 11-5. Note the values entered in the Default value column of the grid and the Variable scope type setting. Run the transformation once; this will create the variables in the Spoon environment. This makes it more convenient to refer to these variables from within other transformations and jobs you might be designing.

NOTE **Note that in the `set_variables` step, the password is entered in plain text. This constitutes a security hazard, as anybody that can read the transformation file can also read the password. This security risk can be mitigated by using *obfuscated passwords*. Obfuscated passwords are discussed in more detail in the section "Using Obfuscated Database Passwords" later in this chapter.**

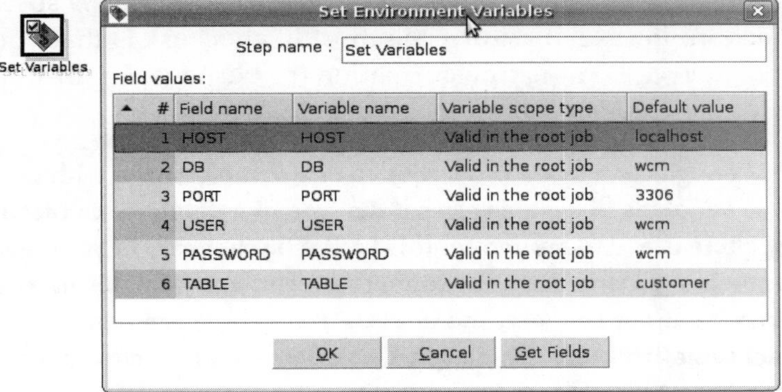

Figure 11-5: Setting variables

2. Create another transformation called `count_rows` and store it in the same location as the `set_variables` transformation. Add a MySQL database connection called `Source` and use variable references for the connection properties, as shown in Figure 11-6.

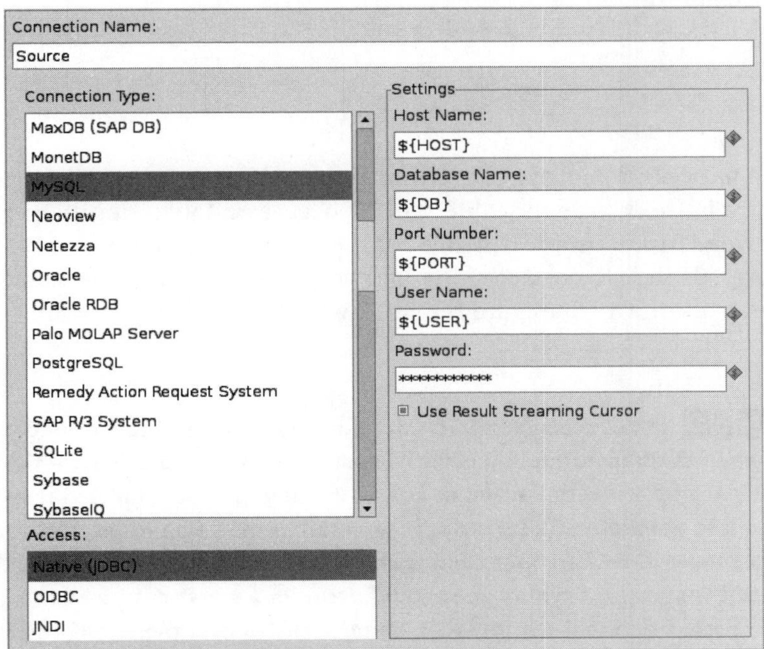

Figure 11-6: A variable database connection

Note that all properties in the Settings frame are parameterized using variable references. (The `Password` property value is shown as a series of asterisks even though its value really is `${PASSWORD}`.) Test the connection. In case of failure, the most likely cause is that you forgot to run the `set_variables` transformation (or perhaps you mistyped one or more of the values).

NOTE **Although connection properties can be parameterized with variables, you cannot use variables to dynamically set the type of a database connection. However, there is a workaround for this limitation that may fit your requirements. You can create a generic database connection, and use variables to parameterize the `Custom Connection URL` and `Custom Driver Class` name properties. This allows you to switch from, say, a MySQL database to an Oracle database depending upon the values of the variables.**

This workaround may not be suitable in all cases. In a specific JDBC connection, the database type setting influences which SQL dialect is used by PDI to communicate to the database. Some steps behave differently depending on the capabilities of the database, and for this reason some functionality is not available for generic database connections.

3. Add a Table input step and configure it to use the `Source` connection. Enter the following SQL statement:

```
SELECT '${TABLE}' AS table_name
,      COUNT(*)   AS row_count
FROM   ${TABLE}
```

The variable `TABLE` appears twice in the SQL statement: once as-is in the `FROM` clause, where its value will be used as a table identifier, and once between single quotes in the `SELECT` list, where it is used as a string literal. Be sure to check the Replace variables in script? checkbox so these instances of a variable are replaced with the value of the `TABLE` variable at runtime.

WARNING **In the preceding SQL statement, variables are substituted by their value when the transformation is initialized. Because variable substitution is basically a simple text replacement action, it can lead to unexpected results when you use it to generate SQL (or script in general). If the value of the `TABLE` variable is not a simple identifier, but contains characters that have a meaning of their own in the SQL language, a syntax error could occur. In a worst-case scenario, the resulting SQL statement may even be harmful and deliver the wrong result or accidentally delete data.**

For this reason, you should avoid using variables in script if possible. For the Table input step, you can often use parameters instead of variables. Parameters are placeholders for value-expressions, and are denoted using a question mark. They

can appear any place where you normally can have a value-expression such as a literal or a column reference. In the case of the preceding example, the variable in the `SELECT` list could have been omitted by using a parameter so that the first part of the statement would read:

```
SELECT ? AS table_name
```

4. Add a Text file output step, and add an incoming hop from the Table input step. Configure the step and edit the `Filename` property so it reads

   ```
   ${Internal.Transformation.Filename.Directory}/${TABLE}
   ```

   as shown in Figure 11-7. Note the two variables separated by a slash. The first is a built-in variable that allows you to build file system paths relative to the location of the transformation. The second is a user-defined variable that was created when you ran the `set_variables` transformation.

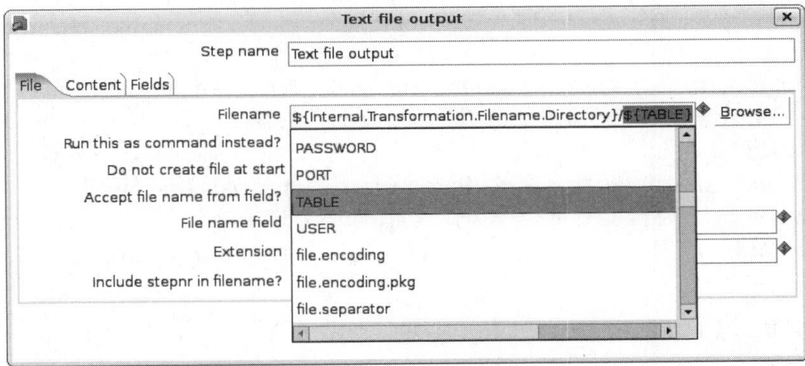

Figure 11-7: Variable file output

TIP You can use the Ctrl+Spacebar keyboard shortcut to bring up a list of existing variables and select them. Conclude the configuration by adding the `table_name` and `row_count` fields by pressing the Get Fields button on the Fields tab.

5. Create a job and store it in the same location as the transformations. Add a START job entry and two Transformation job entries. Configure one of the transformation steps. Rename it to `set_variables` and modify the transformation filename property so that it reads

   ```
   ${Internal.Job.Filename.Directory}/set_variables.ktr
   ```

   Note that this is similar to the `Filename` configuration for the Text file output step in the `count_rows` transformation: this variable has the effect of providing a file system path relative to that of the current job. Create a hop from the START entry to the `set_variables` job entry. Rename the other transformation job entry to `count_rows` and point it to the `count_rows` transformation. Add a hop going from the `set_variables` job entry to the `count_rows` job entry. Your job should now look similar to Figure 11-8. (Note that in the figure, the contents of the transformation job entries are also shown below the actual job. This is added for clarification— on screen, the job looks like the top half of Figure 11-8.) Run the job.

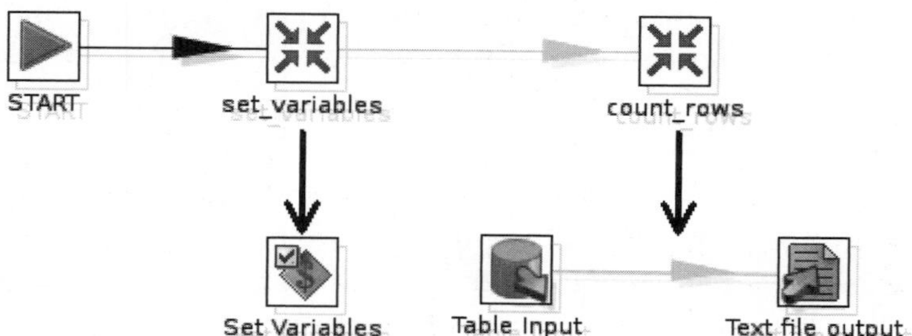

Figure 11-8: A job with a variable database connection

In this example, you created a job that calls two transformations. The first transformation uses the Set Variables step to create a number of user-defined variables. These variables then became available at the level of the calling job. The subsequent transformation picked up the variables and used their values to configure a database connection. In addition, file paths were set up relative to the location of the job and transformation files using built-in variables.

More About the Set Variables Step

From the standpoint of configuration management, it is clear that the usage of built-in variables contributes to ease of configuration management. Relative paths eliminate hard-wired paths from the jobs and transformations, making it easier to transfer files from the development environment to the deployment environment without breaking the data integration solution.

It may be less clear how the user-defined variables created by the Set Variables step improve configuration management. In the example, it seems the configuration properties for the database connection are still hard-coded inside a transformation—they have simply moved from one transformation to the other. However, it is still an improvement if you consider that more transformations such as `row_count` may be added to the job. These other transformations can use the same variables to define their database connections in exactly the same way, allowing all connection parameters for the entire job to be changed by editing only one single transformation.

So, the Set Variables step can be used as a single point of definition to parameterize resources such as database connections for an entire job, or directory and file names. Although this is a good thing, it is still undesirable that the `set_variables` transformation would need to be edited to adjust the transformation to work on another environment.

Fortunately, the Set Variables step is not confined to the default values used in the example. Rather, the normal mode of operation is to use the input stream of the Set Variables step to fill in the values. This way, configuration data can be stored in a resource external to any job or transformation. This allows the configuration to be managed using files or database tables or whatever data source can be read by Pentaho Data Integration.

Set Variables Step Gotchas

An important point to remember is that the Set Variables transformation step is there so that transformations can convey configuration data to jobs and other transformations. You should not attempt to use the Set Variables step to convey information within one and the same job and/or transformation.

You cannot reliably both set and use variables within one and the same transformation because variable substitution takes place in the initialization phase. In the running phase, the value remains fixed until the job or transformation is finished. If you find that you would like to set variables using data from a transformation to configure subsequent steps in the same transformation, the solution is to create a new job with two transformations. This way, you can set the variables in the first transformation, and use them in the other one.

Also remember that the Set Variables step requires exactly one input row. You may find it counterintuitive that the Set Variables step does not support multiple input rows, but try to imagine how it would work out in cases where the transformation is part of a job. The job only sees the variable as it is after the entire transformation is executed. The job cannot see any of the values the variables might have had during the transformation—it can only see whatever value was last assigned to the variable.

Using JNDI Connections

In the previous section, you learned how to use variables for configuration management. Although variables provide the most flexible solution to deal with multiple configurations, they have the disadvantage that the jobs and transformations need to be designed especially to benefit from them.

There is an alternative way to manage database connection configurations. You can consider using JNDI instead of plain JDBC connections.

What Is JNDI?

JNDI (pronounced "gindy") is an acronym for Java Naming and Directory Interface. JNDI is a general way to attach a name to refer to a resource of pretty much any type, such as database connections, URLs, files, and classes.

NOTE **JNDI is part of the Java platform. It is heavily used in many Java applications to solve configuration issues. For example, a sizeable part of the configuration files of the Pentaho BI server use JNDI to manage components. In fact, if you want to run your transformations and jobs inside the Pentaho BI Server, JNDI should be your preferred way of creating PDI connections, as you can hook into the JNDI connections configured at the server level.**

A full discussion of JNDI is outside the scope of this book. If you like, you can find out more about JNDI on Sun's website: `http://java.sun.com/products/jndi/`.

In the context of PDI, a JNDI connection is simply a named JDBC connection for which the exact connection details are stored outside the transformations and jobs. Whenever the transformations and jobs need to refer to the JNDI connection, they do so only by using the connection's name. Whenever the actual connection to the database needs to be established, the name is resolved to the configuration data, which are then used to actually instantiate the connection.

Creating a JNDI Connection

To create a JNDI connection, use a text editor to open the file `jdbc.properties` located in the `simple-jndi` directory beneath the PDI home directory.

NOTE **The `jdbc.properties` file is simply part of a particular JNDI implementation provided by PDI. Other applications, such as the Pentaho BI server, have more advanced JNDI implementations, which require a different configuration procedure.**

Most likely you'll find that the file contains a number of lines already. You'll need to add lines to configure the driver class name, JDBC connect string, username, and password, and a generic line to identify that this JNDI resource is a database connection. The general syntax is shown in Listing 11-1.

Listing 11-1: Syntax for JNDI connections in jdbc.properties

```
<jndi-name>/type=javax.sql.DataSource
<jndi-name>/driver=<Fully qualified JDBC driver class name>
<jndi-name>/url=<Driver and connection specific connectstring>
<jndi-name>/user=<Database user name>
<jndi-name>/user=<Database password name>
```

TIP **If you have trouble figuring out the exact values for the driver class name and/or the `connectstring`, you may find this tip useful. First, create an ordinary JDBC connection in the Database Connection dialog. (This process is described in detail in Chapter 9.) Next, press the Feature List button at the bottom of the**

Database Connection dialog. This brings up a list of properties for the database connection. Look for the properties named Driver Class and URL. Figure 11-9 shows an example of such a feature list.

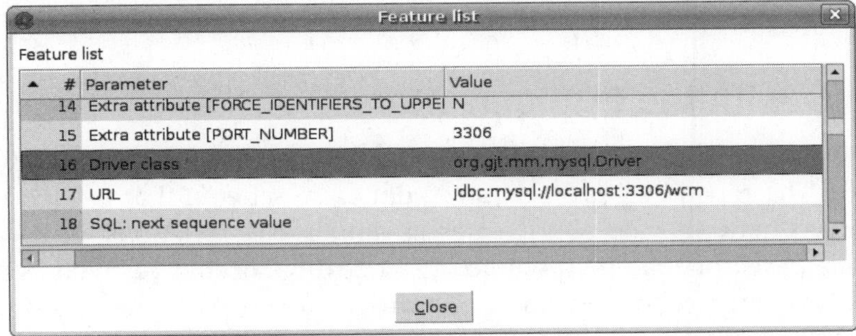

Figure 11-9: Determining the JDBC driver class and URL with the Feature list

Listing 11-2 shows what five such lines might look like to create a JNDI connection called `wcm` to connect to the `wcm` database.

Listing 11-2: An example JNDI connection to the wcm database

```
#
# A JNDI Connection to the wcm database named wcm
#
wcm/type=javax.sql.DataSource          # define a JNDI DB connection
wcm/driver=com.mysql.jdbc.Driver       # Name of the Driver Java Class
wcm/url=jdbc:mysql://localhost/wcm     # JDBC URL (connectstring)
wcm/user=wcm                           # database user name
wcm/password=wcm                       # password for database user
```

WARNING **Be aware that the database password is stored in plaintext in `jdbc.properties`.**

After adding the necessary details to the `jdbc.properties` file, you still need to create the connection at the transformation or job level. In this case, you need to select the appropriate connection type to MySQL (as this information is not part of the JNDI configuration in `jdbc.properties`), set the Access type to JNDI, and then type the JNDI name.

JNDI Connections and Deployment

If you consistently use JNDI connections, you won't need to modify your jobs and transformations, nor will you need to pass the appropriate parameter values at runtime. All you need to do is ensure that both the development environment and the deployment environment are configured to support all used JNDI names.

For example, if you want to run jobs and transformations on the PDI environment on the deployment platform, you'll need to modify the `jdb.properties` file there accordingly. If your deployment platform consists of the Pentaho BI server, you'll need to use the Administration Console to configure the appropriate JNDI names on that end, too.

Working with the PDI Repository

Virtually all components in Pentaho Data Integration can interact with a *repository*. The repository is a relational database schema that is used to store jobs, transformations, and objects such as database connections.

Using a repository can help you to organize development as well as deployment of data integration solutions. The repository can be used by multiple developers simultaneously, thus forming a centralized storage place. Because the repository is just a database, it can be backed up as one, and reports can be run against it.

Using a repository also simplifies configuration management of database connections. In the repository, database connections are stored as separate objects that can be reused in multiple jobs and transformations.

The remainder of this section describes how to use the repository when working with Pentaho Data Integration tools such as Spoon, Kitchen, and Pan. The section "Running Inside the Pentaho BI Server" later in this chapter, describes how to use a PDI repository for running jobs and transformations as action sequence components.

Creating a PDI Repository

You can create a new repository using the Select a repository dialog in Spoon. This dialog opens by default when you start Spoon, unless you modified the options to avoid this behavior. You can control this using the Show repository dialog at startup checkbox in the options dialog. You can also invoke the repository dialog from within Spoon. This is done either through the main menu using Menu ➤ Repository ➤ Connect to repository or by using the keyboard shortcut Ctrl+R. The repository dialog is shown in Figure 11-10.

You can create a new repository by pressing the New button in the repository dialog. A dialog entitled Repository information opens. In this dialog you must specify the database connection to connect to the repository.

Database connections for the repository are no different from ordinary Pentaho Data Integration database connections. There are no special requirements for a particular RDBMS—you should be able to use all popular products such as Microsoft SQL Server, MySQL, Oracle, and PostgreSQL with no issue. See Chapter 9 for information on creating database connections.

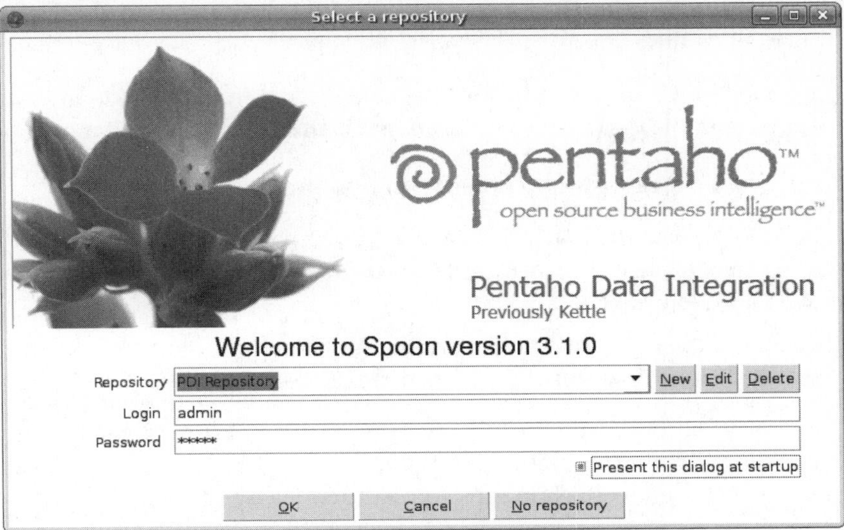

Figure 11-10: The repository dialog

NOTE **At the time of this writing, it is not possible to use SQLite as the underlying database system. If you are looking for an embedded database solution for the repository, you can try H2 or Derby.**

When you've selected the database connection, click the Create button to create the new repository. Or, to upgrade an existing repository, click the Upgrade button. However, there are a number of additional things to consider when upgrading an existing repository. Therefore, upgrading is covered in a separate subsection later in this chapter.

NOTE **Creating the repository involves creation of database tables. You must ensure the account specified in the database connection has sufficient privileges for this task.**

After you confirm that you really want to modify the database, the repository tables are created in the specified database. Note that this will not create a new schema. The repository tables are created in the schema defined at the connection level.

Connecting to the Repository

To use a repository for loading and storing PDI solutions, you must first establish a connection to one. This is done by specifying the credentials of a repository user in the Repository dialog (see Figure 11-10). Specify the name of the repository user in the Login field, and the password in the Password field. Then, click OK.

NOTE **Credentials for the repository user are distinct from the account data associated with the database connection that is used for the repository.**

A newly created repository comes with two predefined users:

- The `admin` user (default password: `admin`) has full privileges for the repository, and should primarily be used to create new repository users for ETL developers.
- The `guest` user (default password: `guest`) can only read from the repository, and should be used to explore the repository.

Typically, you would create other users and configure those to perform specific tasks with the repository. Repository user management is described in detail in the section "Managing Repository User Accounts" later in this chapter.

Once a connection to a repository is established, Spoon will automatically use it. For example, when connected to a repository, the actions File ➤ Save and File ➤ Open correspond to storing to and loading from the repository. When there is no active connection these actions default to storing and loading files from the file system.

You can always disconnect from the repository by choosing the Disconnect repository option from the Repository menu, or by using the keyboard shortcut Ctrl+D.

NOTE **Within Spoon, it can sometimes be confusing when you have to work with multiple repositories. To quickly find out if you are connected and to see which repository you are connected to, look at the window title of the main application window. If you are connected to a repository, the title reads:**

Spoon - [<*repository name*>] [<*repository user*>]

where <*repository name*> stands for the name of the repository, and <*repository user*> stands for the repository user.

Automatically Connecting to a Default Repository

You may find it inconvenient to explicitly log on to the repository. If you usually work with just one single repository, you can configure Pentaho Data Integration to automatically connect to a specific default repository. This setting for the default repository will be used by Spoon, but also the other Pentaho Data Integration tools.

To set up the automatic login for the default repository, use a text-editor to open the `kettle.properties` file located in the `.kettle` directory beneath your home directory. Then, add lines for the variables `KETTLE_REPOSITORY`,

KETTLE_USER, and KETTLE_PASSWORD, and assign values for the name of the repository, the name of the repository user, and the user's password. See Listing 11-3 for an example.

Listing 11-3: Modify kettle.properties to automatically connect to a repository

```
# This is <user-home>/.kettle/kettle.properties
#
# Automatically login in as admin/admin on the Repository PDI_REPO
#
KETTLE_REPOSITORY=PDI_REPO
KETTLE_USER=admin
KETTLE_PASSWORD=admin
```

Note that the value for KETTLE_REPOSITORY must be the name of a repository found in the repositories.xml file, and the values for KETTLE_USER and KETTLE_PASSWORD must correspond to a repository user of said repository.

WARNING **The kettle.properties file is plaintext. Although it resides in the hidden directory .kettle, it can still be read by anybody that can access the file. Because the repository credentials are stored unencrypted, you should be aware that automatically connecting to the repository in this manner poses a security risk.**

The Repository Explorer

If you are connected to the repository, you can open the *Repository Explorer* to examine and manage its contents. You can invoke the Repository Explorer by choosing the Explore Repository option in the Repository menu, or by using the keyboard shortcut Ctrl+E. The Repository Explorer window is shown in Figure 11-11.

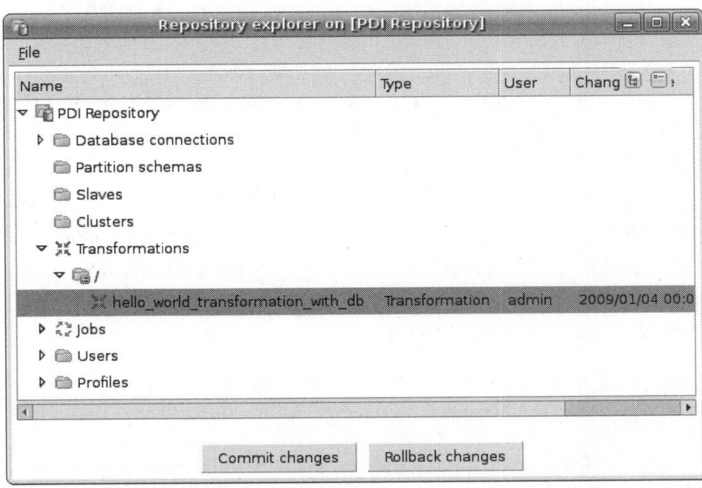

Figure 11-11: The Repository Explorer

The Repository Explorer displays the repository in a tree view. To work with a repository item, right-click on it to open a context menu. From there, choose the appropriate action. In this way you can:

- **Manage database connections**—Database connections are stored on a global level in the repository and can be shared by all transformations and jobs in the same repository. The context menu of the Database connections node lets you create new connections. The context menu for the individual connections enables you to edit or delete the corresponding connection.
- **Manage repository directories**—In the repository, transformations and jobs are always stored in some directory, much like files are stored in a particular directory on the file system. This is useful to structure the data integration solution by keeping related elements together. There is a separate tree of directories for both jobs and transformations. In both cases, the root directory is built-in and named `/` (forward slash character). You can use the directory context menu to create, rename, and delete directories.
- **Export jobs and transformations to file**—Choosing Export jobs or Export transformations will save each individual job or transformation to a separate `.kjb` or `.ktr` file respectively. These actions also recursively export the directory structure and contents downstream of the selected directory.
- **Dump a directory and all of its contents into a single XML file**—You can do this by choosing the Export all objects to an XML file option. This is very convenient in case you need to deploy a branch of your PDI solutions to another repository. You can also dump the entire repository to such an XML file by using the File menu of the Repository Explorer window. In this menu, you will also find an option to import the contents of such an XML dump file.
- **Manage user accounts**—This topic is discussed in more detail in the following subsection.

TIP **You can also export jobs and transformations from the main File. Selecting Menu ➤ File ➤ Export all linked resources to XML is usually the most convenient option, as it will export not only the current job/transformation, but also all transformations and jobs on which it is dependent. When choosing this option, you are prompted to enter the location of a `.zip` file. After storing all linked jobs and transformations in the `.zip` file, a dialog appears to inform you how to open individual jobs or transformations stored in the `.zip` file (without first unzipping the file). This dialog is shown in Figure 11-12.**

Managing Repository User Accounts

We already mentioned that, by default, a new repository provides two user accounts: an `admin` account for repository administration, and a `guest` account for repository introspection. To benefit from the repository when developing data integration solutions, you'll need to create user accounts for data integration developers so they can use the repository to store and retrieve their work.

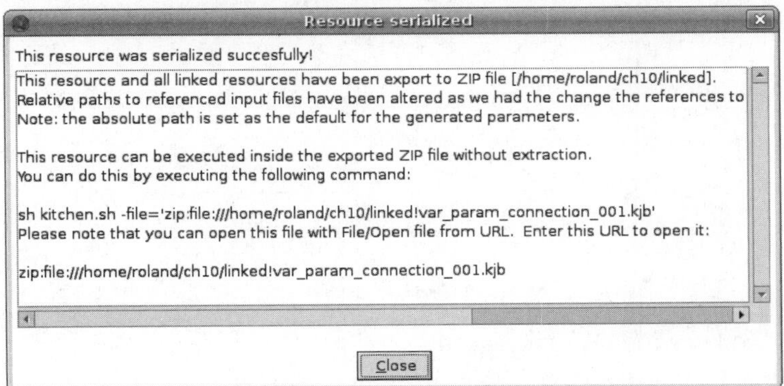

Figure 11-12: Dialog informing you about the job/transformation export

Before we explain in detail how to create new users, it is necessary to consider a few things about user account management in general. In virtually all affairs of user account management, there are two things to consider: identification and authorization. *Identification* is concerned with verifying that a system user corresponds to the actual real-world user. *Authorization* has to do with determining which actions a system user is allowed to perform.

For identification, all real-world PDI Repository users need a username and password, which serve as *credentials*. The real-world user is expected to keep the password secret so that the system may assume that a login request comprising a particular combination of username and password does indeed identify the real-world user.

For authorization, users have an associated *profile*. A profile is a named collection of *permissions* that determine what functionality the user can access. In a newly created repository, three such profiles are already present:

- **Administrator**—This is the default profile for the built-in `admin` user. It allows the user to use all PDI functionality, including user account management.
- **Read-only**—This is the default profile for the built-in `guest` user.
- **User**—This profile is suitable for regular data integration developers.

To create a new repository user, open the Repository Explorer and right-click on the Users node (or a node of a particular user) to bring up its context menu. Choose New user. A little dialog entitled User Information appears. In the User Information dialog, you must specify the username in the Login field, and the password in the Password field. In addition, you can use the Profile list box to assign a profile to the new user. Figure 11-13 shows the Repository Explorer, the Users node context menu, and the User Information dialog.

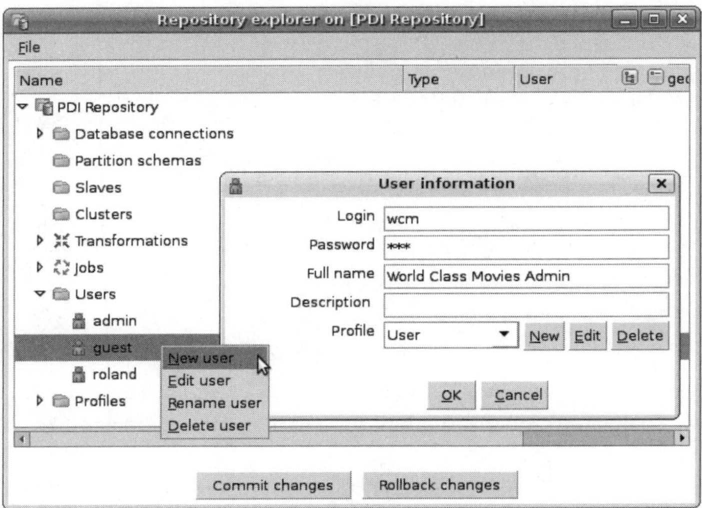

Figure 11-13: Creating a new repository user

The User Information dialog also allows you to create new profiles by grouping one or more individual permissions. However, we find the built-in Profile list to be sufficient for most, if not all, use cases. The actual number of permissions is rather small, and individual permissions are not fine-grained enough to build many more meaningful profiles.

Each user that is connected to the repository can use the Edit current user option in the Repository menu to invoke the User Information dialog to modify their own account. Alternatively, you can use the keyboard shortcut Ctrl+U.

How PDI Keeps Track of Repositories

When PDI tools are requested to connect to a particular repository, they look in the `repositories.xml` file. This file resides in the `.kettle` directory beneath the user's home directory.

NOTE **For Windows-based systems, the most likely location is:**

```
C:\Documents and Settings\<user>\.kettle
```

For UNIX-based systems, the location is:

```
/home/<user>/.kettle
```

Listing 11-4 shows what the (partial) contents of the `repositories.xml` file could look like.

Listing 11-4: Contents of the repositories.xml file

```
<?xml version="1.0" encoding="UTF-8"?>
<repositories>
  <connection>
    <name>Repo Connection</name>
    <server>localhost</server>
    <type>MYSQL</type>
    <access>Native</access>
    <database>pdi_repository</database>
    <port>3306</port>
    <username>root</username>
    <password>Encrypted 2be98afc86aa7f2e4cb79ce7dc781bed6</password>
  </connection>
  <repository>
    <name>PDI REPO</name>
    <description/>
    <connection>PDI Repository2</connection>
  </repository>
</repositories>
```

We mention the `repositories.xml` file because you may want to copy it to another user's home directory, or to another machine—for example, the deployment environment. You may even need to edit it manually to fit the database connection parameters to the deployment environment.

As you can see in Listing 11-4, the format is pretty self-explanatory, and you should have no problem manually editing this.

Upgrading an Existing Repository

If you plan to use Pentaho Data Integration with a repository that was created by a prior version of Spoon, you must upgrade the repository. The process to upgrade an existing repository is identical to that to create a new repository: click the Upgrade button to upgrade an existing repository, or the Create button to create a new one if it does not yet exist.

WARNING **If you intend to upgrade the repository, we strongly advise you to back up the old repository. You can use your database tools to create an ordinary database backup.**

In addition to making a backup of your database, you are strongly advised to export all objects in the repository to an XML file. You can do this using the Repository Explorer described earlier. Another possibility is to use the Pan command-line tool, described later in this chapter. The benefit of exporting all objects to a file is that it allows you to quickly import the solution into a newly created empty repository. This makes it easier to overcome any problems you might encounter upgrading the repository.

Running in the Deployment Environment

You have already seen plenty of examples of running jobs and transformations using Spoon. However, Spoon is not a typical execution environment for deployment purposes. Spoon is completely dependent upon user interaction, and it requires a graphical user interface, both of which are not likely to be available in a deployment environment.

In typical deployment environments, job and transformation execution is automated and often triggered by some kind of timed schedule. In this section, we take a closer look at the tools that can be used for these purposes.

Running from the Command Line

Jobs and transformations can be launched using the command-line tools Kitchen and Pan respectively. Pan and Kitchen are lightweight wrappers around the data integration engine. They do little more than interpret command-line parameters and invoke the engine to launch a transformation or job. These tools are primarily useful for integrating Pentaho Data Integration solutions with operating system–level scripts and scheduling solutions.

Kitchen and Pan are started using shell scripts, which reside in the Pentaho Data Integration installation directory. For Windows, the scripts are called `Kitchen.bat` and `Pan.bat` respectively. For UNIX-based systems, the scripts are called `kitchen.sh` and `pan.sh`.

NOTE **The scripts for UNIX-based operating systems are not executable by default. They must be made executable using the `chmod` command.**

Command-Line Parameters

The Kitchen and Pan user interface consists of a number of command-line parameters. Running Kitchen and Pan without any parameters outputs a list of all available parameters. Basically, the syntax for specifying parameters consists of a forward slash (/) or dash (-) character, immediately followed by the parameter name:

```
[/-] name [[:=] value]
```

Most parameters accept a value. The parameter value is specified directly after the parameter name by either a colon (`:`) or an equals character (=), followed by the actual value. The value may optionally be enclosed in single (`'`) or double (`"`) quote characters. This is mandatory in case the parameter value itself contains white space characters.

WARNING **Using the dash and equals characters to specify parameters can lead to issues on Windows platforms. Stick to the forward slash and colon to avoid problems.**

Although jobs and transformations are functionally very different, there is virtually no difference in launching them from the command line. Therefore, Kitchen and Pan share most of their command-line parameters. The generic command-line parameters can be categorized as follows:

- Specify a job or transformation
- Control logging
- Specify a repository
- List available repositories and their contents

The common command-line parameters for both Pan and Kitchen are listed in Table 11-1.

Table 11-1: Generic command-line parameters for Kitchen and Pan

NAME	VALUE	PURPOSE
`Norep`	`Y`	Don't connect to a repository. Useful to bypass automatic login.
`Rep`	Repository name	Connect to repository with the specified name.
`User`	Repository username	Connect to repository with the specified username.
`Pass`	Repository user password	Connect to repository with the specified password.
`Listrep`	`Y`	Show a list of available repositories.
`Dir`	Path	Specify the repository directory.
`Listdir`	`Y`	List the available repository job/repository directories.
`File`	Filename	Specify a job or transformation stored in a file.
`Level`	`Error` | `Nothing` | `Basic` | `Detailed` | `Debug` | `Rowlevel`	Specify how much information should be logged.
`Logfile`	Filename for logging	Specify to which file you want to log. By default, the tools log to the standard output.
`Version`		Show the version, revision number, and build date of the tool.

Although the parameter names are common to both Kitchen and Pan, the semantics of the `dir` and `listdir` parameters are dependent upon the tool. For Kitchen, these parameters refer to the repositories' job directories. For Pan, these parameters refer to transformation directories.

Running Jobs with Kitchen

In addition to the generic command-line parameters, Kitchen supports a couple of other parameters, shown in Table 11-2.

Table 11-2: Command-line parameters specific to Kitchen

NAME	VALUE	PURPOSE
`Job`	Job Name	Specify the name of a job stored in the repository.
`listjobs`	Y	List the available jobs in the repository directory specified by the `dir` parameter.

Listing 11-5 provides a few examples of typical Kitchen command lines.

Listing 11-5: Typical Kitchen command lines

```
#
# list all available parameters
#
pdi-home> ./kitchen.sh

#
# run the job stored in /home/foo/daily_load.kjb
#
pdi-home> ./kitchen.sh /file:/home/foo/daily_load.kjb

#
# run the daily_load job from the repository named pdirepo
#
pdi-home> ./kitchen.sh /rep:pdirepo /user:admin /pass:admin \
        > /dir:/ /job:daily_load.kjb
```

Running Transformations with Pan

The Pan-specific command-line parameters are completely equivalent to the Kitchen-specific ones. They are shown in Table 11-3.

Table 11-3: Command-line parameters specific to Kitchen

NAME	VALUE	PURPOSE
`Trans`	Job Name	Specify the name of a job stored in the repository.
`Listtrans`	Y	List the available jobs in the repository directory specified by the `dir` parameter.

Using Custom Command-line Parameters

When using command-line tools to execute jobs and transformations, it can be useful to use command-line parameters to convey configuration data. For the command-line tools Kitchen and Pan, you can use Java Virtual Machine properties to achieve the effect of custom command-line parameters. The syntax for passing these ''custom parameters'' is:

```
-D<name>=<value>
```

The following code line illustrates how such a parameter could appear in a Kitchen command line:

```
pdi-home> kitchen.sh /file: -Dlanguage=en
```

In transformations, you can use the Get System Info step to obtain the value of the command-line parameters. You can find this step in the Input category. The Get System Info step generates one output row containing one or more fields having a system-generated value. The Get System Info step is configured by creating fields and picking a particular type of system value from a predefined list (see Figure 11-14).

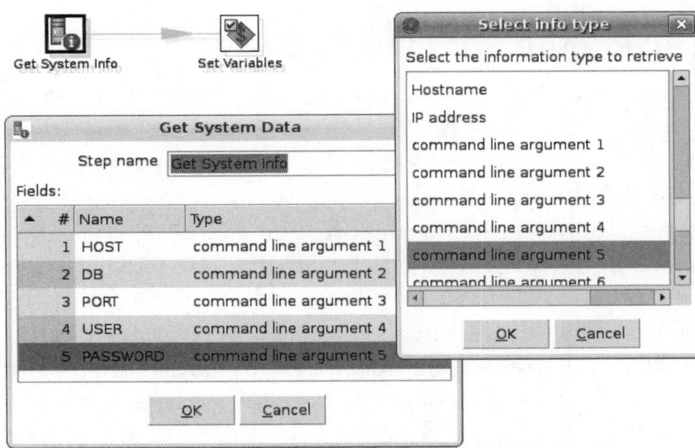

Figure 11-14: Capturing command-line parameters with the Get System Info step

Among the predefined system values, you'll find `command line argument 1` through `command line argument 10`. Fields with one of these types automatically take on the value of the corresponding `D<name>=<value>` command-line parameter.

By using the command-line parameter values as input for a Set Variables step, you can make the command-line parameters accessible to other jobs and transformations. This is also shown in Figure 11-14.

Using Obfuscated Database Passwords

To mitigate the security risk of passing plaintext passwords in the command line of tools like Kitchen and Pan, you can use obfuscated database passwords. You can use this technique to specify the password for the repository connection for the command line tools. You can use the same technique for any database connections that you configured using variables as discussed earlier in this chapter.

To use obfuscated passwords, you first need to run the `Encr.bat` script (for Windows systems) or `encr.sh` script (for UNIX-like systems), passing the plaintext password. Here's an example command to obfuscate the password `wcm`:

```
shell> encr.sh -kettle wcm
```

This command returns the following output:

```
Encrypted 2be98afc86aa7f2e4cb79ce10be85acd7
```

The text output is the actual obfuscated password. You can now use this instead of the plaintext password. Be sure to include the complete obfuscated password, including the readable part, `Encrypted`. This allows PDI to identify the password as obfuscated.

Running Inside the Pentaho BI Server

The Pentaho Platform provides components to integrate Pentaho Data Integration jobs and transformations in action sequences. This allows jobs and transformations to be scheduled using the Quartz scheduler that is built into the server. Another benefit of embedding PDI solutions in action sequences is that it allows for human interaction. For example, the action sequence can prompt the user for input, which can then be used to parameterize a transformation or job.

The integration of PDI into the Pentaho platform doesn't stop with mere execution of jobs and transformations. PDI transformations can transfer a result set to the calling action sequence, allowing reports to draw data directly from the PDI engine. The action sequence can do pretty much everything with the result set: display the data on a report or on a chart, loop through the rows and call a print job, send an e-mail message, use the row data as parameters for a report, and so on and so forth.

Transformations in Action Sequences

Transformations can be incorporated into action sequences using the Pentaho Data Integration process action. The following instructions describe how to use a transformation in an action sequence.

1. Open the action sequence in Pentaho Design Studio. In the Process Actions section, click the Add button or invoke the context menu to add a process action of the Pentaho Data Integration type. You can find this in the Process Action menu by selecting Add ➤ Get Data From ➤ Pentaho Data Integration.
2. Configure the Pentaho Data Integration process action to point it to a transformation. For a transformation stored in a file, use the Browse button to select the appropriate `.ktr` file. For a transformation stored in the repository, check the Use Kettle Repository checkbox, and select the desired directory and transformation using the Directory and Transformation drop-down lists.

NOTE You must configure the BI server to tell it which PDI repository to use. The procedure to do this is described later in this section.

3. If the transformation has a Get System Info step to capture command-line parameters, you can use the Transformation Inputs section to specify which inputs from the action sequence should be passed to the transformation. The Get System Info step is described in detail earlier in this chapter in the section "Using Custom Command-line Parameters".
4. If you want to use the output stream of one of the transformation steps in the action sequence, specify the name of the transformation step in the Transformation Step property. Note that although the property offers a list box, you must still manually type the name of the transformation step. You must also provide a name in the Output Name property to map the result set to an Action Sequence output. This name can then be used by subsequent process actions of the action sequence.

Figure 11-15 shows a simple action sequence containing three process actions: a Secure Filter Description action to prompt the user for a date, a Pentaho Data Integration action to run a transformation, and finally a Pentaho Report action to run a report based on the result set returned by the Pentaho Data Integration action.

Jobs in Action Sequences

The procedure for running a job within an action sequence is very similar to that for transformations. Jobs are executed by the Pentaho Data Integration Job process action. You can find this in the Process Action menu under Add ➤ Execute ➤ Pentaho Data Integration Job.

As with transformations, you can refer to either a file or an item in the repository. You can also specify inputs for a job, just like you can for a transformation. However, a job cannot return a result set to the action sequence.

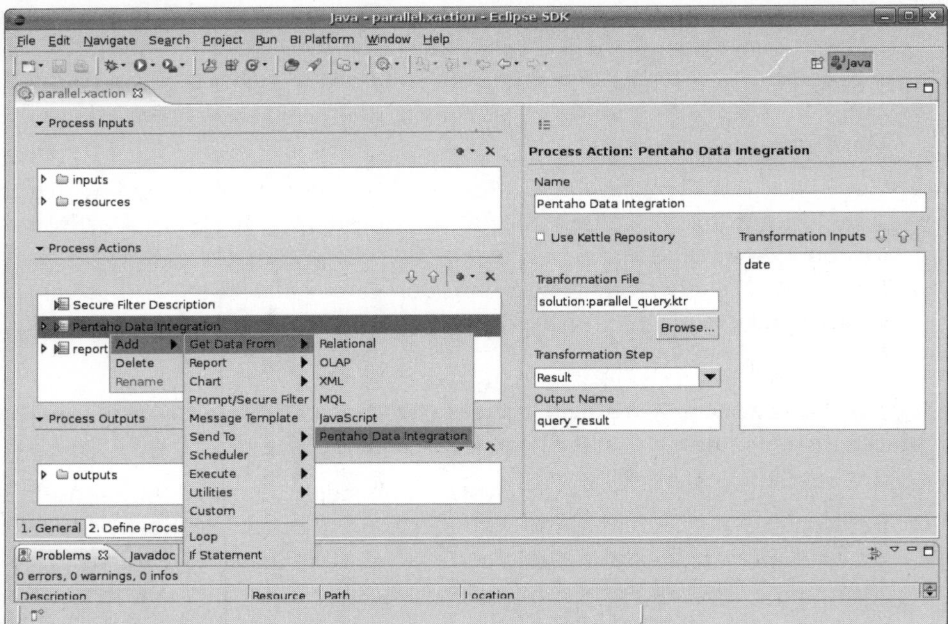

Figure 11-15: Using a transformation in an action sequence

The Pentaho BI Server and the PDI Repository

The Pentaho BI server has a separate configuration file that specifies where to look for jobs and transformations. By default, the server is configured to work with job and transformation files. If you want to use jobs and transformations stored in a PDI repository, you'll need to configure the server accordingly. For example, if you are getting error messages such as the following, you know you'll have to configure this.

```
Kettle.ERROR_0019 - RDBMS access to transformation not allowed when
repository type is 'files'
```

To configure the server to use the PDI repository, use a text editor to open the `settings.xml` file located in the `pentaho-solutions/system/kettle` directory. The contents of this file should look something like Listing 11-6.

Listing 11-6: Contents of the default settings.xml file

```
<kettle-repository>
  <!-- the location of the Kettle repositories.xml file
       leave empty when default (HOME/.kettle/repositories.xml) -->
  <repositories.xml.file></repositories.xml.file>
  <!-- files or rdbms -->
```

```
  <repository.type>files</repository.type>
  <!--  The name of the repository to use -->
  <repository.name></repository.name>
  <!--  The name of the repository user -->
  <repository.userid></repository.userid>
  <!--  The password -->
  <repository.password></repository.password>
</kettle-repository>
```

The comments in the `settings.xml` file are self-explanatory:

- Set the content of the `repository.type` element to `rdbms` if you want to use a PDI repository.
- Put the name of the repository you want to use in the `repository.name` element. This must be the name of an existing repository defined in PDI's `repositories.xml` file.
- Set the `repository.name` element to the name of the repository user that is to connect to the repository.
- Set the `repository.password` element to the password of the repository user.

Contrary to the suggestion in the comments appearing in the `settings.xml` file, it is not possible to specify a particular `repositories.xml` file using the `repositories.xml.file` element. If you do attempt to configure it, an error message like the following indicates it is not yet implemented on your platform:

```
Kettle.ERROR_0017 - Sorry, specifying the repositories.xml file is for
future use, taking the default file for now.
```

Remote Execution with Carte

Carte is a lightweight server that executes jobs or transformations in response to an HTTP request. A Carte server is called a *slave server*, because it responds to requests from elsewhere, and performs the associated work on behalf of the requesting party. Multiple slave servers that are used to collectively execute a single job or transformation are referred to as a *cluster*.

Remote execution and clustering are very powerful features, setting PDI apart as a data integration product that is suitable for cloud computing environments such as Amazon EC2. This means the data integration process can cost-effectively be scaled dynamically according to demand.

In this book, we cannot possibly describe all use cases and advantages of these features. Instead we will describe its architecture and components. This should serve as a good introduction for readers who want to use these features.

Why Remote Execution?

In one way or another, all the reasons to require remote execution or clustering are related to overcoming performance issues. The following list summarizes the most important performance problems that may be solved with remote execution and/or clustering:

- Scalability
- Availability
- Reduction of network traffic
- Reduction of latency

We will now explain these concepts in more detail.

Scalability

Every computer has a processing potential that is ultimately limited by hardware: CPU, memory, disk, and network. As long as none of these components is exhausted by the workload, there is no problem. However, an increasing workload will sooner or later cause one of the resources to be maxed out, thereby limiting the performance of the system as a whole. The term *scalability* refers to how well the system can be grown to keep up with an increasing workload.

There are two fundamental ways to grow a system:

- Upgrade hardware components with others that offer better performance. For example, you can replace a 1 GHz CPU with one that runs at 2 GHz. This strategy is referred to as *scale-up*.
- Add more computers with similar or comparable processing potential. This strategy is referred to as *scale-out*.

With Carte, PDI's remote execution capabilities enable clustering, and this allows the data integration workload to be distributed among a number of computers that work in parallel to get the job done. Parallelization allows more work to be done in the same span of time. This is a typical example of a scale-out architecture.

Availability

Availability of service is usually not the main goal for clustering in a data integration environment. However, when clustering for scale-out purposes, increased availability comes as an extra bonus. This deserves some explanation.

When a process depends on a single computer, that computer becomes a single point of failure. If the computer becomes unavailable for whatever reason, the service it normally provides becomes unavailable too.

A cluster has no such single point of failure. With Carte's clustering capability, in the event that one computer becomes unavailable, the remaining cluster can still be used to process jobs and transformations. The remaining cluster may take a little longer to accomplish the task because there are fewer workhorses to distribute the load to, but the fact remains that the service itself is still available.

Reduction of Network Traffic

If your data integration problem involves large data volumes on remote hosts, or many data sources on remote hosts, pulling the data across the network to one computer to execute a transformation or job can easily overload the network. This may result in longer processing times, or worse, deterioration of other applications that are dependent upon the network.

By pushing all aggregating and filtering transformations as close as possible to the location where the source data is stored, a considerable reduction in the data volume that must be pulled across the network can be achieved, thus offloading the network.

For example, suppose you want to do basic analysis of the access logs of a cluster of web servers. Let's say you want to count the number of visits to each page. Typically, the number of unique pages will be quite small as compared to the total number of requests. Doing the analysis locally on one computer would involve copying the access logs, thereby causing significant load on the network. Remotely executing the analysis on the server where the log is stored using Carte will increase the load on the remote servers, but significantly decrease the load on the network, because only the relatively small result of the analysis will have to travel the network.

Reduction of Latency

Lookup operations on remote data sources take time to travel across the network. If the lookup operation itself is fairly fast, time will be lost waiting for network roundtrips. Using Carte's remote execution capability, you can minimize latency by performing the lookup closer to the source of the lookup data.

Note that this strategy to reduce latency will only work for specific cases. If you need to look up the same data many times, local caching is likely to be a better solution to reduce latency. On the other hand, if almost all lookups are unique, or the amount of lookup data is too large to cache, performing the lookup remotely may help.

Running Carte

Carte is easy to set up. Like the other PDI tools it is started by running a shell script that resides in the PDI home directory. On Windows systems, this script is called `carte.bat`. For UNIX-based systems, the script is called `carte.sh`.

Running Carte without any parameters reveals the available command-line parameters and some example usage (see Listing 11-7).

Listing 11-7: Running carte without parameters

```
shell> ./carte.sh
Usage: Carte [Interface address] [Port]

Example: Carte 127.0.0.1 8080
Example: Carte 192.168.1.221 8081
```

The `Interface address` parameter is used to specify the IP address of the network adapter that is to be used by the Carte server. The `Port` parameter is used to specify on which port the server should listen for requests. Both parameters are mandatory.

NOTE **Be sure to choose a port that is not already used by another server. In the first example provided by the Carte output shown in Listing 11-7, port `8080` is used. Port 8080 is also the default port of the preconfigured Pentaho BI server. You might receive an error message like the following if the port is already taken:**

```
2009-01-23 11:37:39.759::WARN:  failed SocketConnector@127.0.0.1:8080
java.net.BindException: Address already in use: JVM_Bind
```

Creating Slave Servers

Before you can use a remote Carte server to execute your transformation or job, you must create a slave server object. In this context, a slave server is like a database connection: a named descriptor to locate a remote server.

To create a slave server, enable the View mode in the side pane. Expand the current transformation or job, and right-click the Slave server folder in the side pane. In the context menu, choose New, and the Slave Server dialog will appear. In the Service tab page of this dialog, you can define the properties of the Carte server, as shown in Figure 11-16.

Specify a value for the Server name, Hostname or IP address, Port, Username, and Password fields. The Server name will be used to refer to this particular Carte service within PDI. The Hostname/IP address and Port identify the Carte server on the network.

The Username and Password properties are required to provide a basic level of security. By default, you can use `admin` for both. This is sufficient when running in an environment where the network is protected and inaccessible to unauthorized users. If you need to run Carte on a more public network, you can plug in more advanced authentication services to provide better security.

NOTE **You can use variables to parameterize the properties of the slave server. A clear use case for them is when the cloud computing environment does not support fixed IP addresses. This is the case with Amazon's EC2.**

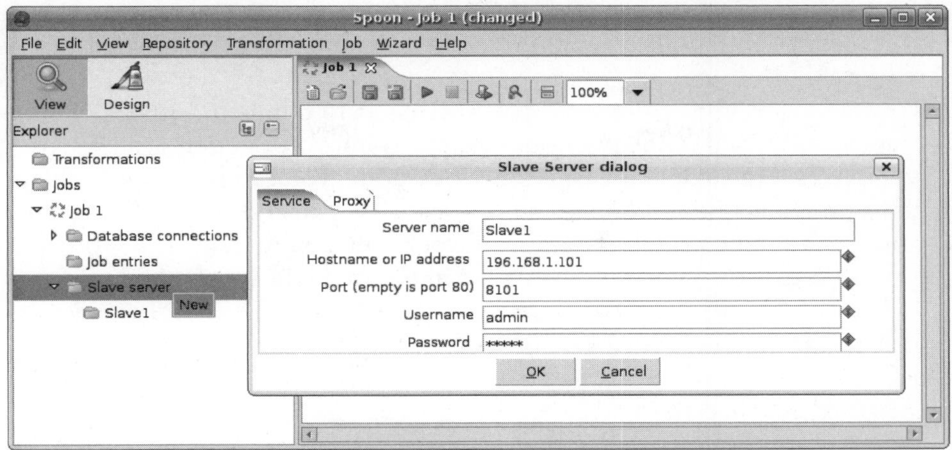

Figure 11-16: Defining a new slave server

Remotely Executing a Transformation or Job

You can use the radio buttons in the Local or remote execution section at the top of the Execute a Job or Execute a Transformation dialogs to choose whether you want to execute the job/transformation on the local host or on one of your slave servers. To execute remotely, check the Execute remotely radio button, and use the Remote host combobox to select the slave server you want to use. This is shown in Figure 11-17.

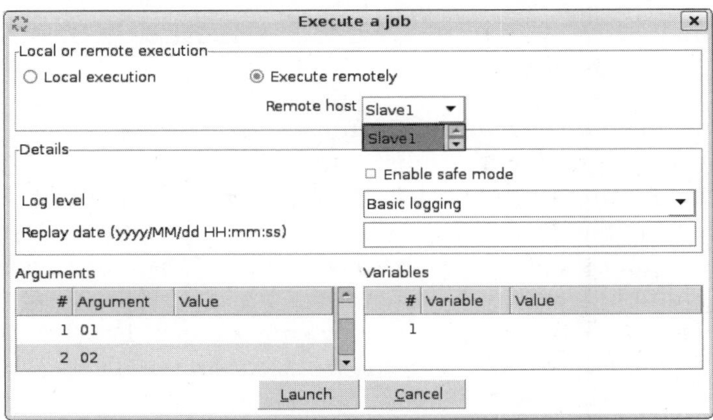

Figure 11-17: Executing a job remotely

Clustering

You can execute transformations on a cluster of slave servers. To use such a cluster, you need to define a *cluster schema*. A cluster schema is simply a named collection of slave servers. After defining the schema, you can assign a cluster to the steps in your transformation, causing that step to be processed on the slaves of that cluster.

To get started with clustering, you first need to define a number of slave servers as discussed in the previous section. Then, you can define a clustering schema. When the side-pane is in the View mode, you can see a Kettle cluster schemas node at the bottom of the tree view. If you right-click that node, a context menu appears; from there you can create a new item. This brings up the Clustering schema dialog, displayed in Figure 11-18.

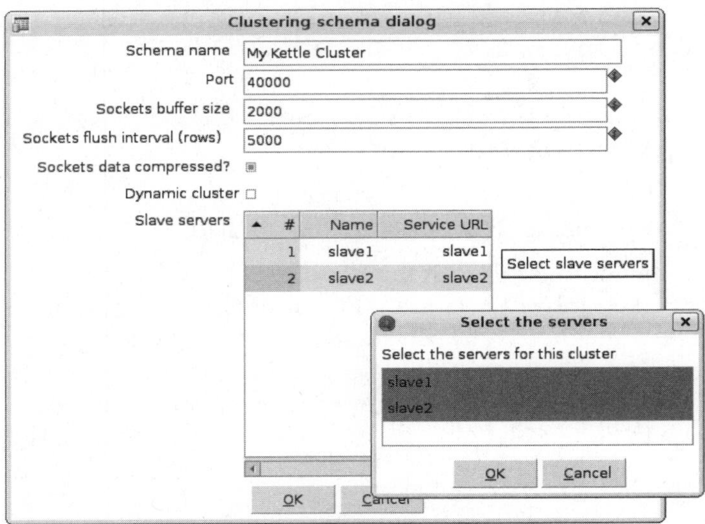

Figure 11-18: The Clustering schema dialog

In the Clustering schema dialog, you must enter a Schema name. The Schema name must be unique for the transformation. You can assign slave servers to the schema by pressing the Select slave servers button. This brings up the Select the servers dialog, listing all the available slave servers. In this dialog, you must select all slave servers that need to participate in the cluster. (You can select multiple items by holding down the control key and clicking on the desired entry.) When you are done picking servers, click the OK button to assign the slave servers. Note that this will clear any previous assignment of slave servers to the cluster.

After defining the clustering schema, you can assign the cluster to your transformation steps. Simply select the step and right-click to bring up the context menu. Choose the Clustering ... option. This brings up a dialog from where you can pick one of the available clustering schemas. Click OK to confirm the dialog and the cluster is assigned to the step. You can clear the association with a cluster by bringing up the dialog again and pressing Cancel.

Summary

In this chapter, you learned different techniques you can use to run and deploy Pentaho Data Integration jobs and transformations on production systems. You learned:

- How to use variables to manage resources like database connections, filenames, and directories
- How to use JNDI connections
- How to work with PDI repositories
- How to use Kitchen and Pan to run transformations and jobs from the command line
- How to run jobs inside the Pentaho BI server using an action sequence
- How to run a job or transformation remotely using Carte
- What clustering is, and what benefits it has
- How to group multiple slave servers into a cluster

Part IV

Business Intelligence Applications

In This Part

CHAPTER 12

The Metadata Layer

Many of the topics related to business intelligence, such as data integration and data warehousing, can be understood as solutions to problems concerning abstraction, accessibility, and delivery of data.

In previous chapters, you learned that the data warehouse provides a substantial deal of abstraction from the raw data accumulated in various data sources. Central to that achievement is the organization of data into subject-oriented star schemas, considerably reducing the complexity of translating questions from the business end to database queries.

Although establishing a data warehouse solves some of the data abstraction and accessibility issues, it is still not ideal for delivering data to reporting tools. Business users trying to get data from the warehouse may struggle to get the information they want in a format they can understand, or the system may need to be tweaked to make sure the data can be accessed in a useful way. In this chapter, you learn how the addition of a metadata layer can help in this respect.

Metadata Overview

In this first section, we explain briefly what kinds of things we are talking about when we use the term "metadata," and what problems it solves. Later in this chapter, we take a closer look at using Pentaho metadata.

What Is Metadata?

The term *metadata* is a bit overused. In a general sense, it means "data about data." Depending upon the context, there are a lot of different things to say ''about'' data, and technically this all qualifies as metadata. For example, most RDBMSes support listing all available databases and schema objects. This is a typical example of metadata as it describes the available types and forms of data stored in the database.

The Pentaho platform offers its own facility for storing and accessing metadata. In the context of this chapter, we use the term *Pentaho metadata* to denote *the metadata facility that is part of the Pentaho platform*.

The Advantages of the Metadata Layer

As mentioned earlier, the data warehouse does not solve all problems in delivering the data to reporting tools. In this section, we take a closer look at these unresolved problems and show how a metadata layer can help to solve them.

Using Metadata to Make a More User-Friendly Interface

From the standpoint of reporting and visualization tools, the data warehouse is ''just'' a relational database. Using it still requires considerable knowledge of and experience with the database query language (which is usually some dialect of the Structured Query Language, SQL). In most cases, this causes report design to be out of reach of the typical business user. The Pentaho metadata layer can alleviate this problem to some extent.

You can use the metadata layer to describe database tables and their columns and relationships. Once this is described, collections of columns can be defined that are likely to appear together in a report. These can then be presented to the user using a wizard interface. This allows the end user to create reports on-the-fly by simply picking the columns of interest and placing them on a report. Because of the metadata defined ''behind the scenes,'' the report engine knows how to generate the appropriate database query to deliver the specified results.

Adding Flexibility and Schema Independence

Suppose you've just built some 50 or more reports directly on your data warehouse. Suddenly, the data warehouse design team decides that in the interest of query performance it makes sense to split off a mini-dimension from the product dimension table. This potentially has an impact on all of the reports you built that are dependent upon the product dimension. In fact, you may need to research exactly which reports will be affected.

The metadata layer may help to limit the impact of database schema changes. Because the metadata layer allows you to specify reports on a predefined collection of tables using known join paths, schema changes can often be solved by mapping the new database schema to the ''abstract schema'' presented to the reports by the metadata layer.

This type of change may go far beyond the simple renaming of tables and columns. For example, if the data warehouse team decides to move from a star schema to a snowflake (or the other way around), the resulting impact can be cushioned completely by a metadata layer. Similarly, solutions that report directly on (a copy of) the source system can gradually be moved to a full-fledged data warehouse environment. These changes would all involve extensive modification of the metadata layer, but this would be a one-shot operation, avoiding the potentially more time- and effort-consuming path of changing all reports.

Refining Access Privileges

Another aspect of data delivery that is not completely solved by the data warehouse is access privileges. Although most RDBMSes provide an access layer that involves user authentication and authorization, this is often not fine-grained enough for applications (including BI applications). The native RDMBS access layer is typically implemented by granting users the privilege for a particular usage (reading, writing, or altering) of designated database objects (such as tables, views, and/or stored procedures). The native RDBMS access layer usually does not provide the ability to control data access on the row level.

The metadata layer allows authorization to be defined on several levels. Authorization can be flexibly controlled on the user or role level, and it can be targeted at objects in their entirety or to individual rows. This allows for fine-grained access policies.

Handling Localization

Report output contains both data as well as metadata. For example, the output of a sales report may show the actual sales figures along with data such as country and state names and sales dates. But in addition, report output usually contains text labels that describe the data being shown. For instance, a sales report with a columnar layout may have a heading that reads ''Country'' right above the column that contains the country names.

The problem with these labels is that they are not language-neutral. This may be a problem in multinational or multilingual organizations. For example, World Class Movies has English- and French-speaking managers. Both need to see the same report data, but the report labels should be localized to the appropriate language, depending on which manager requests the report.

The Pentaho metadata layer supports multiple locales. Descriptive properties such as labels and descriptions of data objects such as tables and columns can be associated with locale-dependent texts. This allows for reports to be tailored for each language.

Enforcing Consistent Formatting and Behavior

Attributes of dimension tables sometimes hold preformatted data. For example, date dimension tables often contain many columns to store different text representations of the calendar date. This is quite different from metrics stored in the fact tables. Metrics are typically numerical, and often, reports show aggregated metric data rather than raw values stored in individual fact rows.

For some types of metric data, special formatting of the data may be desirable. For example, monetary metrics such as cost, profit, and turnover should appear on reports with the appropriate currency symbol and separators for decimals and thousands. Some dimension attributes may still require additional formatting, especially if the desired formatting cannot be achieved by simply storing a value. For example, text representing URLs may need to be rendered in a way that distinguishes them from other data. For some types of report output, such as PDF documents or web pages, it may even be desirable to attach specific behavior to URL data, such as opening the appropriate website when the label is clicked.

The Pentaho metadata layer allows groups of visual and behavioral properties called *concepts* to be attached to data objects such as tables and columns. Concepts can be based on existing concepts from which they inherit their properties. If desired, a concept can override properties from its parent concept. This enables you to build a hierarchy of concepts that can then be used to consistently apply visual and behavioral properties to data items.

Scope and Usage of the Metadata Layer

The following list offers a brief overview of how Pentaho uses the metadata layer in practice. These points are illustrated in Figure 12-1.

- Metadata input from the database, as well as user-defined metadata, is defined using the Pentaho Metadata Editor (PME) and stored in the metadata repository.
- Metadata can be exported from the repository and stored in the form of `.xmi` files, or in a database. The metadata is associated with a Pentaho solution on the Pentaho server, where it can be used as a resource for metadata-based reporting services.

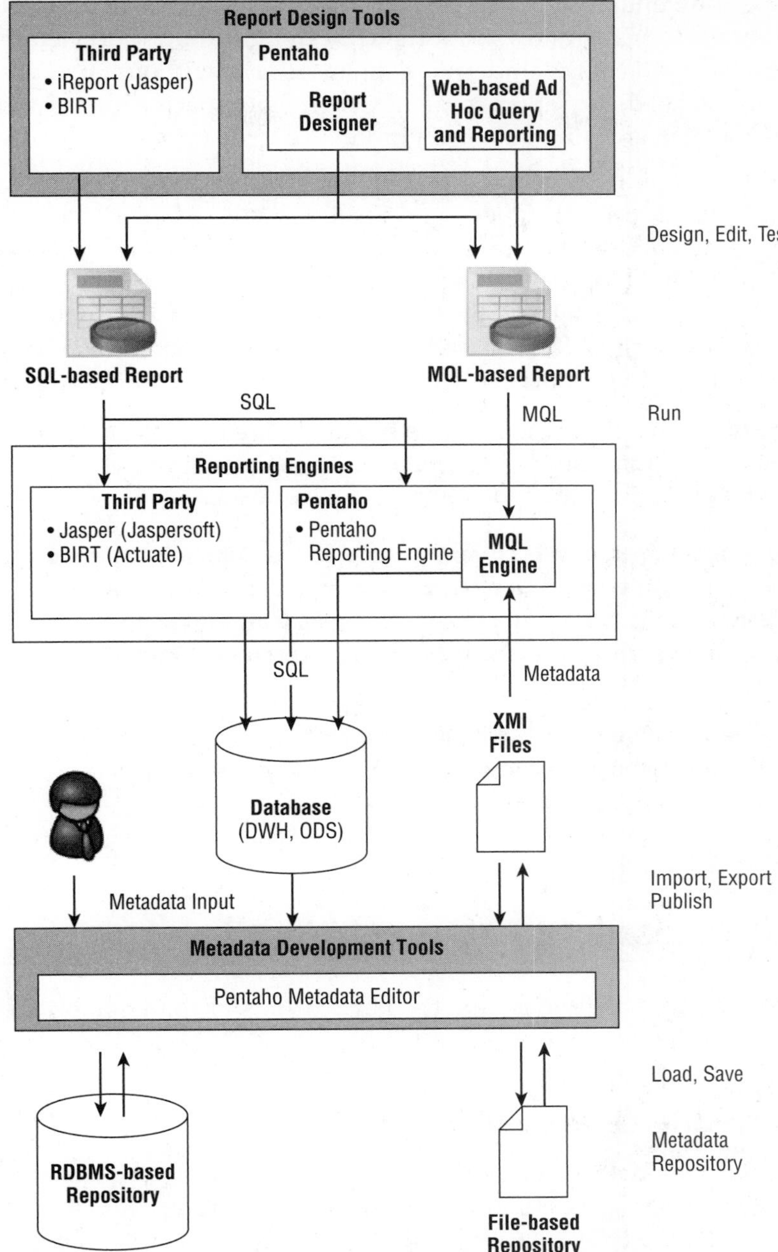

Figure 12-1: High-level overview of the scope and usage of Pentaho Metadata

- Using the Pentaho report design tools, end users can create reports on the metadata. This allows reports to be built without knowledge of the physical details of the underlying database, and without any knowledge of SQL. Instead, the report contains a high-level specification of the query result, which is defined using a graphical user interface.
- When running reports based on Pentaho metadata, the reporting engine interprets the report. Query specifications are stored in the report in a format called Metadata Query Language (MQL), which is resolved against the metadata. At this point, the corresponding SQL is generated and sent to the database. Beyond this point, report processing is quite similar to ''normal'' SQL-based reporting. The database responds to the query by sending a data result, which is rendered as report output.

Currently, the usage of the Pentaho metadata layer is limited to reporting. In the future, metadata support for other components of the platform such as analysis, data mining, and data integration may be added.

NOTE **Pentaho metadata is currently based on the *Common Warehouse Metamodel* (CWM) specification created and maintained by the Object Management Group (OMG). The CWM is an open, platform- and vendor-neutral standard that specifies the exchange and representation of business intelligence metadata.**

For more information on the CWM, please refer to the Catalog of OMG Modelling and Metadata Specifications. You can find it at `http://www.omg.org/technology/cwm/`.

Pentaho Metadata Features

In this section, we briefly describe the key features of the Pentaho metadata layer.

Database and Query Abstraction

The Pentaho metadata layer can contain many distinct types of structural components, and it is easy to lose track of the big picture. Therefore, we will first examine the metadata layer at a high level before diving into the details.

Report Definition: A Business User's Point of View

Consider the requirements of a typical business user—say, the manager of Sales and Rentals at World Class Movies. For each website, the manager would like to see the number of orders placed for each month during 2008 by customers from the United States. Even without any knowledge of the underlying database, most business users are perfectly capable of understanding the structure and items of the report output. A report like this will have:

- One section headed by the website title or URI
- In each section, 12 rows with a label indicating the month
- For each month, the actual subject of the report—that is, the number of orders

Apart from these visible items, the report has two invisible items that are used to make the appropriate selection:

- A year item to select only the orders placed in the year 2008
- A country item used to select only the customers from the United States

Now, we described the structure of the report in terms of sections and section contents, but it is important to realize that this is a matter of presentation: The information conveyed by the report will remain the same regardless of whether it contains one section per month with rows for each website or one section per website containing rows for each month. If we forget about the order of grouping for one moment, we end up with a collection of rows consisting of a website, a month, and the number of orders. In other words, the report data is tabular and contains the items website, number, and number of orders.

Report Implementation: A SQL Developer's Point of View

Suppose you want to retrieve the same report data directly from the World Class Movies data warehouse using SQL. If you have the SQL skills, it certainly isn't hard (although it may be somewhat tedious). Even so, this section walks you through the process step by step to illustrate a few concepts about Pentaho metadata.

A common way of attacking this problem in SQL is to start with the table most central to the question. In this case, the report is about the number of orders, so you start with the `fact_orders` table. You see it contains the `customer_order_id`. If you apply the `COUNT` aggregate function in combination with the `DISTINCT` modifier, you can use this to count the number of individual orders.

From the `fact_order` table, you use a join to "look up" the customer that placed the order in the `dim_customer` table. You need this so you can use the `country_name` column to restrict the result to customers from the United States only. You can use another join between `fact_order` and `dim_website` where you find the `website_title`. Finally, you use another join between `fact_order` and `dim_date` to obtain the order date. You need this so you can restrict the result to orders placed in the year 2008 and to produce labels for each month report item.

Conceptually, the joined tables serve to "widen" the `fact_order` table, extending it with attributes from the joined tables. You can now apply the criteria for the year (must be equal to 2008) and country (must be equal to United States) and then group by website title and month to count the distinct number of orders, which gives you the final result. Figure 12-2 shows a graphical representation of these join paths and the report items.

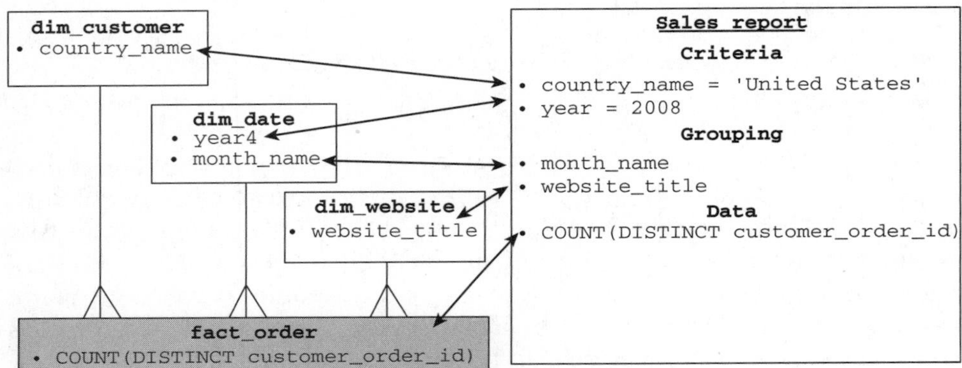

Figure 12-2: Deriving report items from joined tables

For completeness, the SQL statement is shown in Listing 12-1.

Listing 12-1: The SQL statement to retrieve the number of orders, grouped by website title and month

```
SELECT     dim_website.website_title
,          dim_date.month_name
,          COUNT(DISTINCT fact_order.customer_order_id) AS count_orders
FROM       fact_order
INNER JOIN dim_customer
ON         fact_order.customer_key        = dim_customer.customer_key
INNER JOIN dim_website
ON         fact_order.website_key         = dim_website.website_key
INNER JOIN dim_date
ON         fact_order.local_order_date_key = dim_date.date_key
WHERE      dim_date.year4                 = 2008
AND        dim_customer.country_name       = 'United States'
GROUP BY   dim_website.website_title
,          dim_date.month_name
```

Mechanics of Abstraction: The Metadata Layer

It is likely that the steps you just went through are beyond the technical skills of most business users, and certainly beyond their job descriptions. But what if the details of joining the tables had been taken care of in advance? What if you present users with just one set of items from which they can pick whatever they happen to find interesting? What if the `customer_order_id` item was designed to directly represent the `COUNT DISTINCT` operation?

This is, in fact, exactly how Pentaho metadata abstraction works. Business intelligence developers who have the skills and background knowledge of the reporting database or data warehouse can define the existence of actual tables and columns in what is called the *physical layer*. The objects in the physical layer are the building blocks for the logical layer.

In the *logical layer*, the tables from the physical layer are redefined, and sometimes enriched with extra columns that are derived from columns in the physical layer by applying functions and other expressions to them. Another important type of object found in the logical layer is the *relationship*. A relationship essentially defines how two tables in the logical layer can be joined. Sometimes, there are multiple relationships between two tables, which is why you can base multiple tables in the logical layer on one and the same table in the physical layer. This comes in handy when dealing with role-playing dimension tables.

The *delivery layer* is where selections of columns from the logical layer are grouped together in units that make sense to the business user. This is the only part of the metadata layer that will be visible to the business users. From here, they can pick items of interest to build reports. This selection is denoted in a special XML format called MQL (Metadata Query Language).

The MQL ''query'' can be used to generate a SQL query (see Figure 12-1). The origin of the MQL items can be tracked back to the logical layer and from there to the physical layer. Using this information, one can derive which tables must be joined, and which columns must be grouped on.

Properties, Concepts, and Inheritance in the Metadata Layer

In this section, we discuss *concepts* and *properties*, which are fundamental building blocks of the Pentaho Metadata Layer. In addition, we describe how concepts can inherit properties from one another.

Properties

Objects in the metadata layer can have a number of *properties*. Properties are named items which are used to associate different kinds of information with the objects in the metadata layer. Properties can be divided into a number of categories:

- General properties, such as name and description
- Visual properties, such as font, color, and whether the object is visible at all to end users
- Model Descriptors, such as underlying expression, data type, and aggregation rule

Metadata objects can have a collection of properties. Depending on the type of metadata object, some properties are mandatory and always present.

Concepts

In the context of Pentaho metadata, a *concept* is a collection of properties that can be applied as a whole to a metadata object. At most, one concept can be attached to one metadata object in this manner.

An example of a concept would be dollar amount. By adding properties that provide correct visual formatting of dollar amounts, and by specifying a common data type (for example, a decimal type with at least two positions behind the comma) and aggregation rule (for example, summation), you can quickly format all column objects that hold values that represent dollar amounts. By applying the concept rather than locally modifying individual properties on the object level, you ensure that metadata is consistent and easily maintainable.

Concepts are built on top of existing concepts. This is explained in detail in the next section, ''Inheritance.''

Inheritance

Properties can be managed using a feature called *inheritance*. Inheritance occurs by basing an object, the *child* object, on another object, the *parent* object. In case of inheritance, the child's properties and their values are derived by referring to the properties and property values of the parent object. On a higher level, the parent object may itself inherit from its own parent object, establishing a chain or hierarchy of inheritance. This allows changes in properties to cascade down the chain of inheritance.

Objects in the inheritance chain are not required to inherit all properties from their parent object. Rather, they can change some or all of their inherited properties and provide a local value that deviates from the value of the parent object. When an object provides a local value for a property, or defines a property that is not present in the parent object, the inheritance chain is broken with respect to that property, and the child object is said to *override* the properties of its parent object.

The metadata layer has two levels of inheritance:

- Metadata objects inherit properties from their ancestor metadata objects.
- Concepts inherit properties from their ancestor concepts.

Metadata objects inherit the properties of their parent object. For example, logical tables and their columns inherit the properties from their corresponding physical tables and columns. This is very useful as it allows a single point of definition for those properties that generally need to be the same. For example, the data type, data format, and perhaps description defined for a physical column can probably be reused by descendant columns in both the logical layer and the delivery layer. The inheritance ensures that in case the physical model is changed, the change is immediately picked up by the derived objects.

Concepts are based on existing concepts, and inherit the properties from their parent concept. At the root of the concept hierarchy is a special built-in concept, the *Base concept*.

Concept hierarchies allow convenient management of related properties. For example, suppose you want to enforce consistent formatting of numbers. You could start by creating a generic Number concept that inherits from the Base concept. The Number concept would override only one or a few properties of the Base concept that are common to all numeric items. For example, it could override the Text Alignment property and set it to Right instead of Left.

Localization of Properties

General properties such as name and description can be localized so they can be displayed in multiple languages. This is done by first creating all appropriate locales and then specifying the appropriate text for each locale.

Creation and Maintenance of Metadata

This section briefly explains the components that make up the metadata layer as well as the relationships that connect them. In the remainder of this chapter, we describe these components in more detail, and explain how to create them using the Pentaho Metadata Editor.

The Pentaho Metadata Editor

Pentaho offers the Pentaho Metadata Editor to create and edit metadata. You can download this tool from the Pentaho project page at `sourceforge.net`.

The Pentaho Metadata Editor is distributed as a single `.zip` (for Windows platforms) or `.tar.gz` (for UNIX-based platforms) archive. Uncompressing the archive yields a directory containing the software. After uncompressing the archive, you can start the editor by executing the `MetaEditor.bat` (on Windows platforms) or `metaeditor.sh` (for UNIX-based platforms) script.

The Metadata Repository

Pentaho metadata is stored in its own repository, which is distinct from both the Pentaho *solution* repository and the Pentaho *data integration* repository. Currently, the Pentaho Metadata Editor is the only application that is intended to edit the contents of the metadata repository.

By default, the PME uses binary files for storing metadata. These files, called `mdr.btx` and `mdr.btd`, are found in the home directory of the metadata editor.

You can switch from file-based repository storage to a database-based repository fairly easily. When dealing with a large metadata layer, performance of the file-based repository can decrease significantly. In this case, using a database-based repository can increase performance. In addition, a database-based repository is more suitable in case multiple developers are editing the metadata layer simultaneously.

The procedure, described in the `README.txt` file found in the `jdbc` directory beneath the home directory of the metadata editor, is as follows:

1. Make a backup of the `repository.properties` file located in the `jdbc` directory. You can either keep it in the same directory, or move it to a safe place elsewhere. The backup allows you to restore the original file-based repository configuration.
2. The `jdbc` directory contains a number of RDBMS-specific `.properties` files. Overwrite the original `repository.properties` file with a copy of the RDBMS-specific `.properties` file of choice. For example, for storing the repository in a MySQL database, make a copy of `MySQL.properties` and rename it to `repository.properties`.
3. Open the modified `repository.properties` file and edit it to point it to your database. You should provide values for a number of properties. The names of these properties all start with `MDRStorageProperty.org.netbeans.mdr.persistence.jdbcimpl`. This prefix is followed by a dot and a name that configures a property of a JDBC connection. Typical property names (without the prefix) are:
   - `driverClassName`: the Java class name of the driver
   - `url`: the JDBC connection string
   - `userName`: the name of the database user
   - `password`: the password of the database user

NOTE **We found that load and save performance is rather decreased when using the database repository as opposed to the file-based repository. If you are considering using the database-based repository, you should always take some time to measure the impact on performance for your specific situation. It is hard to provide an estimate here, as the actual effect depends on a lot of factors, such as your hardware, the RDBMS, and the size of your metadata layer.**

Metadata Domains

The Pentaho metadata layer as a whole is organized into one or more *metadata domains*. A metadata domain is a container for a collection of metadata objects that can be used together as a source of metadata for one Pentaho solution. (In this context, we use the term ''Pentaho solution'' as defined in Chapter 4: a collection of resources such as reports and action sequences that reside in a single folder in the `pentaho-solutions` directory.)

You can create a new domain file by choosing File ➢ New ➢ Domain File from the main menu. You can delete domains by choosing Delete Domain from the main menu. This will bring up a dialog from where you can choose the domain you would like to remove from the repository.

The Sublayers of the Metadata Layer

The following sections describe the components of the physical, logical, and delivery layers that are included within the metadata layer.

The Physical Layer

The objects that reside in the physical layer of a metadata domain are descriptors that correspond more or less one-to-one with database objects. The following objects reside in the physical layer:

- **Connections**—Database connection descriptors
- **Physical Tables**—Descriptors of database tables and views
- **Physical Table Columns**—Column definitions of a physical table

The following subsections address each of these objects.

Connections

A *connection object* represents a database connection. It is a connection descriptor, much like the ones used by Pentaho Data Integration.

To create a new connection in the metadata editor, you can either use the main menu and choose File ➢ New ➢ Connection, or you can right-click the Connections node in the tree view on the left side of the metadata editor and choose New Connection from the context menu. This brings up a dialog that is, to all intents and purposes, identical to the Pentaho Data Integration Database Connection dialog. (Refer to Chapter 9 for more details on using this dialog to create a database connection.)

Immediately after the connection is created, a dialog box appears. The dialog presents the base tables that reside in the specified database, offering to import them. Cancel the dialog for now. Importing tables will be discussed extensively in the following section.

After a connection is created, the connection appears as a tree node in the tree view in the left panel. You can right-click the connection node to bring up its context menu. The options offered there are again quite similar to those you have seen in Pentaho Data Integration. You can:

- Explore the database connection using the Database Explorer.
- Use the Database Explorer to import database tables (or views).
- Open the SQL editor to run arbitrary SQL statements.
- Duplicate the connection.
- Delete the connection.

If you like, you can configure JNDI connections for the metadata editor. The process is identical to that for adding JNDI connections to Pentaho Data Integration. To use JNDI, you first need to add the connection descriptors to the `jdbc.properties` file located in `simple-jndi` directory directly beneath the home directory of the metadata editor.

Physical Tables and Physical Columns

The metadata layer can describe base tables and views in a database using so-called *Physical Table objects*. Physical Table objects are low-level building blocks of the metadata layer. They offer some abstraction of the actual database tables.

Physical Table objects are direct child objects of connections (discussed in the previous subsection). That is, a Physical Table object is directly dependent upon an existing connection object.

You can import Physical Tables into the metadata layer by right-clicking on a connection and choosing either the Import Tables option or Import from Explorer option from the context menu. The Import Tables option allows you only to import base tables. The Import from Explorer option opens a Database Explorer just like you've seen in Pentaho Data Integration. From here, you can import both base tables and views.

Physical Columns are a direct child of Physical Table objects. A Physical Column object represents an actual database column, just like a Physical Table represents an actual table on the database. Physical Columns are usually added to the metadata layer automatically when importing Physical Tables.

To edit a table (or its columns), right-click it and choose Edit from the context menu. The Physical Table Properties dialog opens, as shown in Figure 12-3. In the left side of the dialog, you can select the table or one of its columns from a tree view. Selecting an item in the tree view loads the appropriate property page on the right side of the dialog. You can navigate to a particular property quickly by selecting it in the properties tree view left of the property page.

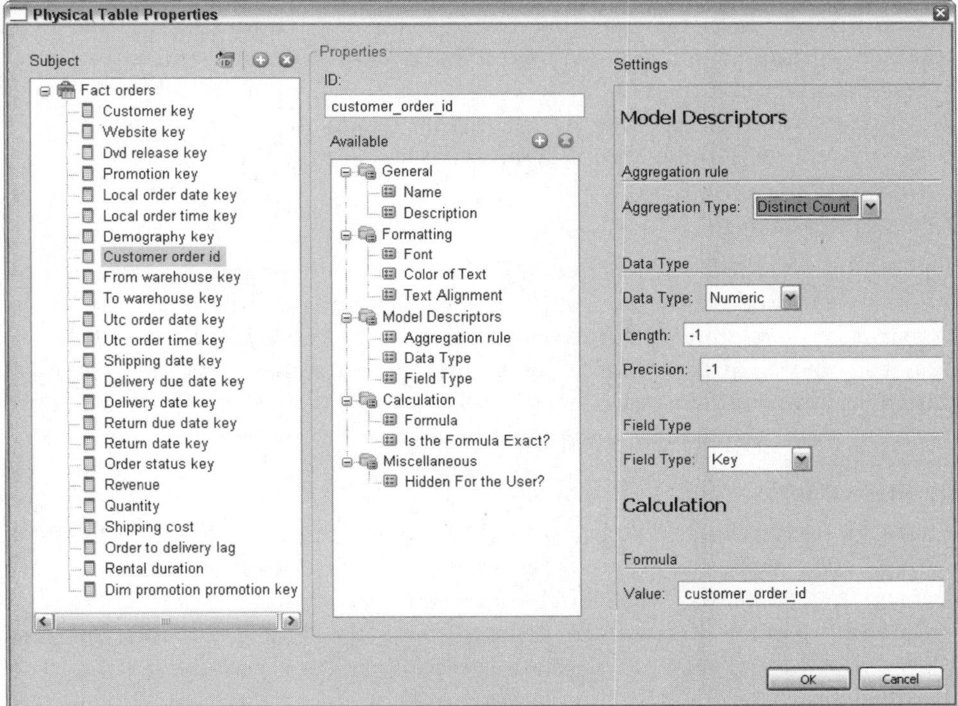

Figure 12-3: The Physical Table Properties dialog

In the dialog, you can also create new, custom columns. This is useful if you want to create a calculated column. For example, the `COUNT(DISTINCT customer_order_id)` that was used in the report example can be added this way.

To create a new column, click the little button with the plus sign that appears at the top of the dialog. Then, edit the properties. You should at least review all properties in the Model Descriptors and Calculation categories:

1. **Aggregation Type**—If applicable, specify the aggregation function. For example, the `fact _order` table in our Sales Report Example would have a Distinct Count aggregator.
2. **Data Type**—The data type of the expression.

3. **Field Type**—This can be used to specify whether the column is a Key column, or a metric or a dimension attribute.
4. **Calculation**—This should contain the SQL expression that defines this column. Typically, this is simply the column name.

If you need custom column definitions, note that you can also define this in the logical layer. In the next section, we will illustrate this for the `COUNT(DISTINCT customer_order_id)` item.

There is no hard and fast rule that tells you where to add these custom columns. In some cases, you may need the custom column in multiple places, in which case it is probably better to add it at the level of a Physical Table. If the custom column is specific to a particular usage of the table, it is probably better to include it in the logical layer at the level of the Business Tables.

The Logical Layer

The logical layer literally sits between the physical layer and the presentation layer. The purpose of the logical layer is to describe how the objects from the physical layer relate to the business. Business users only interact with these business objects, and the logical layer thus insulates them from the technical implementation at the physical level. To some extent this allows a certain degree of database schema independence of reports.

Business Models

The logical layer is organized into *Business Models*. Functionally, you can think of a Business Model as a data mart—that is, a subset of the data warehouse focused on a particular subject of the business.

Business Models contain Business Tables, Relationships, and Business Views. Business Tables and Relationships together form the back-end of the Business Model. Business Tables are models of Physical Tables, and Relationships define how Business Tables can be combined (joined).

Business Views form the front-end of the Business Model, and serve to present the contents of the model to the end-user. A Business View is a container for one or more Business Categories, and as you will see later, a Business Category is functionally similar to a star schema in a data mart.

You can create a new Business Model by right-clicking the Business Models node and choosing the New business model option. In the properties dialog, use the list box that appears on the right top of the dialog to specify the database connection. Currently, only one connection is supported per Business Model.

Business Tables and Business Columns

Business Tables reside in a Business Model and are directly derived from Physical Tables. In the same way, Business Columns are directly derived from Physical Columns.

To some extent, Business Tables faithfully reproduce the structure of their corresponding Physical Table. However, there is an important difference from Physical Tables: A Business Table does not represent the actual table; rather, it represents a particular usage of a Physical Table. This deserves some explanation.

The `dim_date` table is a conformed dimension table. It is used in many different roles throughout the World Class Movies data warehouse. In a Business Model, these role-playing dimension tables would each be represented by their own Business Table. For example, in a Business Model for Customer Orders of the World Class Movies data warehouse, we could have separate Business Tables for the order date, shipping date, delivery date, and return due date.

You can create Logical Tables quickly by dragging a Physical Table to the Business Tables node. The Physical Columns will automatically be imported, too, and will be represented by Business Columns.

As with the Physical Tables, you can also add custom columns for Business Tables. Figure 12-4 shows the Business Table dialog. In the dialog, you can see a customer Order Count column being defined. Its Aggregation Type property is overridden and set to the value Distinct Count. In addition, the Field Type is overridden and set to Fact. These modifications will enable the business user to simply pick the Order Count item instead of explicitly specifying the `COUNT` function and the `DISTINCT` modifier on the `customer_order_id` item.

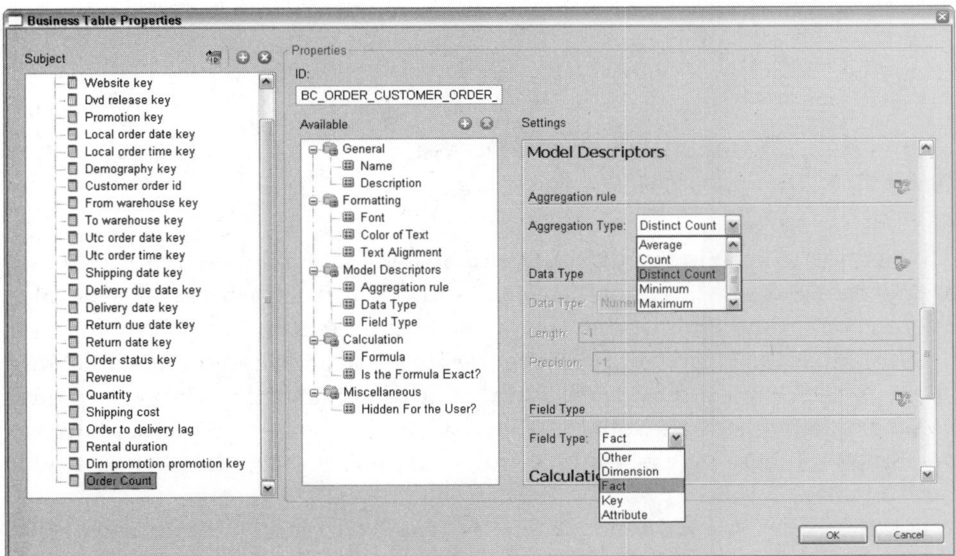

Figure 12-4: The Business Table Properties dialog

Relationships

Relationships define a join path between two Business Tables. Generally speaking, each Business Table that appears in a Business Model should be related to at least one other Business Table in the same Business Model.

There is no logical requirement that dictates that each Business Table must be related to at least another table. However it makes good sense to do so anyway. The reason is that if a Business Model is indeed a proper subset of the data warehouse focused on one particular business aspect, then all of its Business Tables should somehow contribute to it. A Business Table that is not related to any other Business Table has apparently nothing to do with either of the other tables. If that is truly the case, it should probably not be part of this particular Business Model.

You can create a new Relationship by right-clicking on the Relationships node and then choosing New Relationship. In the dialog that pops up, you can select the tables that are related, and specify which columns are to be compared. Figure 12-5 shows the Relationship dialog.

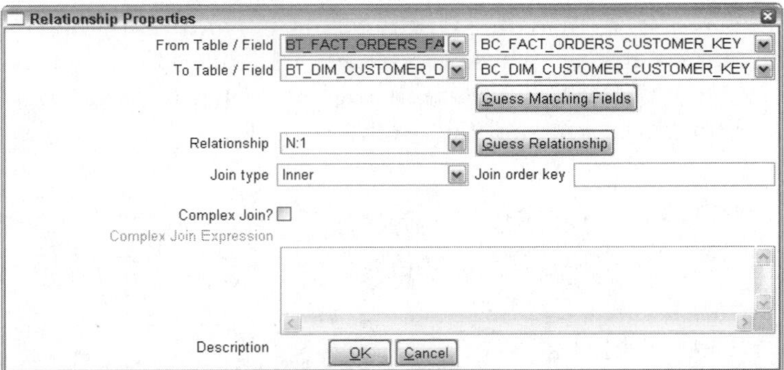

Figure 12-5: The Relationship Properties dialog

One thing to keep in mind about Pentaho metadata relationships is that they are not foreign key constraints. The tables in a relationship have different roles: There is a "From" table and a "To" table but there is no implied direction in the sense that the From table must be the "parent" table and the To table must be the "child" table or vice versa. Rather, the direction of the relationship must be set explicitly using the Relationship list box. In Figure 12-5 this is set to N:1, meaning that there may be multiple rows in the From table for a single row in the To table.

For the sake of maintainability, it is usually a good idea to establish a convention to determine whether the child or the parent table should be entered as the From table (and conversely whether the parent or the child table should be entered as the To table). In Figure 12-5, we have chosen the

Orders business table (which is the child in the relationship, and maps to the `fact_orders` fact table in the data warehouse) as the From table and the Customer business table (which is the parent table in the relationship, and maps to the `dim_customer` dimension table in the data warehouse) as the To table.

The reason for the convention used in Figure 12-5 is a simple one: We try to mimic what would be the case if we would be defining a foreign key constraint. In that case, too, the child table "owns" the foreign key, which is thus pointing from the child table to the parent table. However, if you feel this is not convenient for some reason, you are free to use another convention, as long as you keep in mind that the Relationship property correctly reflects the direction of the relationship.

The Delivery Layer

The Delivery Layer contains the metadata objects that are visible to the end user, such as Business Views and Business Categories.

Business Views

A Business View is a collection of so-called Business Categories. You can think of a Business View as a data mart. A data mart is a collection of functionally related star schemas. Similarly, a Business View is a collection of functionally related Business Categories.

You don't have to explicitly create a Business View. There simply is one Business View in each Business Model.

Business Categories

A Business Category is a coherent collection of related Business Columns. Functionally, a business category can be thought of as a star schema. As such, a business category will usually contain all the items that can be used to report about a single fact table.

That said, Business Categories do not appear to have any internal structure as far as the end user is concerned. The Business Category simply forms a collection of items that can be used together in a report, very much like the Sales Report example introduced earlier in this chapter.

You can create a Business Category by right-clicking on the Business View node and choosing New Category from the context menu. To fill the category with columns, simply drag all columns of interest from the Business Tables and drop them inside the category.

Figure 12-6 shows a screenshot of the Metadata Editor showing a simple Business Model along the lines of the Order report example from earlier in the chapter.

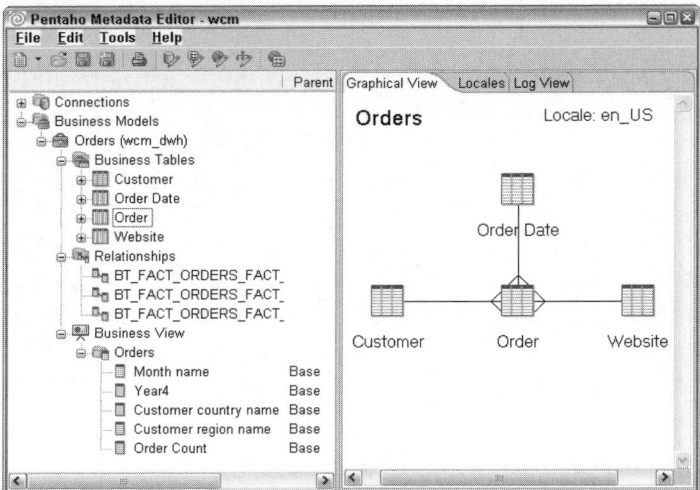

Figure 12-6: A simple Business Model

As you can see, the figure contains the business tables that correspond to the actual tables shown in Listing 12-1. Similarly, the relationships between the tables correspond to the JOIN clauses from Listing 12-1. Once deployed, business users can create all kinds of reports involving orders, order dates, customers, and websites without writing SQL themselves; instead, the Pentaho metadata layer is used to interpret the users' requests for items from the model (MQL) and generate the appropriate database commands (SQL) to produce the report data.

Deploying and Using Metadata

After creating the Business Model(s), you must deploy the data layer before you can use it to create reports. In this section, we describe how to publish the metadata. In the next chapter, you will learn how you can actually build reports on an already deployed metadata layer.

Exporting and Importing XMI files

You can build reports on metadata using the metadata data source. This is explained in detail in Chapter 13. To create a report based on metadata, you must tell the Report Designer where the metadata is.

The Report Designer consumes metadata in the XML Metadata Interchange (XMI) format. To create an XMI file for your metadata, use the main menu and choose File ➤ Export to XMI File. Similarly you can use File ➤ Import from XMI File option to load the metadata layer with existing metadata.

Publishing the Metadata to the Server

If reports are to be run on the server, the metadata must be available to the server. Metadata is stored on the server side as XMI files. You can have one XMI file per Pentaho solution. This file must be called `metadata.xmi`.

You can simply export metadata to an XMI file and then simply copy the XMI file to the appropriate solution directory on the server. However, for a production server, it is not likely that every BI developer has direct access to the server's file system. Therefore, the Pentaho BI server provides a service that allows you to publish metadata from the metadata editor.

You can publish metadata to the Pentaho BI server from the Main menu by choosing File ➤ Publish to server. This pops up the Publish To Server dialog, shown in Figure 12-7.

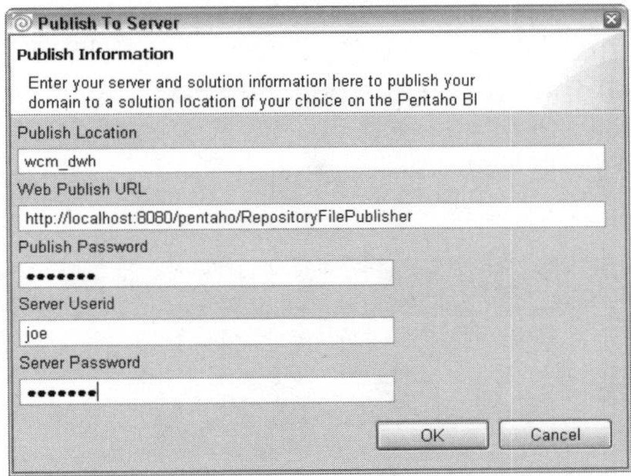

Figure 12-7: The Publish To Server dialog

In order to publish, you must set up your publication configuration. The Publish Location must be the name of an existing directory residing beneath the `pentaho-solutions` directory. The Web Publish URL must be pointed to your Pentaho BI Server. For the Publish Password, you must use the password that was set in the `publisher_config.xml` file. Setting this up is covered in Chapter 3. Finally, you must use the Server user ID and password of a user that has the Admin role (''Joe'' and ''Password'' for a default installation).

Refreshing the Metadata

After publishing or copying the XMI file to the server, you must tell the server to reload the metadata. This can be done from the user console through the menu by choosing Tools ➤ Refresh ➤ Reporting Metadata as shown in Figure 12-8.

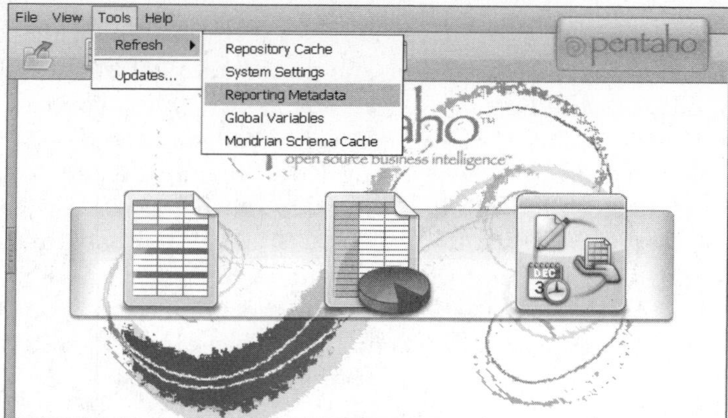

Figure 12-8: Refreshing the metadata with the user console

Alternatively you can refresh the metadata using the Server Administration Console. To refresh the metadata from the Server Administration Console, press the Metadata Models button in the Refresh BI Server panel in the Administration tab page, shown in Figure 12-9.

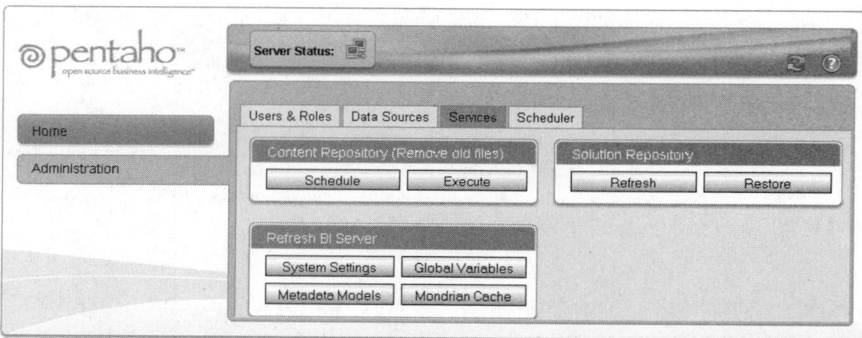

Figure 12-9: Refreshing the metadata with the Server Administration Console

Summary

This chapter introduced the Pentaho metadata layer. The Pentaho metadata layer allows you to present your database or data warehouse in a way that is more understandable to business users. This allows them to make reports without directly writing SQL. The following chapter describes how you can actually use the metadata layer to build reports.

In this chapter you learned:

- What metadata is
- The advantages of a metadata layer
- The features of the Pentaho metadata layer
- How Pentaho metadata is organized in concepts and properties and how inheritance is used to manage them
- How to use the Pentaho Metadata Editor (PME)
- The division of the Pentaho metadata layer into physical, logical and presentation layers
- How the physical layer is organized in database connections, tables, and columns
- How the logical layer is organized in business models, tables, columns, and relationships
- How the presentation layer is organized in business views and categories
- How to publish the metadata layer to the Pentaho server

CHAPTER

13

Using the Pentaho Reporting Tools

The most common way to publish information to end users is to create reports. In fact, when you look at a typical Business Intelligence (BI) environment, about 75 to 80 percent of the usage and delivered content consists of reporting. Another 15 to 20 percent uses analytical tools for OLAP, and only a limited number of people (0 to 5 percent) work with data mining tools. The same 0 to 5 percent is traditionally being used to indicate the size of the user population that uses a management dashboard, but that is changing rapidly. In fact, in a Pentaho solution, most users will likely first access a dashboard that displays the BI content tailored for their needs. Again, a large percentage of this dashboard content will consist of reports, so reporting is a key feature of any BI solution. This chapter introduces you to the two Pentaho reporting tools, the Pentaho Web-based Ad Hoc Query and Reporting Tool and the more advanced Pentaho Report Designer. We have taken a very practical approach by offering many hands-on exercises so that you can follow along while exploring the different tools. It is assumed that you have access to both the Pentaho BI Server and Pentaho Report Designer.

Reporting Architecture

All modern reporting solutions have a similar architecture, as displayed in Figure 13-1. The figure displays the different components of a reporting architecture:

- A report designer to define the report specification
- The report specification in an open XML format

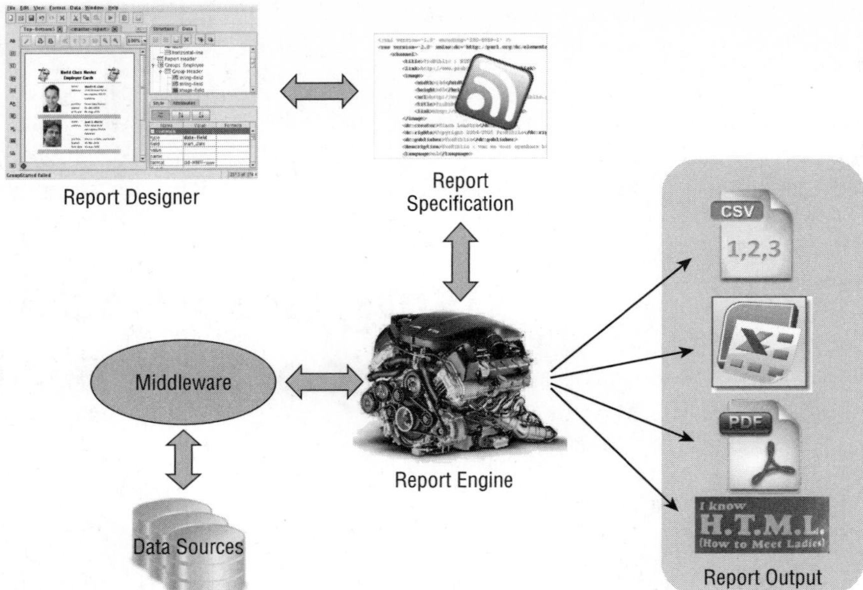

Figure 13-1: Reporting architecture

- A report engine to execute the report according the specification and render the output in different formats
- Database connection definition that can use standard middleware such as JDBC to connect to different data sources. In the latest release of Pentaho Reporting, the queries are directly executed from the reporting engine.

The model in Figure 13-1 is very common for an open source reporting solution. Pentaho contains not only the capabilities to execute Pentaho reports but also includes the libraries for handing JasperReports or BIRT reports. The Pentaho reporting engine was formerly known as JFreeReports; the designer is a completely re-engineered version of the JFree report designer, which is now called the Pentaho Report Designer, or PRD. Although the functionality of other reporting solutions, most notably the BIRT project, previously exceeded that of the Pentaho tool, there have always been some major advantages when working with the Pentaho BI suite that justify favoring PRD and the JFree engine:

- Reports created with PRD can be published directly to the Pentaho BI Server from the PRD menu. This makes deploying new or existing reports as easy as saving a spreadsheet.

- PRD can use the Pentaho metadata layer as a data source, making it an ideal tool for power users without SQL knowledge to create their own advanced reports.
- Reports created by end users using the Pentaho Web-based Ad Hoc Query and Reporting tool can be further extended with PRD (although after modifying them with PRD, they cannot be edited with the web interface anymore).
- PRD is very easy to use once you make the effort to get acquainted with the available options; this chapter is meant to give the inexperienced user a head start in using PRD to create sophisticated reports.

During the first half of 2009, PRD got a complete overhaul and is now functionally on par with the other major open source reporting solutions, and in some respects the feature set even exceeds that of the competing tools.

Web-Based Reporting

The Pentaho web portal is not only for viewing and analyzing content, but also provides ad hoc reporting capabilities. The ad hoc report tool works in an intuitive way by guiding the user through a four-step wizard. The reports that can be created using the web-based report builder are limited to grouped lists without any graphs, charts, or crosstabs. This limits the usability of the web-based tool to create insightful BI-type reports, but it can still be used by end users to quickly get detailed insight into specific issues. The official name of the web tool is *Web Ad Hoc Query and Reporting Client*, or *WAQR* for short. The WAQR can work only with metadata models, which have to be created and published to the server first. This process is explained in Chapter 12.

Creating a report is a straightforward process. You can start in one of three ways: click the New Report button on the Welcome screen, click the Report option icon in the main bar, or select File ➢ New ➢ Report from the menu. All these options start the Ad Hoc Report Wizard, where you begin by selecting a business model and a template. The business model determines which data will be used in the report; the template determines what the report will look like.

NOTE **Be careful when you select a different template after modifying the report settings. Selecting another template resets page layout, paper size, and the report header to the default values.**

After you've selected the business model and clicked Next, Pentaho takes you to the Make Selections part of the wizard. The left side of the screen displays all the available data elements grouped by business view; the right side contains the groups, details, and filter boxes where the selected fields can be placed. Groups allow you to add (sub) headers and (sub) totals and can have five levels of nesting. Fields placed in the details box will become the inner part of the lowest group level. The last box is for filter elements; these fields will not become part of the report output but can be used to filter the data. Filters can also be placed on group and detail fields, but the content of these fields will always be visible in the report.

The simplest report imaginable is adding just a single field to the details box, which is also the minimum requirement for the ad hoc reporter to work. Reports can be previewed in HTML (the default choice), PDF, CSV, or XLS. With these last two options, Pentaho adds a convenient way of extracting data from a data warehouse for analysis in any tool that a user is accustomed to. When all group, detail, and filter fields have been added, you can click Next, which brings up an almost empty screen, apart from the same group, detail, and filter boxes that are now positioned on the left. This Customize Selections screen is where the real work can be done and it contains many options that aren't immediately obvious:

- **Sorting**—Information can be sorted on group and detail fields. WAQR automatically adds the group fields to the sort selection. It is not possible to remove this sorting; the only option is to change the sort order. Detail fields are not automatically added. When you click a detail field, the sort screen appears on the right side of the screen where the field can be added and the sort order can be changed.
- **Filtering**—Any field can be used to filter on, and multiple conditions can be combined using the operators *AND* and *OR*. The conditions available depend on the type of field used in the filter. If it's a character field, conditions such as `begins with` or `contains` are available; for a date, the conditions `on`, `before`, and `after` can be used; and for numeric values, operators such as `=`, `>=`, and `<` are available. A selection option is available where values can be picked from a list of values. This is implemented as a search screen where you can use the `*` character as a wildcard. If you want to display all values from a certain column, enter `*` and press Search.
- **Aggregating and formatting**—Several aggregation functions and field formats are available for the detail fields. Non-numeric values can only be counted, but for numeric values, the standard calculation functions `average`, `count`, `sum`, `min`, and `max` are available. These summaries are placed within each group or subgroup. Just click on a detail field and the formatting options will become visible. Each field can be formatted individually.

- **Grouping and paging**—Each group can be used for setting a page break right after or before a new group starts. You can also choose whether a group total should be added and whether group headers should be repeated on each page. For these settings, you need to select the corresponding level (Level 1 through Level 5), which will display the available grouping and pagination options.

The final screen with the report settings contains page orientation and size and can be used to enter report headers and footers. Print date and page numbers are added automatically. You'll notice that the Next button in the lower right of the screen is grayed out now. This is the correct behavior: saving the report is not part of the wizard but should be done by using the menu or the shortcut buttons in the Pentaho main screen. The report is saved in the format that was the active preview format at the time of saving, so if you selected PDF as the preview option, the saved report will open as a PDF file.

Practical Uses of WAQR

The WAQR option is a great way to start building your first reports with the Pentaho BI Suite, but has several limitations that make it unlikely that WAQR will be your primary reporting tool. As already mentioned, graphs and charts are not available, and the formatting options are quite limited. For example, it is not possible to modify the font type or color of the displayed values in the report unless you modify the settings in the metadata layer. The way we look at it, WAQR can be a good tool in the following two cases:

- **Export data**—Selecting and exporting data to a spreadsheet or CSV file is probably the most widely used option of WAQR. There are, of course, many other ways to get data from a data warehouse into a spreadsheet, but the speed and ease of use of WAQR for this purpose is hard to beat.
- **Quickstart report**—Reports created with WAQR and saved to the server can be opened from the Pentaho Report Designer (PRD) for further modification. Because creating a basic report in WAQR is usually much faster than with the report designer, this can save you a considerable amount of time. One caveat, however: you will need access rights for the folder where the server reports are saved.

TIP **Nearly anything in the Pentaho platform can be altered to your own taste, including the report templates. The templates are stored in the BI server folder** `pentaho-solutions/system/waqr/templates`**. Each template is stored in its own folder, so the easiest way to add your own template is to copy one of the existing folders and rename it. PRD can be used to create and modify templates,**

and the detailed information about the manual modification of templates can be found in the Pentaho Wiki at `http://wiki.pentaho.com/display/ServerDoc1x/Adhoc+Reporting+Templates`.

Pentaho Report Designer

The *Pentaho Report Designer (PRD)* is the graphical front end for creating, editing, and publishing reports for the Pentaho BI platform.

One of the main advantages of using PRD over other report builders is the ability to use Pentaho metadata models as data sources. Reports can also be published directly to the Pentaho server from the designer for usage in the Pentaho User Portal. The new `.prpt` file format is automatically recognized by the Pentaho server application so a PRD report can run in the portal without the need for adding extra wrappers around it.

Basically there are two types of report writers: *banded* and *flow-oriented* tools. Banded tools divide a report in one or more groups of data where report elements can be placed, while flow-based tools allow for a more free-format placement of elements on a page. PRD is a banded report editor, just like the well-known and widely used Crystal Reports. Although banded report writers are stricter in the way different report elements can be used in a report, PRD allows for the use of subreports, which greatly enhance flexibility and layout options.

PRD REPORT FILES

A PRD report is stored as a `.prpt` bundle file. This bundle contains a collection of XML files that define the report. The `layout.xml` file contains all the layout information, whereas the `*-ds.xml` files contain the query definitions. Beware that when a plain JDBC connection is used, passwords are stored as plain text. It's better to use JNDI connections and let the server handle the security definitions.

In addition to the page orientation of the different reporting tools is another important distinction: WYSIWYG versus structure view. *WYSIWYG (What You See Is What You Get)* report designers let you work on a canvas and the end result is immediately visible to the report designer. PRD is not a full WYSIWYG designer, so you mostly work with a design screen that shows the report structure, not the content and final layout. A preview option is available to see how the report will look to an end user. Any report can also be previewed in the different available output formats: PDF, HTML, XLS, RTF, and CSV.

NOTE **Although PRD is not a full WYSIWYG editor, you can change most of the formatting options directly in the properties pane when in preview mode.**

The next sections explain how PRD can be used to create insightful reports. In order to illustrate the different parts of the report designer, we use a very simple example consisting of a report with the years, quarters, and months from a WCM date dimension. Finally, we show how to build a monthly sales report using the full tool set.

The PRD Screen

When you start PRD for the first time, the application presents a Welcome screen as shown in Figure 13-2.

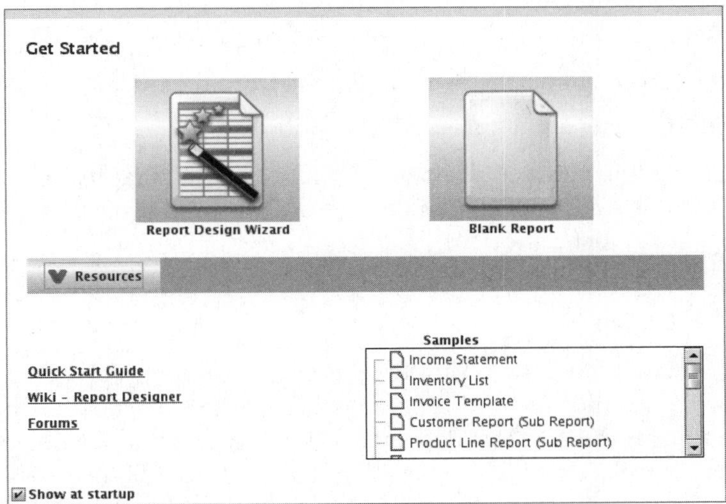

Figure 13-2: Pentaho Report Designer Welcome screen

Figure 13-2 shows the Welcome screen with the Resources tab opened. By default this part of the screen will not be visible. If you close the Welcome screen or you have the option Show at startup switched off, you can re-open the screen by clicking Help ➢ Welcome. The Welcome screen actually comes in handy because it contains all the shortcuts to get you started quickly. Clicking the Resources option displays links to the Quick Start Guide and the Pentaho Wiki with the available product documentation. The Forums link takes you to the Pentaho Forums where you can post and answer questions, or find answers from other users that cannot be found in the documentation. The Resources part of the screen also contains a list of samples to help you get started quickly.

The screen layout of PRD is pretty straightforward and looks a lot like any other reporting tool on the market. There's a menu bar at the top, the gallery with report building blocks on the left, and the properties screen on the right. The central part of the screen is reserved for the design screen itself where you can build the reports and sub-reports. PRD offers two ways of building a new report:

- The New option (or Blank Report in the Welcome screen) creates a new, empty report for you.
- The Report Wizard takes you through the four steps needed to create a complete report.

The Report Wizard works in a similar way to WAQR as described in the section "Practical Uses of WAQR," but its options are a bit different:

1. Select a template for the required report layout.
2. Define the data needed including filters and sorts.
3. Set the grouping and the available items from the query.
4. Set field formats and aggregation functions.

We will skip the wizard in the remainder of this chapter and focus on manually setting up a report. This better builds your understanding of the tool; the wizard is just a shortcut.

Report Structure

A PRD report is divided into multiple sections of different types. Some of these are standard, such as page and report headers; others are flexible and can be added or removed by a report designer. When you start a new, blank report, the basic structure is immediately visible, as is shown in Figure 13-3.

To create Figure 13-3, the Structure tab in the upper right was activated and the Groups and Details Body trees were expanded by clicking on them. When you click an element, such as the master report in the screen shot, the Properties editor appears at the bottom right. Any structure or content element has properties that can be altered either programmatically or by using the designer. Properties are divided into style and attributes, where style properties are used to determine what an element looks like, and the attributes determine the content and behavior of an element.

TIP **To prevent the screen from becoming too cluttered when designing your report, groups and headers can be hidden by clicking them in the Structure navigator and selecting the common Attribute hide-on-canvas, which is a simple checkbox. Selecting or clearing this checkbox has no effect on the report output—it's just a design aid.**

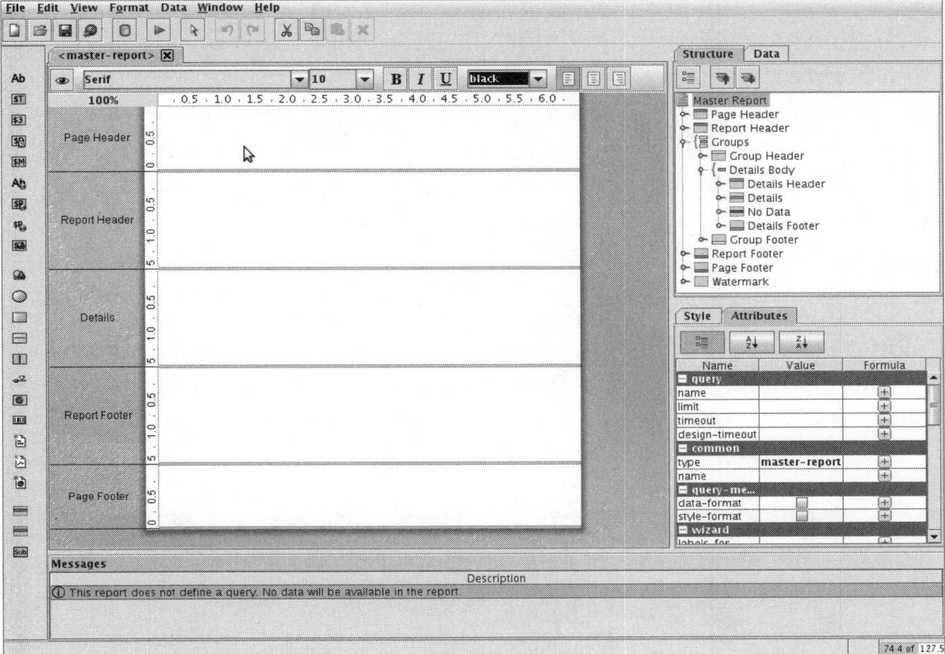

Figure 13-3: Report structure

The basic sections that make up a report are:

- **Page Header/Footer**—Any content placed here will be added to every page of the report. Examples for content are page numbers, print dates, and company logos. The page behavior style properties can be used to indicate whether the page header or footer should be printed on the first or last page or not.
- **Report Header/Footer**—Any content placed here will be displayed only once. Typical use of a report header is a front page with all report parameters, a short report summary, and the title of the report. The footer is often used to display report totals.
- **Group Header/Footer**—A report has at least one group to organize content. Each group has a header and footer for placing group-level labels or subtotals. Groups can be nested in other groups, creating a hierarchical report structure.
- **Details Body**—Only the most inner group contains the Details Body, which contains the Details band where the individual rows from a query result set can be placed. The Details Header and Footer are also part of the Details Body.

- **No Data**—This is a special type of band that can be used to display information when the query result set is empty. It is part of the Details Body group.
- **Watermark**—This special band can be used to add a watermark that will be printed as a background on each page. Common use is to display a text such as "Draft" or "Confidential" or a company logo on each page.

Report Elements

The left side of the design screen in Figure 13-3 contains the palette of basic building blocks for displaying content in a report. Table 13-1 contains a brief description of these elements. All the options are visualized as icons with the text being displayed when the mouse moves over the icon.

Table 13-1: Reporting elements

ELEMENT	DESCRIPTION
label	Most basic element for adding static text and column labels to a report. Contains a labels-for Wizard to easily create column headers.
text-field	Displays text values from a data set.
number-field	Displays numeric values from a data set. Contains format attributes specific to numeric fields.
date-field	Displays date values from a data set. Contains format attributes specific to date fields.
message-field	Most advanced dynamic data field. Can contain combined text, field references and functions in a single cell and allows for formatting the data at the same time. For example: `Customer: $(firstname) $(lastname) member since: $(date_registered,date,MM/dd/yyyy)`
resource-label	Based on a resource file, PRD can translate label texts in other languages.
resource-field	Based on a resource file, PRD can translate field content in other languages.
resource-message	Based on a resource file, PRD can translate messages in other languages.
content-field	Displays image fields from a data set.
image	Displays an image from both a local resource or a URL.
ellipse	Inserts an ellipse.
rectangle	Inserts a rectangle.

ELEMENT	DESCRIPTION
horizontal-line	Inserts a horizontal line.
vertical-line	Inserts a vertical line.
survey-scale	A mini-chart displaying survey results in a scale from 1 to 5. (This is configurable. The actual range is defined via attributes.)
chart	Inserts a chart, which can be edited by the Chart editor.
simple-barcodes	Translates the field content in a barcode that can be read by digital readers.
bar-sparkline	A mini bar chart to be used inline.
line-sparkline	A mini line chart to be used inline.
pie-sparkline	A mini pie chart to be used inline. This field type can also be used to create traffic light indicators in a management summary.
band	Can be used to group and format different elements.
external-element-field	Can be used to load external sub-reports from an URL or path.
sub-report	Inserts a sub-report, which can be opened in its own PRD screen.

Creating Data Sets

The most important part of creating a report is to determine which data should be displayed and, in the case of PRD, how the data is grouped and aggregated. Although grouping and aggregation can be added later, it makes sense to think through the report design before you start to build the data sets. A PRD report can contain only one data set, but reports can contain sub-reports with their own data sets. It is not possible to use or combine data from sub-reports in the main report.

PRD can retrieve data from many data sources; you can even use JavaScript as a data source. The most common way to build queries, however, is to use a JDBC connection or the Pentaho metadata files. When a new report is created, there are three ways to create a data source:

- Using the Add Data Source option from the Data menu option
- Right-clicking the DataSets icon in the Data tab on the right of the screen
- Click on the database icon in the Data tab directly

With any of these methods you get a list of options with JDBC and Metadata on the top. These two options will be used most frequently so they are explained further in the text that follows.

Creating SQL Queries Using JDBC

The screen for defining a JDBC data source consists of a panel with the available connections, available queries, the query name and the actual query itself. You already created the `wcm_dwh` connection in Chapter 3 so it can be selected here. After clicking on the plus sign to the right of the Available Queries text, a new empty query is created with the name `Query 1`. If this is the only query you'll be creating for the report this name is fine, but we advise you to always give a meaningful name to the queries you're building. You can write the SQL query directly in the query pane, but there is a much better alternative, which will show up when you click the little pencil on the right. This opens a graphical Query Designer, which is an embedded version of the open source SQLeonardo project. The Query Designer offers an easy way of creating SQL queries but you'll need some basic SQL knowledge to do so. That's why we included a SQL primer in Chapter 7.

The designer tab, which is opened by default, consists of the visual query representation in the upper left, the available tables and views in the lower left, and a design screen on the right. Figure 13-4 shows an example of the screen with the query that will be used for the images example later in this chapter.

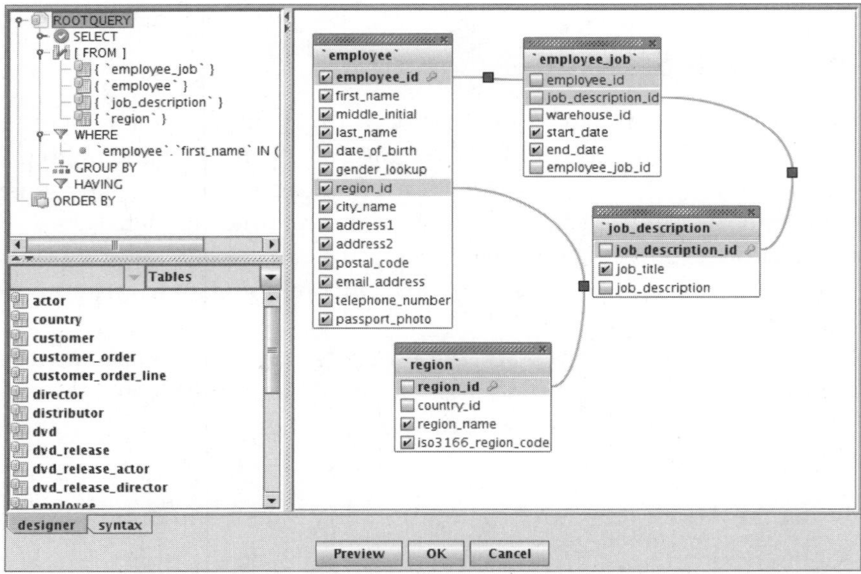

Figure 13-4: SQL Query Designer screen

First you have to decide which tables to use for the query. You can add them to the canvas on the right by dragging them there or just by double-clicking the table name. When you add a second table you'll notice that the Query Designer automatically adds the graphical representation of the foreign key relations if they have been defined in the database. By far the fastest way to select a complete star schema in the Query Designer is to drag a fact table to the canvas, click on the table name and choose Open All Primary Tables from the dropdown menu. This will add all the dimension tables for the star schema because they are the primary key tables for all the `_key` fields in the fact table. By default, all the table fields are selected; to unselect them, click the table name on the canvas and select Deselect All.

Note that this will only work when foreign key constraints have been defined. With MySQL using MyISAM, this is not possible at all so you have to define all the relationships manually.

NOTE Foreign key relationships do not always exist in the database, which means you have to identify the relationships between tables yourself. Simply click on a column in a table, keep the mouse button pressed, and move the mouse to the related column in the other table. When you release the mouse button, the relationship is added. Right-clicking on the little red square in the middle of a relationship enables you to select the edit function. This brings up the join editor where you can change the operator (=, >, <, =>, =<, <>) and indicate the join type by selecting from which table all values should be retrieved.

Selecting the fields that need to be part of the result set is a matter of clicking the check boxes. Adding calculations takes a little consideration, however. If all you want is a sum of a field, do not select the check box but right-click the column and select Add Expression. The aggregate functions `Count`, `Min`, `Max`, and `Sum` are available from the drop-down list. Selecting the `Sum` function for the revenue column in the `fact_orders` table creates the item `sum('fact_orders'.'revenue')` in the result set. Although PRD will accept this as a field name, it's better to add a meaningful alias by right-clicking the function in the Select list, choosing Edit, and adding the text as `Revenue` to the function. From Chapter 7, you may remember that an aggregate requires a `group by` statement as well. The Query Designer doesn't add the fields to the GROUP BY section automatically but these can be easily dragged there. Adding restrictions to the `where` clause works in much the same way as adding expressions. Right-click the column name in the canvas and select the option `add where condition`. This opens the connection editor where restrictions can be defined. There is neither an option to list values nor any other way to view data from a single column so you will have to know the available entries before defining the conditions.

TIP **When you're creating a `where` condition and don't know the right value to enter, do the following:**

1. **Close the Query Designer screen by clicking OK, and add a new query to the data source.**
2. **Open the Query Designer screen and drag the table containing the column whose values you need to know to the canvas.**
3. **Deselect all columns and select the right column.**
4. **Right-click the `SELECT` header right below the `ROOTQUERY` and choose Distinct.**
5. **Press Preview to view the column values; you can copy the values you want by selecting the row(s) and pressing Ctrl+C (there is no right-click option).**
6. **Close the designer, remove the list of values query, and reopen the original query.**
7. **Edit the `where` condition and paste the selected values in. (Don't forget to put double quotes around the value[s] if the selection is on a text column. Numerical values do not require double quotes.)**

You can view both the query results and the SQL that is generated as the result of the query directly from the Query Designer screen. The Syntax tab in the lower left switches the view to the generated SQL, and the Preview option will execute the query and show the result set in tabular form. When finished building your query, press OK to close the Query Designer and subsequently press OK to close the Data Source editor. The new dataset now shows up in the Data tab of PRD with all the column names expanded, as shown in Figure 13-5.

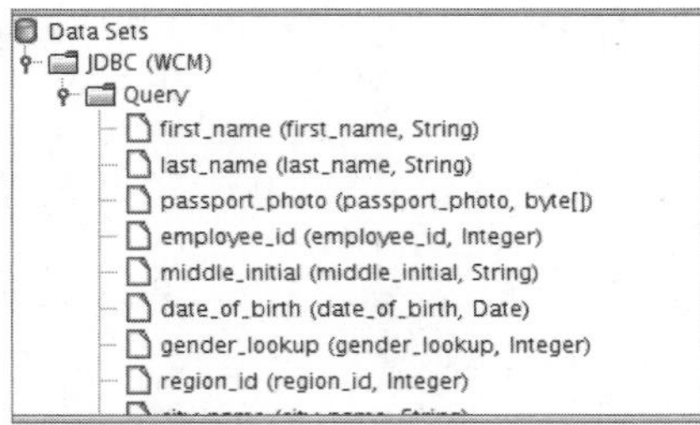

Figure 13-5: JDBC Query result

TIP **When you want to add a table the second time to be used as an alias (for example, to use the date dimension for order date and shipment date), you'll**

notice that PRD generates a warning with the text "Table already loaded and aliasing disabled!" Just close this message and switch to the Syntax tab of the Query Designer after deselecting all columns. Add the alias name to the right of the table name. Do *not* click OK but switch back to the designer tab. You'll get a message saying that the syntax has changed: accept the changes and the table name is now changed into the new alias. Now you can add the same table a second time. Repeat this process if more aliases are needed.

Creating Metadata Queries

When selecting `Metadata` as a data source, a screen similar to the JDBC data source window opens. In addition to the right connection, the Metadata Data Source Editor screen requires the selection of an XMI file. After selecting the XMI file and opening the query editor, the MQL Query Builder opens so that the business model can be selected. The available business views within a model are displayed as folders and fields can be selected by clicking on the field name and subsequently clicking on the arrow to add the field to the Select, Condition, or Order By list.

WARNING **In PRD, the data has to be sorted the way you want it to appear in the report using the sort options in the query. There is no other way to sort the data after it has been retrieved.**

Creating a data set using the MQL editor seems like a very straightforward process and at first sight it is. The same trick for getting values to apply in your conditions can work with the JDBC query editor, but you should be aware of the following limitations:

- No expressions can be added, so when an object is not available in the metadata model you cannot add it in the MQL editor. Instead, the model needs to be expanded and exported as an XMI file again before you can use the new field.
- Conditions cannot be grouped using brackets to force the evaluation precedence but are evaluated according to the logical expression order where `AND` takes precedence over `OR`. You can try this yourself: The expression `a AND b OR c AND d` is evaluated as `(a AND b) OR (c AND d)`, which could be correct, but if you meant it to be `a AND (b OR c) AND d` you have a problem because the MQL editor cannot group conditions this way. The only way to correctly group conditions this way is to rebuild the query in the JDBC editor instead and add the brackets manually.

The result of the MQL query is the same as with any other data source. At the first level is a data set that shows the type of data source (in this case `Metadata`) with the connection name in brackets. Nested below the data set is the query with the query name (in most cases Query 1 or just Query), and at the lowest level the available fields. The difference between a JDBC and Metadata data set is the column description of the Metadata columns, which shows the metadata business column name, not the real database column name.

Example Data Set

For the following instructions you'll use a very simple data set from the `dim_date` table. The example data set can be created by using both the JDBC and Metadata editors and consists of the fields `year4`, `quarter_name`, `month_number`, and `month_name` of any date dimension table. Order the data by `year4`, `quarter_name`, and `month_number` and make sure the Distinct option is chosen. No condition needs to be added yet. Drag the result rows into the Details band and press the Preview button (the little "eye" to the left of the font drop-down list at the top of the design canvas). Figure 13-6 shows the partial result of this exercise. Congratulations—you've just created your first report!

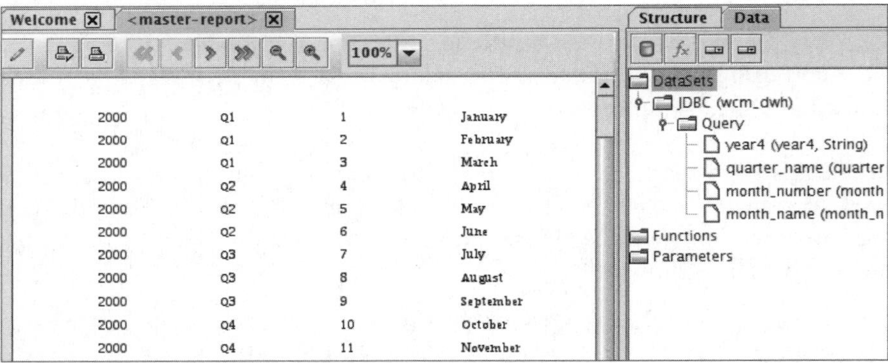

Figure 13-6: First List Report

Adding and Using Parameters

Fixed queries are fine for standard reports, but usually a little more interaction is required. This interaction can be added by using parameters that enable a user to choose certain values each time the report runs. Adding parameters is easy using the PRD Add Parameter function. You can find this under the Data menu, by right-clicking the Parameters tree in the Data tab, or by simply clicking on the shortcut icon at the top of the Data tab. A parameter is usually based on a set of values a user can choose from, but a free text parameter is available as well. All other parameter types require a predefined list of IDs and values. The list of values should come from a data source other than the main query. Any data source can be used here and because JDBC and metadata sources have already been covered, we will introduce a new type of data source here. PRD has the capability to define a custom table, including the content of the table within the report. When you add a parameter and click the plus sign to create a new data source, select Table. This starts the Table Datasource editor, which lets you define custom IDs and values. The ID is the value that will be passed to the query; the value will be displayed as a choice to the user when running the report.

In addition to the basic Text parameter, seven display and selection types are available. The drop-down list, single/multi list, radio button, and checkboxes are basic UI elements that can be encountered in many other applications as well. The last two are quite rare, which is strange considering the clarity and ease of use for end users. These are the single and multi-button types, which display a band of buttons to pick from. For the example report, you will create two parameters, one for selecting a year from a drop-down box, and one for selecting one or more quarters with a multi-button parameter. Each parameter will get its own query. Follow these steps:

1. Add a new parameter for the Year and add a JDBC or metadata data source. The data source contains a query that selects the distinct values from the `year4` field in any date dimension.
2. Give the name `qry_param_year` to the data source and name the parameter `param_year`; enter the text **Select Year** as parameter `Label` and select Drop Down as type. Because the query contains only a single column, `year4`, this is automatically selected for both the ID and Value.
3. Create the `Quarter` parameter. Add a new parameter `param_quarter` and add a new Table DataSource with the name `tbl_param_quarter`. Now enter the values as displayed in Figure 13-7.

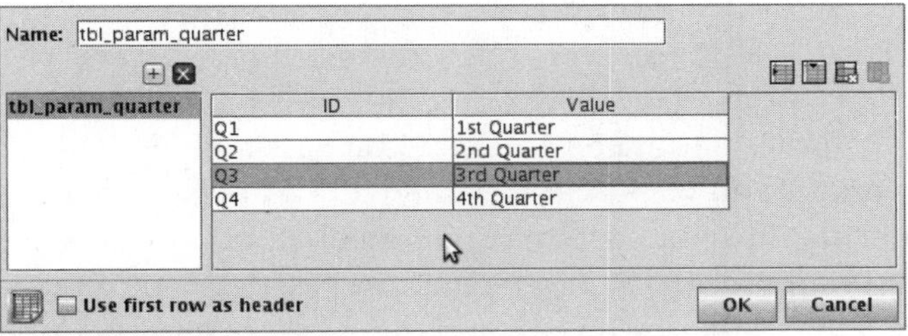

Figure 13-7: Parameter Table editor

4. Select Id as ID/Label and Value as Value from the drop-down lists and make sure that `java.lang.String` is selected as the data type. The Add Parameter screen now looks like the screenshot in Figure 13-8.

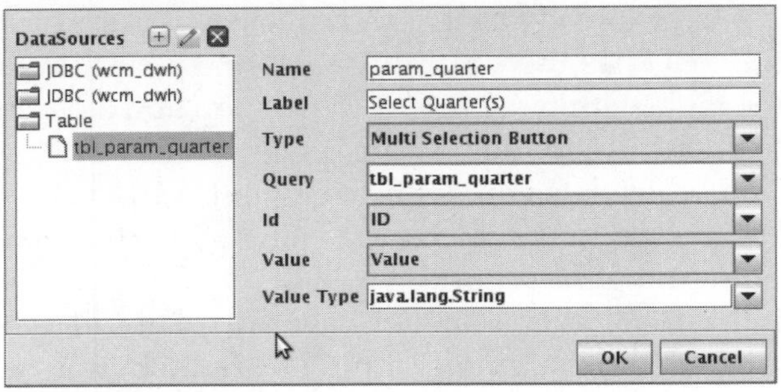

Figure 13-8: Add Parameter screen

The newly created parameters can be tested by running a preview: the parameters will be visible on top of the report screen. You can select and unselect values, but other than that, nothing happens yet. The final step involves linking the parameters to the main query. First you need to know how to reference the parameter in a query. Using a JDBC data source this is simply a matter of enclosing the parameter ID with curly braces and preceding them with a dollar sign, as in `${param_year}`. You can use the graphical designer to add a `where` condition to the columns `year4` and `quarter_name` but the text can also be typed in directly without opening the editor. The complete query should look like the following:

```
SELECT DISTINCT
     'dim_date_en_us'.'year4',
     'dim_date_en_us'.'quarter_name',
     'dim_date_en_us'.'month_number',
     'dim_date_en_us'.'month_name'
FROM
     'dim_date_en_us'
WHERE
     'dim_date_en_us'.'year4' = ${param_year}
 AND 'dim_date_en_us'.'quarter_name' IN (${param_quarter})
```

Because the quarter parameter `param_quarter` can have multiple values you use the `IN` operator and enclose the parameter in brackets. When the query is run, this is translated into a comma-separated list of values. You now have a parameterized report and when selecting the preview option you'll notice an empty screen. After selecting a year, and one or more quarters, and clicking on Update, the selected data appears on the screen. With the Autoupdate option it's also possible to have the query fire automatically when a new value is selected. The result of your work so far is displayed in Figure 13-9.

For clarity, all the queries and parameters have been expanded, which makes it clear why the query and parameter names need to be meaningful. It makes maintaining the report a lot easier when you do.

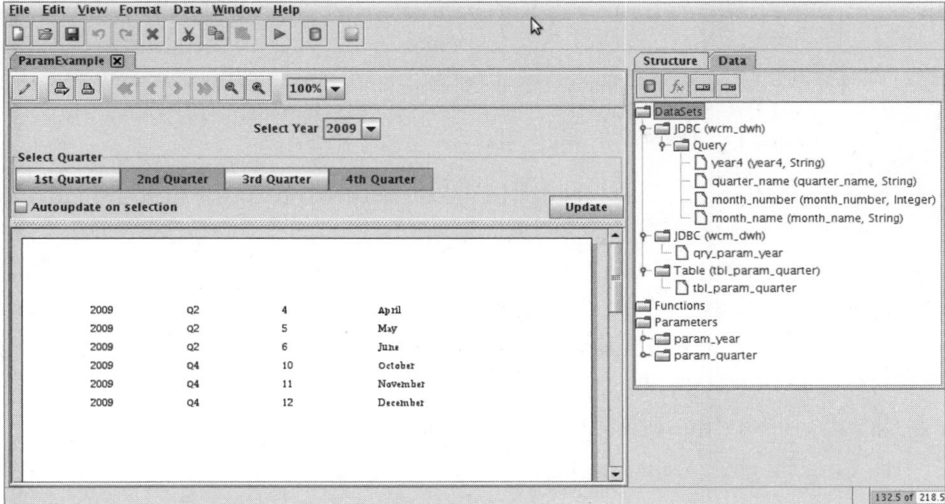

Figure 13-9: Parameter Example report

Layout and Formatting

Most people spend countless hours working on report layout and most reporting tools don't make it very easy either. PRD, however, is based on some smart design principles that make it very easy to quickly change the format of the report. The first and most important principle is *style inheritance* (Chapter 12 contains a basic introduction to the inheritance principles.) When you look at the structure of a report in the Structure pane, you'll notice that the structure is shaped like a nested tree. This isn't a coincidence: PRD follows this hierarchy when changing item properties. The Style property tab contains four columns: Name, Inherit, Value and Formula. The second column, Inherit, is checked for each property by default. This means that the settings for the property are inherited from a higher level in the hierarchy. You can try this in a simple way: Simply select the Details band in the Structure pane. The font family has the checkbox for inherit selected and the value is Serif, which is the default font. Now change the value to Verdana: You'll notice that PRD removes the Inherit check, and all the items that are part of the Details band now have the font family Verdana set automatically by inheritance. The highest level in the hierarchy is the master-report level and here you can change report-wide style properties such as font type, font size, text colors, and so on.

This inheritance principle isn't restricted to the built-in structure levels. The groupings you add yourself work the same way. Suppose you want to create a header for a detail row consisting of four columns. You could add four column labels and format them individually, but it's a lot easier to first create a band by dragging it from the design elements and placing the labels inside the band. Now only the band needs to be formatted—all the labels will inherit the property values of the band. It is impossible to cover all formatting options here so we restrict ourselves to the first steps to help you on your way. We will open the little Year-Quarter-Month report for the examples and start by adding a header for the columns in the report:

1. Navigate to the Details Header in the Structure tree. If the hide-on-canvas checkbox is selected, deselect it to display the band on the canvas.
2. Drag a band from the left object list to the Details Header band and position it at the top.
3. Open the style attributes and set the width, which can be found in the size & position group, to 100 percent.
4. Set the following style attributes for the band:
   - Font family: Arial
   - Font size: 12
   - Bold: checked
   - Text-color: white
   - Bg-color: dark grey
5. Drag four labels into the band. They automatically inherit the style attributes you just created for the band. The positioning guides can be used to place the label exactly above the four columns in the report. That's it: formatting done.
6. The only thing left is to set the right names for the columns. On the Attributes tab you'll see the value `property` to type in the column header, or you can use the labels-for Wizard, which presents a drop-down list with the available columns in the query. If your query column name is exactly what you would like the header to display, use the wizard. In any other case, just type in the values.

In addition to the Style properties, PRD contains a multi-tabbed format screen similar to the formatting dialog screens found in most modern word-processors. Simply select an object in your report and select Format ➢ Font from the main menu.

Alternate Row Colors: Row Banding

To enhance the readability of a list type report, it is a good idea to use alternate row coloring where rows with an even row number get a different color than those with an odd row number. Many reporting tools require that you use something similar to the following: first use a mod calculation, then create a variable, and finally use conditional formatting based on the variable to highlight odd and even rows. With PRD, this process is even simpler. Select the Format Row-Banding option from the menu and select the required colors for the odd and even rows. PRD then creates a row banding function, which is accessible from the Data tab in the Functions folder. Just drag the function to the Details band and make the field invisible. When you click Preview, you'll see the alternating row colors appear, as displayed in Figure 13-10.

Year	Quarter	Month number	Month name
2009	Q1	1	January
2009	Q1	2	February
2009	Q1	3	March
2009	Q2	4	April
2009	Q2	5	May
2009	Q2	6	June
2009	Q3	7	July
2009	Q3	8	August
2009	Q3	9	September
2009	Q4	10	October
2009	Q4	11	November
2009	Q4	12	December
2008	Q1	1	January

Figure 13-10: Row banding applied

Grouping and Summarizing Data

One of the basic principles of PRD (or any banded reporting tool) is the grouped presentation of data. Up to now, you've created the queries needed to select and filter the data for the report. Now it's time to bring structure to the result set by adding groups, headers, and summaries to the report layout.

Adding and Modifying Groups

A group is used to organize content in different levels, where sub-headers and totals can be added. Groups can be added by right-clicking anywhere in the design screen, by right-clicking the Groups section in the report structure, or by clicking the Add Group icon in the Structure tab. When you add a group, a new layer is added to the Groups section. Each group can link to a field in the reports data set, so when you want to create a report with a Year-Quarter-Month grouping, it's best when these fields are already present in the data set first, although this isn't required. One default group is used to group the detail data, as you can see in the structure tree. When you open the group editor (the left-most icon from the left in the structure tab) this empty default group is displayed as an empty line that references an empty field list []. This is the default group; it can be used for grouping but you cannot remove it, although you can remove all the groups from the group editor. After closing the editor and reopening it, you'll notice the empty line with the default group again. Because you don't want to waste resources, you'll use this default group for the Quarter level grouping in your sample report. Using group names is required; otherwise you cannot reference the groups in the report. So add `QuarterGroup` as the name and select the field `quarter_name` as the group field. While you're still in this screen, enter another group and name this `YearGroup`. The field referenced is `year4`. Click on the `YearGroup` line and move it up by clicking on the up arrow. Figure 13-11 shows the result so far.

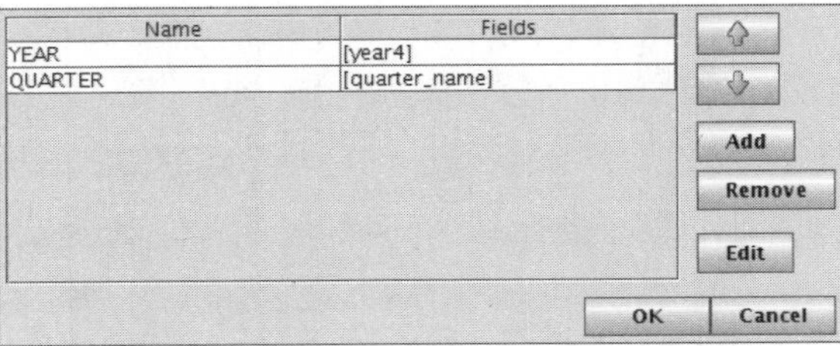

Figure 13-11: Group editor

When you run a preview again you'll notice that the results now have a break at each quarter, and that the details header is repeated for each quarter. Now add a new band in both the year and quarter header and set the band width to 100 percent again. Make sure the color scheme is different for each of the three levels of grouping (Year, Quarter, Details).

NOTE **It is not (yet) possible to drag and drop objects such as labels, fields, or graphs from one band (header) to another, but it is possible to copy or cut from one band and paste them in another.**

Now you could just move the header fields from the details header to the year and quarter header respectively, but let's use a message field instead. The year header message field gets the value `Year: $(year4)`; the quarter header message field gets the value `Quarter: $(quarter_name)`. You can now remove the detail fields for `year4` and `quarter_name` as well. To be able to select more than one year and view the effects of the grouping you added, you can alter the year parameter into a multi-list or multi-button type and change the query condition to `IN`. Don't forget to add the brackets around the parameter. The report should now look something like the example in Figure 13-12.

Year: 2005			
	Quarter: Q3		
		Month nr	Month name
2005	Q3	7	July
2005	Q3	8	August
2005	Q3	9	September
	Quarter: Q4		
		Month nr	Month name
2005	Q4	10	October
2005	Q4	11	November
2005	Q4	12	December
Year: 2006			
	Quarter: Q3		
		Month nr	Month name
2006	Q3	7	July

Figure 13-12: Grouping applied

Using Functions

The final step in creating a grouped report consists of adding the footer texts and summary fields. In order to display summaries such as the total number of months or quarters in a group, you need to create functions. In case you haven't noticed, you already created a function to apply the row banding formatting, but that is done in an almost transparent way. PRD contains many more functions that can be used to enhance your report. The list of available functions can be accessed on the Data tab by clicking the Functions shortcut icon in the top of the data tab, by right-clicking the Functions line inside the Data tab, or by selecting Add Function from the Data menu. The Function list contains expressions for conversions, content layout, and aggregation. Aggregation functions are the ones needed for adding group and total summaries to a report and are divided into Global and Running Aggregation functions. The distinction between these two types of functions is the context in which they are applied: *Global functions* always calculate the aggregation within the group for which they are defined. *Running functions* calculate the aggregation up to the point or sub-group in which they are placed. To illustrate this, let's create four functions to count the number of lines within the report at different levels:

1. Add a Running Item Count function (select Add Function, double-click Running, select the Count [Running] Function, and click Add). Functions get a default name consisting of their function name and an appended sequence number so change the name into `RunningCountYear`. Select `YearGroup` as the Reset Group Name to make sure the counting starts from the beginning for each encountered year.
2. Add a Total Item Count Function, name this **`TotalCountYear`**, and select `YearGroup` as the group name (select Add Function, double-click Summary, select Count and click Add).

3. Now add another Running and Total Item Count Function and name them `RunningCountReport` and `TotalCountReport` but leave the group and reset group names empty to have the aggregation calculated for all the values in the report.
4. Open the Quarter Group Footer and drag the four newly created functions in the footer area. Note that this creates a number field with a reference to the function, which is now part of the field list.
5. Add four labels as well to indicate which value is represented by each field. Figure 13-13 shows what the group of functions and the report footer look like after applying all the previous steps.

Figure 13-13: Aggregation functions example

WARNING **Functions are referenced by name so make sure that every function has a unique name within the report.**

Because the proof of the pudding is in the eating, it's time to hit the Preview button again and find out how these functions are evaluated by PRD. Figure 13-14 displays part of the results with a selection of two years (2008 and 2009) and all four quarters.

Year: 2009			
	Quarter: Q2		
2009	Q2	4	April
2009	Q2	5	May
2009	Q2	6	June
Running Year	*6*		
TotalYear	*12*		
Running Report	*18*		
TotalReport	*24*		
	Quarter: Q3		
		Month nr	Month name
2009	Q3	7	July
2009	Q3	8	August
2009	Q3	9	September
Running Year	*9*		
TotalYear	*12*		
Running Report	*21*		
TotalReport	*24*		

Figure 13-14: Aggregation results

This figure is a good example of how the grouping and aggregation functions work and should give you enough background to build your own reports.

What is shown is that for Q2 2009, the running item count is 6, which is correct because each quarter consists of 3 month lines, and the total within the year group is 12. The Running Report count shows 18 for Q2 2009 because all 2008 lines plus the current 6 of 2009 make 18. Finally the Total Report count displays 24 in each group, which is the number of months over 2 years.

You might be tempted at this point to try to add calculations based on these new function fields, for instance to calculate a row value percentage of a group total. PRD doesn't work that way but provides out-of-the-box functions for these calculations as well. As a last example in the Year-Quarter-Month report, you can add an ItemPercentage function to calculate the month number percentage of the group month number total. As a reference, you can create this month number group total and display it in the Quarter group footer. The ItemPercentage function is part of the running aggregation functions (select Add function, open Running, and select Percent of Total). After the function has been added, the field to create the percentage for and the group for determining the total value needs to be selected. It is also a good idea to change the function name into something meaningful such as MonthPercentage. The complete function specification is displayed in Figure 13-15.

Name	Value
Required	
Function Name	MonthPercentage
Field Name	month_number
Optional	
Reset on Group Name	QUARTER
Rounding Mode	4
Scale	2
Scale Result To 100	False
Dependency Level	0

Figure 13-15: Item Percentage definition

Now the function can be added to the details in the report. To have the column displayed as a percentage, change the format value in the field attributes into `00.0%`. The complete result can be seen in Figure 13-16; although this example is not a very useful calculation in the real world, it does a good job of explaining how the calculation engine of PRD works.

Using Formulas

In the previous section, you learned how to add an ItemPercentage function to calculate the month number percentage of the group month number total. If you already have a function that calculates the month number total, you can achieve the same result using a formula. To do this, you need to create a Number field and specify an expression that calculates the item percentage for the field's `Formula` property. The syntax for Formulas is the same as found in spreadsheet programs like Microsoft Excel and Open Office Calc: you enter an equal sign, followed by the expression. To actually calculate the ItemPercentage, you need to divide the month number by the month total. So, in the formula the expression that appears behind the equals sign would read `[month_number] / [MonthTotal]`. Note that that `[month_number]` and `[MonthTotal]` are themselves also expressions: `[month_number]` references a field from the query, and `[MonthTotal]` refers to a Total Sum function calculating the sum of the month numbers.

Year: 2009				
	Quarter: Q1			
		Month nr	% of group total	Month name
2009	Q1	1	17.00%	January
2009	Q1	2	33.00%	February
2009	Q1	3	50.00%	March
Running Year	3	6		
Total Year	12			
Running Report	15			
Total Report	24			
	Quarter: Q2			
		Month nr	% of group total	Month name
2009	Q2	4	27.00%	April
2009	Q2	5	33.00%	May
2009	Q2	6	40.00%	June
Running Year	6	15		
Total Year	12			
Running Report	18			
Total Report	24			

Figure 13-16: Month number percentages

Expressions in Pentaho Reporting formulas are not limited to fields from the dataset and references to named functions; you can also use constant values, common arithmetical operators like +, -, * and / and logical operators like AND and OR. In addition, there is a host of built-in functions for tasks like date/time calculation and string manipulation. Beware though that this is not a spreadsheet program: you can only reference the current row of data, not the previous or next row. You can, however, use functions to determine minimum or maximum values within a group, for example, and reference the function at the row level. Functions can also reference the results of other functions, so there are practically no limits to what you can do with functions, formulas and expressions.

NOTE **For a complete overview of Pentaho Reporting Formulas, built-in functions, and operators, refer to the Pentaho documentation at** **`http://wiki.pentaho.com/display/Reporting/9.+Report+Designer+Formula+Expressions`.**

Adding Charts and Graphs

A picture is worth a thousand words, and this common wisdom is particularly true in the world of BI. Showing just the numbers is often not enough when you want to get immediate insight into trends or distribution of data. PRD therefore does not only provide an interface for creating Pentaho Reporting, but can be used to integrate JFreeChart as well. Remember that Pentaho Reporting and JFreeChart are two different projects, which have been integrated into a single solution by Pentaho. More information about JFreeChart can be found at `http://www.jfree.org/jfreechart`.

Before a chart can be used, the data to be visualized by the chart needs to be present in the report. PRD cannot use the data fields from a query directly but needs a special data provider called a *collector function* that transforms the data for usage in a chart. There are 6 collector functions and 14 chart types available. Each chart type uses its own collector function, and some chart types can use two of them. For a simple pie chart it suffices to have a series column and a value defined, whereas for a stacked bar chart with a second Y axis more data needs to be passed to the chart. The advantage of using data collectors that are separate from the main data set is the ability to create different charts from a single set of data.

Grasping the way charting works and the different data options available might seem hard at first, so let's start by a simple example to get a sense of how things work. This example is based on the Pentaho Sample database, and will display revenue and quantity by order year and product line in various ways.

NOTE **In a real-life situation, you should first start with the design for the report, which should be based on a business requirement. Only after you've outlined what you want to achieve with the new report can you start thinking about what data would be needed and how the report should be constructed. The following steps assume that the requirements and design phase is already completed so you can now start building the actual report.**

1. After creating a new report, use the PRD Query Designer to add a JDBC data source with `OrderYear`, `ProductLine`, `OrderRevenue`, and `OrderQuantity`. To get the order year, you need the `year()` function.

WARNING **The PRD Query Designer allows you to add the expressions `sum`, `min`, `max`, and `count` but they can be altered later. Beware that when you are using non-aggregate functions such as `year()`, the field needs to be added to the `group by` clause. When you do, it will be added including the alias, which is not correct. The `order by` and `group by` clauses will have to be adjusted manually to generate the correct results. Also, beware that each time you enter the graphical**

Query Designer, SQLeonardo will generate the wrong query syntax again by translating `year(orderdate)` into just `year`.

2. The correct query for getting the result set you need is displayed in the following code block:

```
SELECT      YEAR(o.orderdate) AS orderyear
,           p.productline
,           SUM(d.quantityordered)              AS orderquantity
,           SUM(d.priceeach*d.quantityordered) AS orderrevenue
FROM        orders       AS o
INNER JOIN orderdetails AS d ON o.ordernumber = d.ordernumber
INNER JOIN products     AS p ON d.productcode = p.productcode
GROUP BY    year(o.orderdate)
,           p.productline
ORDER BY    year(o.orderdate) ASC
,           p.productline ASC
```

3. From this result set different charts can be generated at different levels of detail. Charts can be positioned in the report header, but you can also use the created groups in a report. By doing this, you can give a high-level overview at the top of the report and provide detailed information in the group breakdowns. The design idea is the following:
   - Show a bar chart at the top of the report with the total quantity per product line broken down by year to highlight sales trends for each product line over time.
   - For each year, display the revenue and quantity distribution by product line in percentages using pie charts.
   - Display the year, total quantity, and total revenue as group header.
4. To do this, first create a group based on the `OrderYear`. Charts can be added by dragging a chart object from the palette into the design screen, in this case to the report header. In order to have the chart spread over the entire width of the page, click on the chart and set the following style attributes: `x=0`, `y=0`, `width=100%`, and `height=190`.

NOTE **All objects in a report can be sized and positioned in an absolute or a relative way within a report band. The default in PRD is using absolute positioning and sizing in pixels—for example, when a chart is placed somewhere in a band, the *x* and *y* values indicate the absolute position of the upper-left corner of the chart and the `width` and `height` values are in pixels. All values can be changed into relative values by adding the percent (%) sign.**

5. Charts that are placed on the canvas can be edited by right-clicking on the chart and selecting the Chart editor option. This opens the screen that is displayed in Figure 13-17.

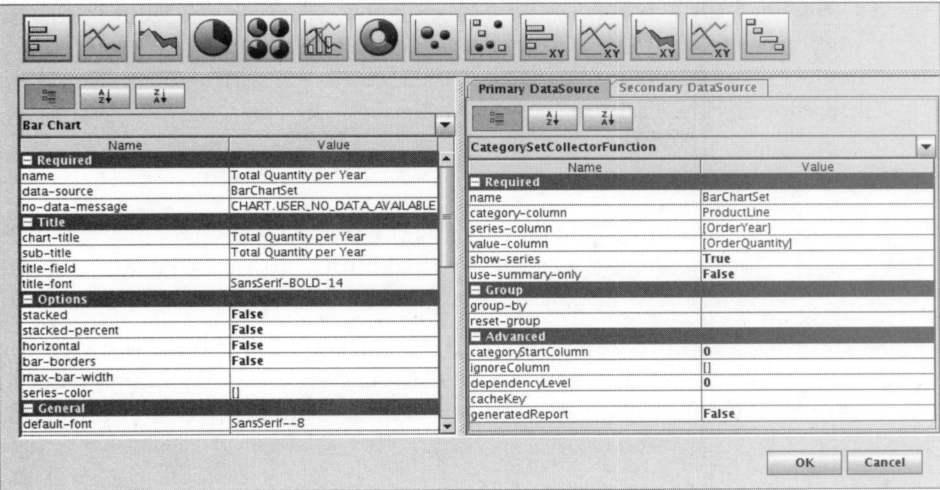

Figure 13-17: Chart editor

The screen shows the different chart types at the top, the chart properties on the left and the data source definition on the right. This data source part is empty when you first create a chart and you will need to select one of the available collector functions to feed the chart. Each chart type has one or two available collector functions, depending on the type of chart. In order to make the right chart choices, you'll need to know what you can do with the various collector functions:

- **PieSet**—Requires a series (the slices of the pie) and a value column. Used for Pie and Ring charts.
- **CategorySet**—Requires a category (the X axis) and a value column. Optionally, a series (breakdown of a category) can be added. Used for bar, line, multi-pie, waterfall, and area charts.
- **PivotCategorySet**—Pivots value columns to use them as categories. Requires you have at least two value columns (for example, actual and budget) that are translated into categories. Used in the same chart types as CategorySets.
- **TimeSeries**—Requires a date/time column to be used as a category (X-axis) and a value. A series can be added optionally. Used in scatter, XY bar, XY line, XY area, and Extended XY line charts.
- **YYSeries**—Allows for two measures to be positioned on the X and Y axis to plot the relative dependency of two variables. A series value is optional. Can be used in the same charts as the TimeSeries collector function.

- **XYZSeries**—Only for the bubble chart; needs three value columns where X and Y determine the position relative to the X and Y axis, and the Z value determines the size of the bubbles. Adding a series allows for a four dimensional visualization.

Adding a Bar Chart

The first chart you want to create is based on a `CategorySet` where `productline` is used as category, `OrderYear` as the series-column, and `orderquantity` as a value column. Note the following:

- Adding the columns for series and values requires a bit more clicking through than opening a separate selection screen. It looks like you could add multiple columns to either a series or a value but when you do, this does not have any effect on the chart, or it just won't display any values at all.
- Make sure that the value for `use-summary-only` is set to `False`. The style attributes on the left can be adjusted to your own liking.
- When a title needs to be displayed, type it in. If you don't want a title, leave the field empty. There is no display title attribute as there is for the legend and the X and Y axis labels.
- The rest of the formatting options are pretty self-explanatory except for the fonts. Fonts can be adjusted by using a three-part format text divided by dashes where the first part consists of the font name, followed by the style and size. A bold, 12 point Arial font is coded as Arial-BOLD-12.
- By using the preview option, you can check whether the chart matches your requirements.

Pie Charts

The pie charts you want to add require a `PieSetCollectorFunction`, and because you want one pie to display quantity and the other one revenue, they both get their own collector function. The nice thing about pie charts is that you can show labels for the slices and indicate which content should be displayed inside the label. Three values can be displayed: the actual label text, the slice value, and the slice percentage. They can be accessed by adding {0}, {1}, or {2} in any order or combination to the label format attribute where you can add text as well. If, for example, you want to display the name of the slice followed by the value in brackets, just type **{0} ({1})**.

The pie charts in the example are placed in the `Year` group header and will display the values for a specific year. The value for the `group by` attribute needs to be set to the `YearGroup` group; otherwise, the charts will not use the grouping and all will display the same overall values.

With pie charts, you can also explode a slice (position it outside the circle by a certain percentage) or display the chart as 3D. A combination of these is not possible: you cannot explode a slice in a 3D pie chart. To select the slice to explode, you will need to know its ID, which is determined by the sort order in the query. ID numbers start with 0 so in this case, the Classic Cars slice has ID 0 and will be exploded. The explode amount is indicated as a percentage between 0 and 1, so 0.1 will give a 10 percent shift of the slice.

You cannot use the Chart editor for sizing and positioning charts; that is part of the main report designer. To place two charts side by side and have them scale automatically, set the x and y value for the left chart to 0 and the width to 50 percent. The right chart will get an x value and a width of 50 percent. Combined, these two charts will now fill the page from left to right. To finish the defined design, there is only one thing left: the group header text with the year, quantity, and revenue in it. If you add a message field and leave a little white space at the top of the group header, set the field to 100 percent, and change the background color into the same light gray as the pie charts, the group header will look like a single block, which gives a very professional appearance to the report. The message field gets the value:

```
Year: $(ORDERYEAR) Total quantity $(ORDERQUANTITY,number,#,###),
  Total revenue $(ORDERREVENUE,number,$#,###.##)
```

The resulting report is displayed in Figure 13-18.

Working with Images

PRD can handle image data from URLs, local files, or database columns. This allows you to embed company logos but also to create reports with product information, including pictures of the product, or employee sheets, including a passport photo if that's available in a corporate database. In order for the following example to work, you will need a logo in any image file format (JPG, PNG, GIF, BMP, WMF or SVG. TIFF will probably work as well but that's not guaranteed) to create a report header, and one or more pictures in a database. The employee table in the sample WCM database contains a `passport_photo` column of type `LONGBLOB` where images can be stored. The table contains some sample pictures, but you can also replace them with your own or use another data source with pictures.

NOTE In most modern databases, a blob field can be defined that can store binary information of an arbitrary kind, including pictures. In MySQL, you need to

define a field of type BLOB (`TINY`, `MEDIUM`, or `LONGBLOB`, depending on the size of the files to be stored). Getting a picture in the database is easy with the MySQL command `LOAD FILE`, which points to the file to be loaded. The statement used for uploading Roland's picture is:

```
UPDATE employee
SET    passport_photo = LOAD FILE('/media/photo/photo_roland.jpg')
WHERE        employee_id = 22612
```

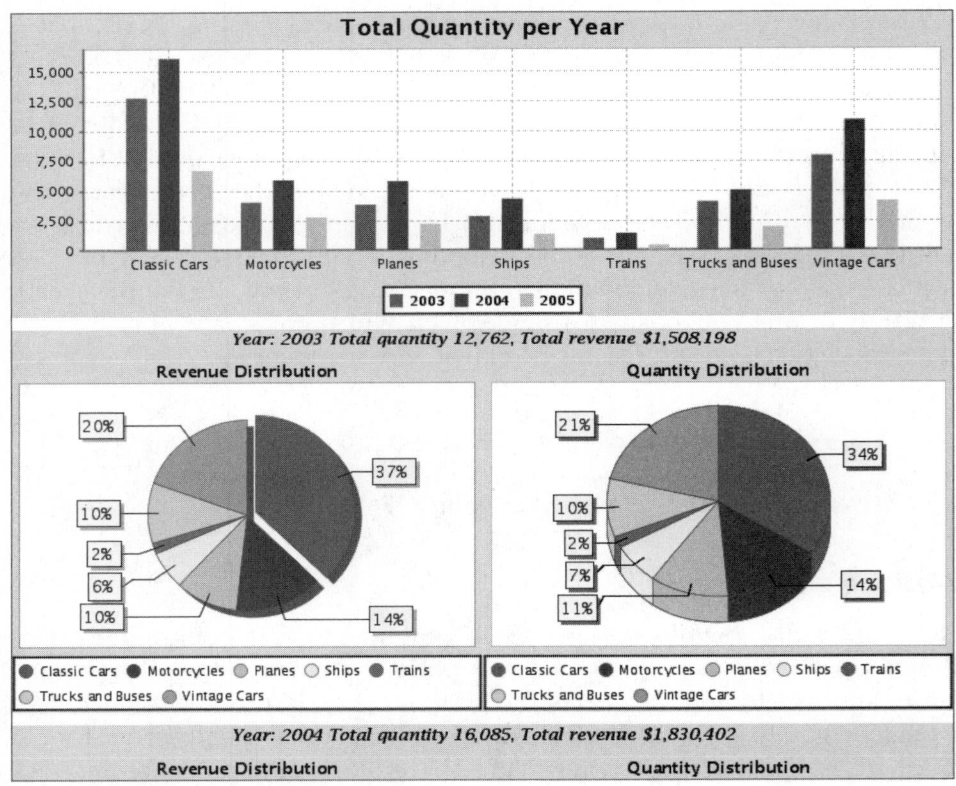

Figure 13-18: Example Chart Report

Follow these steps to create the report shown in Figure 13-19:

1. In PRD, start a new report and create a query to select the employee details from the WCM database, including the column `passport_photo`.
2. To display images from a file or URL, place an image field from the palette in the page header and add a title as well.

3. Right-click the image field and select Edit Content. The File Location editor opens and you can enter a URL or browse to a local file. The example uses the WCM logo.
4. Add a group `Employee` and use `employee_id` as group field. This enables you to organize the report and to start a new page for each employee.
5. Now you can place all the employee detail fields in the group header but make sure you use a content field for the picture.

WARNING **PRD doesn't recognize the blob field automatically so when you just drag the field from the data tab onto the canvas it becomes a text field, not a content field. This is a known bug (PRD-1394).**

6. For both the content object and the content field there are two attributes that probably need to be set: the scale and aspect ratio attributes. Both are readily available when you right-click the fields and are also part of the style attributes in the structure view. Figure 13-19 shows the result of this image exercise.

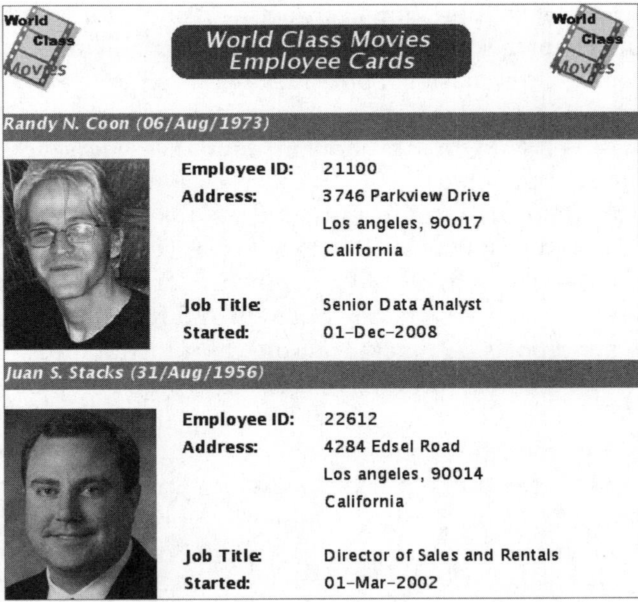

Figure 13-19: PRD Image examples

Here are a few hints for creating these reports:

- Use message fields for names, addresses, or any other information that contains multiple fields from a database. The value for the name field in this example is `$(first_name) $(middle_initial) $(last_name)`. There is no need to explicitly insert spaces; they will be picked up automatically by PRD.
- Date fields need to be formatted; otherwise they will be displayed as full date-time values including the time zone. The date format is entered in the format attribute of the date field. In this example, the value is `dd-MMM-yyyy` (without quotes).
- Fields can be arranged, aligned, and distributed by using the Arrange, Align, and Distribute layout assistants in the Format menu. You can select multiple fields that need to be aligned or distributed evenly by holding down the Shift key and clicking the fields.

Working with Subreports

Subreports can add an extra dimension to your report design and allow for displaying data grouped at a different aggregation level or from different data sources. One word of caution, however, before using subreports: a subreport uses its own data source so it will fire a second query to your database. Using multiple subreports in a master report makes this situation even worse. The best strategy is to design your reports using as few subreports, and thus extra queries, as possible. With this caution in mind, we show you how to use subreports as they are intended.

A PRD master report is used to visualize a single data set. In a sense, the whole report acts as a single table. This means that you cannot filter or display only part of the data set, other than using charts or groups. Displaying two adjacent tables with a similar structure but with different content is not possible without using subreports. A quick example can illustrate this. Suppose you want to display the top and bottom five customers based on their revenue side by side. This would require placing two lists in a single report, which is not possible in PRD (aside from using complex SQL to generate the two lists in the data set). With subreports, it is quite easy to accomplish this: the master report contains both a Top 5 and a Bottom 5 subreport, each with its own query, headers, and details. These subreports can both be placed in the report header, as shown in Figure 13-20.

To build this report, we created a new empty master report without data or layout and added two subreports in the report header. When you drag a subreport onto the canvas and double-click it, a new tab with a report canvas opens. A subreport is similar to a master report. It can contain a data source, different groupings, bands, and charts. There is one notable difference, however: It is not possible to create new parameters for a subreport.

Top 5		Bottom 5	
Name	*Revenue*	*Name*	*Revenue*
Euro+ Shopping ..	908,165	Boards & Toys Co.	9,080
Mini Gifts Distributors ..	651,878	Atelier graphique	24,033
Australian Collectors, ..	200,133	Auto-Moto Classics ..	26,309
Muscle Machine Inc	196,952	Frau da Collezione	28,780
La Rochelle Gifts	179,129	Microscale Inc.	32,946
Total:	*2,136,257*	*Total:*	*121,148*

Figure 13-20: Top 5 and Bottom 5 customers

PRD has two types of subreports: banded and inline. You should choose which type you want as you drag the subreport object from the palette and place it on the canvas. A banded subreport spans the entire width of the band where the subreport is placed, whereas an inline subreport can be placed anywhere. Be careful when using inline subreports because they require more memory and processing power than their banded counterparts. Another thing to be aware of is the band in which the subreport is placed. If the subreport is placed inside the report header or footer, it will be executed only once. When placed inside a group header or footer, it will be executed as many times as there are group values, and if you position a subreport in the details, it will be executed for every line in the report. It is not possible to place a subreport in the page header or footer.

Passing Parameter Values to Subreports

When a parameter is defined in a master report, it should be given a unique ID by which the parameter can be referenced. The subreport can reference the master report parameter by importing it, but no new parameters can be defined in a subreport. You can open the screen for importing parameters by right-clicking the parameter icon in the Data tab of the subreport or clicking on the Sub-report Parameter icon in the Data tab. The screen allows you to map master report parameters to the subreport equivalents. You can use the same name for the master and the subreport, but we prefer to use a different name for clarity. As an example, you can expand the top/bottom-five report from the previous section to include a selection product line that you will pass on to the subreport.

1. First, create both parameters in the master report before opening the subreport.

2. Next, in the subreport, open the Sub-report Parameter editor and enter the outer and inner names of the parameters. The outer names refer to the parent report's parameter names; the inner names will be used in the subreport query. Figure 13-21 shows the parameter editor screen with the values inserted.

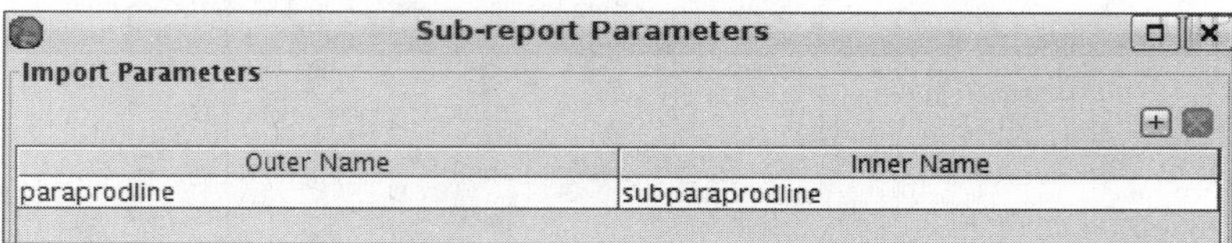

Figure 13-21: Import parameters

3. The query for the Top 5 list can now be extended with the required `where` clauses and parameter entry, as shown in the following code:

```
SELECT      customers.customername
,           SUM(orderdetails.quantityordered*orderdetails.priceeach)
            AS revenue
FROM        orders
INNER JOIN  orderdetails
ON          orders.ordernumber         = orderdetails.ordernumber
INNER JOIN  customers
ON          orders.customernumber      = customers.customernumber
INNER JOIN  products
ON          orderdetails.productcode = products.productcode
WHERE       products.productline       = ${subparaprodline}
GROUP BY    customers.customername
ORDER BY    2 DESC
LIMIT       5
```

4. You can now also include a message field in your master report displaying the selected product line with the expression `Selected Value: $(paraprodline)`. The end result of this exercise is displayed in Figure 13-22.

Publishing and Exporting Reports

You can publish reports to the Pentaho BI Server from the Main PRD menu by choosing File ➤ Publish, or by clicking the Publish icon situated to the right of the Save button in the shortcut bar. This opens the Publish dialog shown in Figure 13-23.

To publish, you must set up your publication configuration. The Publish location must be the name of an existing directory residing beneath the `pentaho-solutions` directory. The Web Publish URL must be pointed to your

Pentaho BI server. For the Publish password, you must use the password that was set in the `publisher_config.xml` file. Setting up this password is covered in Chapter 3. Finally, you must use the Server user ID and password of a user that has the Admin role (''joe'' and ''password'' for a default installation).

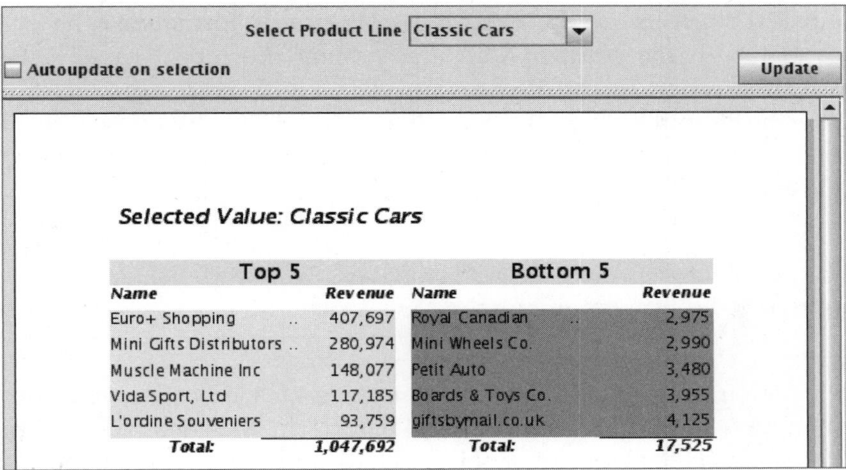

Figure 13-22: Parameterized subreports

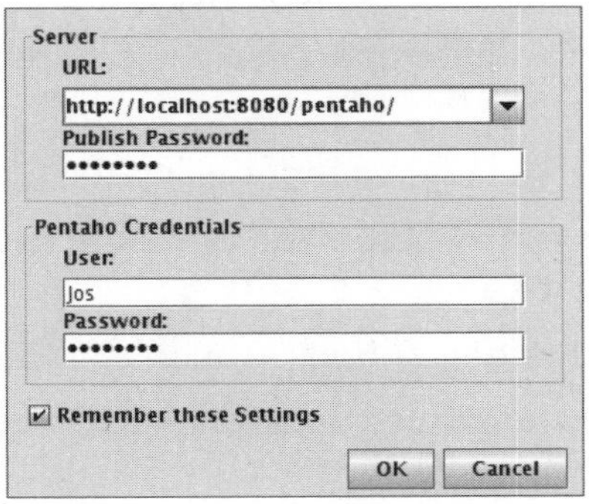

Figure 13-23: The Publish dialog

Refreshing the Metadata

After publishing the report to the server, you must tell the server to reload the metadata to make sure the user will be presented with the latest version of the report when he opens it. This can be done from the user console through the menu by choosing Tools ➤ Refresh ➤ Repository Cache Metadata.

Alternatively, you can refresh the cache using the Server Administration Console. To refresh the cache from the Server Administration console, go to the Services tab and press the Refresh button in the Solution Repository panel.

Exporting Reports

Pentaho PRD reports can be exported in the same formats as the WAQR application, with the extra option of exporting the report as RTF. Before exporting the report, it can be previewed in the desired export format by selecting the output format (HTML, PDF, XLS, RTF, CSV) from the File ➤ Preview menu option. The Preview shortcut icon has one additional option called Preview as Text.

Summary

This chapter introduced the basic architecture of a reporting solution and described two main tools for creating reports in a Pentaho Solution, the Web-based Ad Hoc Reporting tool (WAQR) and the new Pentaho Report Designer (PRD). After offering a brief overview of the WAQR we started building reports using PRD and explained the following topics:

- Different components of the Pentaho Report Designer
- The structure of a Pentaho report and the different elements that can be used inside a report
- Creating JDBC and Metadata queries using the Query Designer
- Adding parameters to give users the flexibility to choose only a subset of the data from a database
- The layout and formatting options available in PRD
- How to group and summarize data inside a report
- Using functions and expressions
- How to visualize information using graphs and charts
- Using images from URLs, files and database tables
- Working with subreports to create complex reporting layouts consisting of multiple datasets
- How to create parameters that can be passed to the data set of a subreport
- How to publish reports to the Pentaho server and make sure that the latest version is displayed to a user

There is a lot more to reporting and the Pentaho Report Designer than we could cover in this chapter. It is intended as a solid foundation to get you started, not as a complete reference or development guide. We encourage you to visit the online Wiki and the forums if you need more technical information about the product.

CHAPTER

14

Scheduling, Subscription, and Bursting

In this chapter, we look at a few of the capabilities of the Pentaho platform to distribute content to the end user. Basically, there are three different ways for users to execute action sequences:

- **Immediate or interactive execution**—In this case, the action is executed immediately after the user requests it, and the user waits for delivery of the action's output, which marks the end of the user's request.
- **Execution in the background**—Upon the user's request, the action is implicitly scheduled to be processed as soon as possible, and instead of waiting for the result, the user's request ends here. The actual execution of the action proceeds asynchronously until it delivers its output, which is then stored so the user can fetch it at a later time.
- **Explicit scheduling**—This is similar to execution in the background, but instead of scheduling the action to take place immediately, it is executed according to a predefined schedule.

You have seen a number of examples of immediate execution in earlier chapters. In this chapter, you explore scheduling and how you can use it to organize content delivery.

Scheduling

Pentaho provides scheduling services through the Quartz Enterprise Job Scheduler, which is part of the Open Symphony project. The scheduler is a component that enables the BI server to perform tasks at a planned time or set time interval.

NOTE **For more information on Quartz and the Open Symphony project, visit the Open Symphony website at `www.opensymphony.com/quartz/`.**

There are a number of use cases for the scheduler:

- Periodical execution of maintenance tasks
- Execution of ETL jobs (such as refreshing aggregate tables)
- Running time-consuming tasks such as large reports in the background
- Distributing server workload over time
- Preparing content for subscribers

Scheduler Concepts

Two items are involved in scheduling:

- A **schedule**, which is a rule or set of rules that specify a moment or series of moments in time
- An **action sequence** (or group thereof) that is executed at the time or times specified by the schedule

We discussed the concept of action sequences in Chapter 4, and you have seen a few examples of them in other chapters of this book. In the remainder of this section, we describe schedules in more detail.

Public and Private Schedules

There are two distinct types of schedules: public and private.

Public schedules are visible to all users. They are mainly used to implement subscription.

Private schedules are available to the server administrator. They are mainly used to implement maintenance tasks. For example, in the Services tab page of the Pentaho Server Administration Console (PAC), there is a Schedule button in the Content Repository pane. Pressing this button will create a private schedule that will be run daily to clean out the content repository. We discuss the content repository in the next section, but the important thing is that this is an example of a scheduled maintenance task that is governed by a private schedule.

Content Repository

Normally, when a user executes an action sequence, the output of the action sequence is immediately delivered to the end user. Scheduled action sequences work differently. The output of scheduled action sequences is generated in the background. The output is saved and preserved in what is called the *content repository*, so the user can inspect the result later on.

Physically, the content repository is simply a directory on the file system where the action sequence output is stored in files. You can find the output files in the `content` directory of the `system` Pentaho solution.

The organization of the content repository is similar to the organization of the solution repository. For each Pentaho solution, there is a separate content repository directory. The structure of the tree beneath each content repository directory mirrors the structure of its corresponding solution repository, but instead of the action sequences there is a directory sharing the name of the action sequence. In those directories you may find a subscriptions directory, which contains the action sequence's output for each time it ran according to a schedule.

In addition to the directories for the Pentaho solutions, the root of the content repository also contains a directory called `background`. This directory is used to store the output of action sequences that run in the background.

In the section ''The User's Workspace'' later in this chapter, you learn how the end user can access the contents of the content repository.

Creating and Maintaining Schedules with the Pentaho Administration Console

You can create and maintain schedules using the Pentaho Administration Console to work with schedules, point your web browser to the PAC home page. Assuming you are running it on the local machine, you can find this at `http://localhost:8099/`. Enable the Administration page and click the Scheduler tab. You can see a list of all public and private schedules maintained by the Pentaho BI server. This is shown in Figure 14-1.

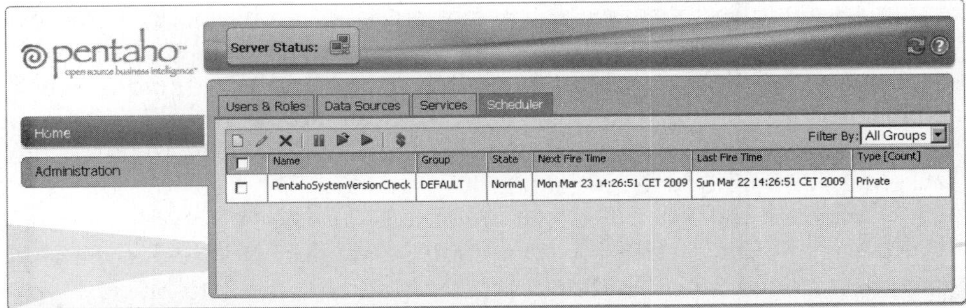

Figure 14-1: The Scheduler tab page in the Pentaho Administration Console

By default, there is one schedule called `PentahoSystemVersionCheck`. This is a private schedule that is used to periodically check if a newer version of Pentaho is available.

Creating a New Schedule

Click on the first toolbar button to create a new schedule. The Schedule Creator dialog appears as shown in Figure 14-2.

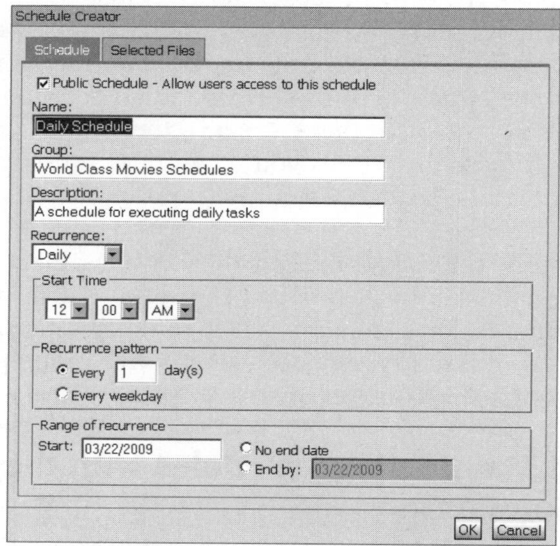

Figure 14-2: The Schedule Creator dialog

If you want to create a public schedule, select the Public Schedule checkbox. This ensures all users can see the schedule and enables them to use this schedule for subscriptions.

Use the Name field to enter a unique name for the schedule. Beware that for public schedules, this name will be presented to end users whenever they have to pick a schedule. Use names that are clear and concise.

Use the Group field to specify a name that describes what kind of schedule this is. For example, you can create groups according to department (warehouse, website), location (Edmonton, Los Angeles), subject area (Sales, Marketing), or timing (daily, weekly).

The toolbar on the Scheduler page (refer to Figure 14-1) includes a list box that enables the administrator to filter for all schedules belonging to the same group. This convenience feature enables the administrator to quickly work with all schedules belonging to the same group.

NOTE Even if you feel you don't need to organize schedules into groups, you are still required to enter something in the Group field. The same goes for the Description field; although it is entirely descriptive, it is still required.

The Description field allows you to enter descriptive text. You should use this field to briefly document the purpose of the schedule. Rather than summing up any properties that have to do directly with the schedule itself (such as timing), this field should describe the kinds of reports that are run according to this schedule and the audience for which the schedule is intended.

The Recurrence list box contains a number of options to specify how often the schedule is triggered. You can choose from a broad range of intervals, all the way from Seconds up to Yearly. There's also a Run Once option to schedule one-shot actions. If the flexibility offered by these options is still not sufficient, you can choose the Cron option to specify recurrence in the form of a `cron` string.

USING CRON EXPRESSIONS

Cron is a well-known job scheduler for UNIX-like systems. For cron, recurrence is specified in the form of a string that denotes six or seven fields of a date/time value, separated by whitespace. The Quartz scheduler used by Pentaho offers support for `cron` expressions.

In `cron` expressions, from left to right the date and time fields are: seconds, minutes, hours, day of month, month, day of week, year. The fields can contain simple integer values, but it is also possible to specify value lists, ranges, and wildcards such as `all`, `last`, and more. For example, the following `cron` expression denotes a recurrence at 1:00 a.m., each second Tuesday of each month:

```
0 0 1 ? * 3#2 *
```

(at zero seconds, zero minutes, 1 hour, regardless of the day of month, each month, the second occurrence of the third weekday, for each year).

You can find more information on `cron` expressions in Quartz at `http://www.opensymphony.com/quartz/wikidocs/CronTriggers Tutorial.html`

For all the available choices of the Recurrence option (except Cron) you can specify a Start Time by choosing the appropriate value in the hour, minute, and second list boxes.

For all Recurrence options except Run Once and Cron, you can specify how often the schedule should be triggered. The appropriate widget to specify the value appears on screen as soon as you select an option in the Recurrence list box. For example, for a Recurrence of seconds, minutes, hours, and days you can enter a number to indicate how many seconds, minutes, and so on are between subsequent executions of the schedule.

The Weekly and Monthly Recurrence options support more advanced possibilities for specifying the interval. For example, the Monthly and Daily Recurrence options pop up a widget that allows you to define the schedule for each Monday of every month, and the Weekly Recurrence option allows you to specify to which weekdays the schedule applies.

Finally, you can specify a start date or a start and end date range. These dates determine the period of time in which the schedule recurs. After specifying the schedule, click OK to save it and close the dialog.

Running Schedules

Although schedules are normally triggered by the passing of time, you can also execute them manually from the Pentaho Administration Console. This is useful for testing purposes, and also to recover from errors.

To manually run the action sequences linked to a schedule, select the checkbox that appears right before each schedule. Then click the Play button (the green triangle) on the toolbar.

Suspending and Resuming Schedules

Sometimes it is useful to temporarily prevent a schedule from running. For example, you may temporarily need the system resources to do some other task, or you may need to deploy multiple new or modified action sequences and you want to prevent the schedule from being triggered while you're in the middle of a deployment.

For these purposes, you can temporarily suspend a schedule. Suspending the schedule prevents its associated actions from being executed. A suspended schedule will remain suspended until you set it to resume. Both these actions can be done from within the PAC.

To suspend one or more schedules, select their respective checkboxes in the Schedules tab page in the server Administration Console. After making the desired selection, press the Pause button in the toolbar. This will suspend the schedules for an indefinite time, and the schedule's `State` will show as `Suspended`. This is shown in Figure 14-3.

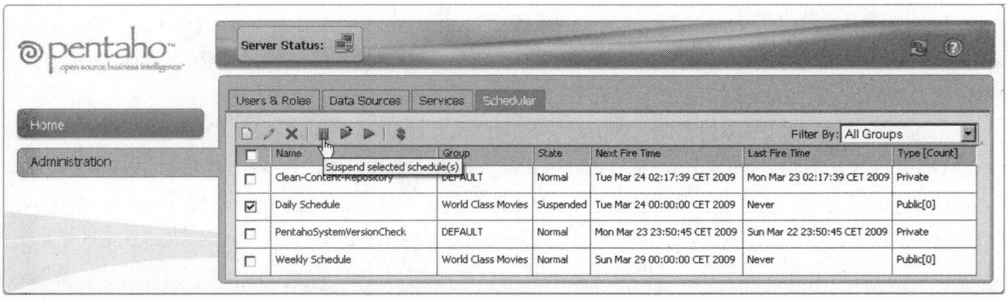

Figure 14-3: Suspending a schedule

Note that the `State` column in the schedules table has the value `Suspended`, whereas all other schedules have the value `Normal`.

To resume suspended schedules, select the schedules you want to resume and press the Resume button (the green triangle with the arrow).

Deleting Schedules

You can delete schedules by selecting the associated checkbox and then pressing the button with the red "X" on the toolbar. Before deleting a public schedule, it is a good idea to first check if the schedule is currently being used by subscribers. You can see this in the schedule overview provided by the PAC, because the column `Type [Count]` shows whether the schedule is public, as well as the number of subscribers.

You are always prompted to confirm the removal of a schedule. Figure 14-4 shows how an attempt to remove the "minute schedule" using the Administration Console triggers a prompt for confirmation, and also shows that there is still one subscriber.

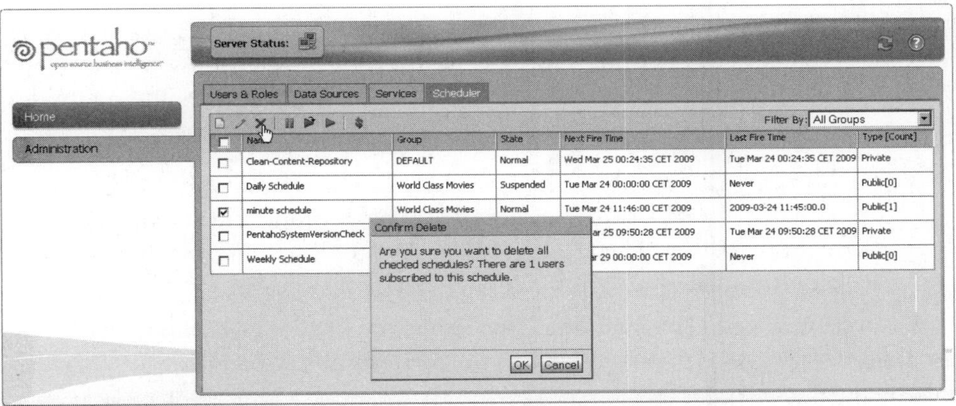

Figure 14-4: Deleting a schedule triggers a prompt for confirmation

Programming the Scheduler with Action Sequences

In addition to the graphical user interface offered by the Administration Console, you can also work with the Scheduler in a more programmatic way through action sequences.

Action sequences offer a number of process actions that allow you to work with the Scheduler. These can all be found in the Scheduler submenu of the Process Action menu. The Scheduler menu is shown in Figure 14-5.

The Scheduler process actions can be used to create an alternative to the Scheduler user interface offered by the Administration Console. A valid use case for rebuilding that kind of functionality is that it would allow end users to exert more control on scheduled content within the server's authorization framework.

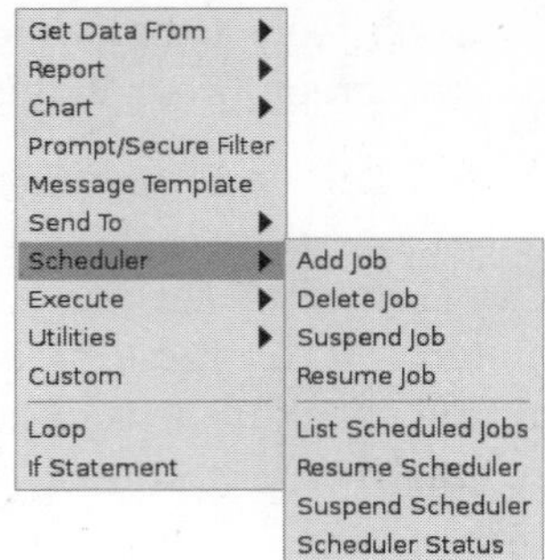

Figure 14-5: The Scheduler process action menu

The following sections briefly describe the Scheduler process actions.

Add Job

The `Add Job` process action creates a new private schedule and associates it with an action sequence. The `Add Job` process action has the following parameters:

- **Job Name**—The name of the Quartz job. This is roughly equivalent to the name of the schedule in Pentaho. (The Pentaho platform adds some abstraction to the Quartz scheduler. A Pentaho schedule is actually a combination of a Quartz job and a Quartz trigger).
- **XAction File**—The filename (including the `.xaction` extension) of the action sequence that is to be associated with this schedule.
- **Solution Name**—The name of the Pentaho solution that contains the action sequence that is associated with the schedule.
- **Solution Subdirectory**—The subdirectory (if any) where the action sequence file resides.
- **Trigger Name**—The name of the Quartz trigger. In Quartz, the trigger contains all timing information that can be used to determine when a job should run. A Quartz trigger refers to one Quartz job (but a Quartz job may be triggered by multiple triggers). In Pentaho, the distinction between trigger and job is hidden. Instead, Pentaho associates one Job with one Schedule and refers to this as a schedule. Also see the description of the Job Name parameter.
- **Trigger Type**—This is a radio button to choose between a simple trigger or a `cron` trigger. Trigger firing for `cron` triggers is specified through a cron string. For simple triggers, firing is determined by an interval value, which determines at what time in the future the trigger fires and a repeat

count. Simple triggers do not support recurrence, and are thus useful only for ''one-shot'' events, such as background execution.

- **Cron String**—Applies to `cron` triggers. Specifies the `cron` string that governs running the job.
- **Trigger Interval**—Applies to simple triggers. This specifies the amount of time before the trigger will be fired, specified in microseconds. For example, one minute from now would be specified as 60000 (60 seconds times 1000), and an hour from now would be specified as 3600000 (60 minutes times 60 seconds times 1000 microseconds).
- **Trigger Count**—Applies to simple triggers. At trigger firing time, the job will be repeatedly executed according to this value. In most cases, this value should be 1 (one) to execute the job only once when the interval has passed.

Figure 14-6 shows the design of a simple action sequence that prompts for job parameters using a `Prompt/Secure Filter` process action and then feeds these parameters into an `Add Job` process action.

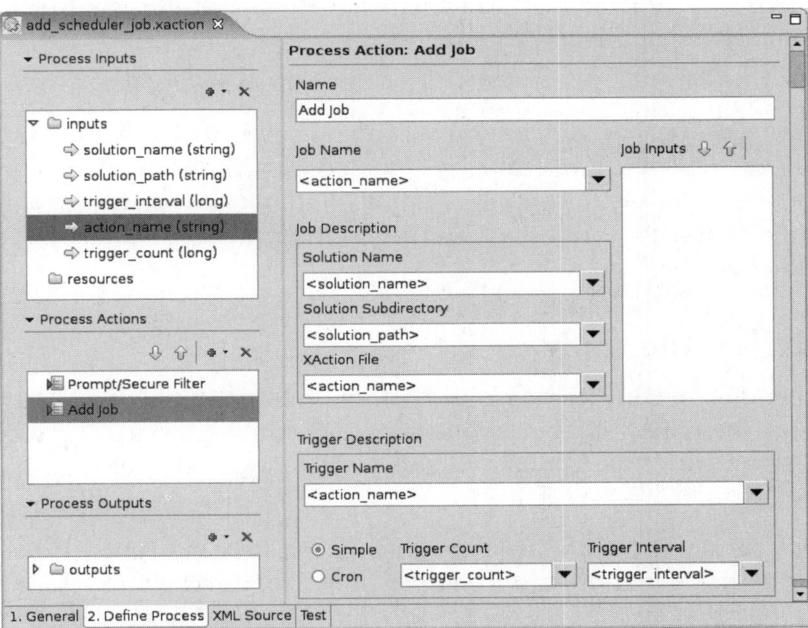

Figure 14-6: A very simple job scheduler that is accessible through an action sequence

This simple action sequence forms a proof of concept for building a scheduling facility that can be made accessible to end users within the authorization framework of Pentaho Server.

Suspend Job, Resume Job, and Delete Job

The `Suspend Job`, `Resume Job`, and `Delete Job` process actions accept only one `Job Name` parameter which must be used to specify the name of a Pentaho schedule. (For a discussion concerning Pentaho schedules and Quartz Jobs, please refer to the previous subsection on the `Add Job` process action). The actions then perform the action implied by their name to the Schedule. The `Suspend Job` process action will pause the specified Schedule, the `Resume Job` process action will continue it, and the `Delete Job` action will permanently remove the Schedule (and all of its associated actions).

Other Scheduler Process Actions

In addition to the process actions just discussed there are a few more Scheduler-related process actions:

- `Suspend Scheduler`—Pauses execution of the entire Scheduler for indeterminate time
- `Resume Scheduler`—Resumes the paused Scheduler
- `Scheduler Status`—Indicates whether the Scheduler is suspended or running.
- `List Scheduled Jobs`—Lists all private schedules

These steps are not very useful when compared to the equivalent functionality offered by the Administration Console. The steps that report the Scheduler's status are quite limited, and if you think you need them to build a custom scheduling user interface, you are probably better off directly querying the Quartz database.

Scheduler Alternatives

The Scheduler built into the Pentaho platform suits many scheduling purposes. However, there may still be advantages to scheduling tasks using tools that are independent of the Pentaho BI server. Here are a few reasons that may apply:

- **ETL jobs**—These can be long-running, and may put severe load on the server. The Platform, the Scheduler, and all of its scheduled tasks all run in the same instance of the Java Virtual Machine, and for performance and availability reasons you may want to separate execution of ETL tasks from the remainder of the BI server.
- **Policy**—For maintainability and sustainability reasons, a company may have standardized on a particular scheduling tool, and this may preclude you from using Pentaho's built-in Scheduler.

If you only need scheduling capabilities for these kinds of purposes and you do not require any of Pentaho's functionalities that build on top of the native Scheduler, you should consider going with a more lightweight solution.

Next we briefly discuss the most common job scheduling solutions for UNIX-like systems and Windows.

UNIX-Based Systems: Cron

UNIX-based systems usually offer some kind of `cron` implementation. Normally, this is set up as part of the installation of the operating system, and you shouldn't have to install anything to get it to work.

You do have to specify the tasks you want to schedule. This is done by simply adding entries for jobs to a special file called the `crontab` (for "cron table"). This file is usually located in `/etc/crontab`, but there may be differences depending upon the UNIX flavor. In many cases, there is a `crontab` utility available which facilitates maintaining `cron` entries.

The actual `cron` entries consist of the `cron` string (which was discussed earlier for Quartz) followed by the command. There is one notable difference between UNIX `cron` strings and Quartz `cron` strings: UNIX `cron` strings do not support a seconds field. Instead, the smallest time field is minutes.

The following line in the `crontab` file would schedule the `daily_load` Pentaho data integration job to run each day at midnight:

```
# m h  dom mon dow    command
  0 0  *   *   *      /opt/pentaho/pdi/kitchen.sh -file /home/wcm/pdi
/daily_load.kjb
```

NOTE For more options on using cron and crontab, refer to your operating system documentation. `man crontab` is usually a good start. There are also many online resources that offer good examples and explanations concerning cron.

Windows: The at Utility and the Task Scheduler

Windows users can use the at utility or the Task Scheduler.

The at utility is available from the command line. Here's a simple example that illustrates how to schedule execution of a batch job to run each day at midnight:

```
at 00:00 /every:M,T,W,Th,F,S,Su "D:\pentaho\pdi\daily_job.bat"
```

Instead of providing a long command directly to the `at` command line, it is usually better to write a batch file (`.bat` file) and have at execute that. (This technique can, of course, be applied also on UNIX-like systems where one would write a `bash` or `sh` script.)

Windows also offers a graphical interface for scheduling. You can find the Windows Task Scheduler in the Control Panel or in the start menu by navigating to Start ➤ Programs ➤ Accessories ➤ System Tools ➤ Task Scheduler.

NOTE **For more information on the `at` command and the Task Scheduler, please go to at `http://support.microsoft.com/` and search for "`at` command" and "Task Scheduler".**

Background Execution and Subscription

Background execution and subscription are two special applications of scheduling. In this section, we describe these features in more detail.

How Background Execution Works

Background execution is a convenient feature that allows users to execute action sequences without waiting for the result. Instead of starting the action sequence and waiting for it to wind down, a private schedule is created to schedule the action to take place as soon as possible. Upon completion, the output of the action sequence is stored so the user can inspect it at a later time.

To execute an action sequence in the background, you can simply right-click it and choose the Run in Background option. This pops up a message box like the one shown in Figure 14-7.

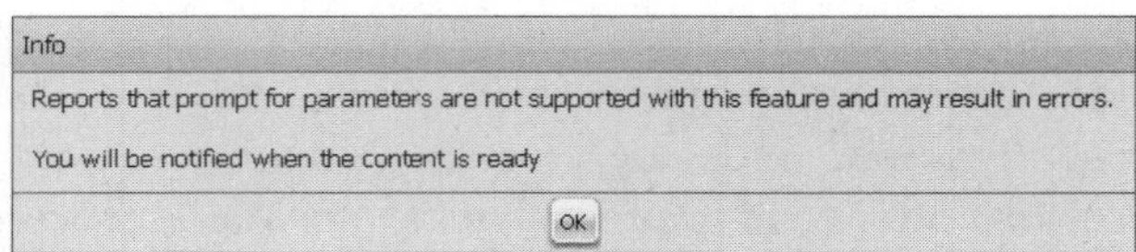

Figure 14-7: A warning before running in the background

As suggested by the message box, running in the background in this way is not supported for action sequences that require input parameters, but there is an alternative.

If you create an action sequence that prompts the user for input parameters using a `Prompt/Secure Filter` Process Action, a radio button is automatically presented that allows the user to choose either immediate or background execution. A simple Prompt/Secure input filter is shown in Figure 14-8. The Run in Background radio button is visible at the bottom.

Report Output
PDF Excel Web Page

Run in Background
Yes No

OK Cancel

Figure 14-8: Prompt for running in the background

How Subscription Works

Subscription is a feature that allows end users to receive BI content according to a predefined schedule. In Pentaho, subscription is built immediately on top of the Scheduler by allowing end users to attach action sequences to public schedules. As such, subscription is an extension of the scheduling feature.

A few requirements must be met to enable subscription:

- The server administrator must define one or more public schedules. We discussed creating schedules using the Server Administration Console in the previous section. Recall that you have to select the Public Schedule checkbox.
- For each action sequence, the administrator must specify which schedules the user is allowed to choose from when subscribing.
- A user that wants to subscribe to a report must have the privilege to execute and schedule the report.

Allowing Users to Subscribe

The server administrator must specify to which public schedules the user may assign a particular action sequence from within the user console. The server administrator can do this from the user console (not the Server Administration Console) by right-clicking the action sequence and choosing Properties.

Choosing the Properties menu item opens the Properties dialog. In the Properties dialog, activate the Advanced tab page. In the Advanced tab page, you have to first check the Use Public Schedules checkbox. Then, you can select a schedule from the Available schedules list on the left side of the tab page and use the button to move it to the Current Schedules list on the right side of the dialog. This is shown in Figure 14-9.

This enables all users that are privileged to do so to schedule this action sequence.

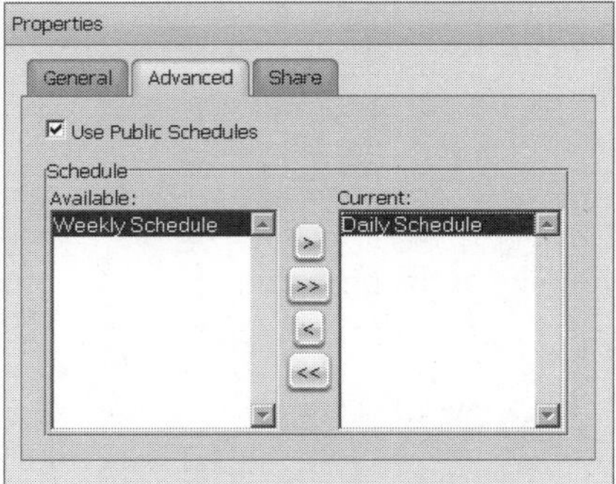

Figure 14-9: Making an action sequence subscribable

Granting Execute and Schedule Privileges

Users need to have at least Execute and Schedule privileges on an action sequence before they can subscribe to it. It does not matter whether these privileges were granted directly or via a role.

To grant privileges on a particular action sequence, right-click it and choose the Share option in the context menu. In the dialog that appears, the Share tab page is already activated. (Another way to get here is to choose the Properties option in the context menu and then manually activate the Share tab page.)

In the top half of the Share tab page in the dialog, you can see all available users and roles. In the bottom half, the privileges that are currently set up for the role or user that is currently selected are displayed. Figure 14-10 illustrates this.

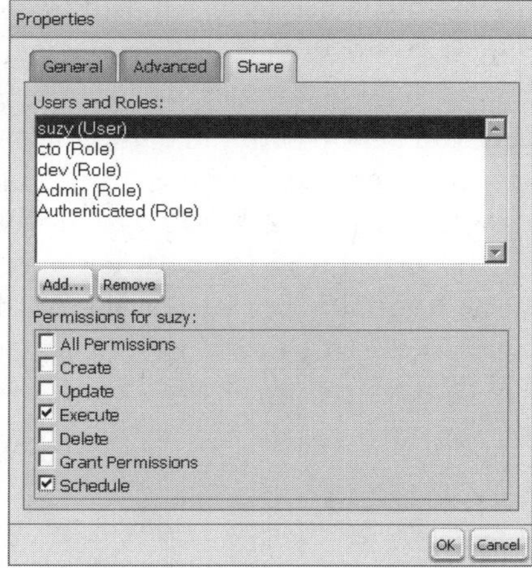

Figure 14-10: Granting the Execute and Schedule privileges

The Actual Subscription

In the user console, end users can create a subscription by right-clicking on an action sequence and choosing the Schedule option from the context menu. If the action sequence is subscribable and the user has sufficient privileges, the web page will load a dialog like the one shown in Figure 14-11.

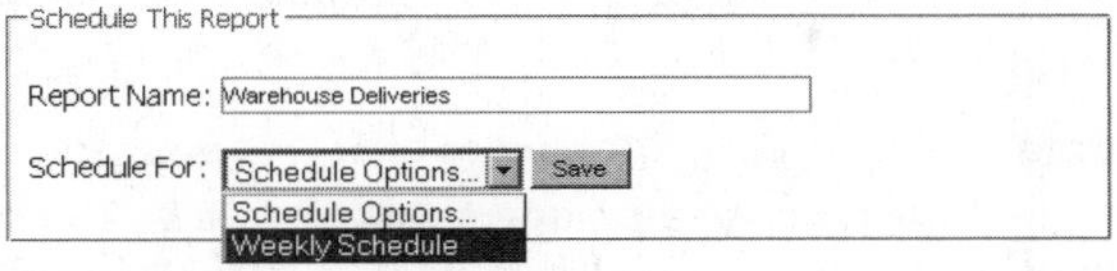

Schedule This Report
Report Name: Warehouse Deliveries
Schedule For: Schedule Options... Save
Schedule Options...
Weekly Schedule

Figure 14-11: A simple subscription dialog

The dialog shown in Figure 14-11 is the simplest possible subscription dialog. In the dialog, the user needs to enter a name in the Report Name textbox to identify the scheduled report. (You can enter at most 25 characters, which isn't an awful lot.)

With the Schedule For list box, the user can select one of the schedules offered. These are all schedules that were associated with the action sequence by the server administrator.

If the action sequence used in the subscription requires user input, the subscription dialog also presents the report parameters, which can then be filled out by the user. For example, Figure 14-12 illustrates how a prompt used to configure the report output format is combined with the prompts for the subscription parameters. The prompt for the output format is explicitly added in the action sequence, whereas the prompt for subscription is presented automatically.

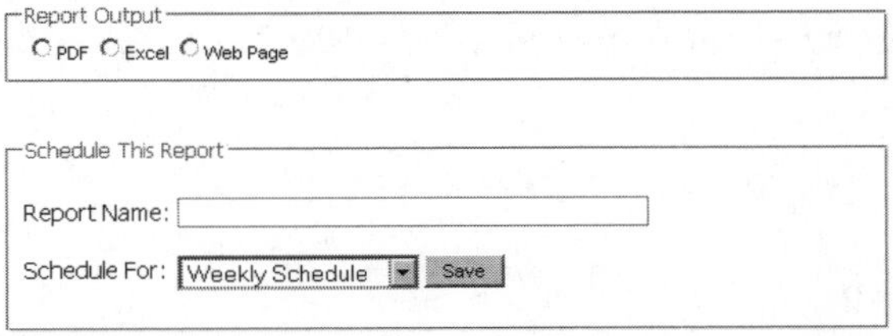

Report Output
PDF Excel Web Page

Schedule This Report
Report Name:
Schedule For: Weekly Schedule Save

Figure 14-12: The regular prompt for parameters is automatically combined with prompts for subscription

The user input is then stored along with the choice of schedule and action sequence in the subscription. When the schedule triggers execution of the action sequence, the stored values are used as parameter values for the action sequence.

As explained in the previous subsection, the user must have both the Execute and the Schedule privilege for the action sequence in order to subscribe to it.

If the user does not have the Schedule privilege, this is indicated by a message box like the one shown in Figure 14-13.

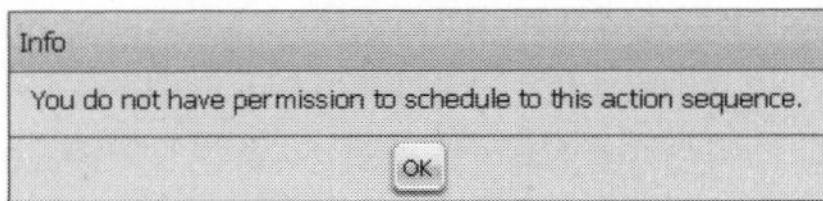

Figure 14-13: A message box indicating the user is not allowed to schedule the report

NOTE **At the time of this writing, it appears as if it is possible to subscribe to action sequences that have not been made subscribable by the server administrator. If you right-click on such an action sequence, you can choose Subscribe, which pops up a Scheduler Creator dialog. However, filling out the dialog and confirming it always leads to an error message.**

The User's Workspace

With the capabilities for scheduling and background execution, the need arises for the user to be able to control and monitor scheduled content. In addition, there has to be some means for the user to access the output generated by any scheduled or background actions.

Pentaho offers a per-user view called the Workspace that allows users to manage their part of the content repository and their schedules.

Viewing the Contents of the Workspace

In the user console, users can review the contents of their personal workspace by choosing View ➢ Workspace from the menu. From the Workspace page, users can monitor and control all action sequences that are scheduled or run in the background on their behalf. Figure 14-14 shows an example user workspace.

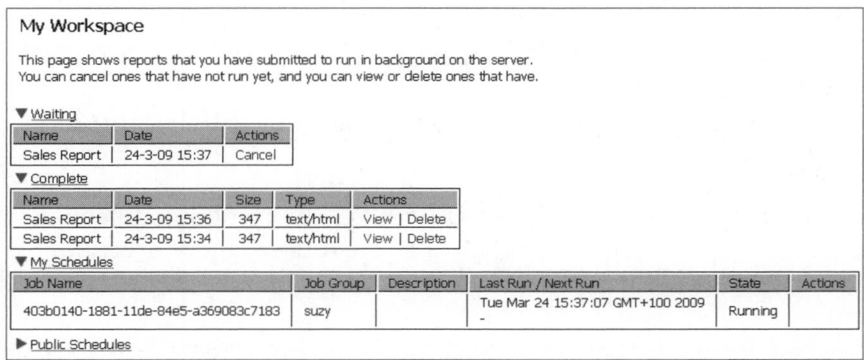

Figure 14-14: A user's workspace

The Workspace page shows a number of panes containing all action sequences scheduled on behalf of the user. Each action pane can be collapsed or expanded by clicking on the triangle immediately before the pane titles.

The Waiting, Complete, and My Schedules Panes

The Waiting, Complete, and My Schedules panes can be used to manage action sequences that are executed in the background.

- The Waiting pane contains one row for each action sequence that is currently executing in the background on behalf of the current user. The name and start date are shown for each job. A Cancel link is available to abort the job. For example, in Figure 14-14 you can see that a job called "Sales Report" started execution in the background on 24-3-09 15:37. At the time the Workspace page was being viewed, the job was still running.
- The Complete pane lists all action sequences that were ordered for execution in the background and that have finished. For each action sequence, the name and execution date are shown. In addition, the result of executing the action is available from the Complete pane: The size column indicates the number of bytes in the output, and the type indicates what type of output was stored. There is also a View link to inspect the result, and a Delete link to permanently remove it from the workspace. In Figure 14-14, two results from prior background execution of the Sales Report are available.
- The My Schedules pane also shows the action sequences that have been started. In addition to the information shown in the Waiting pane, the My Schedules pane shows more detailed information (such as status) regarding the action sequence execution.

The Public Schedules Pane

The Public Schedules pane shows all of the current user's subscriptions. For each subscription, a number of links are available.

- The Run Now link executes the action sequence immediately. This is useful in case there is a sudden need to obtain the result ahead of the regular schedule. Like the Run Now link, the Run and Archive link executes the action sequence ahead of schedule. However, in this case, the action sequence is executed in the background and the result stored in the content repository.
- With the Edit link, you can change the details of the subscription, such as the schedule. If the report accepts parameters, then these can be modified

from this link, too. Figure 14-15 illustrates what happens when you click the Edit link.

- The Delete link permanently removes the subscription. When you click it, a message box pops up and prompts for confirmation to delete the subscription. Confirming this will remove only the current user's subscription, but not the actual public schedule itself.

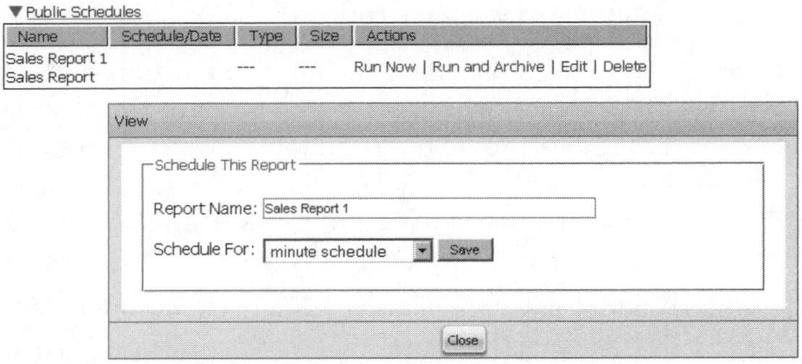

▼ Public Schedules

Name	Schedule/Date	Type	Size	Actions
Sales Report 1 Sales Report		---	---	Run Now | Run and Archive | Edit | Delete

View

Schedule This Report

Report Name: Sales Report 1

Schedule For: minute schedule Save

Close

Figure 14-15: Editing an existing subscription

The subscription output normally appears directly beneath the subscription entry in the Public Schedules pane. Figure 14-16 shows the Sales Report 1 subscription, and immediately below it are three rows that correspond to a successful execution of the action sequence. Using the View link, users can download the result of the action, and with the Delete link, users can permanently remove the content from their workspace.

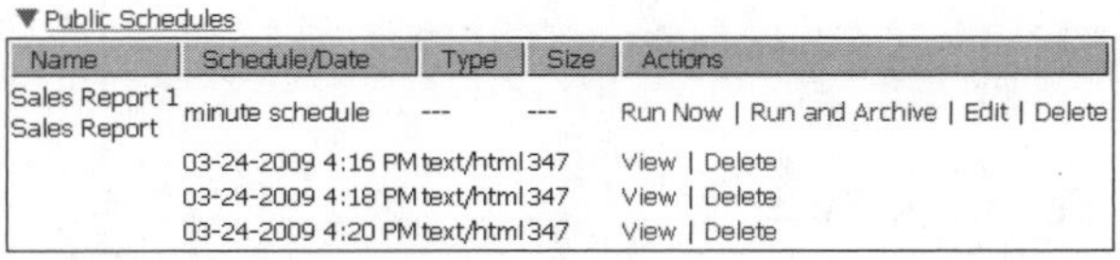

▼ Public Schedules

Name	Schedule/Date	Type	Size	Actions
Sales Report 1 Sales Report	minute schedule	---	---	Run Now | Run and Archive | Edit | Delete
	03-24-2009 4:16 PM	text/html	347	View | Delete
	03-24-2009 4:18 PM	text/html	347	View | Delete
	03-24-2009 4:20 PM	text/html	347	View | Delete

Figure 14-16: A subscription and its output

The Server Administrator's Workspace

The server administrator's workspace, shown in Figure 14-17, has an additional All Schedules panel. This panel shows all schedules and allows them to be run immediately, suspended, and resumed. The same functionality is available from the Server Administration Console, but is duplicated here as a convenience feature.

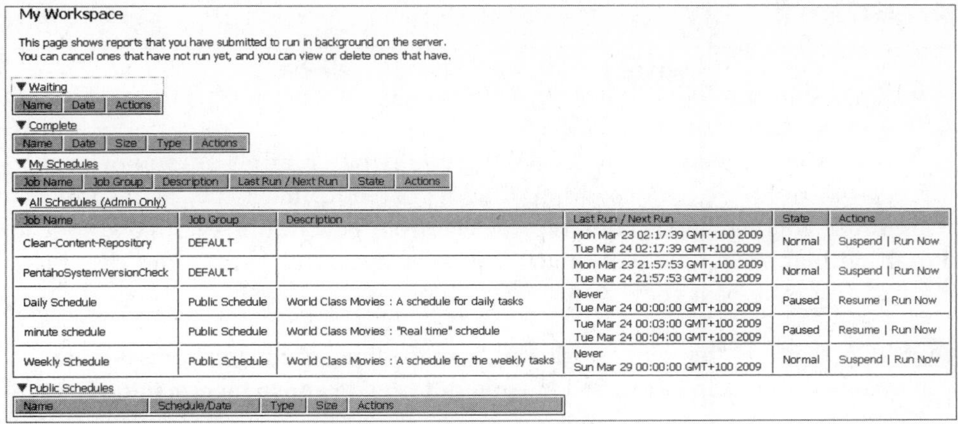

Figure 14-17: The server administrator's workspace

Cleaning Out the Workspace

When left unattended, the content repository will at some point fill up the disk. Users can delete their own items from the content repository, but server administrators must not rely on that. For any production setup, administrators must take care to monitor the content repository.

In the Services tab page of the Administration Console, a few items are available to help manage the content repository. The Content Repository service pane is shown in Figure 14-18.

Figure 14-18: Administration Console services to manage the content repository

Pressing the Execute button will execute the `clean_repository` action sequence located in the `Admin` Pentaho solution. This will remove all files in the content repository that are older than 180 days. If you like, you can edit the `clean_repository` action sequence and modify the number of days.

Pressing the Schedule button will execute the `schedule_clean` action sequence, which also resides in the `Admin` Pentaho solution. This action sequence uses the `Add Job` process action to install a schedule for daily clean-up of the content repository. As you might expect, this falls back on the `clean_repository` to do the actual cleaning.

Bursting

In a BI context, *bursting* is batch-wise, data-driven generation and distribution of BI content such as reports and charts.

A very simple example of bursting would be creating shipment reports for each warehouse, and sending the report output to the corresponding warehouse manager. Another typical example is sending each customer an e-mail with an attachment showing an overview of all rentals and purchases made during the past year.

NOTE The term "bursting" originates from the time when large reports were printed out whole on paper, and the printout would need to be torn into separate pieces for its respective recipients.

In both these examples, the report is run but the content and context of the output is tailored for each recipient.

Implementation of Bursting in Pentaho

The community edition of the Pentaho Server does not offer native bursting features. However, with some creativity and effort, bursting can be implemented by looping through a data set and using the data of the current row to run a report and send the results to the appropriate recipient(s). The following section walks you through a bursting example in Pentaho.

Bursting Example: Rental Reminder E-mails

Consider the use case of rental reminder e-mails: each week, World Class Movies sends e-mail reminders to its customers to notify them which DVDs are due to be returned (or purchased) during the following week. Because this is primarily an operational process, we choose to base this example directly on the WCM database, and not the data warehouse. (In a practical setup, you would most likely still use a separate database instance such as a replication slave in order to offload other operations such as order entry.)

The following steps describe how it works:

1. Obtain a result set of all customers that ordered DVDs that are due to be returned during the following week.
2. Loop over the rows in the result set. For each row:
   - Obtain the actual list of DVD titles that are due to be returned during the following week for the current customer.
   - Run a report that lists the DVD titles and their due dates.

- Attach the report output to an e-mail message and send it to the customer.

In the remainder of this section, we describe how to implement this in a Pentaho action sequence. To follow along with the example, you will need Pentaho Design Studio (to create the action sequence) and the Pentaho Report Designer (to build the report).

Step 1: Finding Customers with DVDs That Are Due This Week

The first step is to find all customers that need to receive a reminder. One way to approach this problem is to look for all DVDs that are due during the following week, and then to look up the corresponding customer data via the order.

Use the SQL in Listing 14-1 to accomplish this.

Listing 14-1: Finding customers with DVDs that are due

```
SELECT      c.customer_id
,           MAX(c.first_name)          first_name
,           MAX(c.last_name)           last_name
,           MAX(c.balance)             balance
,           MAX(c.email_address)       email_address
,           CAST(
              GROUP_CONCAT(
                 col.customer_order_line_id
              ) AS CHAR(512)
            )                           customer_order_lines
FROM        wcm.customer                c
INNER JOIN  wcm.customer_order          co
ON          c.customer_id             = co.customer_id
INNER JOIN  wcm.customer_order_line     col
ON          co.customer_order_id      = col.customer_order_id
WHERE       col.return_due_date
BETWEEN     {report_date}
AND         {report_date} + INTERVAL {report_interval} WEEK
GROUP BY    c.customer_id
```

A few things are worth noting about this query. In the query, you can see `{report_date}` and `{report_interval}`. The curly braces are not valid SQL. Rather, they delimit parameters at the level of an action sequence. Rather than embedding a call to `CURRENT_DATE()` or something like that in the query, we prefer to externalize that into a parameter. This will make it much easier afterwards to start the action sequence a few days ahead or behind schedule. We like to have the `{report_interval}` for a similar reason. By making it available as a parameter, we can easily decide afterwards to send e-mails once every two or three weeks instead of every week. While it is impossible to parameterize everything (or at least it wouldn't be very practical), these items are likely candidates for change because of changing business decisions.

The query uses a `GROUP BY customer_id` clause. Because `customer_id` is the primary key of the `customer` table, this query will yield by definition just one row per customer. In the `SELECT` list, you want to retrieve all kinds of data from the customer, and to avoid confusion, you should explicitly add `MAX` aggregate functions for all other columns you need from the customer. (Technically, you don't need to do that; because of the `GROUP BY` on `customer_id` you can be sure all other columns from the `customer` table will have only one value per distinct `customer_id`. However, you should apply `MAX()` anyway for clarity and portability).

A final aspect of this query is the application of the `GROUP_CONCAT` function. This is a MySQL-specific aggregate function that groups rows using string concatenation, by default separating the values with a comma. In this case, the only argument is the `customer_order_line_id`, which means the `GROUP_CONCAT` function will generate a comma-separated list of the `customer_order_line_ids` that correspond to DVDs that are due to be returned. You will use this later on in the action sequence to execute a query for the report.

To put this in the action sequence, you can use the `Relational` process action. You can find it beneath the Get Data From menu. In the `Query` property, type the SQL statement. For the result set name, you type customers and in addition, you explicitly define every column of the result set in the Result Set Columns grid. This will make it easier to refer to particular items in the result set. You also have to specify action sequence input parameters for the `{report_date}` and `{report_interval}` parameters.

The action sequence is shown in Figure 14-19.

Step 2: Looping Through the Customers

The second step of the action sequence is a `Loop` process action. This iterates through all customers we found in the first step of the action sequence. Figure 14-20 shows how to use the `Loop` process action in your bursting action sequence. In the figure, the `Loop` process action is labeled Action Loop on Customers.

In itself, the `Loop` process action is not very interesting. However, it becomes interesting by virtue of the actions that are placed inside it. These actions are repeated for each iteration of the loop. In Figure 14-20, the remaining three actions appear indented with respect to the loop. So, these actions will be repeated for each row in the `customers` result set.

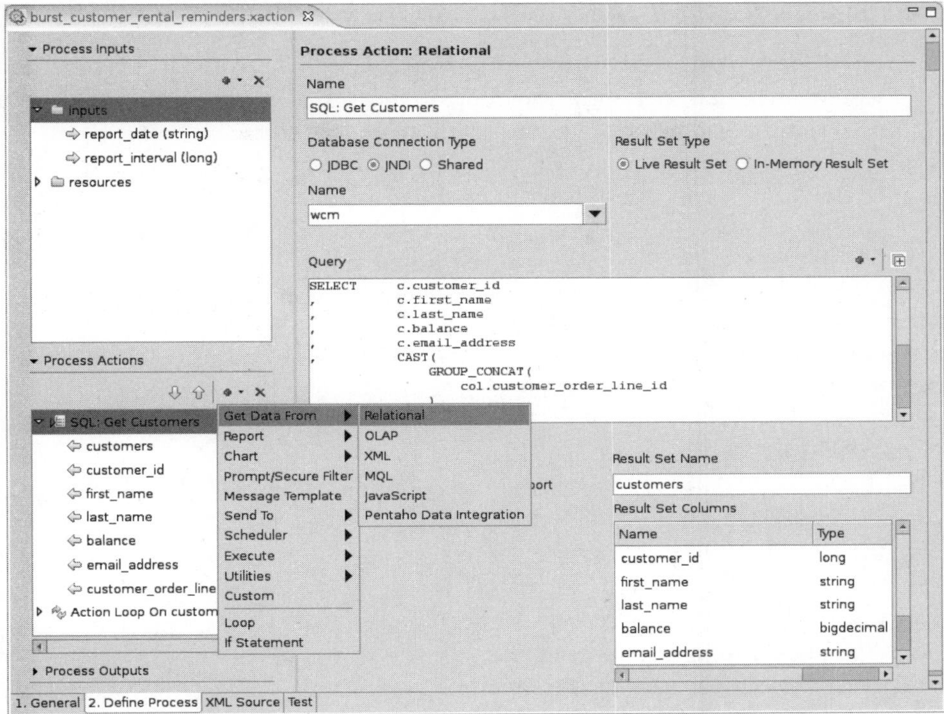

Figure 14-19: Finding customers using a Relational process action step

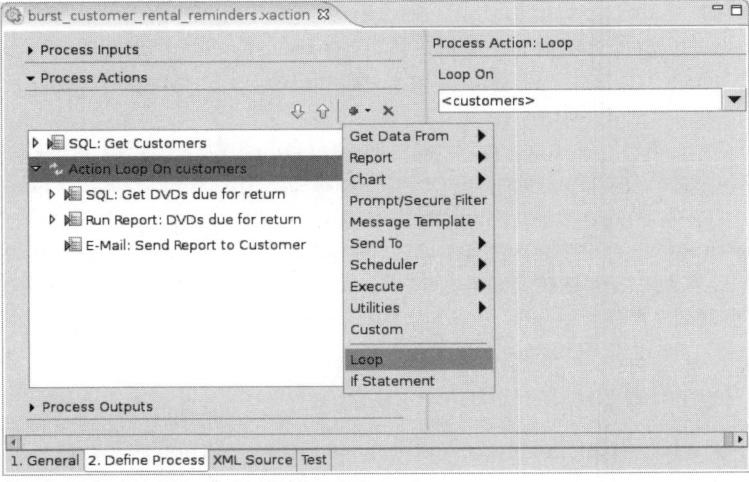

Figure 14-20: Looping through a result set

Step 3: Getting DVDs That Are Due to Be Returned

Inside the loop, you need to find out which DVDs are due to be returned for the current customer iteration. Fortunately, this is quite easy! Because you included the GROUP_CONCAT expression over the customer_order_line_id column in your customers query, you can use a very simple and efficient IN query to look up the pertinent rows from the customer_order_line table. From the customer_order_line table, you can easily look up the corresponding DVDs in the dvd_release table using an INNER JOIN.

Again, you use a Relational process action, as you did for the customers. For the DVDs, we used the query shown in Listing 14-2.

Listing 14-2: Finding DVDs that are due

```
SELECT      {customer_id}   customer_id
,           '{first_name}'  first_name
,           '{last_name}'   last_name
,           {balance}       balance
,           {report_date}   report_date
,           d.title
,           col.return_due_date
,           col.rental_price
,           col.purchase_price
FROM        wcm.customer_order_line col
INNER JOIN  wcm.dvd_release         d
ON          col.dvd_release_id = d.dvd_release_id
WHERE        col.customer_order_line_id IN ({customer_order_lines})
```

In the WHERE clause, you see the {customer_order_lines} parameter, which is used to find the customer_order_line rows. Recall that the GROUP_CONCAT function used in the customer query yields a comma-separated list of customer_order_id values.

Apart from the {customer_order_lines} parameter, you copied the customer data from the current customer iteration into the SELECT list. You need customer data anyway to personalize the report, and although you could retrieve the same information programmatically by extending the SQL statement with INNER JOINs to customer_order and customer, you can just as well benefit from the fact that the work is already performed.

Step 4: Running the Reminder Report

Now that you have data about both the customer and the DVDs, you can render a report. To this end, you need a very simple report, which we have created with the Pentaho Report Designer. We won't describe this process in detail, but the main point about this report is that all data pertaining to the rented

DVDs, such as DVD title, rental due data, rental price, and purchase price are rendered in the Item Band. The repeating data in the Item Band is labeled using static labels that appear in the Report Header. The data pertaining to the report itself (such as the `report_date`) or its receiving customer (such as `first_name`, `last_name`, `balance`, and `report_data`) and are placed in the Page Header. The report design is shown in Figure 14-21.

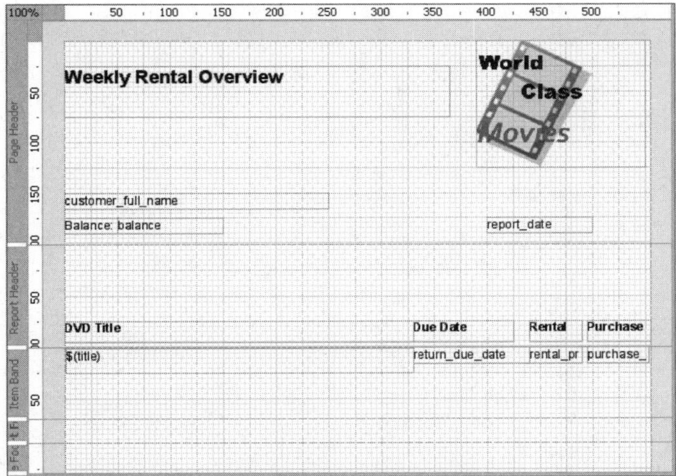

Figure 14-21: The design for the Rental Reminder Report

From the perspective of report design, things are quite straightforward if you send the report as a PDF attachment to an e-mail message. However, if you want to send the report itself as the body of an HTML e-mail, you may want to configure the HTML output especially for that purpose. You can access the report configuration through the report Properties pane shown in Figure 14-22.

Properties

ID	
Name	Report
Appearance	
Page Definition	A4 Portrait
Default Locale	en_US (English (United ...
Resources Path	
Configuration	Default
Max Char Bounds	☑ True

Figure 14-22: Accessing the report properties in the Properties pane

In the properties dialog, you can then activate the `output-table-html` configuration and explicitly suppress external stylesheets, or even force styles to be written inline. For normal web-based reporting, external stylesheets are generally preferable, and inline styling should be shunned. However, external stylesheets and out-of-line styles may prevent some e-mail clients from correctly rendering the report, which is why we explicitly deviate from the default options in this case. Overriding these defaults is shown in Figure 14-23.

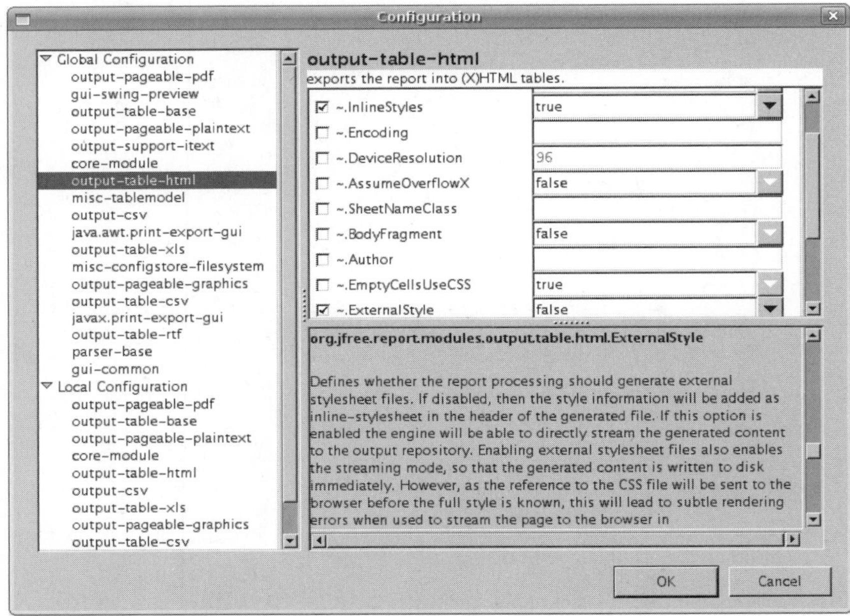

Figure 14-23: Forcing internal stylesheets and inline styles for HTML e-mail

The report is called using the `Pentaho Report` process action, which resides beneath the Report submenu. Figure 14-24 shows what the process action looks like.

Note that the `<dvds>` parameter is used for the Report Data. This is the name of the result set parameter from the previous process action. Note also the Output Report Name, which is set to `rental_reminder_report`. You need to refer to this in the next step, where you'll send the report output in an e-mail.

Step 5: Sending the Report via E-mail

The final step in the action sequence takes care of the delivery to the customer. To do this, you use an `EMAIL` process action. This can be reached from the Send To menu, as shown in Figure 14-25.

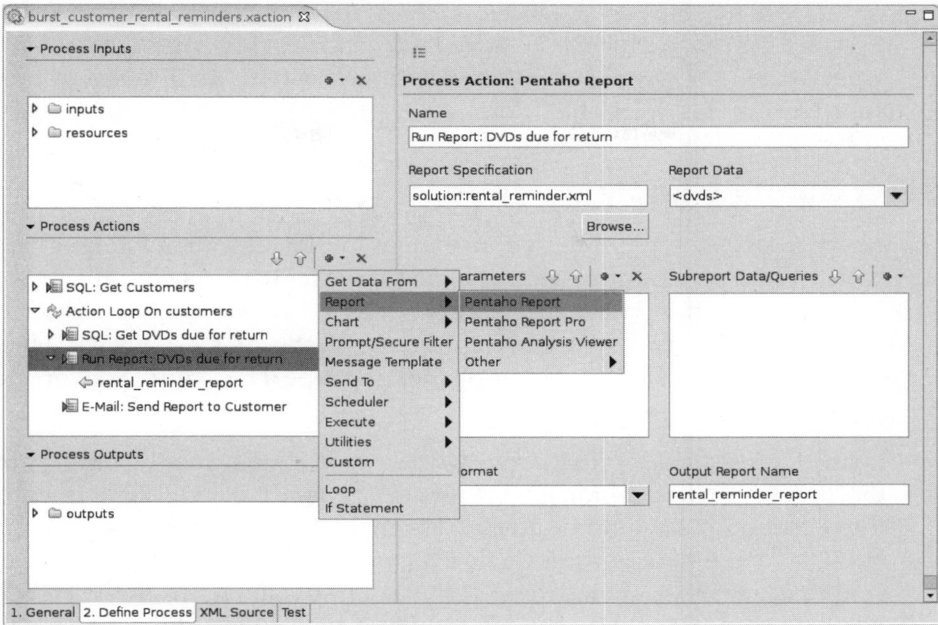

Figure 14-24: Calling the Reminder Report

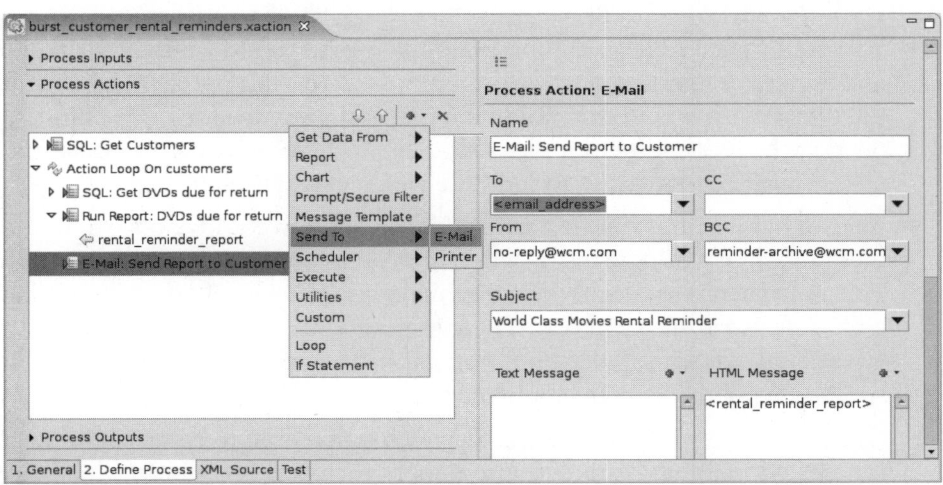

Figure 14-25: Sending the report as HTML e-mail

Note that you use the `<email-address>` from the customer data of the outer result set as a parameter for the To address. For the HTML Message, you use the `<rental-reminder-report>` parameter, which is the actual report output created in the previous process action.

Other Bursting Implementations

The example just shown is simply one way of implementing bursting. There may be cases where this approach works rather well. There may be other cases where this approach is not that useful (such as when the outer resultset is large, and the query for the inner resultset is complex and expensive). Here are just a few other possibilities for implementing report bursting based on the Pentaho BI Suite:

- Instead of sending HTML e-mail, you can configure the report (or the process action calling the report) to generate a PDF. In this case, the report output would be attached to the e-mail rather than sent as the body. With the `Email` process action this change is almost trivial. You can simply move the `<rental-reminder-report>` parameter from the HTML message field to the Attachments grid and type a static text message in the Text Message field.
- If you want to send only a simple e-mail message, you can use the `Message Template` process action to merge a static text template with the result set data coming from elsewhere in the action sequence.
- You could even choose among plaintext e-mail, HTML e-mail, or a PDF attachment depending on user preferences. To do this, you would expand the query with a field that holds the user's preference for PDF, plaintext, or HTML. Depending on the value of that field, you can use an `If Statement` process action to send the right type of e-mail.
- Instead of building complex action sequences, you could choose to implement much of the logic inside a Pentaho Data Integration transformation. This approach is especially worthwhile when you simply need to send an e-mail message, and can bypass generating a full-blown report. An extra advantage of using PDI is that you can use its clustering capabilities to spread the load across multiple machines.
- Once you bring PDI into the mix, you may be able to remove the need for nested database queries altogether. Instead, you could write just one query that includes customer data and DVD titles, and use PDI to transform that directly into a nested structure such as XML or JSON. You would then need to parse that using a Get Data From/XML or JavaScript step, but this may still be faster than waiting for a database query.

Summary

In this chapter, we investigated a few of the more advanced methods of delivering business intelligence content to end users. In this chapter, you learned to:

- Create and maintain schedules using the Administration Console
- Use action sequences to programmatically create schedules
- Use external scheduling solutions such as `cron` and `at`
- Allow action sequences to be subscribable by associating them with a schedule
- Grant the proper privileges to users (and roles) to allow them to subscribe to action items
- Monitor and manage subscribed content in the user's workspace
- Clean out the content repository
- Implement bursting in an action sequence

CHAPTER

15

OLAP Solutions Using Pentaho Analysis Services

Pentaho Analysis Services provides the OLAP capabilities of the Pentaho Platform. Chapter 8 briefly introduced the concepts OLAP, ROLAP, MOLAP, and HOLAP. This chapter is devoted to getting (R)OLAP solutions up and running on the Pentaho BI platform using Pentaho Analysis Services (PAS). PAS allows you to interactively analyze data from the data warehouse by providing a crosstab-style interface on which different dimensions such as time, product, and customer can be placed. Unlike a reporting tool, there is no need to first define a query, retrieve the results and format these, although this is possible if desired. An OLAP front end provides an intuitive point-and-click or drag-and-drop interface that will automatically retrieve and format data based on the selection made by a user. It allows for fast zooming in on certain parts of the data cube, also called *drill down*, or aggregating details to a summary level, also called *drill up*. You can apply conditions to only look at parts of a cube, which is also called *slicing*. Swapping information from rows to columns or vice versa finally is like turning the cube and look at it from different angles, which is also called *dicing*. Performing drill up, drill down, slice and dice, and doing all of this in a high speed, interactive manner is what distinguishes OLAP from other kinds of analysis and reporting and allows a user to quickly analyze data and find exceptions or gain insight in business performance.

In this chapter, we begin by describing the architecture of Pentaho Analysis Services, followed by a brief introduction to MDX, which is the de facto standard OLAP query language. Next, we'll explain in detail how to create and deploy OLAP cubes for the Mondrian ROLAP engine, which is the heart of Pentaho Analysis Services. We also explain how to browse these cubes using the JPivot front end. Finally, we discuss how you can use the Pentaho Aggregate designer to enhance OLAP performance.

Overview of Pentaho Analysis Services

PAS consists of the following four components:

- **JPivot analysis front end**—JPivot is a Java-based analysis tool that serves as the actual user interface for working with OLAP cubes.
- **Mondrian ROLAP engine**—The engine receives MDX queries from front-end tools such as JPivot, and responds by sending a multidimensional result-set.
- **Schema Workbench**—This is the visual tool for designing and testing Mondrian cube schemas. Mondrian uses these cube schemas to interpret MDX and translate it into SQL queries to retrieve the data from an RDBMS.
- **Aggregate Designer**—A visual tool for generating aggregate tables to speed up the performance of the analytical engine.

NOTE **In 2009, a community project was started to build a next-generation Pentaho Analysis Tool (PAT) that aims to replace JPivot in the future. At the time of this writing, PAT is still in its early development phases so for the remainder of this chapter, we stick to JPivot. If you would like to take a look at PAT, visit the project's home page at `http://code.google.com/p/pentahoanalysistool`.**

Architecture

Figure 15-1 shows a schematic overview of the PAS components and their relationships.

First, we summarize the elements and interactions shown in Figure 15-1. The following sequence of events describes what happens when the end user uses a typical Pentaho OLAP application:

1. The end user's web browser does an HTTP request to view, browse, or drill down into an OLAP pivot table. (In Pentaho, this typically results in the execution of an action sequence, which in this case was constructed to call on JPivot.)
2. The JPivot servlet receives the request and translates it into an MDX query. The MDX query is sent to the Mondrian engine.
3. Mondrian interprets the MDX query and translates it into one or more SQL queries. This particular technique is referred to as ROLAP, which stands for Relational OLAP. (In this chapter, we refer to the term OLAP for clarity, although in the context of Mondrian, the actual technique is more properly called ROLAP.)

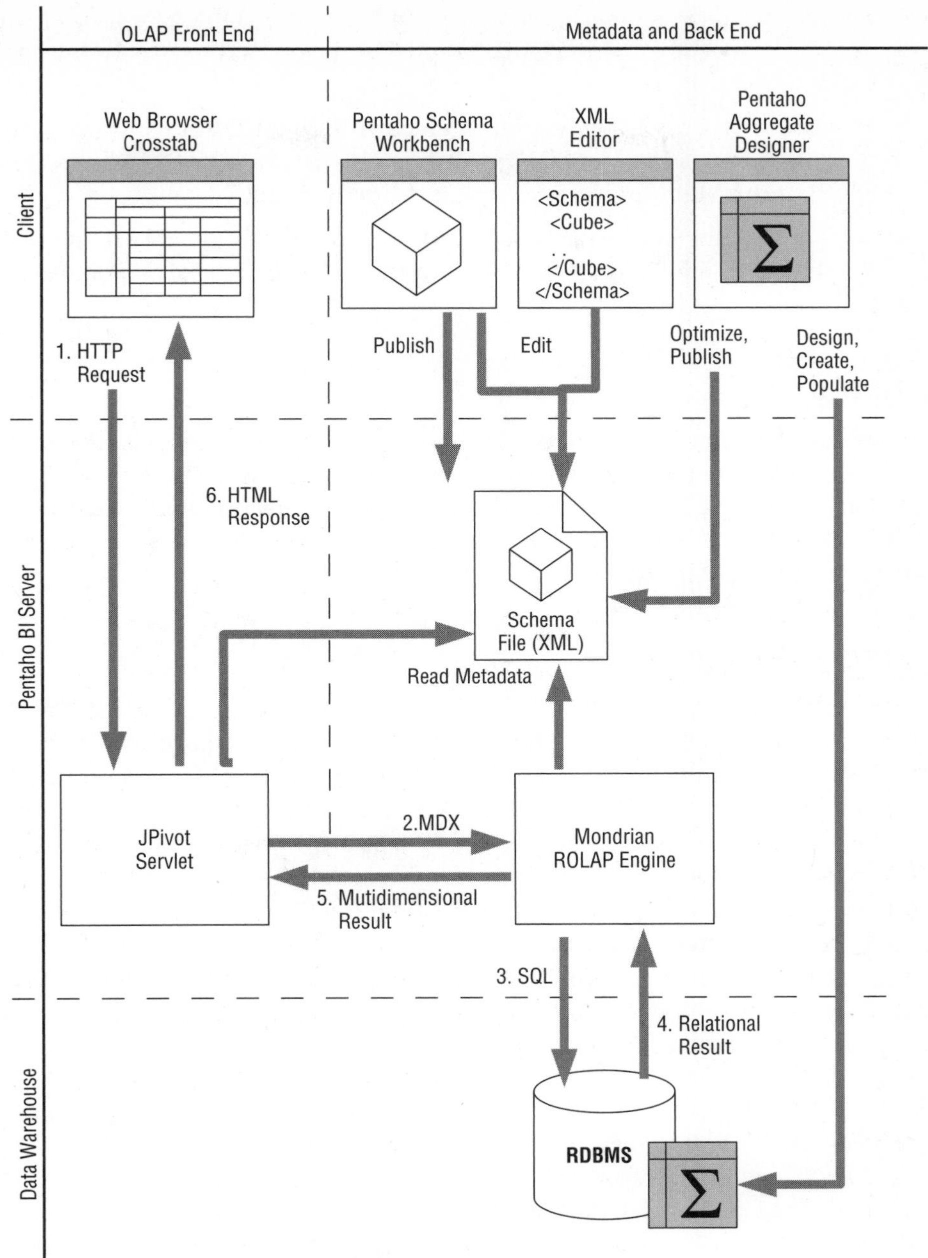

Figure 15-1: Overview of the Pentaho OLAP components

4. The Relational Database Management System (RDBMS) executes the queries issued by Mondrian. Mondrian receives tabular (relational) results.
5. Mondrian processes the results received from the RDBMS and translates them to a multidimensional result-set. This is actually the MDX query result of the MDX query sent to Mondrian in Step 2.
6. JPivot uses the multidimensional result to render an HTML page to display the data. This is then sent to the browser where it is shown to the user.

Schema

A central structure shown in Figure 15-1 is the *schema*. The schema is essentially an XML document that describes one or more multidimensional cubes. The cubes also describe the mapping of the cube's dimensions and measures to tables and columns in a relational database. To Mondrian, the schema is key in translating the MDX query to SQL queries.

Schema Design Tools

The right top part of Figure 15-1 shows a number of components that do not take part directly in the interaction previously summarized. These all represent design and development tools used to construct or enhance Mondrian schemas. A Mondrian schema is the mapping between the relational and the multi-dimensional model. This mapping is used to help translate MDX queries to SQL queries, and to transform relational results received in response to SQL queries to multi-dimensional results. The multidimensional model, consisting of dimensions, hierarchies, and measures, is created first and the relational model is mapped into the schema. Because you'll be working with a star schema as the source of the Mondrian schema, this will be a very straightforward process.

Pentaho Schema Workbench offers a graphical user interface to create Mondrian schemas. In addition, Pentaho Schema Workbench can publish schemas to the Pentaho Server, which then stores them in the solution repository. Once stored in the solution repository, the schemas can be used by the server's Mondrian engine as a back end for OLAP services.

Pentaho Schema Workbench is just one tool you can use to create schemas. You can also use a text editor or XML editor to write the schema manually, which is why we included it in Figure 15-1, right next to Pentaho Schema Workbench. You can publish manually written schemas by using Pentaho Workbench, or by moving the XML file that contains the schema to the desired Pentaho solution directory on the file system.

Aggregate Tables

The Pentaho Aggregate Designer (PAD) is a tool that can assist you in generating and populating aggregate tables. Mondrian can take advantage of aggregate tables to generate efficient SQL queries that can considerably enhance performance. So, PAD analyzes the back-end database, generating the appropriate SQL statements to create and populate the aggregate tables. At the same time, PAD modifies the schema file, which is necessary for Mondrian to use the aggregate tables.

This chapter covers all the tools needed to develop and use OLAP solutions, but before we can do that we need to cover some basic concepts such as MDX and the structure of an OLAP cube.

MDX Primer

MDX is the abbreviation for Multi Dimensional eXpressions, which is a language that is especially designed for querying OLAP databases. MDX is a de facto standard originally developed by Microsoft.

NOTE MDX is an industry standard created and first implemented by Microsoft in the Microsoft Analysis server product, which is shipped as part of the SQL Server RDBMS. After its introduction, MDX was widely adopted by other vendors as the OLAP query language.

Currently no consortium or committee determines standards outside Microsoft, which maintains an MDX specification. Reference documentation is available only as part of the SQL Server product documentation. The current reference documentation can be found at `http://msdn.microsoft.com/en-us/library/ms145506.aspx`.

You can find more information and documentation on the website of one of the inventors of the MDX language, Mosha Pasumansky: `http://www.mosha/.com msolap`. Another excellent source is the MDX Essentials series on `www.databasejournal.com`.

In addition to these online resources, you can read more about MDX in *MDX Solutions: With Microsoft SQL Server Analysis Services 2005 and Hyperion Essbase*, by G. Spofford, S. Harinath, C. Webb, D. Hai Huang, and F. Civardi (Wiley, 2006, ISBN: 978-0-471-74808-3).

In a sense, MDX is to the multidimensional model what SQL is to the relational model. SQL queries define operations on database tables to retrieve a set of rows, whereas MDX queries operate on a *cube* and deliver a multidimensional collection of cells.

Although you don't need to be an expert in MDX, it helps to know the basics before starting to build cubes for Mondrian. Furthermore, if you want to create analytical solutions that exceed the standard drill and filter capabilities of the JPivot front end, you'll need to modify the generated MDX yourself. But before we explore the power of MDX, it's a good idea to cover some basic OLAP concepts to help you to understand the syntax better.

Cubes, Dimensions, and Measures

When you first encounter MDX, one of the most confusing aspects is the terminology used. Some terms may sound familiar and refer to concepts used in dimensional modeling. However, some concepts are totally different and seem awkward at first. In this, and the next few subsections, we take a simplified version of the WCM model and use that to illustrate all these concepts.

The Cube Concept

Most textbooks on OLAP and MDX start by presenting a visual representation of a three dimensional cube. Why should we break with this tradition? So let's introduce some of the main concepts with Figure 15-2, which shows a simple cube built from the WCM data warehouse.

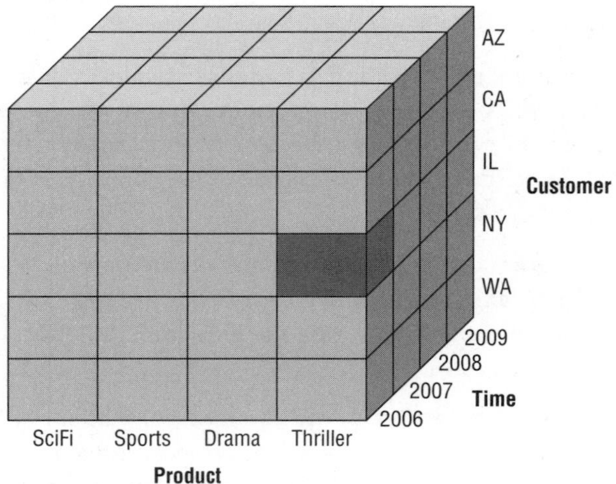

Figure 15-2: Three-dimensional cube

The cube shown in Figure 15-2 consists of a time, product, and customer dimension, each of them placed on one side of the cube. Dimensions are the cornerstone of OLAP cubes: a cube is simply a collection of multiple dimensions.

Besides dimensions with identifying data, you need something to report on, such as sales or rental revenue, cost, or number of rentals. These values are called *measures*. An important aspect of measures is that they do not represent a single value. Rather, they represent an *aggregate* value. The measures just mentioned are typically aggregated by summation. In MDX, the collection of measures forming a special kind of dimension is called the *measure dimension*.

Now take a look at the cube in Figure 15-2; of course, there is more than one product, one customer, and one point in time. In fact, each customer, product, and day in the cube has an intersection called a *tuple*. Each tuple, which can be an individual cell or a section in the cube, can contain one or more measures.

NOTE **Because not every customer buys every product on each available day, a lot of tuples won't physically exist in an OLAP cube. This is called *sparsity* but because data is retrieved from a relational database where only existing data is stored, sparsity doesn't pose a problem.**

Star Schema Analogy

There is an analogy between these MDX concepts and the dimensional modeling and star schema concepts discussed in Chapters 6 and 7 respectively. The term ''dimension'' refers to the same concept in all these domains. An MDX cube is analogous to a star schema, and measures are analogous to facts. For clarity, Figure 15-3 shows how a simple star schema can be mapped to a cube like the one shown in Figure 15-2.

The correspondence between the cube shown in Figure 15-2 and the star schema shown in Figure 15-3 is just a convenient consequence of the star schema modeling technique: although it is possible to organize things so that MDX cubes, dimensions, and measures correspond directly to a star schema, dimension tables, and a fact table respectively, this is not required or implied. We mention the analogy because, in practice, some mapping that describes how a cube can be constructed from the data in the data warehouse always exists. In the case of ROLAP engines such as Mondrian, this mapping is actually quite tight, as the cube data is constructed on-the-fly by querying the database.

Cube Visualization

There is no practical limit to the number of dimensions that can be used to construct a cube. However, most tools that are designed to present visual representations of OLAP cubes to end users can display only two dimensions. Typically, this takes the form of a *cross-table*, also known as a *crosstab* or a *pivot table*.

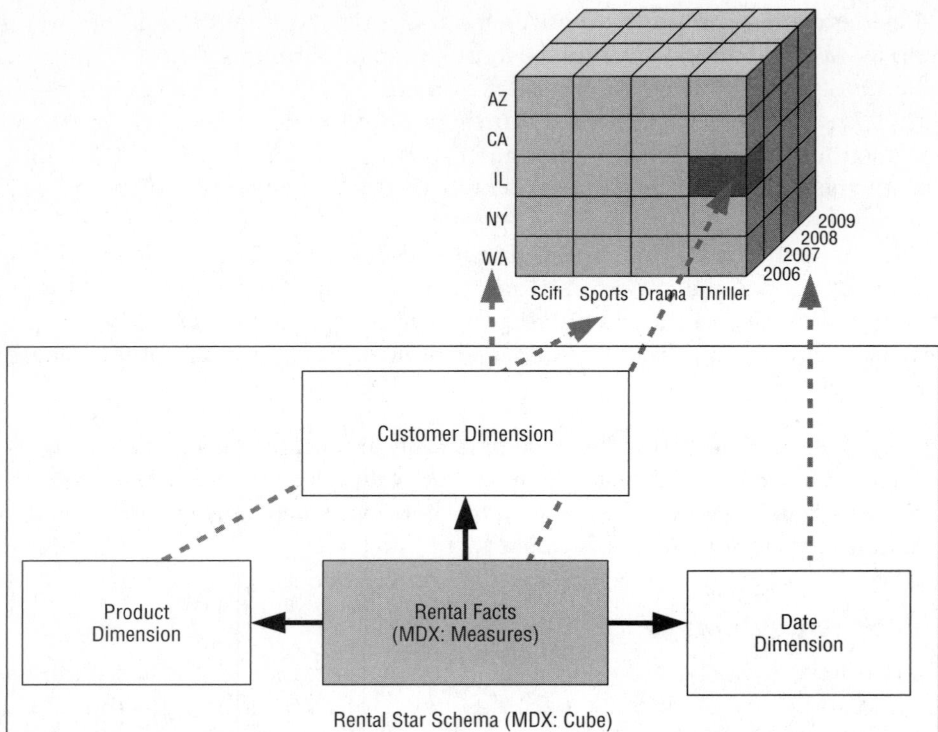

Figure 15-3: A cube as a star schema

In the case of the crosstab, the two display dimensions are the horizontal and vertical axes of the table. Dimensions from a multidimensional cube can be combined, yielding two sets constructed from one or more dimensions. These can then be mapped to the two axes of the crosstab. Figure 15-4 illustrates a possible mapping of the cube shown in Figure 15-2 to a crosstab.

In Figure 15-4, the DVD and Date dimensions are combined and appear as columns of the crosstab (the horizontal axis). The Customer dimension appears as rows in the crosstab (the vertical axis).

Hierarchies, Levels, and Members

For your cube to be useful, you need more than just individual values at the individual dimension intersections. You need a way of aggregating the data across the various dimensions. For this purpose, dimensions are organized into one or more *hierarchies*.

Hierarchies

A hierarchy is a tree-like structure that can be used to retrieve data from the cube at different aggregation levels. The easiest and most often used example is the date dimension with the Year-Quarter-Month-Day hierarchy. To illustrate the hierarchy concept and the corresponding MDX terminology, Figure 15-5 shows a partly expanded Year-Quarter-Month-Day hierarchy of a date dimension.

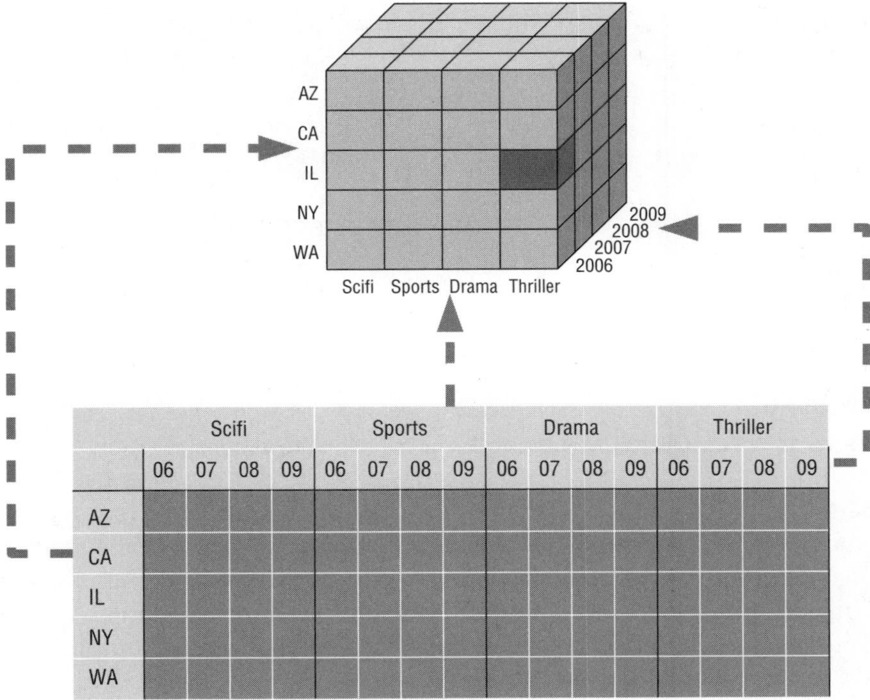

Figure 15-4: Crosstab visualization of a cube

Levels and Members

A hierarchy consists of *levels*, and each level has one or more *members*. So in Figure 15-5, Year, Quarter, Month, and Day are *levels* and the named items within each level are the *members*. For example, the years 2008, 2009, and 2010 are the members at the Year level, and the quarters Q1 through Q4 are members at the Quarter level. The order of levels reflects the hierarchical organization: Year represents a higher level of aggregation than Quarter, and Month represents a lower level of aggregation than Quarter.

An important thing to note is that the members within one level do not overlap: within the Year level, the members are all distinct from one another. But the same is true for the members below the Year level: both the years 2009 and 2010 may have a member called Q1 at the Quarter level, but despite having the same name, these members are distinct from one another. This ensures that data aggregation along a level yields a consistent result.

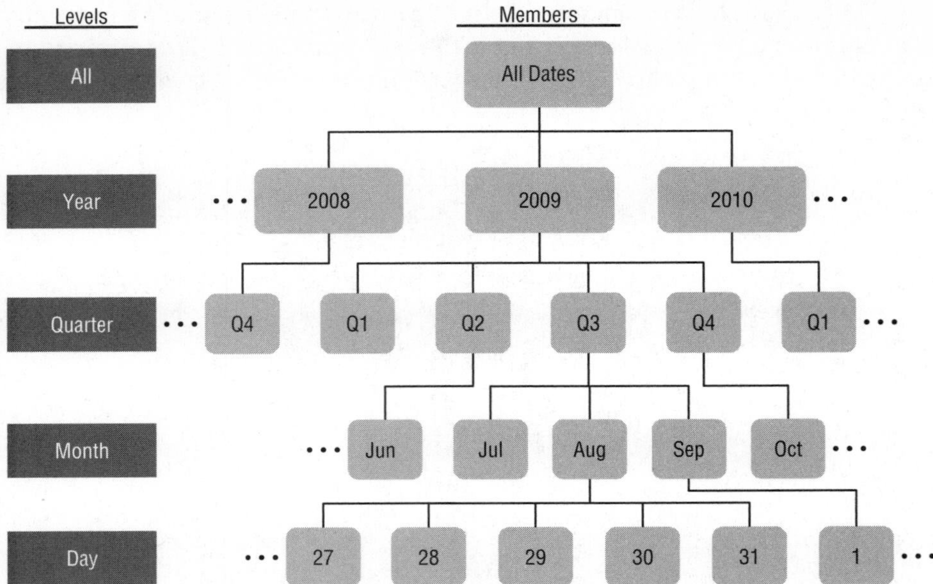

Figure 15-5: A Year-Quarter-Month-Day hierarchy in a date dimension

Using the MDX syntax, a member can always be referenced by using the full member path consisting of the dimension, level and member name, as in `[Date].[Year].[2008]`. Sometimes, members can be referenced within a hierarchy without explicitly naming the level the member belongs to, that is, as long as the member name is unique. So, in the previous example, `[2008]` would work just as well if this is a unique name.

TIP **One of the first things you'll notice when looking at MDX statements is the extensive use of square brackets. This is not required, but if your member names contain spaces or numbers, or if the name is an MDX reserved word, using the [ ] brackets is mandatory. Best practice is to always use the square brackets.**

The All Level, All Member, and Default Member

Hierarchies can have a special *all level* in addition to the explicitly defined levels. The all level is the conceptual root of the hierarchy. It is special because it is not explicitly defined. Instead the OLAP engine rather derives it. It contains exactly one member, the *all member*, which is constructed by unifying all members belonging to the highest defined aggregation level. In Figure 15-5, the all level is labeled All, and the all member is labeled All dates.

Hierarchies can also specify the *default member*, which is used when members are not explicitly specified. This is important to note, as you don't usually explicitly specify all dimensions in an MDX query. Typically, the all member designation is used as default member. The effect of this is that measures are automatically aggregated at the highest level for all dimensions that are not explicitly used in the MDX query.

Member Sets

To retrieve all members of a level, you just add the `MEMBERS` *keyword* to the level, as in `[Date].[Months].[Year].MEMBERS`. This expression evaluates to all members of the Year level as a *member set*. You can also explicitly specify a set by enumerating the member names in a comma-separated list enclosed in curly braces. The curly braces denote the set, as in `{[Year].[2007], [Year].[2008], [Year].[2009]}`.

Multiple Hierarchies

Dimensions can contain multiple hierarchies, offering multiple analytical or navigational paths within a dimension. Typically, multiple hierarchies serve different business needs. For example, in a date dimension, a Year-Quarter-Month-Day hierarchy is used for sales analysis, and an additional Year-Week-Day hierarchy may be used to perform the weekly purchase order analysis. Multiple hierarchies for the same dimension may have a few common levels: in this particular case, the Year level has the same meaning in both hierarchies. However, the level definitions of the hierarchies differ somewhere down the line—this is, in fact, the point of having multiple hierarchies. For example, the two date hierarchies differ from one another for all levels below the Year level.

In MDX you can assign a specific hierarchy to be part of the dimension reference. For example, suppose you have one `Date` dimension with two separate hierarchies: one for Year-Quarter-Month-Day and one for Year-Week-Day, called `Months` and `Weeks` respectively. In this case, the expression `[Date.Months].[2000].[1].[1]` refers to month 1 in quarter 1 in the year 2000, whereas `[Date.Weeks].[2000].[1].[1]` refers to day 1 of week 1 of the year 2000. Note how the hierarchy name is appended to the dimension name directly, using the dot notation inside the square brackets.

If you omit a hierarchy specification, the default hierarchy, which is the first hierarchy specified for the dimension, is used.

Cube Family Relationships

Within each hierarchy in a cube dimension the order of the constituting members is predefined automatically based on their natural alphabetical, numerical or temporal ordering. The levels within a hierarchy are not automatically ordered. They need to be placed in a certain order, going from a summarized to a detailed level. Each member of a lower level in the hierarchy may belong to only one higher level member. As an example, think of products: a product can only be part of one product group, but a product group can contain multiple products. To start with the order in levels, the relationship between different levels is called a *parent-child* relationship. In a date dimension, the Year level is the parent of the Quarter level, which in turn is the child level of Year.

It gets more interesting when you look at the members of the level. Now the year 2009 has four children, Q1, Q2, Q3, and Q4, and each quarter in turn has three children, Jan, Feb, and Mar for Q1, and so forth. Each member can also have *siblings and cousins*. Siblings are related members at the same level but with another parent; they can be addressed only by pointing to the first or last sibling or by retrieving all siblings. A cousin's position in the level corresponds to the referencing member. Suppose that you want to look for the cousin of Q1 2009 in 2008; the resulting member will be Q1 2008. The similarity between children and siblings on the one hand, and cousins on the other, is that children and siblings can be addressed only as a group or by explicitly specifying the first or last members, but cousins need to be addressed by specifying the parent.

Many more ways of referencing related cells are available; you can, for instance, use the keyword *descendants* to retrieve a set of members that descends from the starting member. This would also require that you add the distance to the parent member, so the MDX function `Descendants([2008],2)` retrieves all the months of 2008 if the hierarchy is Year-Quarter-Month. In this case, the Month level is two steps away from the Year level.

Relative Time Relationships

When you are working with a time dimension, special relative functions are available that are based on the preceding family relations between members within a hierarchy. In most BI solutions, users are interested in comparing a period with the same period in a previous year. Although you could use the *cousin* function to get to this comparing period, the `PARALLELPERIOD` function is better suited for this. The function takes three arguments: hierarchy level, number of periods back, and time dimension member. For instance, if you are interested in the parallel period of October 2009 in the previous year, you would use `PARALLELPERIOD([Year],1,[Date].[Month].[200910])`, which would return `[200810]`.

Year-to-date is also a must-have feature for BI solutions, and the `YTD` function delivers that information. From each period in a year, whether you are dealing with quarters or months, you can retrieve the `YTD` members very easily. When you use `YTD([Time].[Month].[200903])`, the members `[200901]`, `[200902]`, and `[200903]` are returned as a set.

MDX Query Syntax

At first glance, MDX might look familiar if you already know the SQL language. Looks can be deceiving, however; there are some similarities but the differences are even greater.

Basic MDX Query

So how do you get data from your cube into an MDX result? Let's start with the simplest of simple MDX queries:

```
SELECT
FROM wcm_sales
```

The query result of this query is the cube total of the default measure of the wcm_orders cube. Of course, this isn't very useful and is only good for testing whether your connection works, but this example does illustrate a few key concepts of MDX, so let's take a closer look at this simple statement.

The cube from which the data is to be retrieved is specified in the MDX FROM clause. As such, it is somewhat analogous to the SQL FROM clause, which specifies a table or intermediate join result that delivers the data for the rest of the query.

The SELECT keyword is specified, but because it is not followed by an expression list, the default measure is used. In this case, the default measure is Revenue. Because measures are aggregated, this query returns the sum of all revenue in the cube called wcm_orders.

Axes: ON ROWS and ON COLUMNS

MDX can represent information on multiple axes. Usually these are the ROWS and COLUMNS axes. Other default axes are PAGES, SECTIONS, and CHAPTERS, but most OLAP visualization tools (including JPivot) cannot work with axes beyond the first two, let alone the 128 possible axes the MDX standard allows.

In most cases, you'll work with only two member sets at a time, one displayed at the columns axis and one at the rows axis. The MDX expression therefore uses the following generic syntax:

```
SELECT <member collection> ON COLUMNS,
       <member collection> ON ROWS
FROM   <cubename>
```

Actually, the keywords ROWS and COLUMNS are aliases for the standard numbered notation, COLUMNS is the alias for AXIS(0), and ROWS stands for AXIS(1). You can even omit the keyword AXIS altogether and simply use 0 and 1. So the previous example could also be written as:

```
SELECT <member collection> ON AXIS(0),
       <member collection> ON 1
FROM   <cubename>
```

Although the actual order of axis specifications is irrelevant, you must specify a gapless consecutive series of axes, starting with AXIS(0) (the COLUMNS axis). So it is possible to specify only the first ON COLUMNS line, but you cannot skip it and only use ON ROWS. Although you could reverse the order of the ON COLUMNS and ON ROWS lines, it would be confusing, which is why we don't recommend using this ordering.

To get a vertical display of only rows with a single measure, use the following query:

```
SELECT [Measures].[Revenue] ON COLUMNS,
       <member collection> ON ROWS
FROM   <cubename>
```

Looking at a Part of the Data

You might ask yourself whether an MDX query can also contain a WHERE clause, and indeed it can. It is called the *slicer* because it restricts data that can be accessed through the cube to a particular subset (a slice). Although the WHERE keyword is the same as in regular SQL, the behavior is quite different, as the name ''slicer'' implies. The following MDX query limits the analysis to the year 2008 by using a slicer:

```
SELECT [Measures].[Revenue] ON COLUMNS,
       <member collection> ON ROWS
FROM   <cubename>
WHERE  [Date].[Year].[2008]
```

So, instead of specifying a condition, as you would in SQL, the MDX WHERE clause requires you to specify the portion of the data that you would like to include in terms of a dimension member specification. You can specify a comma-separated list of member names provided you enclose the list in parentheses. So, the following MDX query limits the result to the year 2008 and the customers from Canada:

```
SELECT [Measures].[Revenue] ON COLUMNS
FROM   <cubename>
WHERE  ([Date].[Year].[2007], [Customer].[Country].[CA])
```

Dimension on Only One Axis

And now the bad news: you cannot use the same dimension on more than one axis. For example, if you use the Date dimension already ON ROWS or ON COLUMNS, it cannot be used in the slicer. The following query therefore fails:

```
SELECT [Measures].[Revenue] ON COLUMNS,
       [Date].[Quarter].Members ON ROWS
FROM   <cubename>
WHERE  [Date].[Year].[2008]
```

Most people used to SQL find this hard to understand, but it's simply one of those MDX intricacies that you'll have to get used to. If you only want to look at quarters in 2008, you can do this by using the CHILDREN keyword on the 2008 member of the year level:

```
SELECT [Measures].[Revenue] ON COLUMNS,
       [Date].[2008].Children ON ROWS
FROM   <cubename>
```

MDX allows you to use multiple dimensions on one axis, but remember that a particular dimension can appear on only one of the axes (or the slicer).

More MDX Examples: a Simple Cube

For the remainder of the MDX explanation and examples, it's best to have a specific model. In the following paragraphs, we build the wcm_orders cube, which has the structure as listed in Table 15-1.

You'll learn how to create a Mondrian cube for this model later, but for now you use it to continue exploring MDX.

The FILTER Function

The FILTER function lets you limit the selection of members in the cube. You can use the WHERE clause only to slice part of the cube, but what if you want to limit the results to DVD titles that have revenue over $10,000 in 2008, or see only movie titles that showed a 10 percent increase in revenue compared to the previous month? These are only two examples where the FILTER function can be useful. FILTER is an MDX function that takes two arguments: a set and a search condition. The first example translates to the following MDX statement:

```
SELECT [Country].Members ON COLUMNS,
       FILTER(
           [Title].Members,
           [Revenue]>10000
       ) ON ROWS
FROM   [wcm_orders]
WHERE  [Year].[2008]
```

The preceding statement includes a filter and a slicer. The latter takes precedence over the other elements, meaning that the filter and the result set are limited to the 2008 slice of the cube.

Table 15-1: WCM_orders_cube

DIMENSION	HIERARCHY	LEVEL
Local Order Date	Months	Year Quarter Month Date
Local Order Date	Weeks	Year Week Date
Customer		Country Region City Zipcode Name
DVD		Genre Title
Measures		Revenue Quantity RentalDuration

The ORDER Function

If you run the query from the previous example, the results retain their natural order, which is alphabetically within the hierarchy. This means that movie titles are ordered alphabetically but the genre ordering always precedes that. (Later in this chapter, when we explain how to build the cube, you learn how to control dimension member order within the cube definition.)

In many cases, you want to order results based on a measure—for example, you might want to order results by revenue, from high to low. You use the `ORDER` function to accomplish exactly that. The `ORDER` function takes three parameters: the set to be ordered, the expression to order by, and the sort order, which can take four possible values: `ASC`, `DESC`, `BASC`, and `BDESC`. The `B` in the last two values forces the hierarchies to break to enable an overall sort order, so if you want to the results in the previous example sorted in descending order, use the following query:

```
SELECT [Country].Members ON COLUMNS,
       ORDER(
           FILTER([Title].Members, [Revenue]>10000),
           [Revenue],
```

```
            BDESC
        ) ON ROWS
FROM    [wcm_orders]
WHERE   [Year].[2008]
```

Now the results will be sorted with the best-selling movies at the top of the list.

Using TOPCOUNT and BOTTOMCOUNT

There is another way to get to the best (or worst) selling movies, and that is by using the TOPCOUNT and BOTTOMCOUNT functions. These functions are actually a shorthand for using the HEAD and TAIL functions that can be used to limit an ordered result set like the one in the preceding example, but make the query a lot simpler to write.

The TOPCOUNT and BOTTOMCOUNT functions take three arguments: a set, the number of members to display, and the measure to order on. Here is the query that retrieves the top 10 movies of 2008:

```
SELECT [Country].Members ON COLUMNS,
       TOPCOUNT(
           [Title].Members
       ,   10
       ,   [Revenue]
       ) ON ROWS
FROM   [wcm_orders]
WHERE  [Year].[2008]
```

Combining Dimensions: The CROSSJOIN Function

MDX isn't limited to displaying one dimension per axis, but to place multiple dimensions on a single axis, you should use the CROSSJOIN function. This function is similar to the CROSS JOIN join type in plain SQL and creates a combination of all values from two dimensions. For example, using CROSSJOIN, you can place both [Customer].[Country] and [DVD].[Genre] on the same axis, and use [Local Order Date].[Year] and [Measures].[Quantity] on the other:

```
SELECT CROSSJOIN(
           {[Local Order Date].[Year].Members}
       ,   {[Measures].[Quantity]}
       ) ON COLUMNS,
       CROSSJOIN(
           {[Customer].[Country].Members}
       ,   {[DVD].[Genre].Members}
       ) ON ROWS
FROM   [wcm_orders]
```

Using NON EMPTY

A commonly used construct in MDX queries is NON EMPTY. It forces the query to return only results that contain a value. Because it's highly unlikely that every customer buys every product on every day in the year, your average MDX query returns a lot of empty results as you start drilling down into details. The NON EMPTY phrase can be placed in front of the set in any of the query dimensions. When a CROSSJOIN is used, the NON EMPTY keyword is placed in front of it, as in the following example:

```
SELECT NON EMPTY CROSSJOIN({[Local Order Date].[Year].Members},
{[Measures].[Quantity]}) ON COLUMNS
```

In fact, this is the default behavior of JPivot in the Pentaho Web platform. The JPivot toolbar contains a button labeled Suppress Empty Rows/Columns that causes the generated MDX queries to include NON EMPTY. By default, this feature is enabled.

Working with Sets and the WITH Clause

Earlier in this chapter, we briefly used the term *sets* and the curly braces needed to specify them. A set is a collection of members within a dimension and is usually defined implicitly. For instance, when you use [Year].MEMBERS on one of the axes, you are using a set because the MEMBERS operator returns a set. In fact, many of the MDX functions you've seen so far return sets: CHILDREN, SIBLINGS, DESCENDANTS, and YTD all behave like that.

The problem with these functions is that they always return the complete collection of members within a level. Sometimes this is not convenient for doing specific analysis on only part of a dimension. Using the WITH clause, you can create your own sets to use in MDX queries. Suppose you want to combine some movie genres into a CoolMovies set containing only some of the genres in the database. CoolMovies is not a known entity in your model, but you could create it anyway using the following syntax:

```
WITH SET [your set name] AS '{set definition}'
```

Translated into a CoolMovies example, this would become

```
WITH
SET [CoolMovies]
AS '{[DVD].[All DVD].[Action/Adventure], [DVD].[All DVD].[Fantasy],
     [DVD].[All DVD].[SciFi], [DVD].[All DVD].[Suspense/Thriller],
     [DVD].[All DVD].[Thriller]}'
SELECT NON EMPTY {[CoolMovies]} ON COLUMNS,
       NON EMPTY CROSSJOIN([Local Order Date].[All Local Order Dates],
                           [Customer].[All Customers]) ON ROWS
FROM  [wcm_orders]
WHERE [Measures].[Quantity]
```

As you can see in the preceding example, you need to use curly braces around your named set when you use it in the SELECT statement; otherwise it is not recognized as a set and an error is generated. Also note that we included the full member definition in the sets. In this case that wouldn't have been necessary because the member `[Thriller]` and the other genres are unique in our cube, so `{[Action/Adventure], [Fantasy], [SciFi], [Suspense/Thriller], [Thriller]}` works as well.

Using Calculated Members

The last part of this MDX primer covers creating calculated members. A *calculated member* is a dimension member whose value is calculated at run-time using a specified expression and can be defined as members of regular dimensions or as members of the measures dimension. Mondrian allows you to add calculated members in the schema directly, but that feature uses standard MDX calculated syntax as well. Only definitions are stored because the value of the expression is determined at run-time. As a consequence, calculated members don't take up space in a cube but do require extra computation power.

A very simple example of a calculated member is a slight variation on the CoolMovies named set you've seen before:

```
WITH
MEMBER [Measures].[CoolMoviesRevenue]
AS '[Action/Adventure]+[Fantasy]+[SciFi]+[Suspense/Thriller]+[Thriller]'
SELECT NON EMPTY {[Measures].[CoolMoviesRevenue],
                  [Measures].[Revenue]} ON COLUMNS,
       NON EMPTY {[Country].Members} ON ROWS
FROM   [wcm_orders]
WHERE  [Year].[2008]
```

You can also use calculated members to group member totals, for instance to create a recent and historical collection of years:

```
WITH
MEMBER [Local Order Date].[All Dates].[Historical]
AS     'SUM([Year].[2000]:[Year].[2005])'
MEMBER [Local Order Date].[All Dates].[Recent]
AS     'SUM([Year].[2006]:[Year].[2010])'
SELECT NON EMPTY {[Local Order Date].[All Dates].[Historical],
                 [Local Order Date].[All Dates].[Recent]} ON COLUMNS,
       NON EMPTY {[Country].Members} ON ROWS
FROM   [wcm_orders]
```

Although there are countless other possible uses and examples of calculated members, this gives you an idea of how you can use them to extend the available content of a cube. For more information about Mondrian-specific MDX, refer to the online documentation at `http://mondrian.pentaho.org/documentation/mdx.php`. And because MDX was originally developed by

Microsoft, a huge number of online references and books are available on this subject, although very few books are devoted to MDX alone.

WARNING **Since its inception and adoption by many OLAP vendors, Microsoft added several extensions to the MDX specification. Some functions and examples may not work with Mondrian. When in doubt, check the online Mondrian MDX reference at `http://mondrian.pentaho.org/documentation/schema.php`.**

Creating Mondrian Schemas

We already discussed the schema and how it relates to the different components of Pentaho Analysis Services when we discussed Figure 15-1. In this section, we show you how to create Mondrian schemas.

Although this section provides detailed information on creating Mondrian schemas, we cannot cover every possible angle. For a complete reference, you should refer to the official documentation. You can find this at `http://mondrian.pentaho.org/documentation/schema.php`.

Getting Started with Pentaho Schema Workbench

We mentioned that Mondrian schemas are defined as XML documents and that Pentaho Schema Workbench (PSW) offers a graphical user interface to edit these schemas. We also mentioned that it's possible to edit the schemas manually using an XML editor, IDE, or even a plain-text editor.

Both of these approaches are equally valid and useful in their own way. For that reason, we pay attention to PSW as well as to the XML format used to denote Mondrian schemas.

Downloading Mondrian

Mondrian is maintained in its own project at `www.sourceforge.net`. You can find it on the SourceForge site simply by searching for Mondrian. The Mondrian project site provides the binaries and source code for the Mondrian engine itself as well as Pentaho Schema Workbench and the Pentaho Aggregate Designer. For now, you need to download only Pentaho Schema Workbench. Later on, you will also take a look at the aggregate designer so you might as well download it now, too.

NOTE **You do not need to download the Mondrian engine software itself: this is already included in the Pentaho BI Server. You need to download the engine itself only if you want to upgrade the Mondrian engine or deploy Mondrian separately without Pentaho Server. However, these use cases are outside the scope of this book, and are not discussed here.**

Installing Pentaho Schema Workbench

Pentaho Schema Workbench is distributed as `.zip` and `.tar.gz` archives. Windows users should download the `.zip` file, and users of UNIX-based system should get the `.tar.gz` file. After downloading, you need to unpack the file. This yields a single directory called `schema-workbench` containing all the software. We refer to this directory as the PSW home directory or simply PSW home. You should move the directory to some place that makes sense for your system. For example, Windows users can move it to `C:\Program Files` and Linux users might move it to `/opt/` or the current user's home directory.

After unpacking PSW, you need to place any JDBC Driver `.jar` files that you may need to connect to the data warehouse in the `drivers` directory. This directory can be found immediately below the PSW home directory.

Starting Pentaho Schema Workbench

Pentaho Schema Workbench is started using a shell script. Shell scripts for different platforms are located directly in the PSW home directory. On Windows systems, you need to double-click the `workbench.bat` file to start PSW. On a UNIX-based system, you need to start the `workbench.sh` script. You may need to make the `workbench.sh` script executable first. If you are running a graphical desktop such as GNOME, you can do this simply by right-clicking the script and choosing Properties. From there you can make the file executable. Alternatively, you can make it executable from the terminal using the `chmod` command:

```
chmod ug+x workbench.sh
```

After starting the script, you should see the PSW application window (see Figure 15-6).

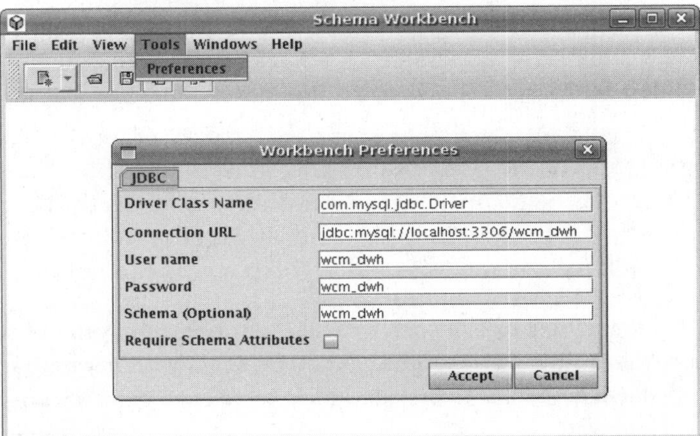

Figure 15-6: The Pentaho Schema Workbench application window

Establishing a Connection

After starting PSW, you should establish a connection to your database. You can invoke the database connection dialog through the main menu by choosing Tools ➢ Preferences. Alternatively, you can press the Preferences toolbar button, which is located at the far right of the application toolbar. A dialog will pop up where you can fill in the JDBC connection parameters. The menu and connection dialog are shown in Figure 15-6.

You need to fill out the following properties in the dialog:

- **Driver class name**—This is the Java classname of the JDBC driver you will be using. For MySQL, this is `com.mysql.jdbc.Driver`.
- **Connection URL**—This is the connectstring used to contact the database server. Assuming you want to connect to the `wcm_dwh` database on a local MySQL instance running at the default port `3306`, the URL is `jdbc:mysql://localhost:3306/wcm_dwh`.
- **Username and password**—The credentials of the database user that connects to the database.

After filling out the dialog, you can click the Accept button to establish the connection. If a message box pops up informing you that the database connection could not be established, you should check parameters you supplied. However, even if you specified the right parameters, you may still get a message informing you that the driver class cannot be found (see Figure 15-7).

Figure 15-7: The error message indicating the JDBC driver wasn't loaded

In this case, you should make sure you placed the `.jar` file containing the JDBC driver you need in the `drivers` directory beneath the PSW home directory (as previously mentioned in the Install subsection). You need to restart PSW to pick up any new `.jar` files you put into the `drivers` directory.

NOTE **If you are unable to establish a database connection, you can still use PSW to define a schema. However, the process will be slightly harder because features such as drop-down list boxes to pick database tables and columns will not work.**

JDBC Explorer

After you establish the connection, you can open a JDBC Explorer window to see the contents of the database. You can open the JDBC Explorer by choosing File ➢ New ➢ JDBC Explorer. This is shown in Figure 15-8.

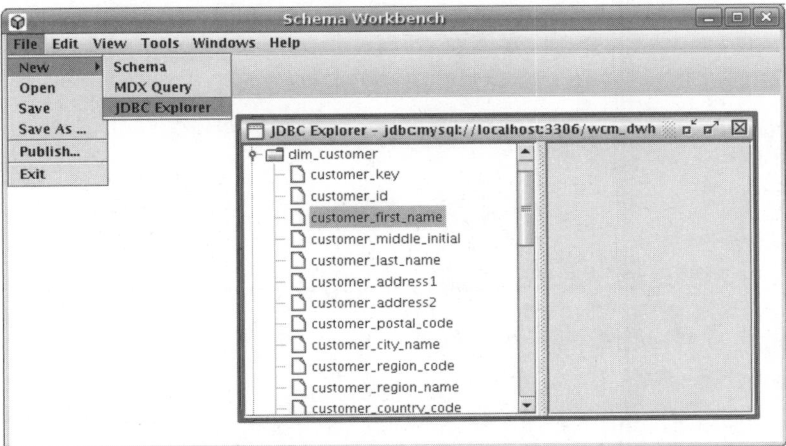

Figure 15-8: Opening the JDBC Explorer

The JDBC Explorer consists of a tree view that displays the tables you can access from the current connection as folders. You can expand the folders to see what columns the table contains. The JDBC Explorer offers no functionality beyond this. However, as you shall see later on, this is just enough to make it a little easier to build your cubes.

Using the Schema Editor

Schemas are created and edited using the schema editor. In this subsection, we'll briefly highlight a few of the features of the schema editor.

Creating a New Schema

Use the menu and choose File ➢ New ➢ Schema to open the schema editor. The schema editor has a tree view on the left side, showing the contents of the schema. Initially, this will be almost empty, save for the Schema node, which is the root of the entire schema. On the right side, the schema editor has a workspace where you can edit elements in the schema. The schema editor is shown in Figure 15-9.

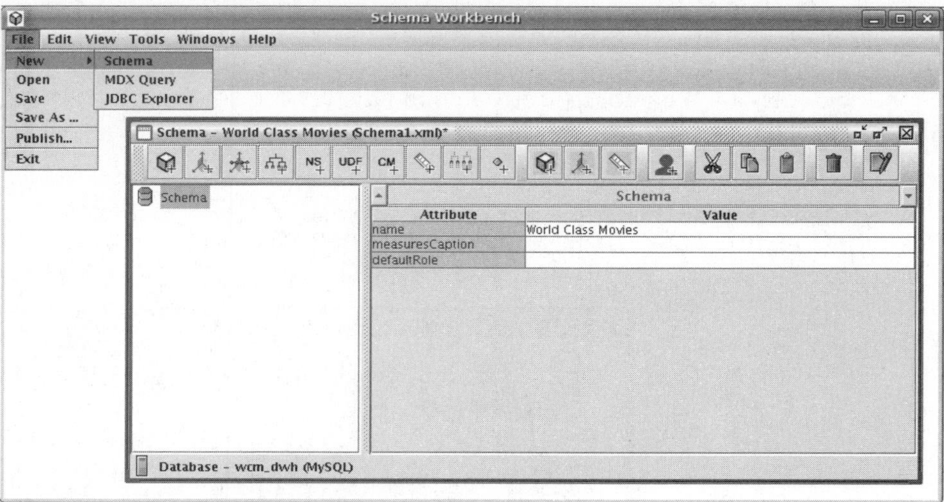

Figure 15-9: The schema editor

In the top of the schema editor a toolbar contains numerous buttons. Most of these buttons are there so you can add new items to the schema. All of these buttons reside on the left side of the toolbar, and you will recognize them by the plus (+) sign in the button icon. At the left side of the toolbar are a few buttons for Cut, Copy, Paste, and Delete. You will be using these buttons a lot in the remainder of this section, but if you would like to learn more now about these buttons, just hover the mouse pointer over the buttons to read the tooltip.

In addition to the toolbar buttons, you can use the context menu from the tree view to accomplish the same tasks. Simply right-click any node in the tree view. The context menu will pop up and offer you all the available actions for that particular node.

Saving the Schema on Disk

After you create a schema, it is a good idea to save it. Just click the floppy icon on the toolbar of the application window and you are prompted to specify a location. For now, just choose whatever filename and location you find convenient—for example, `Schema1.xml`. Your desktop is a reasonable choice while you are working through this chapter.

During the remainder of this chapter, we won't mention that you should save your work all the time. Rather, you should decide for yourself when and whether you should save your work. When developing a schema, it is a good idea to use a version control system such as svn to keep track of changes or to revert to an earlier version should you need to.

Editing Object Attributes

To edit a particular schema item, such as the schema itself, single-click the item in the tree view to select it. Selected items are highlighted in blue. Notice that this is the case for the schema shown in Figure 15-9.

The workspace automatically shows the available attributes for the selected item in an attributes grid. The attributes grid has two columns: the first column is labeled Attribute and lists the attribute names; the second column is labeled Value and contains the attribute value. The attributes grid is also visible in Figure 15-9.

To learn more about a particular attribute, hover the mouse pointer over the attribute name. A tooltip will pop up, displaying a text that describes the purpose of the attribute as well as the default value for the attribute.

To edit an attribute value, place your cursor in the value column of the attributes grid and type the desired value. For example, in Figure 15-9 we entered World Class Movies as the name of this schema.

Changing Edit Mode

The schema is represented as an XML document. If you like, you can switch to inspect the XML representation of the schema at any time by toggling the edit mode. You can do this by clicking the button on the far right side of the toolbar (see Figure 15-10).

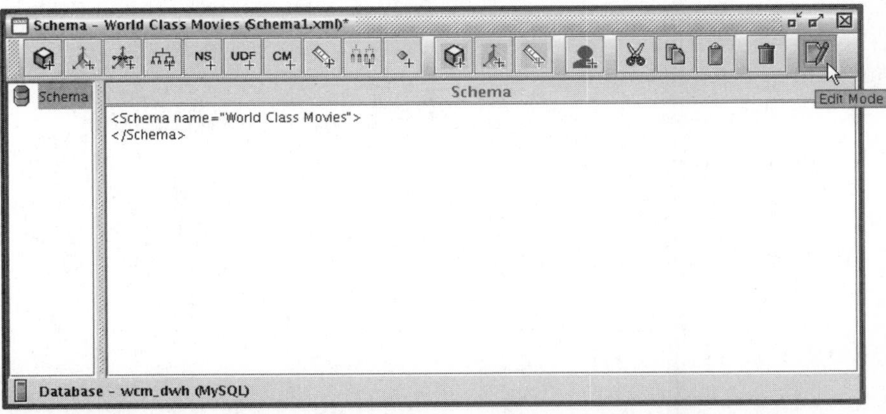

Figure 15-10: Using the edit mode to view the XML representation of the schema

The XML displayed in the workspace corresponds exactly with the selected item in the tree view, which is in this case the schema itself. As you can see, in its present state the XML representation of the schema consists of only the opening and closing tags of a `<Schema>` element.

NOTE **Beware that the XML view is just that—a view. You cannot edit the XML directly from within PSW.**

Creating and Editing a Basic Schema

In this subsection, we will create a schema that contains the cube like we used in the examples of the MDX query syntax. Before we start, you might want to review Figures 15-2 and 15-3 as well as Table 15-1. As we mentioned in our discussion of Figure 15-3, there is an analogy between cubes and star schemas, and for this purpose we will base our cube on the Orders star schema, which was developed in Chapter 8 and shown in Figure 8-6.

Basic Schema Editing Tasks

In the remainder of this section, we describe all common schema editing tasks in detail. Before we do so, it's good to get an overview of the different tasks and subtasks involved, as it's easy to lose sight of the bigger picture.

The tasks can be summarized as follows:

- Creating a schema
- Creating cubes
  - Choosing a fact table
  - Adding measures
- Creating (shared) dimensions
  - Editing the default hierarchy and choosing a dimension table
  - Defining hierarchy levels
  - Optionally, adding more dimensions
- Associating dimensions with cubes

Creating a Cube

You can add a cube by clicking the Add Cube button, which is the first button on the toolbar. The new cube becomes visible in the tree view beneath the schema as a new node having a cube icon. After adding the cube, you can edit its properties (see Figure 15-11).

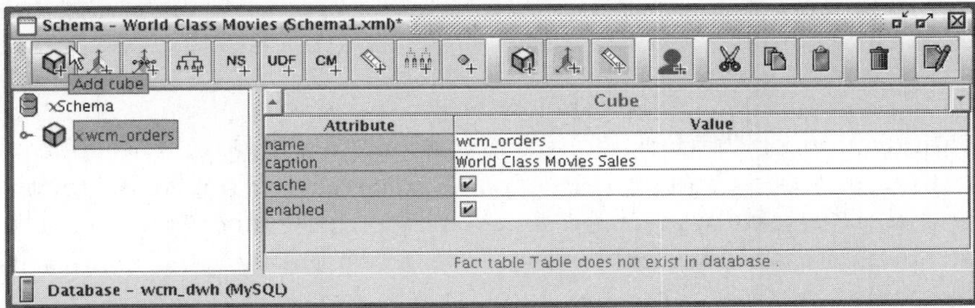

Figure 15-11: Creating a cube

Mondrian cubes can have the following attributes:

- name—Specifies the name that will be used in MDX queries to refer to this cube. This name must be unique within the schema. For our example cube, we must specify wcm_orders here.
- caption—Specifies a display name, which will be used by the user interface to present this cube to the end user. In this case we used World Class Movies Sales.
- cache—Controls whether data from the fact table should be cached.
- enabled—Controls whether Mondrian should load or ignore the cube.

There's another attribute that is currently not supported by PSW:

- defaultMeasure—Optionally, you specify the name of one of the cube's measures here to explicitly make that the default measure.

You can find more information on measures in the next two subsections.

Note that when we added the wcm_orders cube, a little red X icon appeared to the left of the schema and cube icons. The red X icon indicates that there is some error or misconfiguration at or somewhere beneath that particular node. When such a problem is detected by PSW, it ''bubbles up,'' causing any nodes above that node to display the red X icon as well. This allows you to see if something is wrong right away. If a red X icon is displayed, something is wrong.

Whenever you see these X indicators, you should look for the red message at the bottom of the workspace. This message provides a textual description of the problem, and usually it gives you a good idea about what part of the schema you should look at to fix the problem. A different message appears depending on which node is selected in the tree view, so if you want to see the reason why a particular node has a red X icon, select it first.

Choosing a Fact Table

In the case of Figure 15-11, you can tell that there must be something wrong with the cube, or some node beneath it. The error message indicates a misconfiguration of the fact table is the problem's source. The cube node is initially collapsed, and if you expand it, you will notice it contains a table node. This table node represents the fact table upon which the cube is built. In this case, your cube should be based on the `fact_orders` table, which is why you set the table name using the drop-down list box (see Figure 15-12).

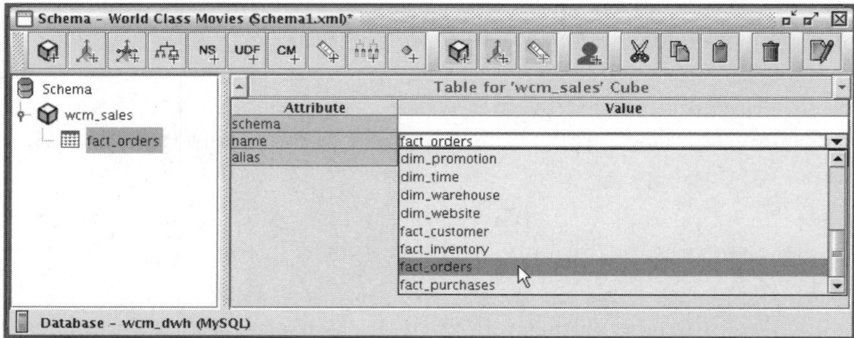

Figure 15-12: Choosing the fact table

Note that the little X icons disappear after you enter the name of an existing table. In this case, the Table element was misconfigured, and by choosing an existing fact table, you fix that problem. This immediately causes the cube and schema nodes above the table node to be fixed as well.

The table name is all you really need to configure for the cube's Table element. However, we include a description of its attributes for completeness:

- `schema`—The identifier of the database schema that contains the fact table. When not explicitly specified, the default schema of the database connection is used.
- `name`—The name of the fact table. When connected to a database, the property editor provides a drop-down list box like the one shown in Figure 15-11, which allows you to pick any of the tables in the default schema. Note that this name is the SQL identifier—unlike the name of the cube, this name property has no bearing whatsoever on any MDX queries.
- `alias`—This is the table alias that will be used for this table when generating SQL statements. It may be useful to specify this in case you want to debug the SQL statements generated by Mondrian.

Adding Measures

Now that you configured a fact table, you can add some measures. To add measures, first select the cube (or its fact table) in the tree view. Then, click the Add Measure button on the toolbar. From the left, this is the first button with the ruler icon and the plus sign. Alternatively, you can right-click the cube and choose the Add Measure option from the context menu (see Figure 15-13).

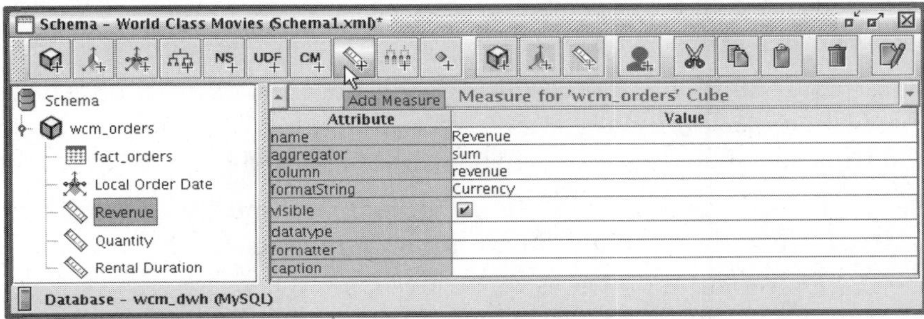

Figure 15-13: Adding measures from the cube's fact table

For now we'll stick closely to the design of the fact table and add the Revenue, Quantity, and Rental Duration measures. These correspond directly to the `quantity`, `revenue`, and `rental_duration` columns in the `fact_orders` table.

The order in which you specify the measures is significant: implicitly, the first measure in the cube is considered the default measure. If you like, you can override this by explicitly specifying the name of the default measure in the `defaultMeasure` attribute of the cube. Currently, this attribute is not supported by PSW, and you'll need to manually edit the schema XML and modify the opening cube tag to include a `defaultMeasure` attribute like so:

```
<Cube defaultMeasure="Quantity" ...>
...
</Cube>
```

Measures themselves can have the following attributes:

- `name`—The identifier that will be used to refer to this measure in MDX queries. This must be unique within the cube.
- `aggregator`—The name of the function that is used to aggregate the measure. The attribute grid offers a drop-down list box from where you can pick one of `sum`, `count`, `min`, `max`, `avg`, and `distinct-count`. For the Revenue and Quantity measures, you should choose the `sum` aggregator. For the Rental Duration Measure, the `avg` aggregator is a more useful choice.

- column—The name of a column from the cube's fact table. When connected to the database, the attribute editor offers a drop-down list box from which you can pick the column.
- formatString—Here you can specify either the predefined format name Currency or a string pattern that specifies how the measure value will be formatted for display. Format strings are discussed in more detail later in this section.
- visible—A flag that specifies whether the measure is displayed to the end user in the user interface.
- datatype—Here you can use a drop-down list box to choose String, Numeric, Integer, Boolean, Date, Time, or Timestamp. When returning data, the specified data type will be used to return data in the MDX result.
- formatter—You can use this attribute to specify a custom formatter. Custom cell formatters must implement the Java interface mondrian.olap.CellFormatter.
- caption—Specifies the display name that is used to present this measure in the user interface. If you leave this blank, the name of the measure is presented instead.

Adding Dimensions

The Mondrian schemas can contain dimensions in two places:

- **Inside the cube that "owns" the dimension**—These dimensions are called private dimensions because they are known only to the cube that contains it and cannot be used outside the enclosing cube.
- **Inside the schema itself**—These are *shared dimensions* and can be associated with multiple cubes, and/or multiple times with the same cube. Shared dimensions are excellent for implementing role-playing dimensions.

Generally, we recommend you always use shared dimensions rather than private dimensions. Although the process of creating private and shared dimensions is similar, the ability to re-use shared dimensions provides a considerable benefit even in the short run.

To create a shared dimension, first select the schema. (To create a private dimension, select the cube that will contain the dimension instead.) Then, click the Add dimension button on the schema editor toolbar. This button is the second button on the toolbar, right next to the Add cube button.

You can define the following attributes for dimensions:

- name—For private dimensions, the name refers to this dimension in MDX queries. For shared dimensions, the name refers to the dimension when you are associating it with a cube. For private dimensions, the name must be unique among all other dimensions used by the cube. For shared dimensions, the name must be unique within the schema. The shared dimension shown in Figure 15-14 uses Date as the name.

- `foreignKey`—If this is a private dimension, this is the name of a column from the cube's fact table that refers to the dimension table that corresponds to this dimension.
- `type`—If your dimension is time or date related, you should use `TimeDimension`. This allows you to use the standard MDX time and date functions. Otherwise, use `StandardDimension`.
- `usagePrefix`—This applies only to private dimensions.
- `caption`—This is a display name used to present this dimension to the end user via the user interface.

Figure 15-14 shows how to add a shared dimension called Date in this manner.

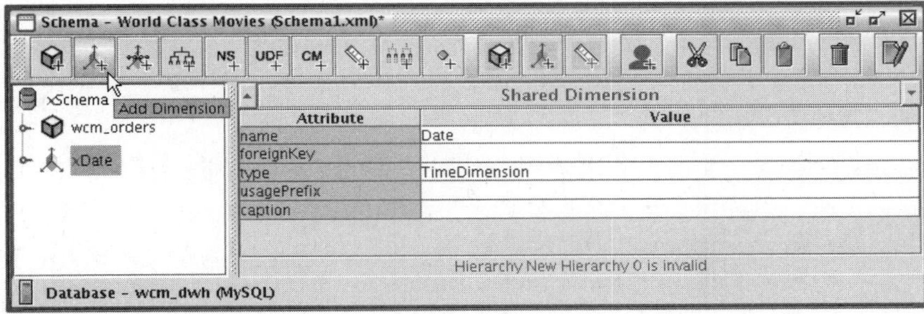

Figure 15-14: Adding a shared Date dimension

Adding the dimension causes red X icons to appear again. The error message at the bottom of the workspace indicates there is something wrong with a hierarchy, so adding and editing hierarchies is the topic of the next subsection.

Adding and Editing Hierarchies and Choosing Dimension Tables

When you create a dimension, a new hierarchy is also created. You can see it when you expand the dimension node. In addition, a table node is automatically created beneath the hierarchy node. Before you edit the hierarchy node, it is best to configure the underlying table node.

The table node represents the dimension table that will deliver the values for the levels of the hierarchy. The procedure to configure the table is exactly the same as the procedure for choosing a fact table for a cube, which was described earlier in this section. For the Date dimension created in the previous subsection, you have to choose the `dim_date_en_us` dimension table.

After choosing the dimension table, you can configure the hierarchy itself. Hierarchies support the following attributes:

- `name`—The name used in MDX queries to refer to the hierarchy. It must be unique within the dimension. Omitting the name causes the hierarchy to get the same name as its dimension. In addition, this hierarchy is the default hierarchy.
- `caption`—The name that is used to present this hierarchy to the end user in the user interface.
- `hasAll`—A flag that indicates whether the hierarchy should have an all level with an all member, for example, a single member in the top of the hierarchy that represents all other members. Usually you should leave this on.
- `allMemberName`—If `hasAll` is enabled, this specifies the MDX identifier that is to be used for the all member. When this is omitted, the all member name is derived automatically as `All` *<name of hierarchy>*.
- `allMemberCaption`—If `hasAll` is enabled, you can use this to specify the name that will be used to present the all member to the end user in the user interface.
- `allLevelName`—The name used to refer to the all level in MDX queries.
- `defaultMember`—The name of the default member. If this is not specified, then the all member will be used as default member if the hierarchy has an All member. This is often exactly the desired behavior. When specified, this member will be used if a member is expected but not explicitly specified in the MDX query. If the default member is not specified and the `hasAll` flag is disabled, the first member of the first level in the hierarchy will be used as default member.
- `memberReaderClass`—Name of a custom member reader class. This specified class must implement `mondrian.rolap.MemberReader`. Typically you would not specify a customer member reader, but let Mondrian read the members from the RDBMS according to the schema's database mappings. Configuring this option is an advanced action that is beyond the scope of this book.
- `primaryKeyTable`—Can be used to specify the name of the table from which this hierarchy queries its members. If not specified, members are queried from the hierarchy's table. You can normally leave this blank if you're creating a cube on top of a star schema as in this example. The flexibility to specify a table name here is required when dealing with snowflake schemas or snowflaked dimensions.

- primaryKey—Typically, you should use this to specify the name of the primary key column of this hierarchy's dimension table. To be exact: this is the column name of the dimension table that is referenced by the rows in the fact table. This should be a column in this hierarchy's dimension table.

To configure the first hierarchy of the Date dimension, you need to specify the following properties:

- name—This should be Months, in accordance with the cube design mentioned in Table 15-1.
- hasAll—This should be enabled.
- primaryKey—This must be set to date_key, which is the primary key of the dim_date_en_us dimension table, which we configured for this hierarchy.

The design for this hierarchy is shown in Figure 15-15.

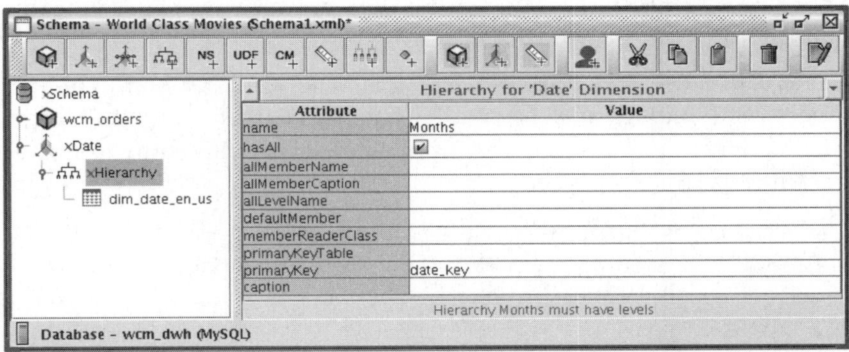

Figure 15-15: The design of the Months hierarchy of the Date dimension

In accordance with the cube design shown in Table 15-1, you should also add a Weeks hierarchy. To add the second hierarchy, you can either select the Date dimension node and then click the Add Hierarchy button on the toolbar, or right-click the Date dimension node and choose the Add hierarchy option in the context menu. As you saw when editing the Months hierarchy, the new Weeks hierarchy already contains a table node. You configure the table node exactly as you configured the Months hierarchy, and point it to the dim_date_en_us dimension table. Finally, the attributes configuration for the Weeks hierarchy should be identical to that of the Months hierarchy, except that the value of its name attribute should be Weeks rather than Months.

Adding Hierarchy Levels

Now that you created the hierarchies, you must define their levels. You can add a level to an existing hierarchy either by selecting it and then clicking the Add Level button on the toolbar, or by right-clicking the hierarchy and choosing the Add Level menu option. After adding a level, you can edit the following attributes:

- `name`—The name that is used to refer to this level in MDX queries.
- `table`—The name of the table that contains the columns where the dimension data is stored for this level. When not specified, the hierarchy's dimension table will be used. This is the normal situation for star schemas like the one used in this example. You need to specify a particular table only when dealing with snowflake schemas.
- `column`—The name of the column that represents the member identifier for this level. This must correspond to this level's table (see the `table` attribute).
- `nameColumn`—The name of the column that contains the name of this level. When not specified, the value of the `name` property is used. Typically you should leave this blank.
- `parentColumn`—This applies only to special kinds of hierarchies called *parent-child* hierarchies. Normally you leave this blank but if you're dealing with a parent-child hierarchy, you use this attribute to specify the column that references the parent member.
- `nullParentValue`—When dealing with a parent-child relationship, you can use this attribute to specify which value indicates the parent member does not exist. Leave this blank when not dealing with parent-child hierarchies.
- `ordinalColumn`—This attribute can be used to specify which column defines how the member values should be sorted by default. You should specify this whenever the natural sorting order of the members themselves does not fit the desired sorting order. If the natural sorting order of the members is also the desired sorting order, you can leave this blank. Sometimes you can still specify a column here if the `ordinalColumn` has a more suitable data type for sorting than the column that provides the member values.
- `type`—The data type of the member values. This is used to control if and how values must be quoted when generating SQL from MDX queries.
- `uniqueMembers`—A flag indicating whether all the members at this level have unique values. This is always true for the first level (not counting the all level) of any hierarchy. If you know it to be true for any of the subsequent levels, you can specify it there, too, and this may enable

Mondrian to generate more efficient SQL queries. Do not enable this if you are not 100 percent sure the values are unique, as it could cause incorrect results to be returned.

- `levelType`—If you leave this blank, it will be assumed this is a regular level, which is the correct value for most dimensions. Dimensions that were configured to be of the type TimeDimension must specify one of the predefined types for TimeDimension levels: TimeYears, TimeQuarters, TimeMonths, TimeWeeks, and TimeDays. For TimeDimensions, specifying the `levelType` is a prerequisite for correct usage of the Mondrian date/time functions such as YTD.
- `hideMemberIf`—This determines in which cases a member should be hidden. Typically, you can leave this blank, which is equivalent to setting the value to `Never`. In this case, the member is always shown.
- `approxRowCount`—The estimated number of members at this level. Specifying a good estimate for this attribute may allow Mondrian to make better decisions on how to query and/or cache the data, which can enhance performance.
- `caption`—The name that will be used to present this level to the user by the user interface. When not specified, the name of the level will be used.
- `captionColumn`—Here you can specify which column of the level's dimension table should be used to present the members to the end user. When not specified, the member identifier will be used. (See the column attribute for more information on this.)
- `formatter`—This can be used to specify a custom formatter, much like we already discussed for the Measures.

Now that we discussed the possible attributes of the levels, we can actually add them. Tables 15-2 and 15-3 show the levels that you need to create for the Months and Weeks hierarchies respectively, and how you should configure their attributes.

Table 15-2: The levels of the Months hierarchy

NAME	LEVELTYPE	COLUMN	CAPTIONCOLUMN	UNIQUEMEMBERS
Year	TimeYears	`year4`		enabled
Quarter	TimeQuarters	`quarter_number`	`quarter_name`	disabled
Month	TimeMonths	`month_number`	`Month_abbreviation`	disabled
Day	TimeDays	`day_in_month`		disabled

Table 15-3 The levels of the Weeks hierarchy

NAME	LEVELTYPE	COLUMN	CAPTIONCOLUMN	UNIQUEMEMBERS
Year	TimeDays	`year4`		enabled
Week	TimeWeeks	`week_in_year`		disabled
Day	TimeDays	`day_in_week`	`day_abbreviation`	disabled

The result should look something like Figure 15-16.

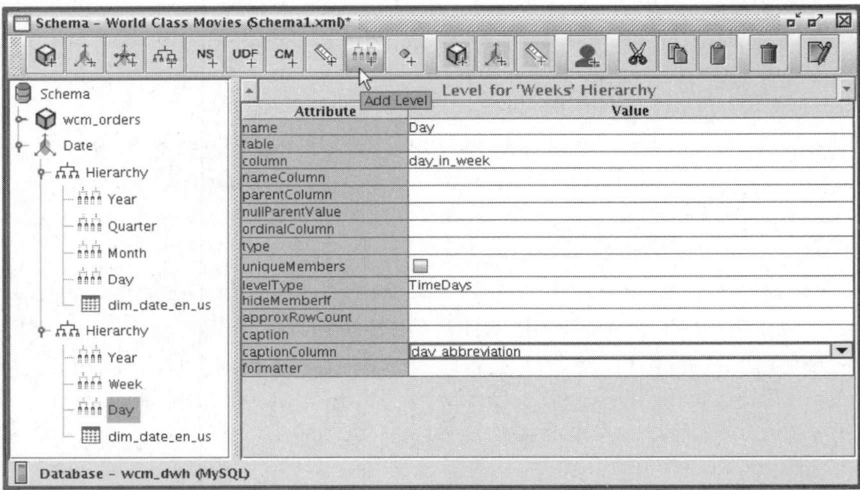

Figure 15-16: Levels for the Months and Weeks hierarchies

Associating Cubes with Shared Dimensions

In the previous sections, you built a shared Date dimension. Before you can use that in the `wcm_orders` cube, you need to associate the dimension and the cube. In Mondrian schemas, the association between a cube and a shared dimension is called a *dimension usage*. To add a dimension usage, either select the cube and click the Add Dimension usage button on the toolbar, or right-click the cube and choose the Add Dimension Usage option from the context menu. You can edit the following attributes for a dimension usage:

- `name`—The name that will be used to refer to the dimension in MDX queries. This name need not be identical to the name of the shared dimension itself. Rather, you should supply a name (or an alias if you will) that reflects the specific purpose of the dimension in relation to the cube. The ability to provide a specific, unique name each time you use a shared dimension is effectively a case of implementing role-playing dimensions.

- foreignKey—The name of the column in the cube's fact table that references the primary key of the dimension table. Recall that you had to specify the primary key column of the dimension table as the primaryKey attribute of the hierarchies; well, this is the counterpart, defining the fact table end of the relationship.
- source—This is the name of the shared dimension.
- level—Here you can specify a level name of the shared dimension that will be joined against the cube's fact table. For star schemas, it should typically be left blank.
- caption—The name used to present the dimension to the end user by the user interface. If left blank, the value of the name attribute will be used.

In case of the Date dimension, you need to configure the dimension usage as follows:

- name—Here you should specify the local order date. The date_dimension table upon which you base the Date dimension in the schema can play a number of roles with respect to the fact_orders table upon which you base the cube. For now, limit it to the local order date, which is reflected in the name.
- foreignKey—Here you must specify the local_order_date_key column of the fact_orders table in accordance with the role played by the Date dimension.
- source—Here you must specify Date, which is the name that identifies your dimension within the schema.

The result is shown in Figure 15-17.

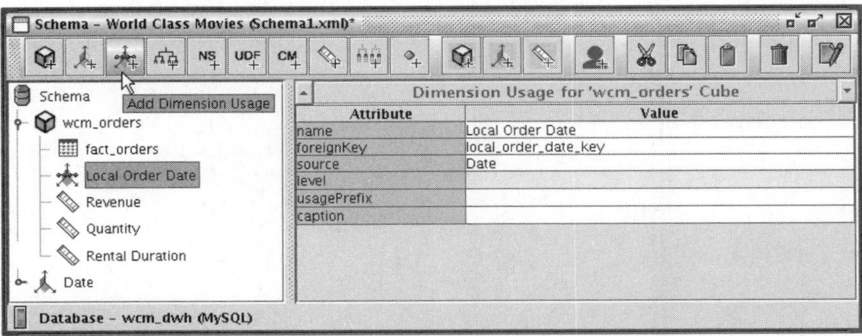

Figure 15-17: The dimension usage associating the cube with the Date dimension as Local Order Date

Adding the DVD and Customer Dimensions

To complete the schema, you need to add shared dimensions for the DVD and Customer dimensions and associate these with the `wcm_orders` cube. By now, you should be able to complete these steps on your own. To summarize, you should repeat the following steps for both dimensions:

- Add and edit a dimension.
- Choose a dimension table.
- Edit the hierarchy.
- Add and edit hierarchy levels.
- Associate the cube with the dimension.

Compared to adding the Date dimension, adding the DVD and Customer dimensions involves a few minor differences that actually simplify things:

- The DVD and Customer dimensions have only one hierarchy instead of two.
- Because these dimensions have only one hierarchy, you should blank out the `name` attribute of their respective hierarchies.
- Their `type` attribute of the dimension should specify `StandardDimension` (the default) rather than `TimeDimension`.
- Similarly, because the levels are also regular, you should not specify their `levelType` attribute.

For completeness, the following list provides an overview of the configuration of the DVD dimension and its association with the `wcm_orders` cube:

- `name`: DVD
- `type`: StandardDimension
- **Dimension Table**:
  - `name: dim_dvd_release`
- **Hierarchy:**
  - `hasAll: true`
  - `primaryKey: dvd_release_key`
  - **Genre Level:**
    - `name`: Genre
    - `column: dvd_release_genre`
    - `uniqueMembers: true`

- **Title Level:**
  - `name`: Genre
  - `column`: `dvd_release_genre`
  - `uniqueMembers`: `false`
- **Dimension Usage:**
  - `name`: DVD
  - `foreignKey`: `dvd_release_key`
  - `source`: DVD

The following list provides an overview of the configuration of the Customer dimension and its association with the `wcm_orders` cube:

- `name`: Customer
- `type`: StandardDimension
- **Dimension Table**:
  - `name`: `dim_customer`
- **Hierarchy:**
  - `hasAll`: `true`
  - `primaryKey`: `customer_key`
  - **Country Level:**
    - `name`: Country
    - `column`: `customer_country_code`
    - `uniqueMembers`: `true`
    - `captionColumn`: `customer_country_name`
  - **Region Level:**
    - `name`: Region
    - `column`: `customer_region_code`
    - `uniqueMembers`: `true`
    - `captionColumn`: `customer_region_name`
  - **City Level:**
    - `name`: City
    - `column`: `customer_city_name`
  - **Postal Code:**
    - `name`: Postal Code
    - `column`: `customer_postal_code`

- **Name:**
  - name: Name
  - column: customer_id
  - captionColumn: customer_last_name
- **Dimension Usage:**
  - name: Customer
  - foreignKey: customer_key
  - source: Customer

XML Listing

For completeness, we include the XML Source of the Mondrian schema here as Listing 15-1. We made a few (insignificant) changes to make the code more compact. You can use this for comparison to your own schema:

Listing 15-1: XML source of the Mondrian schema

```
<Schema name="World Class Movies">
 <Dimension type="TimeDimension" name="Date">
  <Hierarchy name="Months" hasAll="true" primaryKey="date_key">
   <Table name="dim_date_en_us"/>
   <Level name="Year" column="year4" uniqueMembers="true"
          levelType="TimeYears"/>
   <Level name="Quarter" column="quarter_number" uniqueMembers="false"
          levelType="TimeQuarters" captionColumn="quarter_name"/>
   <Level name="Month" column="month_number" uniqueMembers="false"
          levelType="TimeMonths" captionColumn="month_abbreviation"/>
   <Level name="Day" column="day_in_month" uniqueMembers="false"
          levelType="TimeDays"/>
  </Hierarchy>
  <Hierarchy name="Weeks" hasAll="true" primaryKey="date_key">
   <Table name="dim_date_en_us" schema="" alias=""/>
   <Level name="Year" column="year4" uniqueMembers="true"
          levelType="TimeYears"/>
   <Level name="Week" column="week_in_year" uniqueMembers="false"
          levelType="TimeWeeks"/>
   <Level name="Day" column="day_in_week" uniqueMembers="false"
          levelType="TimeDays" captionColumn="day_abbreviation"/>
  </Hierarchy>
 </Dimension>
 <Dimension type="StandardDimension" name="DVD">
  <Hierarchy hasAll="true" primaryKey="dvd_release_key">
   <Table name="dim_dvd_release" schema="" alias=""/>
   <Level name="Genre" column="dvd_release_genre" uniqueMembers="true"/>
   <Level name="Title" column="dvd_release_title" uniqueMembers="false"/>
  </Hierarchy>
 </Dimension>
```

```
 <Dimension type="StandardDimension" name="Customer">
  <Hierarchy hasAll="true" primaryKey="customer_key">
   <Table name="dim_customer" schema="" alias=""/>
   <Level name="Country" column="customer_country_code" uniqueMembers="true"
          captionColumn="customer_country_name"/>
   <Level name="Region" column="customer_region_code" uniqueMembers="true"
          captionColumn="customer_region_name"/>
   <Level name="City" column="customer_city_name" uniqueMembers="false"/>
   <Level name="Postal Code" column="customer_postal_code"
          uniqueMembers="false"/>
   <Level name="Name" column="customer_id" uniqueMembers="false"
          captionColumn="customer_last_name"/>
  </Hierarchy>
 </Dimension>
 <Cube name="wcm_orders" caption="World Class Movies Sales" cache="true"
enabled="true">
  <Table name="fact_orders"/>
  <DimensionUsage source="Date" name="Local Order Date"
foreignKey="local_order_date_key"/>
  <DimensionUsage source="DVD" name="DVD" foreignKey="dvd_release_key"/>
  <DimensionUsage source="Customer" name="Customer" foreignKey="customer_key"/>
  <Measure name="Revenue" column="revenue" formatString="Currency"
           aggregator="sum" visible="true"/>
  <Measure name="Quantity" column="quantity"
           aggregator="sum" visible="true"/>
  <Measure name="Rental Duration" column="rental_duration" formatString="#.00"
           aggregator="avg" visible="true"/>
 </Cube>
</Schema>
```

Testing and Deployment

Now that you created the schema, you are almost ready to use it. You must publish the cube to the Pentaho BI Server before you can use it to build OLAP applications. But before you deploy it, you might want to do some preliminary testing first.

Using the MDX Query Tool

PSW includes a basic MDX query tool. This is not suitable as an end-user reporting tool, but it is quite useful to test whether your cube is functional. You can also use it as an aid in developing MDX queries for direct use in your OLAP solutions.

You can invoke the MDX query tool from the main menu by choosing: File ➤ New ➤ MDX. The MDX editor pops up in its own window. If you happen to have an open schema editor, the MDX query tool attempts to connect to the underlying database as well as load the schema definition.

This is shown in Figure 15-18.

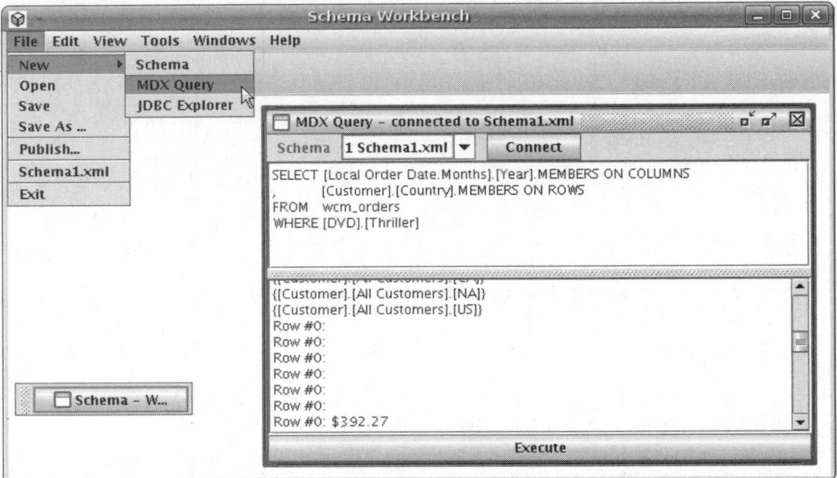

Figure 15-18: The MDX query tool

The MDX query tool has an upper pane and a lower pane. You can enter MDX queries in the upper pane. The MDX query is executed when you click the Execute button that appears at the bottom of the MDX Query tool. The results are shown in the lower pane.

You can now try out some of the MDX queries discussed earlier in this chapter.

Publishing the Cube

When you are satisfied with the cube design, you can publish the cube to the Pentaho BI Server. To invoke the publish dialog, make sure you have a schema opened in the schema editor. Activate the schema editor window. Then choose File ➤ Publish from the main menu, and the dialog pops up, as shown in Figure 15-19.

For the URL, specify the web address of the Pentaho BI Server to which you want to publish the schema. You must use the publisher password that you specified in the server's `publisher_config.xml` file. For the username and password, specify the credentials of any user who is privileged to publish.

When you confirm the dialog, a connection is made with the solution repository, which can take some time. If the connection succeeds, a dialog appears that allows you to browse the server's solution repository. Choose the appropriate path—for example, `/WCM/Analysis`.

In the bottom of the dialog, you can specify which of the server's JNDI data sources to use at the server side to execute the SQL queries. If you enable the checkbox Register XMLA Datasource, the schema is registered as an OLAP data source in the server. This allows the user interface to display a list of schemas.

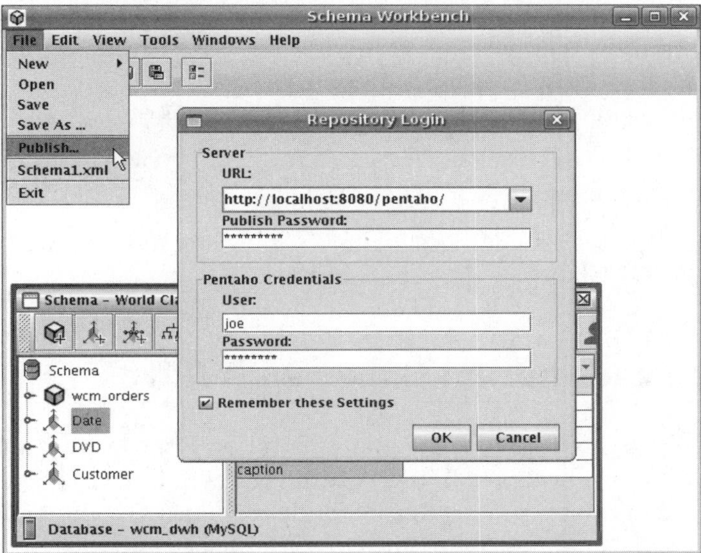

Figure 15-19: Publishing a schema to the solution repository

Schema Design Topics We Didn't Cover

In the previous subsections, you learned how to build a basic Mondrian schema and cube. Although we covered a lot of ground in that respect, there are many topics that we didn't cover. Here's a partial list:

- **Calculated members**—Mondrian cubes can contain definitions of calculated members.
- **Roles and access control**—Schema and cube elements can be associated with roles to grant only certain groups of users access to particular elements of the cube.
- **Working with snowflaked dimensions**—We based our example entirely on a simple star schema, using only one-to-one relationships between each dimension table and its respective cube dimension. But Mondrian is capable of much more advanced mappings that allow you to create cubes on snowflake schemas.
- **Conditional formatting**—We briefly discussed format strings, but formats can actually be specified as formulas that return a particular markup that can be rendered by the user interface. This allows you to do things such as display measures in different colors depending upon their value.

- **Internationalization**—Many of the attributes of schema elements can be given a variable, locale-dependent value of the form `%propertyname%`. The actual values for these properties can then be defined in a separate `.properties` file. This can be used to implement internationalized OLAP applications by using the appropriate `.properties` file for a given locale. You can, for example, use this to pick between an English and a French date dimension table as discussed in earlier chapters..
- **User-defined functions**—You can create your own function as Java classes and import these into your schema.

If you are interested in these features, refer to the original Mondrian documentation at `mondrian.pentaho.org`.

Visualizing Mondrian Cubes with JPivot

After publishing the cube to the Pentaho Solution Repository it can be used to build analysis applications. In this section, you will learn to create dynamic pivot tables to browse and analyze Mondrian cubes. Through these pivot tables, business users can drill up and down, and slice and dice the data.

Getting Started with the Analysis View

The user console of the Pentaho BI Server offers the possibility to create an *analysis view*, which is essentially a JPivot cross table on top of a Mondrian cube, wrapped in a Pentaho process action. To create a new analysis view, click the analysis view icon on the toolbar or on the initial workspace page. You will be prompted to choose a schema, and within the schema, a cube. This is shown in Figure 15-20.

After you choose the schema and cube and confirm the dialog, a pivot table appears. Initially, the default members of all dimensions are displayed on the vertical axis, and the default measure is displayed on the horizontal axis. Remember that normally the default member is the all member, so the result is a table with a single value at the highest possible aggregation level. This is shown in Figure 15-21.

If you like, you can save the analysis view for use later by clicking one of the floppy disk icons on the toolbar of the Pentaho User Console. You will be prompted to supply a location within the repository as well as a name.

In the remainder of this section, we discuss methods that allow you to obtain radically different views on the data in the analysis view. When saving the pivot table, the state of the table will also be saved, allowing you to recall a specific view on the data you are interested in. If you see something you like, save it using a new name.

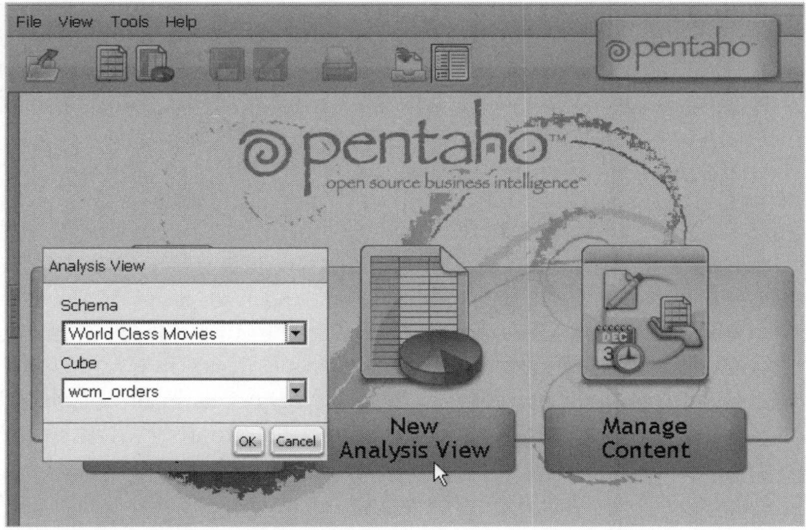

Figure 15-20: Creating an analysis view

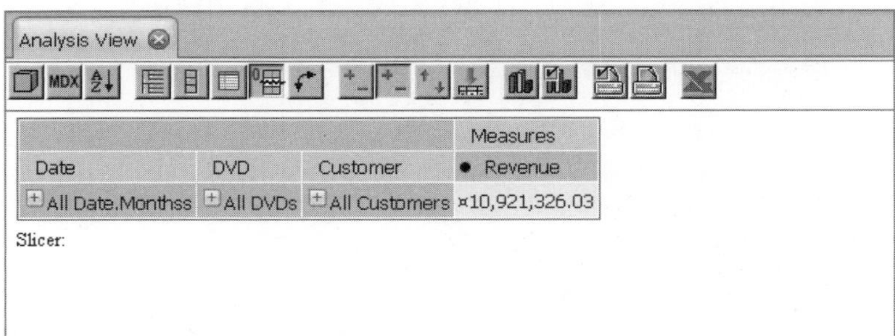

Figure 15-21: The default pivot table

Using the JPivot Toolbar

In addition to the pivot table, JPivot provides a toolbar at the top of the page. On this toolbar you'll find a number of interesting actions. The toolbar is shown in Figure 15-22.

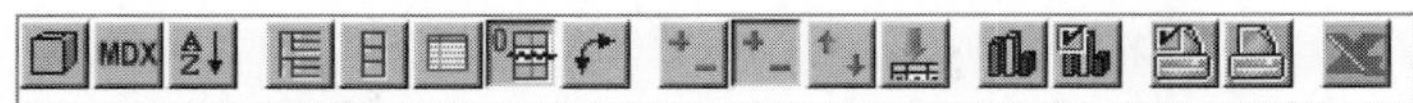

Figure 15-22: JPivot's toolbar

We discuss a few of the toolbar buttons in the following sections.

Drilling

One of the great features of a pivot table is that it is interactive and dynamic. A typical feature in this respect is its *drilling* functionality. Drilling is essentially a form of data browsing where the user navigates from one level of aggregation to another. Support for data browsing is probably the most important reason for requiring a hierarchical organization of dimensions in levels.

In Figure 15-21, you might have noticed the little + icons on the all members of the dimensions. Clicking such a plus icon expands the member, revealing the members at the next level (which represents a lower level of aggregation). At the same time, the measures are re-aggregated to fit the level of the new set of revealed members. This type of action is commonly known as *drilling down*, as you're navigating from the current level of aggregation of one member to a lower level of aggregation applicable to its child members. For example, if you take the Date dimension in the pivot table shown in Figure 15-21 and drill down one level from the All Dates member to the Year level, revealing the individual Year member, you would get something resembling Figure 15-23.

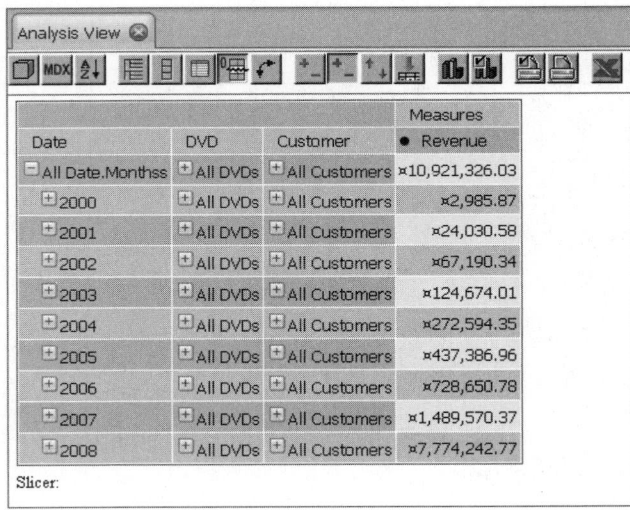

			Measures
Date	DVD	Customer	• Revenue
All Date.Monthss	All DVDs	All Customers	¤10,921,326.03
2000	All DVDs	All Customers	¤2,985.87
2001	All DVDs	All Customers	¤24,030.58
2002	All DVDs	All Customers	¤67,190.34
2003	All DVDs	All Customers	¤124,674.01
2004	All DVDs	All Customers	¤272,594.35
2005	All DVDs	All Customers	¤437,386.96
2006	All DVDs	All Customers	¤728,650.78
2007	All DVDs	All Customers	¤1,489,570.37
2008	All DVDs	All Customers	¤7,774,242.77

Figure 15-23: Drilling down from all to year

Drilling Flavors

There are a number of different ways a user's drilling action can result in a particular drill result. The methods are:

- Drill Member
- Drill Position

- Drill Replace
- Drill Through

The drilling method is controlled through the toolbar buttons shown in Figure 15-24.

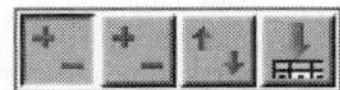

Figure 15-24: The drilling method toolbar buttons

The first three methods are applicable to dimensions. You can use only one of these methods at a time. The fourth method applies to measures. It can be enabled independently of the other three methods.

Drill Member and Drill Position

By default, JPivot uses the *drill member* action. With this action, the drilling on one instance of a member is also applied to all other instances of this member. This behavior is enabled by toggling the first of the drilling method toolbar buttons.

To see drill member in action, ensure that this toolbar button is toggled. Now suppose you start drilling in the table shown in Figure 15-23 at the All Customers member of the year 2000. The drill action will be applied to all other occurrences of All Customers, and the result would look something like Figure 15-25.

			Measures
Date	DVD	Customer	• Revenue
All Date.Monthss	All DVDs	All Customers	¤10,921,326.03
		Canada	¤752,988.55
		United States	¤10,168,337.48
2000	All DVDs	All Customers	¤2,985.87
		United States	¤2,985.87
2001	All DVDs	All Custo	
			,511.48
	DVDs	All Customers	¤1,489,570.37
		Canada	¤80,279.18
		United States	¤1,409,291.19
2008	All DVDs	All Customers	¤7,774,242.77
		Canada	¤658,570.07
		United States	¤7,115,672.70

Figure 15-25: Drill member on All Customers of 2000 will also expand the All Customers member for all other years

As you can see in Figure 15-25, drilling down to All Customers of the year 2000 reveals the Customer members at the next level for all years, not just the year 2000.

The second drill flavor is *drill position*. This can be enabled by toggling the second of the drilling method toolbar buttons. In this case, drilling occurs directly on the member instance and is not applied to any other instances of that member. If you use this method to drill down at the All Customers member during the year 2000 in the table shown in Figure 15-23, only the members below the customers of the year 2000 are revealed, and they would remain hidden for all the other years.

Drill Replace

With the *drill replace* method, the drilled member is replaced with the drill result. You enable this method by toggling the third drill method toolbar button. For example, suppose you have a table like the one shown in Figure 15-21. If you used drill replace on the All Customers member, the result would look like Figure 15-26.

			Measures
Date	DVD	Customer	Revenue
All Date.Monthss	All DVDs	Canada	752,988.55
		United States	10,168,337.48

Figure 15-26: Drill replace removes the drilled member with the drill result

As you can see in Figure 15-26, the All Customers member is gone. Instead you see the members at the new level.

Drill Through

Whereas all the previously discussed drilling methods apply to dimensions, *drill through* applies to the measures. A drill through action retrieves the detail rows (fact table rows) corresponding to the rolled up measure aggregate value, displaying the results in a separate table. Drill through can be enabled by toggling the fourth drill method toolbar button.

The OLAP Navigator

The OLAP Navigator is a graphical user interface that allows you to control how JPivot maps the cube onto the pivot table. You can use it to control which dimension is mapped to which axis, how multiple dimensions on one axis are ordered, and what slice of the cube is used in analysis.

You can open the OLAP Navigator by clicking on the toolbar button with the little cube icon. This is shown in Figure 15-27.

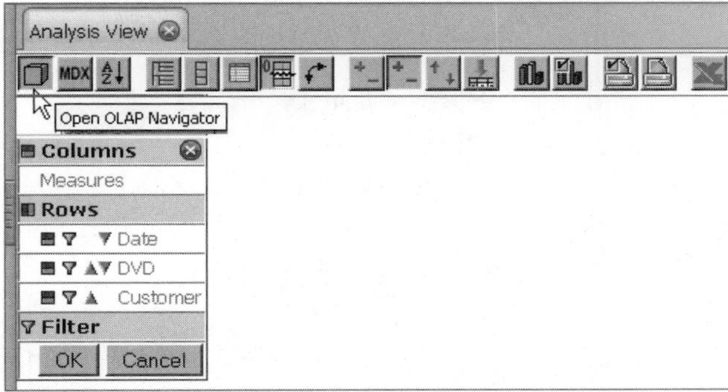

Figure 15-27: The OLAP Navigator

Figure 15-27 has the following elements:

- A Columns section, currently containing only Measures
- A Rows section, currently containing all dimensions
- A Filter section, which is currently empty

In the remainder of this section, we explore these different elements of the OLAP Navigator, and see how you can use them to obtain different cross sections of the cube's data.

Controlling Placement of Dimensions on Axes

In OLAP Navigator, you can move a dimension to another axis by clicking the little square icon before the dimension. For example, clicking the square icon that is displayed right before the Customer dimension moves the Customer dimension from the Rows axis to the Columns axis. (See Figure 15-28.)

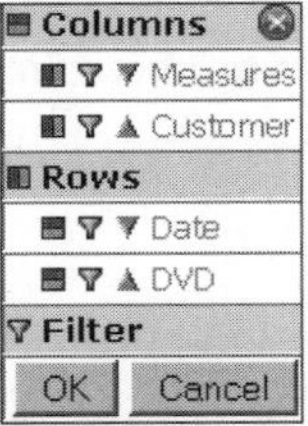

Figure 15-28: Moving the Customer dimension to the Columns axis

You can also change the order of dimensions within one axis. To do that, click the little triangular icons to move the position of a dimension. For example, if you click the little up-pointing triangle icon before the Customer dimension, it is moved up one position. You obtain the same effect by clicking on the little downward triangular icon right before the Measures dimension. The resulting situation is shown in Figure 15-29.

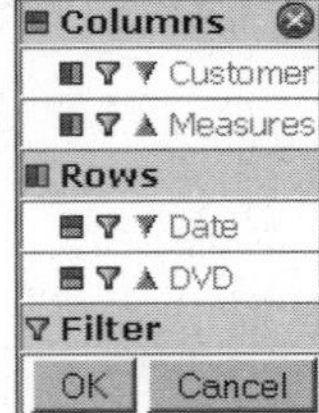

Figure 15-29: Changing the order of the Measures and Customer dimensions

Note that we've only been editing in the OLAP Navigator itself—the pivot table itself hasn't changed. If you now click OK in the OLAP Navigator, the OLAP Navigator is hidden and the page is automatically reloaded to reflect the change in the axes. The result is shown in Figure 15-30.

		Customer
		All Customers
		Measures
Date	DVD	Revenue
All Date.Monthss	All DVDs	¤10,921,326.03
2000	All DVDs	¤2,985.87
2001	All DVDs	¤24,030.58
2002	All DVDs	¤67,190.34
2003	All DVDs	¤124,674.01
2004	All DVDs	¤272,594.35
2005	All DVDs	¤437,386.96
2006	All DVDs	¤728,650.78
2007	All DVDs	¤1,489,570.37
2008	All DVDs	¤7,774,242.77

Figure 15-30: Customer dimension on the horizontal axis

Slicing with the OLAP Navigator

The OLAP Navigator is not limited to column and row axis manipulation. You can also use it to specify the slicer. Recall that the slicer corresponds to the MDX `WHERE` clause and can be used to show only a particular subset or "slice" of the data. Let's use the slice to look only at a particular group of DVDs. To do so, you must first reopen the OLAP Navigator. It should look exactly like Figure 15-29 at this point. Now click the little funnel icon right before the DVD dimension. This causes the DVD dimension to move to the slicer, as shown in Figure 15-31.

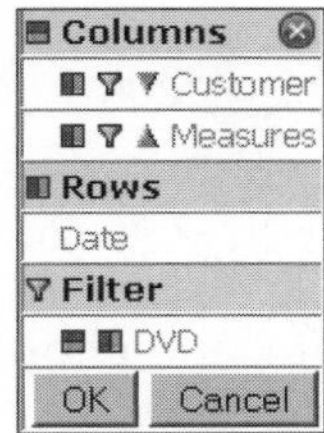

Figure 15-31: Moving the DVD dimension to the slicer

Now, although you moved the dimension to the slicer, your ''slice'' still contains all the DVD data. This is understandable as the all member is the default member and the all member contains all DVDs. To look at a part of all DVDs, you need to specify which members of the DVD dimension you're interested in. To do so, click the word DVD. You get a menu like the one shown in Figure 15-32.

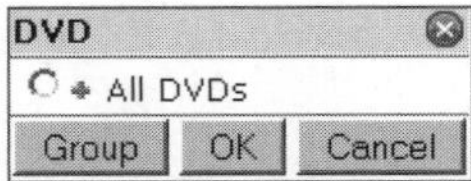

Figure 15-32: The DVD slicer

When you click the plus icon, the DVD dimension expands inside the OLAP Navigator, showing its members. You can then choose one member to define the slice. Select the slice Action/Adventure. This is shown in Figure 15-33.

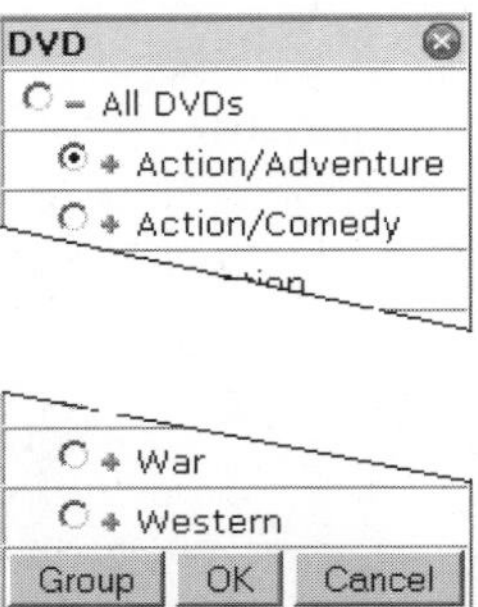

Figure 15-33: Choosing one genre slice

Remember that you must click OK to close the OLAP Navigator before any changes will be visible in the Pivot table.

Specifying Member Sets with the OLAP Navigator

You just learned how you can specify a particular member in the slicer. You can also specify particular members on the columns and rows axes.

1. Open the OLAP Navigator, and click Customer.
2. Expand Customer, and select only Canada and United States.
3. Click OK to confirm.
4. Then, click Date. Expand Date, and choose only 2007 and 2008.
5. Click OK to confirm.

The selections are shown in Figure 15-34.

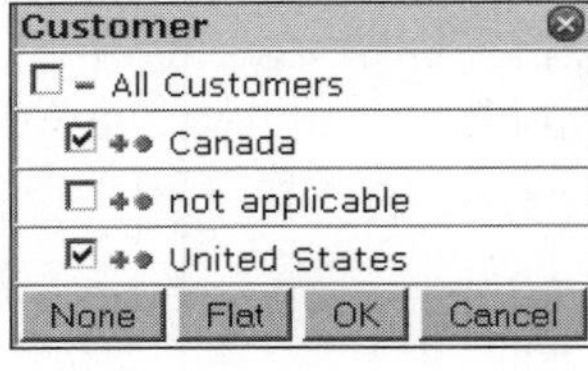

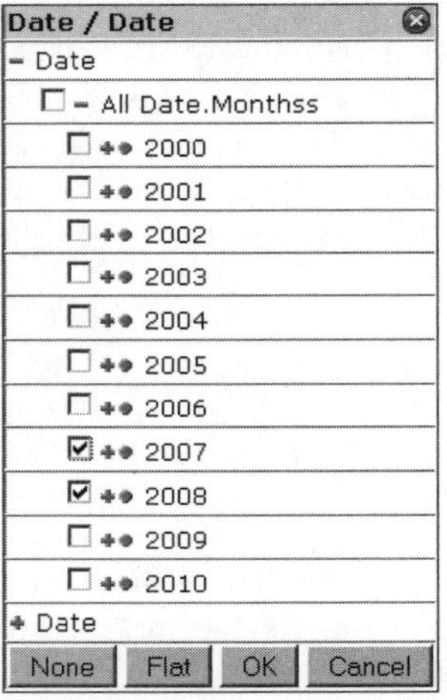

Figure 15-34: Choosing particular members for the axes

If you close the OLAP Navigator, the pivot table is updated to look like Figure 15-35.

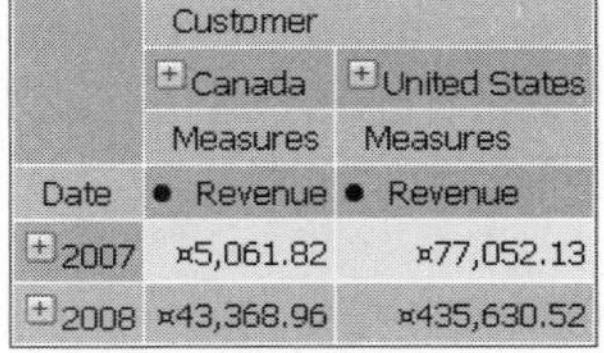

	Customer	
	Canada	United States
	Measures	Measures
Date	• Revenue	• Revenue
2007	¤5,061.82	¤77,052.13
2008	¤43,368.96	¤435,630.52

Slicer: [Genre=Action/Adventure]

Figure 15-35: Years 2007 and 2008, Customers from Canada and the United States, sliced by Action/Adventure

Displaying Multiple Measures

We can use the OLAP Navigator also to show more measures. Open the OLAP Navigator, and click Measures. A menu appears showing all measures defined in the cube (see Figure 15-36.)

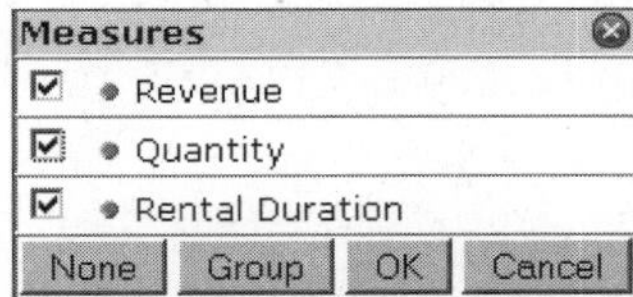

Figure 15-36: Selecting multiple measures

Now select the remaining measures and click OK to close the OLAP Navigator. The result is shown in Figure 15-37.

	Customer					
	Canada			United States		
	Measures			Measures		
Date	• Revenue	• Quantity	• Rental Duration	• Revenue	• Quantity	• Rental Duration
2007	¤5,061.82	614	17.13	¤77,052.13	10,839	17.39
2008	¤43,368.96	4,627	15.35	¤435,630.52	54,218	16.29

Slicer: [Genre=Action/Adventure]

Figure 15-37: A pivot table having multiple measures

Miscellaneous Features

In this section, we briefly discuss a number of useful JPivot features that we haven't covered elsewhere.

MDX Query Pane

You can toggle the visibility of the MDX query pane using the second button on the JPivot toolbar (which says MDX). This query pane contains the MDX query that represents the current state of the analysis view.

The MDX query pane is very useful to explore and learn the MDX syntax. Browsing a pivot table and interpreting the rendered result is quite straightforward for most people—more so than the understanding the text-based results returned by the PSW MDX editor.

You can also use the MDX query pane to temporarily add a definition for a calculated member and immediately inspect the results. You can go back and forth a few times between the MDX pane and the pivot table until you're satisfied. You can then place the code for this calculated member directly inside the cube.

PDF and Excel Export

The analysis view enables you to export the rendered result to both PDF and Microsoft Excel formats with a single mouse click. To export to Excel, just click on the JPivot toolbar button with the Excel icon. This is located at the far right of the JPivot toolbar.

Chart

JPivot also offers a charting feature. You display the chart by toggling the Show Chart toolbar button (the barchart icon at the right half of the JPivot toolbar). You can control the way your chart looks using the Chart Config button, located on the right side of the Show Chart toolbar button. Toggling the Chart Config button displays a Chart Properties form where you can specify all kinds of properties of your chart, such as the type of chart, and chart size. We cannot possibly cover JPivot charting in full. Instead, we encourage you to experiment with this feature. To get started, we provide instructions to create a chart like the one displayed in Figure 15-38.

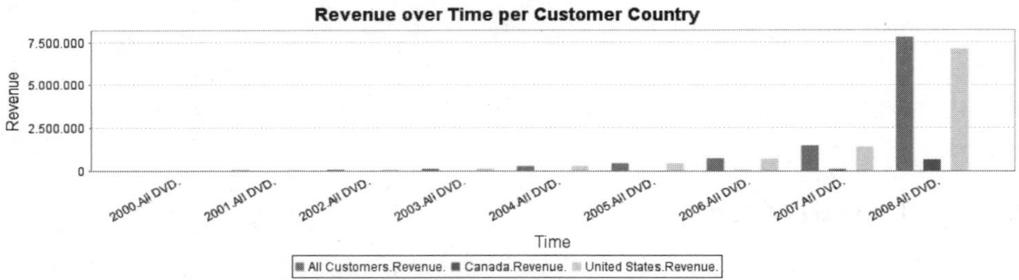

Figure 15-38: A JPivot chart showing revenue over time split by customer country

The chart shown in Figure 15-38 provides an insight in the revenue developments over time, split by country of residency of the customers. The chart data that is visualized in the chart is shown in Figure 15-39.

You can obtain this view on the data by placing the Date and DVD dimensions on the vertical axis and the Customer dimension on the horizontal axis. Be sure to expand the All Customers member to split the data according to the customer's country of residence. In addition, you should remove the All member from the Date dimension. (If you don't remove the All member here, the revenue for the first couple of years will be hardly visible in comparison to the large revenues accumulated for the All Dates member.)

		Customer		
		All Customers	Canada	United States
		Measures	Measures	Measures
Date	DVD	• Revenue	• Revenue	• Revenue
2000	All DVD	2,985.87		2,985.87
2001	All DVD	24,030.58		24,030.58
2002	All DVD	67,190.34		67,190.34
2003	All DVD	124,674.01		124,674.01
2004	All DVD	272,594.35		272,594.35
2005	All DVD	437,386.96		437,386.96
2006	All DVD	728,650.78	14,139.30	714,511.48
2007	All DVD	1,489,570.37	80,279.18	1,409,291.19
2008	All DVD	7,774,242.77	658,570.07	7,115,672.70

Figure 15-39: Data for the chart shown in Figure 15-38

Figure 15-40 shows the Chart configuration. We entered a few properties to configure the chart:

- **Chart Type: Vertical Bar.** There is a wide range of chart types available.
- **Enable Drill Through: checked.** This allows the user to click on the bars in the chart to examine the underlying detail rows.

Chart Properties	
Chart Type	Vertical Bar
Enable Drill Through	☑
Chart Title	Revenue over Time per Customer
Chart Title Font	SansSerif, Bold, 18
Horizontal axis label	Time
Vertical axis label	Revenue
Axes Label Font	SansSerif, Plain, 16
Axes Tick Label font	SansSerif, Plain, 12, 30°
Show Legend	☑ Bottom
Legend Font	SansSerif, Plain, 12
Show Slicer	☑ Bottom, Left
Slicer Font	SansSerif, Plain, 12
Chart Height	300 Chart Width 1000
Background (R, G, B)	255 255 255
	OK Cancel

Figure 15-40: Chart properties for the chart shown in Figure 15-38

- **Horizontal axis label: Time; Vertical axis label: Revenue.** Entering a label makes it much easier for users to interpret the chart.
- **Chart Height, Chart Width:** the height and width in pixels of the chart. You will find that you often need to experiment with these values to get a reasonably readable chart.

Enhancing Performance Using the Pentaho Aggregate Designer

Mondrian does a great job of caching results, giving you fast access to previously retrieved cube members. With large databases, however, it takes considerable time navigate a cube because you are working with a ROLAP tool that needs to retrieve data from large, detailed fact tables. To avoid having to scan millions of rows each time a new dimension level is selected, you can pre-aggregate the data for Mondrian. In Chapter 6, we explained the concepts of aggregate tables and materialized views as performance boosters and mentioned that, to date, none of the open source databases supports the latter. Well, this may be true for the databases themselves, but the behavior of Mondrian using aggregate tables comes very close to having materialized view support. There is one notable difference, however, and that is the automated maintenance of the aggregate tables each time new data is loaded into the data warehouse. One way to solve this issue is to extend your Kettle jobs to update the Mondrian aggregate tables at the end of loading the detailed data into the data warehouse. Using the housekeeping date and time columns or a batch ID makes it easy to identify changed or inserted records and use that as the source for updating or inserting records in the aggregates.

Aggregation Benefits

The sole benefit of using aggregates is to improve query performance, or in the case of Mondrian, ad-hoc analysis speed. Aggregate tables accomplish this by limiting the number of records to be scanned in a query. Take a look at Figure 15-41 to see the effects of aggregation. The left side of the diagram shows a simplified version of the WCM order fact table with 1,359,267 rows in it because the lowest transaction level of the data is stored in this table. Now look at the upper right of the diagram where we created aggregate tables for the detailed fact rows at the level of Month, DVD Genre, and Country. This results in a dramatic decrease in table size because you need only 9,120 rows to store all possible combinations of data at these levels.

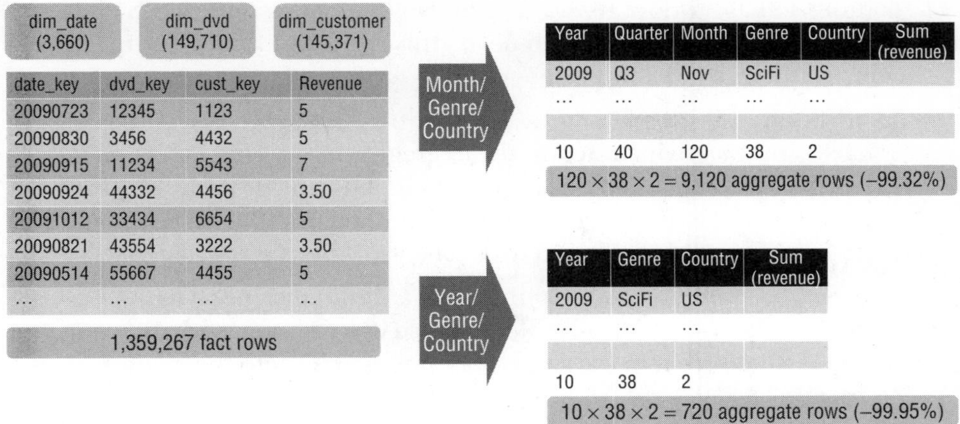

Figure 15-41: Aggregation examples

An additional reduction can be obtained when you omit the quarter and month level altogether. You could still create a valuable cross tab report or analysis view based on these 720 rows of data, which is a reduction in size of almost 99.95 percent. Queries against these aggregate tables produce sub-second response times and very happy users. The question is, how do you incorporate this knowledge in your Mondrian setup?

Extending Mondrian with Aggregate Tables

Before there was an automated tool for designing the aggregate tables, it was a manual process. The next section will cover Pentaho's Aggregate Designer; although you will most likely use this tool for designing and building aggregates, you need to know what's happening under the hood in case something goes wrong. The example we show here is based on the upper-right aggregate table in Figure 15-41. The first step is to create a new table in the data warehouse schema:

```
CREATE TABLE agg_wcm_orders_1 (
    dim_date_Year CHAR(4),
    dim_date_Quarter CHAR(2),
    dim_date_Month CHAR(3),
    dim_customer_Country CHAR(2),
    dim_dvd_release_Genre VARCHAR(35),
    fact_orders_Revenue DOUBLE,
    fact_orders_fact_count INTEGER)
```

As you continue, keep the following points in mind:

- The example aggregate table not only contains the columns you need for analysis but has an extra `fact_count` column as well. The content of this column tells you how many fact rows have been summarized into the aggregate row. Mondrian also needs this extra column to verify that the table is an aggregate and can be used as such.

- In addition to the `dim_date_Month`, the `dim_date_Quarter` and `dim_date_Year` columns are included in the aggregate table. This inclusion allows Mondrian to derive all the required dimension information from the aggregate table and doesn't require you to include the `dim_date` table in the query. This is also referred to as *collapsed dimension* or *conformed rollup*.
- The `fact_orders_Revenue` column is of a different type than the `revenue` column in the `fact_orders` table. Because you are summarizing data, you need to make sure that the summed values still fit into the columns at the aggregate level.
- The diagram in Figure 15-41 shows all dimensions in both aggregate tables. This doesn't need to be the case: the Genre column could have been left out of either aggregate table and it would still be a valid aggregate. By doing this, we would create an aggregate with a *lost dimension* (genre).

The SQL query shown in Listing 15-2 can be used to load the aggregate table.

Listing 15-2: SQL query for loading the aggregate table

```
INSERT INTO agg_wcm_orders_1 (
            dim_date_year
,           dim_date_quarter
,           dim_date_month
,           dim_customer_country
,           dim_dvd_release_Genre
,           fact_orders_revenue
,           fact_orders_fact_count )
SELECT      dim_date.year4                       AS dim_date_year
,           dim_date.quarter_name                AS dim_date_quarter
,           dim_date.month_abbreviation          AS dim_date_month
,           dim_customer.customer_country_code AS dim_customer_country
,           dim_dvd_release.dvd_release_genre  AS dim_dvd_release_genre
,           SUM(fact_orders.revenue)             AS fact_orders_revenue
,           COUNT(*)                             AS fact_orders_fact_count
FROM        fact_orders AS f
INNER JOIN dim_date        AS d ON f.local_order_date_key = d.date_key
INNER JOIN dim_customer    AS c ON f.customer_key         = c.customer_key
INNER JOIN dim_dvd_release AS r ON f.dvd_release_key      = r.dvd_release_key
GROUP BY    d.year4
,           d.quarter_name
,           d.month_abbreviation
,           c.customer_country_code
,           r.dvd_release_genre
```

TIP **An aggregate that is based on another aggregate—for instance, a table with only Year, Country, and Revenue—should be loaded from the aggregate, not from the base fact table. This can result in a considerable performance gain.**

After this has been set up, you can use the PSW again to specify the aggregate table in your existing cube. When you expand the `wcm_orders` cube and right-click on `fact_orders`, a menu opens with three options. The first enables you to declare a new aggregate table and the third enables you to explicitly exclude a table. The second option is actually the more interesting one because it lets you define a pattern that Mondrian uses to determine which tables in the database are aggregates that can be used. Explaining the required regular expressions and how this feature works is beyond the scope of this book but this topic is covered in depth on the Pentaho Mondrian website at `http://mondrian.pentaho.org/documentation/developer_notes.php#Agg_default_rules`.

In this example, stick with the first option, which lets you add the `agg_wcm_orders_1` aggregate name. This changes the `fact_orders` icon and adds a level called Aggregate Name, which in turn offers a right-click menu of its own. Here you need to specify the Aggregate fact count column (in this case: `fact_orders_fact_count`), Aggregate Levels, and Aggregate Measures. The levels and measures have two attributes: the column and the name of the item. The column refers to the column name in the aggregate table, but the name is the MDX specification of the level—for instance `[Customer].[Country]` for the `customer_country` column and `[Local Order Date].[Month]` for the `month_number` column. An example is displayed in Figure 15-42.

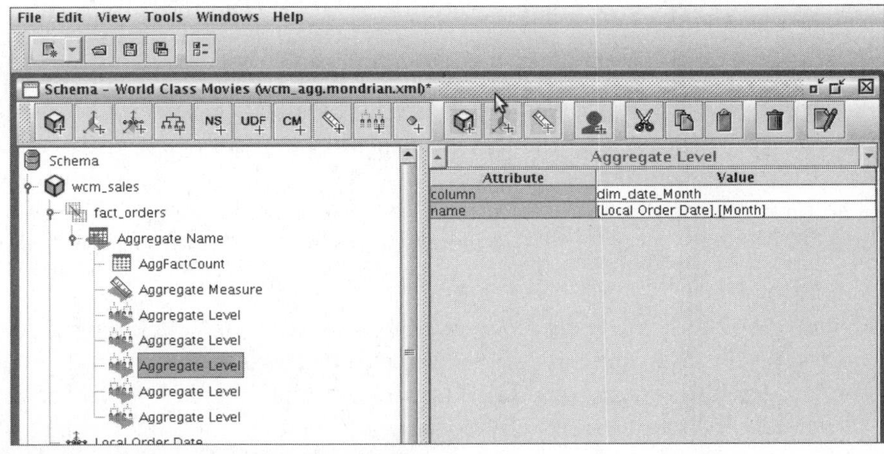

Figure 15-42: Aggregate Level specification

So far we've used only aggregate columns in our aggregate tables, but you can create a summarized table where one or more columns still contain the detailed dimension key. In that case, there's no need to collapse the dimension and include the different levels in the aggregate table as in the Year-Quarter-Month example. If you wanted to be able to drill down to the day level, combined with an aggregate on Country and Genre, you could replace the Year, Quarter, and Month columns with a single `date_key` and specify that as an Aggregate Foreign Key. The agg column would in that case be the `date_key`, and the fact column would be the original `local_order_date_key` column.

> **ENABLING AGGREGATE TABLES**
>
> **The use of aggregate tables in Mondrian is disabled by default. You can enable this feature by setting the values of `mondrian.rolap.aggregates.Use` and `mondrian.rolap.aggregates.Read` to `True` in the Mondrian properties file. This file can be found in the directory `<pentaho install dir>/biserver-ce/pentaho-solutions/system/Mondrian`. If the properties are not present, just add the following lines to this file:**
>
> ```
> mondrian.rolap.aggregates.Use=1
> mondrian.rolap.aggregates.Read=1
> ```

Pentaho Aggregate Designer

The previous paragraph covered the manual setup of aggregate tables within Pentaho. Now that you have a basic understanding of what's going on when you are creating aggregate tables, it's time to make life a little easier by using the Pentaho Aggregate Designer, or PAD. PAD offers a couple of advantages over the manual process of creating aggregate tables. The most important of them is that PAD is capable of automagically selecting the best aggregate tables for the schema you're trying to optimize. When you start PAD, it asks for a database connection. After that's configured, you need to select a Mondrian schema file, and after applying the choice, the cube to work with can be opened. PAD then validates the underlying data model by checking that all tables have primary keys and that no null values are present in the foreign key columns. PAD warns you when the fact table does not contain a primary key. You can use PAD to do any of the following:

- Create your aggregate table definitions manually by clicking the Add button on the right side and subsequently select the aggregation levels on the left. Each new aggregate table is added to the list in the lower right of the screen and can be edited by clicking it.

- Preview, execute, or export the create script for the aggregates from the Export and Publish screen, which can be opened by clicking the Export button.
- Execute or export the load scripts for the aggregate tables from the same Export screen.
- Publish the adjusted Mondrian schema to a Pentaho Server or export the file to a location on disk.

These are all very useful features but the real fun begins when you click the Advisor button. Here you can specify how many aggregates PAD can try to generate and how long the advisor queries are allowed to run. In this simple example you can say 15 aggregates and 60 seconds and click Recommend. PAD then tries to determine all aggregates based on the cube design and the column counts of the underlying data model. Figure 15-43 shows the results of this exercise for the `wcm_orders` cube.

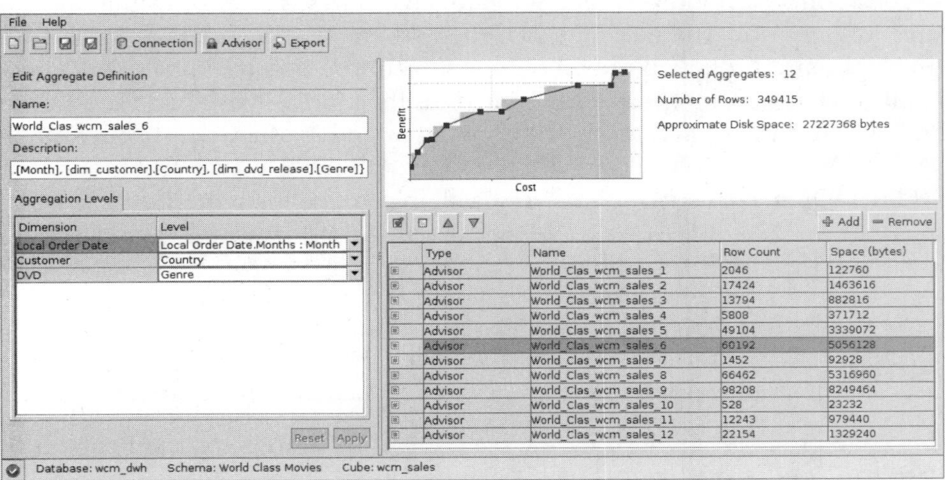

Figure 15-43: Generated Aggregate tables

This is still a recommendation created by PAD, which you can approve or reject. Another option is to manually adjust the Advisor tables or drop the ones you feel won't be necessary. You can watch the effects of your choices immediately in the diagram. So far, we've never found the need to contradict the advisor results and you'll be hard pressed to find a better optimized set of aggregate tables than PAD does.

When you look at the row counts in the advisor tables, you'll probably find that the number for the aggregate created manually in the previous paragraph is much higher than in Figure 15-41 because PAD also takes the (All) levels into consideration, so the numbers displayed are the absolute maximum. The manual `agg_wcm_sales_1` table has a PAD calculated row count of 60,192 whereas in reality the table contains only 4,672 rows, which is even less than the manually predicted number.

After you're satisfied with the created model, you can again use the export and publish options to create and load the tables and publish the updated Mondrian schema to the Pentaho Server.

Alternative Solutions

Using aggregate tables has one considerable drawback: the tables need to be refreshed each time the data in the data warehouse is updated. In smaller environments this is easy to achieve by using the exported load scripts to create simple Pentaho Data Integration jobs. But wouldn't it be nice if all this was unnecessary because your database was fast enough to deliver the desired response times without using aggregate tables? In Chapter 5, we mentioned some of these alternatives but it's good to do that again here. LucidDB, Infobright and MonetDB are all very fast, column-oriented databases. These databases have been especially designed for the kind of workload found in an OLAP environment and are worth looking at and evaluating. At the time of writing there were still issues with the MonetDB JDBC driver and Mondrian, but LucidDB in particular works very well in conjunction with Mondrian. The LucidDB Wiki at `http://pub.eigenbase.org/wiki/LucidDbOlap` describes how to set this up.

Summary

This chapter showed you how to create OLAP solutions for the Pentaho BI Platform. Topics covered included the following:

- Introduction to MDX concepts and syntax
- Building multidimensional solutions using the Pentaho Schema Workbench
- Creating analysis views using the JPivot front end
- Enhancing OLAP performance by using aggregate tables
- Using the Pentaho Aggregate Designer for designing aggregate tables

CHAPTER

16

Data Mining with Weka

Popular books such as *Moneyball*, *Freakonomics*, and *Competing on Analytics* have increased interest in using analytics to get a competitive edge. This chapter explains how some of the more popular analytical techniques work and how they can be applied in real life scenarios. Business analysts and BI professionals are accustomed to reporting on organizational performance. By now, most people are familiar with the use of BI tools and OLAP to report, to identify exceptions, and answer basic questions. The challenge for many people is that new questions require new ways of looking at data. Reporting and OLAP techniques are good when the types of questions are well established, and for explaining past or current activity. These techniques can't be used to understand complex relationships, explore large volumes of detailed data, or predict future activity. Data mining (including visualization and text analytics) provides the means to accomplish tasks that aren't possible with standard BI tools. These advanced analytics are often not used because of their assumed complexity and cost. The truth is that many techniques can be applied simply, and often with relatively inexpensive—sometimes free—tools. One of the more popular tools is Pentaho Data Mining (PDM), better known as Weka (rhymes with "Mecca"), which is the subject of the current chapter.

Although *data mining* is a familiar term used to denote the subject at hand, some people prefer to call it *machine learning* or *(automated) knowledge discovery*. Machine learning is actually a broader subject than data mining but the terms are for a large part interchangeable. For this book, we stick to the term data mining.

Data Mining Primer

Data mining has long been a subject of much confusion and sometimes even mystery: the use of computers for automated decision making or simulating the human thinking process using neural networks has a frightening effect on some people. To tell the truth, there is nothing mysterious or frightening about data mining, but it's true that the perceived complicated nature scares many people away from it. That's a real pity because data mining adds a lot of power to your analytical toolbox, though it does require some learning investment.

What exactly is data mining? Data mining is often considered to be a blend of statistics, artificial intelligence, and database research, but that is not really a definition. A skeptical definition might even be that data mining equals statistics plus marketing. Skepticism aside, the following definition is commonly quoted:

> *Data Mining is the non-trivial process of identifying valid, novel, potentially useful, and ultimately understandable patterns in data.*
>
> **U. M. Fayyad, G. Piatetsky-Shapiro, and P. Smyth, "From Data Mining to Knowledge Discovery: An Overview," in *Advances in Knowledge Discovery and Data Mining,* edited U. M Fayyad, G. Piatetsky-Shapiro, P. Smyth, and R. Uthurusamy, AAAI Press/MIT Press, pp. 1-34, 1996.**

This definition tells us several important things. First, it's about discovering patterns in data that need to be understood. Data mining involves working with large data sets with sometimes millions of rows and hundreds of columns, which are in some way or another related to each other. The patterns we want to discover need to be understandable, so the results must make sense. The results must also be novel, meaning that they should tell us something we didn't know before, and the results should be valid within a specific context. Furthermore, the definition talks about a non-trivial process, which means that we're not doing this for fun but to solve a business, social, or scientific problem. Common business applications for data mining are fraud detection, direct marketing, and customer retention. But did you know that data mining is also an important tool in agriculture, where it is used for diagnosing soybean diseases or scoring the quality of mushrooms? Another example is from the area of life sciences, where data mining is used to predict the survival rate of embryos. In fact, there are many areas where data mining would be useful, but in our case we'll focus on applications for marketing and sales based on the data in the World Class Movies database.

Data Mining Process

An easy way to start is to look at data mining as a *process*. In fact, in 1996 a group of industrial companies decided to develop a data mining methodology currently known as CRISP-DM, short for CRoss Industry Standard Process for Data Mining (a complete reference guide is available online at `http://www.crisp-dm.org`). The basic workflow they agreed upon is displayed in Figure 16-1, which shows the natural flow of the steps that make up a data mining process.

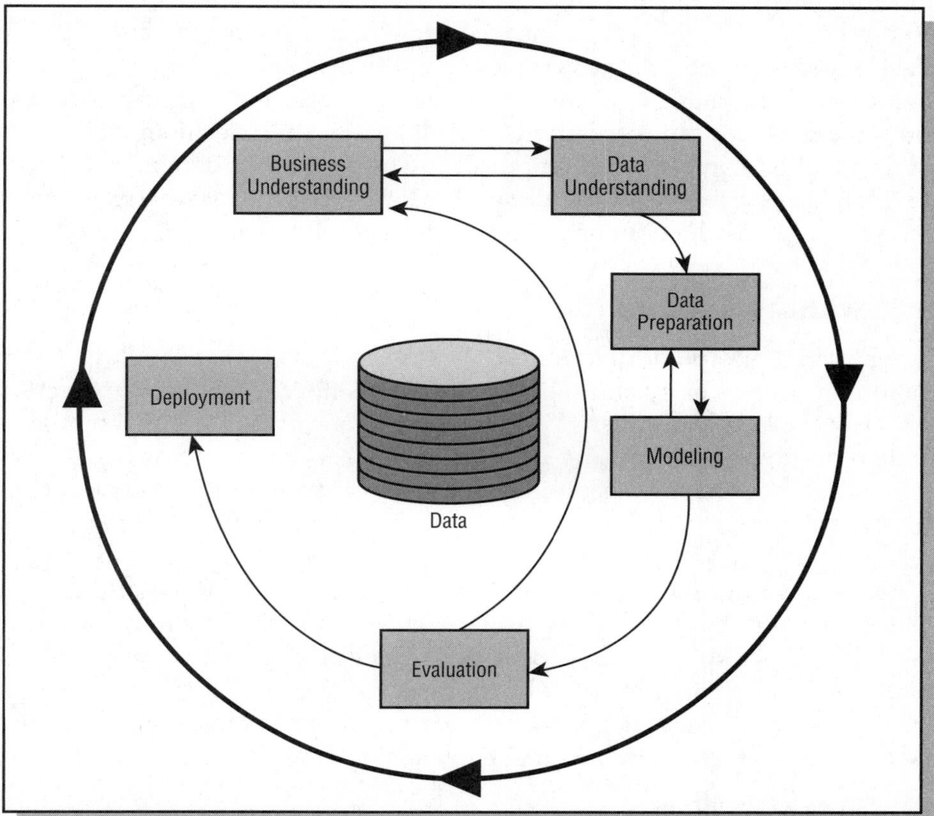

Figure 16-1: Crisp-DM method

This process model shows that there is a lot of overlap between BI and data mining activities:

- Data mining, as with BI, is a continuous loop of activities with the ultimate goal of making better decisions
- Data is the center of all activities; without data, there is no BI and no data mining
- The first three steps of the process model are very similar to building a data warehouse. Business understanding, data understanding, and data preparation were the subject of Chapters 5 to 11, and everything described there can be used for data mining as well.

- As in BI projects, about 70 to 80 percent of the effort is spent on the first three activities. Getting the right data and getting the data right is still the most time-consuming part of any data mining project as it is for a BI project.

The difference starts as soon as you can begin with the modeling phase. Modeling means that you consider different models and choose the best one based on its predictive performance, i.e. you are looking for the best "fit." In a real world scenario this involves testing different solutions with different sample data sets, trying to find a model that produces the most stable results across the different samples. And by results we mean that the model is able to predict an outcome based on input data. The purpose of data mining is not to explain all possible relations within the data, but is more targeted towards finding a practical solution for predicting certain outcomes.

Data Mining Toolset

The predictive nature of data mining is exactly what makes it so appealing to a lot of business users and what distinguishes it from regular BI processes and tools. BI, as we've covered it in the previous chapters in this book, was about reporting and analyzing on past performance, and comparing goals with actual measures. Data mining adds the capability to make *predictions* about future performance within certain limits of confidence. The tools to do this are models and algorithms.

The tasks we want to accomplish with data mining are different from what we've seen so far but most goals can be achieved by using the following four main categories: classification, association, clustering, and regression. Each of these will be explained in the following sections. What all these categories have in common is the fact that they try to predict or explain certain outcomes (the *target* or *unknown* value) based on available data.

Classification

Classification is the process of dividing a dataset into mutually exclusive groups such that the members of each group are as "close" as possible to one another, and different groups are as "far" as possible from one another, where distance is measured with respect to specific variable(s) you are trying to predict. For example, a typical classification problem is to divide a database of customers into groups that are as homogeneous as possible with respect to a retention variable with values `stayer` and `leaver`. You can also try to classify customers based on their revenue class, as you will discover later, in order to predict the possible profitability of a new customer.

Classification starts by defining the outcome variable, in this case, for instance, `retention_group` or `revenue_class`. To train the model, you would need a data set with different variables and a known outcome. In the retention case you would need a data set consisting of loyal customers that have been ordering products for at least two years, combined with customers that terminated their contract at some point in time. For both groups you would need extra information like demographic data, geographic data, and order history. Based on this data you can then determine what variables contribute most to this outcome, for instance last month's customer spending, items bought within a certain period, or maybe income group. Determining the impact of each of these variables or any combination of them is a typical data-mining task. After the process is completed (we *train* the model), you are able to validate the model by running the classification algorithm against a larger data set, which is called *testing the model*. This allows you to check whether the model satisfies your requirements (which could be "customer profitability group is predicted correctly in 95% or more of the cases") and if it does, it can be used to score future customers as well.

Because classification is one of the most used applications of data mining (and the easiest one to get your feet wet), we'll work through a couple of examples later in this chapter.

Clustering

Clustering or database segmentation is very similar to classification in the sense that you try to identify which elements in a data set share common characteristics and group them together based on these characteristics. The most notable difference, however, is that with clustering you let the algorithm determine the groups based on a selection or even all available data, whereas with classification you already have the groups defined. This difference is also identified as *supervised* (classification) versus *unsupervised* (clustering) learning. Clustering has a more explorative nature because when the data-mining algorithm has determined which clusters of items belong together, you can look at the reasoning behind it. The data-mining tool will show how it made its decision and which variables contributed mostly to the different groups. Now it's up to the analyst to investigate the different groups, why they are different, and how this can be used to make better decisions. If the clusters found prove to be useful, they can then be used as classes in a classification analysis.

Association

With association you try to find out what the relation is between two or more data elements in a data set. One of the best known applications of association is market basket analysis, where large numbers of transactions are scanned to determine which articles are bought in which combination. A famous example of this is the diaper and beer case that you might have heard or read about. A large retail chain analyzed millions of sales transactions from the point of sales system and found a strong correlation between the sales of beer and diapers. The explanation they came up with was that young fathers on their way home from work picked up the groceries. And since they couldn't go out with their friends because of the baby, they picked up a package of beer to drink at home. As a result, the retail chain started to position the two products close to each other in the shops to boost sales and service their customers better. Or at least, that's the story. It turned out eventually that there was indeed a correlation, but not a causal relationship in the form ''buys diaper ➤ buys beer.'' The lesson here, and one of the most frequent mistakes made in data mining, is confusing correlation for causality.

Numeric Prediction (Regression)

The previous three categories of data mining applications predict specific classes (nominal values); these are non-numeric values such as `good`, `bad`, `stayer`, or `leaver`. Often you want to predict a numeric outcome based on past events, which is a different style of application because now you don't have discrete values as outcome but an infinite range of possible numeric values. Think of predicting the performance of a computer based on the components and configurations used, or the yearly revenue estimate of a customer based on customer characteristics and buying behavior. We won't cover regression in this chapter but the ''Further Reading'' section at the end of the chapter contains some excellent references if you want to dive deeper into the subject.

Data Mining Algorithms

The four categories of data-mining applications introduced in the previous sections are a high level classification of the tools available for data mining. You might find different categorizations in other sources, but the categories we use here are based on the division that the designer of Weka chose. The Weka tools therefore also contain these same four basic data mining categories.

Categories are not enough though; for each category several algorithms are provided to do the actual work. So classification is a specific kind of data mining but to classify data we need instruments such as decision trees or rule algorithms. Algorithms are what make a data-mining tool powerful. In general, data miners don't care about fancy interfaces or nice visualization tools, as long as the algorithms are sufficiently powerful from a predictive standpoint. Most of the popular algorithms are available in the public domain as they are the result of publicized scientific research. Weka contains over 45 such algorithms.

Proprietary data mining tools often contain improved or extended versions of publicly available algorithms. A good example is the decision tree algorithm, known as C4.5, which is the basic workhorse of any data miner. An adjusted version of this algorithm is available in Weka as the J48 tree classifier, but the successor of C4.5, which is known as C5.0, is only available from a commercial vendor. Because this new version has improvements both in speed and memory consumption (and small improvements in accuracy), many organizations decide to acquire this software to obtain better results from their data-mining efforts. Although C5 has boosting built-in, you can get a similar performance boost with Weka by combining J48 and the AdaBoost meta classifier.

Training and Testing

Two terms that are often confused with each other will be used extensively when you start with a data-mining process: training and testing. *Training* is the process of setting up the data mining model; *testing* is using a model obtained from the training phase to validate the quality of the model. The data used for these two activities should not be the same. To take this even further: there shouldn't be any overlap in the data set used for training and the data set used for testing. (There are possible exceptions to this rule but they will not be covered here.) And to make it even more complicated: the data used for training should be a random selection of considerable size from the total data set. A good rule of thumb is that two-thirds of the data should be used for training, and the remainder (one-third) for testing. This is usually referred to as the "holdout" method of model evaluation.

You may face further challenges when selecting the right data to train your model. For example, although you might like to, it is not feasible to use 100 billion rows of data to build a model, so if your data set is really big you should consider taking a sample from it before you start building your model. In this chapter we will show you how this can be achieved by using Pentaho Data Integration (PDI).

Stratified Cross-Validation

Data sets have a couple of possible issues that make it tricky to use them to build a model from. The first issue is the randomness of selected data and the possibility that the class values are unevenly distributed between the training and the test set. The solution for this is to *stratify* the data, which ensures that both the training and test sets have the same distribution of class values as in the data as a whole. The second issue occurs when data is limited. The holdout method (with stratification) only goes part of the way to safeguard against uneven representation of input and output values in training and test sets. A more general way to compensate for any bias caused by the particular sample chosen for holdout is to use a statistical technique called *cross-validation*. In cross-validation, the data is divided into a fixed number of mutually exclusive partitions or *folds*. Suppose you use four folds which means that the data is divided into four approximately equal chunks. One fold is then used for testing and the other three for training. This process is repeated using a different fold for testing and the other three for training until all folds have been used in each role. Using stratified ten-fold cross-validation has become the standard way of predicting the performance of a learning algorithm in machine learning. Extensive tests on many benchmark data sets have shown that ten is about the right number of folds to get the best estimate of accuracy.

The Weka Workbench

Weka is a data-mining tool originally developed at the University of Waikato in New Zealand. The name is an acronym for Waikato Environment for Knowledge Analysis, but also it's the name of a bird, which is now the project mascot. Weka started as a government-funded project in 1993 and its aim was to "develop a state of the art workbench of data mining tools." Although Pentaho has adopted the Weka tool as its data-mining engine, it is the only part of the BI platform that isn't yet available from the regular Pentaho download sites. In addition, Weka is not yet part of the nightly builds on Hudson, and the source code cannot be downloaded from the Pentaho SVN repositories. The integration in the Pentaho platform is limited to a special plugin for Kettle to call a Weka scoring algorithm. However, because the tool is in a class of its own, and will most likely be used by specialists, this won't pose a big problem. In 1996, the first public version (2.1) was released and in 1999 version 3 (100 percent written in Java) was released. The current version 3.6 is an incremental release still based on the 3.0 code, making Weka probably the most mature part of the Pentaho BI platform.

Weka consists of three different tools, each of which can be used independently, but, when combined, make a very powerful data mining platform. (Actually there are four tools but we doubt you'll ever use the Simple Client, which is a command line interface for Weka.) The main tools are the following:

- **Explorer**—The starting point for getting acquainted with Weka and data mining. Explorer allows for an easy, explorative (hence the name) way of working with data sets. It also offers a wide range of functionality.
- **Experimenter**—Meant for setting up and executing larger experiments where multiple data sets and multiple algorithms can be added simultaneously. The results of the experiment can then be compared with each other to determine which outcomes were (statistically) better than others.
- **KnowledgeFlow**—The latest addition to the Weka tool suite can be used to build complete data mining workflows similar to the flows you are familiar with in Pentaho Data Integration or the Design Studio.

Weka Input Formats

Before you can analyze the data, it must be prepared for use in Weka. Weka can read data from multiple sources, including directly from a JDBC database and CSV files. Weka also has its own, native file formats. The first is called ARFF (Attribute Relation File Format), which is a text-based file format but with added metadata so that Weka knows what kind of data is in the file. Listing 16-1 shows an example of an ARFF file. As you can see, it contains the relation (the subject of the analysis), all the attributes used including either the possible values or the data type, and the data itself.

Listing 16-1: ARFF format with the weather data

```
@relation weather

@attribute outlook {sunny, overcast, rainy}
@attribute temperature real
@attribute humidity real
@attribute windy {TRUE, FALSE}
@attribute play {yes, no}

@data
sunny,85,85,FALSE,no
sunny,80,90,TRUE,no
overcast,83,86,FALSE,yes
rainy,70,96,FALSE,yes
rainy,68,80,FALSE,yes
rainy,65,70,TRUE,no
overcast,64,65,TRUE,yes
sunny,72,95,FALSE,no
sunny,69,70,FALSE,yes
rainy,75,80,FALSE,yes
sunny,75,70,TRUE,yes
overcast,72,90,TRUE,yes
overcast,81,75,FALSE,yes
rainy,71,91,TRUE,no
```

The second format is called XRFF (eXtensible attribute-Relation File Format) and is an XML-based extension of the ARFF format. Both ARFF and XRFF files can be opened in an archived form as well. XRFF has an advantage over standard ARFF in that it allows the class attribute to be specified in the file. Standard ARFF files do not specify a class attribute and leave it to the user to select one via the graphical user interface or via an option if using Weka's command line interface. In Listing 16-1, the attribute `play` is considered to be the class (the outcome variable)—the user would have to be aware of this and choose this attribute explicitly. XRFF, on the other hand, allows a default class attribute to be defined in the file. This attribute then gets chosen automatically in Weka's GUI or command line interface. Of course, this doesn't prevent the user from manually selecting another attribute to be treated as the class if they desire. Finally, XRFF allows for adding both attribute and instance weights (ARFF only supports instance weights), which enables balancing the importance of each attribute in an outcome.

There are also a couple of other file formats that Weka can handle, such as C4.5, which is a standard file format similar to ARFF but the attribute descriptions and data are split into two separate files. With the LibSVM (Library for Support Vector Machine), SVM Light, and SBI (Serialized Binary Instances), Weka is capable of handling output data from other data mining or statistic packages as well.

Setting up Weka Database Connections

As mentioned, Weka provides the option to read data from databases using the JDBC interface. Before you can use this feature some extra setup effort is required because there is no out-of-the-box database support. To view the standard behavior of Weka when attempting to use a database, start Weka from the command line first.

TIP **A Java program can usually be started by opening a terminal screen or pressing Alt+F2 and entering the command**

```
java - jar <jarfile name>
```

In the case of Weka, this would become

```
java -jar weka.jar
```

If you select Explorer from the GUI Chooser, you'll notice the following errors in the console:

```
---Registering Weka Editors---
Trying to add JDBC driver: RmiJdbc.RJDriver - Error, not in CLASSPATH?
Trying to add JDBC driver: jdbc.idbDriver - Error, not in CLASSPATH?
Trying to add JDBC driver: org.gjt.mm.mysql.Driver - Error, not in CLASSPATH?
Trying to add JDBC driver: com.mckoi.JDBCDriver - Error, not in CLASSPATH?
Trying to add JDBC driver: org.hsqldb.jdbcDriver - Error, not in CLASSPATH?
```

This means that Weka cannot find these drivers, which is fine as long as you don't need to connect to a database. You'd like to read data from the WCM data warehouse, so a few modifications need to be made. First, you need to extend the *class path*. The class path is an environment variable called `CLASSPATH` where the program can find the required Java classes for a certain task. In this case you need to specify the location of a JDBC driver, so add the

MySql driver to the CLASSPATH variable. Use the driver that's already available in the Pentaho BI Suite and enter the following command on the command line (note that the entire command should be on a single line):

```
export CLASSPATH=$CLASSPATH:/opt/pentaho/biserver-ce/
tomcat/common/lib/mysql-connector-java-5.0.7.jar
```

If you want to use another database you can replace the mysql connector for the driver for your database. Adding more than one database requires extending the class path with the extra drivers. Just add them to the command as previously shown, separated by a colon (:).

NOTE **Linux class path entries are separated by a colon; on Windows a semi-colon (;) is used.**

The next thing is to make sure that Weka can translate all the MySQL datatypes used in our data warehouse. Because we defined some integer columns as unsigned (which Weka cannot read by default), you need to modify the database settings in a file called DatabaseUtils.prop. And while you're at it, you can also get rid of the annoying class path error messages. Weka looks for the .prop file in the following three locations, and in the following order: the current directory, the user's home directory, and finally, in the experiment subdirectory of the weka.jar file. Although you could change this last one directly, we strongly advise against it; as soon as you reinstall or update the current Weka installation all modifications will be lost. The first option is also not the best one because this would force you to always start Weka from the Weka directory. You therefore need to create the file in your home directory.

Although you don't want to modify the jar file, it does contain sample DatabaseUtils.props files for the most common databases, including MySQL. The easiest way to get this file in your home directory is to open the weka.jar file and browse to the DatabaseUtils files as displayed in Figure 16-2.

The file you need is the one with the .mysql extension, and because it cannot be copied from the jar directly, open it first by double-clicking the file. The file opens in a standard text editor so you can make the required modifications. The line with the JDBC driver should be changed to:

```
jdbcDriver=com.mysql.jdbc.Driver
```

and the JDBC URL to

```
jdbcURL=jdbc:mysql://localhost:3306/wcm_dwh
```

This assumes you are running the database server on the local machine. Below the URL you'll see the specific data types that have been commented out. These are the Weka defaults and you don't want to change these. Now you should add the unsigned integer mappings somewhere below this section with the following lines:

```
TINYINT_UNSIGNED=3
SMALLINT_UNSIGNED=4
INTEGER_UNSIGNED=5
```

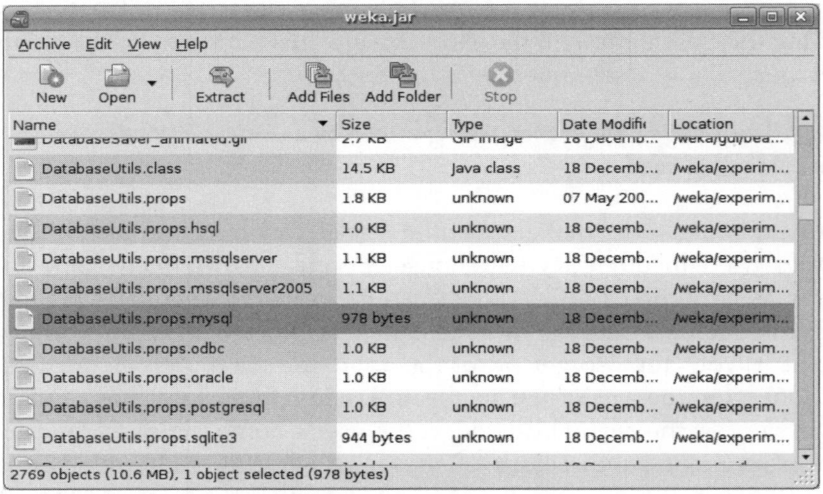

Figure 16-2: Weka.jar DatabaseUtils files

Next, you should save the file as `DatabaseUtils.props` in your home directory. A complete description of the properties of the `DatabaseUtils.props` file can be found online at `http://weka.wiki.sourceforge.net/weka_experiment_DatabaseUtils.props`. In the next section, we explain how Weka should be started using a customized class path.

Starting Weka

If you followed the instructions in the previous paragraph and you start Weka again by running the `java - jar weka.jar` command, and select Explorer from the GUI chooser, you will notice that there is still one error message left:

```
---Registering Weka Editors---
Trying to add JDBC driver: com.mysql.jdbc.Driver - Error, not in CLASSPATH?
```

Again, there is nothing to worry about—it is just a warning that the database drivers are not in the class path yet. `CLASSPATH` is an *environment variable*, which means it can easily be extended. Because you want to read data from a MySQL database, you should add the MySQL driver to the class path. Use the driver that's already available in the Pentaho BI Suite and enter the following command on the command line (the command should be on a single line):

```
export CLASSPATH=$CLASSPATH:/opt/pentaho/biserver-ce/
tomcat/common/lib/mysql-connector-java-5.0.7.jar
```

In order to use the adjusted class path, you have to explicitly refer to it when starting Weka. If you use the `-jar` option again, the `CLASSPATH` variable will be overwritten. You also need to specify the main class Weka should start with, and you can set the amount of memory to reserve for Weka at the same time. The GUI chooser can now be started with the following command but you need to be in the `weka` directory for it to work:

```
java -Xmx128m -classpath $CLASSPATH:weka.jar weka.gui.GUIChooser
```

A better way is to use the following command with the complete Weka pathname included (again, this command should be on a single line):

```
java -Xmx128m -classpath $CLASSPATH:/opt/pentaho/
weka-3-6-0/weka.jar weka.gui.GUIChooser
```

Now when you start the Explorer from the GUI chooser, the MySQL error is gone and you can use the Open DB option to connect to the WCM Data Warehouse database. The last command can also be copied into a new launcher to make it part of the Pentaho menu. The `-Xmx` parameter used in the command specifies the amount of memory that Weka will use. When working with large datasets, you should set this value at a high level to prevent the error message in Figure 16-3.

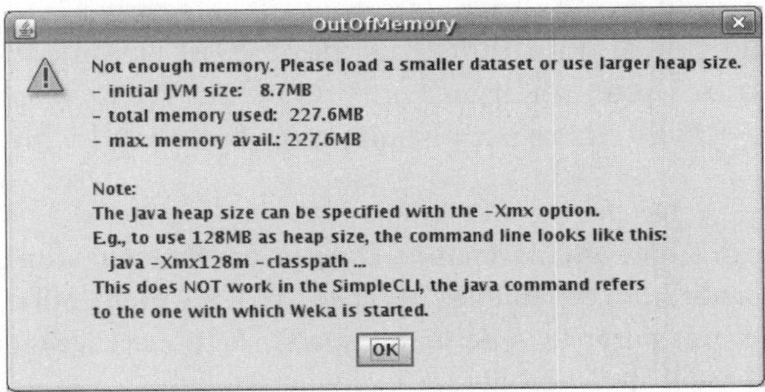

Figure 16-3: Weka memory error

After this error, Weka closes, and none of the data is saved, so it's best to use as much memory as you can spare (for example, use `-Xmx1024m` for starting with a gigabyte of RAM).

The Weka Explorer

The Weka Explorer can be started from the GUI chooser or directly from the command line using the following command:

```
java -Xmx128m -classpath $CLASSPATH:/opt/pentaho/
weka-3-6-0/weka.jar weka.gui.explorer.Explorer
```

Now you'll probably want to know whether the database connection has been set up correctly, so click Open DB to start the SQL Viewer. If everything works the way it should, the database URL is now visible in the Connection panel. Next you need to specify the user and password by clicking the User option, after which you can connect to the database. The Info box at the bottom of the SQL Viewer will show a message that the connection succeeded, and you can enter a query in the Query panel. Because this panel doesn't support you in writing your query in any way at all, it's perhaps a good idea to develop your query first in another environment such as the MySQL Query Browser, Squirrel, or SQLeonardo. As an example, enter the query **`select * from dim_date`**. If everything was set up correctly, the results should be displayed now in the bottom panel. If not, please review the previous setup steps.

The Weka Explorer is a complete data mining application in its own right and allows you to get data from files in various formats, from a database query, or from a URL. It even includes an option to generate an artificial set of data to work (play) with, which can be useful if you want to compare different approaches and algorithms without getting distracted by the content or meaning of the data. Preprocessing also includes the ability to apply filters on the data, both on attributes (columns) and on instances (rows). For classification, clustering, association, and numeric prediction, the workbench offers special tabs where the four data mining categories can be used, each with its own collection of algorithms and options. The classification and cluster models can also be saved for usage outside of the Weka workbench, as we will show later. Finally, there's a visualization option, which is displayed in Figure 16-4.

NOTE **Although a nice add-on feature, chances are that you won't pick Weka for its stunning visualization capabilities because there are many other tools that are better suited for this purpose. A better alternative is to use RWeka, which contains both Weka and the R statistical library, including RGraph.**

In the final example of this chapter, you'll see the Explorer used to create a model for the Weka PDI Scoring plugin.

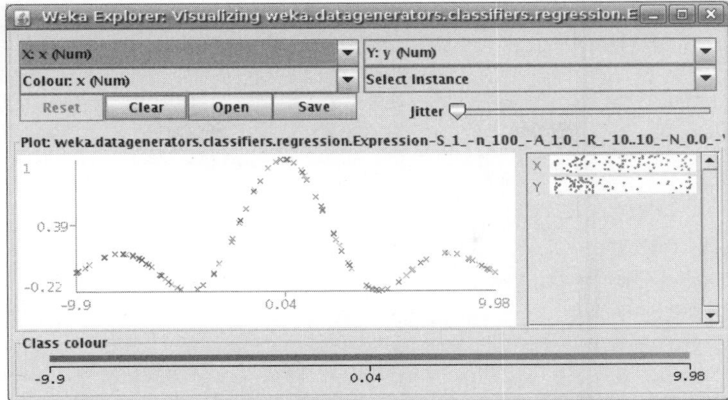

Figure 16-4: Regression visualization

The Weka Experimenter

The Experimenter has two operation modes, simple and advanced, and allows you to run a series of data mining algorithms any number of times against a number of data sets. This also means that it is a tool for more advanced users because it doesn't give you immediate feedback about the results of an experiment. There are a number of advantages to using this tool:

- Multiple operations can be run in a single batch.
- An iteration number can be set, forcing the algorithm to run multiple times. Running ten iterations with a ten-fold cross-validation results in executing the same classifier one hundred times, making for more statistically valid results.
- All results are written to a file (CSV or ARFF) or database table for easy analysis and comparison of the different algorithms.
- Results can be analyzed and tested using any comparison field of the results file. Figure 16-5 shows the Analyse screen after running a ZeroR and J48 algorithm on the same data set. It is easy to see that the decision tree algorithm provides much better results.
- Experiment configurations can be saved and modified.
- Notes can be added to each experiment.

Although the Experimenter won't be the first part of the Weka toolset that you'll be using, it is a powerful addition and surely something worth further investigation.

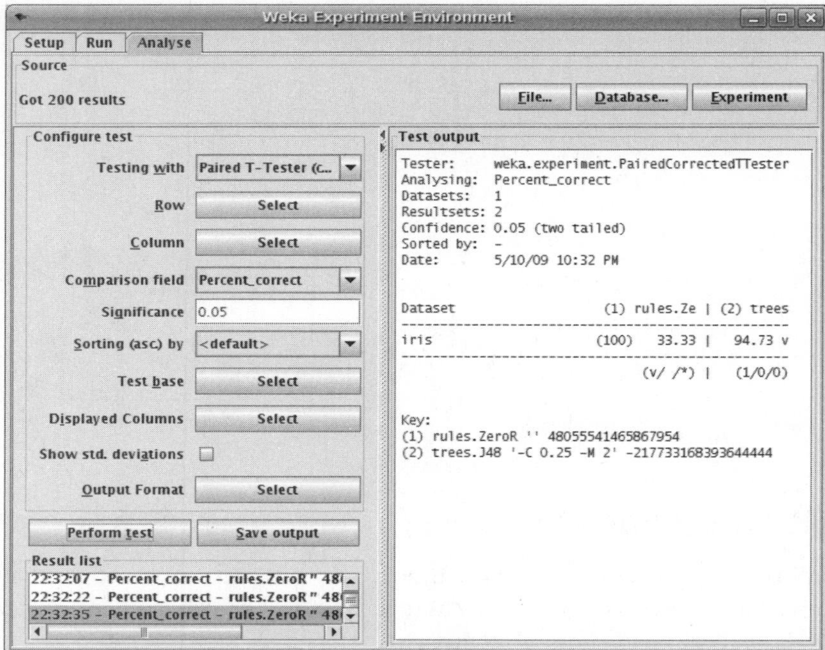

Figure 16-5: Experimenter analysis

Weka KnowledgeFlow

The Weka KnowledgeFlow is like an Explorer on steroids; in fact, it resembles the way some of the leading commercial data mining tools support building workflows and data mining processes. When you know your way around Explorer, KnowledgeFlow will hold few secrets as the arrangement of the available tools is set up in the same way and all of the Explorer's algorithms are also available in the KnowledgeFlow tool. The main difference is the graphical layout of the workflow, which also allows for more complex branching than supported by the Explorer. Figure 16-6 shows a simple example of a classification flow.

The development of KnowledgeFlow is still ongoing but in addition to the visually appealing interface there are a few other things that differentiate it from the Explorer:

- KnowledgeFlow can process multiple streams in parallel.
- Data can be processed incrementally as well as in batch.
- Filters can be chained together (Explorer can handle only one at a time).
- A plugin architecture is available, just like PDI, which makes it an extensible environment.

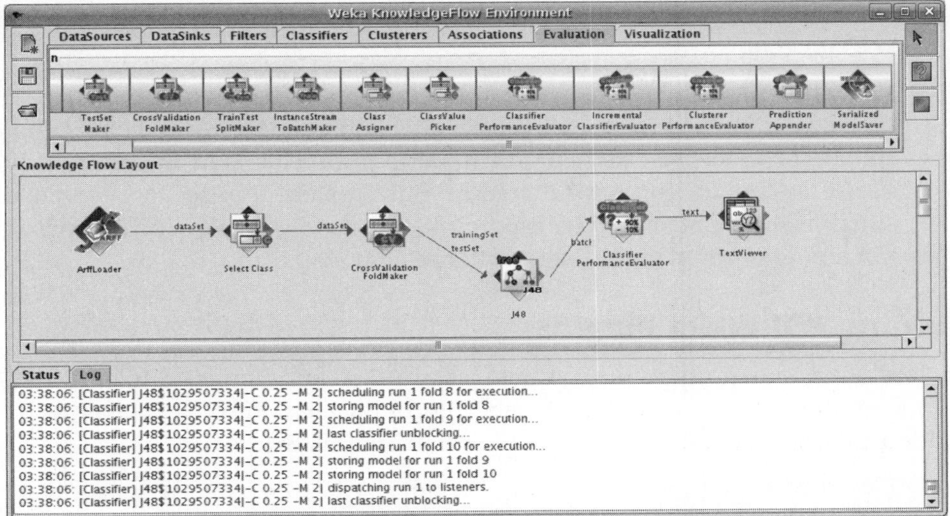

Figure 16-6: KnowledgeFlow example

More information about KnowledgeFlow can be found in the Weka Wiki.

Using Weka with Pentaho

As we explained in the introduction to this chapter, Weka is a loosely coupled part of the Pentaho BI platform. There are two parts of the platform where some form of integration exists, with PDI having the most support for Weka functionality provided by extra plugins. Although there is only one plugin that actually uses the models built with the Weka Explorer, there are two others that help you prepare and deliver data mining data:

- **Weka Scoring**—Enables you to use a Weka model from within a PDI transformation. It is a tool that allows classification and clustering models created with Weka to be used in a PDI transformation. *Scoring* simply means that incoming rows of data are scored (the outcome variable is determined) during the transformation. The scoring plugin is able to attach a predicted label (classification/clustering), number (regression), or probability distribution (classification/clustering) to a row of data.
- **ARFF Output**—Creates a file in ARFF format (see Listing 16-1) to be used in Weka. The incoming field formats from PDI are mapped to ARFF format using the following rules:
  - String: nominal

- Number, Integer: number
- Date: date

- **Reservoir Sampling**—A tool that allows you to get a random selection of rows from an incoming Kettle data stream. All rows have equal chance of being selected (uniform sampling). This step is particularly useful in conjunction with the ARFF output step in order to generate a suitable-sized data set to be used by Weka. As of PDI version 3.2, this is not a plugin anymore but part of the regular steps.

Adding PDI Weka Plugins

Before you can use any of the plugins described so far, they need to be added to an existing PDI installation. Furthermore, the `weka.jar` file needs to be added as well. The following steps describe how this works.

1. Download the plugins from the Pentaho Wiki at `http://wiki.pentaho.com/display/EAI/List+of+Available+Pentaho+Data+Integration+Plug-Ins`.
2. Unpack the zip files; each zip file will create a new subdirectory in the current location.
3. Create a new subdirectory for each plugin under the `/opt/Pentaho/data-integration/plugins/steps` directory and name each one according to the plugin.
4. Copy the files from the deployment subdirectory of the unzipped downloaded files into the newly created subdirectories from Step 3.
5. Copy the file `weka.jar` from the main Weka directory (in our case, `/opt/Pentaho/weka-3-6-0`) into the subdirectories of the plugin steps for the Weka Scoring and ARFF Output steps.
6. Restart Spoon (PDI).

Spoon should now have the new steps available: the Output folder contains the ARFF output step, the Transform folder contains the Weka Scoring step, and the Statistics folder contains the Reservoir Sampling step.

NOTE **The zipped plugin files contain more than just the Deployment extension. The user documentation for the step is available as a PDF file in the subdirectory `/doc`.**

Getting Started with Weka and PDI

The final part of the chapter consists of a complete workflow involving data preparation using PDI, model creation using Weka, and data processing using the Weka scoring plugin. The `WekaScoring.pdf` document included in the plugin zip file contains a simple example of how to use the scoring functionality in PDI and works with a sample data set (pendigits), which is also part of the zip file. You can use this document as a reference because we will use the same workflow and functionality here, although we will use a different data set that more resembles the data we have available in the WCM data warehouse.

Data Acquisition and Preparation

As in BI, most of the data mining effort is spent on getting good quality data to work with. Fortunately, you can skip a few steps and build on the work already done by others. The data set you will use is extracted from the U.S. Census data and already contains a meaningful selection. It can be retrieved from `http://archive.ics.uci.edu/ml/datasets.html` (or from the website for this book) and is called the Adult data set.[1] It is fairly large, which allows you to split it first using the Reservoir Sampling step, and is in an unusable format, which forces you to use PDI to prepare the data and convert it to an ARFF format first. The data set contains 14 demographic attributes, plus the class variable, and can be used to predict whether a person with certain characteristics makes more or less than $50,000 per year. You need three files for this exercise:

- `adult.names` contains the description of the data and the results from previously used algorithms. Note that Weka's J48 algorithm is not listed here so you can actually compare this to the original C4.5.
- `adult.data` contains the data you will use for training the model.
- `adult.test` contains the test set to validate the model.

Download all three files into a directory of choice (or create a Job and use the HTTP step to read them directly from the URL). We've added a data directory to the Pentaho root for this exercise (`/opt/pentaho/data`). You want to do the following:

- Merge the data and test file.
- Use the Reservoir Sampler to extract 10,000 rows.
- Export the sample data as an ARFF file.

The complete transformation is shown in Figure 16-7.

We'll explain briefly how to create this; the complete transformation can be found on the website for this book at `www.wiley.com/go/pentahosolutions`.

1. First, start Spoon and create a new transformation. Start by creating a CSV input with the `adult.data` file (you'll see why later on). Because this file doesn't have a header row, you will have to specify the field names

[1]Asuncion, A. & Newman, D. J. (2007). UCI Machine Learning Repository [http://www.ics.uci.edu/~mlearn/MLRepository.html]. Irvine, CA: University of California, School of Information and Computer Science.

manually. They can be found in the `.names` file. Now adjust the CSV Input step as follows:

- Delete the `Enclosure` specification.
- Clear the `Header row present?` checkbox
- Select the value `both` for all fields under `Trim type`.

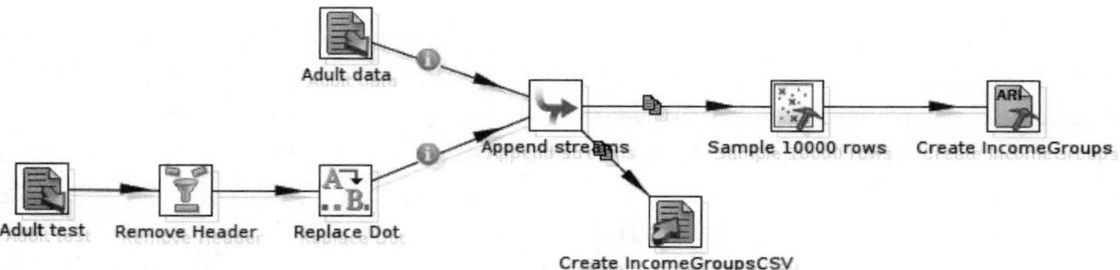

Figure 16-7: Adult2IncomeGroup

2. Duplicate the step and change the input file of the duplicate to `adult.test`. The first row of this file is a single text value, which makes it impossible for PDI to determine the file specification. You've already specified that in the original input step, and because the files have an identical structure, you don't have to do anything else here.
3. Now the `adult.test` file has two problems. The first is the almost empty row at the top, and the second is the class field that has a dot at the end, meaning that if you don't get rid of that you'll end up with four instead of two class values. The header can be removed by using a Filter Rows step with the condition `income-group IS NOT NULL` (in fact, any field except the first one will do here).
4. To get rid of the dot, use a Replace in string step and simply set the In stream field to `income-group` and the Search value to "." and leave the Replace with value empty. Now the two streams can be appended and the output can be sent to both a CSV output step (this one contains all rows in CSV format) and a Reservoir Sample step. This last is set to 10,000.
5. Finally, the ARFF output can be inserted as the final step of the transformation. All you need to do in this last step is enter the file and the relation name. After running the transformation, you should have a CSV file called `IncomeGroups.csv` with 48,842 rows and an ARFF file called `IncomeGroups.arff` with 10,000 data rows.

NOTE There is a simple explanation for the fact that the WCM customer data could not be used for this example: It is randomly generated. As a result, any attempt to cluster or classify customers based on revenue, movie information, or other characteristics will fail.

Creating and Saving the Model

You can now start the Weka Explorer, either by choosing Explorer from the GUIChooser or by starting it directly from the command line. Click Open File and select the `IncomeGroups.arff` file you created earlier. The file will be loaded and summary statistics for the attributes shown in the Preprocess panel, as you can see in Figure 16-8.

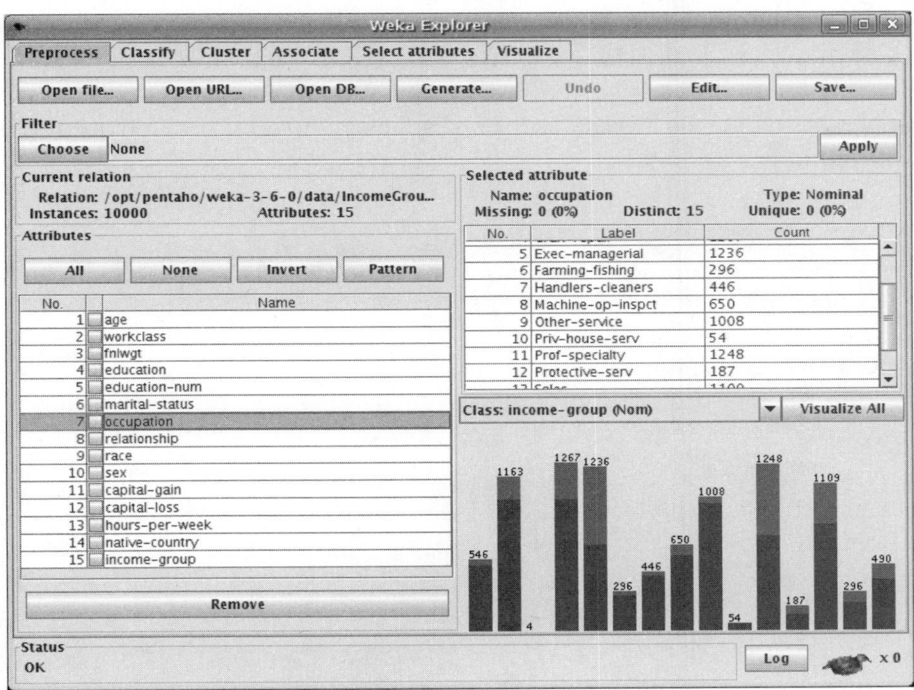

Figure 16-8: Loaded ARFF file in Explorer

You can also see that the name Explorer for this tool is a proper one, as it allows you to browse through the data and make some assumptions about it. For instance, if you want to make more than $50K per year (remember, this is data from 1995!), you had better be an executive or a professional because they have the highest (> $50K) ranges. Another area of interest is the sex division at roughly one-third female and two-thirds male, which means that more men than women earn a salary. What you'll also notice is that more men than women make more than $50K per year. Being a married man also helps. So even without running a classifier, you can already tell that these attributes have a large impact on the outcome class. This is not always the case, however; in many cases, data mining provides the insight that cannot be obtained otherwise.

The next step is to select a classifier. Remember that this is a classification data set with a known outcome (the class). If it was unclear what we were looking for, we could use the Cluster option to find which instances of the data are ''closer'' to each other than others. The classifier we'll choose is J48, which is in the `weka-classifiers-trees` folder when you click Choose. After selecting the classifier, the parameters for the algorithm can be set by clicking on the classifier name, which opens an object editor. Leave all values at their default settings here. In the Test options, select Cross-validation with 10 folds (the default value), verify that the `income-group` is selected as the class, and click Start to execute the classifier. The status bar at the bottom of the window will show the fold that is currently executed and after running ten times (the number of folds), the results will be displayed in the Classifier output, as displayed in Figure 16-9.

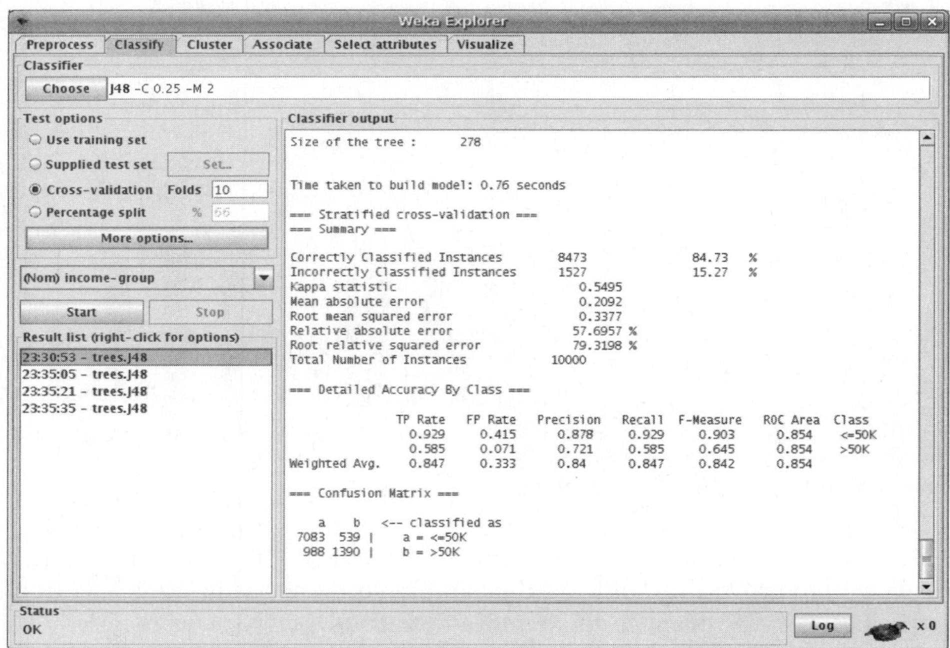

Figure 16-9: J48 Classifier output

Besides the ten-fold cross-validation, you can experiment with other Test options to check whether better quality results can be obtained by using a percentage split or by just using the training set. Actually, the training set yields better results in this case: it classifies a higher percentage correctly but the results are not very reliable because we use the same data for training and testing. As we explained earlier, you should try to avoid this whenever possible.

Exporting the trained classifier is now only a few mouse clicks away. When you right-click on the Result list entry of the model you'd like to export, a submenu is shown with the option to Save the model somewhere in the middle. Save the model in the Weka data directory and name it J48. The `.model` extension is added automatically.

Using the Weka Scoring Plugin

Using the trained model in PDI to score new data is simply a matter of configuring the Weka scoring plugin to load and apply the model file you created in the previous section.

1. You will use the complete adult data set you saved as a CSV file earlier. To do this, create a new transformation in Spoon and add a CSV input step that reads the `IncomeGroups.csv` file from your data directory.
2. The Weka Scoring step needed next can be dragged from the transforms to the canvas. Then, edit the Weka Scoring step and select the `J48.model` file as the load/import model. After selecting the model, the Fields mapping tab shows how the fields from the CSV input step have been mapped to the J48 model attributes. In this case, there are no errors, but if there were, the field types should be adjusted in the CSV input step, not here. The Model tab will show the Tree that was the result of the model training.

NOTE **The class attribute `income-group` is part of the CSV file but it isn't needed for the scoring to work; it is the value that will be determined by the model but is not part of the model itself.**

3. You can now click the Preview button (or right-click the Weka Scoring step and select Preview). There is now an extra field available with the same name as the class with a `_predicted` suffix, as displayed in Figure 16-10.
4. If you want to have the Output probabilities added to each output row instead of the predicted class, tick the corresponding checkbox on the Weka Scoring model file tab. In that case, an extra column will be added for each distinct class value with the calculated probability for each value, as shown in Figure 16-11.

Note that this last option is only available for models that have been trained on a discrete class problem.

TIP **When a transform is executed, the Weka scoring plugin will load the model from disk using the path specified in the File tab. It is also possible to store the model in PDI's repository and use this instead when the transform is executed. To do this, first load a model into the Weka Scoring step as described previously. Once you are satisfied that the fields have been mapped correctly and the model is correct, you can clear the Load/import model text box and click OK. When the transform is saved, the model will be stored in the repository.**

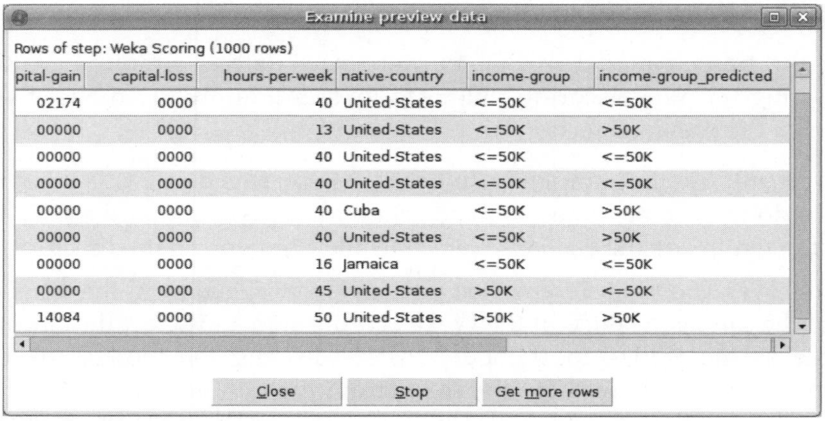

Examine preview data

Rows of step: Weka Scoring (1000 rows)

pital-gain	capital-loss	hours-per-week	native-country	income-group	income-group_predicted
02174	0000	40	United-States	<=50K	<=50K
00000	0000	13	United-States	<=50K	>50K
00000	0000	40	United-States	<=50K	<=50K
00000	0000	40	United-States	<=50K	<=50K
00000	0000	40	Cuba	<=50K	>50K
00000	0000	40	United-States	<=50K	>50K
00000	0000	16	Jamaica	<=50K	<=50K
00000	0000	45	United-States	>50K	<=50K
14084	0000	50	United-States	>50K	>50K

Close Stop Get more rows

Figure 16-10: Prediction results

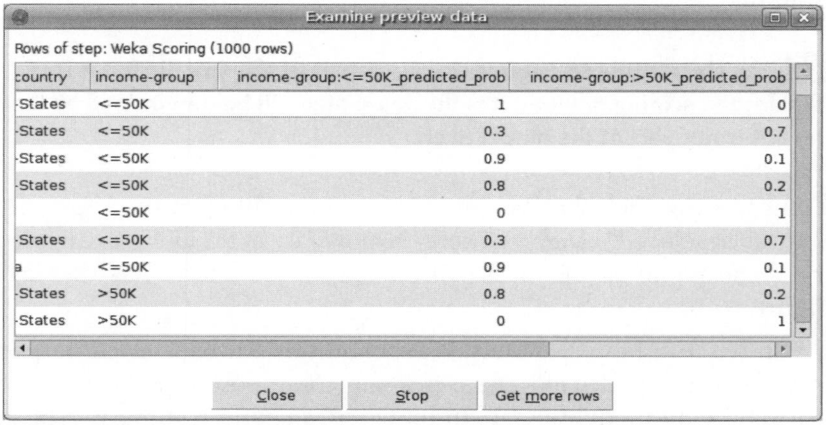

Examine preview data

Rows of step: Weka Scoring (1000 rows)

country	income-group	income-group:<=50K_predicted_prob	income-group:>50K_predicted_prob
-States	<=50K	1	0
-States	<=50K	0.3	0.7
-States	<=50K	0.9	0.1
-States	<=50K	0.8	0.2
	<=50K	0	1
-States	<=50K	0.3	0.7
a	<=50K	0.9	0.1
-States	>50K	0.8	0.2
-States	>50K	0	1

Close Stop Get more rows

Figure 16-11: Output probabilities

Other tips and notes pertaining to the Weka scoring plugin are available in the documentation that's part of the zipped plugin.

Further Reading

Data mining is a very well-documented field of research, so the Internet has an unfathomable amount of information on the subject. Some of the most useful sources of information are listed here:

- Online Pentaho Weka documentation—`http://wiki.pentaho.com/display/DATAMINING/Pentaho+Data+Mining+Community+Documentation`
- Weka homepage—`www.cs.waikato.ac.nz/ml/weka/`
- Pentaho Weka forum—`http://forums.pentaho.org/forumdisplay.php?f=81`
- A complete online statistics handbook—`www.statsoft.com/textbook/`
- Homepage of Data Miners Inc., the authors of four Wiley books on data mining, Michael Berry and Gordon Linoff—`www.data-miners.com`
- Data mining community—`www.kdnuggets.com`

Summary

This chapter was a short introduction to the vast topic of data mining. Because of the diversity and complexity of the subject, we could show only the tip of the iceberg, but we tried to touch on the most important points and provide a hands-on example of how data mining models can be used in the Pentaho BI Suite, especially PDI. Future versions of Pentaho will further enhance the integration between the analytic power of Weka and the BI capabilities of the Pentaho platform. A logical next step would be to call a Weka model from an action sequence (although that can already be achieved by using the Scoring plugin and calling the PDI transformation from an action sequence). Another option to enhance the analytical capabilities of Pentaho is the integration of the R statistical library, which is already available as a solution from one of the Pentaho partners.

This chapter covered the following topics:

- Introduction to data mining
- Overview of the Weka Workbench
- Additional installation and configuration options for Weka and the Weka PDI plugins
- A complete example of how data mining can be integrated into the Pentaho platform

CHAPTER

17

Building Dashboards

In the context of Business Intelligence, a dashboard is an application that is used to present high-level BI content to the end users. Dashboards contain only a few key indicators of the performance of some business aspect (''Sales'') or even the business as a whole.

Dashboard content is almost invariably graphical in nature: instead of figures, metrics are symbolized with pictures, meters, dials, and sometimes graphs. The purpose is to provide a very condensed overview of a large area of business, allowing managers to assess business status at a glance.

Typically, the high-level graphical indicators that appear on dashboards provide some interactivity that allows the user to drill down to more detailed business intelligence content such as reports or OLAP cubes.

The Community Dashboard Framework

The Community Dashboard Framework (CDF) is a set of open source technologies that allows BI developers to build dynamic dashboards for the Pentaho BI Server. CDF dashboards are essentially web pages that use AJAX technology to dynamically combine BI components such as reports, charts, OLAP tables, and maps. Although the CDF is by default included in the Pentaho BI Server, it is developed and maintained by members from the Pentaho Community rather than the Pentaho Company.

CDF, the Community, and the Pentaho Corporation

The CDF is a great example of synergy between the goals of a commercial open source software company like Pentaho and its community.

The Pentaho Corporation includes the CDF in both the Community and the Enterprise Edition of the BI server as a plugin. For users of the Enterprise Edition, Pentaho also provides a dashboard builder that can simplify building dashboards. You can find a section on the CDF under the BI Developer Examples solution, which contains useful documentation, sample dashboards, and background information (see Figure 17-1).

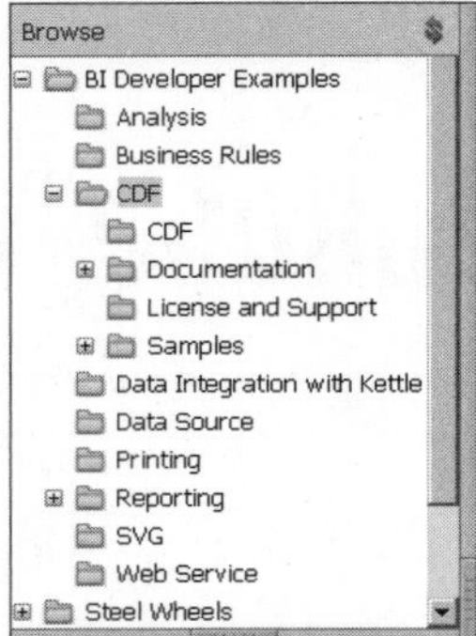

Figure 17-1: The CDF in the BI Developer Examples section

Although the Pentaho Corporation is not formally involved in the CDF, a number of Pentaho's developers are active contributors to the project. In addition, Pentaho offers hosting for the CDF project's issue management, Wiki documentation, and forum.

The CDF is freely distributable under the LGPL license. The project's source code and resources are hosted as a Google code project (`http://code.google.com/p/pentaho-cdf/`).

CDF Project History and Who's Who

The CDF project is led and maintained by a number of prominent members from the Pentaho community.

The roots of the CDF lead back to 2007 when Ingo Klose presented an AJAX-based dashboard solution as an alternative to the prior existing Java servlet–based dashboarding technology provided by Pentaho. Ingo's primary motive was the desire for a dashboarding solution that was easier to use and deploy.

Ingo's work was quickly adopted by Pedro Alves. He collaborated in an early stage with Ingo. Together, he and Ingo founded the CDF project to centralize development and allow for other community members to contribute. Since then, he has added many features and reworked several aspects of the architecture.

Apart from these key contributors, many other community members have worked to create sample dashboards, dashboard templates, and new dashboard components.

Issue Management, Documentation, and Support

CDF issue management is hosted on the `jira.pentaho.com` website. It can be found in the Community Section at `http://jira.pentaho.com/browse/CDF`.

Project documentation is currently available in a number of places. First, the Pentaho Wiki includes an area that is devoted entirely to the CDF at `http://wiki.pentaho.com/display/COM/Community+Dashboard+Framework`.

Apart from the documentation Wiki pages, CDF samples distributed in the Pentaho BI server also contain a lot of valuable documentation.

For community support, there is a forum at `forums.pentaho.com`, which is dedicated to CDF topics. For commercial support, you can contact the WebDetails company at `http://www.webdetails.pt/`.

Skills and Technologies for CDF Dashboards

Two different types of skills are required to build CDF dashboards:

- **General Pentaho development skills**—You need to be able to build action sequences and the BI content such as reports, charts, and so on that you want to visualize on the dashboard. This book should get you well started in this direction.
- **Web development skills**—A focus on web developments skills is beyond the scope of this book. This is primarily a book about Business Intelligence, and there are plenty of high quality books and resources available on web development.

It is not mandatory to unify these rather different skills in the same person. On the contrary, it may be more productive to create dashboards using pairs of BI developers and web developers, or a team of BI developers, Web developers, business domain experts, and end users.

The required web development skills include:

- **HyperText Markup Language (HTML)**—HTML is the standard language used to create web pages. In the early nineties, it emerged and quickly became the dominant format for Internet pages, owing its popularity to a combination of simplicity and features such as hyperlinks and images. Currently HTML is an open standard maintained by the W3C. Detailed information about HTML can be found at `http://www.w3.org/TR/REC-html40/`.

- **Cascading Style Sheets (CSS)**—CSS has emerged as the dominant language for defining document presentation. Like HTML, it is an open standard that is maintained by the W3C. Detailed information on CSS can be found at `http://www.w3.org/TR/CSS21/`.
- **JavaScript; knowledge of the JQuery framework is recommended**—JavaScript is a programming language that was designed especially for adding interactivity to web pages. Over the years, the importance of JavaScript has increased. Slowly it gained standing, and during the past few years, the proliferation of a particular programming technique called AJAX (sometimes identified with the so-called Web 2.0) helped establish its position as a serious programming language.

  A standardized version of JavaScript called ECMAScript is specified by the ECMA International. More information on ECMAScript can be found at `www.ecma-international.org/publications/standards/Ecma-262.htm`.

  JavaScript itself is just a programming language. Much of its value for creating interactive web pages is not part of the language proper, but of the execution environment (sometimes dubbed "runtime"). The most important standards with regard to manipulating HTML documents is the DOM specification, or rather its mapping to ECMAScript. The DOM specification is an open standard maintained by the W3C. More information on this topic can be found at `www.w3.org/TR/REC-DOM-Level-1/ecma-script-language-binding.html`.

If you are not familiar with these technologies, don't let all this scare you off. Mastery is not required to build simple dashboards. Even if you are a BI developer and are working together with web developers to create your dashboards, we still recommend you go ahead and work through this chapter. At the very least, it will show you what technologies are involved and what their possibilities and limitations are.

CDF Concepts and Architecture

CDF dashboards are essentially web pages (HTML documents) that contain areas called "components," which are used to visualize BI content. Figure 17-2 illustrates what happens behind the scenes when a dashboard is opened by the user.

1. The end user uses a web browser to navigate to a dashboard. This causes an ordinary HTTP request to be sent to the Pentaho BI server.

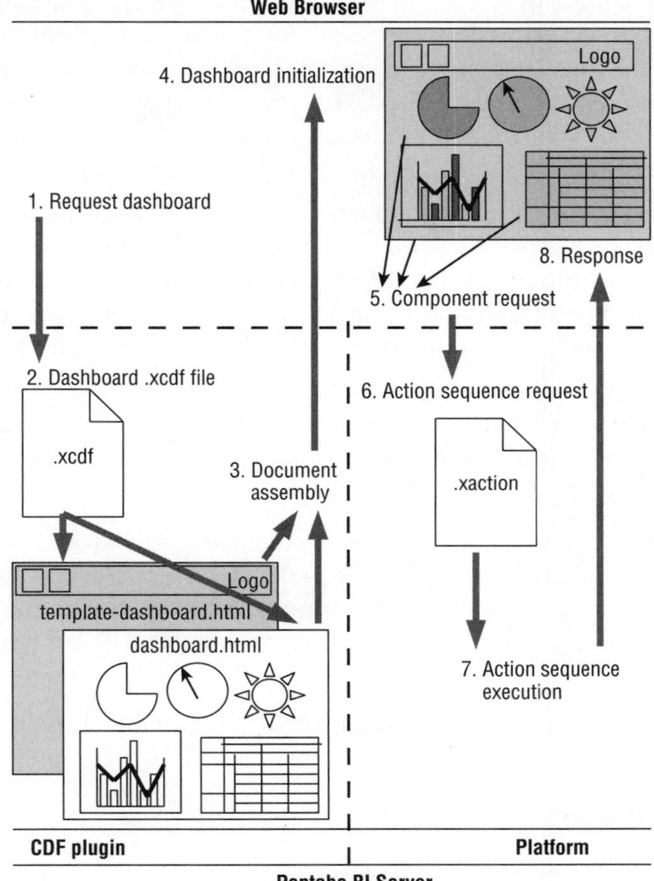

Figure 17-2: Bird's eye view of CDF dashboarding

2. The Pentaho BI server receives the request and recognizes that it should serve a dashboard. The request contains the name and solution path of the dashboard, which is sufficient to locate the dashboard's `.xcdf` file.
3. The `.xcdf` file specifies the *dashboard content template*. This is a (partial) HTML file that contains placeholders for the dashboard components and JavaScript instructions to fill them with dashboard components. The dashboard content template is combined with a *dashboard document template* (sometimes called *outer template*) to assemble a web page (an HTML document). The outer template can be explicitly specified in the `.xcdf` file, but if it is not, a default is used.

4. The web page is received by the browser where it is read and rendered for display. As part of this process, the dashboard is initialized. This is done as the JavaScript instructions in the document are executed, leading to the actual creation of the dashboard components. In the web page, the dashboard components exist as JavaScript objects that are added to a `Dashboards` object, which is also created with JavaScript.
5. After dashboard initialization, the components respond to commands issued by the `Dashboards` object. The basic command is `update`, which orders the components to collect their BI content and place it in their corresponding placeholder(s) in the document. Typically, components react to the `update` command by sending a web request to the Pentaho Server.
6. The Pentaho Server receives requests sent by the components. Typically, the components request the execution of an action sequence.
7. The Pentaho Server executes the action sequence.
8. The content generated by the action sequence is sent back to the requesting component. There, the response is parsed by the component for inclusion in the web page. Finally, the component places the content inside its placeholder(s) in the document, thus making the BI content visible on the page.

We will now discuss the key elements in the CDF architecture in more detail.

The CDF Plugin

Dashboard requests are handled by a Pentaho plugin. This plugin is a piece of Java software that knows how to handle web requests to get a dashboard.

The Pentaho plugin system is the preferred way for third parties to extend the Pentaho Server and to add custom functionality. A full discussion about plugins is beyond the scope of this book, but in this section, we touch upon a few concepts that we hope will help you understand how an addition like the CDF can be integrated with the Pentaho platform. You can find detailed information regarding Pentaho plugins in the Pentaho Wiki documentation at `wiki.pentaho.com/display/ServerDoc2x/1.+Developing+Plugins`.

The CDF Home Directory

The plugin and all related files reside in and beneath the `pentaho-cdf` directory beneath the directory that houses the `system` Pentaho solution. In the remainder of this chapter, we refer to this location as the *CDF home directory*, or simply *CDF home*.

There are a couple of subdirectories in the CDF home directory:

- The `lib` directory contains the java binary files that contain the actual software that makes up the plugin.
- The `js` directory contains the JavaScript and CSS files (as well as some other resources) that make up the client-side software of the CDF. You will see later how these files end up in the actual dashboard web pages.
- The `resources` directory contains various resources such as images and CSS stylesheet files.

The plugin.xml File

The actual plugin definition is contained in the file `plugin.xml`. The contents of this file are shown in Listing 17-1.

Listing 17-1: The CDF plugin.xml file

```
<?xml version="1.0" encoding="UTF-8"?>
<plugin title="Pentaho Community Dashboard Framework">
 <content-types>
  <content-type type="xcdf" mime-type="text/html">
   <title>Dashboard</title>
   <description>Community Dashboard File</description>
   <icon-url>content/pentaho-cdf/resources/cdfFileType.png
   </icon-url>
   <operations>
    <operation>
     <id>RUN</id>
     <command>content/pentaho-cdf/RenderXCDF?solution={solution}&amp;
path={path}&amp;action={name}&amp;template=mantle</command>
    </operation>
    <operation>
     <id>NEWWINDOW</id>
     <command>content/pentaho-cdf/RenderXCDF?solution={solution}&amp;
path={path}&amp;action={name}&amp;template=mantle</command>
    </operation>
   </operations>
  </content-type>
 </content-types>
 <content-generator scope="local" id="pentaho-cdf" type="xcdf" url="">
  <classname>org.pentaho.cdf.CdfContentGenerator</classname>
  <fileinfo-classname>org.pentaho.cdf.CdfFileInfoGenerator</fileinfo-
```

```
classname>
   <title>CDF Display Handler</title>
  </content-generator>
</plugin>
```

If required, you can change this configuration file to modify the behavior of CDF dashboards. For example, you can add additional content types to allow files having a particular extension to be recognized as CDF dashboards. To learn more about Pentaho plugins, refer to the official Pentaho documentation. The relevant information can be found at `http://wiki.pentaho.com/display/ServerDoc2x/Developing+Plugins`.

WARNING **You should ensure you make a back-up of the `plugin.xml` file before you make any changes.**

CDF JavaScript and CSS Resources

The CDF dashboard makes extensive use of JavaScript to create and control components and make calls to the Pentaho BI server. The CDF JavaScript files are located in the `js` subdirectory of the CDF Home directory. There are a number of different JavaScript files in the `js` directory, as well as supporting resources such as CSS files and images:

- `jquery.js`—The CDF is built on top of the popular JQuery AJAX framework. All files that have a name that starts with `jquery` are from this framework. The JQuery framework offers functionality for handling the low-level details of changing HTML documents at runtime (called DOM manipulation) as well as programmatically doing web requests and processing the returned content. Combined, these two functionalities are usually referred to by the term *AJAX* (which stands for Asynchronous JavaScript and XML).
- `jquery.<name>.js` and `jquery.<name>.css` files— In addition to delivering low-level AJAX functionality, JQuery also offers a lot of extensions that implement user interface elements (often called *widgets*) such as date pickers, autocomplete textboxes, and so on. These JavaScript files and supporting CSS files implement various widgets, as well as supporting functionality for actions such as positioning content. There are also a number of subdirectories in the `js` directory. These contain yet more JQuery widget plugins.
- `Dashboards.js`—This is the core of the CDF. This file instantiates a `Dashboards` JavaScript object, which is the actual dashboard implementation.

- `<name>Components.js`—These files contain the object definitions of the various component types that can appear on CDF dashboards. In the actual dashboard, instances of these component types are created and added to the `Dashboards` object. `CoreComponents.js` contains definitions for frequently used dashboard components. `MapComponents.js` contains two components for working with geographical maps. `Navigation Components.js` contains special dashboard components that can be used to generate navigation interaction.
- `resources.txt`—This text file lists all JavaScript and CSS files that are to be included in the resulting dashboard HTML document that is to be sent to the client.

During document assembly, the CDF plugin reads the `resources.txt` file and injects references to the listed JavaScript and CSS files into the dashboard HTML document in the form of `<script>` and `<link>` elements. This ensures these resources will be loaded by the browser when it receives the dashboard, which is necessary for the dashboard and its components to work correctly.

The .xcdf File

The `.xcdf` file is a small XML file containing information that describes the dashboard. These files can be placed in any folder in the solution repository to allow users to navigate to the dashboard.

Some information contained in the `.xcdf` file, such as display name, description, and icon are used by the user console to offer an item so the user can navigate to the dashboard. The `.xcdf` file also refers to a partial HTML file that acts as a dashboard content template. Optionally, the `.xcdf` file can also specify a dashboard document template. These templates are discussed in detail in the next subsection.

Listing 17-2 shows the contents of a sample `.xcdf` file:

Listing 17-2: A sample .xcdf file

```
<?xml version="1.0" encoding="UTF-8"?>
<cdf>
 <title>Pentaho Home Dashboard</title>
 <author>Webdetails</author>
 <description>Pentaho Home Dashboard</description>
 <icon></icon>
 <template>dashboard.html</template>
 <style>mantle</style>
</cdf>
```

As shown in Listing 17-1, all content in the `.xcdf` file is contained in `<cdf>` and `</cdf>` tags. The `cdf` element contains a list of tags that describe the various properties of the dashboard.

The most important tags are `<title>`, `<template>`, and `<style>`:

- `<title>` is a mandatory element that defines the name of the dashboard as it appears to the user in the user console.
- `<template>` identifies the dashboard content template. The value can be a file name in case the content template resides at the same location in the solution repository as the `.xcdf` file. If so desired, the content template can be placed at another location within the repository, but then the path needs to be specified as well. For example, `<template>foo/bar.html </template>` specifies `bar.html` located in the child folder of the current location called `foo` as the content template.
- `<style>` identifies a particular document template. This is an optional tag. If present, it identifies an HTML file wherein the dashboard contents will be placed. If this tag is not specified, the default document template will be used.

Note that the extension `.xcdf` is required. Without this extension, the file won't be recognized as a dashboard definition. The extension is controlled through the `plugin.xml` file discussed in the previous subsection. To be precise, there are two elements in the `plugin.xml` file that control the extension:

- The `type="xcdf"` attribute in the `<content-type>` element
- The `type="xcdf"` attribute in the `<content-generator>` element

Templates

We mentioned already that dashboards are essentially HTML documents. The CDF generates these documents by merging a generic skeleton HTML document with another (partial) HTML document that contains the actual dashboard content definition.

We refer to both these HTML documents as templates, and to the final merged web page as the dashboard. We call the generic skeleton document the *document template* (sometimes called *outer template*). We use the term *document content template* for the file that defines the actual dashboard. Figure 17-3 illustrates the process of document assembly.

Document Template (a.k.a. Outer Template)

Document templates are designed to allow recurring content to be reused by multiple dashboards. Typical examples of reusable content include:

- <link> and/or <style> elements to define cascading style sheets for maintaining a consistent look and feel
- <script> elements for adding custom interaction or importing extension dashboard components
- Navigation structures such as links, toolbars, and/or menus
- Structural elements to obtain a generic document layout

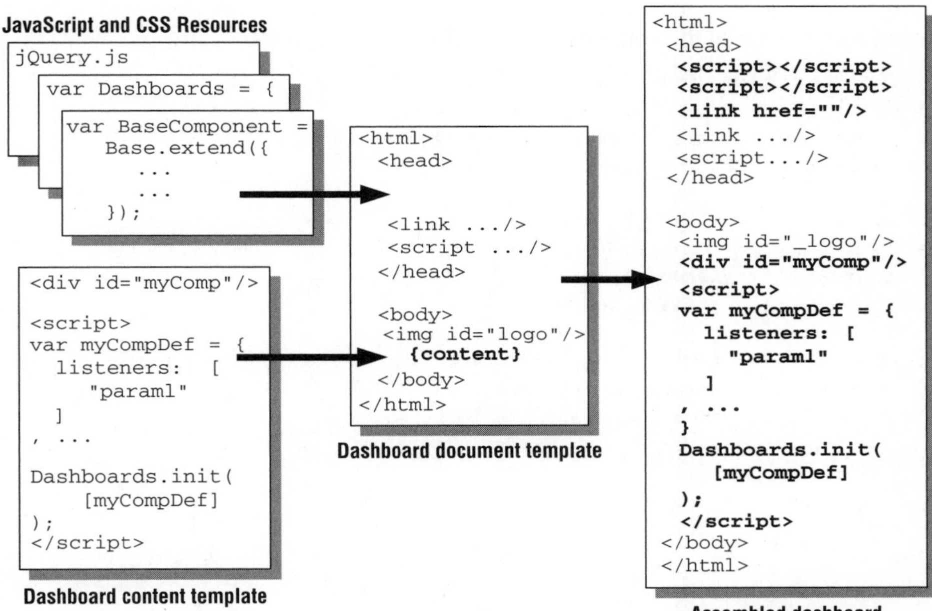

Figure 17-3: Document assembly

CDF document templates reside in the CDF home directory. The default Pentaho Community Edition server ships with two dashboard document templates:

- `template-dashboard.html`—This is the default document template. If the dashboard's `.xcdf` file does not specify a `<style>` element, this template will be used. It includes some navigational elements to allow dashboards to be run outside of the Pentaho user console environment.
- `template-dashboard-mantle.html`—This template is a slightly modified version of `template-dashboard.html` that does not include any navigation elements. This document template is intended for dashboards that run inside a tab page of the Pentaho user console (which is called *mantle*, hence the `mantle` suffix).

In addition to the generic, reusable HTML elements, the document template also contains placeholders, which are substituted by the CDF plugin during document assembly. These placeholders are denoted using the following syntax:

```
{placeholder-name}
```

Listing 17-3 shows some of the contents of the default document template `template-dashboard.html`.

Listing 17-3: Some of the contents of a CDF document template

```
<html xmlns="http://www.w3.org/1999/xhtml">
  <head>
    <link type="text/css" rel="stylesheet"
      href="resources/style/template.css"/>
  </head>
  <body>
    <script type="text/javascript">
      isAdmin = "{isAdmin}";
      isLoggedIn = "{isLoggedIn}";
    </script>
    <div id = "content">
      <div id = "primaryContentContainer">
        <div id="primaryContent">
          {content}
        </div>
      </div>
    </div>
  </body>
</html>
```

In Listing 17-3, you can see a number of placeholders:

- `isAdmin`—Can be replaced with `true` in case the current user is the Pentaho administrator.
- `isLoggedIn`—Can be replaced with `true` in case the current user is Authenticated.
- `content`—Can be replaced with the contents of the dashboard content template. The dashboard content template is discussed in detail in the next subsection.

The file names of the standard document template files in the CDF home directory start with `template-dashboard` and end with `.html`. This file name pattern is a requirement for all document templates. Between the `template-dashboard` prefix and the `.html` suffix there can optionally appear a template name, which must be prepended by a dash. For example, in the file name of the `template-dashboard-mantle.html` template, the text `-mantle` appears between the prefix and suffix. In this case, `mantle` is the actual template name.

To specify the document template, you can set the value of the `<style>` element in the dashboard's `.xcdf` file to the template name. For example, Listing 17-2 uses `<style>mantle</style>` to specify that the `mantle` template should be used—this would map to the `template-dashboard-mantle.html` file.

If no document template is specified in the `.xcdf` file, the default template (`template-dashboard.html`) will be used. For these dashboards, the document template can also be set dynamically by passing the template name in the `template` parameter in the query part of the dashboard's URI.

Content Template

The content template is a partial HTML file that contains the actual dashboard definition. During dashboard assembly, the `{content}` placeholder in the document template is replaced by the contents of the content template. The content template is referenced from the `.xcdf` file using the `template` element. Normally, you would put the dashboard content template in the solution directory along with the `.xcdf` file.

The content template typically contains the following things:

- JavaScript object definitions for the dashboard components and some code to initialize the `Dashboards` JavaScript object.
- HTML placeholders for component content.
- Optionally, static HTML content to achieve a layout for dashboard components.

Listing 17-4 shows an example of a very simple content template that sets up a dashboard with only one component.

Listing 17-4: A very simple CDF content template

```
<div id="component_placeholder">
<!-- This component placeholder will be filled by the component -->
</div>
<!--  This script defines a component and initializes the dashboard -->
<script language="javascript" type="text/javascript">
/*
*   Define the component and configure its properties.
*/
var component = {
```

```
    name: "component_name", type: "xaction",
    htmlObject: "component_placeholder",
    solution: "wcm", path: "/dashboards/customers",
    action: "dashboard_component.xaction",
    parameters: [],
    executeAtStart: true
}
/*
*   Initalize the Dashboard and add the component.
*/
Dashboards.globalContext = false;
var components = [component];
Dashboards.init(components);
</script>
```

Listing 17-4 contains only two HTML elements: a `div` element that is used as component placeholder and a `script` element that contains the JavaScript code to set up the dashboard and its component. Normally, dashboard content templates would have some more components as well as some HTML to place the components on the page.

There are a few things of note in Listing 17-4 that apply to all dashboard content templates:

- Content placeholders are typically `div` or `span` elements. The placeholders are given an `id` attribute, which is used to assign a unique identifier. This is required to allow the components to find the area where they can display their output. In the example, we used a `div` element and assigned the ID `component_placeholder`.
- The component definition is an object literal, which is—at least from the perspective of the dashboard builder—little more than a set of name/value pairs. We will discuss components in detail in the next subsection.
- The dashboard is initialized with a call to `Dashboards.init()`. This initializes the dashboard and can add multiple components, which are passed as an array.

Example: Customers and Websites Dashboard

In this section, we walk you through building an example dashboard. For the example, assume you need to build a dashboard that allows the managers from the World Class Movies company to quickly obtain an overview of their customers and how they relate to the various World Class Movies websites. Figure 17-4 shows the final result of this effort:

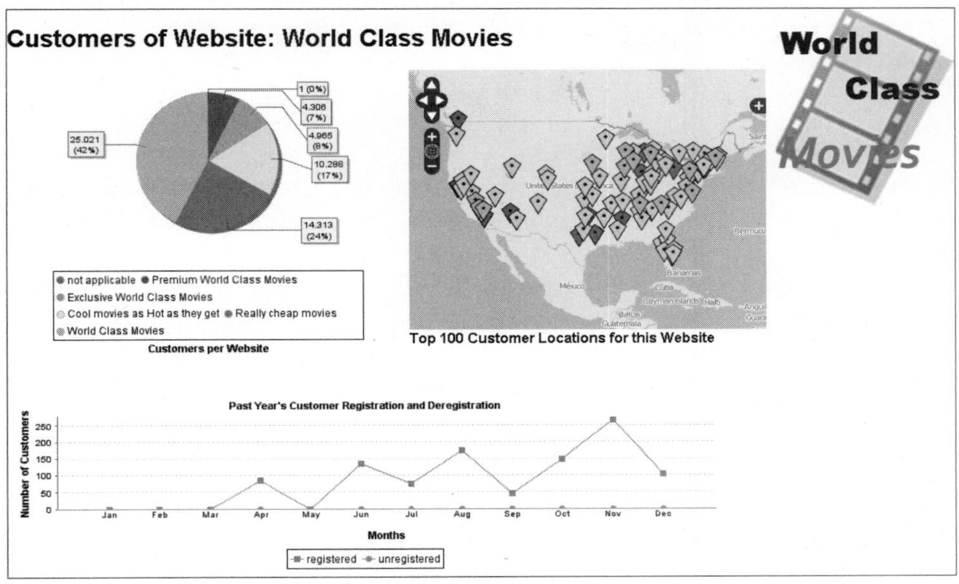

Figure 17-4: A customers and websites dashboard

The dashboard contains the following components:

- On the top left, a pie chart that shows the total number of customers per website. This provides a quick and intuitive overview of the business potential of each website. End users can click on the pie slices to drill down and obtain per-website information.
- The dashboard title displays the value of the current selection made on the pie chart. This is shown at the top of the dashboard.
- A map that shows where the customers from a particular website are located.
- A line chart displaying customer registrations and de-registrations. We won't include the actual details for adding this, but leave this as an exercise to the reader. You should be able to add it on your own if you succeeded adding the prior components.

The remainder of this section describes step by step how to create this dashboard.

NOTE **Note that no special tools are required to create the dashboard. All you need is Pentaho Design Studio to create action sequences, and a text editor to create the dashboard-specific files. There are also no tools involved to deploy the**

dashboard. It is simply a matter of placing files into the solution repository file system. For this example, we assume you are working as Administrator with a locally running Pentaho BI server. This way, you can simply place the files you create for the dashboard directly into the appropriate Pentaho solution subdirectory.

Setup

Before you can build the dashboard, it is a good idea to create a separate folder to keep all items related to the dashboard. This is probably best done from the user console.

We recommend you create a separate `dashboards` folder in the `wcm` solution, and beneath that, a `Customers` folder for this specific example dashboard.

Creating a separate `dashboards` folder is a matter of convenience. It provides a space to keep all kinds of resources shared by multiple dashboards, and it also makes it easier to create a new dashboard, simply by copying and pasting an existing one. It is by no means a requirement to do so.

Creating the .xcdf File

The first step in creating a dashboard is to set up the `.xcdf` file.

1. Create a new text file called `customers.xcdf` directly in the file system directory that corresponds to the `Customers` folder in the Pentaho solution repository.
2. Open the `customers.xcdf` file, and add the contents shown in Listing 17-5.
3. Save the changes to the file.

Listing 17-5: The customers.xcdf file

```
<?xml version="1.0" encoding="UTF-8"?>
<cdf>
  <title>WCM Customers Dashboard</title>
  <author>World Class Movies - Randy Coon</author>
  <description>
    The WCM Customers Dashboard provides
    a quick overview of the distribution of
    - WCM customers over websites
    - customer location
    - customer registration/deregistration
  </description>
  <icon></icon>
  <template>customers-template.html</template>
</cdf>
```

Creating the Dashboard HTML File

In the previous subsection, you created the customers.xcdf file. This file includes the <template> tag and uses it to specify that customer -template.html is your dashboard content template:

```
<template>customers-template.html</template>
```

From our earlier discussion of the .xcdf file, you may remember that the template element specifies the path and name of the dashboard content template. In this case, no path is specified, and the CDF plugin will look for a file called customer-template.html in the current directory. So, you can simply create the customer-template.html file in the same directory as the customer.xcdf file.

1. Open the customer-template.html file and add the contents shown in Listing 17-6.
2. Save your changes when you're done.

Listing 17-6: The customer-template.html file

```
<h1>The WCM Customers Dashboard</h1>
<script language="javascript" type="text/javascript">
  // Get the solution and path of this current location
  var solution = Dashboards.getQueryParameter("solution");
  var path = Dashboards.getQueryParameter("path");

  // Dashboard Parameters
  Dashboards.globalcontext = false;
  //parameter definitions go here

  // Component Definitions
  var components = [];

  // Dashboard initialization
  Dashboards.init(components);
</script>
```

Boilerplate Code: Getting the Solution and Path

The initial contents of the customer-template.html file are just a skeleton—boilerplate code that you can now gradually expand to build the dashboard. We want to mention a few things about this code.

The first two statements define the solution and path global variables. These are used to hold the name of the current Pentaho solution and solution repository path respectively. This is a matter of convenience: you need to configure a number of components that call upon an action sequence. In addition to the name of the `.xaction` file, these components need to know the name of the Pentaho solution and solution repository path where the `.xaction` file resides.

You can obtain the values for the solution and path variables from the URI of the current web page. This works because your dashboard itself is served up from the solution repository, and the name of the solution and path are present in the query part of the URI. The `Dashboards` object provides the `getQueryParameter` method, which is especially created to parse the current URI and grab the value of the query parameter specified by the argument.

For example, the query part of the URI of our example dashboard is:

```
?solution=wcm&path=/dashboard/customers&action=customers2.xcdf
```

By calling `Dashboards.getQueryParameter("path")`, we obtain the value `/dashboard/customer`, and calling `Dashboards.getQueryParameter( "solution")` results in the value `wcm`.

Boilerplate Code: Dashboard Parameters

The statement in the boilerplate code `Dashboards.globalcontext = true;` marks the start of a section you will use to define dashboard parameters and their initial values.

Dashboard parameters are used to drive dashboard component updates. There aren't any parameter definitions in the boilerplate code yet, and you will add them as needed, but it is always a good idea to reserve a section in advance. Once you find that you do need parameters, this will help you to keep them in one place. We place the parameters section before the components, because this will make it easier to configure those components that need to refer to any dashboard parameters.

For now, the only line in this section sets the `globalcontext` property of the `Dashboards` object to `false`. By default, this property is `true`, which allows the dashboard to use all global variables as parameters. For several reasons, we recommend that you always set this to `false`.

Boilerplate Code: Dashboard Components

The final sections of the boilerplate code are there to make component addition a little more convenient. The typical pattern is to create all the component definitions and add them all at once to the `Dashboards` object with a call to its `init` method.

Listing 17-6 created a global variable called `components`, and assigned a new empty array to it. As you create new component definitions, one by one, you will add them to this array. Finally, in the last line of the code, you pass the components array to `Dashboards.init`.

The advantage of this approach is that it allows you to keep the code that creates each component definition together with the code that causes it to be added to the dashboard. An additional advantage is that the actual line that adds the components does not have to list variable names of the individual components. In our experience, this makes it easier and less error prone to add and remove components.

Testing

Although the dashboard itself does not yet contain any real content, you can already access it from the user console. It is, in fact, wise to test this right now, just to make sure we got the initial steps right.

1. Because the `customers.xcdf` and `customer-template.html` files reside in the solution repository, you must refresh it in order to test the dashboard. You can do this either from the Pentaho Administration Console or directly from the user console—the latter option is probably the most convenient. (Remember—you can refresh the repository from the user console menu by choosing Tools➤ Refresh➤ Repository Cache, or you can click the little refresh icon in the top-right corner of the Browse pane).
2. After you refresh the repository, you should be able to invoke the dashboard from the user console. Figure 17-5 shows a screenshot of what the dashboard might look like at this point.

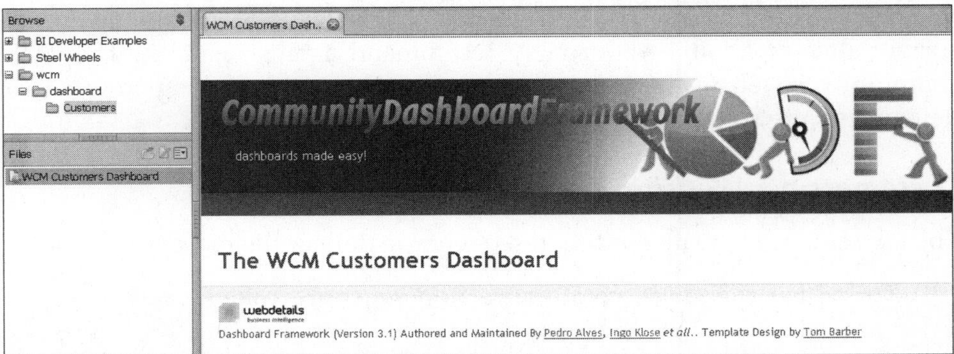

Figure 17-5: An empty customers dashboard

Now that you have an empty dashboard, you can start adding components. For now, this is best done one step at a time. Testing the dashboard after each addition makes it easy to spot any problems early on.

Customers per Website Pie Chart

You will first add the Customers per Website pie chart. There are two ways to include charts on dashboards:

- Build an action sequence that delivers the chart, and include that in the dashboard using CDF's `XactionComponent`.
- Create a CDF `JFreeChartComponent` and configure it to load data directly from a SQL or MDX query or PDI transformation.

For this example, you will stick to the first option. There are a number of reasons for this choice.

First of all, a separate action sequence will be reusable throughout the platform. This may not be the best reason for everyone, but if the chart is likely to be reused in other action sequences or even other dashboards, then a separate action sequence will add to the maintainability of the BI solution as a whole.

The second reason to prefer an action sequence is that there are important security issues involving all components that allow data to be obtained directly from a query. Currently, these queries are executed by the server, but the query text is controlled from the client side. Even though the component definition stems from whatever was specified in the content template at the server side, the query text can be manipulated by the client, leading to SQL and/or MDX injection. (This can easily be achieved using a browser JavaScript debugger such as Firebug or scripting plugin such as Greasemonkey.)

For MDX queries, the ramifications are perhaps not as serious as for SQL, because the Mondrian cubes that are targeted by MDX can be secured with role-based authorization. For SQL queries, this is virtually impossible. In the current state of affairs, we strongly recommend against using it. The CDF community is well aware of these issues and is currently working on a way to deliver a secure solution for this problem.

Customers per Website: Pie Chart Action Sequence

The next step is to create the action sequence to deliver the pie chart.

1. To deliver the chart, create an action sequence called `customers_per_website_piechart.xaction` and store it in the `wcm/dashboards/Customers` directory along with the other dashboard files. The action sequence design is shown in Figure 17-6.
2. The first step in the action sequence is called `Get Customer Count per Website`. This is a Relational process action. (You can find this type of action in the Get Data From submenu.) The SQL query that is used to retrieve the data for the pie chart is shown in Listing 17-7.

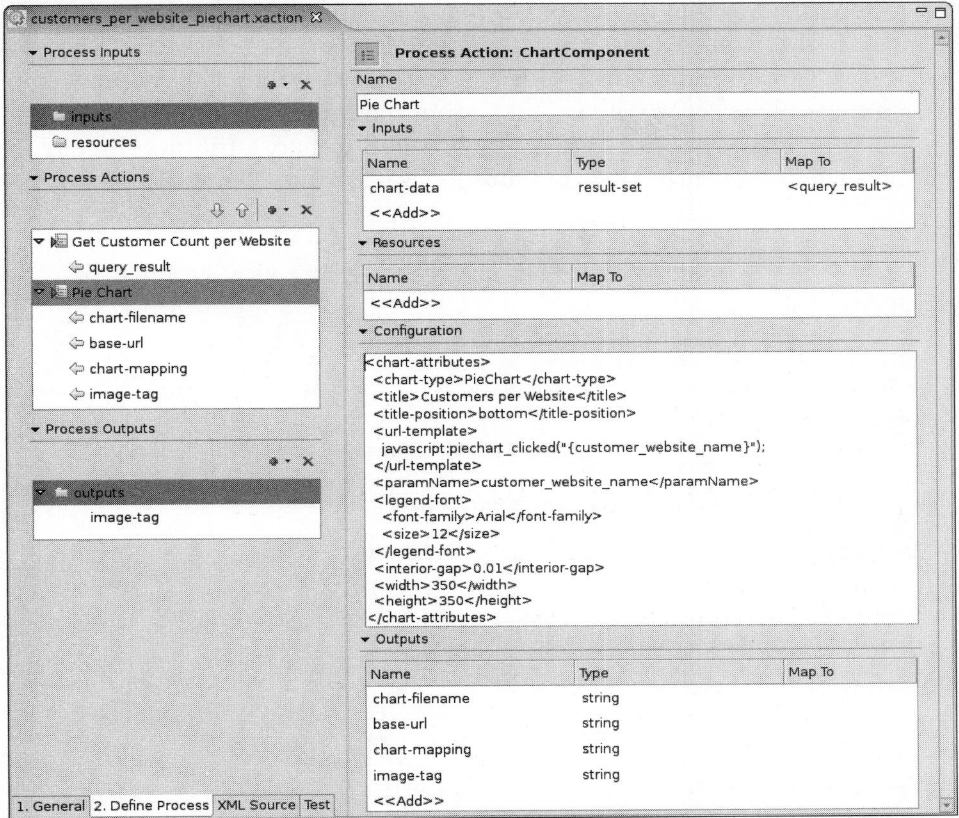

Figure 17-6: The action sequence design for the Customers per Website pie chart

Listing 17-7: The SQL query for the Customers per Website pie chart

```
SELECT    customer_website_name,
          COUNT(*) AS customer_count
FROM      dim_customer
WHERE     current_record = 1
AND       customer_date_unregistered > CURRENT_DATE()
GROUP BY customer_website_name
ORDER BY 2
```

This is a fairly straightforward query that fetches the current row from each registered customer, and groups the rows to count the number of customers by website. Finally the result is ordered by the `customer_count`. The ordering is important and will affect the order of the slices on the pie chart. In the action sequence, the result of the query is made accessible to the rest of the action sequence in the `query_result` output parameter.

3. The second step in the action sequence is simply called `Pie Chart`. You can find this process action in the menu in the Chart submenu. The `Pie Chart` process action accepts the `query_result` from the previous step and uses it to set the `chart-data` input parameter. In addition, some of the `Pie Chart`'s options are set by specifying chart attributes directly in the action sequence. The configuration is shown in Listing 17-8.

Listing 17-8: Configuring the Pie Chart process action

```
<chart-attributes>
  <chart-type>PieChart</chart-type>
  <title>Customers per Website</title>
  <title-position>bottom</title-position>
  <url-template>
    javascript:piechart_clicked("{customer_website_name}");
  </url-template>
  <paramName>customer_website_name</paramName>
  <legend-font>
    <font-family>Arial</font-family>
    <size>12</size>
  </legend-font>
  <interior-gap>0.01</interior-gap>
  <width>350</width>
  <height>350</height>
</chart-attributes>
```

NOTE The configuration XML used in Listing 17-8 may look a bit daunting at first. However, it looks harder than it really is. The Pentaho Wiki contains excellent information on creating and configuring charts. The relevant documentation can be found in:

`http://wiki.pentaho.com/display/ServerDoc2x/Chart+Reference`

The bolded lines from Listing 17-8 are of particular interest. These lines allow the HTML document that contains the chart to react in case a slice from the chart is clicked. A full discussion regarding how this configuration affects the generated HTML is beyond the scope of this book. For now it is enough to realize that the `url-template` element causes a JavaScript function called `piechart_clicked()` to be called whenever a slice of the pie is clicked. The `paramName` element and the `{customer_website_name}` placeholder ensure that the name of the website that corresponds to the pie slice is passed as an argument to the function. Note that the name `customer_website_name` is identical to the name of the first column from the result set delivered by the first step in the action sequence.

The `image-tag` output parameter is used to deliver the result of the Pie Chart process action to the caller of the action sequence. This will generate the necessary HTML to render a pie chart in your dashboard.

After creating the action sequence, it is a good idea to test it. If you accidentally made a mistake in the sequence but did not test it beforehand, you can waste a lot of time debugging your dashboard only to find out that the problem occurred upstream.

So, refresh the solution repository. You should see a new item pop up in the user console. Open it to verify that the pie chart is displayed. It should look like the pie chart shown earlier in Figure 17-4.

Customers per Website: XactionComponent

Once you have verified your action sequence, you need to modify the `customer-template.html` file to include it in your dashboard. You need to:

- Add an HTML placeholder element that acts as container wherein output from the action sequence can be displayed.
- Create a JavaScript object that knows how to call the action sequence. This object is the actual dashboard component.
- Add the component to the dashboard.

1. To accomplish this, open the `customers-template.html` file and add a `div` element to act as a placeholder. Insert it right after the closing tag of the initial `h1` element, but before the `script` element, as shown here:

```
<h1>The WCM Customers Dashboard</h1>
<div id="customersPerWebsite"></div>
<script language="javascript" type="text/javascript">
...rest of file...
```

   Note the `id` attribute on the `div` element. As you will see, you need to pass its value to the component definition so it knows where to place its output.

2. Now you can add a new section inside the script element to define your component. First, find the line that reads:

```
var components = [];
```

Immediately after this line, add the code listed in Listing 17-9 and then save your changes.

Listing 17-9: The Pie Chart Component definition

```
// Customers per website Pie Chart Component
components[components.length] = {
  name: "customersPerWebsite", type: "XactionComponent",
  solution: solution, path: path,
  action: "customers_per_website_piechart.xaction",
  parameters: [],
  htmlObject: "customersPerWebsite",
  executeAtStart: true
};
```

The code in Listing 17-9 is an assignment statement. To the right of the equals sign, you have an object literal (this is the piece from the opening curly brace immediately after the equals sign to the closing curly brace at the end of the listing), which will be used by the `Dashboards` object to create and configure the actual component. To the left of the equals sign, you have `components[components.length]`. As a whole, the statement has the effect of appending a new component configuration to the end of the components array (which is stored in the `components` variable). At this stage, the object literal itself is little more than a bag of name/value pairs. Here's a brief explanation of their purposes:

- `name`—A string value. This must uniquely identify the component among all other components on the page.
- `type`—A string value. Internally, this is used to do the actual instantiation of one of the component classes. In this particular case, you want to get a result from an action sequence, which is why you used the string `XactionComponent`. Alternatively, you can also use `xaction` or `Xaction`—these are all mapped to the `XactionComponent` component in the `CoreComponents.js` file.
- `solution`—A string value. This is the name of the Pentaho solution where the action sequence we want to call resides. Simply assign the `solution` variable, which we covered in our discussion of the boilerplate code.
- `path`—A string value. This is the solution repository path where the action sequence we want to call resides. Simply assign the `path` variable, which we covered in our discussion of the boilerplate code.
- `action`—The name of the `.xaction` file.
- `parameters`—This is an array to specify which parameters should be passed when invoking the action sequence. The `Pie Chart` action sequence does not require (nor expect) any parameters, which is why the array is empty. When you configure other components, you will learn how to configure the `parameters` member.

- `htmlObject`—A string value. Here, you assign the value of the ID attribute of the component's place holder. This establishes a link between the component's JavaScript object and the HTML document and allows the component to show its output on the dashboard.
- `executeAtStart`—A Boolean value. Setting this to `true` causes the component to be rendered as soon as all components are added to the dashboard. Otherwise, the component will be updated only in response to a parameter change. This is discussed in the next subsection.

Now that you changed the dashboard to include a component, you should refresh the solution repository and test the dashboard. When you invoke the dashboard you should see that the pie chart has been added to the dashboard.

Dynamically Changing the Dashboard Title

In this section, we explain how to allow dashboard components to interact with each other. This involves three distinct additions to `customer-template.html`:

- The `piechart_clicked()` function, which will be called whenever the user clicks a slice of the pie chart
- The `website` dashboard parameter, which is used to communicate the name of the clicked pie chart slice to the `Dashboards` object
- The HTML placeholder and JavaScript code for a `TextComponent` that reacts to a change in the `website` parameter by displaying its value

Adding the website_name Dashboard Parameter

Because both the `piechart_clicked()` function and the new `TextComponent` need to refer to the `website` parameter, it's best to create that first.

Append the following code to the `parameter` section so it reads:

```
//parameter name
var param_website = "website";
//initial value of the parameter
Dashboards.setParameter(param_website, "World Class Movies");
```

This new snippet of code does two things:

- Assigns the parameter name `website` to the global variable `param_website`
- Actually creates the parameter in the `Dashboards` object and supplies it with a default value, in this case `"World Class Movies"`

As you can see, the name of the parameter is stored in a global variable so you can use that to refer to the parameter name. The advantage of this approach is that you do not need to repeatedly type the parameter's literal name all over the code. If you were to use the literal string `"website"`, there is the risk of accidentally mistyping the name. You can, of course, also make a mistake when typing the variable name `param_website`, but this will result in a clear runtime error wherever you refer to the non-existing variable. Problems caused by mistyping the literal parameter name are much harder to troubleshoot: any runtime errors are likely to arise at a much later stage, after dashboard initialization, and it is also likely that components will appear to fail silently.

Note that you are required to create the parameter using `setParameter` because you explicitly set the `globalcontext` member of the `Dashboards` object to `false`. If you left `globalcontext` enabled, you would still be required to "create" the parameter, but it would have boiled down to creating a global `website` variable, like so:

```
//initialize website parameter
var website = "World Class Movies";
```

Although this may look simpler at first, using global variables makes it harder to maintain the dashboard code. For one, it is harder to distinguish between those global variables that are "just" global variables and the ones that are used as parameters. It is very easy to accidentally overwrite the value of a global variable, which makes it difficult to debug problems. By disabling `globalcontext`, you are forced to explicitly use calls to `Dashboards.setParameter()` and `Dashboards.getParameterValue()`, which makes it immediately clear what the intention is.

Reacting to Mouse Clicks on the Pie Chart

The second step is to create the `piechart_clicked()` function. Remember that when you configured the `url-template` property of the chart (see Listing 17-8), you only caused the `piechart_clicked()` function to be called. You never defined the function itself. You will now add the code for the `piechart_clicked()` function.

Listing 17-10 shows a possible implementation of the `piechart_clicked()` function. Add this code to the `customer-template.html` file, directly beneath the definition of the pie chart component.

Listing 17-10: The piechart_clicked function

```
//function that handles the mouse clicks on the pie slices
function piechart_clicked(website){
  var curr_param_website = Dashboards.getParameterValue(param_website);
  if (curr_param_website != website){
      Dashboards.fireChange(param_website, website);
  }
}
```

When `piechart_clicked()`is called, the category name that belongs to the respective slice is passed via the function's `website` argument. This is an immediate consequence of the way you configured the `url-template` property of the `Pie Chart` action sequence. This code is shown in full in Listing 17-8.

In the body of the function, you first determine the current value of the `website` dashboard parameter. This is done by calling the `getParameterValue()` method of the `Dashboards` object, passing the `param_website` variable, which holds the parameter name.

Next, check whether the current value of the `website` parameter differs from the new value passed in as the argument. This is used by an `if` statement to decide whether to call the `fireChange()` method of the `Dashboards` object. The `fireChange()` method of the `Dashboards` object expects to be passed two parameters:

- **The name of an existing dashboard parameter**—Again, you can use the global variable `param_website`.
- **The new value for the specified parameter**—This is the argument value you receive from the pie chart.

The purpose of the `fireChange()` method is to communicate the change to the `Dashboards` object, which will then notify the other components of the change.

NOTE **Note that "fireChange" is a bit of a misnomer as the `fireChange()` method does not necessarily fire a change. If you really want to ensure you are only signaling change, you have to explicitly make sure yourself. This is why our implementation of the `piechart_clicked()` method uses an `if` statement to prevent spurious signaling of changes that didn't occur.**

Adding a TextComponent

The final step is to add a dashboard component that can display the value of the `website` parameter. The `TextComponent` is intended for precisely this type of task.

1. To include this dashboard component, you need to add an HTML element placeholder where the component can render its text. You will use a `span` element for this purpose, which you will place in the already existing `h1` element:

   ```
   <h1>Customers of Website: <span id="websiteName"></span></h1>
   ```

   You use a `span` element to ensure the text rendered by the component will appear "inline" with the text of the containing `h1` element. Note that we included an `id` attribute and assigned the value `websiteName`. The `id` attribute will be used by the `TextComponent` to manipulate the HTML document, in this case to render some text. This is similar to our prior usage of the `id` attribute in the placeholder corresponding to the `XactionComponent` we used to display the pie chart.

2. After adding the placeholder, you can add JavaScript code to create the component. The code for the `TextComponent` is shown in Listing 17-11. Add this code right beneath the `piechart_clicked()` function:

Listing 17-11: Code for the TextComponent to dynamically change the name of the website parameter in the dashboard title

```
// Website name Textcomponent
components[components.length] = {
  name: "website", type: "TextComponent",
  listeners: [param_website],
  expression:
    function(){
      return Dashboards.getParameterValue(param_website);
    },
  htmlObject: "websiteName",
  executeAtStart: true
};
```

The code in Listing 17-11 reveals a number of similarities to the code for the `XactionComponent` used to display the pie chart (which is shown in Listing 17-9). The `name`, `type`, `htmlObject` and `executeAtStart` members were all shown there, and have a similar meaning for this type of component. Unlike the `XactionComponent` shown in Listing 17-9, the `TextComponent` does not invoke an action sequence, and thus the member variables `solution`, `path`, and `action` and parameters are not applicable. There are two member variables we didn't encounter before:

- `expression`—A string function. For the `TextComponent`, this function will be called to deliver the text value that will be placed in the element identified by the `htmlObject` member. In Listing 17-11, we chose to attach a so-called anonymous function inline directly to the member. If there is a named function already available, you can simply assign the function name itself. If you do use a named function, note that you must not append the parentheses after the function name as that has the effect of calling the function, which will cause the return value of the function to be assigned, not the function itself.
- `listeners`—An array of parameter names. This member can be configured for all component types. Listing a dashboard parameter name

here causes the component to listen to that parameter. In practice this means that the component will be called to update itself whenever the `fireChange()` method of the `Dashboards` object is called with the respective parameter name as its first argument. In Listing 17-11, we configured the component to listen to the `website` parameter by including the `param_website` variable in its listeners array.

After completing these steps, you should test to see if everything works. So refresh the solution repository and then open the dashboard. Click on the pie to ensure that the clicks are captured. Also check to see if the dashboard title is updated automatically when clicking the pie chart.

Showing Customer Locations

Now that you have a dashboard parameter that is controlled through mouse clicks on the pie chart, you can add more components and set up listeners for it.

In this subsection, you will learn how to add a CDF `MapComponent` to display geographical distribution of customers. You will use this to display a map of the United States that marks the top 100 (by number of customers) locations of the World Class Movies company's customers for the current website.

NOTE **The CDF `MapComponent` is based on the OpenLayers JavaScript library. Unlike other popular web page map solutions, OpenLayers is open source and available under a BSD license. It is shipped together with the CDF. You can find more information on OpenLayers at `http://openlayers.org`.**

In addition to the OpenLayers library, the CDF `MapComponent` also uses web requests to `www.openstreetmap.org`, which provides the data to draw street overlays for an OpenLayers map.

The CDF `MapComponent` can also make web requests to `http://www.geonames.org/`, which is used to do longitude/latitude lookups for location names.

CDF MapComponent Data Format

The CDF `MapComponent` can be used to indicate locations on the world map. The component uses an action sequence to obtain the data that is to appear on the map. The data set has the following format:

- `id`—A unique identifier for a location.
- `latitude`—The geographical latitude of the location. This defines the distance of a location from the equator, expressed as a number of degrees. Latitude ranges from +90 (at the North Pole) to –90 (the center of Antarctica). If the latitude is not available, you can supply an empty string.

- `longitude`—The geographical longitude for the location. This defines the distance of a location from the prime meridian, expressed as a number of degrees. Longitude ranges from +180 to −180. If the longitude is not available you can supply an empty string.
- `name`—A string that represents a human-readable name of the location.
- `value`—The value of the metric you want to map.
- `title`—This optional value can be used by the `MapBubbleComponent`. (This is a component that can be popped up from a location on the map to show details concerning that specific location.)

If you look at the format of the dataset, you may notice a redundancy: Location can be specified by name, but also by longitude/latitude. If the longitude and latitude are not present, the location name is used to search a web service provided by `www.geonames.org`. This works well if you are interested in mapping a few locations, but can become quite slow when mapping hundreds of locations. In addition, a single name can map to multiple locations, so it is best to always explicitly supply longitude and latitude data.

Later in this section we describe how to create the action sequence to provide the data for the `MapComponent`.

Adding a Geography Dimension

Before you can create an action sequence to deliver the data to the `MapComponent`, you need to obtain the longitude and latitude for all locations you want to map. To keep things simple, we chose not to include a geography dimension in our World Class Movies data warehouse. However, for the purpose of demonstrating the `MapComponent` in this dashboard, we need to provide longitude and latitude data for the customer locations.

NOTE **A geography or location dimension is a common feature in many data warehouse designs. In the World Class Movies data warehouse, a geography dimension table could be used to browse the `fact_customer`, `fact_order`, and `fact_inventory` fact tables. In addition, it could serve to snowflake the `dim_customer` and `dim_warehouse` dimension tables. The only reason to not include it was to maintain simplicity. However, incorporating a geography dimension table into the `wcm_dwh` database (and modifying the ETL process accordingly) is an excellent exercise left to the reader.**

Listing 17-12 shows the layout of the geography dimension table.

Listing 17-12: The layout of the dim_geography dimension table

```
CREATE TABLE dim_geography (
  geography_key          INTEGER      NOT NULL,
  geography_country_code CHAR(2)      NOT NULL,
```

```
  geography_country_name VARCHAR(50) NOT NULL,
  geography_region_code  CHAR(2)     NOT NULL,
  geography_region_name  VARCHAR(50) NOT NULL,
  geography_longitude    DOUBLE      NOT NULL,
  geography_latitude     DOUBLE      NOT NULL,
  geography_city_name    VARCHAR(50) NOT NULL,
  PRIMARY KEY ('geography_key'),
  INDEX
(geography_city_name,geography_region_code,geography_country_code)
)
```

Data for the dim_demography table can be obtained from several sources. We used the "world cities population" dataset provided by MaxMind. You can download it as worldcitiespop.txt.gz from http://geolite.maxmind.com/download/worldcities. Alternatively, you can use the data from geonames.org. We already mentioned that this web service is used by the CDF MapComponent to obtain longitude/latitude data online, but the same site also provides compressed files that are available for download from http://download.geonames.org/export/dump.

We won't discuss the loading of the dim_geography dimension in detail as the process is pretty straightforward. We loaded the data with PDI. First we used the Text Input and Table Output steps to load the data in a table in the staging area database. We then indexed this table to allow an efficient lookup on country, state (region), and city. In a separate transformation, we used a Table Input step to load all current rows from the customer table in the wcm database. We added Database Lookup steps to find the corresponding rows in the region and country tables, and this allowed us to look up longitude and latitude by city name, region code (state), and country code. The result was then dumped into the dim_geography table.

Location Data Action Sequence

Now that you have the necessary data, you can create an action sequence that can deliver the data to a MapComponent. In this case, you can use a very simple action sequence, containing just one Get Data From/Relational step. The design of the action sequence is shown in Figure 17-7.

Note that the action sequence has an input parameter called customer_website_name. This will be used to get the locations for customers of the currently selected website. The result of the process action is mapped to the query_result output parameter. This ensures the data can be parsed from the response after doing a web request for the action sequence.

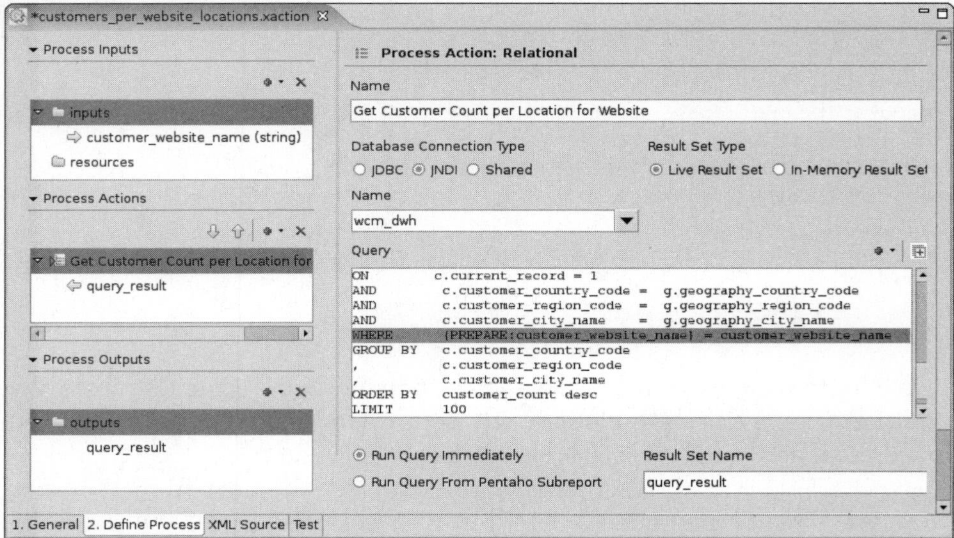

Figure 17-7: An action sequence to deliver the location data

The SQL is shown in Listing 17-13.

Listing 17-13: A SQL query to get customer locations

```
SELECT      g.geography_key
,           CASE WHEN g.geography_key IS NULL THEN ''
                 ELSE g.geography_latitude END        AS latitude
,           CASE WHEN g.geography_key IS NULL THEN ''
                 ELSE g.geography_longitude END       AS longitude
,           CONCAT( c.customer_city_name
            , '  ', c.customer_region_code
            , ' (', c.customer_country_code, ')')     AS location_name
,           COUNT(*)                                  AS customer_count
,           CONCAT(c.customer_city_name)              AS location_title
FROM        dim_customer   c
LEFT JOIN   dim_geography  g
ON          c.current_record = 1
AND         c.customer_country_code =  g.geography_country_code
AND         c.customer_region_code  =  g.geography_region_code
AND         c.customer_city_name    =  g.geography_city_name
WHERE       {PREPARE:customer_website_name} = customer_website_name
GROUP BY    c.customer_country_code
,           c.customer_region_code
,           c.customer_city_name
ORDER BY    customer_count desc
LIMIT       100
```

NOTE **If the `wcm_dwh` design had featured the `dim_geography` table, the `dim_customer` table would probably have been snowflaked, allowing for a straightforward `INNER JOIN` using the `geography_key`.**

Putting It on the Map

You can now add the code to include the `MapComponent` in your dashboard.

1. Open the `customer-template.html` file, and add the following line right after the placeholder for the pie chart.

   ```
   <div id="map" style="width:400px; height:300px;"></div>
   ```

   This will be the placeholder for the `MapComponent`. There are two things of note in this placeholder HTML element:

   - Currently, the CDF supports exactly one map per dashboard, and it must be in a placeholder with the `id="map"`.
   - Width and height are explicitly specified using a `style` attribute. Typically, it's advisable to refrain from using inline style attributes because it makes it harder to theme dashboards afterwards. However, in this case, you need to explicitly specify the dimensions of the placeholder, or else the map won't be visible.

2. You can now add the `MapComponent` JavaScript code to the `components` section. The code is shown in Listing 17-14.

Listing 17-14: The map component

```
//customer locations map component
components[components.length] = {
  name: "customerLocations", type: "map",
  solution: solution, path: path,
  action: "customers_per_website_locations.xaction",
  listeners: [param_website],
  parameters: [ ["customer_website_name", param_website] ],
  htmlObject: "map",
  executeAtStart: true,
  initPosLon: -37.370157, initPosLat: -100.458984,
  initZoom: 1,
  expression:
    function(){
      return "'js/OpenMap/OpenLayers/img/marker.png'";
    }
};
```

A number of the members we configured in Listing 17-14 were introduced in Listing 17-9 (the pie chart component code) and 17-11 (the dashboard title component code). The following member configurations merit some more discussion:

- `type`, `name`, and `htmlObject`—String values. Currently, the `MapComponent` is dependent upon a few global variables that restrict all these properties from having a value different from `"map"`. Note that this also applies to the value of the `id` attribute of the placeholder HTML element.
- `listeners`—Note that the member is configured exactly as you saw in Listing 17-11. It ensures that the map will be updated in response to a change in the `website` parameter.
- `parameters`—An array of arrays. You already encountered the `parameters` member in Listing 17-9. This time, you pass a *component parameter definition* to bind the dashboard parameter to the input parameter of the action sequence. As shown in Listing 17-13, a parameter definition for a component is itself an array with two entries. The first entry is an expression that evaluates to the name of the action sequence parameter. In Listing 17-13, this is the literal string `"customer_website_name"`. Note that that is exactly the name of the input parameter of the `customers_per_website_locations.xaction`. The second entry in the component parameter definition is the variable `param_website`, which contains the name of the `website` dashboard parameter. Together, this ensures that whenever the map component is called to update itself, it will use the value of the `website` dashboard parameter to parameterize the `customer_website_name` of the action sequence.
- `initPosLon` and `initPosLat`—`double` values. These members are specific to the `MapComponent`. They control what location should initially be the center of the map. In this case, the map will use the center of the USA as the focal point.
- `initZoom`—`integer`. Specifies the initial zoom factor for the map.
- `expression`—A string function returning an expression. For each point in the data set, this function will be called. The function is expected to return an expression that evaluates to a URI (as a string value). The URI is used to create a picture that is to be placed on the map at the corresponding location. In Listing 17-14, we always return the URL of a little marker picture that is bundled with OpenLayer.

This is all there is to it. You can now refresh the repository cache and test the dashboard again. Click on the pie chart, and notice that both the title and the map are updated.

Using Different Markers Depending on Data

In the previous subsection we explained how to add a `MapComponent` to the dashboard to visualize the geographical distribution of customers. However, you didn't actually do anything with the actual metric, the number of customers. In this subsection, you'll add some code to show different markers depending on the amount of customers residing in that particular location.

For our example, assume that you are interested in distinguishing between locations that have few, moderate, or large amounts of customers. For now let's settle for a few simple rules:

- Locations with 100 or fewer customers are considered small, and will get a green marker.
- Locations having more than 250 customers are considered large and will get a red marker.
- Remaining locations (with more than 100 but no more than 250 customers) are considered moderate and get a yellow marker.

Let's first try and try to come up with something that more or less works. You can then gradually improve the code if you like. A very simple implementation of the new requirement involves writing a modified expression for the `expression` member to pick the right marker image URI.

If you keep things simple and settle for the images bundled with OpenLayer, the code in Listing 17-15 implements your requirements.

Listing 17-15: Modified code for the expression member

```
expression:
  function(){
    return "value <=100 ? 'js/OpenMap/OpenLayers/img/marker-green.png'"
    + ":     value > 250 ? 'js/OpenMap/OpenLayers/img/marker.png'"
    + ":                   'js/OpenMap/OpenLayers/img/marker-gold.png'"
    ;
  }
```

However, this code leaves a lot to be desired. First of all, it is pretty hard to read, due to the fact that you have to put your code into a literal string. If you do the mental exercise of calling the function assigned to the expression member and then imagine the code that it evaluates to, you end up with something equivalent to the following snippet:

```
  value <= 100 ? 'js/OpenMap/OpenLayers/img/marker-green.png'
: value >  250 ? 'js/OpenMap/OpenLayers/img/marker.png'
:                'js/OpenMap/OpenLayers/img/marker-gold.png'
```

Now that we unwrapped the code, you can see that there's a variable called `value` that holds the value of the metric. This variable is made available to the components internally. The unwrapped code enables you to spot a few problems:

- The code refers to the images using string literals. There is no way to configure what images will be shown. This is bad because it hard-wires a presentational aspect (the marker image) to the logic that is chosen for a particular presentation.

- The logic itself, with the threshold values of 100 and 250, is also hard-wired. If your concept of ''large'' and ''small'' locations are likely to change over time, this type of code prevents the dashboard from adapting to that kind of change.

The solution to both problems is to make the literal values configurable. Fortunately, the `MapComponent` was designed to have a facility to configure the marker images. This can be configured through the `markers` member, which can be set to an array of URI strings. Just like the `value` variable, the `markers` member is magically made available to the expression. This means you can use the following code to extract the literal URI strings from the expression code:

```
components[components.length] = {
  name: "customerLocations", type: "map",

  ...other members...,

  markers: [
    "js/OpenMap/OpenLayers/img/marker-green.png",
    "js/OpenMap/OpenLayers/img/marker.png",
    "js/OpenMap/OpenLayers/img/marker-gold.png"
  ],
  expression:
    function(){
      return "value <=100 ? markers[0]"
      + ":    value > 250 ? markers[1]"
      + ":                  markers[2]"
      ;
    }
}
```

This is definitely better, as we can now change the marker images without changing the code that performs the logic. That said, there is still some room for improvement. Right now, the threshold values 100 and 250 are still hard-wired into the code. Now, these values are not immutable—our idea of what a large number of customers is may change over time, or in this case, we may develop the opinion that the threshold values should actually be dependent upon the website. Another reason why we're not so happy with the hard-wired constants is that we cannot simply apply the same logic in other dashboards—that is, not without duplicating the code. Combine this with a requirement to change the values at some point in the future, and you're looking at maintenance hell.

Fortunately, there is a simple way to deal with this. All you really have to do is replace the occurrence of the constant values with references to dashboard parameters. So, first add two new parameters for the threshold values in the parameters section:

```
var low_customer_count = "low_customer_count";
Dashboards.setParameter(low_customer_count, "100");
var high_customer_count = "high_customer_count";
Dashboards.setParameter(high_customer_count, "250");
```

Note that currently, the CDF supports only string value parameters. The modified expression member is shown here:

```
expression:
  function(){
  return "value <=parseInt(Dashboards.getParameterValue
    (low_customer_count))?markers[0]"
+ ":       value >parseInt(Dashboards.getParameterValue
    (high_customer_count))?markers[2]"
+ ":
    markers[1]"
  ;
  }
```

As you can see, the threshold variables are now parameterized. Note how the built-in `parseInt()` function is used to convert the parameter values to the integer type. This is required for a proper (numerical) comparison.

Note that we did not (yet) add the `low_customer_count` and `high_customer_count` parameters to the `listeners` array of the `MapComponent`. It would make good sense to do so if the threshold values were dependent on the website, or if the dashboard allowed the end user to enter a new threshold value to enable a what-if analysis. This is left as an exercise for the reader.

Styling and Customization

In the previous sections, you created a dashboard, components, and interaction. So far, we deliberately suppressed the temptation to have you make the dashboard look nice. This allowed you to focus on the technical details of making dashboard components work without having to deal with the distraction of layout issues and the like. Another consideration is that the skills required to create dashboards and building dashboard components are really quite different from the ones you need to make a layout and create an aesthetically pleasing whole. The former tasks are best done by a BI developer with just a few web development skills, whereas the latter are best done by a web developer, perhaps in conjunction with a usability expert.

In this section, we show a few techniques you can use to add a layout to your dashboard. A detailed discussion of this topic is beyond the scope of this book, but we can at least show the first few steps of the process. We're quite confident that you should be able to start here and follow your own route, provided you have some skills in styling web pages, or if you can rely on a web developer to help you.

Styling the Dashboard

There are two things to consider when styling a dashboard:

- **Layout**—Arranging placement of components. This pertains mainly to individual dashboards.
- **Theming**—Ensuring a consistent look and feel is used across dashboards, or an entire application.

By definition, component layout will largely be specific to an individual dashboard. For this reason, style and document structure to control layout belongs mostly in the content template. Theming, on the other hand, involves recurrence of presentational elements and attributes such as colors and fonts. Because the document template can be reused for several dashboards, it makes good sense to control theming at that level. (Using custom document templates is the topic of the next subsection.)

You can use two different devices to control layout:

- Document structure—By using specific HTML elements, and usage of element nesting
- Cascading Style Sheets (CSS)

A full discussion of these methods and the techniques involved would be well out of scope for this book. We'll settle for the point of view that both methods are valid and useful, and often the desired effect can best be achieved by combining both methods.

HTML tables are still the easiest way to quickly achieve a robust layout. A simple layout that places the dashboard title on the top of the dashboard, and beneath that, the pie chart on the left-hand side and the map on the right-hand side, is shown in Listing 17-16.

Listing 17-16: Using an HTML table to lay out the components

```
<table>
  <!-- row 1: header -->
  <tr>
    <!-- cell spans width of table -->
    <td colspan="100%">
      <h1>Customers of Website: <span id="websiteName"></span></h1>
```

```
      <br/>
    </td>
  </tr>
  <!-- row 2: components -->
  <tr>
    <!-- left column -->
    <td>
      <div id="customersPerWebsite"></div>
    </td>
    <!-- right column -->
    <td>
      <div id="map" style="width:400px; height:300px;"></div>
    </td>
  </tr>
</table>
```

This method uses the `table`, `tr` (for table row) and `td` (for table data) elements to create a tabular layout. Although this method is easy to set up and works in a reasonably similar way across browsers, it is usually frowned upon by modern web developers because the layout is basically a side effect of the document structure (i.e., the elements). This makes it harder to understand HTML documents because it cannot be determined whether the document structure is there for its own sake (to render tabular data) or to achieve a layout effect. Therefore, modern best practices dictate that layouts should be controlled using CSS rather than document structure.

In Listing 17-17, you'll find the HTML code that achieves a similar layout as that resulting from the code in Listing 17-16.

Listing 17-17: Using CSS to lay out the components

```
<style>
  #customersPerWebsite {
      position: absolute;
      top: 75px;
      left: 20px;
      width:250px;
      height:250px;
  }
  #map {
      position: absolute;
      top: 75px;
      left: 400px;
      width:400px;
      height:300px;
  }
</style>
<h1>Customers of Website: <span id="websiteName"/></span></h1>
<div id="customersPerWebsite"></div>
<div id="map"></div>
```

NOTE The layout in Listing 17-17 does not work particularly well with the default CDF templates, as these do not anticipate absolute positioning of elements. In the next section, we develop a content template that is better suited for this type of layout.

Creating a Custom Document Template

So far, you have been using the default document template for your Customers dashboard. This means your dashboard always featured the standard header with the CDF logo, and the footer with the link to the WebDetails site.

If you like, you can use your own document template to customize the appearance of your dashboard further. The possibilities for adding your own backgrounds, layouts, and navigation are quite unlimited. A detailed discussion on all the things and techniques you could apply is beyond the scope of this book. However, we can at least show you how to create your own document template.

To add your own document template, create a new file called `template-dashboard-wcm.html` directly in the CDF home directory. Remember that the file name is important; it must start with `template-dashboard-` and have the `.html` extension. Add the contents shown in Listing 17-18 to the file.

Listing 17-18: The template-dashboard-wcm.html file

```
<!DOCTYPE html PUBLIC "-//W3C//DTD XHTML 1.0 Strict//EN"
"http://www.w3.org/TR/xhtml1/DTD/xhtml1-strict.dtd">
<html xmlns="http://www.w3.org/1999/xhtml">
 <head>
  <meta http-equiv="content-type" content="text/html; charset=utf-8" />
  <title>Community Dashboard Framework for Word Class Movies </title>
  <script language="javascript">
    isAdmin = "{isAdmin}";
    isLoggedIn = "{isLoggedIn}";
  </script>
 </head>
 <body>
 <div id="header"></div>
 <div id="content">
  <div id = "primaryContentContainer">
   <div id="primaryContent">
   {content}
   </div>
   </div>
  </div>
  <div id="footer"></div>
 </body>
</html>
```

Remember, the `{content}` placeholder will be replaced by the dashboard content template during document assembly.

You must modify the `.xcdf` file in order to use the custom document template. Simply add a line like the following between the `cdf` opening and closing tags:

```
<style>wcm</style>
```

Note that the value, `wcm`, corresponds directly to the `wcm` postfix in the file name of the example document template, `template-dashboard-wcm.html`. Please refer to Listing 17-2 for an example of an `.xcdf` file that specifies a document template.

Summary

In this chapter, we covered creating dashboards based on the Community Dashboard Framework. In this chapter, you learned the following things:

- The CDF is created and maintained by the Pentaho community.
- The Pentaho Corporation includes the CDF in the server.
- Dashboards are actually web pages built on technologies such as HTML, CSS, and JavaScript, and use AJAX built on JQuery.
- CDF dashboard requests are handled by a plugin that assembles the dashboard from a document template and a content template.
- The `.xcdf` file contains the information on what document and content template to use.
- Document and content templates are actually HTML files.
- Dashboard components are added with JavaScript and often require an HTML placeholder to display their content.
- Dashboard components can listen for changes in dashboard parameters, which acts as a cue to automatically update them.
- Components can signal a parameter change with the `fireChange` method.
- Dashboard components can rely on action sequences to deliver the actual BI content.
- The `XactionComponent` can be used to display the contents of an arbitrary action sequence.
- Dynamic text can be implemented using the `TextComponent`.

We also discussed the following:

- How to capture mouse clicks on a `JFreeChart`
- How to use the `MapComponent` to display geographical distribution of date
- How to display different markers on a `MapComponent` depending on the value of metrics
- How to style your dashboards
- How to create and use a custom document template

Index

A

B

C

D

E

Q

S

T

U

V

W

X